Lecture Notes in Computer Science

Commenced Publication in 1973
Founding and Former Series Editors:
Gerhard Goos, Juris Hartmanis, and Jan van Leeuwen

Massimo De Gregorio   Vito Di Maio
Maria Frucci   Carlo Musio (Eds.)

Brain, Vision, and Artificial Intelligence

First International Symposium, BVAI 2005
Naples, Italy, October 19 – 21, 2005
Proceedings

 Springer

Volume Editors

Massimo De Gregorio
Vito Di Maio
Maria Frucci
Carlo Musio
Istituto di Cibernetica "Eduardo Caianiello"
CNR Via Campi Flegrei 34, 80078 Pozzuoli, Napoli, Italy
E-mail: {m.degregorio, v.dimaio, m.frucci, c.musio}@cib.na.cnr.it

Library of Congress Control Number: 2005933473

CR Subject Classification (1998): I.4, I.5, I.2, G.2, F.1, F.2, J.3, J.4

ISSN   0302-9743
ISBN-10   3-540-29282-9 Springer Berlin Heidelberg New York
ISBN-13   978-3-540-29282-1 Springer Berlin Heidelberg New York

Springer is a part of Springer Science+Business Media

springeronline.com

© Springer-Verlag Berlin Heidelberg 2005
Printed in Germany

Typesetting: Camera-ready by author, data conversion by Scientific Publishing Services, Chennai, India
Printed on acid-free paper   SPIN: 11565123   06/3142   5 4 3 2 1 0

Preface

The 1st International Symposium on "Brain, Vision & Artificial Intelligence" (BVAI, Naples, Italy, October 19–21, 2005) was a multidisciplinary symposium aimed at gathering scientists involved in study of the Brain, Vision and Intelligence, from both the natural and artificial points of view. The underlying idea was that to advance in each of the above research topics, integration with and attention to others is necessary. The overall rationale of the BVAI symposium was based on a multidisciplinary approach of biophysics and neurobiology, visual and cognitive sciences and cybernetics, dealing with the interactions of natural and artificial systems.

BVAI was conceived and organized by a group of researchers — active in the BVAI topics — of the Institute of Cybernetics "E. Caianiello" of the Italian National Research Council, Pozzuoli, Naples (ICIB-CNR), with the support of the Italian Institute for Philosophical Studies (IISF), and the help of the Macroscopic Quantum Coherence and Computing Association (MQC2). BVAI was sponsored by the EBSA (European Biophysics' Societies' Association) which in particular provided travel grants for deserving young participants from outside Italy. The symposium was held under the auspices of the AI*IA (Italian Association of Artificial Intelligence), GIRPR (Italian Group of Researchers in Pattern Recognition), SIBPA (Italian Society of Pure and Applied Biophysics) and SINS (Italian Society for Neurosciences). BVAI addressed the following main topics and subtopics:

Brain Basics: neuroanatomy and physiology; development, plasticity and learning; synaptic, neuronic and neural network modelling.
Natural Vision: visual neurosciences; mechanisms and model systems, visual perception, visual cognition.
Artificial Vision: shape perception, shape analysis and recognition, shape understanding.
Artificial Intelligence: hybrid intelligent systems, agents, cognitive models.

The scientific program included the participation of six invited speakers, selected among international leading scientists in the above mentioned fields: Igor Aleksander, Imperial College, UK; Dana Ballard, University of Rochester, USA; Cristiano Castelfranchi, Institute of Cognitive Sciences and Technologies — CNR, Italy; Péter Érdi, Kalamazoo College, USA; Kevan A.C. Martin, Institute of Neuroinformatics, ETH/UNIZ, Switzerland; and Enrica Strettoi, Institute of Neurosciences — CNR, Italy. Furthermore, the program included about 50 contributions from worldwide participants, presented in plenary sessions. The peer-reviewing process for the papers was performed by the members of the Scientific Committee of the symposium, including distinguished persons of the scientific community, together with a number of additional reviewers, appointed by the Scientific Commitee members. The accepted contributions were selected among more than 80 papers submitted to BVAI.

We believe that the papers in this volume and the discussions during the symposium will provide new insights and constructive thoughts. In particular we are confident that young researchers will usefully benefit in their work from their attendance at the symposium and from reading these contributions. We hope that we made BVAI an enjoyable event both from the scientific point of view and through the social activities that are also a way to provide new research stimuli in a more relaxed atmosphere.

We would like to thank the contributors who responded to the Call for Papers in a very positive way, the invited speakers, the members of the Scientific Commitee as well as the additional reviewers and, of course, all the participants. A grateful acknowledgement is due to EBSA, to the Regione Campania, to IISF, and to ICIB-CNR for their financial contribution that helped us to make BVAI successful. Finally, we would warmly aknowledge the symposium's Steering Committee and the Scientific Secretariat members: without their advice and constant support, BVAI could not have been realized. A special thanks goes to the symposium's Local Committee and Secretariat members for their precious work.

August 2005   Massimo De Gregorio and Vito Di Maio
                                                    Maria Frucci and Carlo Musio

Organization

BVAI was organized by ICIB-CNR, with the support of IISF, and the help of MQC2.

Conference Chairs

General Chairs   Massimo De Gregorio and Vito Di Maio
                                             ICIB-CNR, Pozzuoli (Naples), Italy
Program Chairs   Maria Frucci and Carlo Musio
                                             ICIB-CNR, Pozzuoli (Naples), Italy

Steering Committee

Vittorio Guglielmotti (ICIB-CNR)   Gabriella Sanniti di Baja (ICIB-CNR)
Francesco Mele (ICIB-CNR)   Francesco Ventriglia (ICIB-CNR)

Scientific Committee

Internal Members

Antonio Calabrese (ICIB-CNR)
Veeramani Maharajan (ICIB-CNR)
Giuliana Ramella (ICIB-CNR)

External Members

Carlo Arcelli (Italy)   Luigi P. Cordella (Italy)
Marina Bentivoglio (Italy)   Adriana Fiorentini (Italy)
Gunilla Borgefors (Sweden)   Marco Gori (Italy)
Roman Borisyuk (UK)   Benjamin B. Kimia (USA)
Alfred Bruckstein (Israel)   Petr Lansky (Czech Republic)
Horst Bunke (Switzerland)   Gyula Lazar (Hungary)
Ernesto Burattini (Italy)   Michele Migliore (Italy)
Terry Caelli (Canada)   Takako Nishi (Japan)
Leo Chalupa (USA)   Nicolai Petkov (The Netherlands)
Santi Chillemi (Italy)   Shunsuke Sato (Japan)

Peter Shiller (USA)
Carles Sierra (Spain)
Kostas Stathis (UK)
Cloe Taddei-Ferretti (Italy)
Settimo Termini (Italy)
Francesca Toni (UK)
Giuseppe Trautteur (Italy)

Henry Tuckwell (USA)
Shimon Ullman (Israel)
Leslie G. Ungerleider (USA)
Alessandro E.P. Villa (France)
Vincent Walsh (UK)
Barbara Webb (UK)

Additional Referees

H.C. Aras (USA)
E. Armengol (Spain)
M. Barbi (Italy)
A. Bell (USA)
G. Boccignone (Italy)
M.C. Chang (USA)
P. Coraggio (Italy)
A. d'Avila Garcez (UK)
K. de Raedt
    (The Netherlands)
C. De Stefano (Italy)
A. Del Bimbo (Italy)
A. Di Garbo (Italy)
V. Di Maio (Italy)
P. Érdi (USA)
P. Garcia-Calvés (Spain)
M. Ghanem (UK)

A. Gosh
    (The Netherlands)
S.J. Gotts (USA)
P. Gualtieri (Italy)
F. Hadj-Bouziane (USA)
V. Jain (USA)
F. Lesmes (Spain)
A. Machì (Italy)
F. Mele (Italy)
M.C. Morrone (Italy)
C. Musio (Italy)
P. Napoletano (Italy)
G.K. Ouzounis
    (The Netherlands)
O.C. Ozcanli (USA)
R. Prevete (Italy)
G. Sanniti di Baja (Italy)

C. Sansone (Italy)
S. Santillo (Italy)
L. Serino (Italy)
E.N. Subramanian
    (The Netherlands)
O. Talamo (Italy)
R. Toledo (Spain)
F. Tortorella (Italy)
M. Trinh (USA)
A. Tuson (UK)
E.R. Urbach
    (The Netherlands)
F. Ventriglia (Italy)
W. Vinje (USA)

Scientific Secretariat

Silvia Santillo (ICIB-CNR)
Luca Serino (ICIB-CNR)
Oliviero Talamo (ICIB-CNR)

Local Committee

Publicity: Salvatore Piantedosi   Local Arrangements: Antonio Cotugno

Secretariat

Paolo Coraggio, Luigia Cristino, Silvia Rossi

Sponsoring and Endorsing Institutions

BVAI was financially supported by: ICIB-CNR, IISF, Regione Campania, and EBSA.

BVAI was endorsed by: AI*IA, GIRPR, SIBPA, and SINS.

Table of Contents

Brain Basics

Natural Vision

Artificial Inteligence

Artificial Vision

Towards a Dynamic Neuropharmacology: Integrating Network and Receptor Levels

Péter Érdi[1] and János Tóth[2,*]

[1] Center for Complex Systems Studies, Kalamazoo College, Kalamazoo, MI 49006, USA
and Department of Biophysics, Research Institute for Particle and Nuclear Physics of the
Hungarian Academy of Sciences
perdi@kzoo.edu
[2] Department of Analysis, Institute of Mathematics, Faculty of Sciences,
Budapest University of Technology and Economics,
Egry J. u. 1., H-1111 Budapest, Hungary
jtoth@math.bme.hu

Abstract. Computational modeling by integrating compartmental neural technique and detailed kinetic description of pharmacological modulation of transmitter - receptor interaction is offered as a method to test the electrophysiological and behavioral effects of putative drugs. Even more, an inverse method is suggested as a method for controlling a neural system to realize a prescribed temporal pattern. Generation and pharamcological modulation of theta rhytm related to anxiety is analyzed. Integrative modeling might help to find positive allosteric modulators of $GABA_A$ α_1 subunits as potential candidates for being selective anxyolitics.

Systems Biology is an emergent movement to combine system level description with microscopic details. It might be interpreted as the renaissance of cybernetics [3] and of system theory [4], materialized in the works of Robert Rosen [5]. (For an excellent review on applying the system theoretical tradition to the new systems biology see [6]).

To have a system-level understanding of biological systems [1,2] we should get information from five key features:

- function,
- architecture,
- dynamics,
- control,
- design.

* Thanks to Global Partnership to sponsor JT's visit to Kalamazoo College. We benefited fromDiscussions with Jean-Pierre Rospars (JT), and Ildiko Aradi (PE). Thanks for the motivation and experimental data to Mihály Hajos (Department of Neuroscience, Pfizer, Groton) and to Tamás Kiss, Gergõ Orbán and Balázs Ujfalussy, who made the lion share of the model building and testing both in Kalamazoo and Budapest/Csillebérc. Partial support of the National Scientific Research Council (Hungary) (Nos. T037491, T047132) are also acknowledged by JT. PE thanks the Henry R. Luce Foundation the general support.

Function. From proteins via genes, cells and cellular networks to the function of our body and mind.

Architecture. From network of gene interactions via cellular networks to the modular architecture of the brain.

Dynamics. Dynamical system theory offers a conceptual and mathematical framework to describe spatiotemporal patterns of concentrations of biochemical components, cellular activity, global dynamical activities (such as measured by electroencephalogram, EEG). Bifurcation analysis and sensitivity analysis reveal the qualitative and quantitative changes in the behavior of the system.

Control. There are internal control mechanisms which maintain the function of the system, while external control (such as chemical, electrical or mechanical perturbation) of an impaired system may help to recover its function.

Design. There are strategies to modify the system architecture and dynamics to get a desired behavior at functional level. A desired function may be related to some "optimal temporal pattern".

While Systems Biology is now generally understood in a somewhat restricted way for proteins and genes, its conceptual and mathematical framework could be extended to neuroscience, as well. Trivially, there is a direct interaction between molecular and mental levels: chemical drugs influence mood and state of consciousness. "Almost all computational models of the mind and brain ignore details about neurotransmitters, hormones, and other molecules." [7].

In this paper we show how to realize the program of Systems Biology in the context of a new, dynamic neuropharmacology. Also, we offer a methodology to integrate conventional neural models with detailed description of neurochemical synaptic transmission in order to develop a new strategy for drug discovery. The procedure is illustrated on the problem of finding selective anxiolytics.

First, we briefly review the functional aspects of our system to be investigated, namely the neuropsychology of anxiety. The septohippocampal system is known to be involved in anxiety. Second, the architecture of the real and the model skeleton network of the septohippocampal system are discussed. Third, since there seems to be a positive correlation between the theta rhythm (i.e. the dynamics of the system), and the level of anxiety, the mechanism of theta rhythm generation is reviewed. Fourth, we review the available data on $GABA_A$ receptor kinetics to be integrated to the septohippocampal network.

Finally, we conceptually formulate the inverse problem to have a method for design. Having sufficient data for building a detailed kinetic model, we should be able to give advice to drug designers pointing out which subprocess should be modulated to obtain a desired behavior. The specific goal we are focusing on now is to design anxiolytic drugs acting on the α_2 subunit of $GABA_A$ receptors without effecting α_1 subunits related to sedative and hypnotic effects.

1   Function: Anxiety vs Mood Regulation

"Anxiety is a complex combination of the feeling of fear, apprehension and worry often accompanied by physical sensations such as palpitations, chest pain and/or shortness of breath. It may exist as a primary brain disorder or may be associated with other medical problems including other psychiatric disorders.

A chronically recurring case of anxiety that has a serious affect on your life may be clinically diagnosed as an anxiety disorder. The most common are Generalized anxiety disorder, Panic disorder, Social anxiety disorder, phobias, Obsessive-compulsive disorder, and posttraumatic stress disorder..." [11]

While the historically used mood regulators acting on the barbiturate or benzodiazepine sites of GABA receptors, these drugs have both anxiolytic and hypnotic activity. They enhance the action of GABA via an action at separate binding sites of the $GABA_A$ receptor.

(Both barbiturates and benzodiazepines shift the GABA concentration-response curve to the left, but barbiturates also increase the maximum response. They act on different states, consequently they have different kinetic effects: average open time of the channel, but not the channel opening frequency is increased significantly by barbiturates. As opposed to benzodiazepines, barbiturate receptors do not contain γ subunits (see later). One more difference is that at high concentration GABA receptor channels can directly be opened by barbiturates. For a summary see [45]. Anxiolytic activity was not a particular disadvantage when these drugs were used as hypnotics, hypnosis was a definite disadvantage when they were used as anxiolytics. Recent discoveries made possible the separation between hypnotic and anxyolitic activity and selective hypnotic agents (e.g. zolpidem) are already on the market. Selective anxiolytics are on the preclinical and/or in clinical trial stage.

2 Architecture: The Septohippocampal Skeleton Network

It was demonstrated (see e.g. the seminal book of Gray and McNaughton [12] that the septohippocampal system is strongly involved in anxiety and related disorders.

In a joint pharmacological and computational work [13,14] effects of the injection of the positive and negative $GABA_A$ allosteric modulators diazepam and FG-7142, respectively, were studied. To investigate the dynamical and functional effects of different pharmacological agents by computational tools a skeleton model of the septohippocampal system was established.

The *skeleton network* model (Fig. 1) of the hippocampal CA1 region and the septal GABAergic cells consisted of five cell populations. The hippocampal CA1 pyramidal cells model was a multicompartmental model modified from [17] and supplemented with hyperpolarization activated current I_h based on [18]. Besides I_h the cell model contained sodium (I_{Na}), delayed rectifier potassium (I_K), A-type potassium ($I_{K(A)}$), muscarinic potassium ($I_{K(M)}$), C-type potassium ($I_{K(C)}$), low threshold calcium (I_{Ca}) and calcium concentration dependent potassium ($I_{K(AHP)}$) currents. Active and leakage currents were described using the Hodgkin–Huxley formalism. For online supplementary materials, see: http://geza.kzoo.edu/theta/theta.html.

In the hippocampal CA1 region basket neurons and two types of horizontal neurons were taken into account. Basket neurons formed the fast spiking neuron population of the pyramidal layer, containing I_{Na} and I_K currents. These model neurons were previously used in [20,21] to account for the population of fast, regularly spiking neurons.

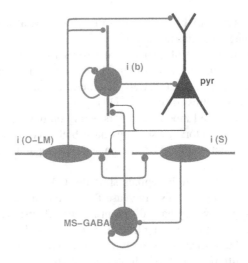

Fig. 1. *Left*: Computer model of the hippocampal CA1 circuitry. Neuron populations hypothesised to be responsible for the generation of theta oscillation are shown (pyr – pyramidal cells; i(O-LM) – horizontal cells projecting to the distal dentrites of pyramidal cells in the lacunosum moleculare layer; i(b) – basket interneurons; i(S) – septally projecting hippocampal horizontal interneurons; MS–GABA – septal GABAergic cells, triangles denote excitatory, dots inhibitory synapses). Connections originating and ending at the same population denote recurrent innervation.

The two types of horizontal neurons represented those interneuron populations whose somata resided at the oriens/alveus border [19]. These neurons were described by the same set of equations as their observed physiological properties are similar and contained sodium, potassium, a high-threshold calcium and hyperpolarization-activated currents [29]. The basket and O-LM neurons were able to generate repetitive action potentials autonomously, and O-LM neurons showed adaptation and low-frequency autonomous firing in the theta band.

Medial septal GABAergic neurons were previously described using single compartment models by Wang [19]. This cell type evokes action potentials repeatedly in clusters. Between any two clusters the cell exhibits subthreshold oscillation but no action potentials due to a slowly inactivating potassium current, which was added to this model neuron besides the Hodgkin–Huxley type sodium and potassium currents.

Connections within and among cell populations were created faithfully following the hippocampal structure. The main excitatory input to horizontal neurons is provided by the pyramidal cells via AMPA (alpha-amino-3-hydroxy-5-methyl-4-isoxazolepropionic acid) mediated synapses [22]. Synapses of the septally projecting horizontal cells [25] and synapses of the O-LM cell population innervating distal apical dendrites of pyramidal cells [23] are of the $GABA_A$ type. O-LM neurons also innervate parvalbumin containing basket neurons [24]. Basket neurons innervate pyramidal cells at their somatic region and other basket neurons [27] as well. Septal GABAergic cells innervate other septal GABAergic cells and hippocampal interneurons [26,28] (Figure 1).

3   Dynamics: Generation of Theta Rhytms

Theta frequency oscillation of the septohippocampal system has been considered as a prominent activity associated with cognitive function and affective processes. It is well documented that anxiolytics and hypnotics reduce amplitude of septohippocampal oscillatory theta activity, which contributes to their therapeutic effect but causes unwanted side effects, e.g. cognitive impairment as well [16,15].

This detailed, realistic model was used to examine the generation and control of theta oscillation in the hippocampal CA1 region. As shown on Figure 2 (A), firing of neurons of the four populations were not evenly distributed in time, but time intervals in which firing was significantly reduced were alternated by intervals where enhanced firing was observed. This synchronized state of neural firing was further confirmed by the field potential, which exhibited a prominent ≈5 Hz oscillation as reflected in the power spectrum (Figure 2 (B)).

Simulation results showed that key components in the regulation of the population theta frequency are membrane potential oscillation frequency of pyramidal cells, strength of pyramidal cell–O-LM cell innervation and strength of recurrent basket cell connections. Membrane potential oscillation of pyramidal cells is determined by their averages, passive membrane parameters and parameters of the active currents. Average depolarization in our model results from septal cholinerg innervation. An important

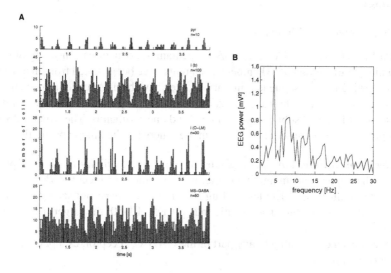

Fig. 2. Appearance of theta frequency population activity in the firing of cells and the Fourier spectrum of the field potential. *A*, firing histograms were calculated by binning firings of all cells of one of the four populations (pyr – pyramidal cells, i(b) – basket cells, i(O-LM) – oriens-lacunosum moleculare interneurons, MS-GABA – septal GABAergic cells) into discrete bins. Resulting graph shows the total activity of the respective population. *B*, power spectrum of the field potential. Theta frequency population activity is reflected by temporal modulation of firings in (*A*) and the ≈5 Hz peak in the power spectrum (*B*).

factor is the presence and maximal conductance of the hyperpolarization activated current. If I_h is present it shortens response times of pyramidal cells to hyperpolarizing current pulses and more importantly decreases its variance: I_h acts as a frequency stabilizer. Synaptic strengths in our description are set by convergence numbers and maximal synaptic conductances.

An explanation of intrahippocampal theta oscillation generation—based on this model—includes *i*, signal propagation in the pyramidal cell → O-LM cell → basket cell → pyramidal cell feed-back loop, *ii*, synchronization of neural activity via the recurrent, inhibitory $GABA_A$ connections within the basket cell network and *iii*, synchronization of pyramidal cell firing due to rebound action potential generation. It is that the propagation of a single signal throughout this trisynaptic loop would not require the amount of time characteristic to the theta oscillation (≈ 0.2–0.25 sec), thus in the present case the population oscillation is created not by the propagation of single signals but rather the propagation of a "synchronized state" in the network. The observed periodic population activity is brought about by alternating synchronization and desynchronization of cell activities due to the interplay of the above mentioned synchronizing forces and some desynchronizing forces (such as heterogeneity of cell parameters and diversity of synaptic connections), as observed in previous works [21,30].

4 Control: Integrating GABA Receptor Kinetics to the Receptor Model

4.1 Pharmacological Elements

Receptor Structure. $GABA_A$ receptors are pentameric structures consisting of multiple subunits. At this moment [31] nineteen subunits have been cloned from mammalian brain. According to their sequence similarities, they have been grouped into seven families: $\alpha, \beta, \gamma, \delta, \epsilon, \pi$ and θ. Only a few dozen among the many combinatorial possibilities exist. The most frequent subtyes two α, two β and one γ subunits. The structural variations imply functional consequnces [31], among others for the kinetic properties.

Drug-Receptor Interaction. A drug/substance may have *affinity* for the receptor: it may have the capacity to maintain contact with or bound to receptor. *Potency* is the the absolute number of molecules of drug required to elicit **response**. *Efficacy* is the maximum effect obtainable. Therapeutic index: LD50/ED50; the larger it is the safer the drug is.

All the substances binding to any part of the $GABA_A$ receptor, except GABA, will be called *modulators* below.

Agonists: Chemicals to open or to facilitate opening the Cl^- channels thereby enhancing or creating the inhibitory actions. These are also termed as *positive allosteric modulators*.

- *Endogeneous agonist:* the GABA itself.
- *Full agonists:* of the benzodiazepine family with sedative effects: e.g. diazepam, zolpidem.
- *Partial agonists:* e.g. bretazenil.

Inverse Agonists: Chemicals to close or to inhibit opening the Cl^- channels (e.g.) thereby decreasing the inhibitory actions. These are also termed as *negative allosteric modulators.*

- *Full inverse agonist* of the benzodiazepine type with anxiogenic effect: e.g. FG-7142.
- *Partial inverse agonists:* e.g.

Antagonists: Compounds which bind but have no effect on GABA inhibition. They have affinity, but no efficacy, e.g. bicuculline.

1. Desenzitization
    - prolonged/continuous use of agonist,
    - inhibition of degradation or uptake of agonist,
    - cell may attempt to bring its response back to normal by decreasing the number of receptors or binding affinity of receptors.
2. Senzitization
    - prolonged/continuous use of receptor blocker,
    - inhibition of transmitter synthesis or release,
    - cell may attempt to bring its response back to normal by increasing the number of receptors or binding affinity of receptors.

4.2 The Conventional Tool of Computational Neuroscience

One way to describe synaptic transmission is to use a gating variable similar to the well known Hodgkin–Huxley formalism:

$$I_{syn} = \bar{g}_{syn}s(V - E_{syn}) \tag{1a}$$

$$\frac{ds}{dt} = \alpha F(V_{pre})(1 - s) - \beta s \tag{1b}$$

$$F(V_{pre}) = \frac{1}{1 + \exp\left(\dfrac{V_{pre} - \Theta_{syn}}{K}\right)} \tag{1c}$$

with I_{syn} being the synaptic current, $\bar{g}_{syn}$ the maximal synaptic conductance, s the gating variable of the synaptic channel, E_{syn} the synaptic reversal potential, $F(\cdot)$ is an activation function, α and β rate functions describing opening and closing of the gate of the synaptic channel, Θ_{syn} is a threshold.

Figure 3. illustrates the general form of effects of $GABA_A$ receptor modulators.

4.3 An Intermediate Level Strategy: The Pharmacokinetic - Pharmacodynamic Approach

A theoretical framework with intermediate complexity based on pharmacokinetics - pharmacodynamics (PK/PD) was suggested to model the effects of GABA modulators on EEG in a series of papers [32,33]. *Pharmacokinetics* generally is supposed to describe drug disposition and biophase equilibration, diffusion included. In the applied

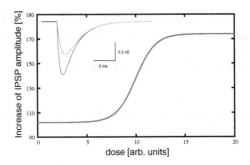

Fig. 3. Modelling the effects of allosteric GABA$_A$ receptor modulators. In a simple description of synaptic transfer the strength of synapses was modulated via the $\bar{g}_{syn}$ parameter in eq. (1a) in a dose dependent manner. *Inset*: modelled inhibitory postsynaptic potentials before (smaller amplitude) and after (larger amplitude) administration of positive GABA$_A$ allosteric modulator.

framework *pharmacodynamics* might consist of two stages: one for drug-receptor interaction, and another one for the signal transduction processes or stimulus-response relationship. The stimulus - response function is empirically determined, and intentionally neglects the architecture of the system under investigation. While this approach proved to be an efficient method, we believe that the architecture of the neural circuits should be taken into account explicitly to get a better understanding of the underlying neural mechanisms.

4.4   Kinetic Modeling of α_1 and an α_2 Modulators: A Plan

From Pharmacodynamics to Detailed Kinetic Scheme. A more effective, but certainly most expensive, modelling tool to evaluate the pharmacological effects of the different modulators, or even to give help for offering new putative molecules for drug discovery, is the inclusion of more detailed kinetic studies of GABA receptor modulation.

Suppose the dose response curve of GABA$_A$ is given and we also have the dose response curve of a modulator or a drug-modulator pair. Then, one can draw a few qualitative consequences.

It is important to fix, if the effect is measured as a function of drug concentration which is usually a hyperbola (naturally, without any inflexion point), or, as a function of the logarithm of the concentration in which case again a saturation curve is obtained but with an inflexion point at ED$_{50}$.

The effect of different modulators is as follows. If the effect is that the saturation point (the limit of the dose response curve at infinite modulator concentration) is smaller then without the modulator, then the modulator is a partial agonist. If the modulator has no effect (although it binds to the same binding site or to a site which hinders the endogenous agonist to act), i.e. the dose effect curve is constant zero, then we have an antagonist. If the effect of the modulator is a monotonously decreasing curve then we have an inverse agonist. One may also have a dose response curve shifted to the right (left); the modified system (modulator, or modulator + endogeneous agonist) has a smaller (larger) potency, i.e. a larger (smaller) number of drug molecules are required to elicit the same response. If the modified system's curve goes parallel with the original but below it (i.e. not only its limit is smaller), then the efficacy is decreased.

Kinetic Schemes. Jones and Westbrook [8] established a model for describing the rapid desensitization of the $GABA_A$ receptors. More specific kinetic models should be studied to describe the effects of the different (full and partial) agonists and antagonists. Baker et al. [34] explained the functional difference between the effects of protophol (which has hypnotic effect) and of midazolam (a sedative - amnestic drug) based on a detailed kinetic model.

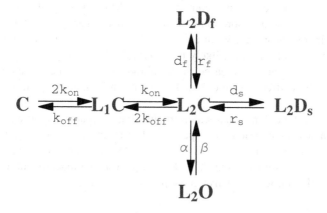

Fig. 4. Basic scheme of $GABA_A$ receptor kinetics. C, L_1C, L_2C denote closed states with zero, one and two bound ligands respectively. L_2O is the open state, while L_2D_f, L_2D_s are the desenzitized states. Modulators may effect different steps of these complex chemical reaction.

The main difference is that protophol modifies the desenziation processes, more dramatically the slow desenzitation steps and the modified kinetic parameters. These differences imply distinct behavior of the network (synchronization, frequency of oscillation) and therefore also in function.

4.5 Models of Anxioselective Actions: Search for Data

Recently it became clear that α subunits exhibit a remarkable functional specificity. Genetic manipulations helped to show that α_1 subunits are responsible for mediating sedative effects, while α_2 subunits mediates anxiolytic effects [10]. Preliminary experimental data and modelling studies for the the effects of the preferential $GABA_A$ α_1 and α_2 positive allosteric modulator, zolpidem and $L838, 417$ for the septohippocampal theta activity have been reported [9].

In this study we examined the effects of the α_1 and α_2 subtype-selective benzodiazepine site ligand zolpidem and $L838, 417$ on the septohippocampal system. In electrophysiological experiments extracellular single unit recordings were performed from medial septum/diagonal band of Broca with simultaneous hippocampal (CA1) electroencephalogram (EEG) recordings from anesthetized rats. Both of the drugs eliminated the hippocampal theta oscillation, and turned the firing pattern of medial septal cells from periodic to aperiodic, but only the zolpidem reduced the firing rate of the these neurons. In parallel to these experimental observations, a computational model has been constructed to clearly understand the effect of these drugs on the medial septal pacemaker cells. We showed that the aperiodic firing of hippocampo-septal neurons can reduce the periodicity of the medial-septal cells, as we have seen in the case of the $L838, 417$. The reduction of firing rates in the case of zolpidem is attributed to the increase of the synaptic conductances and the constant inhibition of these cells. We modelled these drug effects by modifying (i) the synaptic maximal conductances of the GABA synapses. (ii) the constant excitatory drive of the median septal cells and (iii) the hippocampal input. The incorporation of a more detailed synaptic model is in progress.

Zolpidem increases by concentration-dependent manner the duration and amplitude of the postsynaptic current, most likely by enhancing the affinity of the receptors for GABA [35]. It significantly increased the amplitude and frequency of the postsynaptic current, but these effects were diminished or absent in neurons from α_1 knock-out mice [36].

There seem to be compounds, which might have comparable binding affinity but different efficacies at the various subtypes, thereby preferentially exerting its effects at subtypes thought to be associated with anxiety. $L838, 417$ seems to be an an example for efficacy selective compounds [37], but kinetic or even pharmacodynamic data could not be found (at least not very easily) in the public domain.

4.6   Modulation of Synaptic and Extra-Synaptic $GABA_A$ Receptors

There are different mechanisms for postsynaptic modulation. It might be a long-term change in the number of receptors, a change in the affinity of a ligand, or a change on ionic conductances [38]. Recently it was emphasized that in addition to the conventional ("phasic") synaptic transmission the extrasynaptic "tonic" GABAergic cell-cell communication also has a significant functional role [39,40,31]. GABA can activate receptors on presynaptic terminals or at neighboring synapses ('spillover'). The phasic and tonic inhibitions are spatially and temporally discrete, and continuous, respectively. (For a review on non-synaptic communication see [46].) The two distinct mechanisms of the $GABA_A$ -receptor mediated inhibition implies different functional roles. Also, most likely different receptor subtypes mediate the two types of inhibition, and might be modulated by different kinetic schemes. Future works will show the similarities and differences among the different kinetic schemes behind the modulatory mechanisms of the phasic and tonic inhibition.

4.7   Direct Problem: To Simulate Modulatory Effects

Kinetic modeling of synaptic transmission has a flexibility in the level of detailed description from chemical kinetic to simplified representation [41]. The development of new pharmacological, electrophysiological and computational techniques make possible to investigate the modulatory effects of putative drugs for synaptic currents, and consequently for local field potentials and even behavioral states. Putative drugs with given kinetic properties can be tested *in silico* before (instead of?) real chemical and biological studies.

5   Design (Inverse Problem): From System Identification to Optimal Temporal Patterns

We have shown that in a moderately complex conductance-based model of the hippocampal CA1 region theta rhythm generation can be observed and major interactions between cell populations and within cells responsible for the phenomena can be identified. These results qualify the model for consideration as a useful tool in the hands of pharmacologists, physiologists and computational neuroscientists to complete their repertoire of available tools in the search for efficient and specific drugs.

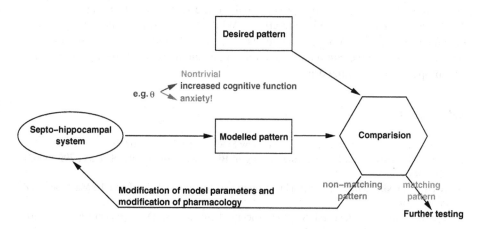

Fig. 5. Computational neuropharmacology—an idealized method for drug discovery. See text for a description.

Figure 5 is an oversimplified scheme offered for finding finding a modulator to set optimal septohippocampal EEG pattern.

In order to decrease anxiety first a desired EEG pattern shold be defined. Anxyolitics should reduce the amplitude the theta amplitude (but preserving the cognitive performance and avoiding sedative hypnotic side effects). Computational analysis should offer a best kinetic scheme and rate constant to modulate te fixed network to minimize the deviation from the desired "optimal pattern". (Network architecture is supposed to be fixed. By neglecting this assumption we should turn from neuropharmacology to neurosurgery...) Most likely there are more than one possibilities to reach the goal, and model discrimination and parameter estimation techniques may help to narrowing the alternatives.

As it is known from chemical kinetics [43,47] sensitivity analysis shows that in a kinetic scheme there are "more and less important" components and reactions. It helps to answer the question, whether how to modify the structure of a given drug to change the reaction rate constants in the desired direction—and leaving everything else intact.

6 Discussion, Further Research

The aim of the present paper is to offer conceptual and mathematical frameworks to integrate network and receptor level descriptions for investigating the effects of potential drugs for the global electrical patterns of a neural center, and and for the behavioral states (mood, consciousness etc.). Once we have understood (i) the basic mechanisms of rhythm generation, (ii) the elementary steps of the modulatory process, we shall a be able to give advice to drug designers pointing out which subprocess and how to be modulated to reach a given goal.

Specifically, we briefly reviewed some aspects of $GABA_A$ receptor kinetics, and the effects of (full and partial) agonists, antagonists and inverse antagonists to septo-hippocampal theta rhytms. The specific goal we are focusing is to design anxiolytic drugs with as small as possible side effects. While is is known that positive allosteric modulators acting on $GABA_A$ α_1 subunits are potential candidates for being selective anxyiolitics, integrative computational modeling would help to find the appropriate kinetic properties of potential drugs.

References

1. Kitano H.: Systems biology: a brief overview Science **295** 2002) 1662-1664
2. Csete ME., Doyle JC.: Reverse Engineering of Biological Complexity. Science, **295** (2002) 1664-1669
3. Wiener N: Cybernetics: or Control and Communication in the Animal and the Machine. MIT Press, 1948.
4. Von Bertalanffy L: General Systems Theory: Foundations, Development, Applications. George Braziller, New York/NY, 1969
5. Rosen R: Anticipatory Systems. Philosophical, Mathematical and Methodological Foundations. Pergamon Press, 1985
6. Wolkenhauer O: Systems biology: The reincarnation of systems theory applied in biology? Briefings in Bioinformatics, **2** (2001) 258-270
7. Thagard, P. : How molecules matter to mental computation. Philosophy of Science, **69** (2002) 429-446.
8. Jones B, Westbrook GK Desensitized states prolong gabaa channel responses to brief agonist pulses. Neuron, **15** (1995) 181–191.
9. Ujfalussy B, Orbán G, Kiss T, Hoffmann WE, Érdi P, and Hajós M" Anxiolytics and septo-hippocamapal oscillation: Pharmacological and computational analysis of action of gaba$_a$ α_1 and α_2 receptor allosteric modulators. *Conf. Hungarian Neuroscience Association, abstract,* 2005.
10. Rudolph U and Mohler H. Analysis of gaba$_a$ receptor function and dissection of the pharmacology of benzodiazepines and general anesthetics through mouse genetics. *Annu. Rev. Pharmacol. Toxicol.*, 44, 475-498, 2004.
11. From Wikipedia, the free encyclopedia. Anxiety. http://en.wikipedia.org/wiki/Anxiety
12. Gray, J.A., McNaughton, N., (2000) The Neuropsychology of Anxiety: An Enquiry into the Functions of the Septo-hippocampal System, 2nd ed., *Oxford University Press, Oxford*

13. Hajós M, Hoffmann WE, Orbán G, Kiss T, and Érdi P.: Modulation of septo-hippocampal θ activity by GABA$_A$ receptors: An experimental and computational approach. *Neuroscience*, 126(3):599–610, 2004.

14. Kiss T, Orbán G, Érdi P.: Modelling hippocampal theta oscillation: applications in neuropharmacology and robot navigation. *International Journal of Intelligent Systems* (in press)

15. Lees G and Dougalis A.: Differential effects of the sleep-inducing lipid oleamide and cannabinoids on the induction of long-term potentiation in the ca1 neurons of the rat hippocampus in vitro. *Brain Research*, 997(1):1–14, 2004.

16. A Maubach K, Martin K, Choudhury HI, and Seabrook GR.: Triazolam suppresses the induction of hippocampal long-term potentiation. *Neuroreport*, 15(7):1145–1149, 2004.

17. Varona P, Ibarz M, López-Aguado L, and Herreras O.: Macroscopic and subcellular factors shaping population spikes. *Journal of Neurophysiology*, 83:2192–2208, 2000.

18. Magee JC.: Dendritic hyperpolarization-activated currents modify the integrative properties of hippocampal CA1 pyramidal neurons. *Journal of Neuroscience*, 18(19):7613–7624, October 1998.

19. Wang XJ.: Pacemaker neurons for the theta rhythm and their synchronizati on in the septo-hippocampal reciprocal loop. *Journal of Neurophysiology*, 87(2):889–900, 2002.

20. Wang XJ and Buzsáki G.: Gamma oscillation by synaptic inhibition in a hippocampal interneuron network model. *J Neurosci*, 16:6402–6413, 1996.

21. Orbán G, Kiss T, Lengyel M, and Érdi P.: Hippocampal rhythm generation: gamma-related theta-frequency resonance in CA3 interneurons. *Biol Cybern*, 84(2):123–132, 2001.

22. Lacaille JC, Mueller AL, Kunkel DD, and Schwartzkroin PA.: Local circuit interactions between oriens/alveus interneurons and ca1 pyramidal cells in hippocampal slices: electrophysiology and morphology. *J Neurosci*, 7:1979–1993, 1987.

23. Lacaille, J.C., Williams, S. (1990) Membrane properties of interneurons in stratum oriens-alveus of the CA1 region of rat hippocampus in vitro. *Neuroscience* 36:349–359.

24. Katona I., Acsády L., Freund T.F. (1999) Postsynaptic targets of somatostatin-immunoreactive interneurons in the rat hippocampus. *Neuroscience* 88:37–55.

25. Jinno S and Kosaka T.: Immunocytochemical characterization of hippocamposeptal projecting gabaergic nonprincipal neurons in the mouse brain: a retrograde labeling. *Brain Res*, 945:219–231, 2002.

26. Freund TF and Antal M.: Gaba-containing neurons in the septum control inhibitory interneurons in the hippocampus. *Nature*, 336:170–173, 1988.

27. Freund TF and Buzsáki G.: Interneurons of the hippocampus. *Hippocampus*, 6:347–470, 1996.

28. Varga V, Borhegyi Zs, Fabo F, Henter TB, and Freund TF. In vivo recording and reconstruction of gabaergic medial septal neurons with theta related firing. *Program No. 870.17. Washington, DC: Society for Neuroscience.*, 2002.

29. Maccaferri G and McBain CJ:. The hyperpolarization-activated current (Ih) and its contribution to pacemaker activity in rat CA1 hippocampal stratum oriens-alveus interneurones. *Journal of Physiology*, 497:119–130, 1996.

30. Kiss T., Orbán G., Lengyel M., Érdi P. (2001) Intrahippocampal gamma and theta rhythm generation in a network model of inhibitory interneurons. *Neurocomputing* 38–40:713–719.

31. Farrant, M. and Nusser, Z.: Variations on an inhibitory theme: phasic and tonic activation of GABAA receptors. Nature Reviews Neuroscience. 6, 215-229. 2005.

32. Visser SA, Smulders CJ, Reijers BP, Van der Graaf PH, Peletier LA, Danhof M.: Mechanism-based pharmacokinetic-pharmacodynamic modeling of concentration-dependent hysteresis and biphasic electroencephalogram effects of alphaxalone in rats. *J. Pharmacol Exp Ther.* 302(3):1158-67. 2002

33. Visser SA, Wolters FL, Gubbens-Stibbe JM, Tukker E, Van Der Graaf PH, Peletier LA, Danhof M.: Mechanism-based pharmacokinetic/pharmacodynamic modeling of the electroencephalogram effects of GABAA receptor modulators: in vitro-in vivo correlations. *J Pharmacol Exp Ther.* 2304(1):88-101. 2003

34. Baker PM, Pennefather PS, Orser BA, Skinner FK.: Disruption of Coherent Oscillations in Inhibitory Networks With Anesthetics: Role of GABAA Receptor Desensitization *J. Neurophysiol.* 88:2821-33. 2002

35. Perrais D, Ropert N: Effect of Zolpidem on Miniature IPSCs and Occupancy of Postsynaptic GABAA Receptors in Central Synapses. J. Neuroscience, 19:578-588. 1999

36. Goldstein PA, Elsen FP, Ying SW, Ferguson C, Homaincs GE, Harrison NE: Prolongation of Hippocampal Miniature Inhibitory Postsynaptic Currents in Mice Lacking the GABAA Receptor α_1 Subunit. Neurophysiol 88: 3208-3217, 2002;

37. Atack, J. R.: Anxioselective Compounds Acting at the GABAA Receptor Benzodiazepine Binding Site. Curr Drug Target CNS Neurol Disord. **2.4** (Aug) (2003) 213–232

38. Cooper JR, Bloom FE and Roth RH: The Biochemcial Basis of Neuropharamcology., 8 th edition, Oxford University Press 2003.

39. Mody I: Distinguishing between GABA(A) receptors responsible for tonic and phasic conductances. Neurochem Res 26:907-913.

40. Mody, I., and Pearce, R.A.: Interneuron diversity series: Diversity of inhibitory neurotransmission through GABAA receptors. Trends in Neuroscience 27:569-575 (2004).

41. Destexhe, A., Mainen, Z. A., Sejnowski, T. J.: Kinetic Models of Synaptic Transmission. In: Koch, C., Segev, I. (eds.): Methods in Neuronal Modeling (2nd ed). MIT Press, Cambrdige, MA (1998) 1–30

42. Deupree, J. D., Bylund, D. B.: Basic Principles and Techniques for Receptor Binding. Tocris Review **18** (March) (2002)

43. Érdi, P., Tóth, J.: Mathematical Models of Chemical Reactions. Theory and Applications of Deterministic and Stochastic Models. Princeton University Press, Princeton, and Manchester University Press, Manchester (1989)

44. Jones, J. W., Westbrook, G. L.: Desensitized States Prolong $GABA_A$ Channel Responses to Brief Agonist Pulses. Neuron **15** (1995) 181–191

45. Martin, I. L., Dunn, S. M.: GABA Receptors. Tocris Review **20** (March) (2002)

46. Vizi ES: Role of High-Affinity Receptors and Membrane Transporters in Nonsynaptic Communication and Drug Action in the Central Nervous System Pharmacol. Rev. 52,63-90. 2000.

47. Turányi, T.: Sensitivity Analysis of Complex Kinetic Systems: Tools and Applications. J. Math. Chem. **5** (1990) 203–248

Cortical Architecture

Tom Binzegger[1,2], Rodney J. Douglas[1], and Kevan A.C. Martin[1]

[1] Institute of Neuroinformatics, University Zürich and ETH Zürich,
Winterthurerstrasse 190, 8057 Zürich, CH
[2] Institute of Neuroscience, Henry Wellcome Building,
University of Newcastle Upon Tyne, NE2 4HH, UK

Abstract. The evolution of the structure of the neocortex is one of the most important events in the chain that led to the human brain. The paleontological evidence shows that the human brain expanded two-fold in size over three million years, while modern chimpanzees still have brains about the size of the earliest hominids. The brains of chimpanzees and modern humans have a similar anatomy, so the vast difference in their size (400ml vs 1400ml) is due to an expansion of the cerebral cortex, rather than the development of entirely novel brain structures. Here we explore in what way the neocortical circuits are common to all mammalian species. We define a canonical structure that can be identified in all cortical areas and in all land-based mammalian species where data are available. This structure has recurrent excitatory and inhibitory loops formed by local neurons as a feature of its design. Quantitative studies from our laboratory show that the input from the sensory periphery forms less than one percent of the total input to the primary visual cortex in the cat. Thus the major synaptic input to a cortical neuron comes from its neighbors. We provide a conceptual model that offers an operational view of how the canonical circuit of the neocortex might operate.

1 Out of Africa

We all come from Africa, although some of us perhaps more recently than others. It is in Africa where we find the chain of evidence that shows how we inherited such a large brain. Three million years ago, Australopithecines walked upright in Africa. These early members of the hominid branch had small bodies, and brains about the size of modern chimpanzee (400ml). One and a half million years later, the fossil record shows that the brain size of Homo erectus was about 800ml, which already shows a remarkably fast expansion in brain size. Modern humans, however, have an even larger brain sizes (1400ml), although curiously, modern brains are smaller than their immediate ancestors - early modern Homo sapiens and Homo neanderthalis (1550ml). When normalized for body weight, we find that the size of the hominid brain has nearly doubled in a brief three million years (see [1]). The usual question that arises is, why? What drove evolution so fast, since evidently, the hominid line branched from the line that led to modern apes very recently (within the last 10 million years)? A rather less frequently asked

M. De Gregorio et al. (Eds.): BVAI 2005, LNCS 3704, pp. 15–28, 2005.

question is, how do you make a brain expand so much in so few generations, yet have it still work so well? Not only has it continued to work well, but it has added capacities that make human brains seem qualitatively different from all other primates. It is competent to a degree that is simply not seen in our cousins the apes, yet gene mapping suggest that modern apes and humans have 95% of their DNA in common ([2]). It is evident that the way in which we use our brains is radically different from apes. This is evident in humans' unique ability to use language and manipulate symbols, and is also clearly evident in the invention and use of tools.

For most of this time of brain expansion, the ancestors of modern humans made stone tools, the earliest of which were found in the Oldovai gorge in Tanzania and date from about 2.5 million years. These Oldowan tools were essentially of two types: a crude chopper or scraper, and sharp flakes that were produced by making the chopper. They offer an intriguing view of their maker's intelligence and how the homids of the time were thinking and behaving. But, after the invention of these first stone tools, there was a period of stasis: the same basic tools were used for over a million years unchanged. Only with the emergence of Homo erectus about 1.7 million years ago, did a new tool technology develop, called 'Acheulian' after the site St. Acheul in France where they were first discovered. Homo erectus started making larger tools than those of the Oldowan's, like a pick, a cleaver, and most characteristically, a tear-drop shaped hand axe. Once these Acheulian tools had been invented, there was again one million years of stasis and it was only in the last 250,000 years that new tools were invented by the archaic Homo sapiens. Thus, there is no strict correlation between the size of the brain and the development of more varieties of tools. Rather, it seems that as their brain size increased hominids discovered new ways of using it. These new ways of using the brain may also have driven the evolution of the morphology of the hand, which in turn allowed more sophisticated tools to be made.

But this is speculation. What is more certain is that the endocranial casts taken from the fossil skulls show that the increase in the size of the brain was mainly due to an increase in the size of the cerebral cortex. The question to ponder is how in 150,000 generations or so, over the 3 million years, can the size of the brain be doubled? If the neuron density in the early brains was the same as modern humans, then the 400ml brain would contain about three billion neurons compared to the eleven billion in human brains. Over 3 million years, 8 billion new neurons have to be added to achieve current human brain sizes. If we take a generation to be 20 years, this means that every generation would have to have add, on average, 60,000 cells to their brain. Since each cubic mm of the neocortex contains about 50,000 to 100,000 neurons, this addition makes a tiny addition to the total volume. How would such an increment in neuron numbers be achieved? Since it takes only 33 divisions to generate eight billion neurons from a single neuroblast, double this number of neurons can be generated if each neuroblast just went through one more division before differentiating. Thus an increment of even 60 000 neurons requires that only a few neuroblast continue in the cell cycle during neurogenesis. It is worth noting in passing that human neurogenesis occurs over about three months and so on average the human brain adds 1400 new neurons per second, and about one and a half million synapses per second during this phase. In the face of this plenitude and speed, it seems more a problem to not make too many neurons (although many neurons do die) than to make exactly the required number.

In the event, the raw size of the brain is not the issue, since we see that it correlates poorly with the invention of new tools. What is more critical is how the new neurons are wired together. Here there is a potential generation gap, for 3 million years seems too short to accept that all the new neurons have been required because novel circuits have evolved. We seem to share all the same neural structures as non-human primates. What seems to be the major difference is one of quantity ([3] pp. 390). We don't seem to have a differently designed brain from our cousin primates, but one that is three times bigger than it should be for a primate of our weight. It seems more likely therefore that since most of the new neurons added over the past 3 million years have been used in the construction of more cerebral cortex, the additional cortical circuits were modeled on the existing designs.

The appalling thought is then that the success of hominid evolution is due to chance mutations that led to the construction of more pieces of the same evolutionary successful and well-tested circuit. The additional new pieces would form new or expanded cortical areas, and would be connected into the older pieces according to prevailing rules of connectivity. In this sense they were following exactly the same pattern that was seen during the evolution of mammals. From its modest beginnings in the first mammals, the cerebral cortex became larger and more and more differentiated, in the sense that it could carry out a wider range of functions. Similar trends are evident in modern mammals, where in rodents the cerebral cortex that forms a volume of about 40% of their brain, whereas in monkeys its forms about 70%, and in humans it forms about 85% of the entire brain. Thus, while the reasons for the rapid expansion of the hominid brain remain a mystery, most of the new neurons were most likely built into circuits whose design had already proved their worth during the evolution of the mammalian brain.

2   Cortical Foundation

The question is of course, what is so special about the cerebral cortical circuits? In particular, what is so special about the circuits of the neocortex, which form the greater part of the cerebral cortex? The comparative anatomy of these circuits still remains sketchy and the detailed anatomy of any has until recently been unknown. However, an important insight into the organization of these circuits was provided by experiments that recorded the intracellular response of the cortical neurons to an electrical pulse stimulus applied to the incoming fibers (Fig. 1). These experiments ([4,5,6]) were performed in cat primary visual cortex in vivo. The response for neurons through the depth of the cortex was,

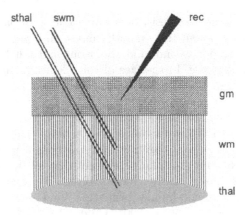

Fig. 1. Configuration of the experiment [6] that generated the data described in Fig. 2. Two pairs of fixed stimulating electrodes (*sthal, swm*) were placed in the thalamus (*thal,* grey ellipse), and in the white matter (*wm,* vertical lines) immediately beneath the grey matter (*gm,* hatched) respectively. Individual cortical neurons were impaled by a mobile glass microelectrode (*rec,* black). This electrode recorded the intracellular voltage of the neuron, and its response to stimulation of cortical afferents, whose somata lie in the thalamus, and whose axons ascend to *gm* via *wm*.

at first glance, stereotypical. The pulse elicited at short latency (1-2ms) a depolarization of short duration (5ms), followed by a long lasting hyperpolarization (200ms duration) (Fig. 2). This pattern of excitation followed by inhibition has been detected in all other cortical areas where this experiment has been done ([7,8,9,10]).

Although these physiological results agreed with those of a number of previous studies, what made this study different from pervious ones was that the neurons were not only recorded intracellularly, but they were labeled with a dye (horseradish peroxidase) during the recording. This meant that the type of neuron could be determined and that the position of the neuron in the cortical layers was known exactly. This information turned out to be critical for what followed, for a closer look revealed that the time taken to reach to maximum hyperpolarization was far longer for neurons lying in the superficial layers of the cortex (layers 2 and 3) than those of the deeper layers (layers 5 and 6). Our interpretation of these results is that the initial excitatory response of all cortical neurons is rapidly quenched by inhibition, but that the inhibition is stronger in the deep layers. This explained the much shorter time-course of the initial depolarization in the deep layer neurons.

These combined physiological and anatomical data provided the essential observations for the first version of a model of the cortical circuitry that attempted to capture this functionality. Its diagrammatic form is shown in Fig. 3. The circuit captured the laminar differences in the responses of the excitatory neurons through the depth of the cortex. It also captured a key computation feature of the cortical circuit - its recurrence. This feature is reflected in all three groups of

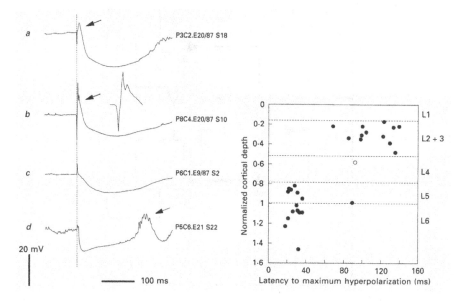

Fig. 2. Results derived from the experimental configuration described in Fig. 1 ([6]). The four intracellular recordings at left are typical of those obtained following subcortical stimulation (whose time of application is indicated by stimulus artefact). Traces a,b were recorded from histologically identified pyramidal neurons in the superficial layers of cortex, whereas c,d were recorded from deep pyramidal cells. In all cases the response is dominated by an approximately 300ms period of hyperpolarizing inhibition. The latency to maximum hyperpolarization is correlated with the depth of the neuron in the cortex (right sub-figure). The latency to this maximum is longer in the superficial pyramids than in the deep ones. A single inhibitory neuron recorded in layer 4 (open circle) exhibited a hyperpolarizing response that was qualitatively similar to the pyramidal neurons of the superficial layers. In superficial pyramids the inhibition is preceded by a phase of excitation (arrowed) lasting some 20ms. This phase often contains a few sub-peaks (b, enlarged inset), suggesting that the stimulation evokes superimposed waves of excitation. In some neurons (at all depths) there may be a late phase of excitation (arrowed in d). The source of this event is unknown.

neurons depicted in the model: the superficial and deep layer excitatory neurons, and the class of inhibitory neurons. Clearly this model is a radical simplification of the complexity of the real cortical neurons. Nevertheless, even in its simplicity it provided the key step from the abstract recurrent networks explored by Hopfield and others, to a biologically-based model of a cortical recurrent network. As the first such network based on in vivo functional data, its value was in providing a bench-mark model for the local circuit. It provided a canonical cortical circuit for theoretical explorations of a wide number of issues, including orientation tuning, direction tuning, working memory, chaos, etc. ([5,11,12,13,14,15]).

One important point to establish was to what extent the canonical circuit from sensory cortex was generalizable. To explore this, we have undertaken an

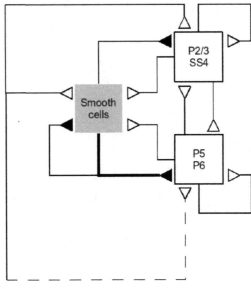

Thalamus

Fig. 3. The 'canonical microcircuit' is the minimal circuit necessary to explain experimental results reported in [4,5], as exemplified in Fig. 2. The circuit is composed of two populations of recurrently connected excitatory neurons; one superficial (pyramidal neurons of layer 2/3 and spiny stellate neurons of layer 4); and one deep (pyramidal neurons of layer 5 and 6). A third population of inhibitory neurons exerts a stronger effect on the deep excitatory population than the superficial one.

extensive search of the comparative literature to understand the nature of the anatomical evidence for similar excitatory circuits in other cortical areas and other species ([16]) These common feature concern not only the connections between local circuits, but also the connections to circuits in other areas. Although there are nominally 6 cortical layers, little is known of the connections of layers 1 and 2, and here they are essentially subsumed under layer three. Layer 4, the major thalamorecipient layer, shows the most variation. Area 17 of the old world monkey is now divided into 4 sublayers, but one of these (layer 4B) is not a thalamorecipient layer and should probably be considered a subdivision of layer 3. In the motor cortex, layer 4 is residual, and the thalamic afferents terminate mainly in the lower part of layer 3. However, if debates about what are actually the homologous layers in different areas and different species is set aside for the moment, the basic pattern of interlaminar and interareal connections is as shown in Fig. 4.

There are a number of common features in addition to the thalamic projection to layer 4 that can be noted. One is that the output from a local circuit to subcortical structures, such as the thalamus or superior colliculus, arises principally from the deep layers in all areas. The layer 6 pyramidal neurons provide a feedback to the thalamic relay nuclei, whereas the layer 5 pyramidal neurons

Area A   Area B

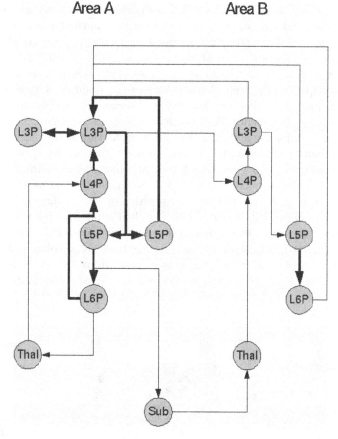

Fig. 4. Graph of the dominant interactions between significant excitatory cell types in neocortex, and their sub-cortical relations ([16]). The nodes of the graph are organized approximately spatially; vertical corresponds to the layers of cortex, and horizontal to its lateral extent. *Directed edges (arrows)* indicate the direction of excitatory action. *Thick edges* indicate the relations between excitatory neurons in a local patch of neocortex, which are essentially those described originally by Gilbert and Wiesel [17,18] for visual cortex. *Thin edges* indicate excitatory connections to and from subcortical structures, and inter-areal connections. Each node is labeled for its cell type. For cortical cells, *Lx* refers to the layer in which its soma is located. *P* indicates that it is an excitatory neuron (generally of pyramidal morphology). *Thal* denotes the thalamus, and *Sub* other subcortical structures, such as the basal ganglia.

project to the pulvinar and motor structures, such as the spinal cord and superior colliculus. A stereotypical projection pattern is also seen for the interareal connections (see e.g. [19]). The rule of thumb for the interareal networks is that projections resembling those of the thalamocortical projections, i.e. terminating principally in the middle layers of cortex, originate from layer 3 and layer 6 neurons and are called 'feedforward' projections. Interareal projections that terminate outside layer 4 are called 'feedback' projections. The same neurons whose axons form the local circuits also form the long distance connections between areas. Thus, the local network is embedded in a large scale cortical network. However, the contribution of excitatory synapses by a given cortical area to another is exceedingly small, amounting to less than one percent of the total excitatory synapses in an area. An estimate of the number of synapses found for any given projection has been extremely difficult to come by and there are very few direct measurements. We have recently made the first complete inventory of all the synapses contributed by the neurons that form the local circuit in the cat's primary visual cortex ([20]). To make this estimate, neurons were recorded intracellularly in vivo, and filled with horseradish peroxidase, which labels the entire dendritic and axonal tree. The single neurons were then reconstructed in 3-D, (Fig. 5) and the laminar position of every synaptic bouton and every segment of of dendrite was mapped. We then applied a simple rule ('Peters rule') that the different classes of neurons connect with each other in proportion to which they contribute dendrites or synapses to a given volume of neuropil. Applying this simple rule to all the classes of neurons that had been recovered in the intracellular recordings, we derived a series of synaptic maps for the

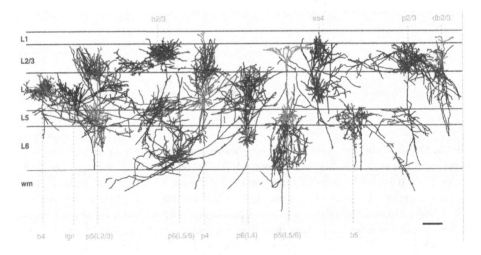

Fig. 5. Coronal view of reconstructed cells representing the different cell-types present in the visual cortex of the cat ([20]). Axons are shown in black, dendrites in grey. Boutons are ignored for visibility. Cell-types are indicated at the top. Abbreviations: 'b2/3', 'b4', 'b5' basket cells in layer 2/3, 4 and 5; 'db2/3' double bouquet cell in layer 2/3; 'p2/3', 'p4', 'p5', 'p6' pyramidal cells in layer 2/3, 4, 5 and 6. 'ss4' spiny stellate cells in layer 4. Spiny stellate cells and pyramidal cells in layer 5 and 6 were further distinguished by the preferred layer of the axonal innervation ('ss4(L4)' (not shown), 'ss4(L2/3)', 'p5(L2/3)', 'p5(L5/6)', 'p6(L4)' and 'p6(L5/6)'). 'X/Y' thalamic afferents of type X and Y. Horizontal lines indicate the approximate cortical layers L1, L2/3 (layer 2 and 3 were merged), L4, L5, L6. Also indicated is the white matter ('wm'). Scale bar is $300\mu m$.

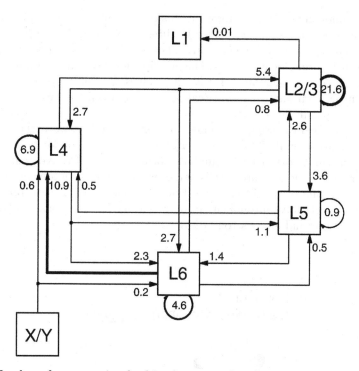

Fig. 6. Number of synapses involved in the connections between excitatory neurons between layers, including the X-type and Y-type afferents from the dLGN ([20]). A-D: Each arrow is labeled with a number indicating the proportion of all $15 \cdot 10^{10}$ excitatory synapses in area 17 that are formed between only excitatory neurons. The proportion of all asymmetric unassigned synapses that the excitatory neurons in each layer receive is 0.01% (layer 1), 5% (layer 2/3), 3% (layer 4), 4% (layer 5), and 16% (layer 6). These synapses are presumably formed by the afferents originating outside area 17.

various classes. Figure 6 shows for example the map for the connections between the major classes of excitatory neurons, where the numbers given express the percentage of the total population of excitatory synapses found in area 17, as assessed by quantitative methods ([21]). This map of excitatory connections reveals that even within the local circuits, there are multiple sources of excitation, and that most of them involve only a few percent of the synapses. Considered numerically, most connections are 'weak', as indicated by the thin connecting lines in Fig. 6. However, there are notable exceptions, particularly within layers, as indicated by the bold connecting lines.

The excitatory cells in layer 4 consist of two major classes, the spiny stellate cells and the star pyramidal cells. The data show that the thalamus, which provides the major drive to the visual cortex, provides only 0.6% of the synapses made with these layer 4 excitatory cells. This estimate seems extraordinarily low, expecially given the textbook model that the pattern of thalamic input provides the major excitatory drive to layer 4, which, it should be re-emphasized, is the major thalamorecipient layer. However, this estimate of such a small fraction of thalamocortical synapses is supported by direct experimental studies (e.g. [22]). These estimates and experimental data indicate that the major excitatory input to layer 4 comes from local neurons. The principal local excitatory inputs to layer 4 neurons are from other layer 4 cells themselves, and of course the strongest connection between any of the cortical layers is between the layer 6 pyramidal cells and neurons in layer 4.

The (numerically) strongest connections are formed between the layer 2/3 pyramidal neurons. Fully 22% of the excitatory synapses are made between these neurons. The inhibitory neurons similarly form a plexus of convergent input to each other and to the excitatory cells of cortex (described in more detail below). Thus, the anatomical weight of connections is already sufficient to provide the skeleton for a rich polyneuronal circuit of excitatory neurons consisting of many weak connections and a few strong connections.

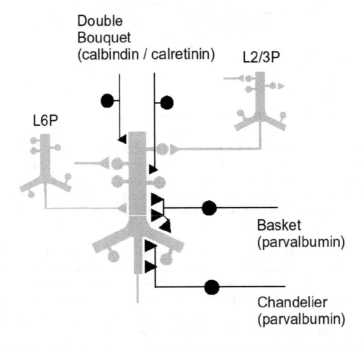

Fig. 7. Schematic showing the proposed distinction between the effects of 'horizontal' and 'vertical' smooth cells [16]. Parvalbumin positive 'horizontal' smooth cells make multiple synaptic contacts on the crucial dendritic output path (apical dendrite, soma, and initial segment) of a representative superficial pyramidal neuron. The trajectories of calbindin / calretinin positive double bouquet axons pass vertically through the dendritic fields, making contact with some of them at various locations ranging from proximal to distal.

3   Differential Inhibition

The inhibitory neurons have smooth dendrites, use the neurotransmitter gamma amino butyric acid (GABA) and are found in all layers, where they form about 20% of the neurons and about 15% of the synapses. Unlike the pyramidal cells, their dendritic trees are local and usually confined to one layer. Their axonal trees are also local, and even the basket cells which have the most laterally extensive axons, spread far less laterally than the axons of spiny stellate and pyramidal neurons. However, lateral inhibition can be effected di-synaptically, via the long lateral collaterals of the spiny stellate or pyramidal cells, which have smooth neurons as a small fraction (20%) of their targets. Other smooth cell types, particularly the double bouquet cells, have axons that extend vertically through several layers in a columnar fashion.

Amongst the excitatory cells, all but the layer 6 pyramidal cells form their synapses mainly with dendritic spines. The smooth neurons, by contrast, form synapses with all parts of the neuron, including the cell soma, the initial segment of the axon, the dendritic shaft and dendritic spines (Fig. 7). However, this targeting is not indiscriminate, for the basket cells and chandelier cells target the proximal regions of pyramidal neurons (soma, proximal dendrites and axon initial segment), whereas the double bouquet cells target the distal dendrites. These two classes of smooth neurons can be distinguished on the basis of their expression of calcium-binding proteins. The basket cells and chandelier cells express parvalbumin, while the double bouquet cells express calbindin or calretinin. The reasons for this different expression of calcium-binding proteins is unknown, but the differences in the site of action of the inhibition may have important computational consequences.

The dendrites are the only sites of excitatory input to a cortical neuron and are the means whereby synaptic integration occurs, both locally on single dendrites and collectively at the soma. The double bouquet cells, whose inhibitory synapses form on the distal dendrites, can therefore act to reduce the excitatory current that flows down individual dendrites towards the soma. The soma and the axon hillock are the sites at which the action potential is initiated, and so the basket and chandelier cells can act to reduce the net spike output of the neuron. This dual control allows for separable fine tuning of both inputs and outputs.

The role of inhibition is critical for our thinking about the range of operations of the cortical circuits. Since, qualitatively the rules of connection seem common to all areas so far studied, the claim for canonical circuits, rather than a series of very different specialized circuits, seems reasonable. We have thus extended the notion of the canonical circuit towards a generic computational circuit that is strongly biologically based (Fig. 8) ([16]). In this circuit, the pyramidal cells of layers 2 and 3 are the major site of integration of the inputs arising from subcortical (e.g. thalamic) streams and from other cortical areas. Thus they can combine information arriving from the sensory periphery as well as processed information arriving from the recurrent circuits within the same area and from other cortical areas. The goal of this superficial sub-circuit is to resolve salient

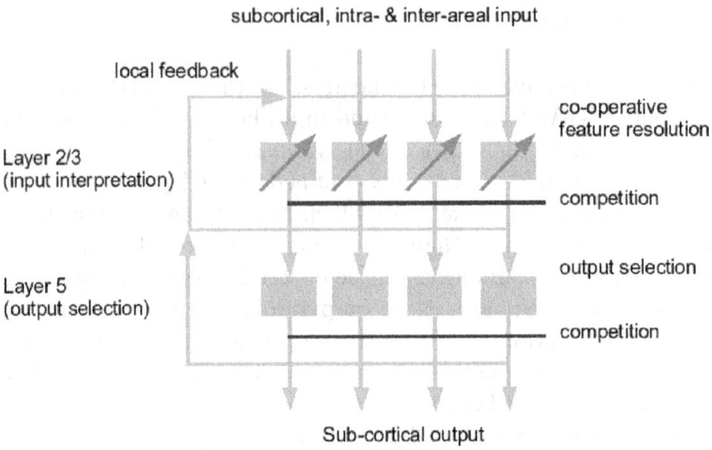

Fig. 8. Simple model of cortical processing incorporating the principal features of cortical circuits ([16]). A patch of superficial pyramidal neurons receive feedforward input from sub-cortical, inter-areal, and intra-areal excitatory sources. They also receive recurrent input from other local superficial and deep pyramidal cells. These inputs are processed by dendrites of the superficial pyramidal neurons (*upper gray rectangles*, Layer 2/3) whose signal transfer properties are adjusted dynamically by the pattern of 'vertical' smooth cell inputs (*oblique dark gray arrows*). The outputs of the superficial pyramids participate in a selection network (e.g. soft winner-take-all), mediated by the 'horizontal' smooth cells (*upper horizontal dark gray line*). These outputs of the superficial pyramids adjust the pattern of vertical smooth cell activation. In this way, the superficial layer neurons within and between patches, and within and between areas, co-operate to resolve a consistent interpretation. The layer 5 pyramids (*lower gray rectangles*) have a similar soft selection configuration (*lower dark gray line*) to process local superficial signals and decide on the output to motor structures.

features of the input. The vertically-oriented arcades of the double bouquet cell axons act to adjust dynamically the signal transfer properties of the distal dendrites, while a selection network, mediated by the inhibitory basket cells, allows a co-operative computation between the pyramidal cells to resolve the features through a soft winner-take-all (WTA) mechanism. In this way, the superficial circuit may thought to explore alternative interpretations of current data against a priori knowledge stored in its connections. The prevailing best hypothesis is held in the deep sub-circuit, where again a co-operative selection obtains consistent motor output to be signaled by the layer 5 pyramidal cells to subcortical motor nuclei.

The concept of canonical cortical circuits is a powerful one, in that it provides not only an explanation for the laminar structure of the cortex but also offers universal functions for these canonical circuits in the different cortical areas. Thus, while each cortical area has a unique set of connections to subcortical and cortical structures, nevertheless the fundamental way it acts on its inputs may be common to all areas.

Acknowledgements

As always, we acknowledge John Anderson for his able assistance. We also acknowledge the financial support of an EU grant to KM and RJD; and a Newcastle University Academic Fellowship to TB.

References

1. McHenry, H.: Tempo and mode in human evolution. PNAS **91** (1994) 6780–6786
2. Britten, R.: Divergence between samples of chimpanzee and human DNA sequences is 5%, counting indels. PNAS **99** (2002) 13633–13635
3. Passingham, R.E.: The Human Primate. Freeman (1982)
4. Douglas, R., Martin, K., Witteridge, D.: A canonical microcircuit for neocortex. Neural Comput **1** (1989) 480–488
5. Douglas, R.J., Martin, K.A.: A functional microcircuit for cat visual cortex. J Physiol **440** (1991) 735–69
6. Douglas, R.J., Martin, K.A., Whitteridge, D.: An intracellular analysis of the visual responses of neurones in cat visual cortex. J Physiol **440** (1991) 659–96
7. Phillips, C.: Intracellular records from betz cells in the cat. Q.J.Exp. Physiol. **44** (1959) 1–25
8. Li, C., Ortiz-Galvin, A., Chou, S., Howard, S.: Cortical intracellular potentials in response to stimulation of the lateral geniculate body. J. Neurophysiology (1960) 592–601
9. Dreifus, J., Kelly, J., Krnjevic, K.: Cortical inhibition and gamma-butyric acid. Exp. Brain Res. **9** (1969) 137–154
10. Fuentealba, P., Crochet, S., Timofeev, I., Steriade, M.: Synaptic interactions between thalamic and cortical inputs onto cortical neurons in vivo. J Neurophysiol **91** (2004) 1990–8
11. Douglas, R.J., Koch, C., Mahowald, M., Martin, K.A., Suarez, H.H.: Recurrent excitation in neocortical circuits. Science **269** (1995) 981–5
12. Somers, D.C., Nelson, S.B., Sur, M.: An emergent model of orientation selectivity in cat visual cortical simple cells. J Neurosci **15** (1995) 5448–65
13. Ben-Yishai, R., Bar-Or, R.L., Sompolinsky, H.: Theory of orientation tuning in visual cortex. Proc Natl Acad Sci U S A **92** (1995) 3844–8
14. Wang, X.J.: Discovering spatial working memory fields in prefrontal cortex. J Neurophysiol **93** (2005) 3027–8
15. Sompolinsky, H., Crisanti, A., Sommers, H.J.: Chaos in random neural networks. Physical Review Letters **61** (1988) 259–262
16. Douglas, R.J., Martin, K.A.: Neuronal circuits of the neocortex. Annu Rev Neurosci **27** (2004) 419–51
17. Gilbert, C.D.: Microcircuitry of the visual cortex. Annu Rev Neurosci **6** (1983) 217–47
18. Gilbert, C.D., Wiesel, T.N.: Functional organization of the visual cortex. Prog Brain Res **58** (1983) 209–18

19. Barone, P., Batardiere, A., Knoblauch, K., Kennedy, H.: Laminar distribution of neurons in extrastriate areas projecting to visual areas V1 and V4 correlates with the hierarchical rank and indicates the operation of a distance rule. J Neurosci **20** (2000) 3263–81

20. Binzegger, T., Douglas, R.J., Martin, K.A.: A quantitative map of the circuit of cat primary visual cortex. J Neurosci **24** (2004) 8441–53

21. Beaulieu, C., Colonnier, M.: A laminar analysis of the number of round-asymmetric and flat-symmetric synapses on spines, dendritic trunks, and cell bodies in area 17 of the cat. J Comp Neurol **231** (1985) 180–189

22. Latawiec, D., Martin, K.A., Meskenaite, V.: Termination of the geniculocortical projection in the striate cortex of macaque monkey: A quantitative immunoelectron microscopic study. J Comp Neurol **419** (2000) 306–19

Unsupervised Recognition of Neuronal Discharge Waveforms for On-line Real-Time Operation

Yoshiyuki Asai[1,5,6], Tetyana I. Aksenova[2,4], and Alessandro E.P. Villa[2,3,5,6]

[1] National Institute of Advanced Industrial Science and Technology (AIST),
Tsukuba, Japan
yoshiyuki.asai@aist.go.jp
[2] Laboratory of Preclinical Neuroscience, INSERM U318, France
tatyana.aksyonova@ujf-grenoble.fr
[3] Laboratoire de Neurobiophysique, Université Joseph Fourier Grenoble 1, France
alessandro.villa@ujf-grenoble.fr
[4] Institute of Applied System Analysis, Ukrainian Academy of Sciences
[5] Neuroheuristic Research Group, INFORGE, University of Lausanne, Switzerland
{oyasai, avilla}@neuroheuristic.org
[6] Institute for Scientific Interchange Foundation, Villa Gualino, Torino

Abstract. Fast and reliable unsupervised spike sorting is necessary for electrophysiological applications that require critical time operations (*e.g.*, recordings during human neurosurgery) or management of large amount of data (*e.g.*, recordings from large microelectrode arrays in behaving animals). We present an algorithm that can recognize the waveform of neural traces corresponding to extracellular action potentials. Spike shapes are expressed in a phase space spanned by the first and second derivatives of the raw signal trace. The performance of the algorithm is tested against artificially generated noisy data sets. We present the main features of the algorithm aimed to on-line real-time operations.

1 Introduction

The study of brain functions has been mainly performed by electrophysiological means in the past decades. There is an increasing interest in using multisite microelectrode recordings thanks to the miniaturization of the hardware. The study of cognitive functions by arrays of microelectrodes introduced in the brain of behaving animals [7] and clinical applications such as human neurosurgeries embedding a chronic electrode for deep brain stimulation [2] require a quick analysis of the biological signals. Following appropriate signal filtering the extracellular recordings correspond to the compound activity of the neurons located near the microelectrode tip. Under stationary recording conditions, it can be assumed that a neuron generates action potentials–spikes– with similar dynamics of the membrane potential. Then, the extracellularly recorded waveforms of the spikes generated by one same neuron are assumed to be nearly identical, as they depend on the type of the neuron and some environmental parameters such as the location of the neuron with respect to the microelectrode,

M. De Gregorio et al. (Eds.): BVAI 2005, LNCS 3704, pp. 29–38, 2005.

the density of the neuropil, *etc.* . This means also that different waveforms should be assumed to correspond to action potentials generated by different neurons. Spikes which are similar in shape to each other should be clusterized into an homogeneous group such that the group is assumed to include all spikes generated by one same neuron. The principal idea of spike sorting consists to detect as many groups as possible on the basis of the signal waveform analysis. The first step in most spike sorting techniques is the detection of waveforms that correspond to spikes in the raw signal. The classification of detected spikes into specific clusters requires the characterization of the shape of each spike. To this aim several procedures have been used, such as principal component analysis [8], independent component analysis [6], wavelet transform[4], and probabilistic model[5]. The classification directly corresponds to spike sorting in most algorithms, implying that these methods are well suited for off-line analysis. Critical time constraints, like those imposed by human neurosurgery aimed to select the optimal target for implanting chronic electrodes, push towards the development of on-line spike sorting techniques. Template-based spike sorting algorithms are adequate to the on-line task. However, most of the commercially available techniques of this kind require manual operation by experienced user for selection of templates, which reduce the advantages of this approach. In the present paper we present a template-based spike sorting algorithm which can recognize spikes and find templates automatically after unsupervised learning. Representative "signature" signals are defined as the spikes which are the nearest to the center of gravity of the respective clusters. Clusterization is performed with an improved heuristic version of a technique where distances between spikes are defined in the phase space spanned by the first and second derivatives of the raw signals [1].

2   Methods

2.1   Architecture of the Application

We developed a software application to implement and test our algorithm. The application is composed of two parts, *i.e.* , the computation engine and the user interface. The computation engine was written in ANSI C, and the graphical user interface was built with multi-platform compatibility on Labview 7.1 (National Instruments Corp., Austin, TX, USA). We also developed a command-line user interface written in ANSI C, which can be included for off-line batch processing. Mac OSX (10.3.6) on G5 Power Mac (Dual 2.5 GHz PowerPC G5 with 2.5 GB DDR SDRAM) and an A/D data acquisition board (NI-PCI-6250, by National Instruments) were used to develop the application.

2.2   Unsupervised Spike Recognition Algorithm

Detection of Events. The detection of the neuronal spikes in the raw signal is the first step of the algorithm. At this stage the term "spike" is ambiguous because it assumes that the algorithm can recognize what a "spike" means. In fact the algorithm cuts out segments of the raw signal which satisfy several criteria. The set of these segments should contain all potential spikes but some segments could be noisy traces that satisfy the criteria by chance. Let us call such potential spikes *events*. The first and second derivatives of the raw signal were used to detect the events. Since the method of computing derivatives has a filtering effect [1], the derivatives are less affected by noise, in particular with respect to lower frequency components that may be generated by muscles twitch or cardiac artifacts. The first and second derivatives express the underlying nonlinear dynamics of the membrane potential of neurons, which are generally described in theoretical neuron models which can reproduce neuronal discharges successfully. The trajectory of a spike in the phase space contains richer information about its dynamics than its waveform. Let us define a threshold as $m \pm k\sigma$ where m and σ represent the mean and square root of the variance of the first derivatives, respectively. k is a coefficient set by the the user. Whenever the first derivative of the raw signal crosses either the upper or lower threshold, then the threshold crossing is considered as an occurrence of an event.

Templates Selection. A segment of raw signal which represents a typical shape of an extracellularly recorded neuronal spike is referred to as a "template" in this manuscript. The spikes generated by one particular neuron are supposed to be characterized by shapes similar to the template of that neuron. In addition, the spikes of the same neuron are assumed to form an homogeneous cluster in a phase space, given a measure of dissimilarity between two spikes. Then, the number of clusters should correspond to the number of different neurons near the tip of the microelectrode that generate an action potential whose extracellular trace is large enough to be discriminated from the background noise.

A learning procedure based on an iterative computation is implemented to form clusters of detected events and to select the templates, defined as the events nearest to the center of gravity of their corresponding clusters. At the first round, an arbitrary event is taken as a provisional template. Provisional templates are assumed to converge towards "optimal" and stable templates after the following iterative procedure. The distances between the i-th event to all provisional templates are computed, such that if the i-th event fell inside a super sphere with a certain radius centered on a provisional template, the i-th event is assigned to the cluster represented by that provisional template. This test is sequentially performed for all events. Notice that in the case an event lies at the intersection of several super spheres, then that event is counted as a member of all those clusters. Conversely, in the case an event lies outside any previously described super spheres, then the event is itself considered as a new provisional template. At the end of a round of the iteration, each event nearest to the center of mass of its corresponding cluster is considered as the renewed provisional template to be used for distance calculation at the next round of the iteration. The radius of the super spheres is estimated from the distribution of the distances between all-to-all events. The first local peak of this histogram is fitted by a Gamma probability density function. Then, the distance corresponding to the peak of the fitted Gamma p.d.f. is used as the default radius, which is kept fixed throughout the iterative procedure.

Templates Optimization. The procedure of templates selection described so far did not include any *a priori* knowledge information about the waveforms of bioelectrical signals. Events with strange profiles satisfying the above described procedure could be included as potential templates until the end of the procedure, leading to the degradation of the overall performance of the algorithm. Furthermore, since the procedure allows an event to be a member of more than one cluster, several templates could be defined from clusters with overlapping events. One way to solve this problem consists to merge those clusters that represent closely related populations of signal traces. Such overall post-processing, called template optimization procedure, includes the three following steps. (1) The elimination of spurious templates consists to discard the waveforms without a clear positive peak or with a peak appearing at the extremes of the event. (2) The two nearest templates, *i.e.* those characterized by the minimal distance, are merged if their distance is less than the default radius. Thus, the two clusters associated to these templates are merged and a new template is determined by the event closest to the center of gravity of the newly formed cluster after merging. This procedure is repeated until all templates are separated by a distance larger than the default radius. (3) In the third step, the specific radius is calculated for each template based on the statistics of the events in the cluster. The specific radius is then used for spike sorting.

2.3 Spike Sorting

The above two processes, *i.e.*, templates selection and templates optimization, can be performed off-line. Spike sorting is the task applied to the data stream. It consists to associate a newly detected event with one of the templates. If the source of the data stream is the data acquisition board, the task can be performed as on-line real-time operation because spike sorting can be achieved very quickly. The distances between any new event to all templates are evaluated. In the case the shortest distance is smaller than the specific radius of the template that gives the minimal distance, then the new event is assigned to that template. Otherwise, the new event is discarded and thrown into a 'noise' cluster formed by those events not assigned to any template. According to this procedure an event can be sorted only into one cluster and double detection artifacts are avoided.

2.4 Measure of the Dissimilarity

The dissimilarity between two events $x_k(t)$ ($k = 1, 2$) was defined as the distance d_{x_1, x_2} in the phase space spanned by time, and by the first and second derivatives of the raw signal. Let $x_k^{(1)}(t)$ and $x_k^{(2)}(t)$ represent the first and second derivatives of $x_k(t)$ ($k = 1, 2$), respectively. The first and second derivatives were normalized before calculation of the distance (denoted as $\tilde{x}_k^{(1)}(t)$ and $\tilde{x}_k^{(2)}(t)$). Let us consider $W(t)$ a user-defined piecewise-linear bell-shaped weight function ranging from 0 to 1, corresponding to the knowledged weight of the 'phase' of an extracellular spike (*e.g.*, steepness of the depolarization, repolarization, after-potential hyperpolarization, *etc.*) in the sense of the neurophysiology. Let k_t be a phase shift factor. The distance was defined by the following equation

$$d_{x_1, x_2} = \sqrt{\sum_{t=0}^{T} \left\{ (\tilde{x}_1^{(1)}(t) - \tilde{x}_2^{(1)}(t + k_t))^2 + (\tilde{x}_1^{(2)}(t) - \tilde{x}_2^{(2)}(t + k_t))^2 \right\} W(t)} \quad (1)$$

We considered three measures of the distance, referred to as 'normal distance', 'minimal distance', and 'aligned distance'. In the case of *normal distance*, $k_t \equiv 0$. In the case of *minimal distance* (as defined in [1]) k_t in Eq. 1 is an integer value in [-2, 2] which gives the minimal value of

$$\sqrt{(\tilde{x}_1^{(1)}(t) - \tilde{x}_2^{(1)}(t + k_t))^2 + (\tilde{x}_1^{(2)}(t) - \tilde{x}_2^{(2)}(t + k_t))^2}, \quad k_t \in [-2, 2] \quad (2)$$

for each t. In the case of *aligned distance*, k_t in Eq. 1 corresponds to a constant value, that is a phase shift factor calculated for t at the peak of raw signal of $x_1(t)$.

3   Results

3.1   Application of Unsupervised Spike Recognition

In the application with graphical user interface (GUI) the users can select the operation mode according to the type of data stream, *i.e.*, off-line mode for the analysis of WAV formatted files that contain the raw signal, and on-line mode

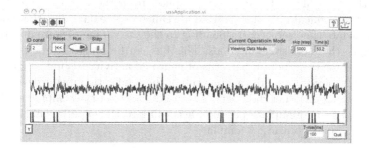

Fig. 1. Main window of the application with graphical user interface. There are several buttons to control the application at the top of the window. The waveform shows the raw signal. The small chart, just below the waveform, indicates the time series corresponding to the occurrences of detected events.

(a)   (b)

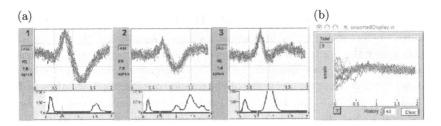

Fig. 2. (a) Status view of spike sorting. Three charts display the sorted events, grouped in different clusters. Below of each chart, the histogram of distances is displayed. (b) A window shows all events which were not classified as members of any clusters.

for the analysis of a signal recorded with the data acquisition board. Users can easily shift from one mode to the other without restarting the application. In each operation mode, the application provides three utilities: a signal viewer showing only the event detection, the template learning utility including the template-to-all error distributions and the spike sorting utility. The application with GUI can be operated by users intuitively. The main window of the application (Fig. 1) shows the waveform of the raw signal. During spikes sorting, the application provides a window to display all spikes which were sorted into clusters. Those events are superimposed on templates (Fig. 2a). In this window, the users can vary and tune the value of the template-specific radius for each template individually. An additional window displays the events which are not sorted to any clusters (Fig. 2b). The application can be used through a command line interface that provides the possibility to work in batch mode and process large amounts of data in a semi-automatic way. In this mode the application loads a configuration file that contains all required parameters and the path to access and load the WAV formatted files. The data is processed at first to find templates following the unsupervised learning procedure. Then, the application rewinds the data file and starts sorting spikes from the begin of the file. The output of the application is a formatted file called "spike data file" that contains the multivariate time series corresponding to the the timing of spike occurrences according to the inter-spike-intervals. This file can be processed for time series analysis, *e.g.* for the study of patterns of neuronal activity in clinically recorded data. The templates found during one run of the application might be of interest for spike sorting on other data sets. The users can save the templates as XML formatted files (one template per file), according to the experimental condition or date, and build libraries of templates.

3.2   Performance Test

The performance of the unsupervised spike sorting (USS) was tested with artificially generated data. The base test set, noiseless, included three types of templates (T1, T2 and T3) distributed randomly in time at a mean rate of

Table 1. Dependency of unsupervised spike sorting performance on the threshold for the event detection. Sorting errors were shown in percentage with respect to the event number involved in the test data set. σ represents the deviation of the data. Type III error never occurred and was not shown in the table. The template-specific radius was fixed at 99%. The aligned distance was used for the measure of dissimilarity of events. T1, T2 and T3 represent templates type 1, 2 and 3 of the test data set.

		Low Noise			High Noise		
Threshold		1.9σ	2σ	2.3σ	1.9σ	2σ	2.3σ
	T1	0.1	0.1	0.1	3.1	3.1	4.2
Type I error	T2	0.5	0.1	0.3	0.4	0.4	0.4
	T3	1.0	1.0	1.1	1.4	3.7	5.2
	All	0.5	0.4	0.5	1.6	2.4	3.3
	T1	0.2	0.2	0.2	0.1	0.1	0.1
Type II error	T2	0.0	0.0	0.0	0.0	0.0	0.0
	T3	0.0	0.0	0.0	0.0	0.0	0.0
	All	0.1	0.1	0.1	0.1	0.1	0.1
Total unsorted events		4660	4296	3663	5164	4474	3530

7.5 spikes/s for each template. The total duration of the data was 3 min. From this set we generated two more test sets by adding two different levels of noise, *i.e.* high noise (SNR=2.51 dB) and low noise (SNR=3.55 dB) [3]. The evaluation was based on three potential sorting mistakes. Type I error were due either to undetected events or to detected events that were not classified into the templates clusters. Type II error corresponded to noisy traces wrongly classified into one of the templates. Type III error corresponded to a misclassification, *i.e.* spikes belonging to a given template that were sorted in a wrong cluster. Table 1 shows the dependency of USS performance on the threshold for event detection. In the test set with low noise, both Type I and Type II errors occurred very seldom (0.5% and 0.1%, respectively). With higher levels of noise we observed that larger thresholds led to an increase in Type I errors (up to 5.2% for template T3) but Type II error remained as lows as 0.1%. Notice that we observed no Type III errors in the test set used here. The noise distribution also affects the measure of dissimilarity between events because this measure was based on the shape of signal trace of the events. The calculation of dissimilarity between events played an important role in the template learning since the radii used to form clusters were calculated according to the distribution of the distances between events. Since the test data was generated by adding noise uniformly to the original noiseless data set, all three types of templates in the test data were supposed to be equally distorted by noise. If the algorithm is sufficiently robust against noise, it is expected that the distribution of the distances become smoothly broader according to probability theory and the radii estimation become larger than that for noiseless test data. In this latter case there is a high peak with zero width at distance zero in the histogram of distance distribution, since all events assigned to the same cluster are identical, *i.e.*, the distance be-

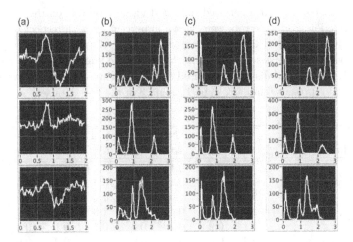

Fig. 3. Dependency of the distance distribution on the definition of the dissimilarity. (a) Signal traces of templates. The top, middle and bottom panels correspond to templates T1, T2 and T3, respectively. Panels (b), (c) and (d) show the histogram of distances calculated by the *normal distance*, *minimal distance* and *aligned distance* methods, respectively.

tween them is zero. Figure 3 shows that USS could discriminate correctly the templates T1, T2 and T3 of the test data with high level of noise and allows to compare the methods for computing the template-to-all distances. Notice three small peaks between 0 to 1 in the top panel of Fig. 3b, *i.e.* histogram calculated following *normal distance* . The events corresponding to these three peaks were very similar in waveform to each other meaning that events originally belonging to the same template in the noiseless test data were perturbed by the noise and split into three sets. This perturbation affects the estimation of the radius and provokes an unstable evaluation of dissimilarity between events. The same tendency could be seen in the bottom panel in Fig. 3b. In case the error distribution were calculated by *minimal distance* and *aligned distance* , a sharp peak appeared near to the left end of each panel (Fig. 3c and 3d) which suggested that these methods are more robust for the error estimation.

3.3   Example of Clinical Data

The unsupervised spike sorting was applied to the analysis of electrophysiological data recorded from patients with Parkinson's disease, during the surgical operation aimed to implant a microelectrode for chronic deep brain stimulation of STN in the University Hospital of Grenoble[2]. The event detection threshold was fixed at 2σ. The aligned distance was used for the measure of dissimilarity of events, and the template-specific radius was set at 99%. Figure 4 shows templates after learning and optimization.

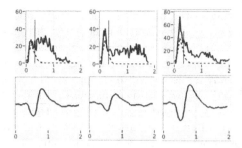

Fig. 4. Three clusters identified from an electrophysiological recording in the human subthalamic nucleus. The raw signal trace is shown in Fig. 1. Each panel in the upper row shows the statistical distribution of the distances from the template to all other events (the solid curve), and its fit by a Gamma p.d.f. (dotted curve) used to calculate the template-specific threshold indicated by a vertical tick. The raw signal profiles of the representative neural spikes of each cluster are shown in the lower row.

4   Discussion

We have presented a new algorithm for unsupervised spike sorting (USS) and demonstrated its performance with test data that included two levels of noise. The formation of clusters during the learning procedure is clearly separated from the spike sorting in the present algorithm. This architecture is important for the development of a real-time on-line oriented application. The template learning is a computationally intensive task because it requires to calculate the dissimilarity between all-to-all events. The user can define the duration of the learning interval. In the test case this duration was set equal to 30 seconds and 1395 events were detected. This means that at least $1395 \times 1394/2 = 972315$ times calculations of the dissimilarity are required. The sorting of a newly detected event does not require much calculation power (*e.g.*, the distances between the new event and, at most, six templates), and suits the requirements of on-line real-time applications.

The USS method achieved good performance levels by combining a good detection quality, avoiding detection of spurious events, and quality of classification, avoiding misclassification of detected events. Even if additional events which are not neural signals were detected, this would not cause serious trouble if those events can be eliminated by the classification procedure. Spurious events require more computation resource for processing, but this is a liminal problem with ever-growing processing power. However, if events which are neural signals are not detected, this immediately pulls down the performance of the spike sorter, because it increases the Type I error. In the case shown in Table 1, the highest error was observed for T3 in data with high noise and with large threshold. This is due to the shape of the signal trace of T3 (*c.f.* Fig. 3a bottom panel), characterized by a small elevation of the membrane potential in the phase of depolarization, leading to small increasing of the value of the first derivative.

In such case the crossing of the upper threshold might not occur and provoke the undetection of the event. If we consider the lower threshold crossing, events belonging to T3 satisfy the criterion of the event detection (data not shown). The feature of selecting upper threshold crossing, lower threshold crossing, or both of them, was already implemented in the proposed USS application. It was shown that minimal and aligned distances as the definition of the dissimilarity between events could provide good result with robustness against noise. From the viewpoint of the required computation resources, the calculation with the minimal distance took about 1.5 times longer processing time than the one with the aligned distance. Since we aimed at developing real-time on-line USS application the dissimilarity defined by the aligned distance was preferred as it provided good performance and faster computation.

Acknowledgment. The authors wish to thank Dr. Jan Eriksson and Dr. Javier Iglesias for technical suggestions. This research was partly supported by the Canon Foundation in Europe Research Fellowship, and JSPS Research Fellowships for Young Scientists No. 0407735.

References

1. Aksenova TI, Chibirova O, Dryga AO, Tetko IV, Benabid Al, Villa AEP. An unsupervised automatic method for sorting neuronal spike waveforms in awake and freely moving animal. Methods (2003) 30: 178–187.
2. Benabid AL, Pollak P, Gross C, Hoffmann D, Benazzouz A, Gao DM, Laurent A, Gentil M, Perret J. Acute and long-term effects of subthalamic nucleus stimulation in Parkinson's disease. Stereotact Funct Neurosurg (1994) 62: 76–84.
3. Chibirova OK, Aksenova TI, Benabid A-L, Chabardes S, Larouche S, Rouat J, Villa AEP. Unsupervised Spike Sorting of extracellular electrophysiological recording in subthalamic nucleus of Parkinsonian patients. BioSystems (2005) 79: 159–171.
4. Letelier JC, Weber PP. Spike sorting based on discrete wavelet transform coefficients. Journal of Neuroscience Methods (2000) 101: 93–106.
5. Lewicki MS. Bayesian modeling and classification of neural signals. Neural Comp (1994) 6: 1005–1030.
6. Takahashi S, Anzai Y, Sakurai Y. A new approach to spike sorting for multi-neuronal activities recorded with a tetrode – how ICA can be practical. Neuroscience Research (2003) 46: 265–272.
7. Villa AEP, Tetko IV, Hyland B, Najem A. Spatiotemporal activity patterns of rat cortical neurons predict responses in a conditioned task. Proc. Natl. Acad. Sci. USA (1999) 96: 1006–1011.
8. Zhang PM, Wu JY, Zhoub Y, Liang PJ, Yuan JQ. Spike sorting; Template-matching; χ^2-Test; Overlapping; Principal component analysis; Subtractive clustering. Journal of Neuroscience Methods (2004) 135: 55–65.

Neural Connectivity and Dynamical Regimes of Neural Activity in a Network of Interactive Populations

Roman Borisyuk[1,2]

[1] Centre for Theoretical and Computational Neuroscience,
University of Plymouth, Plymouth, PL4 8AA, UK
`rborisyuk@plymouth.ac.uk`
[2] Institute of Mathematical Problems in Biology of the Russian Academy of Sciences,
Pushchino, Russia, 142290

Abstract. We study the dynamics of neural activity in networks of interactive neural populations with periodic forcing. Two extreme cases of connection architectures are considered: (1) regular and homogeneous grid with local connections and (2) sparse random coupling. In the network of the first type, a propagating wave has been found for excitatory-to-excitatory local connections. It was shown that in the network with random excitatory and inhibitory connections about 60% of neural populations work in the oscillatory regime and some of these oscillations are synchronous. We discuss the regime of partial synchronization in the context of the cortical microcircuit.

1 Introduction

Rhythms, waves and synchronization of neural activity have been observed in different brain structures for many years (e.g. [7, 10]). Oscillations and/or synchronization accompany sensory processing such as visual recognition, auditory processing, and odor detection (e.g. [1, 8, 11]). Behavioral data also show oscillations (e.g. [2]). The state of awareness, for example, can be related to wave patterns (e.g. [15]).

Current theories and models of information processing in the brain include those that postulate that neurodynamics of interactive populations, rhythms, and synchronization of neural activity play a fundamental role (e.g. [12, 18]). The principle of synchronization of neural activity is also used as a basic hypothesis when modeling the associative memory (e.g. [4]); feature binding (e.g. [3]) and attention (e.g. [5]).

In this paper we study the relationship between the connection architecture and neural dynamics of a network, a correspondence between the coupling structure of neural elements and the functional behavior of the network. We consider two different cases of connection architecture:

(1) Homogeneous local connections on a grid. In this case we have found several interesting dynamical regimes: wave propagation, bump-like activity, persistent activity caused by a short stimulus presentation.

(2) Sparse random coupling. In this case we have found that about 60% of neural populations work in an oscillatory regime of irregular (chaotic) oscillations and the other approximately 40% of neural populations demonstrate stable sta-

M. De Gregorio et al. (Eds.): BVAI 2005, LNCS 3704, pp. 39–48, 2005.
© Springer-Verlag Berlin Heidelberg 2005

tionary neural activity. Forcing by a periodic input signal results in a regime of **partial synchronization**: some oscillators are synchronized (phase locked) with the input signal and other oscillators either demonstrate stationary activity or anti-phase oscillations.

We hypothesize that the regime of partial synchronization is extremely important for the modeling of microcircuits, which are the main building blocks of information processing in the brain. Let us consider a neural population of excitatory and inhibitory neurons with a specific coupling architecture, connection strengths, inputs, etc. Such a neural population which performs a specific function is often called a microcircuit (cortical microcircuit, functional microcircuit, local microcircuit, cortical column, etc). A microcircuit (MC) is defined by its internal connection architecture and the external input which delivers an input signal to the MC. The MC can demonstrate different dynamical responses (specific neural activities) to the presentation of a specific set of input signals which the MC learns during the developmental stage. For example, the MC of the visual cortex, that is responsible for identification of a vertical bar, will show a high neural activity on presentation of input signals corresponding to a vertical bar or a bar with almost vertical orientation and the response rate of this MC will be significantly lower on presentation of an input signal related to another bar orientation. We suppose that according to a stimulus driven learning process, the MC adjusts its parameters to demonstrate a regime of **partial synchronization** to presentation of an appropriate set of stimuli. In the regime of partial synchronization some sub-population of neurons works coherently and the MC shows a significant increase in population firing rate. The number of coherently spiking neurons in the regime of partial synchronization should be large enough to provide a firing rate which can be identified at the next level of information processing. The detailed mechanism of adjustment of the coupling architecture, connection strengths, connection delays, and other parameters is still unclear. It is known that two processes are important: (1) the genetically defined processes of "local rules" which controls axon growth and synapse formation by markers, labels, etc; (2) a random component of developmental process which allows probabilistic choice of particular direction of axon growth and synapse formation. Of course, both processes are input driven. The resulting structure which appears during the development period depends on the interplay of these two processes and it is important to understand the relation between deterministic and stochastic components.

In fact in this paper we consider two extreme cases of connection architecture: highly organized regular and homogeneous local connections and random sparse connections and we study the dynamics of neural activity under periodic stimulation. We believe that the connection architecture of the MC includes both a sub-net with local connections and subnet with random connections. Interplay of these two sub-networks defines the resulting dynamics of neural activity. Models of interactive neural populations with different connection architectures represent an important paradigm in the description of the dynamics and synchronisation of neural activity (e.g. [9, 14]). These models shed some light on our understanding of neural mechanisms of information processing in the nervous system.

2 Model Description

We consider the Wilson-Cowan model of interactive neural populations [16]. In particular, this model of a neural oscillator contains both an excitatory neural population $E_n(t)$ and an inhibitory neural population $I_n(t)$. Let us suggest that identical oscillators are arranged in a 2D grid with local connections between neighboring oscillators of the first and second order. The dynamics of the network is described by the equations:

$$\frac{dE_n}{dt} = -E_n + (k_e - E_n) * S_e(c_1 E_n - c_2 I_n + P_n + V_n),$$

$$\frac{dI_n}{dt} = -I_n + (k_i - I_n) * S_i(c_3 E_n - c_4 I_n + W_n), \qquad n = 1,2,...,N.$$

(1)

Here c_1, c_2, c_3, c_4 are the coupling strengths between populations of the nth oscillator; P_n is the external input to excitatory population; $S_p(x) = S_p(x; b_p, \theta_p)$, $p \in \{e,i\}$ is the monotonically increasing sigmoid-type function given by the formula: $S_p(x) = 1/(1 + \exp(-b_p(x - \theta_p))) - 1/(1 + \exp(b_p \theta_p))$; $k_p = 1/S_p(+\infty)$. Parameter values are: $c_1 = 16, c_2 = 12, c_3 = 15, c_4 = 3$, $\theta_e = 4, b_e = 1.3, \theta_i = 3.7, b_i = 2$, $P_n = 1.5$ and the choice of these values corresponds to the oscillatory regime of a single neural oscillator studied in [6]. In this regime, a single neural oscillator has one attractor in two-dimensional phase space, which is a stable limit cycle.

Coupling between oscillators is described by the terms V_n and W_n which define the type of connections. For example, for **excitatory-to-excitatory** connections these terms are:

$$V_n = \beta \sum_{j \in N_n^1} E_j + \alpha \sum_{j \in N_n^2} E_j,$$

$$W_n = 0.$$

(2)

Here N_n^1 is a set of first order neighboring nodes of the nth excitatory population (this set includes the eight closest nodes of the grid); N_n^2 is a set of second order neighboring nodes of the nth excitatory population (this set includes the sixteen nodes of the grid which are next to the closest ones); β and α are the strengths of homogeneous connections of the first and second order respectively.

We consider the boundary conditions on the opposite sides of the grid to be identical and the resulting surface is a torus.

3 Wave Propagation in a Network of Locally Coupled Neural Oscillators

Spatio-temporal patterns of neural activity were studied for both a 1D network with local connections (a chain of oscillators) and a 2D network on the toroidal surface. It

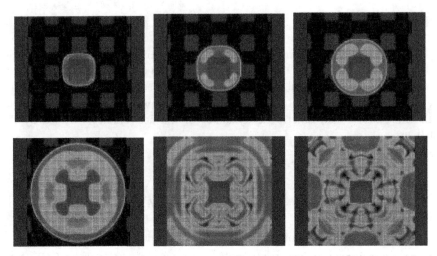

Fig. 1. 2D wave propagation. There is a constant source of oscillatory activity- a square region at the centre contains oscillators in the oscillatory mode. All other oscillators are in the regime of low stationary activity. Six moments of wave propagation on the torus (opposite sides of the grid are considered to be identical) are shown. The last frame shows a complex and irregular pattern of spatial activity.

was shown that the regime of propagating waves exists in the case of excitatory to excitatory connections. In the case of other connection types (excitatory to inhibitory, inhibitory to excitatory and inhibitory to inhibitory) the regime of propagating waves was not found.

Fig. 1 shows wave propagation over a 2D grid on the torus surface. Each oscillator receives excitatory local connections from excitatory populations of oscillators allocated in the first and second order nodes (equations 1 and 2). External input to each oscillator is chosen to produce a low stationary activity ($E_n = 0$) in independently working oscillators ($P_n = 0.8$) and this means that the total grid is a passive medium with a low stationary activity. To initiate the wave propagation we change the external input value ($P_n = 1.5$) of oscillators allocated in a square region in the centre of the grid. This value of external input corresponds to the oscillatory regime but due to excitatory-to-excitatory connections the total excitation received by an oscillator of this group is large enough to keep this oscillator in a stationary state of high activity. Thus, the square region in the centre of the grid is considered as a source of propagating waves. It is interesting to note that inside of a propagating wave, neural activity has a complex and fast changing structure (e.g. see left-bottom frame in Fig. 1). On the boundary, the wave interacts with itself and this result in a complex spatial pattern of neural activity. Fig. 1 shows activities of excitatory populations at 6 sequential time steps. A video clip of the propagating wave is available from the following webpage: http://www.tech.plym.ac.uk/soc/staff/roman/home2.htm.

The wave's speed and distance of propagation depends on strengths of local connections (α, β). For example, in the case of weak coupling, the wave propagates a short distance only, the wave's amplitude decays, and the wave disappears. In the case of medium values of connection strengths, the speed of wave propagation can be

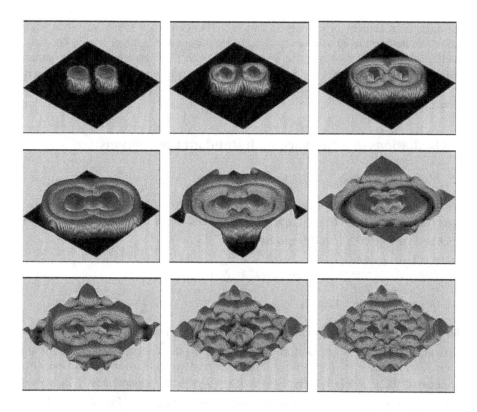

Fig. 2. 2D waves propagation and interaction. There are two identical sources of propagating waves. Wave interaction results in a complex pattern of spatial activity. Different frames show spatial activity patterns of excitatory populations at sequential times.

very slow and a bump-like structure of neural activity exists for a long time. This kind of persistent activity is traditionally considered as a model of short-term memory.

Wave propagation is stimulus-dependent and it has been found that short time stimulation can also result in the appearance of a permanent source of propagating waves. Let us suppose that similar to the stimulation procedure described above, the external input to the oscillators allocated in the central square region of the grid have been changed to $P_n = 1.5$ for a short time only and after that they have been returned to $P_n = 0.8$, which corresponds to a low stationary activity of a single oscillator. Thus, a short-term stimulation has been applied to a passive medium and it results in the emergence of persistent spatio-temporal mode of propagating waves.

Fig. 2 shows interaction of two propagating waves. As in Fig. 1, we consider the 2D grid on the torus with local connections of excitatory-to-excitatory type and the same parameter values. The only difference is that in this case we have two permanent sources of propagating waves. The waves demonstrate non-linear interaction resulting in the appearance of a complex spatial pattern of neural activity. Fig. 2 shows activities of excitatory populations progressing with time. Two propagating waves interact and generate a ring-like structure (see right-top frame in Fig.2) which surrounds both sources of propagating waves. This combined source of propagating waves can be considered as a new source of propagation of a larger wave. The wave reaches the boundaries of the grid and interacts with itself giving rise to a complex spatio-temporal pattern. A video clip of propagating and interacting waves is available from the following webpage: http://www.tech.plym.ac.uk/soc/staff/roman/home2.htm.

4 Oscillations in a Network with Random Connections

4.1 Model Description

Here we consider a neural network of interactive Wilson-Cowan neural populations $x_n(t)$ with all-to-all connections and random values of connection strength, external input, and parameters of the sigmoid function:

$$\frac{dx_n}{dt} = -x_n + (k - x_n) * S(\sum_{j=1,N} \alpha_j^n x_j + P_n),$$

$$n = 1,2,...,N.$$

(3)

Here α_j^n is the connection strength from population j to population n, values of these parameters are random and uniformly distributed in the interval $[-20,20]$; P_n is the external input to the nth population, values are random and uniformly distributed in the interval $[0,2]$; $k = 1/S(+\infty)$; $S(x) = S(x;b_n,\theta_n)$ is the monotonically increasing sigmoid-type function which has already been used in Equation (1); values of b_n are random and uniformly distributed in the interval $[1,7]$; values of θ_n are random and uniformly distributed in the interval $[2,10]$, $N=300$.

   Connection strength values are distributed in a range which includes both positive and negative values, therefore the influences of the nth neural population to other populations are either excitatory or inhibitory. We do not prescribe specific connections which can result in oscillatory activity; instead we expect that oscillations will emerge as a result of the interplay between excitation and inhibition.

4.2 Distribution of the Fraction of Oscillating Populations

Simulation of neural activity of a network with random parameters shows that each neural population has either stationary neural dynamics or irregular oscillations. Fig. 3 (left frame) shows typical dynamics of neural populations in the network with random parameters. The right frame in Fig. 3 shows the dynamics of the network with random and sparse connections. In this case 97% of randomly selected connections have been deleted (the connection strength has been made equal to zero). It is interesting to note that increased sparseness results in a more regular oscillatory pattern.

   Let μ be the fraction of populations with an oscillatory dynamical regime (regular or irregular) in a network with all-to-all connections and random parameters. This characteristic μ is a random variable because any repetition of simulation generates a

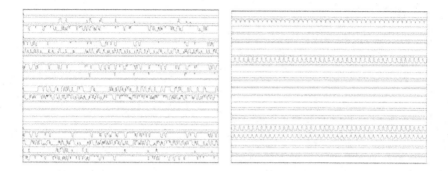

Fig. 3. Examples of neural activity dynamics in the network with random parameters (*left frame*). *The right frame* shows dynamics in the network with sparse random parameters.

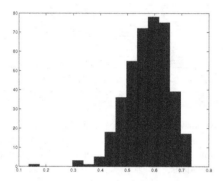

Fig. 4. The distribution of the fraction of oscillating populations in the network with randomly selected connections, input parameter values, and parameters of the sigmoid function

new value of μ. The histogram of the μ-distribution is shown in Fig. 4. The mean of random variable is 0.6 and it means that about 60% of neural populations demonstrate the oscillatory regime and the other populations (about 40%) show stationary activity.

4.3 Partial Synchronization by Periodic Input

Here we consider the model of interactive populations with all-to-all connections and randomly chosen parameters (equation 3). Connection strengths α_j^n are random and uniformly distributed in the interval [-2,2]; P_n are random and uniformly distributed in the interval [0,0.5] for all oscillators except ten oscillators (shown in the central part in Fig. 5) which have the periodic input $P(t) = 10 * \sin(2 * \pi * t / 40)$; b_n are random and uniformly distributed in the interval [1,7]; values of θ_n are random and uniformly distributed in the interval [2,10], $N=200$.

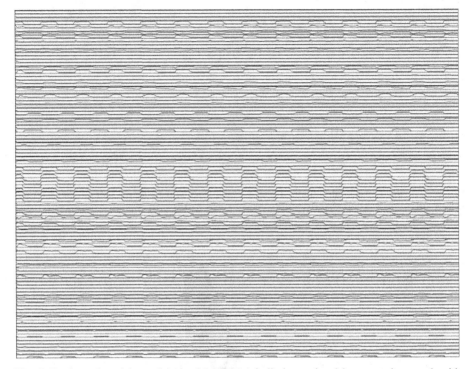

Fig. 5. Regime of partial synchronization with periodic input signal in a neural network with very sparse random connections. Periodic forcing was applied to ten neural populations (*in the centre of the frame*) and some populations work in phase with the periodic signal. There are anti-phase and quiescent populations.

We study the dynamics of this network with random connections and a strong periodic forcing with period 40 ms. We have found that the dynamics of any population belongs to one of the following 4 classes: (1) regular periodic oscillations in-phase with the periodic input signal; (2) regular periodic anti-phase oscillations; (3) irregular chaotic dynamics without any visible period; (4) steady state activity. Neural populations which demonstrate in-phase oscillations are in the regime of partial synchronization. We have found that decreasing the number of connections (or increasing sparseness) results in decreasing the number of irregular oscillations. Fig. 5 shows dynamics of 100 neural populations with random connections, periodic forcing, and 90% of connection strengths equal to zero. In this case of very sparse connections, the regime of partial synchronization is easily visible. It is interesting to note that repetition of the same simulation with different initial conditions and other parameters fixed demonstrates another pattern of partial synchronization.

5 Discussion

The study of spatio-temporal patterns of neural activity is a fundamental problem of theoretical neuroscience. For example, it is important to investigate how the spatio-temporal activity depends on coupling parameters and external stimulation. Such study can be considered as an initial step in the investigation of neural network learning procedures which adjust parameter values in such a way that the resulting pattern of spatio-temporal activity corresponds to a desirable pattern. Here we have studied the dynamical behavior of average activity of neural populations. This type of model's activity is related to EEG experimental recordings as well as to local field potential experiments.

To study spatio-temporal patterns we use an approach of discrete interactive neural populations allocated in the grid nodes (compare with other approaches based on intergro-differential equation model [13, 17]). Advantages of our approach are: (1) easy to implement; (2) requires a low computational power; (3) flexible in adjustment of connection types (connections between excitatory and inhibitory populations). Our study of wave propagation shows that a wave propagates in the system of interactive oscillators in the case of excitatory-to-excitatory connections. Similar simulations with other connection types show that the wave's amplitude rapidly decays (compare with [14]).

Simulations of neural networks with random connections show that even in the case of random and sparse connections, the oscillatory regime is typical for many neural populations. The regime of partial synchronization has been found in networks with random and sparse connections and periodic forcing. We consider this result to be a first step in modelling of the MC development. Further process of self-organization of connection architecture and parameter calibration by stimulus driven learning will result in the appearance of the regime of partial synchronization of a significant amount of neural populations as a MC's response to the presentation of a specific stimulus. These results will be discussed in another publication.

References

1. Ahissar, M., Ahissar, E., Bergman, H., Vaadia E.: Encoding of sound-source location and movement: activity of single neurons and interactions between adjacent neurons in the monkey auditory cortex. J Neurophysiol. 67 (1992) 203-215
2. Bertrand, O., Tallon-Baudry, C.: Oscillatory gamma activity in humans: a possible role for object representation. Int J Psychophysiol. 38 (2000) 211-23
3. Borisyuk, G., Borisyuk, R., Kazanovich, Y., Strong, G.: Oscillatory neural networks: Modeling binding and attention by synchronization of neural activity In: Brown, V., Levine, D., Shirey, T. (eds.): Oscillations in Neural Systems, Lawrence Erlbaum Assoc. Inc. (1999) 261-283
4. Borisyuk, R., Hoppensteadt, F.: Memorizing and recalling spatial-temporal patterns in an oscillator model of the hippocampus BioSystems. 48 (1998) 3-10
5. Borisyuk, R., Kazanovich, Y.: Oscillatory model of attention-guided object selection and novelty detection. Neural Networks. 17 (2004) 899-915
6. Borisyuk, R.M., Kirillov, A.B.: Bifurcation analysis of a neural network model. Biol. Cybernet., 66 (1992) 319-325
7. Castelo-Branco, M., Goebel, R., Neuenschwander, S., Singer, W.: Neural synchrony correlates with surface segregation rules. Nature. 405 (2000) 685–689

8. Fries, P., Schroeder, J.-H., Roefsema, P.R., Singer W., Engel A.K.: Oscillatory neural synchronisation in primary visual cortex as a correlate of stimulus selection. J. Neurosci. 22 (2002) 3739-3754

9. Golomb, D., Ermentrout, G.B.: Effects of delay on the type and velocity of travelling pulses in neuronal networks with spatially decaying connectivity. Network. 11 (2000) 221-246

10. Gray, C.M., Konig, P., Engel, A.K., Singer, W.: Oscillatory responses in cat visual cortex exhibit intercolumnar synchronisation which reflects global stimulus properties. Nature. 388 (1989) 334-337

11. Laurent, G., Stopfer, M., Friedrich, R.W., Rabinovich, M.I., Volkovskii, A., Abarbanel H.D.I.: Odor encoding as an active, dynamical process: experiments, computation, and theory. Annu. Rev. Neurosci. 24 (2001) 263-297

12. Loebel, A., Tsodyks, M.: Computation by ensemble synchronization in recurrent networks with synaptic depression. J Comput Neurosci. 13 (2002) 111-24

13. Pinto, D., Ermentrout, B. Spatially structured activity in synaptically coupled neuronal networks: I. Travelling fronts and pulses. SIAM J Appl Math. 62 (2001) 206-225

14. Rinzel, J., Terman, D., Wang, X.J., Ermentrout, B.: Propagating activity patterns in large-scale inhibitory neuronal networks Science 279 (1998) 1351-1355

15. Wexler, M. Waves of visual awareness. Trends Cogn Sci. 5 (2001) 417

16. Wilson, H., Cowan, J.: Excitatory and inhibitory interactions in localized populations of model neurons. Biophys. J, 12 (1972) 1-24

17. Wilson, H., Cowan, J.: A mathematical theory of the functional dynamics of cortical and thalamic nervious tissue. Kybernetik. 13 (1973) 55-80.

18. Winfree, A.T.: On emerging coherence. Science. 298 (2002) 2336-2337

Signal Transmission and Synchrony Detection in a Network of Inhibitory Interneurons

Angelo Di Garbo, Alessandro Panarese, Michele Barbi, and Santi Chillemi

Istituto di Biofisica CNR, Sezione di Pisa,
Via G. Moruzzi 1, 56124 Pisa, Italy
{angelo.digarbo, alessandro.panarese, michele.barbi,
santi.chillemi}@pi.ibf.cnr.it
http://www.pi.ibf.cnr.it

Abstract. Fast Spiking GABAergic interneurons, also coupled through gap junctions too, receive excitatory synaptic inputs from pyramidal cells and a relevant problem is to understand how their outputs depend on the timing of their inputs. In recent experiments it was shown that Fast Spiking interneurons respond with high temporal precision to synaptic inputs and are very sensitive to their synchrony level. In this paper this topic is investigated theoretically by using biophysical modelling of a pair of coupled Fast Spiking interneurons. In particular it is shown that, in agreement with the experimental findings, Fast Spiking interneurons transmit presynaptic signals with high temporal precision. Moreover, they are capable of reading and transferring high frequency inputs while preserving their relative timing. Lastly, a pair of Fast Spiking interneurons, coupled by both inhibitory and electrical synapses, behaves as a coincidence detector.

1 Introduction

Experimental findings suggest that networks of inhibitory interneurons contribute to brain rhythms by synchronizing their firing activities and that of the principal cells [1, 2]. Moreover, it was found that they are interconnected also by electrical synapses and play a key role in the emergence of network oscillations [3-14, 22]. Here, by starting from the experimental results reported in [4] and by using a biophysical modelling of each Fast Spiking (FS) interneuron we study the spike transmission properties of these cells.

2 Methods

FS interneurons are not capable of generating repetitive firing of arbitrary low frequency [15]; thereby they have type II excitability property [16]. Experiments carried on FS cells reveal that they have high firing rates (up to ~ 200 Hz), average resting membrane potential of $-72\ mV$ and input resistance ~ 89 $M\Omega$; their action potential has a mean half-width ~ 0.35 ms, average amplitude ~ 61 mV and after-hyperpolarization amplitude ~ 25 mV [3-5, 17, 22].

M. De Gregorio et al. (Eds.): BVAI 2005, LNCS 3704, pp. 49–58, 2005.

2.1 Model Description

Our HH-like biophysical model of an FS interneuron, well accounting for the features quoted above, is defined by the following equations:

$$CdV/dt = I_E - g_{Na} m^3 h(V-V_{Na}) - g_K n(V-V_K) - g_L (V-V_L),$$ (1a)

$$dx/dt = (x_\infty - x) / \tau_x, x_\infty = \alpha_x / (\alpha_x + \beta_x), \tau_x = 1 / (\alpha_x + \beta_x), (x = m, h, n),$$ (1b)

where $C = 1\mu F/cm^2$ and I_E is the external stimulation current. The maximal specific conductances and the reversal potentials are respectively: $g_{Na} = 85$ mS/cm^2, $g_K = 70$ mS/cm^2, $g_L = 0.15$ mS/cm^2 and $V_{Na} = 60$ mV, $V_K = -95$ mV, $V_L = -72$ mV. The kinetic of the Na^+ current was modeled by using recordings from hippocampal FS interneurons [18]: $m_\infty(V) = 1/\{1+exp[-(V+V_m)/k_m]\}$, $h_\infty(V) = 1/\{1+exp[(V+V_h)/k_h]\}$, $\tau_m(V) = 0.03+1/\{3exp[(V+V_m)/13]+ 3exp[-(V+V_m)/17]\}$, $\tau_h(V) = 0.5+1/\{0.026exp[-(V+V_m)/8]+ 0.026exp[(V+V_m)/7]\}$, with $V_m = 25.1$ mV, $V_h = 58.3$ mV, $k_m = 11.5$ mV, $k_h = 6.7$ mV. The kinetics of the fast-delayed rectifier component of potassium current was taken from [19]: $\alpha_n = [-0.019(V-4.2)]/\{exp[-(V-4.2)/6.4]-1\}$, $\beta_n = 0.016exp(-V/v_{AHP})$. The value of parameter v_{AHP} was modified to get an after-hyperpolarization amplitude of the action potential of ~ 25 mV: the adopted value was $v_{AHP} = 13$ mV. In this model the onset of periodic firing occurs through a subcritical Hopf bifurcation for $I_E \approx 1.42$ $\mu A/cm^2$ with a well defined frequency (~ 14 Hz), according to type II excitability property (data not shown) [16].

2.2 Synaptic Coupling Modeling

The electrical and chemical synapses are modeled as follows. The inhibitory postsynaptic current at time $t > t_N$ is defined by $I_{Sy}(t) = g_{Sy} s_T(t) (V_{Post}(t)- V_{Rev}) = g_{Sy} \Sigma_j s(t - t_j)$ $(V_{Post}(t) - V_{Rev})$, where g_{Sy} is the specific maximal conductance of the synapse (in mS/cm^2 unit), $s(t) = [exp(-t/\tau_{Decay}) - exp(-t/\tau_{Rise})]/ Max_{\{t\}}[exp(-t/\tau_{Decay}) - exp(-t/\tau_{Rise})]$, t_j ($j = 1, 2,...,N$) are the times at which the presynaptic neuron generated spikes, τ_{Decay} and τ_{Rise} are the decay and rise time constants of the inhibitory postsynaptic current. The electrical synapse is modeled as $I_{El} = g_{El} (V_{Pre} - V_{Post})$, where g_{El} is the maximal conductance of the gap junction (in mS/cm^2 unit). In the following the adopted conductance values for the inhibitory and electrical synapses are (for both cells), respectively, $g_{Sy} = 0.1$ mS/cm^2 and $g_{El} = 0.02$ mS/cm^2.

2.3 Synaptic Background Activity Modeling

To reproduce the in vivo conditions the synaptic background activity was modeled according to [20]. The total noisy synaptic current is the sum of two currents, one excitatory and the other inhibitory, described as follows:

$$I_{Syn}(t) = g_e (V(t)- V_e)+ g_i (V(t)- V_i),$$ (2a)

$$dg_{e,i}(t)/dt = -(g_{e,i}(t) - g_{e0,i0})/\tau_{e,i} +D_{e,i}^{1/2} W_{e,i},$$ (2b)

where $g_{e0,i0}$ are average conductances, $\tau_{e,i}$ are time constants, $D_{e,i}$ are noise diffusion coefficients, $\sigma_{e,i}^2 = 0.5D_{e,i}\tau_{e,I}$ and $W_{e,i}$ denotes Gaussian white noise of unit standard deviation and zero mean. The values of the other parameters are: $V_e = 0$ mV, $V_i = -75$ mV, $g_{e0} = 0.0121$ mS/cm^2, $g_{i0} = 0.0573$ mS/cm^2, $\sigma_e = 0.025$ mS/cm^2, $\sigma_i = 2.5\sigma_e$, $\tau_e = 10.49$ ms, $\tau_i = 2.728$ ms [20].

3 Results

Let us first study how excitatory synaptic inputs affect the firing rate of the FS cell model in the presence of synaptic background bombardment. The excitatory postsynaptic current (EPSC), which depolarizes the FS interneuron (see panel a of figure 1), is modeled as follows: $I_{EPSC}(t) = g_{EPSC}[exp(-t/\tau_{Decay}) - exp(-t/\tau_{Rise})]/Max_{\{t\}}[exp(-t/\tau_{Decay}) - exp(-t/\tau_{Rise})]$. The parameter values, $\tau_{Rise} = 0.4$ ms and $\tau_{Decay} = 2$ ms, are chosen to mimic the experimental time course of the EPSC from a pyramidal cell to an FS cell [4]. To increase the discharge rate arising from the synaptic background activity, the FS cell is injected with constant depolarizing current to get a firing frequency of ~ 22 Hz in absence of EPSC (see panel b of figure 1). As expected, the presence of EPSCs lead to increasing the discharge rate of the postsynaptic cell and this can be seen by inspecting the panels c) and d) of figure 1. The spike histogram exhibits a sharp peak located just to the right of the peak of the EPSC (panel e). The estimated latency between the peak of the EPSC and that occurring in the histogram is ~ 2 ms and is of the same order of magnitude as the experimental one of ~ 1.7 ms [4]. Each spike histogram reported in this paper was obtained as follows: the times of occurrence of spikes t_j^{Fir} ($j=1,2,...,N$), falling in a given time window were recorded for all trials (N_{Trials}), then the histogram of the t_j^{Fir} values was built by using a bin size of 0.2 ms (with N up to 33000). The impact of the EPSC on the postsynaptic firing rate was quantified by the temporal precision of spike transmission according to [4]. With this aim in mind we fitted the shape of the peak of the spike histogram by a Gaussian function and the spike precision was defined as twice the standard deviation of this distribution. Such a measure is shown in panel f) of figure 1 against the amplitude of the EPSC showing that the precision of spike transmission improves as g_{EPSC} increases (the estimated average value of spike precision was ~ 1.02 ms ± 0.3 ms). These findings agree with the corresponding experimental results [4]. In conclusion these results imply that FS cells are capable of representing the pattern of the presynaptic spikes with high fidelity as suggested in [4].

Now, to investigate the response to high frequency inputs, the cell is injected with two EPSCs separated by a time delay of 4 ms, and the results are displayed in the left panel of figure 2. The spike histogram exhibits two distinct peaks and this means that the cell model is able to transmit high frequency signals (up to 250 Hz) while preserving the presynaptic timing. The height of the second peak is smaller than that of the first one, and this phenomenon is a direct manifestation of paired-pulse depression (in agreement with experimental results). By increasing the time delay between the two pulses the difference between the two heights decreases (data not shown). As shown in [4] the velocity of membrane depolarization can affect the probability that one cell generates a spike. To reproduce this phenomenon, the FS cell model was injected with two EPSCs having different rise time constants and the results are shown in the right panel of figure 2. The peak corresponding to the slow rise EPSC is lower and larger

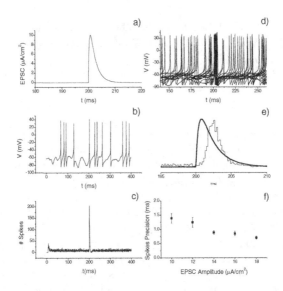

Fig. 1. Transmission properties of excitatory presynaptic inputs by the FS cell model. a) Time course of the EPSC; b) spike firing of the FS interneuron model in the presence of synaptic background activity; c) spike histogram for a cell receiving an EPSC pulse at time $t = 200$ *ms* with $N_{Trials} = 250$; d) superposition of the time courses of the cell membrane potentials obtained in several trials; e) latency between the EPSC peak (thick line) and that of the histogram; f) spike precision against the EPSC amplitude. For panels (a-e) it is $g_{\text{EPSC}} = 10 \ \mu A/ \ cm^2$.

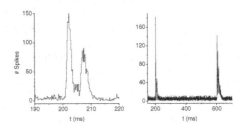

Fig. 2. Spike histograms of the FS cell output. Left: $\tau_{\text{Rise}} = 0.4 \ ms$, $\tau_{\text{Decay}} = 2 \ ms$, the time delay between the two EPSC pulses is 4 *ms*. Right: the time delay between the pulses is 400 *ms*, but they have different rise time constants. For the first pulse (at $t = 200 \ ms$) the parameters values of the EPSC are $\tau_{\text{Rise}} = 0.4 \ ms$, $\tau_{\text{Decay}} = 6 \ ms$, for the other one (at $t = 600 \ ms$) they are $\tau_{\text{Rise}} = 5.8 \ ms$, $\tau_{\text{Decay}} = 6 \ ms$. For both panels it is $g_{\text{EPSC}} = 12 \ \mu A/ \ cm^2$ and $N_{Trials} = 1500$.

than the other. This means that the spike precision depends on the rising kinetics of the presynaptic pulse: the faster the rising phase of the pulse the higher the temporal precision of spike transmission.

Also, in order to investigate how the decay time constant of the EPSC affects the transmission properties of the presynaptic inputs, the cell model is injected with

EPSCs which have different values of τ_{Decay} and for each value of this parameter the number of trials was $N_{Trials} = 1500$. When the decay time constant of the EPSC pulse is 2 *ms* the spike histogram exhibits a single peak; as τ_{Decay} increases, other peaks of lower amplitude appear (data not shown). This phenomenon arises due to the depolarizing effect of the EPSC, which now covers a larger time window. For each τ_{Decay} the time separation between these peaks is of the same magnitude and their appearance can be explained as follows. Once the cell has fired a spike there is a time interval T_{Off} (the recovery phase) where, in spite of the depolarizing effect of the EPSC, the probability that a new spike is generated is low. Obviously the value of T_{Off} depends on the kinetics of the ionic currents defining the model, and its value provides an estimation of the time separation between the peaks observed in these numerical experiments. Moreover, as τ_{Decay} increases, the corresponding T_{Off} value slightly decreases (data not shown). Therefore these results show, in agreement with the experimental results, that the kinetics of the EPSC strongly affects the transmission of the information contained in the presynaptic signals.

Within the context of neural information coding an interesting problem is to understand how the output of a population of coupled FS cells depends on the synchrony level of the inputs they receive. In fact, as experiments suggest, the synchronization of the discharges of a population of neurons could be relevant for cognitive tasks [21]. Moreover FS cells, receiving strong inputs from thalamus, could be implicated in the transfer of the sensory information to the cortex [22]. Thus, it is important to check whether FS cells behave as coincidence detectors. Recently this issue was addressed experimentally and it was shown that a pair of FS interneurons, coupled through inhibitory and electrical synapses, is sensitive to the relative timing of their inputs [4].

In particular, a time separation between the inputs of the order of 1 *msec* promotes a synchronous generation of action potentials in both cells, whereas for larger separations (~ 5 msec) the firing of one of them is strongly reduced [4]. Therefore, a pair of FS cells is capable of distinguishing synchronous from asynchronous inputs, i.e. behaves as a coincidence detector. Here the problem is approached by investigating the capability of a pair of FS cell models, connected by a single inhibitory synapse plus the electrical one (i.e. the same network architecture as that investigated experimentally [4]), to detect synchronous excitatory inputs. In this case, in keeping with the experiments, the simulations are carried out in absence of background synaptic activity. To reproduce the membrane potential fluctuations occurring in *in vitro* conditions, each cell model is injected with a Gaussian random current of small amplitude ($\sigma = 0.3 \ \mu A/cm^2$). The two EPSC pulses are of the same amplitude, but separated by a time delay Δt, with cell 1 receiving the first EPSC pulse. According to the experiment performed in [4] only cell 2 is inhibited and the results are shown in figure 3 for several Δt values. Let us first consider the case in which, in absence of any coupling, each EPSC pulse elicits a spike with probability 1. When the time delay, Δt, between the two pulses is lower than ~ 2 *msec* both cells discharge with high probability, whereas for Δt values ~ 5 *msec* the firing probability of cell 2 is close to zero. This effect is mainly due to the inhibition that cell 2 receives from cell 1. In fact, as the time delay between the pulses is further increased ($\Delta t = 18$ *msec*), the magnitude of the inhibitory input received by cell 2 is reduced and its firing rate is restored.

The overall results shown in figure 3 imply that if the inputs to the two cells occur synchronously ($\Delta t < 2$ *msec*) both cells generate action potentials. When the time interval between the pulses increases ($\Delta t > 2$ *msec*) the firing rate of cell 2 becomes smaller and smaller until cell 1 alone is discharging.

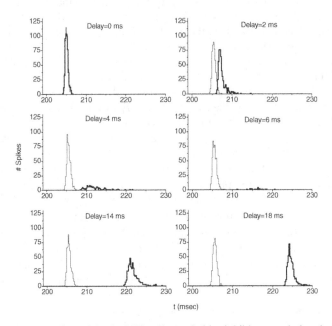

Fig. 3. Spike histograms of two identical FS cell coupled by inhibitory and electrical synapses in the presence of a time delay between the EPSC pulses. For all panels it is $g_{Sy} = 0.1 mS/cm^2$, $g_{El} = 0.02$ mS/cm^2, $g_{EPSC} = 7$ $\mu A/ cm^2$, $I_E = 0.5$ $\mu A/cm^2$, $\sigma = 0.3$ $\mu A/cm^2$ and $N_{Trials} = 500$. The rise and the decay time constants of the EPSC pulses are, $\tau_{Rise} = 0.4$ ms, $\tau_{Decay} = 2.$ ms, respectively, while the corresponding quantities for the inhibitory synapse are $\tau_{Rise} = 0.25$ ms, $\tau_{Decay} = 2.6$ ms.

This means that the network of coupled FS cells behaves as a coincidence detector when the firing probability of each cell is 1 in absence of coupling. To better understand these findings the firing probabilities of both cells are displayed in figure 4 against the time delay and in several coupling conditions. The firing probability of each cell is defined as $p = N_S / N_{Trials}$, where N_S is the total number of spikes generated by the cell during the trials. From the middle panel it follows that in absence of inhibitory coupling both cells discharge with probability one, independently of the value of the time delay between the pulses. In this case our system does not behave as a coincidence detector. However, the data displayed in the right panel of figure 4 clearly show that it is the presence of inhibitory coupling that confers the capability of behaving as a coincidence detector to the network of coupled FS cells. However, as we will see, this explanation of the behaviour of the network does not hold in general. In particular, we investigate how the network of coupled FS cells behaves in more realistic conditions: i.e. when, in the absence of coupling, the firing probability of each cell is lower than 1. With this aim in mind the amplitude of the EPSC is decreased until the firing probability of each cell, in absence of coupling, becomes ~ 0.77. The corresponding firing probabilities are displayed in figure 5 against the time delay between the two EPSC pulses. From the left panels it follows that the network behaves as a coincidence detector: both cells fire when the time delay between the two EPSC pulses is a few milliseconds (1-3 *ms*). As Δt is further increased (3 *msec* < Δt < 6-7 *msec*) the firing rate of cell 1 decreases drastically and for longer time delays the firing rate of both cells is strongly depressed. This behaviour, as can be deduced from the results reported in figure 5, is determined by the presence of the electrical coupling. A qualitative explanation of this behaviour is the following: when the electrical coupling between the two cells is on the depolarization amplitude of cell 1 reduces. This occurs because the presence of the electrical coupling lowers its input resistance.

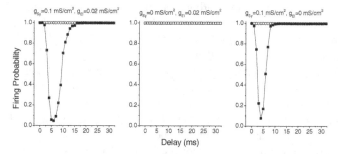

Fig. 4. Firing probabilities of a pair of identical FS cells receiving EPSC pulses of amplitude $g_{EPSC} = 7$ $\mu A/$ cm^2 separated by a variable time delay. Parameter values are the same as those used for figure 3. The values of the inhibitory and electrical coupling conductances are reported at the top of each panel. For all panels the open circles represent the firing probability of cell 1, the solid squares that of cell 2, and $N_{Trials} = 500$.

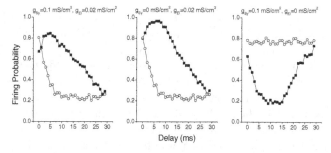

Fig. 5. Firing probabilities of a pair of identical FS cells receiving EPSC pulses of amplitude $g_{EPSC} = 5.5$ $\mu A/$ cm^2 separated by a variable time delay. The remaining parameter values as in figure 4. The values of the inhibitory and electrical coupling conductances are reported in the top of each panel. For all panels the open circles represent the firing probabilities of cell 1, while the solid squares those of cell 2, and $N_{Trials} = 500$.

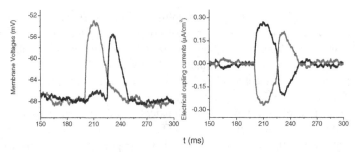

Fig. 6. Time course of the membrane potentials and of the electrical coupling currents of a pair of identical FS cells coupled by inhibitory and electrical synapses, with $g_{Sy} = 0.1 mS/cm^2$, $g_{El} = 0.02\ mS/cm^2$, $g_{EPSC} = 5.5\ \mu A/\ cm^2$, $\Delta t = 25\ msec$. Gray lines: cell 1; black lines: cell 2.

In other words when the current through the gap junction flows from cell 1 to cell 2 ($V_1 > V_2$) the membrane potential of cell 1 is less depolarized for the presence of an outward current, while that of cell 2 is more depolarized. This explain why the firing probability of cell 2 is higher than that of cell 1 for $3\ msec < \Delta t < 27\ msec$ (see left and middle panels of figure 5). Thus, the firing probability of cell 1 is smaller than that in absence of electrical coupling (see the left and right panels of figure 5). As an example, figure 6 shows the time course of the membrane potential and the electrical coupling current for both cells in the case $\Delta t = 25\ msec$ and for $N_{Trials} = 1$. It can be seen that during the depolarization phase of both cells (see the left panel) their corresponding electrical coupling currents are outward (right panel) as predicted. For Δt values higher than 27 $msec$ each cell strongly depresses the firing activity of the other cell and, as before, this occurs for the presence of the electrical coupling (see the left and middle panels of figure 5).

4   Conclusions

In this paper, by using a biophysical model of an FS interneuron, the capability of these interneurons of reading and transmitting their presynaptic inputs were investigated by simulations. Initially we studied how EPSC pulses from a pyramidal cell to an FS one affect its firing properties in the *in vivo* conditions. To do that the model cell was injected with a noisy current generated with the algorithm proposed in [20] and then we showed that, in agreement with the experimental results, an FS cell is capable of representing with high fidelity the pattern of the presynaptic spikes (see figures 1, 2, 3). In particular it was shown that both the rise and decay time constants of the EPSC affect the transmission properties of the presynaptic inputs. Moreover we found that high frequency presynaptic signals are encoded with high fidelity.

Next we investigated whether a small network of coupled FS cells is capable of distinguishing synchronous from asynchronous inputs by using the same network architecture as experimentally investigated in [4]. We found that the output of this network is sensitive to the relative timing of the inputs. In particular, when the time separation between the inputs is less than 1-2 *msec*, the probability that both cells generate action potentials is high, while for larger separations (~ 5 *msec*) the firing of one of them is strongly reduced. These simulation results suggest, in keeping with the experimental results in [4], that a network of coupled FS cell models operates as a coincidence detector.

References

1. Cobb SR, Buhl EH, Halasy K, Paulsen O, and Somogyi P. Synchronization of neuronal activity in hippocampus by individual GABAergic interneurons. Nature 378: 75–78, 1995.
2. Pouille, F. and Scanziani, M. Enforcement of temporal fidelity in pyramidal cells by somatic feed-forward inhibition. Science 293, 1159–1163, 2001.
3. Galarreta, M., & Hestrin, S. Electrical synapses between GABA-releasing neurons. Nature Neurosci., 2, 425–433, 2001.
4. Galarreta M and Hestrin S. Spike transmission and synchrony detection in networks of GABAergic interneurons. Science, 292, 2295–2299, 2001.
5. Gibson J.R., Michael Beierlein M., Connors B.W. Functional Properties of Electrical Synapses Between Inhibitory Interneurons of Neocortical Layer 4, J Neurophysiol., 93, 467–480. 2005.
6. Jonas P., Bischofberger J., Fricker D., Miles R. Interneuron Diversity series: Fast in, fast out – temporal and spatial signal processing in hippocampal interneurons, TRENDS in Neurosciences, 27, 30-40, 2004.
7. Whittington M.A., Traub R.D., Jefferys J.G. Synchronized oscillations in interneuron networks driven by metabotropic glutamate receptor activation. Nature 373:612–615, 1995.
8. Wang, X. J., Buzsaki, G. Gamma oscillation by synaptic inhibition in a hippocampal interneuronal network model. J. Neurosci. 16, 6402–6413, 1996.
9. Bartos M., Vida I., Frotscher M., Meyer A., Monyer H., Geiger J.R., Jonas P. Fast synaptic inhibition promotes synchronized gamma oscillations in hippocampal interneuron networks. PNAS, 99, 13222–13227, 2002.
10. Lewis T.J., Rinzel J. Dynamics of spiking neurons connected by both inhibitory and electrical coupling. J Comput Neurosci., 14, 283–309, 2003.
11. Bem T., Rinzel J. Short Duty cycle destabilizes a half-center oscillator, but gap junctions can restabilize the anti-phase pattern. J Neurophysiol., 91, 693–703, 2004.
12. Kopell N.,Ermentrout B. Chemical and electrical synapses perform complementary roles in the synchronization of interneuronal networks. PNAS, 101, 15482–15487, 2004.
13. Pfeuty B., Mato G., Golomb D., Hansel D. The Combined Effects of Inhibitory and Electrical Synapses in Synchrony. Neural Computation, 17, 633–670, 2005.
14. Di Garbo A., Panarese A., Chillemi S. Gap junctions promote synchronous activities in a network of inhibitory interneurons. BioSystems, 79, 91–99, 2005.
15. Erisir A., Lau D., Rudy B., Leonard C. S. Function of specific K^+ channels in sustained high-frequency firing of fast-spiking neocortical interneurons. J. Neurophysiology, 82, 2476-2489, 1999.
16. Rinzel J., Ermentrout B. Analysis of neural excitability and oscillations, Eds. Koch and Segev, Methods in neural modelling (1989), The MIT Press, Cambridge.
17. Galarreta M., Hestrin S. Electrical and chemical Synapses among parvalbumin fast-spiking GABAergic interneurons in adult mouse neocortex. PNAS, 99, 12438-12443, 2002.

18. Martina M, Jonas P. Functional differences in Na^+ channel gating between fast spiking interneurons and principal neurons of rat hippocampus. J. of Physiol., 505.3, 593-603, 1997.

19. Lien C. C., Jonas P. Kv3 potassium conductance is necessary and kinetically optimized for high-frequency action potential generation in hippocampal interneurons. J. of Neurosci., 23, 2058-2068, 2003.

20. Rudolph M., Destexhe A. The discharge variability of neocortical neurons during high-conductance states. Neuroscience, 119, 855-873, 2003.

21. Singer W. Search for coherence: a basic principle of cortical self-organization. Concepts in Neurosci. 1, 1-26, 1990.

22. Gibson J. R., Belerlein M., Connors B. W., 1999. Two networks of electrically coupled inhibitory neurons in neocortex. Nature 402, 75-79.

Stimulus-Driven Unsupervised Synaptic Pruning in Large Neural Networks

Javier Iglesias[1,3,4], Jan Eriksson[3], Beatriz Pardo[2], Marco Tomassini[1], and Alessandro E.P. Villa[1,3,4]

[1] Information Systems Department, University of Lausanne, Switzerland
{Javier.Iglesias, Marco.Tomassini}@unil.ch
http://inforge.unil.ch/
[2] Centro de Biologia Molecular Severo Ochoa, Universidad Autonoma, Madrid, Spain
bpardo@cbm.uam.es
[3] Laboratory of Neuroheuristics, University of Lausanne, Switzerland
jan@lnh.unil.ch
http://www.nhrg.org/
[4] Inserm U318, Laboratory of Neurobiophysics, University Joseph Fourier, Grenoble, France
Alessandro.Villa@ujf-grenoble.fr

Abstract. We studied the emergence of cell assemblies out of locally connected random networks of integrate-and-fire units distributed on a 2D lattice stimulated with a spatiotemporal pattern in presence of independent random background noise. Networks were composed of 80% excitatory and 20% inhibitory units with initially balanced synaptic weights. Excitatory–excitatory synapses were modified according to a spike-timing-dependent synaptic plasticity (STDP) rule associated with synaptic pruning. We show that the application, in presence of background noise, of a recurrent pattern of stimulation let appear cell assemblies characterized by an internal pattern of converging projections and a feed-forward topology not observed with an equivalent random stimulation.

1 Introduction

Massive synaptic pruning following over-growth is a general feature of mammalian brain maturation [11]. Pruning starts near time of birth and is completed by time of sexual maturation. Trigger signals able to induce synaptic pruning could be related to dynamic functions that depend on the timing of action potentials. Spike-timing-dependent synaptic plasticity (STDP) is a change in the synaptic strength based on the ordering of pre- and postsynaptic spikes. This mechanism has been proposed to explain the origin of long-term potentiation (LTP), i.e. a mechanism for reinforcement of synapses repeatedly activated shortly before the occurrence of a postsynaptic spike [8,2]. STDP has also been proposed to explain long-term depression (LTD), which corresponds to the weakening of synapses strength whenever the presynaptic cell is repeatedly activated shortly after the occurrence of a postsynaptic spike [7]. The relation

M. De Gregorio et al. (Eds.): BVAI 2005, LNCS 3704, pp. 59–68, 2005.

between synaptic efficacy and synaptic pruning [3,9], suggests that the weak synapses may be modified and removed through competitive "learning" rules. Competitive synaptic modification rules maintain the average neuronal input to a postsynaptic neuron, but provoke selective synaptic pruning in the sense that converging synapses are competing for control of the timing of postsynaptic action potentials [12,13].

This article studies the emergence of cell assemblies out of a locally connected random network of integrate-and-fire units distributed on a 2D lattice. The originality of our study stands on the size of the network, between 8,100 and 12,100 units, the duration of the experiment, 500,000 time units (one time unit corresponding to the duration of a spike), and the application of an original bio-inspired STDP modification rule compatible with hardware implementation [4]. In this study the synaptic modification rule was applied only to the exc–exc connections. This plasticity rule might produce the strengthening of the connections among neurons that belong to cell assemblies characterized by recurrent patterns of firing. Conversely, those connections that are not recurrently activated might decrease in efficacy and eventually be eliminated. The main goal of our study is to determine whether or not, and under which conditions, such cell assemblies may emerge from a large neural network receiving background noise and content-related input organized in both temporal and spatial dimensions.

2 Model

The complete neural network model is described in details in [5]. Some aspects that were not discussed in that reference are presented here, along with a sketch description of the model. Integrate-and-fire units (80% excitatory and 20% inhibitory) were laid down on a squared 2D lattice according to a space-filling quasi-random Sobol distribution. Network sizes of [90 × 90], [100 × 100], and [110 × 110] were simulated. Sparse connections between the two populations of units were randomly generated according to a two-dimensional Gaussian density function such that excitatory projections were dense in a local neighbourhood, but low probability long-range excitatory projections were allowed [5]. Edge effects induced by the borders were limited by folding the network as a torus.

All units of the network were simulated by leaky integrate-and-fire neuromimes. The state of the unit (spiking/not spiking) was a function of the membrane potential and a threshold. After spiking, the membrane potential was reset, and the unit entered an absolute refractory period set to 3 ms for excitatory units, and 2 ms for inhibitory units. Each unit received a background excitatory input (corresponding to a depolarization of 60 mV) that followed an independent and uncorrelated Poisson process of mean $\lambda = 5$ spikes/s.

It is assumed *a priori* that modifiable synapses are characterized by discrete activation levels that could be interpreted as a combination of two factors: the number of synaptic *boutons* between the pre- and postsynaptic units and the changes in synaptic conductance as a result of Ca^{2+} influx through the NMDA receptors. In the current study we attributed a fixed activation level (meaning no synaptic modification) $A_{ji}(t) = 1$, to exc–inh, inh–exc, and inh–inh synapses while activation levels were allowed to take one of $A_{ji}(t) = \{0, 1, 2, 4\}$ for exc–exc synapses, $A_{ji}(t) = 0$ meaning that the projection was permanently pruned out (see [5] for more details).

3   Stimulus Protocol

Each simulation was running for $5 \cdot 10^5$ discrete time steps (1 ms per time step), corresponding to about 8.5 minutes. After a stabilization period of 1 s without any external input, a stimulus was presented every 2 seconds. Overall this represented 250 presentations of the stimulus along one simulation run. Three stimulus durations were used: 50 ms followed by 1,950 ms without any external input, 100 ms followed by 1,900 ms without any external input, 200 ms followed by 1,800 ms without any external input. The stimulus was composed of vertical bars uniformly distributed over the 2D lattice surface, each bar being 1 column wide. The number of bars composing the stimulus was a function of the simulated network sizes: 9 bars for $[90 \times 90]$ networks, 10 bars for $[100 \times 100]$ networks, and 11 bars for $[110 \times 110]$ networks, such that the bars were always distant of 10 columns one from another and spanning all over the available surface. At each time step during stimulus presentation, the bars were simultaneously moved one column to the right, such that each bar slipped over the entire surface of the network.

The stimulus was applied only to a fraction of the population formed by excitatory units; these units are called *input units* . The number of input units used for the simulations was a ratio (i.e. 3, 5, 7, or 10%) of the initial number of excitatory units. For a $[100 \times 100]$ network, 10% of input units corresponds to 800 input units, i.e. 10% of the 80% excitatory units of the 10,000 units. The stimulus applied on a particular input unit provoked a depolarization on its membrane with amplitudes equal to 0 (i.e. no stimulation), 30, 40, 50, and 60 mV, depending on the protocol. Notice that the stimulus amplitude was selected in the beginning and did not vary during the simulations.

The three following presentation protocols were applied: (i) *'No stimulation'* : this condition corresponds to a stimulation of zero amplitude which is necessary to check computing artefacts that might be associated to the programming routines used to "stimulate" the units; (ii) *'Random stimulation'* : at each stimulus presentation, the input units were randomly chosen, such that the input units changed at any new stimulus presentation; (iii) *'Fixed stimulation'* : the input units were selected in the beginning of the simulation run and remained the same at any new stimulus presentation. The total amount of applied stimulation is equal in both random and fixed protocols.

To summarize the stimulation procedure, let us consider the following example. For each of the input units, randomly selected among the 10% of excitatory units, of a $[100 \times 100]$ network stimulated with a 100 ms stimulus, one stimulus presentation resulted in a sequence of 10 external inputs equally distributed in time every 10 ms. At the network level, each stimulus presentation corresponded to a spatiotemporal sequence characterized by 10 groups of 80 synchronously excited units stimulated 10 times during 10 ms.

4   Computer Implementation

The simulator was a custom C program that relies on the GNU Scientific Library (GSL) for random number generation and quasi-random Sobol distribution implementations. With our current implementation and setup at the University of Lausanne, a 10,000 units network simulation for a duration of 500 seconds lasted approximatively 3 hours, depending on the network global activity. We performed simulations with both fixed and random input stimulations, using the same model parameters and pseudo-random number generator seed, and compared the cell assemblies that emerged. Network activity was recorded as a multivariate time series akin of multisite multiple spike train recordings at a resolution of 1 ms. The firing pattern of each unit could be characterized by first- and second-order time domain analyses using the programs and tools accessible from the OpenAdap.Net[1] project.

The complete status of the network was dumped when the simulations were stopped, providing information on the strength of the connections after the STDP-driven synaptic plasticity and pruning. A set of custom scripts were used to extract emerged cell assemblies from the dumped status. The extracted weighted and oriented graphs were further analyzed by means of a tool built on top of the Java Universal Network/Graph Framework (JUNG[2]). Some typical graph measurements were computed, including the number of incoming projections (k_{in}, *in-degree*) and outgoing projections (k_{out}, *out-degree*) for each vertex of the graph.

5   Results

The pool of excitatory units whose incoming and/or outgoing excitatory projections were not entirely pruned and that were *not* directly depolarized by the external stimulus was identified at time $t= 500$ seconds (from the beginning of the simulation). Among the units of this pool a subset of units is selected on the basis of their connection pattern to– and from the pool itself. The units with at least three strong incoming ($k_{in} \geq 3$) and three strong outgoing projections ($k_{out} \geq 3$) within the pool are dubbed *strongly interconnected units*   (*SI*-units).

The activity of all the *SI*-units was affected by the *fixed stimulation*   presentation. Fig. 1 shows the response of two *SI*-units to an external stimulus lasting 200 ms, during the fixed stimulus presentation. About 22% of the *SI*-units were strongly inhibited during the stimulus presentation (e.g. Fig. 1a), despite the fact that the stimulus was delivered only to excitatory units. This effect is due to the activity of the local inhibitory units that receive excitatory projections from

---

[1] http://www.openadap.net/

[2] http://jung.sourceforge.net/

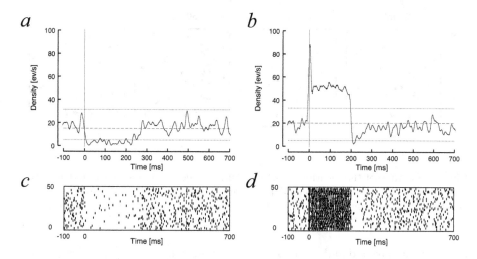

Fig. 1. Response of two strongly interconnected sample units to 50 presentations of the *fixed stimulation* between time $t = 450$ and $t = 500$ seconds from the simulation start. Network size: $[100 \times 100]$; background activity: 5 spikes/s; stimulus duration: 200 ms; stimulus intensity: 60 mV; ratio of input units: 10%; *fixed stimulation* protocol. *(a, b):* peri-event densities (PSTH) for the last 50 presentations of the stimulus; smoothed with a Gaussian kernel, bin=5ms. *Dashed line* corresponds to the mean firing rate; *dotted lines* represent the 99% confidence limits assuming a Poissonian distribution. Time zero corresponds to the stimulus onset; *(c, d):* corresponding raster plots.

the input units. The peristimulus histogram of the other *SI*-units showed that the firing rate strongly increased during the stimulus presentation (e.g. Fig. 1b) with a "primary-like" response pattern, despite the fact that none of the units belonging to this pool was directly stimulated.

The effect of the different stimulation protocol was complex. The overall number of *SI*-units found in absence of stimulation was similar to the number of *SI*-units found with *random stimulation* ($n \approx 400$, 6% of excitatory units not directly stimulated). In the *fixed stimulation* protocol, the number of *SI*-units was much smaller (about 2%), but depended on the stimulus-induced depolarization amplitude (Fig. 2). Conversely, in the *random stimulation* protocol condition, we did not observe a significant change of the number of *SI*-units in response to stimulus intensity.

During the process of pruning only the modifiable connections that kept a sufficient level of activity driven by the STDP rule could "survive". Then, the first step for searching an oriented topology after 500 seconds consisted to detect the *excitatory neighbourhood* of the *SI*-units. This neighbourhood corresponds to the set of those excitatory units that send a projection to the *SI*-units, receive a projection from the *SI*-units, or both send and receive projections. Thus, this neighbourhood may also include input units, i.e. the units that are directly receiving the stimulus. The ratio between the number of input units belonging

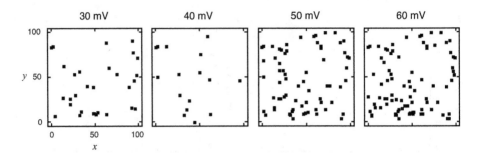

Fig. 2. Example of the location of strongly interconnected units as a function of the amplitude of the stimulus-induced depolarization. Network size: $[100 \times 100]$; stimulus duration: 200 ms; input units: 10% of the excitatory units; *fixed stimulation* protocol.

to the neighbourhood and the number of *SI* -units defines the *index of connected units* (ICU). The larger the ICU, the larger the influence of the input units on the *SI* -units.

The value for the ICU was computed for different network dimensions, stimulus durations and ratio of input units during the *fixed stimulation* protocol (Fig. 3). With a ratio of input units equal to 3%, we observed that the value of ICU was almost zero and independent of the other parameters, because the amount of stimulus delivered to the network was not sufficiently large to let appear a noticeable stimulus-driven pruning. Such pruning appeared with 5% of input units and became clearly visible with 7 and 10% of input units. It is worth to note that a stimulus lasting 200 ms provoked an effect similar to a stimulus lasting 50 ms. The "network size" effect is not so interesting by itself, as it is consistent with the fact that the smaller the network, the larger is the impact of a certain ratio of the input units. Besides, the application of a parameter scaling factor introduced in [5] almost suppressed the size effect (compare Fig. 3a and b).

The evolution of k_{in} and k_{out} for the *SI* -units and their neighbourhood was studied as a function of the simulation duration for a $[100 \times 100]$ network. The state of the network was analysed at $t = 50$, $t = 200$ and $t = 500$ seconds (Fig. 4). In the beginning of a simulation, an average excitatory unit receives and sends projections to about 190 other excitatory units, i.e. $k_{in} = k_{out} \approx 190$ (see Fig. 4a). The variability comes from the projection two-dimensional Gaussian density function (see Model description). As no new connections are established during the simulation, k_{in} and k_{out} can only decrease under the pressure of the pruning process. Some units tend to loose their incoming connections first, others tend to loose their outgoing connections first. The existence of other processes combining different speeds for the loss of input and output connections results in the smear of points visible in Fig. 4b-d.

We observed that as soon as $t = 50$ seconds, corresponding to 25 stimulus presentations with the *fixed stimulation* protocol (Fig. 4d), the evolution of the *SI* -neighbour units k_{in} and k_{out} was different from the other two protocols.

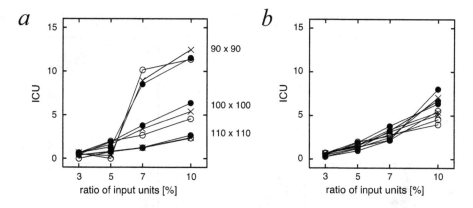

Fig. 3. The index of connected units (ICU), i.e. the ratio between the number of input units and the number of SI-units, as a function of the ratio of input units, stimulus duration, and network dimensions. Labels of stimulus duration: o: 50 ms; ×: 100 ms; •: 200 ms. *(a)*: simulations performed with unscaled parameter values for all network sizes; *(b)*: like *(a)* except for the size-specific scaled variables defined in [5]. Stimulus intensity: 60 mV; *fixed stimulation* protocol.

Plots for $t = 200$ and $t = 500$ seconds show that most units have $k_{out} \ll k_{in}$, which indicates that the pruning modified the topology of the connections and favored the emergence of a converging pattern. The comparison of these degrees between $t = 200$ and $t = 500$ s (Fig. 4e-g *vs.* Fig. 4h-j) shows that the tendency to loose outward projections continued during the last part of the simulation. In particular, notice that a large part of the neighbourhood population lost all its input connections ($k_{in} = 0$); these units 'survived' only because the background noise maintained some of their outward connections timely tuned with the discharges of their targets.

Figure 4 shows that the distribution patterns, for the *random stimulation* protocol (Fig. 4c,f,i) and in absence of stimulation (Fig. 4b,e,h) are very similar. A random stimulus could not drive any significant effect, which was somehow expected, but it was necessary as a control experiment to detect any bias introduced in the simulation program. In the *fixed stimulation* protocol (Fig. 4g,j), we observed $n = 415$ units with $30 \leq k_{in} \leq 130$ at $t = 200$ s that are maintained at $t = 500$ s. There are only 26 units with these properties in the other two conditions. This population is composed of 407 input units belonging to the neighbourhood. These input units maintained a large k_{in}, because of the synchronization of their activity during the stimuli presentations. The vast majority of the input units (> 85%) were presynaptic with respect to the SI-units, thus confirming that the topology organized towards a feed-forward converging pattern of connections.

In the *fixed stimulation* protocol, the number of incoming and outgoing projections of the SI-units was $k_{in} \approx 180$ and $3 \leq k_{out} \leq 20$. It is important to notice that the distribution of the k_{in} of the SI-units did not change in time.

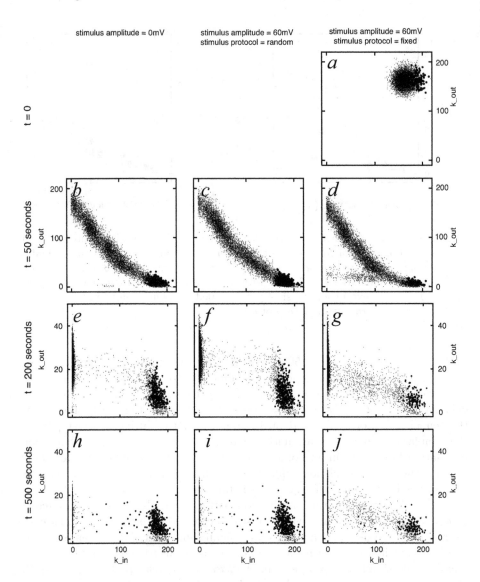

Fig. 4. Evolution of the out-degrees (k_{out}) vs. in-degrees (k_{in}): (•) SI-units; (·) SI-neighbour units. *(b, e, h):* in absence of any input (362 SI-units, 6,954 neighbours); *(c, f, i): random stimulation* protocol (425 SI-units, 6,996 neighbours); *(a, d, g, j): fixed stimulation* protocol (123 SI-units, 6,762 neighbours). *(a):* initial situation at $t = 0$ is identical for all three protocols; *(b, c, d):* at $t = 50$ seconds; *(e, f, g):* at $t = 200$ seconds; *(h, i, j):* at $t = 500$ seconds; Note the scale of vertical axis k_{out} is 200 in panels *(a-d)*, and 40 for panels *(e-j)*. Network size: [100×100]; stimulus duration: 100 ms; input units ratio: 10%.

In fact, the *SI*-units were characterized by an input pattern very close to that they had since the very beginning of the simulation. Different random seeds generated different populations of *SI*-units but the number of these units did not vary much as a function of the random seed.

6 Discussion

The main result has been to show that the application, in presence of background noise, of a recurrent pattern of stimulation let appear cell assemblies of excitatory units when associated to STDP-driven pruning. The vast majority of the connections that are modifiable by the spike-timing dependent plasticity rule were eliminated during the first thousands time steps of the simulation run [5]. Among the remaining active synapses, almost all were characterized by the highest possible activation level, in accordance with previous results [12].

We observed that the unsupervised pruning mechanisms tended to organize a feed-forward cell assembly of strongly interconnected units on top of the input units selected by the pruning process. Inhibitory responses observed in the pool of the *SI*-units are due to a balanced network reaction to the overall increased firing rate by increasing the activity within the pool of inhibitory units. The connectivity pattern of *SI*-units, initially set at random, appeared to match some requirements for maintaining almost all the input connections. The interpretation is that the cell assembly formed by the *SI*-units was initially determined by chance and when the pruning process started to select the active connections, these were maintained because of their connectivity pattern, thus letting emerge a particular circuit that was embedded in the network at time $t = 0$. However, the emergence of the diverging projections was much more difficult to observe than the convergence.

The self-organization of spiking neurons into cell assemblies was recently described in a study featuring large simulated networks connected by STDP-driven projections [6]. They studied the spatiotemporal structure of emerging firing patterns, finding that if axonal conduction delays and STDP were incorporated in the model, neurons in the network spontaneously self-organized into neuronal groups, even in absence of correlated input. The study [6] emphasizes the importance of axonal conduction delays that we did not initially consider in our model.

The choice of our neuromimetic model was justified by its compatibility with a novel hardware architecture [14]. Instead of leaky integrate-and-fire neuromimes, the use of biophysical models of neuromimes based on the Hodgkin-Huxley framework with multistate neurons and the associated multidimensional synapses [10] could bring better insight into the biological rationale of the emergence of cell assemblies by synaptic pruning.

Acknowledgments. The authors thank Dr. Yoshiyuki Asai for discussions and comments on the results and the manuscript. This work was partially funded by the European Community Future and Emerging Technologies program, grant #IST-2000-28027 (POETIC), and Swiss grant OFES #00.0529-2 by the Swiss government.

References

1. Abeles, M.: Corticonics: Neural Circuits of the Cerebral Cortex. Cambridge University Press (1991)
2. Bi, G. Q., Poo, M. M.: Synaptic modifications in cultured hippocampal neurons: dependence on spike timing, synaptic strength, and postsynaptic cell type. J Neurosci. **18** (1998) 10464-72
3. Chechik, G., Meilijson, I., Ruppin, E.: Neuronal Regulation: A Mechanism for Synaptic Pruning During Brain Maturation. Neural Computation **11** (1999) 2061–80
4. Eriksson, J., Torres, O., Mitchell, A., Tucker, G., Lindsay, K., Rosenberg, J., Moreno, J.-M., Villa, A.E.P.: Spiking Neural Networks for Reconfigurable POEtic Tissue. Lecture Notes in Computer Science **2606** (2003) 165–73
5. Iglesias, J., Eriksson, J., Grize, F., T., Marco, Villa, A.E.P.: Dynamics of Pruning in Simulated Large-Scale Spiking Neural Networks. Biosystems **79** (2005) 11–20
6. Izhikevich, E. M., Gally, J. A., Edelman, G. M.: Spike-timing Dynamics of Neuronal Groups. Cerebral Cortex **14** (2004) 933–44
7. Karmarkar, U. R., Buonomano, D. V.: A model of spike-timing dependent plasticity: one or two coincidence detectors? J Neurophysiol. **88** (2002) 507–13
8. Kelso, S. R., Ganong, A. H., Brown, T. H.: Hebbian synapses in hippocampus. Proc. Natl. Acad. Sci. USA **83** (1986) 5326–30
9. Mimura, K., Kimoto, T., Okada, M.: Synapse efficiency diverge due to synaptic pruning following over-growth. Phys Rev E Stat Nonlin Soft Matter Phys **68** (2003) 031910
10. Quenet, B., Horcholle-Bossavit, G., Wohrer, A., Dreyfus, G.: Formal modeling with multistate neurones and multidimensional synapses. Biosystems **79** (2005) 21–32
11. Rakic, P., Bourgeois, J. P., Eckenhoff, M. F., Zecevic, N., Goldman-Rakic, P. S.: Concurrent overproduction of synapses in diverse regions of the primate cerebral cortex. Science **232** (1986) 232–5
12. Song, S., Miller, K. D., Abbott, Larry F.: Competitive Hebbian learning through spike-timing-dependent synaptic plasticity. Nature Neuroscience **3** (2000) 919–26
13. Song, S., Abbott, Larry F.: Cortical Development and Remapping through Spike Timing-Dependent Plasticity. Neuron **32** (2001) 339–50
14. Tyrrell, A., Sanchez, E., Floreano, D., Tempesti, G., Mange, D., Moreno, J.M., Rosenberg, J., Villa, A.E.P.: POEtic: An Integrated Architecture for Bio-Inspired Hardware. Lecture Notes in Computer Science **2606** (2003) 129–40

Inverse First Passage Time Method in the Analysis of Neuronal Interspike Intervals of Neurons Characterized by Time Varying Dynamics

Laura Sacerdote and Cristina Zucca

Dept. of Mathematics, University of Torino
Via Carlo Alberto 10, 10123 Torino, Italy
laura.sacerdote@unito.it
cristina.zucca@unito.it

Abstract. We propose a new method to analyze time series recorded by single neuronal units in order to identify possible differences in the time evolution of the considered neuron. The effect of different dynamics is artificially concentrated in the boundary shape by means of the inverse first passage time method applied to the stochastic leaky integrate and fire model. In particular, the evolution in the dynamics is recognized by means of a suitable time window fragmentation on the observed data and the repeated use of the inverse first passage time algorithm. The comparison of the boundary shapes in the different time windows detects this evolution. A simulation example of the method and its biological implications are discussed.

1 Introduction

Time series recorded from neuronal units are generally studied via statistical methods, with correlograms and higher order descriptions, or with the help of mathematical models. In these last instances the typical approach describes the spiking activity as a renewal process and attributes all the recorded data to a single dynamics. For example, in the stochastic leaky integrate and fire (LIF) model the classic assumptions require that, after each spike, the membrane potential is reset to its resting value while its underthreshold dynamics are described via the same diffusion process during the entire observational time. The Ornstein-Uhlenbeck (OU) process is largely used for this purpose [1,4,7,8,9,18,19] but also diffusion processes with time dependent drift term appear in the literature [16]. The interspike time intervals (ISI) are then described via the first passage time (FPT) of the process through a boundary, possibly time depending, and the comparison of the theoretical and experimental distributions is used to validate the model or to explain the observed dynamics [14,15]. A second application of the models in this context has been recently proposed in [13] where the inverse first passage time (IFPT) method is applied to determine the shape of the

M. De Gregorio et al. (Eds.): BVAI 2005, LNCS 3704, pp. 69–77, 2005.

boundary that generates the observed data when the underthreshold dynamics are modeled via an OU process.

Generally stochastic models are built to analyze experimental data and use the same model to describe the totality of the observed data. Indeed all the data are attributed to a single sample without differentiating between possible different dynamics. One admits a non stationary behavior, by considering a time dependent input or a time varying threshold, but all the ISI are considered as generated by the same dynamics. On the contrary, the use of classical methods for time series analysis shows, in some experimental instances, a change of the neuronal dynamics during the observational time [10]. The necessity to recognize changes in the neuronal dynamics during the observational time clearly arises when one considers recordings from a neuron that alternates periods of spontaneous and stimulated activity. The use of the time series methods can reveal the existence of different dynamics but loses the interpretation of these dynamics that can be obtained with the use of mathematical models. Here we propose a method to analyze recorded ISI on sufficiently large time intervals with the help of stochastic models and of the IFPT method [20]. The leading idea of this new method is to determine suitable successive shifting time windows and to analyze the observed data applying the IFPT method to the moving window. The underlying diffusion process is not changed during all the analysis in order to detect differences between the different dynamics by means of discrepancies in the shapes of the boundary. The repetition of the analysis with different time windows and with different shifting times for the window can detect the times when the neuronal dynamics have changed.

This work is devoted to validate the proposed method, hence the results presented in Sect.4 consider only simulated data while the application of the method to experimental data will be the topic of a future work.

2   Model and Mathematical Background

Here we sketch the main features of the so called stochastic LIF model while we refer to the literature [11,18] for its derivation and its biological motivation. In a LIF model the time evolution of the membrane potential between two consecutive neuronal firing is described through a stochastic process $X = \{X_t; t \geq 0\}$ and the ISI are identified with the FPT of the process X through a threshold $S(t)$

$$T = \inf\{t > 0|X_t \geq S(t)\}, \tag{1}$$

whose probability density function is

$$g(t) = \frac{d}{dt}P(T \leq t). \tag{2}$$

Different diffusion processes have been used to model the membrane potential evolution [8], here we focus on the OU process that is one of the most largely used thanks to its mathematical manageability. Hence, we describe the subthreshold time evolution of the membrane potential by means of a stochastic process, fulfilling the stochastic differential equation

$$\begin{cases} dX_t = \left(-\frac{X_t}{\theta} + \mu\right) dt + \sigma dW_t \\ X_0 = 0 \end{cases} \tag{3}$$

where the constant μ characterizes the neuronal input, $\theta > 0$ reflects the spontaneous voltage decay in absence of input and $\sigma > 0$ is a constant related with the variability of the neuron input. A spike is elicited any time that the process crosses the boundary $S(t)$, then the process X starts again according to a renewal process. This assumption is necessary to identify the time series of successive spike times $(T_1, ..., T_N)$ as a sample of size N extracted from a population with distribution $g(t)$. Therefore the stochastic LIF model is completely described when one knows the OU parameters and the boundary shape function with its parameters. According to this approach one can determine the FPT distribution using one of the numerical [12] or simulation [5,6] methods proposed in the literature and this formulation of the problem is called direct first passage time problem. Alternatively, if the process with its parameters and the FPT distribution are assigned, one can determine the corresponding threshold shape. This is the inverse first passage time problem formulation and one of the numerical algorithms [20] for its solution are the basis of the method that we propose in Sect.3. The IFPT algorithm applied here requires the knowledge of the FPT distribution that can be approximately obtained from experimental data via the kernel method or via other numerical approaches.

3   Moving Window Inverse FPT Method

The study of the ISI trains of a neuron by means of the FPT of the OU process generally considers the observed ISI as a part of a single sample. This assumption tacitly implies that the dynamics of the neuron do not change during the observational time. However, also under spontaneous activity, different inputs from neighborough neurons can activate the observed neuron determining different dynamics on successive time intervals. This fact becomes extremely relevant when the data comes from a neuron of a network activated with external input during the recording interval.

Here we want to determine changes in the neuron dynamics during the observational period from the simple analysis of the ISI trains recorded from the neuron, assuming the absence of further information on the inputs and on the external stimulations during the observational period. We also want to recover the times when these changes happened and to describe the different dynamics on the different intervals.

To obtain these features, in analogy with the classical methods of time-frequency analysis [3], we consider a window of fixed amplitude. The amplitude can be alternatively defined or by fixing a time interval or by fixing the number of spikes considered in the sample. We apply the IFPT method and we introduce a shift of assigned lag. Also the lag can be alternatively defined as a fixed time interval or as a fixed number of spikes. Then we repeatedly shift the window of this assigned lag, performing each time the study with the IFPT method. If no change in the boundary shapes is observed on successive shifted windows, we conclude that a unique behavior characterizes the observational time. In this case no remarkable differences arise between the shape of the boundary computed using the observed data all together or using the set of windows. On the other hand if the process changes its dynamics inside the observed interval, the shapes of the boundary corresponding to different windows change. A careful choice of the shifting lag and of the windows amplitude, or a suitable rescaling of the window amplitude, suggests the times when the dynamics of the neuron change. Note that the choice of the window amplitude is constrained by the necessity to have a sufficiently large sample to apply the IFPT method. However a large window increases the risk to lose the dynamics change. This fact could be balanced introducing smaller shifting times. Difficulties can arise when there are frequent changes in the dynamics and one deals with rare events. It is clear that a careful choice of windows amplitude and shifting lags requests a detailed preliminary study on their role but our goal here is principally to describe and to test the proposed approach. Examples discussed in this paper use lag and window amplitude defined through the number of spikes. This choice simplifies the analysis and allows a first check on the reliability of the method. Note that this choice implies the use of windows characterized by different time amplitudes.

The application of the IFPT method on each window, maintaining the same diffusion process for all the analyses, compacts all the information on the evolution of the process dynamics into the boundary shape. The advantage of this choice is the possibility to compare deterministic functions in spite of comparing stochastic processes. However as one has recognized two different boundaries on successive windows one can reinterpret the result in terms of two different diffusion processes crossing the same constant boundary. Indeed a space transformation can always send differences in the boundary shape into differences between the processes [11].

Since the IFPT method requests the use of a smooth approximation of the FPT probability density function here we approximate it via the kernel method on the data [2,17]. Since the IFPT method is highly sensible to an error on the right tail of the FPT density we apply the method on the 90% of the probabilistic mass.

4   Results

In order to check the reliability of the proposed method we apply it to simulated data. Different choice can be made for the boundary shape of the simulated process but for this first investigation we will limit ourselves to the case of a boundary that assume different constant values. We simulate 3 samples, with sample size $N = 10^5$, from an OU process with $\theta = 1$ ms^{-1}, $\mu = 0$ mVms^{-1} and $\sigma^2 = 2$ mV^{2}ms^{-1} and boundaries $S_1 = 2$, mV $S_2 = 2.5$ mV and $S_3 = 2$ mV, respectively. Note that for simplicity we use a standardized process but a simple space time transformation makes the considered parameters values biologically compatible [11]. Since the IFPT algorithm converges after some iterations, the boundary estimates are not reliable for small time. Hence, we plot the computed boundaries starting when the method becomes stable.

As a first step in our analysis we apply the IFPT method to the total sample of size $3 \cdot 10^5$. Figure 1a shows the resulting histogram and its continuous approximation obtained via the Epanechnikov kernel method [17] while in Fig.1b the boundary obtained with the IFPT method is plotted. Note that the merging of all the data determines misleading results on the boundary that appears linearly increasing. This fact is due to the merging of the three samples as it is shown in Fig.2 where the histograms and the corresponding boundaries, computed via the IFPT method, for the three separate samples of size 10^5 are plotted. This last figure confirms the reliability of the IFPT method discerning the three boundaries used in the simulations.

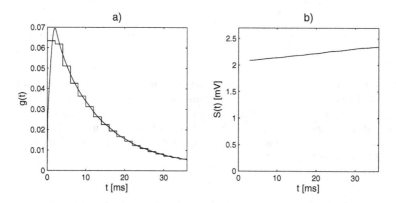

Fig. 1. a) Normalized histogram and its continuous approximation obtained via the kernel method (Epanechnikov kernel) of the data. Three samples of size $N = 10^5$ generated as the FPT of an OU process with parameters $\theta = 1$ ms$^{-1}, \mu = 0$ mVms^{-1} and $\sigma^2 = 2$ mV^{2}ms^{-1} through the boundaries $S_1 = 2$ mV, $S_2 = 2.5$ mV and $S_3 = 2$ mV respectively, are merged in a single sample. **b)** The boundary obtained with the IFPT method.

Figures 3 and 4 illustrate the application of the moving window IFPT method. We show the different boundaries obtained shifting a window of size $N = 10^5$ of a lag step $L = 10^4$. In Fig.3, from the bottom to the top, we illustrate the boundaries corresponding to the successive windows obtained with a shift of lag $k \cdot L, k = 0, 1, ..., 10$ while in Fig.4 from top to bottom, we illustrate the boundaries corresponding to the successive windows obtained with a shift of lag $k \cdot L, k = 10, 11, ..., 20$. Note that the bottom boundaries in Figs.3 and 4 consider only samples from the process with boundary to $S = 2$ mV, while the top boundaries in these figures correspond to the sample from the process with boundary $S = 2.5$ mV and are correctly recognized constant. The instances

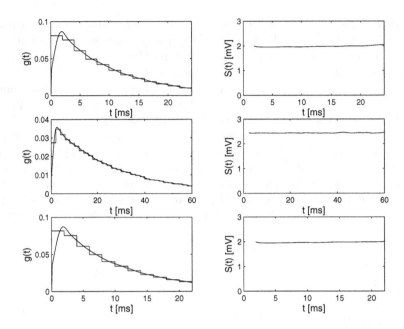

Fig. 2. Normalized histograms and its continuous approximation obtained via the kernel method (Epanechnikov kernel) for the three separate samples of size 10^5 generated as the FPT of an OU process with parameters $\theta = 1$ ms^{-1}, $\mu = 0$ mVms^{-1} and $\sigma^2 = 2$ mV^{2}ms^{-1} through the boundaries **a)** $S_1 = 2$ mV, **c)** $S_2 = 2.5$ mV and **e)** $S_3 = 2$ mV and the corresponding boundaries obtained applying the IFPT method **b)** $S_1 = 2$ mV, **d)** $S_2 = 2.5$ mV and **f)** $S_3 = 2$ mV.

when the sample contains a mixture from two different samples determine linear boundaries with a slope depending on the weight of each sample in the mixture.

The changes of the boundary shapes as we shift the window indicate a change in the observed dynamics. In order to detect the time when this change happens, the analysis can be repeated with smaller windows sizes and/or smaller shift lag.

Different shapes of the boundary will be tested in a more comprehensive future work where the method will also consider experimental data. Here we limit our analysis to the constant boundary instance. Linear boundaries have been determined in [13] using experimental data. In that paper the nature of the boundary was used to obtain a classification method for ISI simultaneously recorded from a set of neurons. The results illustrated in Figs.3 and 4 suggest that a linear boundary can be determined by a change of the dynamics involving two different constant boundaries.

The method has been also checked with simulated samples of size $N = 1000$ obtaining similar results.

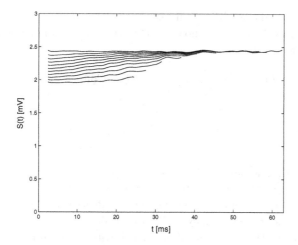

Fig. 3. From bottom to top, boundaries corresponding to successive windows of size $N = 10^5$ obtained with a shift lag $k \cdot L, k = 0, 1, ..., 10$ with $L = 10^4$. The boundary shape computation is stopped when the 90% of the probability mass of $g(t)$ is reached.

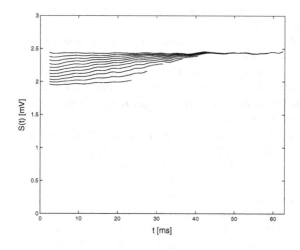

Fig. 4. From top to bottom, boundaries corresponding to successive windows of size $N = 10^5$ obtained with a shift lag $k \cdot L, k = 10, 11, ..., 20$ with $L = 10^4$. The boundary shape computation is stopped when the 90% of the probability mass of $g(t)$ is reached.

5   Conclusions

The example discussed here validates the new proposed method in the case of a sample generated with different constant boundaries. In order to have a more complete vision of the power of the method other cases should be considered. In particular, we plan to analyze the case of periodically oscillating boundaries, with different periods on disjoint intervals. Furthermore, a planned extensive theoretical study will help the choice of the window and of the shift lag in the case of experimental data.

Acknowledgments. Work supported by PRIN-Cofin.

References

1. Capocelli R.M., Ricciardi L.M.: Diffusion approximation and first passage time problem for a model neuron. Kybernetik **8**(6) (1971) 214–223

2. Devroye, L.: A course in density estimation. Birkhauser. Boston (1987)

3. Cohen, L.: Time-frequency analysis. Prentice Hall. (1995)

4. Feng J.F., Brown D.: Integrate-and-fire models with nonlinear leakage. Bull. Math. Biol. **62** (3) (2000) 467–481

5. Giraudo, M.T., Sacerdote, L.: An improved technique for the simulation of first passage times for diffusion processes. Commun. Statist. Simul. **28** (4) (1999) 1135–1163

6. Giraudo, M.T., Sacerdote, L., Zucca, C.: A Monte Carlo method for the simulation of first passage times diffusion processes. Methodol. Comput. Appl. Probab. **3** (2) (2001) 215–231

7. Lansky P., Sacerdote L.: The Ornstein-Uhlenbeck neuronal model with signal-dependent noise. Phys. Lett. A **285** (3-4) (2001) 132–140

8. Lansky P., Sacerdote L., Tomassetti F.: On the comparison of Feller and Ornstein-Uhlenbeck models for neural activity. Biol. Cybern. **73** (5) (1995) 457–465

9. Pakdaman K.: Periodically forced leaky integrate-and-fire model. Phys. Rev. E **63** (4) (2001) Art. No. 041907 Part 1

10. Priestley, M.B.: Spectral analysis and time series. Academic Press. London (1987)

11. Ricciardi, L.M.: Diffusion Processes and related topics in biology. Lectures Notes in Biomathematics **14**. Springer-Verlag. Berlin-New York (1977)

12. Ricciardi, L.M., Di Crescenzo, A., Giorno, V., Nobile, A.G.: An outline of theoretical and algorithmic approaches to first passage time problems with applications to biological modeling. Math. Japon. **50** (2) (1999) 247–322

13. Sacerdote, L., Villa, A.E.P., Zucca, C.: On the classification of experimental data modeled via a stochastic leaky integrate and fire model through boundary values. Preprint (2005)

14. Sacerdote, L., Zucca, C.: Threshold shape corresponding to a Gamma firing distribution in an Ornstein-Uhlenbeck neuronal model. Sci. Math. Jpn. **58**(2) (2003) 295–305

15. Sacerdote, L., Zucca, C.: On the relationship between interspikes interval distribution and boundary shape in the Ornstein-Uhlenbeck neuronal model. In: Capasso, V. (ed) Mathematical modelling & computing in biology and medicine. Esculapio, Bologna. (2003) 161–168

16. Shimokawa, T., Pakdaman, K., Takahata, T., Sato, S.: A first-passage-time analysis of the periodically forced noisy leaky integrate-and-fire model. Biol. Cybern. **83** (2000) 327–340

17. Silverman, B.W.: Density Estimation for Statistics and Data Analysis. Chapman and Hall. New York (1986)
18. Tuckwell H.C.: Introduction to Theoretical Neurobiology: I. Cambridge University Press, Cambridge (1988)
19. Tuckwell H.C., Wan F.Y.M., Rospars J.P.: A spatial stochastic neuronal model with Ornstein-Uhlenbeck input current. Biol. Cybern. **86** (2) (2002) 137–145
20. Zucca, C., Sacerdote, L. and Peskir, G.: On the Inverse First-Passage Problem for a Wiener Process. Quaderno del Dipartimento di Matematica-Università di Torino n.2

Coding by Neural Population Oscillations?

Francesco Ventriglia

Istituto di Cibernetica "E. Caianiello",
CNR Via Campi Flegrei,
34, 80078 - Pozzuli (NA), Italy
franco@ulisse.cib.na.cnr.it

Abstract. The search of the code underlying the transmission of information through the different stages of integration of the brain is a very active investigation field. Here, the possible involvement in the neural code of global population oscillatory activities has been discussed. The behaviorally important rhythmic activities of the hippocampal CA3 field have been analyzed to this aim. The genesis and the features of such activities have been studied by the computer simulation of a model of the entire CA3. The simulation demonstrated the ability of the network of inhibitory interneurons to control nicely the transmission of activity through the pyramidal population. The results suggested that the hippocampal formation and the CA3 field—in particular—could be organized in a way to allow the passing of excitatory activities only during specific and narrow time windows, confined by inhibitory barrages possibly linked to attentional processes.

1 Introduction

The neural information flows in brain along the multiple stages of the neural circuitry, starting from the primary (sensorial) cortices, till the Hippocampus and superior areas and back. The problem of the modalities according which the information is coded within the neural populations of brain, is very elusive and yet there are no clear indications about its nature. The most common hypotheses about such code, the "rate code" and the "temporal code", received contrasting evidence and the issue remains controversial. The rate code hypothesis assumes that the neurons, basically noisy, can transmit information only via the mean rate of spiking. This hypothesis is based on the common observation that recorded sequences of spike intervals in cortical pyramidal neurons are so highly irregular to support the existence of important random influences on its genesis [13,14,15,24]. The more recent temporal-code view, partially based on the assumption that the rate code proposal produces a too poor code, retains that the information is conveyed by the precise order of the inter-spike time intervals, or in a weaker form, it is related to the precise time of the first spike after an event [1,2,16,17].

The base of a new hypothesis on the rules governing the transmission of information in brain is discussed here. This hypothesis considers the global oscillatory

M. De Gregorio et al. (Eds.): BVAI 2005, LNCS 3704, pp. 78–88, 2005.

activities in neural populations as the possible base of a temporal code, very different from that outlined above. Synchronous oscillatory activities constitute one of the most characteristic aspects of the brain activity and are associated closely to behavioral states. Rhythmic oscillations in the gamma (20-80 Hz) and theta (4-15 Hz) ranges are among the most prominent patterns of activity in Hippocampus [3] and both rhythms are believed to be essential products of the hippocampal machinery. The theta rhythm is commonly supposed to be produced in the hippocampus by activity coming from medial septum and entorhinal cortex. Recent experimental and theoretical articles support the hypothesis that the network of inhibitory interneurons in the Hippocampus generates intrinsically the gamma rhythm. Both rhythms are present during the exploratory activity in awake animals and are related to learning, memory processes and to cognitive functions [19,4]. Some fast (80-200 Hz) [6] and ultra-fast (200-500 Hz) [10] oscillations have been also recorded in the hippocampus (and cortex) of several animals and in man.

The CA3 field of the Hippocampus, one of the most significant components of the limbic system, has been used here as a case study to evaluate the new hypothesis. In particular, the global reactions of CA3 to its inputs and the precise spatio-temporal behavior of excitatory and inhibitory waves invading the CA3 field have been closely investigated. The results suggested that this field is organized as an inhibitory filter which allows the passing of excitatory activities only during narrow time windows. They are strictly confined by inhibitory barrages possibly linked to attentional processes.

2 The Kinetic Model

Based on a kinetic theory of neural systems, formulated several years ago [20,22], a set of differential equations was constructed for the description of the activity of the CA3 neural field. This theory translates the action potentials traveling within the neural fields along the axonic branches in massless particles. They move freely within the neural systems until they collide with a neuron. The collision can result in the absorption of the impulse by the neuron and in this case the subthreshold excitation of the neuron increases or decreases according to the quality, excitatory or inhibitory, of the absorbed impulse. When the subthreshold excitation reaches the threshold value (here assumed equal to 1 for simplicity) the firing occurs and a stream of new impulses is emitted within the neural field. After the firing the neurons go in refractoriness state, for a period of time τ. The functions $f_s(\mathbf{r}, \mathbf{v}, t)$ and $g_{s'}(\mathbf{r}, e, t)$ describe, respectively, the impulse velocity distribution and the distribution of the subthreshold neuronal excitation within the neural field. Whereas, $\psi_{s'}(\mathbf{r})$ denotes the local density of neurons. The variables $\mathbf{r}, \mathbf{v}, e$ and t are associated to the position, the velocity, the subthreshold excitation and the time, respectively. The index s refers to the different action potentials traveling within the neural field (CA3 pyramidal short range, CA3 pyramidal long range, CA3 inhibitory fast and CA3 inhibitory slow, Enthorinal Cortex pyramidal, Mossy Fibers from Dentate Gyrus,

Medial Septum (cholinergic or inhibitory)) and the index s' is associated to the different families (pyramidal, inhibitory fast and inhibitory slow) of neurons present in CA3. Moreover, s_e denotes a generic impulse coming from external sources and $s_{\bar{e}}$ denotes a CA3 generated impulse. The time evolution of the two distribution functions is governed by the following set of coupled differential equations:

$$\nabla_t f_s(\mathbf{r}, \mathbf{v}, t) + \mathbf{v} \cdot \nabla_\mathbf{r} f_s(\mathbf{r}, \mathbf{v}, t) + f_s(\mathbf{r}, \mathbf{v}, t)(\Sigma_{s'} \psi_{s'}(\mathbf{r}) \mid \mathbf{v} \mid \sigma_{s's}) =$$

$$S_s(\mathbf{r}, \mathbf{v}, t)\delta(s - s_e) + f_s^*(\mathbf{r}, \mathbf{v})N_{s'}(\mathbf{r}, t)\delta(s - s_{\bar{e}})$$

$$+f_s^0(\mathbf{v}) \int_A \xi_{s's}(\mathbf{r}, \mathbf{r}') \, d\mathbf{r}' \int f'(v')N_{s'}(\mathbf{r}', t - \frac{|\mathbf{r} - \mathbf{r}'|}{v'}) \, dv' \delta(s - s_{\bar{e}}) \qquad (1)$$

$$\nabla_t g_{s'}(\mathbf{r}, e, t) + \mu(e_r - e)\nabla_e g_{s'}(\mathbf{r}, e, t) = [g_{s'}(\mathbf{r}, e - \epsilon, t) - g_{s'}(\mathbf{r}, e, t)]$$

$$+N_{s'}(\mathbf{r}, t - \tau_{s'})\delta(e - e_r)$$

$$+M_{s'}(\mathbf{r}, t)\theta(\epsilon)\delta(e - e_0) \qquad (2)$$

where the functions $\delta(.)$ and $\theta(.)$ denote the Dirac and the step functions, respectively; e_r and e_0 are the resting potential and the maximum hyperpolarization level of the neurons and $\sigma_{s's}$ is the absorption coefficient, μ is the decay constant of the subthreshold excitation, and A is the surface covered by CA3. The functions $f^*(\mathbf{r}, \mathbf{v})$, $f^0(\mathbf{v})$ are linked to the velocity spectra of impulses emitted in different conditions. The function $\xi_{s's}(\mathbf{r}, \mathbf{r}')$ is an origin/destination matrix for long-range impulses, and $f'(v')$ denotes the velocity distribution along these paths. $S(\mathbf{r}, \mathbf{v}, t)$ is a source term denoting the impulses entered in CA3 from external sources. When this source term is present in equation 1 (for specific values of the index), the other two source terms on the right member (related to CA3 generated impulses) must be considered null. The other functions present in the above equations have the following expressions and meanings:

$$N_{s'}(\mathbf{r}, t) = \int_{1-\epsilon(\mathbf{r},t)}^{1} g_{s'}(\mathbf{r}, e, t) de \qquad (3)$$

denotes the probable number of neurons in $\mathbf{r}$ firing at time t;

$$\nabla_t M_{s'}(\mathbf{r}, t) = \int_0^{-\epsilon(\mathbf{r},t)} g_{s'}(\mathbf{r}, e, t) de - M_{s'}(\mathbf{r}, t)\theta(\epsilon) \qquad (4)$$

is a differential equation associated to the probable number of neurons in $\mathbf{r}$ which stay in maximum hyperpolarization level at time t;

$$I_{s's}(\mathbf{r}, t) = \frac{\int f_s(\mathbf{r}, \mathbf{v}, t)\psi_{s'}(\mathbf{r})\sigma_{s's} \mid \mathbf{v} \mid dv}{\psi_{s'}(\mathbf{r})} \qquad (5)$$

is the excitation absorbed by the neurons in $\mathbf{r}$ at time t (mean number of absorbed impulses of type s). Denoting by $E_s(\mathbf{r}, t)$ the mean Post Synaptic Potential associated to excitatory or inhibitory impulses—a positive function for excitatory impulses, negative for inhibitory ones—the following convolution equation furnishes the time course of the net excitatory effect on the subthreshold neurons in $\mathbf{r}$ at time t:

$$\epsilon_{s'}(\mathbf{r}, t) = \Sigma_{s=1}^n \int_0^t E_s(\mathbf{r}, t) \cdot I_{s's}(\mathbf{r}, t - t')dt'. \tag{6}$$

In the above equations, use is made of the conditions that the function $g_{s'}(\mathbf{r}, e, t) = 0$ if $e \leq 0$ or if $e > 1$.

This mathematical model has been utilized to carry out a series of computational experiments. The space-time course of some macroscopic parameters (local frequency of spikes, local mean sub-threshold excitation, number of firing neurons), which have close analogy with the *in vivo* recorded activity of the CA3 field (population spike trains, local field potentials), has been analyzed to obtain information on its ability to simulate oscillating hippocampal activity.

3 Oscillatory and Spiraling Activity

The genesis of the above mentioned rhythmic oscillations in gamma and theta ranges has been investigated by computational experiments which simulated the reaction of the CA3 model to external stimuli. All the results described in this paper were based on a model having the space dimensions of the entire CA3 field of the rat. From the Atlas of Rat Brain [12] CA3 has space dimensions of $8mm$ long (septo-temporal axis) and $3mm$ large (transverse axis). Also the neuronal densities and parameters of connectivity have been computed by values from literature (see [23], where the values of the impulse velocity spectra, of ξ and of the absorption coefficients $\sigma_{s's}$ are also reported). Based on the neuronal density values about 300.000 pyramidal neurons and 30.000 fast and 30.000 slow inhibitory neurons constituted the simulated CA3 field. Excitatory stimuli originated from Entorhinal Cortex both via Dentate Gyrus (through the Mossy Fibers) and by a direct path have been simulated. Also, in some simulations, inhibitory or excitatory influences from Medial Septum have been studied. Dentate Gyrus input was assumed to be conveyed by layered mossy fibers distributed along parallel strips of pyramidal neurons (stratum lucidum), each strip being $3mm$ long and $50\mu m$ large and containing about 6.250 mossy fibers and 87.500 mossy synapses. The amplitude of the strip ($50\mu m$) was dictated by the space step utilized in the simulation (see the Appendix where the values of other basic parameters are presented). The Dentate Gyrus input to each strip was constituted by random volleys, whose arrival times were distributed according to a Poisson distribution, while the duration and the amplitude were Gaussian distributed. Often the volleys along the different strips were correlated. The CA3 field was also reached

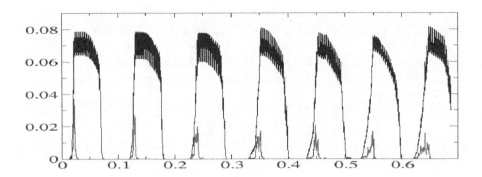

Fig. 1. Time course of the firing frequencies of the excitatory (smaller values) and inhibitory (higher values) neuronal populations in CA3. The ordinates denote the percentage of firing neurons, with reference to the respective total populations. The time is in *sec*.

by Poissonian inputs originating from the direct Entorhinal Cortex path. In experiments in which a concurrent input from Medial Septum was simulated, some inputs inhibited selectively the inhibitory neural populations of CA3. The most interesting activities were shown when the inhibition conveyed by the neural population producing slow inhibitory effects was considered constantly inhibited by inputs coming from Medial Septum. In these simulations the frequency of the global activity, both for excitatory and inhibitory neural populations, was in the range of the theta rhythm. A typical time course is presented in figure 1. A theta rhythm with a frequency of about $10Hz$ is evident from this figure. Interestingly the percentage of pyramidal cells involved in the firing activity is only a small fraction of the total population, about 2% in mean. Small ripples, at very high frequency, are also shown by the oscillations associated to the firing of the fast inhibitory neuronal population. The interest of these results is linked also to an ongoing debate about the drive to the global activity of CA3 field [18], which motivated some authors to suggest the necessity of gap junctions among pyramidal axons to sustain such activity. That this is not necessary has been demonstrated herein. In fact, the excitatory activity flowing along the long range pyramidal axons (Schaffer collaterals), with a velocity low enough to produce delays of $10-20ms$, and the slow decay of the Post Synaptic Potentials in the excitatory synapses on inhibitory neurons (massively charged by the pyramidal population discharge) can sustain the firing of the inhibitory population for about 50 milliseconds. The excitatory and inhibitory activity had a patterned displaying on the entire CA3 field. The time course can be described as follows. At some time, depending on the assumed characteristics of the Poisson distribution governing the Dentate Gyrus and the Entorhinal Cortex inputs, the first volleys of impulses began to propagate in one or more strips of CA3. The absorption of impulses drove some pyramidal neurons to fire action potentials. This induced firing in other pyramidal and in fast inhibitory neurons (the slow inhibitory neurons being assumed inhibited). In some milliseconds a patterned,

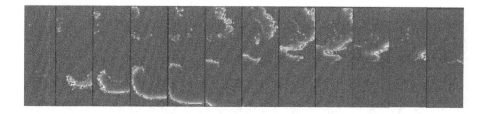

Fig. 2. Time course of the density of impulses produced by the whole pyramidal neuronal population in CA3 (about 300.000 neurons). Two, not complete, reverberations are shown invading the entire CA3. The duration of the displayed activity is 12.5*ms*. After 2 more milliseconds all the excitatory activity vanishes. The white is related to the maximum value of the intensity.

self-organized activity began to appear in the neuronal firing, which stabilized and propagated throughout the entire CA3 field, involving both the pyramidal and the inhibitory neurons. The induced firing of fast inhibitory neurons produced a so high level of inhibition that the pyramidal neurons were reduced to a silent state. In such a way they remained unable to react to new inputs originating from the simulated sources. The patterned activity of the inhibitory neural population remained active for several periods of time, as long as they had sufficient drive on their excitatory synapses. After some time, the decaying of the residual excitation on inhibitory neurons reduced gradually their firing. The decaying of the inhibition permitted the inputs to ignite again some of the neurons of the pyramidal strips. A new cycle began with a patterned activity that could be slightly or strongly different form the previous one. In figure 2 the activity of pyramidal neurons is presented by using the local density of impulses. [To show with greater precision the time course of the activity, in this figure and in the subsequent ones, the interval of time among the frames is not constant. In some parts the time is accelerated, in others it is lagged.] In figure 3, the waves associated to the propagation of fast inhibitory impulses are presented. The results presented in these two figures are very attracting, since spiraling activities are manifested. In fact, while spiral waves are not difficult to find in natural, not-neural systems [26], in neural systems the evidence is scarce. Only some rare articles report the observation of spiral waves in neural tissues [7] and [8]. As asserted by [7], the difficulty arise because, to demonstrate a true spiral wave, the medium under study must be relatively smooth and isotropic and a "phase singularity" should be observed at the center of the activity. This is a distinctive sign that differentiates spiral waves from other kinds of rotating waves. In a previous work [21], based on a simpler version of the kinetic theory, some rotating waves of neural activity, traveling outward from a center, have been found. But to produce them a very particular stimulation had to be utilized. In the present case the production of spiraling activity occurs in a very natural way, since it is due to the interference of two different activities, which spread on the neural field.

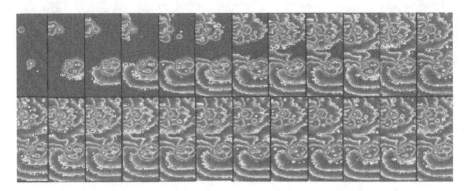

Fig. 3. Time course of the density of impulses produced by the whole fast inhibitory neuronal population in CA3 (about 30.000 neurons). A spiraling activity is shown invading the lower sector of CA3 field. The starting time is the same of Figure 2. $7ms$ of additional activity are shown in the lower row. 9 frames in this row, by starting from the third, are separated only by $\frac{1}{8}ms$. The spiraling waves stop only after further $44ms$ of activity (not shown).

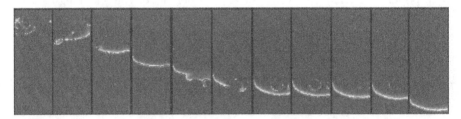

Fig. 4. Time course of the density of impulses produced by pyramidal neurons in CA3. The total time displayed is $18ms$. After the last frame the pyramidal activity vanishes in about $2ms$.

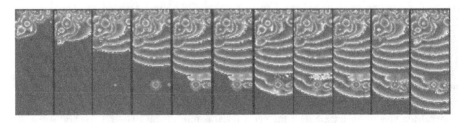

Fig. 5. Time course of the density of impulses produced by inhibitory neurons in CA3. The total time displayed is $18ms$. After the last frame the inhibitory oscillating activity persists for further $42ms$.

A different kind of activity is shown in figures 4 and 5. It occurred at times subsequent to those of figures 2–3. Also these figures show activities related to pyramidal (figure 4) and fast inhibitory (figure 5) neuronal populations. In the present case, a single traveling wave is shown by pyramidal population firing which induces an oscillating activity in the inhibitory neural population. It, gradually, invades the entire CA3 field. Intriguingly, a backwash behavior is shown in the lower right zone of figure 5, where a local nucleus of oscillation interferes with activity coming from the upper zone of the field.

4 Discussion

From the study by computer simulation of the neural activity of the CA3 field of Hippocampus, some remarkable features of the neural dynamics have been observed. Under appropriate driving inputs, some activity self-organized within the pyramidal neuron population and spread to the entire CA3 region. In the wake of the excitatory activity, stable and well-organized oscillatory activities occurred within the inhibitory neural population. They presented a sort of complex and persistent remnant, or trace, of the spatio-temporal behavior of the previous pyramidal activity. These oscillations continued for periods of time much longer than the activity in driving pyramidal neurons. During this time, the pyramidal neurons being very efficiently inhibited could not generate new activities. The inhibition of the slow inhibitory neurons could modulate the duration of the inhibitory periods. This was obtained by simulating an input originating from Medial Septum. In such a way, the frequency of the global pyramidal activity could range from 1.5Hz to 11Hz (results not shown). Hence, the global activity of the CA3 field was organized in such a way to present specific time windows for the generation of excitatory activities, conveyed by pyramidal neurons. These activities were separated by long periods of inhibition. This suggests that a sort of temporal coding—with a meaning quite different from the common view—is associated to the function of the entire CA3, that seems to operate in the following way. Among all the inputs from cortical regions arriving to CA3 field, only those which reach it in appropriate time intervals, that can be also under the control of activities in behavior-linked sub-cortical nuclei (like Locus Coeruleus and Median Raphe), are able to trigger global activities and can produce effects on the brain regions driven by CA3. Other volleys, which arrive either too late or too early, are not able to filter through the inhibitory barrage, and in such a way they are neither able to induce global reactions of CA3, nor can modify the evolving patterned inhibitory activity. Hence, the information they convey is not allowed to pass to other brain stages. In such a way, a free period of time with a duration of $50 - 80ms$ is reserved to the successful inputs, during which they can drive activities in cortical regions without interferences by competing inputs. These activities may result in learning, memory and other cognitive effects. A link between the theta rhythm and an attention mechanism has been hypothesized also by the long experimental activity of Vinogradova [25]. A similar, but weaker hypothesis on the inhibitory activity in Hippocampus has been proposed in [5]. These authors suggest that oscillating inhibitory networks may provide temporal windows for single cells to suppress or facilitate their synaptic inputs in a coordinated manner.

This kind of functioning, which seems to be characteristic of the Hippocampus being produced by its specific organization and by the peculiar connectivity of the CA3 field, could be also present in cerebral cortex. This hypothesis, however, can not be extended to all the cortical areas, since the primary cortices show a different organization [9,11]. The primary visual cortex—for example—seems to be organized in a large number of more or less identical elementary processing units, the *columns* , each of which contains the complete machinery for the analysis of a small part of the visual field with respect to all possible stimulus features. An incomplete list contains columns specialized for orientation, ocular dominance, color selectivity, direction of movement, spatial frequency, disparity, and stimulus on- or offset. Since the primary cortices seem to use a different coding, a global neural population oscillatory code could be only hypothesized for cortical structures at higher stages (multimodal and associative cortices). The difficulty to unveil such a code at those levels could be due to the complexity of the cerebral cortex and of its activities, which could mask it. Moreover, the inhibitory barrage could be more smoothly controlled at the cortical level and more subtle effects could result.

References

1. Abeles M. Role of the cortical neuron: integrator or coincidence detector? Isr J Med Sci. **18** (1982) 83–92
2. Abeles M *Corticonics: neural circuits of the cerebral cortex.*(1991). New York: Cambridge
3. Buzsaki G, Chrobak JJ. Temporal structure in spatially organized neuronal ensembles: a role for interneuronal networks. Curr Opin Neurobiol. **5**(1995) 504–10
4. Cohen N. J. and Eichenbaum H. *Memory, amnesia, and the hippocampal system.* (1993) The MIT Press, Cambridge-London
5. Csicsvari J, Hirase H, Czurko A, Mamiya A, Buzsaki G. Oscillatory coupling of hippocampal pyramidal cells and interneurons in the behaving Rat. J Neurosci. **19**(1999) 274–87
6. Draguhn A, Traub RD, Bibbig A, Schmitz D. Ripple (approximately 200-Hz) oscillations in temporal structures. J Clin Neurophysiol. **17** (2000) 361–76
7. Harris-White ME, Zanotti SA, Frautschy SA, Charles AC. Spiral intercellular calcium waves in hippocampal slice cultures. J Neurophysiol. **79** (1998) 1045–52
8. Huang X, Troy WC, Yang Q, Ma H, Laing CR, Schiff SJ, Wu JY. Spiral waves in disinhibited mammalian neocortex. J Neurosci. **24**(2004) 9897–902
9. Hubel DH, Wiesel TN. Early exploration of the visual cortex. Neuron **20**(1998) 401–12

10. Kandel A, Buzsaki G. Cellular-synaptic generation of sleep spindles, spike-and-wave discharges, and evoked thalamocortical responses in the neocortex of the rat. J Neurosci. **17** (1997) 6783–97

11. Mountcastle VB. The columnar organization of the neocortex. Brain **120** (1997) 701-722

12. Paxinos G. and Watson C. *The rat brain in stereotaxic coordinates.* (1986) Academic Press, San Diego-Toronto

13. Shadlen MN, Newsome WT. Noise, neural codes and cortical organization. Curr Opin Neurobiol. **4**(1994) 569–79

14. Shadlen MN, Newsome WT. Is there a signal in the noise? Curr Opin Neurobiol. **5**(1995) 248–50

15. Shadlen MN, Newsome WT. The variable discharge of cortical neurons: implications for connectivity, computation, and information coding. J Neurosci. **18**(1998) 3870–96

16. Softky WR. Simple codes versus efficient codes. Curr Opin Neurobiol. **5** (1995) 239–47

17. Stevens CF, Zador AM. Input synchrony and the irregular firing of cortical neurons. Nat Neurosci. **1** (1998) 210–7

18. Traub RD, Bibbig A, LeBeau FE, Cunningham MO, Whittington MA. Persistent gamma oscillations in superficial layers of rat auditory neocortex: experiment and model. J Physiol. **562** (2005) 3–8

19. Traub RD, Cunningham MO, Gloveli T, LeBeau FE, Bibbig A, Buhl EH, Whittington MA. GABA-enhanced collective behavior in neuronal axons underlies persistent gamma-frequency oscillations. Proc Natl Acad Sci U S A. **100** (2003) 11047–52

20. Ventriglia F. Kinetic approach to neural systems.I. Bull. Math. Biol. **36** (1974) 534–544

21. Ventriglia F. Activity in cortical-like neural systems: short-range effects and attention phenomena. Bull Math Biol. **52** (1990) 397–429

22. Ventriglia F. Towards a kinetic theory of cortical-like neural fields. In *Neural Modeling and Neural Networks* (ed. Ventriglia F.) (1994) pp. 217-249. Pergamon Press, Oxford-New York

23. Ventriglia F. Computational experiments support a competitive function in the CA3 region of the hippocampus. Bull Math Biol. **60**(1998) 373–407

24. Ventriglia F, Di Maio V. Neural code and irregular spike trains. [*Same volume*]

25. Vinogradova OS. Hippocampus as comparator: role of the two input and two output systems of the hippocampus in selection and registration of information. Hippocampus **11** (2001) 578–598

26. Winfree AT *The geometry of biological time.*(2001). New York: Springer

Appendix

The following values have been utilized by the numerical procedure solving the kinetic equations: time step: $\delta t = 0.125 ms$, space step: $\delta x = \delta y = 50 \mu m$.

In this way each grid point was representative of a small square of neural matter with a side length of $50 \mu m$ in which 30 excitatory neurons, 3 fast and 3 slow inhibitory neurons, in mean, were contained and the entire model simulated the activity of 60x160 modules. The resting levels $e_{rs'}$ of different neurons were: $e_{rp} = 0.34$ (corresponding to $-75mV$)—pyramidal neurons, $e_{rf} = 0.67$ (corresponding to $-62.5mV$)—fast inhibitory neurons, $e_{rs} = 0.34$ (corresponding to $-75mV$)— slow inhibitory neurons. The periods of absolute refractoriness and the synaptic delays were: $\tau_p = 15ms$, $\tau_f = \tau_s = 1.75ms$ and $t_{0p} = t_{0f} = t_{0s} = 0.5ms$, respectively. The slow-IPSP onset time had value $\bar{t}_s = 30ms$. The long-distance impulses in the absorption-free zone assumed a constant velocity $v' = 60cm/s$.

Neural Code and Irregular Spike Trains*

Francesco Ventriglia and Vito Di Maio

Istituto di Cibernetica *E. Caianiello*,
CNR Via Campi Flegrei 34, 80078 - Pozzuoli (NA), Italy
`franco@ulisse.cib.na.cnr.it`

Abstract. The problem of the code used by brain to transmit information along the different cortical stages is yet unsolved. Two main hypotheses named the *rate code* and the *temporal code* have had more attention, even though the highly irregular firing of the cortical pyramidal neurons seems to be more consistent with the first hypothesis. In the present article, we present a model of cortical pyramidal neuron intended to be biologically plausible and to give more information on the neural coding problem. The model takes into account the complete set of excitatory and inhibitory inputs impinging on a pyramidal neuron and simulates the output behaviour when all the huge synaptic machinery is active. Our results show neuronal firing conditions, very similar to those observed in *in vivo* experiments on pyramidal cortical neurons. In particular, the variation coefficient (CV) computed for the Inter-Spike-Intervals in our computational experiments is very close to the unity and quite similar to that experimentally observed. The bias toward the rate code hypothesis is reinforced by these results.

1 Introduction

The problem of how information is coded in brain is perhaps the hardest challenge of modern neuroscience. The general agreement on this issue is that information in brain is carried by neuronal spike activity, although the way in which the information is coded in the series of spikes, generated both directly by subcortical nuclei and indirectly along the several areas of the brain's neural hierarchy, remains controversial. Two main hypothesis face each other in this respect. The first assumes that information can be coded by spike frequency and, accordingly, it has been defined as *rate* (or *frequency*) *code*. This hypothesis rests on the fact that the time sequences of spikes produced by cortical (pyramidal) neurons are so highly irregular to support the idea of a predominant influence of randomness on their genesis [20,21]. In fact, a Poisson process (a typical example of stochastic processes) can adequately describe the spike sequences observed in cortical pyramidal neurons. A rich investigation field, based on stochastic models of neuronal activity, arose from this finding [8,14,15,18,27,28]. The randomness of the Inter Spike Intervals (ISIs) implies that information cannot be coded in

---

* This work has been partially supported by a project grant given by Istituto di Cibernetica *E. Caianiello* for the year 2005.

M. De Gregorio et al. (Eds.): BVAI 2005, LNCS 3704, pp. 89–98, 2005.

the precise temporal pattern of spikes in the sequence. Neurons are then considered as integrate-and-fire devices which integrate all the inputs (excitatory and inhibitory) arriving to neurons from dendritic and somatic synapses. A fine balancing of excitatory and inhibitory inputs determine the firing probability of the neuron as well as the ISIs. Hence, only the firing frequency (averaged on appropriate time intervals) can be considered as the candidate for coding information [22]. Viceversa, a more recent view assumes that the precise spike times, or the inter-spike interval patterns, or the times of the first spike (after an event) are the possible bases of the neural code. This constitutes the *temporal code* or *coincidence detector* hypothesis. The main motivation for this view is the belief that the transmission of information is based on the synchronous activity of local populations of neurons and, consequently, the detection of coincidences among the inputs to a neuron is the most prominent aspect of the neuronal function [1,2,23].

Several attempts, both computational and experimental, have been carried on to identify the causes of the high irregularity of the firing patterns. In some experiments on brain slices, synthetic electrical currents, constructed in a way to simulate the true synaptic activity, have been applied to somata of pyramidal neurons in order to obtain the irregular ISIs produced by neurons naturally stimulated by synaptic activity [25]. On the other side, several computational models, with different level of complexity, have been proposed for the same purpose ([13], among many others). In some models the variability of synaptic input has been singled out as the cause of the output variability. In others, the main focus has been given to the structure and the *status* of the neuron receiving the stimuli. Comparison both of experimental and computational results, still gives contradictory interpretations and this could be due to the contrasting approaches used for modeling and simulation. The lack of a precise definition of the *code machinery* induced recently some authors to consider the possibility that brain uses not a single coding system but a continuum of codification procedures ranging from rate to temporal [26]. In the present paper, we made an attempt to study ISIs variability by using a computational model of a pyramidal neuron having a complete synaptic structure featuring that of an hippocampal neuron. To this aim, we simulated the activity of the entire set of synapses (inhibitory/excitatory) connected both to dendrites and soma, by using experimental data on glutamatergic and gabaergic synaptic currents and data obtained in our previous studies on single synaptic activities [29,30].

2   Model

To study the coding properties of the pyramidal firing we constructed a model of neuron by using anatomical information from pyramidal neurons in CA1 (and CA3) field of the hippocampus for which a fairly complete description both of the dendritic structure and of the synaptic distribution is available. A general description of such a neuron can be made by dividing it in compartments according to the anatomical position of the components in the hippocampal fields.

In this way our neuronal model has a set of modules called respectively: *stratum lacunosum-moleculare, shaft, stratum radiatum, stratum lucidum, soma, stratum oriens* and *axon*. Each of the above modules has its set of functional (inhibitory and excitatory) synapses which are arranged according to data from literature.

2.1 Model of Pyramidal Neuron

Information on the the main structure of hippocampal pyramidal neurons obtained from literature divided dendrites of pyramidal neurons in CA1 field of Hippocampus into three main layers: *oriens, radiatum* , and *lacunosum-moleculare* . In the CA3 field, a *lucidum* layer (formed by the mossy synapses of axon terminals coming from granular neurons of Dentate Gyrus) must be added. Different authors have carefully computed the length and spatial distribution of these dendrites and have computed also the number of synapses in each stratum, their quality (inhibitory or excitatory) as well has the number and quality of synapses on the soma and the axon [3,7,16,17]. The gross, total numbers for CA1 are: 31000 excitatory synapses and 1700 inhibitory synapses. About their distribution within the strata, the following values can be obtained: 12000 excitatory synapses in *stratum oriens* , where the inhibitory synapses are estimated to be about 600; 17000 and 700 respectively excitatory and inhibitory in the *stratum radiatum* ; and respectively 2000 excitatory and 300 inhibitory in *stratum lacunosum-moleculare* . The article in [16] reports only space densities for the two classes of synapses for pyramidal neurons in CA3. These values can be utilized to compute the distribution of synapses on a single neuron by using the result that 88% are excitatory and 12% are inhibitory. Also the percentages of excitatory synapses in different strata have been computed and so we know that they are almost 30% *in lacunosum-moleculare* , 28% *in radiatum* , 18% in the *lucidum* , 1% on *soma*, and 23% in *oriens*. Percentage of inhibitory synapses are: 33% in *lacunosum-moleculare* , 19% in *radiatum* , 10% in *stratum lucidum* , 9% on the *soma* and 29% in *stratum oriens* . The distribution of the inhibitory synapses discloses that about 89% are positioned on dendritic *shafts*, 9% on *soma*, and 2% directly act on the initial segment of the *axon* (i.e., very close to the hillock). If we use the total value obtained for the synapses on pyramidal neurons of CA1, and divide it in 88% excitatory and 12%, from the above percentage we can compute the following numbers for a pyramidal neuron of the CA3 field of the hippocampus. The numbers for the excitatory synapses in different strata are: 9300 in *lacunosum-moleculare* , 8700 in *stratum radiatum* , 5500 in the *stratum lucidum* , 300 on the *soma*, and 7000 in the *stratum oriens* . The inhibitory synapses results to be : 1300 in *stratum lacunosum-moleculare* , 750 in *stratum radiatum* , 400 in the *stratum lucidum* , 350 on the *soma* and 1150 in the *stratum oriens* .

2.2 Mathematical Description

To compute the Excitatory (and Inhibitory) Post Synaptic Potential (EPSP and IPSP) produced at the axon hillock by a generic excitatory (and inhibitory) synapse located at a specific position on some dendrite (or shaft or soma) we based ourselves on the method described by Kleppe and Robinson [10]. They computed the activation time course of the AMPA receptors of a generic excitatory synapse located on a dendrite by analyzing the time course (recorded at the soma) of the co-localized NMDA receptors. They assumed that the opening time of single NMDA ionic channels is so short (only about $1\mu s$) that it could be considered as a step function. Hence, they computed the filter response of the dendrite to an impulse function (Dirac's δ) and to a step function. In such a way they were able to obtain, by the time course of currents recorded at the soma, that of AMPA phase currents at the synapse. We inverted this procedure and, by knowing the time course of AMPA currents produced at each synapse, we computed the time course of currents at the hillock. From our previous computational experiments on synaptic diffusion and EPSP-AMPA generation [29,30] and from experimental data in literature [6] we could establish the time course of AMPA currents produced at excitatory synapses. Similar behaviors were surmised for inhibitory currents. The current time course at the synapses has been described by the following equation:

$$I(t) = K \left(\exp\left[\frac{-t}{\tau_2}\right] - \exp\left[\frac{-t}{\tau_1}\right] \right) \tag{1}$$

where τ_1 is the activation time constant, τ_2 is the decay time constant and K is a scaling constant. The contribution of each inhibitory and excitatory synapse to the membrane voltage at the hillock was computed by the following equation which provide the filtered time curse at the soma:

$$I(T) = \frac{kL}{2\sqrt{(\pi)}} \int_o^T \frac{\exp\left[\frac{u-T}{\tau_1}\right] - \exp\left[\frac{u-T}{\tau_2}\right]}{u^{\frac{3}{2}} \exp\left[u + \frac{L^2}{4u}\right]} du \tag{2}$$

where L is the distance between the site of the synapse and the point of the axonic hillock, in units of λ (the space constant of the dendrite), T is the time in units of τ_m (the membrane time constant), and k is an appropriate constant related to the peak amplitude of the AMPA current. From the summed synaptic current at the soma and by using the following differential equation, we computed the Post Synaptic Potential (PSP) :

$$C\frac{d}{dt}V(t) + [V(t) - V_r]G - I(t) = 0 \tag{3}$$

where $V(t)$ is the membrane potential, C is the membrane capacitance, G is the membrane conductance, and $V_r(= -70mV)$ is the resting potential. Typical values for these parameters can be found in [11]. Dividing by G, this equation translated into:

$$\tau_m \frac{d}{dt}V(t) = -[V(t) - V_r] - \frac{I(t)}{G}. \tag{4}$$

At the last, the following discrete time equation was used to compute the PSP, $V(t)$, by the synaptic current $I(t)$:

$$V(t + \Delta) = V(t)\left[1 - \frac{\Delta}{\tau_m}\right] + \frac{\Delta}{G\tau_m}I(t) + V_{r\Delta} \tag{5}$$

where $V_{r\Delta}$ is the constant $\frac{V_r\Delta}{\tau_m}$.

3 Simulation

From a geometrical point of view, we considered the pyramidal neuron as composed of the compartments described in the following. A *soma* of spherical shape from which depart a *shaft* and an *axon*; the starting portion of the *shaft* forms the *stratum lucidum*. With the apex on the starting portion of the *shaft*, a first set of dendrites arise and are disposed in a conical volume forming the *stratum radiatum*. A second set of dendrites forms the *stratum lacunosum-moleculare* arranged in a semi-conical volume positioned on the top of the *stratum lucidum*.

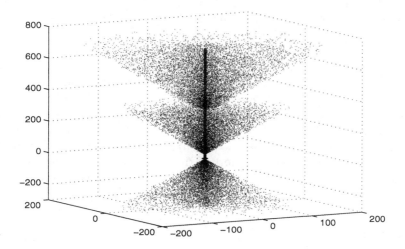

Fig. 1. A pyramidal neuron. The shape is obtained by plotting the synaptic positions in 3D. The units are in μm.

On the opposite side of the soma with respect to the shaft, the *stratum oriens* is arranged in a conical volume. Synapses, both inhibitory and excitatory, are arranged randomly according to an uniform distribution on the different dendritic structures but respecting the proportion and the number as reported in [16,17]. An example of the geometry of a pyramidal neuron is shown in Figure 1 as it is obtained by plotting in 3D the synaptic positions. Once synapses have been positioned, their distances from the hillock have been computed and converted in units of λ. The times of activation of each excitatory and inhibitory synapse have been computed according to a Poisson distribution, with a mean frequency (chosen from data in the literature) which could vary across the computational experiments. The amplitude of current peak at each synapse for each activation time has been chosen depending on a positive skewness distribution which considered both experimental data [6] and computational results obtained in our previous work [29,30]. At any time step $(0.01ms)$ the contribution of each synapse to the current arriving at the hillock, computed by using equation 2, was summed up and the voltage was computed by equation 5. Each time the voltage was equal or exceeded the threshold value (which for simplicity has been considered constant), the neuron produced a spike. In a first approximation, spikes are not modelled according to Na^+ and K^+ channel activation and deactivation as in the Hodgking and Huxley model, nevertheless each spike is not simply considered as a discontinuity point in the membrane voltage time series as usually assumed in simplified models of leaky integrated-and-fire (LIF) neurons [5]. The following procedure has been assumed for its simulation. When the membrane potential crossed the threshold value, the voltage was raised to a fixed positive $(+30mV)$ value and, after, it went in an hyperpolarization state. During the subsequent refractory period, with a duration of $15ms$, the neuron remained unable to react to the incoming synaptic current but the membrane potential increased according to equation 5. The complete procedure mimicked an hyperpolarizing after potential (see Fig. 3). At the end of the refractory period the neuron became again able to react to the synaptic activity. For each computational experiment our simulator computed the ISI distribution, the mean ISI, the standard deviation and the C.V. (i.e., the coefficient of variation of the distribution of ISIs), defined as the standard deviation σ divided by the mean μ: $CV = \frac{\sigma}{\mu}$. This last parameter is considered as an evaluator of the neuronal firing irregularity. At the end of the computational experiment, currents, voltages, activation of single synapses (chosen as control) and the number of active synapses at each time were produced. A report of the more important parameters used for simulation and of the most salient results (mean, sd and C.V. of ISIs and of spiking frequency) was also generated.

4   Results

In this paper we present results which were obtained in computational experiments in which the number and the position of the synapses have been kept fixed and so, the biological structure of the neuron remained constant. In a first series of computer simulations, the numbers of excitatory and inhibitory synapses reported in [16,17] have been considered as reference values to compute the firing activity of the simulated pyramidal neurons. Several computations have been carried on by modifying some meaningful parameters. In particular, the mean and the standard deviation of the peak amplitudes for Excitatory and Inhibitory Post Synaptic Currents (EPSC and IPSC) or the frequency of Poissonian inputs to excitatory and inhibitory synapses changed in the different simulations. The currents produced at the synaptic level, arrived delayed and reduced at the axon

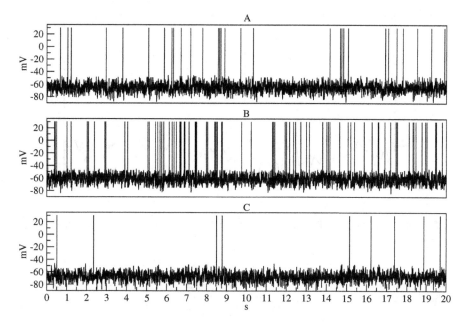

Fig. 2. 20s of simulated CA3 pyramidal neuron activity for 3 different combination of synaptic input frequency: A) excitatory $0.526Hz$ and inhibitory $22.2Hz$; B) excitatory $0.526Hz$ and inhibitory $20Hz$; C) excitatory $0.5Hz$ and inhibitory $22.2Hz$

hillock, in conformity with the equation 2 which takes into account the distances of each synapse from the hillock. The experiments have been compared only by changing the frequency of activation of the synaptic input. The synaptic currents, both excitatory and inhibitory, had peak amplitude of $30 \pm 30pA$ (mean $\pm$ standard deviation). The panels of Figure 2 show an example of three different runs where the synaptic input frequency changed, while the structure and position of synapses did not varied. The mean spike frequency of the simulated neuron was $4.34Hz$ and the CV of ISIs was 1.11 for the panel A. In the simulation producing the output of the panel B only the activation frequency of inhibitory synapses has been changed slightly with respect to the previous example. In this case the mean spike frequency of the simulated neuron was $10.5Hz$ and the CV of ISIs was 0.98. For the panel C, the result was obtained by decreasing a little the activation frequency of excitatory synaptic input and increasing that of the inhibitory one. The obtained results give a mean spiking frequency of $1.26Hz$ with a CV for ISIs of 0.98. The difference in the spiking activity was obtained by small variations of excitatory and/or inhibitory synaptic activation frequency. In all the above cases the CV of ISIs was very close to the unit and within the range of values reported for *in vivo* recordings of cortical pyramidal neurons [24]. Figure 3 shows the membrane potential in the proximity of a spike generation (2nd spike of panel C in Fig. 2). It has to be noted the large, irregular fluctuations of the membrane potential which occasionally can produce the threshold crossing and hence the firing of the neuron. This high irregularity is due to the

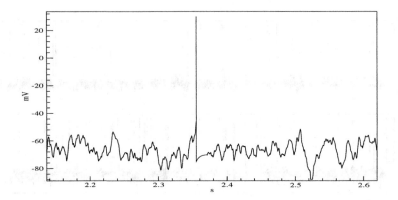

Fig. 3. Membrane potential at the hillock for a time period encompassing the generation of a spike

complete contribution of excitatory and inhibitory synapses and depends greatly on the respective frequency of activation.

5   Discussion

In the present paper we exhibit a model of pyramidal neuron which accounts for many biological parameters. The structure of a single pyramidal neuron of the CA3 field of Hippocampus has been geometrically determined. Up to 30802 excitatory and 4280 inhibitory synapses have been positioned onto dendritic tree, shaft, soma and axon. By combining the distance of each synapse with the cable properties of the dendrites and the contribution given by each filtered synaptic current at any time, the membrane potential at the hillock has been computed. The stochastic fluctuations due to a non-synchronous activation of synapses (produced by a stochastic Poissonian process) determine a large fluctuation in the current arriving at the hillock. The direct consequence of this is a random fluctuation of the potential at the hillock which range from hyper-polarizing values up to the threshold value which is occasionally reached (see Fig. 3). The resulting randomness in the time occurrence of spikes gives origin to spike patterns comparable with those observed in *in vivo* experiments [24]. Of great relevance is that the C.V. we obtain in our simulation is very close to the unit which is that computed from in *in vivo* recordings [24]. This shows that, in spite of the simplifications, the model can be considered robust and biologically plausible. Also, we want to stress that although the pyramidal neuron model used in the present investigations reflects structural data from hippocampal pyramidal neurons, its input and its basic activity are quite similar to pyramidal neurons of cortical areas. Hence, the results describe adequately the behavior of the last neurons. In this preliminary study we present data derived by computational experiments in which the response of the neuron to small variations of the synaptic input frequency is considered. Analysis of data seems to show that such a system is very sensitive to small changes of the synaptic input frequency both in inhibitory and in excitatory synapses (compare panels A,B, and C of Fig. 2). A system with such characteristics would suggest that codification of information in the brain is arranged in such a way that small variations of input frequencies on single neurons result in large (amplified) variations of their output spiking frequency. Highly irregular spike trains seem to be a characteristic of pyramidal neurons of superior cortical areas. The indications about the code underlying the transmission derived from our computational results reinforce the bias toward the rate code hypothesis. However, we want to stress the fact that this indication can not be extended to the activity of primary cortices, which seem to be organized in a different way. In fact, results from primary visual and auditory cortices denote much more tuned responses to specific features of the input [4,9].

References

1. Abeles M. Role of the cortical neuron: integrator or coincidence detector? Isr J Med Sci. **18** (1982) 83–92
2. Abeles M (1991) Corticonics: neural circuits of the cerebral cortex. New York: Cambridge.
3. Amaral D.G., Ishizuka N. and Claiborne B. (1990) Neurons, number and the hippocampal network. In *Progress in Brain Research* (ed.s Storm-Mathisen J., Zimmer J. and Otterson O. P.), Vol. 83, pp. 1-11. Elsevier, Amsterdam-New York-Oxford
4. DeWeese MR, Wehr M, Zador AM. Binary spiking in auditory cortex. J Neurosci. **23** (2003) 7940–7949
5. Di Maio V, Lansky P and Rodriguez R. Different types of noise in leaky-integrate and fire model of neuronal dynamics with discrete periodical input. General Physiology and Biophysics **23** (2003) 21–28
6. Forti L, Bossi M, Bergamaschi A, Villa A, Malgaroli A. Loose-patch recordings of single quanta at individual hippocampal synapses. Nature. **388** (1997) 874–878
7. Gonzales RB, DeLeon Galvan CJ, Rangel YM, Claiborne BJ. Distribution of thorny excrescences on CA3 pyramidal neurons in the rat hippocampus. J Comp Neurol. **430** (2001) 357–368
8. Gerstein GL, Mandelbrot B. Random walk models for the spike activity of a single neuron. Biophys J. **71** (1964) 41–68
9. Hübener M, Shoham D, Grinvald A, Bonhoeffer T. Spatial relationships among three columnar systems in cat area 17. J Neurosci **17** (1997) 9270–9284
10. Kleppe IC, Robinson HP. Determining the activation time course of synaptic AMPA receptors from openings of colocalized NMDA receptors. Biophys J. **77** (1999) 1418–1427
11. Segev I, Fleshman JW, Burke RE. (1989) Compartment models of complex neurons. In: *Methods in Neuronal Modeling* (edited by C. Koch and I. Segev), p. 63-96. Cambridge, MA: MIT Press
12. Konig P, Engel AK, Singer W. Integrator or coincidence detector? The role of the cortical neuron revisited. Trends Neurosci. **19** (1996) 130–137
13. Kuhn A, Aertsen A, Rotter S. Neuronal integration of synaptic input in the fluctuation-driven regime. J Neurosci. **24** (2004) 2345–2356
14. Lansky P. On approximations of Stein's neuronal model. J Theor Biol. **107** (1984) 631–647

15. Lansky P, Lanska V. Diffusion approximation of the neuronal model with synaptic reversal potentials. Biol Cybern. **56** (1987) 19–26

16. Matsuda S, Kobayashi Y, Ishizuka N. A quantitative analysis of the laminar distribution of synaptic boutons in field CA3 of the rat hippocampus. Neurosci Res. **49** (2004) 241–252

17. Megias M, Emri Z, Freund TF, Gulyas AI. Total number and distribution of inhibitory and excitatory synapses on hippocampal CA1 pyramidal cells. Neuroscience. **102** (2001) 527–540

18. Ricciardi LM, Ventriglia F. Probabilistic models for determining the input-output relationship in formalized neurons. I. A theoretical approach. Kybernetik. **7** (1970) 175–183

19. Salinas E, Sejnowski TJ. Impact of correlated synaptic input on output firing rate and variability in simple neuronal models. J Neurosci. **20** (2000) 6193–6209

20. Shadlen MN, Newsome WT. Noise, neural codes and cortical organization. Curr Opin Neurobiol. **4** (1994) 569–579

21. Shadlen MN, Newsome WT. Is there a signal in the noise? Curr Opin Neurobiol. **5** (1995) 248–250.

22. Shadlen MN, Newsome WT. The variable discharge of cortical neurons: implications for connectivity, computation, and information coding. J Neurosci. **18** (1998) 3870–3896.

23. Softky WR. Simple codes versus efficient codes. Curr Opin Neurobiol. **5** (1995) 239–247

24. Softky WR, Koch C. The highly irregular firing of cortical cells is inconsistent with temporal integration of random EPSPs. J Neurosci. **13** (1993) 334–350.

25. Stevens CF, Zador AM. Input synchrony and the irregular firing of cortical neurons. Nat Neurosci. **1** (1998) 210–217

26. Tsodyks MV, Markram H. The neural code between neocortical pyramidal neurons depends on neurotransmitter release probability. Proc Natl Acad Sci U S A. **94** (1997) 719–23

27. Tuckwell HC. Determination of the inter-spike times of neurons receiving randomly arriving post-synaptik potentials. Biol Cybern. **18** (1975) 225–237

28. Tuckwell Henry C. (1989) Stochastic Processes in the Neurosciences. Soc for Industrial and Applied Math, Philadelphia, Penn. USA

29. Ventriglia F. Saturation in excitatory synapses of hippocampus investigated by computer simulations. Biol Cybern. **90** (2004) 349–359

30. Ventriglia F, Di Maio V. Synaptic fusion pore structure and AMPA receptor activation according to Brownian simulation of glutamate diffusion. Biol Cybern. **88** (2003) 201–209

31. Zador A. Impact of synaptic unreliability on the information transmitted by spiking neurons. J Neurophysiol. **79** (1998) 1219–1229

Basic Retinal Circuitry in Health and Disease

Enrica Strettoi and Vincenzo Pignatelli

Istituto di Neuroscienze del CNR, Area della Ricerca,
Via G. Moruzzi 1 56100 Pisa, Italy
enrica.strettoi@in.cnr.it

Abstract. Because it is a highly approachable part of the brain, the retina is by far one of the best known regions of the Central Nervous System. The systematic application of modern neuroanatomical and quantitative techniques has provided the complete catalogue of retinal cells, while electrophysiological experiments are gradually revealing their functions. Retinal complexity is achieved through serial and parallel connections of about 50 different types of neurons. Among retinal circuits, the best known is the rod pathway, a chain of neurons by which rod-generated signals are grafted onto an evolutionary more antique cone system. About ten types of cone bipolar cells provide parallel channels conveying to the brain information related to colour, temporal domain, motion etc. This elegant and complex circuitry becomes severely corrupted in retinal degeneration causing the progressive death of photoreceptors for genetic causes. Retinitis Pigmentosa and related disorders are more than just photoreceptor diseases, as inner retinal cells are severely affected by the loss of their major input neurons.

1   Retinal Rod and Cone Pathways

Vision starts in the retina, one of the best known regions of the Central Nervous System. Thanks to the retinal highly regular structure and to the systematic employment of sophisticated neuroanatomical and electrophysiological techniques, we know now by name each of the some 50 types of neurons contributing to retinal architecture.

In mammals, retinal organization is remarkably conserved; albeit differences in the relative proportions of rods and cones, and regional specializations such as the primate fovea, information processing is achieved basically through the same neuronal networks.

Considerable computation of the visual signal is performed in the retina, a true piece of the brain, and not simply a relay station of electric responses initiated in photoreceptors. This is obtained by means of two basic types of photoreceptors (rods and cones), two classes of second order neurons (bipolar cells and horizontal cells), specialized interneurons (amacrine cells) and output neurons (ganglion cells). A fundamental role is also played by Müller glial cells, dedicated, among other functions, to the retrieval of glutamate used for neuronal transmission. The basic wiring diagram of the mammalian retina is schematized in Figure 1.

M. De Gregorio et al. (Eds.): BVAI 2005, LNCS 3704, pp. 99–107, 2005.
© Springer-Verlag Berlin Heidelberg 2005

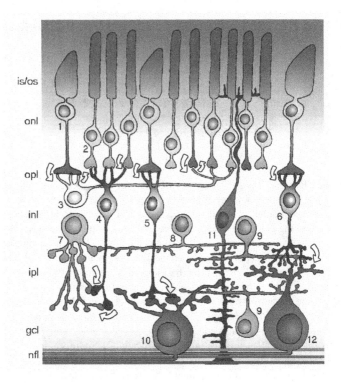

Fig. 1. Schematic drawing of the major classes of retinal cells and their connections. is/os: inner and outer segments of photoreceptors; onl and inl: outer and inner nuclear layers; opl and ipl: outer and inner plexiform layers; gcl: ganglion cell layer; nfl: nerve fiber layer. 1-2: cones and rods. 3: horizontal cell. 4: rod bipolar cell. 5 and 6: ON and OFF cone bipolar cells, respectively. 7, 8 and 9: examples of amacrine cells. The neuron n.7 is an AII amacrine cell. 10 and 12: ON and OFF ganglion cells. 11: Müller glial cell.

Remarkably, each of the six classes of neuronal cells is fragmented in different types, each of them constituting parallel circuits, anatomically equipotent, presumably dedicated to different functions. Each cellular type is characterized by a collection of properties, all together conferring unique signatures: morphology, stratification pattern, tiling over the retinal surface, number, physiology. Hence, one can distinguish 1-3 types horizontal cells, about a dozen bipolar cells, thirty types of amacrine cells and 12-15 types of ganglion cells [1]. Albeit well defined on the basis of morphological features, the physiological properties of each cell types are only beginning to be unravelled.

One of the best known retinal neuronal networks is the so-called rod pathway, meaning by that the dedicated chain of neurons responsible for the elaboration of visual signals initiated in rod photoreceptors and carried up to ganglion cells toward the exit of the retina.

It is long known from electrophysiological findings that a single set of ganglion cells is used for both vision in scotopic as well as in photopic conditions (starlight and sunlight, respectively); this represents an obvious example of retinal efficiency in the absence of duplication. However, because rod photoreceptors far outnumber cones in most mammalian retinas, it was a surprise to learn, by means of quantitative neuroanatomy, that cone bipolars outnumber rod bipolars even in the retina of mice, nocturnal animals in which cones are only 3% of all the photoreceptors [2-3]. The reason is that more rods converge onto a single rod bipolar than cones onto cone bipolars; thanks to convergence, the rod system achieves high sensitivity.

The circuitry associated with rods is simpler than that of cones. There is only one type of rod photoreceptor and rods are connected to only a single type of bipolar cell. The latter synapses on a specialized amacrine cell, termed AII, which can be considered an hallmark of the mammalian retina. Thanks to the bi-stratified morphology, the AII transmits the output of rod bipolar cells to ganglion cells stratified at various depth in the inner plexiform layer. Output occurs by either chemical synapses or via gap junctions established by AII dendrites onto axon terminals of various types of cone bipolar cells, which then excite the ganglion cells [4-5].

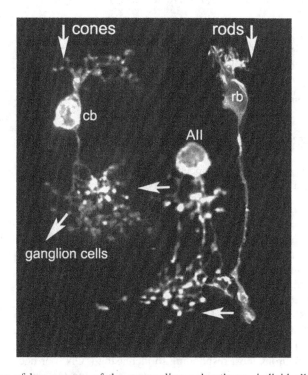

Fig. 2. Montage of key neurons of the mammalian rod pathway, individually labeled with fluorescent dyes. The light signal generated in rods is conveyed to a single type of rod bipolar cell (rb), that, in turn, is presynaptic onto the dendrites of AII amacrine cells. The latter establish connections with the axonal arborizations of cone bipolar cells (cb); these, finally, deliver the signal to ganglion cells, and thus to the exit from the retina.

Figure 2 schematizes the key players of the principal rod pathway. The illustrated cells have been individually labelled with lipophilic fluorescent dyes with the aid of a gene gun, and assembled in a montage. Only one type of cone bipolar cells is represented, although up to a dozen types have been described in the retina of various mammals. AII amacrines establish connections with most of them; hence, the principal rod pathway is composed of a chain of 5 neurons, comprising rods, rod bipolars, AII amacrines, cone bipolars and, finally, ganglion cells.

The reason of this particular arrangement can be explained in evolutionary terms: because rods appeared in evolution after cones [6], the possibility exists that the rod circuitry was grafted onto the pre-existing cone pathways, ultimately exploiting its complexity. By connecting to the axon terminals of the cone bipolar cells, the rod pathway gains access to the elaborate circuitry of the cone pathway, including its associated amacrine network [7]. For example, the directionally selective type of ganglion cell, sensing the particular direction of motion of a visual stimulus, can function in scotopic conditions, even though it receives no direct synapses from the rod bipolar cells. One can say that the rod system piggybacks on the cone circuitry rather than accessing a dedicated, re-invented neural pathway solely dedicated to rods.

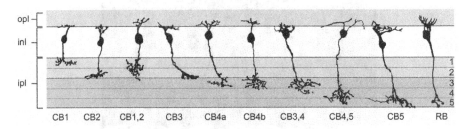

Fig. 3. Schematic representation of bipolar cells types of the mouse retina. There is one single type of rod bipolar cell (RB) and nine types of cone bipolar cells (CB).

Molecular cloning of the visual pigments (opsins) supports the conclusion that cone pigments evolved long before rhodopsin, the rod pigment [6]. Cones are associated with a complex variety of postsynaptic cells, as demonstrated by the fact that most mammalian retinas have 8 to 12 cone-driven bipolar cells. Our laboratory has recently provided a detailed classification of bipolar cells of the mouse retina, individually labelled with fluorescent molecules delivered with a gene gun to living retinal slices [8]. An example of the classification is given in Figure 3. Cone bipolars can be divided into two large group, based on the level of ramifications in the outer or inner laminae of the inner plexiform layers. In all vertebrates, these correspond to the termination of neurons most responding to increasing ("ON") or decreasing ("OFF") light levels. It is well known that the dichotomy between ON and OFF channels is established by the presence of different types of glutamate receptors on the dendrites of diverse types of cone bipolar cells. In the retina of the mouse, we found 4 types of presumptive OFF-cone bipolar cells and 5 types of presumptive ON-cone bipolar cells. This is quite similar to the results of Ghosh et al. [9] who provided a similar classification by means of intracellular injections of fluorescent dyes. It also agrees with previous studies on monkeys, rabbits and rats, confirming the existence of a largely conserved structural plan in the retina of mammals [10-13].

The different types of OFF and ON cone bipolar cells can provide separate channels for high-frequency and low-frequency information. This is made possible by the presence on the dendrites of the bipolar cells of different types of AMPA and kainate receptors [14]. Experimental data demonstrate that different glutamate receptors recover from desensitization quickly in the transient cells and more slowly in the sustained cells [14].

Besides the ON and OFF subdivision, cone bipolars can be further discriminated according to the morphology of their axonal arbors, size, and relative abundance. Pharmacological and biochemical studies demonstrate that individual bipolar cell types have characteristic sets of neurotransmitter receptors and calcium-binding proteins [15]. These molecular signatures reflect different modes of intracellular signaling and different types of excitatory and inhibitory inputs from other retinal neurons, either at their inputs from cones or from amacrine cells that synapse on their axon terminals. At the cone synapses, different glutamate receptors are present. At their axon terminals, different bipolar cells can receive inhibitory glycinergic or GABAergic input via one of two different kinds of GABA receptors. The different receptors and their channels have different affinities and rates of activation and inactivation, which give the cells different postsynaptic responsiveness.

Thus, the two broad classes of ON and OFF bipolars are each further subdivided, providing, among others, separate channels for high-frequency (transient) and low-frequency (sustained) information. Two obvious consequences of splitting the output of the cones into separate temporal channels are to expand the overall bandwidth of the system and to contribute creating temporally distinct types of ganglion cells. The result is that the output of each cone is split into several bipolar cell types to provide many parallel channels, each communicating a different version of the cone's output to the inner retina.

Although artificial vision does not have necessarily to mimic the retinal operating mode, the articulated cone pathways and the existence of a piggy-backing rod network provide an elegant example of parallel and serial processing, representing a formidable and challenging template for devising artificial prostheses.

2 Alterations of Retinal Circuitry in Disease

Photoreceptor-specific genes undergo an exceptionally high number of mutations; more than 100 of them have been identified for the sole gene of rhodopsin, the light sensitive molecules of rods. The resulting phenotype is usually a retinal degeneration starting in rods at various ages and then propagating to cones as well.

In humans, mutations in photoreceptor specific genes might cause Retinitis Pigmentosa (RP), a family of genetic disorders leading to progressive blindness, with an incidence of about 1:3,500. Although RP is presently without cure, experimental work is in progress in the hope to prevent the progressive death of photoreceptors or in the attempt to repair and replace these highly specialized cells.

In view of the growing body of therapeutic approaches being developed to cure RP, it is important to focus the attention not only onto photoreceptors (the cells traditionally studied in this family of diseases) but on the fate of the whole retina; particularly, it is important to understand whether secondary degeneration affects the synaptic partners of photoreceptors, and namely the bipolar and horizontal cells.

Preservation of second order neurons, in fact, is a pre-requisite for retinal repair based on transplantation of photoreceptor precursors, on gene-therapy or on retinal exogenous stimulation achieved with electronic prostheses [16-18].

Up to few years ago, it was generally accepted that photoreceptor degeneration had minor effects upon inner retinal cells. Staining of histological sections with general methods did not reveal particular changes in retinal architecture; this was thus considered to be preserved except at the very late stages of the disease, anyway considered not suitable for attempting a cure.

The application of cell-type specific methods of staining to pathological retinal tissue allowed the study of individual cell types at various stages of the disease progression. Few groups of investigators (including ours) examined systematically the retina of mammals (mostly rodents) with various forms of inherited retinal degeneration and brought to light impressive changes occurring among inner retinal cells as a consequence of the death of rods and cones [19].

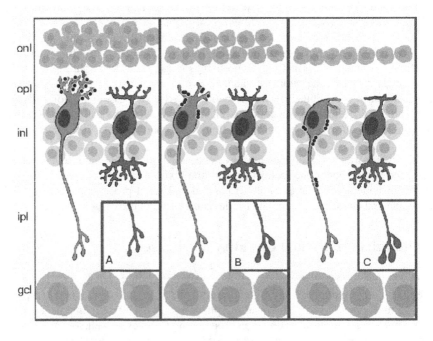

Fig. 4. Diagram illustrating some of the effects of photoreceptor degeneration upon rod (left) and cone bipolar cells (right). As long as photoreceptors die off, the dendrites of bipolar cells undergo progressive retraction, up to complete atrophy. Neurotransmitter receptors, such as the metabotropic glutamate receptor mGluR6 (black dots) are down regulated and misplaced to the cell bodies and axons of the bipolar cells. The axonal arborizations, normally growing to their adult size during postnatal retinal development, show a structural failure and remain atrophic.

Our laboratory demonstrated that, the wave of photoreceptor death is accompanied by a stereotyped series of changes in second order neurons: this series is independent of the genetic abnormality underlying the disease and it is common to different animal species. Abnormalities include progressive and wide-spread dendritic retraction in rod and cone bipolar cells, misplacement and loss of glutamatergic postsynaptic receptors, aberrant neurite sprouting and, in the most aggressive mutations, secondary neuronal loss [20-23]. A diagram illustrating major remodelling events in bipolar cells of mouse models of RP is shown in Figure 4.

Other investigators have described extensive gliosis, ectopic cellular migration and self-excitation of neuronal and glial cells in advances stages of the disease [19].

Studies on reactive changes of ganglion cells are in progress in our laboratory; they are made possible by the recent development of mice expressing the fluorescent protein GFP in a small number of ganglion cells. By crossing these animals with mice carrying a mutation causing photoreceptor degeneration, one can correlate the anatomy and physiology of individual types of ganglion cells to the stage of the disease. This is very important in view of the recent development of intra-ocular electronic devices which transform light energy into electric impulses that then should excite ganglion cells directly, completely bypassing the retinal circuitry. An apparent limitation of such a prosthetic approach to treat retinal degeneration is the experimental finding that the threshold of electrical stimulation of ganglion cells in human patients suffering from RP is surprisingly high [24]. Our results on secondary remodelling of bipolar cells in mice rise the possibility that the effects of photoreceptor death propagate as a cascade to the innermost retinal layers, ultimately leading to the progressive atrophy and loss of excitability of ganglion cells.

More studies are necessary to understand the biology of Retinitis Pigmentosa; however, this should be considered a disease affecting the retina as a whole, more than just a dysfunction of photoreceptors.

The possibility of studying retinal neurons individually by means of cell-type selective methods has considerably increased our knowledge of retinal architecture and specialized circuitry. Now it is time to extend the same panel of methods to retinal disorders, to study with equal detail how the refined retinal architecture becomes corrupted in degenerating diseases. The challenge and the hope are to prevent and cure them.

Acknowledgements. Funded by the Italian National Research Council (CNR) and the National Eye Institute of the USA (R01-EY 12654).

References

1. R.H. Masland. Neuronal diversity in the retina. Current Opinion in Neurobiology, 11:431-436, 2001.
2. E. Strettoi, R.H. Masland. The organization of the inner nuclear layer of the rabbit retina. The Journal of Neuroscience. 15:875-881, 1995.
3. E. Strettoi, M. Volpini. Retinal organization in the bcl-2-overexpressing transgenic mouse. Journal of Comparative Neurology,446(1):1-10, 2002.

4. E. Strettoi, E. Raviola and R.F. Dacheux. Synaptic connections of the narrow-field, bistratified rod amacrine cell (AII) in the rabbit retina. Journal of Comparative Neurology, 325(2):152-168, 1992.
5. E. Strettoi, R.F. Dacheux and E. Raviola. Cone bipolar cells as interneurons in the rod pathway of the rabbit retina. Journal of Comparative Neurology 347:139-149, 1992.
6. J. Nathans. The evolution and physiology of human color vision: insights from molecular genetic studies of visual pigments. Neuron, 24(2):299-312, 1999.
7. M.A. MacNeil, J.K. Heussy, R.F. Dacheux, E. Raviola and R.H. Masland. The shapes and numbers of amacrine cells: matching of photofilled with Golgi-stained cells in the rabbit retina and comparison with other mammalian species. Journal of Comparative Neurology, 413:305-326, 1999.
8. V. Pignatelli , E. Strettoi. Bipolar cells of the mouse retina: a gene gun, morphological study. Journal of Comparative Neurology, 476(3):254-66, 2004.
9. K.K. Ghosh, S. Bujan, S. Haverkamp and A. Feigenspan, H. Wassle. Types of bipolar cells in the mouse retina. Journal of Comparative Neurology,469(1):70-82, 2004.
10. B.B. Boycott, H. Wassle H. Morphological Classification of Bipolar Cells of the Primate Retina. European Journal of Neuroscience, 3:1069-1088, 1991.
11. E. Cohen, P. Sterling. Demonstration of cell types among cone bipolar neurons of cat retina. Philosophical Transaction of the Royal Society London, B Biological Sciences, 330:305-321, 1990.
12. T. Euler, H. Wassle H. Immunocytochemical identification of cone bipolar cells in the rat retina. Journal of Comparative Neurology, 361:461-478, 1995.
13. G.S. McGillem, R.F. Dacheux. Rabbit cone bipolar cells: correlation of their morphologies with whole-cell recordings. Visual Neuroscience, 18:675-685, 2001.
14. S.H. DeVries. Bipolar cells use kainate and AMPA receptors to filter visual information into separate channels. Neuron, 28:847-856, 2000.
15. D. Krizaj, S.J. Demarco, J. Johnson, E.E. Strehler and D.R. Copenhagen. Cell-specific expression of plasma membrane calcium ATPase isoforms in retinal neurons. Journal of Comparative Neurology, 451:1-21, 2002.
16. G.M. Acland, G.D Aguirre, J. Ray, Q. Zhang, T.S Aleman, A.V Cideciyan, S.E Pearce-Kelling, V. Anand, Y. Zeng, A.M. Maguire, S.G Jacobson, W.W. Hauswirth and J. Bennett. Gene therapy restores vision in a canine model of childhood blindness. Nature Genetics, 28:92-95, 2001.
17. N.S. Peachey, A.Y. Chow. Subretinal implantation of semiconductor-based photodiodes: progress and challenges. Journal of Rehabilitation Research ad Development, 36: 371-376, 1999.
18. R.D. Lund, A.S Kwan, D.J. Keegan, Y. Sauve, P.J. Coffey and J.M. Lawrence. Cell transplantation as a treatment for retinal disease. Progress in Retinal and Eye Research, 20: 415-449, 2001
19. R.E. Marc, B.W. Jones, C.B. Watt and E. Strettoi. Neural remodeling in retinal degeneration. Progress in Retinal and Eye Research, 22:607-655, 2003.
20. R.N. Fariss, Z.Y Li and A. H. Milam. Abnormalities in rod photoreceptors, amacrine cells and horizontal cells in human retinas with retinitis pigmentosa. American Journal of Ophthalmology, 129: 215-223, 2000.
21. E. Strettoi, and V. Pignatelli. Modifications of retinal neurons in a mouse model of retinitis pigmentosa. Proceedings of the Naional. Academy of Science U.S.A., 97:11020-11025, 2000.

22. E. Strettoi, V. Porciatti, B. Falsini, V. Pignatelli, and C. Rossi. Morphological and functional abnormalities in the inner retina of the rd/rd mouse. Journal of Neuroscience, 22:5492-5504, 2002.
23. V. Pignatelli, C.L. Cepko and E. Strettoi . Inner retinal abnormalities in a mouse model of Leber's congenital amaurosis. Journal of Comparative Neurology, 469(3):351-359, 2004.
24. J.F. Rizzo 3rd, J. Wyatt, J. Loewenstein , S. Kelly and D. Shire. Methods and perceptual thresholds for short-term electrical stimulation of human retina with microelectrode arrays. Investigative Ophthalmology and Visual Sciences, 44(12):5355-5361, 2003.

Does a Plane Imitate a Bird?
Does Computer Vision Have to Follow
Biological Paradigms?

Emanuel Diamant

VIDIA-mant, P.O. Box 933, 55100 Kiriat Ono, Israel
emanl@012.net.il

Abstract. We posit a new paradigm for image information processing. For the last 25 years, this task was usually approached in the frame of Triesman's two-stage paradigm [1]. The latter supposes an unsupervised, bottom-up directed process of preliminary information pieces gathering at the lower processing stages and a supervised, top-down directed process of information pieces binding and grouping at the higher stages. It is acknowledged that these sub-processes interact and intervene between them in a tricky and a complicated manner. Notwithstanding the prevalence of this paradigm in biological and computer vision, we nevertheless propose to replace it with a new one, which we would like to designate as a two-part paradigm. In it, information contained in an image is initially extracted in an independent top-down manner by one part of the system, and then it is examined and interpreted by another, separate system part. We argue that the new paradigm seems to be more plausible than its forerunner. We provide evidence from human attention vision studies and insights of Kolmogorov's complexity theory to support these arguments. We also provide some reasons in favor of separate image interpretation issues.

1 Introduction

It is generally acknowledged that our computer vision systems have been and continue to be an everlasting attempt to imitate their biological counterparts. As such, they have always faithfully followed the ideas and trends borrowed from the field of biological vision studies. However, image information processing and image understanding issues have remained a mystery and a lasting challenge for both of them. Following biological vision canons, prevalent computer vision applications apprehend image information processing as an interaction of two inversely directed sub-processes. One is – an unsupervised, bottom-up evolving process of low-level elementary image information pieces discovery and localization. The other – is a supervised, top-down propagating process, which conveys the rules and the knowledge that guide the linking and grouping of the preliminary disclosed features into more large agglomerations and sets. It is generally believed that at some higher level of the processing hierarchy this interplay culminates with the required scene decomposition (segmentation) into its meaningful constituents (objects).

M. De Gregorio et al. (Eds.): BVAI 2005, LNCS 3704, pp. 108–115, 2005.

As said, the roots of such an approach are easily traced to the Treisman's Feature Integrating Theory [1], Biederman's Recognition-by-components theory [2], and Marr's theory of early visual information processing [3]. They all shared a common belief that human's mental image of the surrounding is clear and full, and point by point defined and specified. On this basis, a range of bottom-up proceeding techniques has been developed and continues to flourish. For example, super-fast Digital Signal Processors (DSPs) with Gigaflop processing power, which were designed to cope with input data inundation. Or Neural Nets that came to solve the problems of data patterns discovery, learned and identified in massive parallel processing arrangements. Or the latest wave of computational models for selective attention vision studies [4].

With only a minor opposition [5], the bottom-up/top-down processing principle has been established as an incontestable and dominating leader in both biological and computer vision.

2 Denying the Two Stage Approach

The flow of evidence that comes from the latest selective attention vision studies encourages us to reconsider the established dogmas of image processing. First of all, the hypothesis that our mental image is entirely clear and crisp does not hold more, it was just an inspiring illusion [6]. In the last years, various types of perceptual blindness have been unveiled, investigated and described [7].

Considering selective attention vision studies, it will be interesting to note that the latest investigations in this field also come in contradiction with the established bottom-up/top-down approaches. After all, it was a long-standing conviction that the main part of the incoming visual information is acquired via the extremely dense populated (by photoreceptors) eye's part called fovea. Because of its very small dimensions, to cover the entire field of view, the eyes constantly move the fovea, redirecting the gaze and placing the fovea over different scene locations, thus enabling successful gathering of the required high-resolution information. A more scrutinizing view on the matters reveals that the decision to make the next saccadic move precedes the detailed information gathering performed at such a location. That leads to an assumption that other sorts of information must be involved, supporting attention focusing mechanisms.

Considering the empirical evidence (and the references that we provide are only a negligible part of an ample list of recent publications), juxtaposing it with the insights of Kolmogorov Complexity theory (which we adopt to explain these empirical biological findings), we have come to a following conclusion: the bottom-up/top-down principle can not be maintained any more. It must be replaced with a more suitable approach.

Recently, we have published a couple of papers ([8], [9]) in which we explain our view on the issue. For the clarity of this discussion, we will briefly repeat their main points. First, we reconsider the very notion of image information content. Despite of its widespread use, the notion of it is still ill defined, intuitive, and ambiguous. Most often, it is used in the Shannon's sense, which means information content assessment averaged over the whole signal ensemble (an echo of the bottom-up approach).

Humans, however, rarely resort to such estimates. They are very efficient in decomposing images into their meaningful constituents and then focusing attention to the most perceptually important and relevant image parts. That fits the concepts of Kolmogorov's complexity theory, which explores the notions of randomness and information. Following the insights of this theory, we have proposed the next definition of image contained information: image information content can be defined as a set of descriptions of the visible image data structures. Three levels of such description can be generally distinguished: 1) the global level, where the coarse structure of the entire scene is initially outlined; 2) the intermediate level, where structures of separate, non-overlapping image regions usually associated with individual scene objects are delineated; and 3) the low level description, where local image structures observed in a limited and restricted field of view are resolved.

The Kolmogorov Complexity theory prescribes that the descriptions must be created in a hierarchical and recursive manner, that is, starting with a generalized and simplified description of image structure, it proceeds in a top-down fashion to more and more fine information details elaboration performed at the lower description levels.

A practical algorithm, which implements this idea, is presented, and its schema is depicted in the Figure 1.

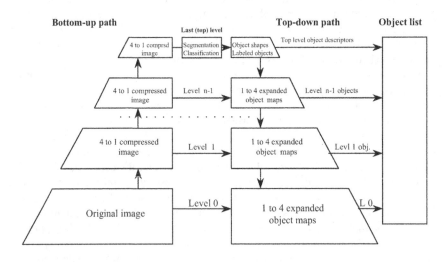

Fig. 1. The Schema of the proposed approach

As it can be seen from the figure, the schema is comprised of three processing paths: the bottom-up processing path, the top-down processing path and a stack where the discovered information content (the generated descriptions of it) are actually accumulated.

As it follows from the schema, the input image is initially squeezed to a small size of approximately 100 pixels. The rules of this shrinking operation are very simple and fast: four non-overlapping neighbour pixels in an image at level L are averaged and the result is assigned to a pixel in a higher $(L+1)$-level image. This is known as "four children to one parent relationship". Then, at the top of the shrinking pyramid, the image is segmented, and each segmented region is labeled. Since the image size at the top is significantly reduced and since in the course of the bottom-up image squeezing a severe data averaging is attained, the image segmentation/classification procedure does not demand special computational resources. Any well-known segmentation methodology will suffice. We use our own proprietary technique that is based on a low-level (local) information content evaluation, but this is not obligatory.

From this point on, the top-down processing path is commenced. At each level, the two previously defined maps (average region intensity map and the associated label map) are expanded to the size of an image at the nearest lower level. Since the regions at different hierarchical levels do not exhibit significant changes in their characteristic intensity, the majority of newly assigned pixels are determined in a sufficiently correct manner. Only pixels at region borders and seeds of newly emerging regions may significantly deviate from the assigned values. Taking the corresponding current-level image as a reference (the left-side unsegmented image), these pixels can be easily detected and subjected to a refinement cycle. In such a manner, the process is subsequently repeated at all descending levels until the segmentation/classification of the original input image is successfully accomplished.

At every processing level, every image object-region (just recovered or an inherited one) is registered in the objects' appearance list, which is the third constituting part of the proposed scheme. The registered object parameters are the available simplified object's attributes, such as size, center-of-mass position, average object intensity and hierarchical and topological relationship within and between the objects ("sub-part of...", "at the left of...", etc.). They are sparse, general, and yet specific enough to capture the object's characteristic features in a variety of descriptive forms.

Finally, it must be explicitly restated: all this image information content discovery, extraction and representation proceeds without any involvement of any high-level knowledge about semantic nature of an image or any cognitive guidance cues mediating the process. However, that does not preclude a human observer to grasp the gist of the segmented scene in a clear and unambiguous way. (Which confirms that all information needed for gist comprehension is extracted and is represented correctly.)

3 Illustrative Example

To illustrate the qualities of the image information extraction part we have chosen a scene from the Photo-Gallery of the Natural Resources Conservation Service, USA Department of Agriculture, [10].

Figure 2 represents the original image, Figures 3 – 7 illustrate segmentation results at various levels of the processing hierarchy. Level 5 (Fig. 3) is the topmost nearest level (For the image of this size the algorithm has created a 6-level hierarchy). Level 1 (Fig. 7) is the lower-end closest level. For space saving, we do not provide all the samples of the segmentation succession, but for readers' convenience each presented example is expanded to the size of the original image.

Fig. 2. Original image, size 1052x750 pixels   **Fig. 3.** Level 5 decompos., 8 region-objects

Fig. 4. Level 4 decompos., 14 region-objects   **Fig. 5.** Level 3 decompos., 27 region-objects

Fig. 6. Level 2 decompos., 49 region-objects   **Fig. 7.** Level 1 decompos., 79 region-objects

Extracted from the object list, numbers of distinguished (segmented) at each corresponding level regions (objects) are given in each figure capture.

Because real object decomposition is not known in advance, only the generalized intensity maps are presented here.

4 Introducing Image Interpretation

Eliminating information content extraction from the frame of the bottom-up/top-down approach and declaring its independent, self-consistent and unsupervised top-down manner of information processing, immediately raises a question: and what is about high-level cognitive image perception? Indeed, none at any time has ever denied the importance of cognitive treatment of image content. But the autonomous nature of image information content preprocessing (that we have just above defined and approved) does not leave any choices for an anticipated answer: understanding of image information content, that means, its appropriate interpretation, must come from the outside, from another part of the processing system. Contrary to the bottom-up/top-down approach, this part has no influence on its predecessor.

The consequences of acceptance of such a two-part processing concept are tremendous. First of all, the common belief that the knowledge needed for high-level information processing can be learned from the input data itself is totally invalidated. Now, all of the so cherished training and learning theories, neural nets and adaptive approximators – all that must be put in junk. And then... Regarding image interpretation duties (the functionality of the second system's part), several questions must be urgently considered: 1) how the knowledge, packed into a knowledge base that supports the interpretation process, is initially acquired? How and from where does it come? 2) how it must be presented? What is the best representation form of it? 3) how the interaction with the information content (the image stuff subjected to interpretation and contained in the preceding system's module) is actually performed?

We hope that we have the right answers. At least, we will try to put them unambiguously. For the first question, we think that the knowledge must come from the system designer, from his image context understanding and his previous domain-related experience. As in humans, the prime learning and knowledge accumulation process must be explicit and declarative. That means, not independently acquired, but deliberately introduced. As in humans, the best form for such introduction, its further memorization for later recall, its representation and usage – is an ontology [11]. (And that is the answer for the second question.) By saying this, we don't mean the world's ontology that a human gradually creates in his life span. We mean a simplified, domain-restricted and contextualized ontology, or as it is now called – domain interpretation schema [12]. Which can be very specific about image information content and context, and does not have to share knowledge with other applications. This makes it very flexible, easily designed by the application supervisor, which thus becomes a single source for both the required knowledge and its representation in a suitable form (of an interpretation schema).

A known way to avoid complications in ontology maintenance and updating (in accordance with the changing application environment) is to create additional partial interpretation schemas, which take into account the encountered changes. To make the whole system workable, a cross mapping between partial schemas must be established. Such mapping is a part of a local representation, and, as we see that, must be also provided by the system designer. However, he has not to do this in advance, he can gradually expand and increase the system's interpretation abilities adding new ontologies as the previous arrangement becomes insufficient.

Finally, and that is the first time when the idea is announced, we propose to see the description list at the output of the first module (the early described information processing module) as a special kind of a partial ontology, written in a special description language. By the way, this language can be shared with attribute description languages utilized in the partial ontologies. Once more, providing the mapping between them paves the way for the whole system integration. And that is the answer for the third question.

The proposed framework does not solve the whole image interpretation problem. It must be seen only as a first step of it, where segmented in an unsupervised manner image regions become meaningfully regrouped and bonded into human accustomed objects with human familiar lexical names and labels. The latter can be used then in further more advanced interpretations of image spatio-temporal content.

5 Conclusions

In this paper, we have presented a new paradigm for image information content processing. Contrary to the traditional two-stage paradigm, which rely on a bottom-up (resource exhaustive) processing and on a top-down mediating (which requires external knowledge incorporation), our paradigm assumes a two-part approach. Here, one part is responsible for image information extraction (in an unsupervised top-down proceeding manner) and the other part is busy with interpretation of this information. Such subdivision of functional duties more reliably represents biological vision functionality, (albeit, it is still not recognized by biological vision research community).

The two-part paradigm forces reconsideration of many other image information related topics. For example, Shannon's definition of information, as an average over an ensemble, versus Kolmogorov's definition of information, as a shortest program that reliably describes/reproduces the structure of image objects. A new viewpoint must be accepted regarding information interpretation issues, such as knowledge acquisition and learning, knowledge representation (in form of multiple parallel ontologies), and knowledge consolidation via mutual cross-mapping of the ontologies.

A hard research and investigation future work is anticipated. We hope it would be successfully fulfilled.

References

1. A. Treisman and G. Gelade, "A feature-integration theory of attention", *Cognitive Psychology*, 12, pp. 97-136, Jan. 1980.
2. I. Biederman, "Recognition-by-components: A theory of human image understanding", *Psychological Review*, vol. 94, No. 2, pp. 115-147, 1987.
3. D. Marr, "Vision: A Computational Investigation into the Human Representation and Processing of Visual Information", Freeman, San Francisco, 1982.
4. L. Itti, "Models of Bottom-Up Attention and Saliency", In: *Neurobiology of Attention*, (L. Itti, G. Rees, J. Tsotsos, Eds.), pp. 576-582, San Diego, CA: Elsevier, 2005.
5. D. Navon, "Forest Before Trees: The Precedence of Global Features in Visual Perception", *Cognitive Psychology*, **9**, pp. 353-383, 1977.

6. A. Clark, "Is Seeing All It Seems? Action, Reason and the Grand Illusion", *Journal of Consciousness Studies*, vol. 9, No. 5/6, pp. 181-218, May – June 2002.

7. D. J. Simons and R. A. Rensink, "Change blindness: past, present, and future", *Trends in Cognitive Science*, vol. 9, No. 1, pp. 16 – 20, January 2005.

8. E. Diamant, "Image information content estimation and elicitation", *WSEAS Transactions on Computers*, vol. 2, issue 2, pp. 443-448, April 2003.

9. E. Diamant, "Searching for image information content, its discovery, extraction, and representation", *Journal of Electronic Imaging,* vol. 14, issue 1, article 013016, January-March, 2005.

10. NRCS image collection. Available: http://photogallery.nrcs.usda.gov/ (Iowa collection).

11. M. Uschold and M. Gruninger, "ONTOLOGIES: Principles, Methods and Applications", *Knowledge Engineering Review*, vol. 11, No. 2, pp. 93-155, 1996.

12. P. Bouquet, F. Giunchiglia, F. van Harmelen, L. Serafini, and H. Stuckenschmidt, "C-OWL: Contextualizing Ontologies", *Second International Semantic Web Conference (ISWC-2003)*, LNCS vol. 2870, pp. 164-179, Springer Verlag, 2003.

A Neural Model of Human Object Recognition Development

Rosaria Grazia Domenella and Alessio Plebe

Department of Cognitive Science, University of Messina, Italy
{rdomenella, aplebe}@unime.it

Abstract. The human capability of recognizing objects visually is here held to be a function emerging as result of interactions between epigenetic influences and basic neural plasticity mechanisms. The model here proposed simulates the development of the main neural processes of the visual system giving rise to the higher function of recognizing objects. It is a hierarchy of artificial neural maps, mainly based on the LISSOM architecture, achieving self-organization through simulated intercortical lateral connections.

1 Introduction

Object recognition is the most astonishing capability of the human visual system, and in the last decades many researches has been carried out to simulate it by means of artificial computational models. However, the majority of these attempts have just addressed the achievement of performances comparable with human vision, regardless of how the performances would be achieved. The point of how the human brain may gain recognition abilities has been much less investigated, since it may appear inessential to the understanding of how the adult visual system works. In part this is still heritage of Marr's epistemology, with the underlaying principle of engineering design as discloser of the natural evolutionary strategies in forging vision.

On the contrary, here is held that the understanding of how the brain areas involved in recognition gradually succeed in developing their mature functions would be a major key in revealing how humans and primates in general can recognize objects. This is the motivation of studying artificial models of vision where the main focus is in reproducing basic developmental mechanisms, avoiding the explicit design of any of the processing steps involved in the classical algorithmic approach to artificial vision.

The background assumption is that most of the processing functions involved in recognition are not genetically determined and hardwired in the neural circuits, but are the result of interactions between epigenetic influences and some very basic neural plasticity mechanisms. This view is clearly not a prerogative of visual recognition only, but is extended as the most general explanation of the representational power of the neural system [20], in line with the constructivism in philosophy [28] and biology [29]. Visual recognition is indeed an exemplar case,

M. De Gregorio et al. (Eds.): BVAI 2005, LNCS 3704, pp. 116–125, 2005.

where the idea of cortical functions as emerging organizations of neural maps is supported by a particularly strong ground of neuroscientific [12, 2, 13, 11], neurocognitive [8], and psychological [4, 23, 16] evidences.

2   Modeling Cortical Development with Self-organization

In the neurocomputational community several computational tools has been suggested for modeling the development of functions in population of neurons, especially in vision. One of the most attractive mathematical principle is the so-called *self-organization* of cortical maps, first applied to the development of visual areas in [27]. In this approach the final functions are achieved by the combination of self-reinforcing local interaction of neurons, supporting Hebbian principle, and some sort of competitive constraint in the growth of synaptic connections keeping constant the average of cell activities. Using variants of this principle von der Malsburg was able to simulate visual organizations like retinotopy, ocular dominance and orientation sensitivity. His original formulation was fairly realistic in mimicking cortical computations, limited to the two mentioned effects, but the resulting system of differential equation was not too manageable and therefore had little further developments.

On the contrary a later mechanism called SOM (*Self-Organizing Maps*) [14] become quite popular because of its simplicity. The learning rule is on a *winner-take-all* basis: if the input data are vectors $v \in \mathbb{R}^N$, the SOM will be made of some M neurons, each associated with a vector $x \in \mathbb{R}^N$ and a two dimensional (in vision applications) coordinate $r \in \{< [0,1], [0,1] >\} \subset \mathbb{R}^2$. For an input v there will be a winner neuron w satisfying:

$$w = \arg \min_{i \in \{1,...,M\}} \{\|v - x_i\|\}. \tag{1}$$

The adaptation of the network is ruled by the following equation:

$$\Delta x_i = \eta e^{-\frac{\|r_w - r_i\|^2}{2\sigma^2}} (v - x_i), \tag{2}$$

where w is the winner, identified thanks to the (1), η is the learning rate, and σ the amplitude of the neighborhood affected by the updating. Both parameters η and σ are actually functions of the training epochs, with several possible schemes of variations.

The SOM is a useful tool for modeling in an abstract sense brain processes emerging from input interactions and represented as topological organization, but it is clearly far from reproducing realistic cortical mechanisms.

A recent model called LISSOM (*Laterally Interconnected Synergetically Self-Organizing Map*) attempts to preserve the simplicity of the SOM with a more realistic simulation of the basic plasticity mechanisms of cortical areas [22, 1]. The main differences from the SOM are the inclusion of intercortical connections, and the resort to plasticity as interaction between Hebbian growth and competitive constraints. In this model each neuron is not just connected with the afferent input vector, but receives excitatory and inhibitory inputs from several neighbor neurons on the same map. The activation $a_i^{(k)}$ of a neuron i at discrete time k is given by:

$$a_i^{(k)} = f\left(\gamma_X \boldsymbol{x}_i \cdot \boldsymbol{v} + \gamma_E \boldsymbol{e}_i \cdot \boldsymbol{y}_i^{(k-1)} + \gamma_H \boldsymbol{h}_i \cdot \boldsymbol{z}_i^{(k-1)}\right),\tag{3}$$

where the vectors $\boldsymbol{y}_i$ and $\boldsymbol{z}_i$ are the activations of all neurons in the map with a lateral connections with neuron i of, respectively, excitatory or inhibitory type. Vectors $\boldsymbol{e}_i$ and $\boldsymbol{h}_i$ are composed by all connections strengths of the excitatory or inhibitory neurons projecting to i. The vectors $\boldsymbol{v}$ and $\boldsymbol{x}_i$ are the input and the neural code. The scalars γ_X, γ_E, and γ_H, are constants modulating the contribution of afferents. The map is characterized by the matrices $\mathbf{X}, \mathbf{E}, \mathbf{H}$, which columns are all vectors $\boldsymbol{x}, \boldsymbol{e}, \boldsymbol{h}$ for every neuron in the map. The function f is any monotonic non-linear function limited between 0 and 1. The final activation value of the neurons is assessed after a certain settling time K.

The adaptation of the network is done by Hebbian learning, reinforcing connections with a coincidence of pre-synaptic and post-synaptic activities, but is counterbalanced by keeping constant the overall amount of connections to the same neuron. The following rule adapts the afferent connections to a neuron i:

$$\Delta \boldsymbol{x}_i = \frac{\boldsymbol{x}_i + \eta a_i \boldsymbol{v}}{\|\boldsymbol{x}_i + \eta a_i \boldsymbol{v}\|} - \boldsymbol{x}_i.\tag{4}$$

The weights $\boldsymbol{e}$ and $\boldsymbol{h}$ are modified by similar equations.

3   The Object Recognition Model

The model is made of several maps of artificial neurons, named in analogy with the brain areas, locus of the corresponding function; the overall scheme is visible in Fig. 1. The environment of the experiments is the set of natural images in the COIL-100 benchmark library [19], a collection of 100 ordinary objects, each seen under 72 different perspectives. In the model there are two distinct pathways, one monochromatic connected to the intensity retinal photoreceptors, and another sensitive to the green and red photoreceptors. For simplicity the short band photoreceptors has been discarded, it is known that short waves are less important for the representation of colors in the cortex [30]. The lower maps are called LGN with relation to the biological Lateral Geniculate Nucleus, the function performed includes in fact also the contribution of ganglion cells [5]. There are three pairs of on-center and off-center sheets, the former activated by a small central spot of light, and inhibited by its surround, conversely for the latter. One pair is for intensity, the other two collect alternatively the activation or the inhibition portions from the red and the green planes, producing the red-green opponents. It is known that also in LGN the functions performed are the result of early neural development, however since this work is aimed at investigating functions taking place in the cortex, for simplicity this component was not left to develop naturally, but was simulated using predefined difference of Gaussian functions.

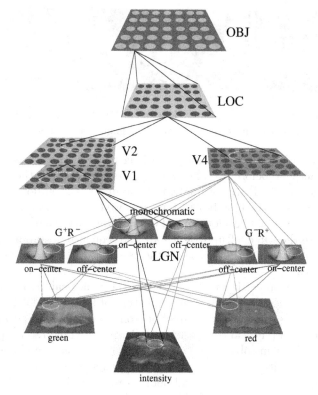

Fig. 1. Scheme of the model architecture

The cortical map named V1 collects its afferents from the monochromatic sheets pair in the LGN, and is followed by the map V2, which has a lower resolution and larger receptive fields. The relationship between brain areas and maps of the model is clearly a strong simplification: the biological V1 is known to be the place of an overlap of many different organizations: retinotopy [25], ocularity [18], orientation sensitivity [26], color sensitivity [15], contrast and spatial frequency [24]; the main phenomena reproduced by this model is the development of orientation domains, small patches of neurons especially sensitive to a specific orientation of lines and contours. Several studies suggest that the natural

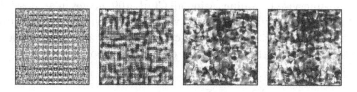

Fig. 2. Development of orientation domains in V1. The gray-scale in the maps is proportional to the orientation preference of the neuron, from black→horizontal to withe→vertical.

Fig. 3. Development of color-constancy domains in V1. The gray-scale in the maps is proportional to the sensitivity of the neurons to a single specific hue.

development of orientation sensitivity is a long process starting as response to spontaneous activity before eye opening, and continuing with the exposure to external images [9, 3, 21]. Accordingly, the training has been done using artificial elliptical blobs in the first 10000 steps, followed by natural images for other 10000 steps. The gradual development of orientation sensitive domains is shown in Fig. 2, where the three leftmost maps are the sequence of training using synthetic blobs only, the rightmost final is the result of the training using all the 7200 real images.

The color path proceeds to V4, named as the biological area especially involved in color processing [30]. The main feature of the cortical color process is color constancy, the property of group of neurons to respond to specific hue, despite the changes in physical composition of the reflected light. This property is important in recognizing objects, giving continuity to surfaces, and has also been proven to be an ability emerging gradually in infants [4]. During the training of V4 at the beginning there is a normal neural response, therefore with very low sensitivity to pure hue, and is peaked in the middle range between red and green, at the end the color sensitivity of all patches is uniformly distributed along the hue range. The development of color constancy domains is shown in Fig. 3.

The paths from V4 and V2 rejoin in the cortical map LOC, which has larger receptive fields, and is the last area of LISSOM type. It is known that knowledge of non-visuotopic areas in humans is currently poor [7], and scarcely comparable with primates [6]. An area that recently has been suggested as strongly involved in object recognition is the so-called LOC (Lateral Occipital Complex) [17, 10]. The response properties of cells in this area seems to fulfill the requirement for an object-recognition area: sensitivity to moderately complex and complex visual stimuli, and reasonable invariance with respect to the appearance of objects. The most difficult and unconstrained variability in appearance is inherent to the physics of vision: the 2D projection on the retina of 3D objects. The model LOC achieves by unsupervised training, using all COIL-100 images in all possible view, a remarkable invariance with respect to viewpoint, as visible in some examples in Fig. 4. Table 1 summarizes the numerical results over all images, measured by cross-correlation between base view and other views, both in the input images and in the LOC maps:

$$\rho\left(I_1, I_2\right) = \frac{\sum_{0<r<N} \sum_{0<c<M}(x_{r,c} - \mu_1)(y_{r,c} - \mu_2)}{\sigma_1 \sigma_2 M N}, \tag{5}$$

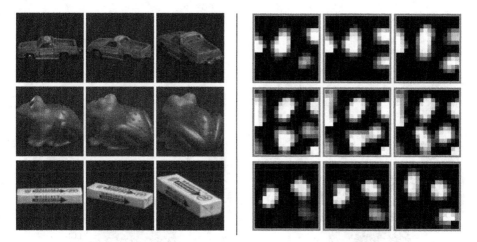

Fig. 4. Invariance properties of the LOC map. In the right block is displayed the activations of the LOC map in response to the corresponding input images in the left block. Rotations are in steps of $30°$.

Table 1. Correlations between images under viewpoint transformation (middle column), and the corresponding LOC map (right column), averaged over all 100 objects

type of transformation	input image	LOC map
rotation of $30°$	0.781	0.903
rotation of $60°$	0.648	0.756
size downscaling of 80%	0.637	0.794
size downscaling of 70%	0.547	0.655
translation of 10%	0.463	0.586
translation of 20%	0.207	0.397

where I_1 and I_2 are two images, as matrices $N \times M$ of pixels x and y, σ is the standard deviation and μ the mean value. In Fig. 5 are shown all visuotopic maps of the model, from the retina up to LOC, excluding OBJ, for two sample images. It can be seen how, traveling from the bottom to the top of the model, the map responses gradually loose a definite correspondence with the retinal input, and assume more the nature of distributed coding.

The highest map in the model is called OBJ. It processes as vector input the whole content of LOC, ignoring the spacial organization of the data. This map is an abstraction of the semantic organization of the visual scene, it is not related to any defined brain locus, but performs functions spread in many areas, not only the occipital lobe. For this reason it is not modeled with the LISSOM architecture, but takes advantage of the synthetic categorization capabilities of the SOM map. In a minimal interpretation it can be just intended as a way of visualizing the categorizations that are implicitly available in the neural coding of responses elicited in the LOC map by the various objects.

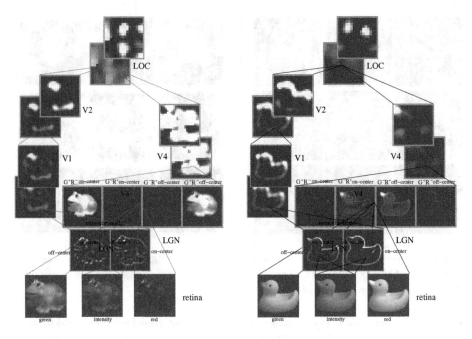

Fig. 5. Two sample processes through all the visual areas of the model. For all cortical areas there is a first activation map, and overlapped the final settled map.

The results of the organization in OBJ are shown using a labeling technique: being o an object of the COIL set $\mathcal{O}$, $I_i^{(o)}$ one of its view, and x a neuron in the OBJ map, the labeling function $l(\cdot)$ is given by:

$$l(x) = \arg\max_{o \in \mathcal{O}} \left\{ \left| \left\{ I_i^{(o)} : x = w\left(I_i^{(o)}\right) \right\} \right| \right\}, \tag{6}$$

where $w(\cdot)$ is the model function giving the winner in OBJ for an input image, and being $|\cdot|$ the cardinality of a set. The image used for labeling an object o is its base view. The organization of all objects in OBJ, revealed by the labeling (6), is shown in Fig. 6. For most objects the prevailing neurons are clustered close together, in some cases even in a single unit. The neighborhood of different objects is based on the overlap of several coexisting ordering principles: color, shape, symmetries. For the large majority of the objects this topological relationship represents a consistent spontaneous categorization. There are also cases of objects in two positions far away in the map, like the electrical plug, in the middle of the top row and in central part of the second and third columns, or the house-shaped piece of wood. In all those cases there are two clusters corresponding to very different appearance of the object under different perspectives, in general at orthogonal angles. This is consistent with the image-based view of invariant recognition.

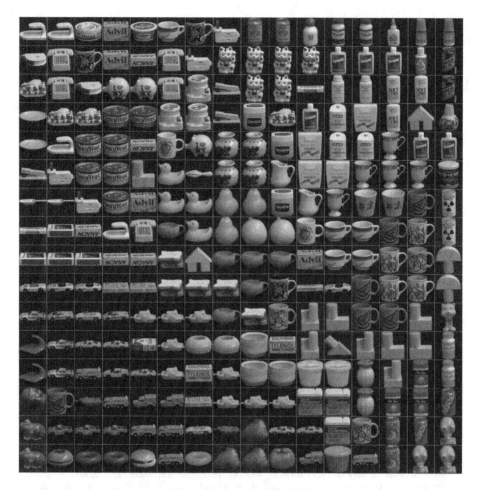

Fig. 6. Organization of objects in the OBJ map of the model. Each neuron of the map is labeled using the base view of the object prevailing on that neuron.

4   Conclusions

A neural model of visual object recognition has been presented. As every model, it includes several simplifications with respect to the biological vision. Some are really drastic: the segregation of processes in areas, the lack of backprojections, and the simplification of the neural computations. Probably it is even more simple than other models available in literature. But it pursues a precise goal: not to simulate the functions involved in object recognition, to simulate instead the mechanisms giving rise spontaneously to these functions. In this objective, the model succeeds in reproducing some of the fundamental computational steps, known to be essential for visual recognition, without any explicit modeling of the processing functions necessary, only thanks to the basic neural self-organization plasticity.

References

[1] J. A. Bednar. *Learning to See: Genetic and Environmental Influences on Visual Development.* PhD thesis, University of Texas at Austin, 2002. Tech Report AI-TR-02-294.

[2] A. Burkhalter, K. L. Bernardo, and V. Charles. Development of local circuits in human visual cortex. *Journal of Neuroscience,* 13:1916–1931, 1993.

[3] B. Chapman, M. P. Stryker, and T. Bonhoeffer. Development of orientation preference maps in ferret primary visual cortex. *Journal of Neuroscience,* 16:6443–6453, 1996.

[4] J. L. Dannemiller. A test of color constancy in 9- and 20-weeks-old human infants following simulated illuminant changes. *Developmental Psychology,* 25:171–184, 1989.

[5] J. E. Dowling. *The Retina: An Approachable Part of the Brain.* Cambridge University Press, Cambridge (UK), 1987.

[6] D. C. V. Essen, J. W. Lewis, H. A. Drury, N. Hadjikhani, R. B. Tootell, M. Bakircioglu, and M. I. Miller. Mapping visual cortex in monkeys and humans using surface-based atlases. *Vision Research,* 41:1359–1378, 2001.

[7] M. J. Farah and G. K. Aguirre. Imaging visual recognition: Pet and fmri studies of the functional anatomy of human visual recognition. *Trends in Cognitive Sciences,* 3:179–186, 1999.

[8] P. Gerhardstein, I. Kovacs, J. Ditre, and A. Feher. Detection of contour continuity and closure in three-month-olds. *Vision Research,* 44:2981–2988, 2004.

[9] I. Gödecke and T. Bonhoeffer. Development of identical orientation maps for two eyes without common visual experience. *Nature,* 379:251–254, 1996.

[10] K. Grill-Spector, Z. Kourtzi, and N. Kanwisher. The lateral occipital complex and its role in object recognition. *Vision Research,* 41:1409–1422, 2001.

[11] C. Hou, M. W. Pettet, V. Sampath, T. R. Candy, and A. M. Norcia. Development of the spatial organization and dynamics of lateral interactions in the human visual system. *Journal of Neuroscience,* 23:8630–8640, 2003.

[12] L. C. Katz and E. M. Callaway. Development of local circuits in mammalian visual cortex. *Science,* 255:209–212, 1992.

[13] A. Kirkwood and M. F. Bear. Hebbian synapses in visual cortex. *Journal of Neuroscience,* 14:1634–1645, 1994.

[14] T. Kohonen. *Self-Organizing Maps.* Springer-Verlag, Berlin, 1995.

[15] C. E. Landisman and D. Y. Ts'o. Color processing in macaque striate cortex: Relationships to ocular dominance, cytochrome oxidase, and orientation. *Journal of Neurophysiology,* 87:3126–3137, 2002.

[16] L. I. Leushina and A. A. Nevskaya. Development of vision and visual notions in infants. *Journal of Evolutionary Biochemistry and Physiology,* 39:67–76, 2003. Translated from *Zhurnal Evolyutsionnoi Biokhimii i Fiziologii.*

[17] R. Malach, J. B. Reppas, R. R. Benson, K. K. Kwong, H. Jiang, W. A. Kennedy, P. J. Ledden, T. J. Brady, B. R. Rosen, and R. B. Tootell. Object-related activity revealed by functional magnetic resonance imaging in human occipital cortex. *Proceedings of the Natural Academy of Science USA,* 92:8135–8139, 1995.

[18] K. D. Miller, J. B. Keller, and M. P. Stryker. Ocular dominance column development: Analysis and simulation. *Science*, 245:605–615, 1989.

[19] H. Murase and S. Nayar. Visual learning and recognition of 3-d object by appearence. *International Journal of Computer Vision*, 14:5–24, 1995.

[20] S. R. Quartz and T. J. Sejnowski. The neural basis of cognitive development: a constructivist manifesto. *Behavioral and Brain Science*, 20:537–596, 1977.

[21] F. Sengpiel and P. C. Kind. The role of activity in development of the visual system. *Current Biology*, 12:818–826, 2002.

[22] J. Sirosh and R. Miikkulainen. Topographic receptive fields and patterned lateral interaction in a self-organizing model of the primary visual cortex. *Neural Computation*, 9:577–594, 1997.

[23] L. B. Smith. Children's noun learning: How general learning processes make specialized learning mechanisms. In B. MacWhinney, editor, *The Emergence of Language*. Lawrence Erlbaum Associates, Mahwah (NJ), 1999. Second Edition.

[24] B. H. Tootell, M. S. Silverman, S. L. Hamilton, E. Switkes, and R. De Valois. Functional anatomy of the macaque striate cortex. V. spatial frequency. *Journal of Neuroscience*, 8:1610–1624, 1988.

[25] B. H. Tootell, E. Switkes, M. S. Silverman, and S. L. Hamilton. Functional anatomy of the macaque striate cortex. II. retinotopic organization. *Journal of Neuroscience*, 8:1531–1568, 1988.

[26] W. Vanduffel, R. B. H. Tootell, A. A. Schoups, and G. A. Orban. The organization of orientation selectivity throughout the macaque visual cortex. *Cerebral Cortex*, 12:647–662, 2002.

[27] C. von der Malsburg. Self-organization of orientation sensitive cells in the striate cortex. *Kibernetic*, 14:85–100, 1973.

[28] E. von Glasersfel. *The construction of Knowledge: Contributions to Conceptual Semantics*. Intersystems Publications, Seaside (CA), 1987.

[29] J. von Uexküll. *Umwelt und Innenwelt der Tiere*. Springer-Verlag, Berlin, 1921.

[30] S. Zeki. Colour coding in the cerebral cortex: The reaction of cells in monkey visual cortex to wavelenghts and colours. *Neuroscience*, 9:741–765, 1983.

Photoelectric Response of Bacteriorhodopsin in Thin PVA Films and Its Model

M. Frydrych[1], L. Lensu[2], S. Parkkinen[3], J. Parkkinen[4],
and T. Jaaskelainen[5]

[1] Lab. of Computational Engineering, Helsinki University of Technology, Finland
frydrych@lce.hut.fi
[2] Lab. of Information Processing, Lappeenranta University of Technology, Finland
[3] Dept. of Biology, University of Joensuu, Finland
[4] Dept. of Computer Science, University of Joensuu, Finland
[5] Dept. of Physics, University of Joensuu, Finland

Abstract. Bacteriorhodopsin is a protein in the purple membrane of the archaean *Halobacterium salinarum*. Its natural function is to act as a light-driven proton pump contributing to the energy balancing mechanism in the archaean. Bacteriorhodopsin retains its proton pumping property even when isolated from the purple membrane and incorporated into an artificial membrane or polymeric film. Such bacteriorhodopsin films have been studied as a potential material for information technology. We built optical elements based on bacteriorhodopsin and measured their spectral properties. Here we describe a model of photoelectric response of the elements and compare it to the experimentally measured values.

1 Introduction

Very-large-scale integration (VLSI) technology dominates construction of contemporary artificial vision systems in every part, including photodetectors, amplifiers, and processors. In contrast, nature has evolved rather different computing architectures, such as highly parallel neural structures. Consequently, there are suggestions to closely emulate biological systems. In molecular computers, for example, silicon circuits are replaced by a molecular material [5]. In those computers, molecules have a key functional role.

One protein that has received considerable attention as a potential material for molecular optical devices is bacteriorhodopsin (BR), a light-transducing protein found in the purple membrane of the archaean *Halobacterium salinarium* [18]. BR resembles both vertebrate and invertebrate photoreceptor rhodopsins both structurally and functionally, yet all three molecules evolved independently. As with all rhodopsins, BR is composed of seven transmembrane alpha-helices of aminoacids and a functional retinal chromophore, derivative of vitamin A. The protein part (opsin) is bound to the chromophore with a Schiff base linkage.

M. De Gregorio et al. (Eds.): BVAI 2005, LNCS 3704, pp. 126–136, 2005.

The purpose of BR in the archaean is to take part to the energy balancing mechanism. Under anaerobic conditions, BR produces a proton gradient across the cell membrane by the light-induced photocycle [2,10], which together with electric potential difference between the cytoplasm and the outside makes it possible for ATPases in the cell to convert ADP to ATP [1].

BR retains the photocycle even when isolated from the purple membrane and incorporated into an artificial membrane [7,12,21] or thin polymer-based film [3,22]. BR responds to light with a differential sensitivity common in motion detection and edge enhancement [4,11]. Such capabilities are also found in natural sensors, for example, the receptive field structure of the ganglion cells in the human eye [20].

To study the functionality of BR, or to use it in an application, purple membrane fragments can be incorporated into an artificial membrane. Both thin and thick films[1] of BR can be used for this purpose. BR films have properties that make them well suited for optical and photoelectric applications. Films produced by immobilizing wild-type BR in gelatin or polyvinylalcohol (PVA) are highly stable. A film of BR molecules produces a photoelectric response (PER) when illuminated, caused by the translocation of protons in the film. Therefore, it can be used in making photodetectors.

Beside the naturally occurring form, BR can also be modified by methods of bioengineering. Among the modifications of BR are variants with shifted absorption spectra, and consequently, combination of the variants in one photosensing device can be used for color discrimination. The sensor in which three BR types, wild-type BR, and 4-keto and 3,4-didehydro variants, were combined into one matrix was described in [23] and its color detection capabilities were demonstrated in [9].

In our previous work [8], we reported the wavelength dependencies of BR films with different absorption properties, their PERs, and we compared the modeled PERs with the measurements for the elements containing wild type BR and its two retinal analogs. BR for the elements was used in a form of purple membrane isolated from *Halobacterium salinarum* wild type (S9), the membrane was isolated as described by Oesterhelt and Stoeckenius [19]. Two variants of wild type BR were prepared by reconstituting bleached BR with synthetic retinal analogues: 4-keto and 3,4-didehydro retinals. Opto-electric elements were produced from the three proteins as follows: PVA films were prepared by mixing PVA with BR solution and spread onto a conductive glass substrate. After drying 24 hours, a gold layer of about 40 nm was sputtered on the PVA film to form a counter electrode for the conductive glass. A thin wire was attached to the corner of gold layer by silver paint to form an electric connection from the gold layer; a system containing altogether six such elements was made [23]; the elements were in pairs, each pair containing one of the three proteins. In this study, we used a set of new BR PVA elements as described in [14], and used signal conditioning electronics to achieve good signal-to-noise ratio in the PER.

---

[1] A coating of less than 5 μm thick is a thin film, whereas coatings of 5 μm or thicker are thick films.

2   Model of Photoelectric Response

Absorption of a photon by BR excites the retinal chromophore to a higher energy state which causes structural changes in the molecule. The excitation is followed by a series of thermal relaxations during which the molecule returns to the ground state. The absorption coefficient of BR depends on the photon energy. The energy E_p depends on the frequency ν or wavelength λ of the photon, that is,

$$E_p = h\nu = \frac{hc}{\lambda}$$

where h is Planck's constant, and c is the velocity of light. When the spectral energy P of a single pulse from the light source is known, the number of photons at a given wavelength λ is

$$N_p(\lambda) = \frac{\lambda P(\lambda)}{hc}. \tag{1}$$

The quantum yield of BR, that is, the average number of protons moved per incident photon has been studied by optical measurements indirectly from the number of molecules in the M intermediate. The minimum value of quantum yield has been determined to be 0.64±0.04 [24]. Knowing the number of photons from the light source at each wavelength and the spectral sensitivity or absorptance α of BR, the total number of moved charges is as follows:

$$N_e = \Phi_{B \longrightarrow J} \int \alpha(\lambda) * \frac{\lambda P(\lambda)}{hc} d\lambda \tag{2}$$

where $\Phi_{B \longrightarrow J}$ is the quantum yield of photo-induced transition from the ground state to the first identified intermediate of the photocycle. Often, the absorbance function is provided instead of absorptance. Absorptance $\alpha(\lambda)$ can then be directly calculated from absorbance $A(\lambda)$ as [26]

$$\alpha(\lambda) = 1 - 10^{A(\lambda)} \tag{3}$$

Elementary charges generate an electric field to their environment. When charges move, they induce charge and current to electrodes within their proximity. Since BR molecules move protons during their light-induced photocycle, a BR film enclosed between two electrodes generates a photoelectric response [25].

To estimate the number of moved charges, it is necessary to know spectral energy of the light pulse and spectral absorbance of the retinal. Obtaining both functions is not straightforward. Although spectral absorbance of BR elements can be measured with a spectrophotometer, the measured functions are not absorbance functions of retinals — the elements contain also other light absorbing matter in addition to the retinals, such as protein, glass, gold, PVA, indium-tin-oxide, and some impurities. The absorbances of some nonretinal matter cannot be measured independently. Therefore, we need a way how to derive the spectral absorbance of retinals. The absorbance function of BR containing the retinal also differs from the absorbance function that could be derived by simple super-position of absorbance funtions of bleached BR, that is, BR without retinal, and the retinal alone.

In the following section, we will describe a method to account for the non-retinal absorption and to find an approximation of retinal absorbance functions.

2.1   Template Fitting

Building on structural and functional similarity between BR and photoreceptor rhodopsins, we can derive the absorptance function of retinals indirectly from the so called absorption template introduced by Dartnall [6]. The functional form of the template has been proposed by Lamb [13]. The template is parameterized by the wavelength of maximum absorption λ_{max}. The template function is normalized, so generally the fitting requires scaling of the template. Multiplicative scaling will, however, make the curve either broader or narrower. To match the correct width, we can offset the template by a constant. The justification to offset the absorbance is found from the fact that the measured spectral absorbances include absorbance of nonretinal matter.

First, let us examine whether it is possible to use the λ_{max} found directly from spectrophotometric measurements. The absorption spectra of the three types of BR, wild-type BR, 4-keto BR, and 3,4-didehydro BR in aqueous solution are shown in Fig. 1a, and the absorption spectra of elements are shown in Fig. 1b. The spectral absorbances of PVA, conductive glass, and gold are plotted in Fig. 2, respectively. Note, that the spectral absorbance of nonretinal matter is nearly flat near the absorbance peaks of all three BR variants in aqueous solution, and for elements with wild-type BR and 4-keto BR variants. Therefore, positions of the peaks λ_{max} will not be strongly affected in those cases.

Next, we find the template scaling factor and a constant absorption offset. Since the measured spectral absorption should fit the fixed invariant curve, both values can be determined using the fact that the wavelength λ_{max} of the peak is related to the wavelength of half the maximum absorbance $\lambda_{0.5}$ through a

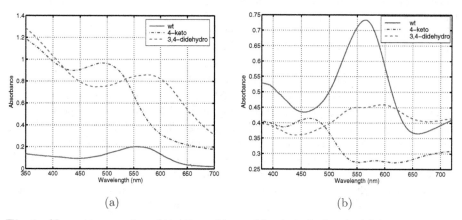

(a)   (b)

Fig. 1. Absorption spectra of the three types of bacteriorhodopsin (a) in aqueous solution, and (b) in polyvinylalcohol films

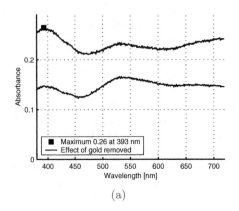

(a)

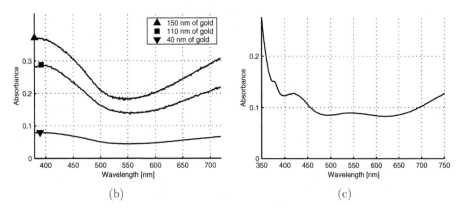

(b)   (c)

Fig. 2. Absorption spectra of (a) polyvinylalcohol film of 48 nm, (b) gold layers with different thicknesses, and (c) conductive glass

constant [17]. For retinal-based pigments the constant is $1/1.0948$ following from Dartnall's data (see also [16]). Since we use Lamb's curve as a template, the ratio of $\lambda_{0.5}/\lambda_{max} = 1.0899$. The described method was used to fit the templates to spectral absorbances of BR elements in [8].

Due to the close attachment of new BR elements to signal electronics and shielding casing in [14], light has to pass through a gold layer before it interacts with BR. The spectral absorbance of the BR film is affected by the gold absorption in such a way that the measurement of $\lambda_{0.5}$ will not be reliable because the spectral absorption curve of gold has a high slope at long wavelength tail of BR absorption. Nevertheless, since the template has a fixed shape for given λ_{max} and measurements of spectral absorbance are made at sufficiently small intervals, we can find the proper scaling (and width) from the relation of λ_{max} to the wavelength of another fraction of the peak absorbance than half. The ratio of 0.9 yielded rather good fitting results. This is because $\lambda_{0.9}$ is close to λ_{max} so it remains in the region where the gold absorbance is nearly flat.

Clearly, a measure of goodness of the fit of each individual absorbance function to the "ideal" invariant form is needed. MacNichol [17] proposed to use the

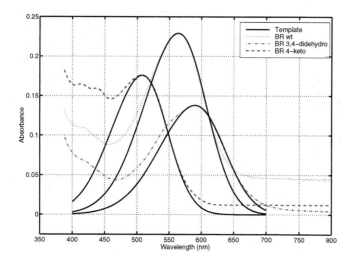

Fig. 3. Absorption spectra of the three variants of bacteriorhodopsin and the fitted templates for the elements described in [8]

product of slope tangent s to the curve at $\lambda_{0.5}$ multiplied by $\lambda_{0.5}$, $Q = s * \lambda_{0.5}$. If the spectral absorbance function is invariant when plotted on a relative wavelength scale, then the slope tangent s will be linearly dependent on $\lambda_{0.5}$. From this follows that Q will be constant. If the experimental curve is broader than the invariant template, the slope and Q will be smaller than in the ideal case. Similarly, if the experimental curve is narrower, Q will be larger. MacNichol found a Q of about 8.5 for the retinal based visual pigments. Q calculated from the invariant form of Lamb is about 8.78.

The value of Q was 7.44 for wild-type BR, 8.34 for 3,4-didehydro BR, and 8.81 for 4-keto BR for the fitted spectral absorbance templates shown in Fig. 3.

2.2 Measured and Modeled Photoelectric Responses

The measurement of photoelectric properties requires a light source and an instrument to register the electric response. In [8], we used a photographic flash as the source of light pulses. A pulsed Oriel series Q xenon flash lamp was used as the source of short light pulses (1.6 μs) for measuring the elements described in [14]. The wavelength dependence of photoresponse was measured using a set of Oriel narrow band interference filters placed between a light source and the elements. The transmittance peaks of the filters were every 20 nm from 400 to 700 nm, the half width of the transmittances was about 10 nm. The wavelength dependences for all the three types of elements was measured. The measured responses were compensated for the irradiance of the photographic flash or flash-lamp, respectively, and for the transmittances of the narrow-band filters. In [8], to measure the wavelength dependence of element response, the elements were connected to a standard digital oscilloscope. The maximum compensated re-

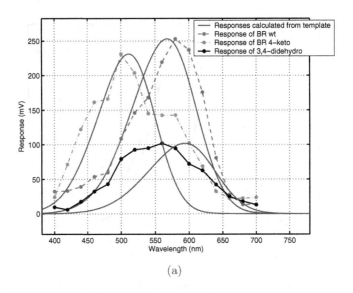

(a)

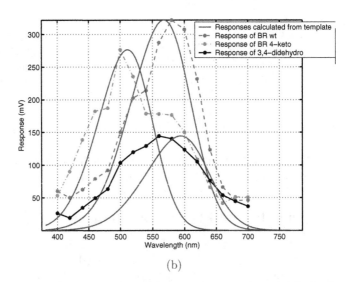

(b)

Fig. 4. Compensated responses for wild type, 4-keto, and 3,4-didehydro bacteriorhod-opsin compared to responses calculated from template. (a) The elements described in [8], and (b) the elements described in [14].

sponse for the element with wild-type BR was at 580 nm, for the element with 4-keto BR was at 500 nm, and for the element with 3,4-didehydro BR was at 560 nm, respectively. The compensated photoelectrical responses are compared to responses calculated from the templates in Fig. 4a. To measure elements described in [14], signal conditioning electronics to achieve good signal-to-noise ratio in the PER was used between the elements and the oscilloscope, and the elements were installed into aluminum cases to reduce electromagnetic interference from the environment [15]. The maximum compensated response for the element with wild-type BR was at 580 nm, for the element with 4-keto BR was at 500 nm, and for the element with 3,4-didehydro BR was at 560 nm, respectively. The responses are compared to responses calculated from templates in Fig. 4b.

3 Conclusions

The templates fit to the measured spectral absorbances well as can be seen both from the figure and from the values of coefficient Q measuring the goodness of fit. This suggests that the template functions can be used in place of measured spectral absorbances in the model of PERs. The modeled spectral response functions are in good agreement with experimentally measured values for the elements containing wild-type and 4-keto BR. The measured and modelled response functions for 3,4-didehydro BR, however, differed significantly. We cannot give a full plausible explanation of this disparity at present state, two major issues confound the modeling: the spectral absorption of gold and conductive layers were considered constant and the measurement of the spectral irradiance of the light source is not reliable enough for the pulsing frequencies used in the measurements.

Determining the spectral irradiance of the pulsed xenon light source was problematic. The optical power meter used for the measurement was applicable to pulsing frequencies above 20 Hz, but the PERs had to be measured at 1 Hz. The narrow-band irradiance from the source was observed to contain abrupt changes when the pulsing frequency and/or discharge energy was altered. Therefore, the spectrum should be measured with identical settings of the light source as the ones used for measuring the photoelectric responses. Primary concern in the future research will be to obtain accurate information concerning the spectral irradiance of the light source.

Acknowledgement

The research project has been supported by Finnish Technology Agency TEKES and Academy of Finland. We wish to thank prof. Dieter Oesterhelt for the bacteria, Ph.D. Pertti Silfsten for his help with the measurements, and M.Sc. (Tech.) Marko Palviainen and research assistant Chayma Aschi for their efforts in the project.

References

1. S. Bickel-Sandkötter, W. Gärtner, and M. Dane. Conversion of energy in halobacteria: ATP synthesis and phototaxis. *Archives of Microbiology*, 166:1–11, 1996.
2. C. Bräuchle, N. Hampp, and R. Drabent. Optical applications of bacteriorhodopsin and its mutated variants. *Advanced Materials*, 3:420–428, 1991.
3. K. Bryl, G. Váró, and R. Drabent. The photocycle of bacteriorhodopsin immobilized in poly(vinyl alcohol) film. *FEBS Letters*, 285(1):66–70, 1991.

4. Z. Chen and R. Birge. Protein-based artificial retinas. *Trends in Biotechnology*, 11:292–300, 1993.

5. M. Conrad. Molecular computing. In M. C. Yovits, editor, *Advances in Computers*, volume 31, pages 235–324. Academic Press: San Diego, 1990.

6. H. J. A. Dartnall. The interpretation of spectral sensitivity curves. *British Medical Bulletin*, 9(24):24–30, 1953.

7. I. Eroğlu, B. M. Zubat, and A. M. Yücel. Modelling and kinetics of light induced proton pumping of bacteriorhodopsin reconstituted liposomes. *Journal of Membrane Science*, 61:325–336, 1991.

8. M. Frydrych, L. Lensu, and J. Parkkinen. Model of photovoltage response of bacteriorhodopsin in PVA films. In *Technical Proceedings of the 2001 International Conference on Computational Nanoscience, ICCN*, pages 17–20, Hilton Head Island, South Carolina, U.S.A., March 19-21, 2001.

9. M. Frydrych, P. Silfsten, S. Parkkinen, J. Parkkinen, and T. Jaaskelainen. Color sensitive retina based on bacteriorhodopsin. *Biosystems*, 54(3):131–140, 2000.

10. N. Hampp, R. Thoma, C. Bräuchle, F.-H. Kreuzer, R. Maurer, and D. Oesterhelt. Bacteriorhodopsin variants for optical information processing: a new approach in material science. In *AIP Conference Proceedings*, pages 181–190, 1992.

11. F. Hong. Molecular sensors based on the photoelectric effect of bacteriorhodopsin: origin of differential responsivity. *Materials Science and Engineering C: Biomimetic Materials, Sensors and Systems*, 5(1):61–79, 1997.

12. M. Ikonen, H. Lemmetyinen, A. Alekseev, B. I. Mitsner, V. Savransky, and A. Prokhorov. A flash photolysis study of all-trans-retinal in Langmuir-Blodgett films and in liposomes. *Chemical Physics Letters*, 164:161–165, 1989.

13. T. D. Lamb. Photoreceptor spectral sensitivities: common shape in the long-wavelength region. *Vision Research*, 35(22):3083–3091, 1995.

14. L. Lensu, M. Frydrych, J. Parkkinen, S. Parkkinen, and T. Jaaskelainen. Photoelectric properties of bacteriorhodopsin analogs for color-sensitive optoelectronic devices. *Optical Materials*, 27(1):57–62, 2004.

15. L. Lensu, J. Parkkinen, S. Parkkinen, M. Frydrych, and T. Jaaskelainen. Photoelectrical properties of protein-based optoelectronic sensor. *Optical Materials*, 21(4):783–788, 2003.

16. L. E. Lipetz and T. W. Cronin. Application of an invariant spectral form to the visual pigments of crustaceans: implications regarding the binding of the chromophore. *Vision Research*, 28(10):1083–1093, 1988.

17. E. F. MacNichol, Jr. A unifying presentation of photopigment spectra. *Vision Research*, 26(9):1543–1556, 1986.

18. D. Oesterhelt and W. Stoeckenius. Rhodopsin-like protein from the purple membrane of *Halobacterium Halobium*. *Nature New Biol*, 233(39):149–152, 1971.

19. D. Oesterhelt and W. Stoeckenius. Isolation of the cell membrane of *Halobacterium Halobium* and its fractionation into red and purple membrane. *Methods Enzymol*, pages 667–686, 1974.

20. C. W. Oyster. *The Human Eye*. Sinauer Associates, Inc., Sunderland, Massachusetts, U.S.A., 1999.

21. J.-L. Rigaud, M.-T. Paternostre, and A. Bluzat. Mechanisms of membrane protein insertion into liposomes during reconstution procedures involving the use of detergents. 2. incorporation of the light-driven proton pump bacteriorhodopsin. *Biochemistry*, 27:2677–2688, 1988.

22. P. Silfsten, S. Parkkinen, J. Luostarinen, A. Khodonov, O. Demina, T. Jaaske-lainen, and J. Parkkinen. Opto-electrical properties of bacteriorhodopsin and its analogs in polyvinylalcohol films. In Z. Yaacov, editor, *Proceedings of the 7th International Conference on Retinal Proteins*, Isreal, June 23-28, 1996.

23. P. Silfsten, S. Parkkinen, J. Luostarinen, A. Khodonov, T. Jaaskelainen, and J. Parkkinen. Color sensitive biosensors for imaging. In *Proceedings of the 13th International Conference on Pattern Recognition, ICPR'96*, volume 3, pages 331–335, Vienna, Austria, 1996.

24. J. Tittor and D. Oesterhelt. The quantum yield of bacteriorhodopsin. *FEBS Letters*, 263(2):269–273, 1990.

25. H.-W. Trissl. Photoelectric measurements of purple membranes. *Photochemistry and Photobiology*, 51(6):793–818, 1990.

26. J. W. Verhoeven. Glossary of terms used in photochemistry. *Pure and Applied Chemistry*, 68(12):2223–2286, 1996.

Non-image Forming Function
of the Extraocular Photoreceptors in the Ganglion
of the Sea Slug *Onchidium*

Tsukasa Gotow[1], Kyoko Shimotsu[1], and Takako Nishi[2]

[1] Department of Neurology, Kagoshima University Graduate School of Medical
and Dental Sciences, 8-35-1 Sakuragaoka Kagoshima 890-8520, Japan
`tsukasa@m.kufm.kagoshima-u.ac.jp`
[2] Laboratory of Physiology, Institute of Natural Sciences,
Senshu University, 2-1-1 Higashimita Kawasaki 214-8580, Japan
`nishi@isc.senshu-u.ac.jp`

Abstract. Several identified photoresponsive neurons (or extraocular photore-ceptors) exist in the ganglion (CNS) of the sea slug *Onchidium*. The named A-P-1/Es-1 of these neurons responded to light with a depolarization, caused by closing of the cGMP-gated K^+ channels, as in vertebrate phototransduction. The hyperpolarizing photoresponse of the others Ip-2/Ip-1 was produced by opening of the same cGMP-gated K^+ channels as above following activation of a G-protein, Go coupled with guanylate cyclase. The amount of light required to stimulate these neurons covered *in situ* could be easily provided by the trans-mission of living daylight through the animal's body wall. The first order pho-tosensory cells, A-P-1/Es-1 and Ip-2/Ip-1 were not only the second order in-terneurons relaying several kinds of sensory inputs, but also motoneurons in-nervating the mantle and the pneumostome. Thus, it is suggested that the depo-larizing photoresponse of A-P-1/Es-1 plays a role in facilitating the synaptic transmission of sensory inputs and the following outputs, i.e. the mantle move-ments and that the hyperpolarizing one of Ip-2/Ip-1 in depressing a transmission similar to above and the following pneumostome ones. Similarly, it is possible that the photoresponse of photoresponsive neurons, ipRGCs in mammalian ret-ina operates also in the general regulation of synaptic transmission and behav-ioral activities.

1 Introduction

Extraocular photoreception is mediated through photoresponsive neurons in the caudal ganglion of the crayfish [17], [24] and in the abdominal or pleuro-parietal ganglion of the sea slugs, *Aplysia* [1], [2] and *Onchidium* [8], [16], but not through photoreceptor cells (photoreceptors) included in well-developed bilateral eyes (ocu-lars) on their head. Such neurons will be referred to as extraocular photoreceptors, because they are directly responsive to light without the aid of any above-mentioned eye photoreceptors. We will also call those neurons simple photorecep-tors, in view of their lack of microvilli or cilia characteristic of vertebrate and inver-tebrate eye photoreceptors.

M. De Gregorio et al. (Eds.): BVAI 2005, LNCS 3704, pp. 136–146, 2005.

Of four identified simple photoreceptors in the *Onchidium* ganglion, the named A-P-1 and Es-1 respond to a brief light stimulus with a long-lasting depolarization [9], [19], while the others Ip-2 and Ip-1 respond to the same light with a long-lasting hyperpolarization [20]. In addition, these neurons (the primary photosensory cells) have also been second order interneurons relaying some sensory stimuli. A considerable amount of information has since been obtained about the phototransduction mechanisms of the above simple photoreceptors [9], [12], [13], and [21]. However, little has yet been definitely established about the functional significance of those extraocular photoreceptors *in situ*.

Recently, extraocular photoreceptors, called the intrinsically photosensitive retinal ganglion cells (ipRGCs) which differ radically from the rod and cone eye photoreceptors have been also discovered in the rat or mouse retina [3], [15] (for review, see [4]). According to these authors, the simple ipRGCs without microvilli or cilia showed a remarkably sustained depolarization following a suitably brief light and also these primary photosensory neurons functioned as secondary interneurons in the retinal pathway. Considering a characteristic of such a sustained photoresponse and an arrangement as interneurons of ipRGCs, one supposes that the simple ipRGCs may be homologous to the same simple photoreceptors, *Onchidium* A-P-1/Es-1 and Ip-2/Ip-1. At present, the phototransduction and precise role of ipRGCs has not yet been determined. Related matters will be discussed later. Here, we survey the phototransduction and light-dependent channels of the *Onchidium* simple photoreceptors studied to date. We further examined and discussed with reference to non-visual function of those photoreceptors.

2   Materials and Methods

Experimental animals, the opisthobranch (or pulmonate) mollusc *Onchidium verruculatum* weighting 10 - 15 g, were collected from the intertidal zone of Sakurajima, Kagoshima, Japan. The molluscs were kept in a natural seawater aquarium (20-23°C), and were fed with dried natural sea weeds occasionally. The circumesophageal ganglia were exposed by dissecting through the mid-dorsal surface of the animal and were isolated after overlying connective tissue had been removed (Fig. 1A, B). The procedure for preparing and conditioning extraocular photoreceptors, the photoresponsive neurons in the abdominal ganglion of this animal was similar to that described previously [9], [20]. In some experiments, a whole animal, the semi-intact preparation was used to examine the possible electrophysiological correlates of the behavioral phenomena observed. This preparation was similar to that described previously [6].

The normal solution, artificial seawater (ASW) used for continuous perfusion of each preparation had the following composition (mM): NaCl, 450; KCl, 10; CaCl$_2$, 10; MgCl$_2$ 50; Tris buffer, 10. The pH was 7.8. Various modified perfusing solutions used for optional experiments intended have been described previously (e.g., see [9], [13], [20].

For electrophysiology, an individual, identified neuron was inserted with up to four microelectrodes for the recording of membrane potential or current, passing current, the ionophoresis and the pressure injection under visual control. The general techniques of current-, voltage-, and patch-clamp recordings have been fully described previously [9], [10], [13], [20].

The standard procedure for photostimulation has been described in detail elsewhere [9], [20]. The light stimulus energy was measured with a radiometer (4090, SJI) whose sensor was placed at the position of the preparation.

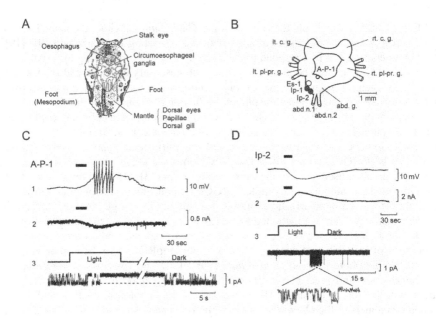

Fig. 1. The depolarizing and hyperpolarizing photoresponses of extraocular photoreceptors in the *Onchidium* CNS. A diagram (dorsal aspect) showing the location of central ganglia in the intact animal. B: The diagram of the dorsal surface of the expanded central ganglia. Approximate location of photoresponsive neurons (A-P-1, Es-1, Ip-2, Ip-1) is indicated. C: Depolarizing photoresponse of A-P-1. C1: the depolarizing receptor potential. C2: an inward current, voltage clamped at -40 mV. C3: single-channel currents closed by light illumination (upper trace). An open channel level in a dotted line. D: Hyperpolarizing photoresponse of Ip-2. D1: the hyperpolarizing receptor potential. D2: an outward current, voltage-clamped at -40 mV. D3: single channel currents opened by light. The expanded unitary currents in the insets. The 15 s light stimuli are indicated by horizontal bars (1, 2 in C and D).

3 Results

3.1 Neural Photoreception of the Extraocular Photoreceptors in the *Onchidium* Central Ganglion (CNS)

Several extraocular photoreceptors, the photoresponsive neurons are identified on the dorsal aspect of the abdominal ganglion of the sea slug *Onchidium* (fig. 1A, B). Of these simple (extraocular) photoreceptors, the named A-P-1/Es-1 responded to light with a depolarizing receptor potential, caused by a decrease in K^+ conductance (Fig. 1C-1; see also [9]), while a hyperpolarizing photoresponse of the others named Ip-2/Ip-1 resulted from an increase in K^+ conductance (Fig. 1D-1; see also [20]). When those simple photoreceptors were voltage-clamped at resting revel, light induced inward (Fig. 1C-2) and outward (Fig. 1D-2) photocurrents, corresponding to the above depolarization and hyperpolarization.

As shown, it should be characterized that these both photoresponses can last for many minutes following only tens of seconds of light stimuli.

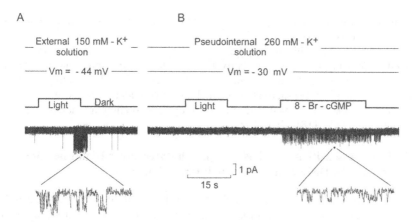

Fig. 2. Single-channel recordings showing changes from the cell-attached patch (A) to the inside-out patch (B) excised from the intact simple photoreceptor Ip-2. The bottom in A shows light-dependent single-channel currents, and the bottom in B, cGMP-activated single-channels, but no light-dependent channels in the excised inside-out patch. The upward steps of the above recordings in A and B show the light stimuli, and an application of 8-Br-cGMP. Parts of the channel recordings at the point marks, the expanded time scale. For details, see also [12].

A further analysis for the single channel recordings showed that the depolarizing and hyperpolarizing responses of A-P-1/Es-1 and Ip-2/Ip-1 are produced by the closing (Fig. 1C-3) and opening (Fig. 1D-3) of the same light-dependent K$^+$ channels, respectively (see also [11], [13]).

3.2   A Phototransduction Mechanism of the Simple A-P-1/Es-1 and Ip-2/Ip-1

To determine whether cGMP can directly activate the above light-dependent K$^+$ channels in the cell-attached patches of the simple photoreceptors their patch membranes were excised, forming inside-out patches and allowing access to the intracellular face (Fig. 2A). An application of cGMP to the excised inside-out patches newly activated a channel that disappeared on removal of cGMP (Fig. 2B). However, an application of cAMP, IP$_3$, or Ca^{2+} failed to activate any channels (not shown). This cGMP-activated channel was indistinguishable from the light-dependent K$^+$ channels recorded earlier in the same intact patches on the basis of K$^+$-selectivity, conductance and kinetics of the channels [11], [13]. The above results show direct evidence that cGMP acts as a second messenger involved in the final stages of transduction process

Table 1. Threshold of wavelength (λ) in a spectral peak sensitivity of the extraocular photoreceptors (A-P-1, Es-1, Ip-1, Ip-2)

	λ (nm)	Threshold (photons/cm$^2 \cdot$s)
A-P-1	490	3×10^{11}
Es-1	580	7×10^{13}
Ip-2/Ip-1	510	2×10^{12}

activating or gating the light-dependent K^+ channels, the cGMP-activated channels of the simple photoreceptors.

Finally, we have concluded that the depolarizing photoresponse of A-P-1/Es-1 is produced by closing of the cGMP-activated channels, as in vertebrate rod or cone cGMP cascade theory [28] and that the photoresponse of Ip-2/Ip-1 is hyperpolarized by opening the same cGMP-activated channels following an activation of a G-protein, Go (but not Gq nor Gt) coupled with guanylate cyclase to allow an increase in cGMP levels [10], [11], [13], [18], [20], [22].

3.3 Is the Photosensitivity of Those Simple Photoreceptors High Enough to Overcome the Deficiencies of Their Internal Location?

A-P-1, Es-1, Ip-1, and Ip-2 *in situ* which are well buried in the CNS and covered by the body wall are unsuitable for a functional photosensory system; but it may be that those simple photoreceptor type has been adapted to serve as a sensory photoreceptor unit in other forms.

To test whether the absolute sensitivity of the above internal photoreceptors is thus sufficient to activate those photoresponses or not, we measured the amount (energy) of light transmitted through the body wall (mantles and feet, mesopodia) and compared with the absolute sensitivity, the threshold energy. In table 1, the threshold is defined as an energy of light wavelength for a minimally detectable photoresponse of each simple cell. The light wavelength showed a maximally effective light for each photoresponse [9], [19], [20].

Tλ (transmittance) in Table 2 shows the rate (%) of spectral incident light transmitted vertically at the dorsal mantle or ventral foot surface of animals from the outside to the inside. Each Tλ in the mantle and foot was obtained from spectral scanning through the almost middle circle area having a radius of 4 mm in the surface of

Table 2. Transmittance (Tλ) of the spectral illumination through the animal's body wall (mantle and foot sides)

Tλ	Mantle	Foot
T490	2.3 - 10 %	6.0 - 20 %
T580	7.0 - 25 %	15.4 - 35 %
T510	3.3 - 13.3 %	8.0 - 23.3 %

Table 3. The incident energy in the spectrum of sunlight in Kagoshima, Japan with a fine weather at noon on August 13, 2002, measured by using a spectroradiometer (MS-700; EKO, Inc.)

Wavelength (λ, nm)	Energy (photons/cm^2 •s)
490	2.4×10^{15}
580	2.6×10^{15}
510	2.4×10^{15}

mantles or mesopodia of 3 to 5 individuals. As a whole, Tλ of each spectral light was about 2 times higher through the translucent white mesopodia than the dark-brown mantles. Further, we measured the spectral energy of incident sunlight in the center of Kagoshima by using a spectroradiometer (Table 3). Each energy value of the concerned wavelength in sunlight was almost comparable to that at Sakurajima beach, the home of *Onchidium*.

Taken together, the results suggest that light transmittance of the animal's body wall covered by both mantle and foot is high enough to activate (stimulate) the internal *Onchidium* extraocular photoreceptors *in situ*.

3.4 Morphology and Electrophysiological Properties

3.4.1 The Depolarizing A-P-1 and Es-1

The axonal branchings and spatial arrangement of both A-P-1 and Es-1 in the same ganglion was visualized by an intracellular cobalt or Lucifer yellow injection technique and confirmed by the simultaneous recording of the evoked somatic spike and the subsequent axonal spike in the nerves leaving the ganglion (not shown, [7], [9], [19]). The simultaneous recordings of A-P-1 and Es-1 in the membrane potential showed that both cells are connected by inhibitory chemical synapses from A-P-1 to Es-1 [19]. Further, previous study [6] showed that the primary simple photoreceptor, Es-1 is not only a second order interneuron receiving (relaying) tactile or other sensory synaptic input from the mantle, but also a motoneuron innervating the mantle and foot, leading to the mantle-elevating movements.

On the other hand, we investigated effects of light on the synaptic transmission of the tactile sensory inputs.

Under dark conditions, the single electrical stimuli to a given afferent nerve, instead of the tactile mechanical stimulation, were adjusted so as to be subthreshold for the spike generation of Es-1. The light intensity was also adjusted to a subthreshold value. Here, if the subthreshold electrical stimuli were applied under the condition of the subthreshold light intensity, all or nothing spikes (impulses), following the graded EPSPs were generated in Es-1 (not shown).

This suggest that the depolarizing photoresponses of A-P-1/Es-1 play a role in facilitating the transmission of the tactile or other sensory information (see also Fig. 5B).

3.4.2 The Hyperpolarizing Ip-1 and Ip-2

Two whitish colored somata of Ip-1 and Ip-2 lie close together in the lower edge of the abdominal ganglion, so that they can be easily distinguished from those of the orange colored A-P-1 and Es-1, as shown in Fig. 1B. The axonal processes of Ip-2/Ip-1 in the CNS have been partly known by the intracellular staining of Lucifer Yellow [20]. Both Ip-1 and Ip-2 in the ganglion branch into 2 or 3 main axons and at least two of their branches go into abd. n. 1 and abd. n. 2, respectively (scheme of Fig. 3B). Further, an anatomical analysis showed that abd. n. 1 and abd. n. 2 innervate the pneumostome and pulmonary sac ([14], see also Fig. 5A).

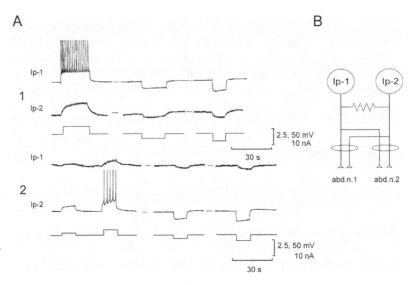

Fig. 3. Simultaneous recordings showing electrical synapses between Ip-1 and Ip-2. A1: Depolarizing and hyperpolarizing current injections (the lowest step marks) for Ip-1. A2: Current injections for Ip-2. B: A scheme showing electrical synapses and axonal branchings of Ip-1 and Ip-2. abd. n.1: abdominal nerve 1. For details, see text.

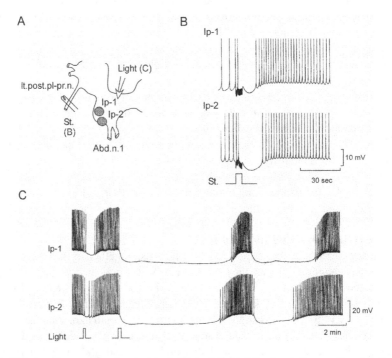

Fig. 4. Effects of a presynaptic electrical (B) and light (C) stimulation on the simultaneous membrane potential activities of Ip-1 and Ip-2. A: A sketch map showing experiments, B, C. lt. post pl-pr. n.: left posterior pleuro-parietal nerve.

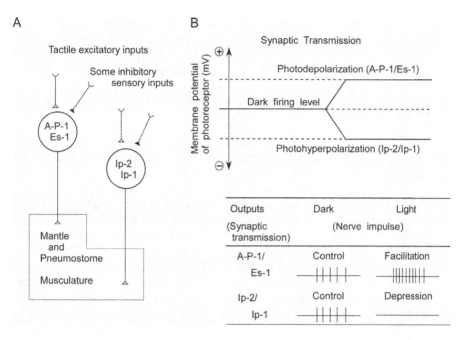

Fig. 5. Proposed scheme for the functions of the simple, non-specialized photoreceptors, A-P-1/Es-1 and Ip-2/Ip-1. A: A-P-1/Es-1 and Ip-2/Ip-1 innervating mantle and pneumostome, respectively. B-upper: Dark and light levels of synaptic transmission. B-lower: Dark and light effects of nerve impulse on synaptic transmission. For details, see text.

To examine the functional properties of these simple hyperpolarizing photoreceptors, we tried simultaneous intracellular recordings of the membrane potential of Ip-2 and Ip-1 (Fig. 3). Fig. 3B shows that the two Ip-2 and Ip-1 are interconnected by electrical synapses which do not rectify. A slow de- or hyper-polarization in one cell was transformed in a smaller polarizing change of the same polarity in the other. However, spikes in one cell were never transmitted, instead reflected only by small spike-like deflections of less than 1 mV in the other, suggesting the low-pass filtering synapses (fig. 3A). Those electrical coupling ratios ranged from 0.05 to 0.1 in 3 to 5 experiments. Similar results were obtained from Ca^{2+}-deficient ASW (not shown). Thus, these low-pass filter properties of the electrical synapse suggested that each spike in a sustained beating or bursting discharges of Ip-2/Ip-1, is never transmitted, but that only the periodical slow changes of membrane potential underlying the beating or bursting are well transformed, thereby leading to the synchronous beating or bursting discharges along both axonal branches (outputs) of Ip-2 and Ip-1 (see also Fig. 4B, C).

Fig. 4 shows effects of a presynaptic electrical stimulation on the membrane potential activity of Ip-2/Ip-1. When the left posterior pl- pr. nerve containing afferent fibers was stimulated, the post synaptic Ip-2/Ip-1 produced a synchronous long-lasting IPSP with blockade of the beating or bursting discharges (Fig. 4B). This suggested that the primary extraocular photoreceptors, Ip-2/Ip-1 are also second order interneurons relaying some synaptic inputs from various nerves leaving the ganglion

(CNS). On the other hand, synchronous bursting discharges in Ip-1 and Ip-2 were inhibited and hyperpolarized by illumination (Fig. 4C).

These results suggest that the hyperpolarizing photoresponses of Ip-2/Ip-1 play a role in depressing the transmission of inhibitory or excitatory sensory inputs (see also Fig. 5B).

4 Discussion

We should like to claim that extraocular photoreceptors in the *Onchidium* CNS are referred as 'simple' or 'non-specialized' photoreceptors, for lack of any morphologically specialized structures such as microvilli and/or cilia, characteristic of most eye photoreceptors. In other words, it should be understood that the above specialization or its vestigial structure in the eye photoreceptors is not always required for a photosensory cell to become photoresponsive. This is well supported by the most recent discovery [4] of the non-specialized ipRGCs in the mammalia retinas, similar to the *Onchidium* extraocular photoreceptors. It has been also proved that melanopsin is a functional sensory photopigment of these ipRGCs, instead of rhodopsin in the eye photoreceptors [25, 26]. Unfortunately, such a photopigment has not yet been found in the *Onchidium* simple cells, although it is suggested to be a rhodopsin-like photopigment for the *Aplysia* simple photoreceptor, R2 [27].

On the other hand, the present study show that the simple Ip-2/Ip-1 use a phototransduction included activation of a Go, G-protein coupled with guanylate cyclase, which differs from that of a cGMP cascade theory [28] in another simple A-P-1/Es-1. It is likely that the mammalian simple ipRGCs use also a phototransduction similar to that of Ip-2/Ip-1, from a similarity between their photoresponse and their morphological arrangements as described in the Introduction. Of course, it has been reported that the phototransduction of ipRGCs may differ from that of Ip-2/Ip-1 [23, 26].

Function of Extraocular Photoreceptors, the Photoresponsive Neurons or the Simple, Non-specialized Photoreceptors, A-P-1, Es-1, Ip-1 and Ip-2

Onchidium are intertidal and amphibian molluscs, so that they use gill at high tide and interchange with lung (pneumostome) for ventilation at low tide. Thus, these molluscs could very easily be affected by the incident sunlight (light/dark cycles). However, the functional importance of the simple photoreception remains unclear, because of the deep-lying positions of the central ganglia.

The present study showed that the incident sunlight transmittance of the animal's body wall is high enough to elicit a photoresponse of the internal simple photoreceptors. Further, the same units performing these primary simple photoreceptors were not only interneurons relaying various sensory inputs, but they were also motoneurons innervating the mantle and pneumostome with pulmonary sac.

Thus, Fig. 5 shows a tentative scheme to explain functions of the *Onchidium* simple photoreceptors, A-P-1/Es-1 and Ip-2/Ip-1. The depolarizing photoresponses of A-P-1/Es-1 may play a role in facilitating the synaptic transmission of the tactile sensory inputs and in enhancing more the following mantle movement activities. The hyperpolarizing photoresponses of Ip-2/Ip-1 may play a role in depressing the transmission of inhibitory or excitatory inputs and in diminishing more the following pneumostome movement activities. Similarly, it is possible that the mammalian ipRGCs operate also in the general regulation of synaptic transmission and behavioral activity (see also [5]).

We wish to thank Professors H. Akasaka and K. Soga, Dept. of Architecture, Faculty of Engineering, Kagoshima Univ., for supplying us with the data of sunlight spectrum energy. This study is supported by Senshu University research grant for study of *Onchidium* nervous system in 2004.

References

1. Andresen, M.C., Brown, A.M.: Photoresponses of a Sensitive Extraretinal Photoreceptor in *Aplysia*. J. Physiol. 287 (1979) 267-282
2. Arvanitaki, A., Chalazonitis, N.: Nervous Inhibition. In: Florey, E. (ed): Excitatory and Inhibitory Processes Initiated by Light and Infra-red Radiations in Single Identifiable Nerve Cells (Giant Ganglion cells of *Aplysia*). Pergamon, Oxford (1961) 194-231
3. Berson, D.M., Dunn, F.A., Takao, M.: Phototransduction by Retinal Ganglion Cells that Set the Circadian Clock. Science 295 (2002) 1070-1073
4. Berson, D.M.: Strange Vision: Ganglion Cells as Circadian Photoreceptors. Trends Neurosci. 26 (2003) 314-320
5. Dacey, D.M., Liao, H.W., Peterson, B.B., Robinson, F.R., Smith, V.C., Pokorny, J., Yau, K.-W., Gamlin, P.D.: Melanopsin-expressing ganglion cells in primate retina signal colour and irradiance and project to the LGN. Nature 433 (2005) 749-754
6. Gotow, T., Tateda, H., Kuwabara, M.: The Function of Photoexcitive Neurones in the Central Ganglia for Behavioral Activity of the Marine Mollusc *Onchidium verruculatum*. J. Comp. Physiol. 83 (1973) 361-376
7. Gotow, T.: Morphology and Function of the Photoexcitable Neurons in the Central Ganglion of *Onchidium verruculatum*. J. Comp. Physiol. 99 (1975) 139-152
8. Gotow, T.: Decrease of K^+ Conductance Underlying a Depolarizing Photoresponse of a Molluscan Extraocular Photoreceptor. Experientia 42 (1986) 52-54
9. Gotow, T.: Photoresponses of an Extraocular Photoreceptor Associated with a Decrease in Membrane Conductance in an Opisthobranch Mollusc. Brain Res. 479 (1989) 120-129
10. Gotow, T., Nishi, T.: Roles of Cyclic GMP and Inositol Trisphosphate in Phototransduction of the Molluscan Extraocular Photoreceptor. Brain Res. 557 (1991) 121-128
11. Gotow, T., Nishi, T., Kijima, H.: Single K^+ Channels Closed by Light and Opened by Cyclic GMP in Molluscan Extra-ocular Photoreceptor Cells. Brain Res. 662 (1994) 268-272
12. Gotow, T., Nishi, T.: Cyclic GMP-activated K^+ Channels of the Molluscan Extra-ocular Photoreceptor Cells. In: Taddei-Ferretti, C., Musio, C. (eds.): From Structure to Information in Sensory Systems. World Scientific, Singapore New Jersey London Hong Kong (1998) 357-371
13. Gotow, T., Nishi, T.: Light-dependent K^+ Channels in the Mollusc *Onchidium* Simple Photoreceptors are Opened by cGMP. J. Gen. Physiol. 120 (2002) 581-597
14. Gotow, T., Nishi, T., Nakagawa, S.: Membrane Properties as Interneurons of the Extraocular Photoreceptors in the *Onchidium* Ganglia. Neurosci. Res. 50 (2004) S190
15. Hattar, S., Liao, H.-W., Takao, M., Berson, D.M., Yau, K.-W.: Melanopsin-Containing Retinal Ganglion Cells: Architecture, Projections, and Intrinsic Photosensitivity. Science 295 (2002) 1065-1070
16. Hisano, N., Tateda, H., Kuwabara, M.: Photosensitive Neurones in the Marine Pulmonate Mollusc *Onchidium verruculatum*. J. Exp. Biol. 57 (1972) 651-660
17. Kennedy, D.: Physiology of Photoreceptor Neurons in the Abdominal Nerve Cord of the Crayfish. J. Gen. Physiol. 46 (1963) 551-572

18. Nishi, T., Gotow, T.: A light-induced Decrease of Cyclic GMP is Involved in the Photo-response of Molluscan Extraocular Photoreceptors. Brain Res. 485 (1989) 185-188
19. Nishi, T., Gotow, T.: A Neural Mechanism for Processing Colour Information in Mollus-can Extra-ocular Photoreceptors. J. Exp. Biol. 168 (1992) 77-91
20. Nishi, T., Gotow, T.: Light-increased cGMP and K^+ Conductance in the Hyperpolarizing Receptor Potential of *Onchidium* Extra-ocular Photoreceptors. Brain Res. 809 (1998) 325-336
21. Nishi, T., Gotow, T.: Depolarizing and Hyperpolarizing Receptor Potentials of the Mol-luscan Extra-ocular Photoreceptor Cells. In: Taddei-Ferretti, C., Musio, C. (eds.): From Structure to Information in Sensory Systems. World Scientific, Singapore New Jersey London Hong Kong (1998) 341-356
22. Nishi, T., Gotow, T.: An Activation of Guanylate Cyclase Coupled with G protein, Go Mediates the Hyperpolarizing Photoresponse of the *Onchidium* Extra-ocular Photorecep-tors. Neurosci. Res. 46 (2003) S40
23. Panda, S., Nayak, S.K., Campo, B., Walker, J.R., Hogenesch, J.B., Jegla, T.: Illumination of the melanopsin signaling pathway. Science 307 (2005) 600-604
24. Prosser, C.L.: Responses to Illumination of the Eyes and Caudal Ganglion. J. cell comp. Physiol. 4 (1934) 363-378
25. Provencio, I., Jiang, G., De Grip, W.J., Hayes, W.P., Rollag, M.D.: Melanopsin: An Op-sin in Melanophores, Brain, and Eye. Proc. Natl. Acad. Sci. USA 95 (1998) 340-345
26. Qiu, X., Kumbalasiri, T., Carlson, S.M., Wong, K.Y., Krishna, V., Provencio, I., Berson, D.M.: Induction of Photosensitivity by Heterologous Expression of Melanopsin. Nature 433 (2005) 745-749
27. Robles, L.J., Breneman, J.W., Anderson, E.O., Nottoli, V.A., Kegler, L.L.: Immunocyto-chemical Localization of a Rhodopsin-like Protein in the Lipochondria in Photosensitive Neurons of *Aplysia californica*. Cell Tissue Res. 244 (1986) 115-120
28. Yau, K.-W., Baylor, D.A.: Cyclic GMP-activated Conductance of Retinal Photoreceptor Cells. Annu. Rev. Neurosci. 12 (1989) 289-327

A Population-Based Inference Framework for Feature-Based Attention in Natural Scenes

Fred H. Hamker

Allgemeine Psychologie, Psychologisches Institut II,
Westf. Wilhelms-Universität, 48149 Münster, Germany
fhamker@uni-muenster.de
http://wwwpsy.uni-muenster.de/inst2/lappe/Fred/FredHamker.html

Abstract. Vision is a crucial sensor. It provides a very rich collection of information about our environment. However, not everything in a visual scene is relevant for the task at hand. Feature-based attention has been suggested for guiding vision towards the objects of interest in a visual search situation. Computational models of visual attention have implemented different concepts of feature-based attention. We will discuss these approaches and present a solution which is based on population-based inference. We illustrate the proposed mechanism with simulations using real world-scenes.

1 Introduction

Visual Search and other experimental approaches have demonstrated that attention plays a crucial role in human perception. Understanding attention and human vision in general could be beneficial to computer vision, especially in vision tasks that are not limited to specific and constrained environments. Previous models of attention have suggested different underlying computational mechanisms of how feature cues (e.g., color) affect visual processing. In most models attention is solely defined by determining the locus of a unique spatial focus [24,13,28,1,19,10]. Feature-based attention is left to only guide the selection process by weighting the input into the saliency map [16,18]. For example, the search for the blue lighter is typically implemented by enhancing the input into the saliency map for cells encoding the target color (Fig. 1A). The selective tuning model implements feature-based attention by enhancing the value of the interpretive nodes which in turn biases the winner-take-all (WTA) competition for projection into the next layer [26]. A cascade of top-down directed WTA processes prune away all irrelevant connections within successively smaller receptive fields. As a result, features such as the color blue allow to segment a target object in the scene (Fig. 1B). Technically the top-down biasing nodes form an independent top-down path, but present implementations of the selective tuning model do not distinguish between feature and spatial attention in the sense that feature-based attention induces competition only through the spatially selective WTA.

Treue and Martínez Trujillo [25] have proposed a Feature-Similarity Theory of attention. Their single cell recordings in area MT revealed that directing attention to one stimulus enhances the response of a second stimulus presented elsewhere in the visual field, but only if the features of both stimuli match (e.g. upward motion). They proposed

M. De Gregorio et al. (Eds.): BVAI 2005, LNCS 3704, pp. 147–156, 2005.

that attending towards a feature could provide a global, spatially non-selective feedback signal. The same effect has been found in a similar experiment using fMRI [22]. In an earlier experiment that presumably revealed feature-based attention as well, the knowledge of a target feature increased the activity of V4 cells [17].

Inspired by these findings, computational approaches have been used to investigate the mechanisms of feature-based attention [14,12,27,4,21,3]. We have developed a model to investigate the putative feedforward and feedback interactions between area V4, TE and the frontal eye field [6,8]. In this model attention emerges by interactions in the vision process. To find an object in a crowded scene our model predicts a feature-specific component that highlights all cells encoding target features in parallel and a spatially directed, serial component that is linked to the planning of an eye movement. This prediction of our model has been recently confirmed in neural cell recordings [2]. However, only little has been done to demonstrate that the proposed mechanisms even hold for large networks, e.g. for natural scene processing.

Thus, we have further developed our aprochach and extended it to a large scale network for natural scene processing [7,9] (Fig. 1C). We now explain the population-based inference framework and its relation to feature-based attention. Then, the model is introduced and specifically its feature-based attention effects are illustrated.

2   Population-Based Inference

Population coding has been frequently used as a theoretical basis for describing computation in the brain. Much emphasis has been given to investigate how a population encodes a stimulus. Our population-based inference approach provides a framework to continuously update the conspicuity of an internal variable using prior knowledge in form of generated expectations. The population is represented by a set of cells. The selectivity of each cell is defined by its location $i \in \{1..20\}$ in the population and its activity r_i reflects the conspicuity of its preferred stimulus. Each cell is simulated by an ordinary differential equation, that governs its average firing rate over time. Thus, the model allows to describe the temporal change of activity induced by top-down inference. In abstract terms, the top-down signal represents the expectation $\hat{r}$ to which the input (observation) $r^{\uparrow}$ is compared. If the observation is similar to the expectation the conspicuity is increased. This increase is implemented as a gain control mechanism on the feedforward signal. The population-based inference approach has been proven to be a suitable computational framework for simulating spatial [5] and feature-based attention effects [6]. As far as feature-based attention is concerned a cell's response over time $r_{d,i,\mathbf{x}}(t)$ at location $\mathbf{x}$, selective dimension d and preferred feature i can be computed by a differential equation (with a time constant τ):

$$\tau \frac{d}{dt} r_{d,i,\mathbf{x}}^{V4} = I_{d,i,\mathbf{x}}^{\uparrow} + I_{d,i,\mathbf{x}}^{N} + I_{d,i,\mathbf{x}}^{A} - I_{d,\mathbf{x}}^{inh} \tag{1}$$

The activity of a V4 cell is primarily driven by its bottom-up input $I^{\uparrow}$. Inhibition $I_{d,\mathbf{x}}^{inh}$ introduces competition among cells and normalizes the cell's response by a shunting term. $I_{d,i,\mathbf{x}}^{N}$ describes the lateral influence of other cells in the population. Feature-based attention is a result of the bottom-up signal $I_{d,i,\mathbf{x}}^{\uparrow}$ modulated by the feedback

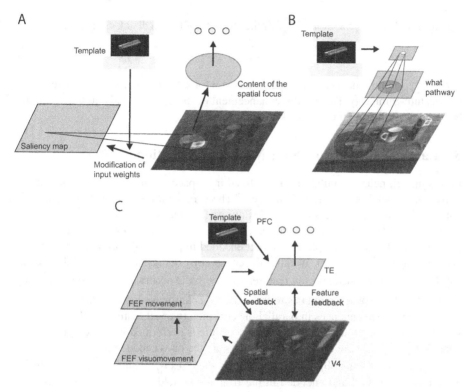

Fig. 1. Three models of attention for real world scenes and their implementation of feature-based attention. The goal directed search for the blue lighter requires some knowledge of the target object, called a template, to be represented. Most models assume that just simple, "preattentive" features (e.g. color, orientation) are part of such a template. A) In the classical approach of visual attention, feature-based attention only modifies the input of the saliency map. For example, all weights into the saliency map of cells encoding blue are globally increased, such that the lighter has a higher chance being selected. A neural correlate of feature-based attention would therefore only be visible in a pronounced activation in the saliency map. A winner-takes-all process then determines the location of the highest activity, which in turn can be used to compute a focus of attention such that the area around the blue lighter is processed preferably . B) The selective tuning model uses top-down directed feature cues to guide competition in the what pathway. Present implementations of this model, however, do not distinguish feature-based and spatial attention, since a cascade of winner-take-all processes immediately generates an attentional beam that segments the lighter from its background and generates an inhibitory surround. C) A model of distributed processing with spatial and feature feedback. Here, attention emerges by the interactions in the network. A template, which can contain any object information, is send downwards, enhances the sensitivity of specific populations encoding the features of interest and lateral interactions normalize the activity. As a result, the model shows feature-based attention. For example, the search template of the lighter selectively enhances cells encoding blue in parallel prior to any spatial selection, as indicated by the brighter parts of the image. Other parts are relatively suppressed as illustrated by the darkened areas in the scene. This modulated activity in V4 guides areas responsible for eye movements, which in turn send a spatially selective signal back to enhance populations encoding stimuli at a specific location - spatial attention emerges.

signal from TE $r_{d,j,\mathbf{x}'}^{\text{TE}}$ with $w_{i,j,\mathbf{x},\mathbf{x}'}^{\text{IT,V4}}$ as the strength of the feedback connection:

$$I_{d,i,\mathbf{x}}^{A} = I_{d,i,\mathbf{x}}^{\uparrow}\sigma(\alpha - r_{d,i,\mathbf{x}}^{\text{V4}}) \cdot \max_{j,\mathbf{x}'}(w_{i,j}^{\text{TE,V4}} \cdot r_{d,j,\mathbf{x}'}^{\text{TE}}) \tag{2}$$

$\sigma(\alpha - y_{d,k,\mathbf{x}}^{\text{V4}})$ implements a saturation of the gain for salient stimuli [7]. Consistent with the Feature-Similarity Theory, the enhancement of the gain depends on the similarity between the input and the feedback signal.

3 Large Scale Approach for Modeling Attention

In this model, neural populations are defined in a space spanned by the feature selectivity i and spatial selectivity $\mathbf{x}$ of the cells. The variable d refers to different channels computed from the image such as orientation (O), intensity (I) or red-green (RG), blue-yellow (BY), or spatial resolution (σ). The conspicuity of each encoded feature is altered by the target template. A target encoded in prefrontal cortex defines the expected features $\hat{r}_{d,i}^{\text{PFC}}$ (Fig. 2). We infer the conspicuity of each feature in TE denoted as $r_{d,i,\mathbf{x}}^{\text{TE}}$ by comparing the expected features $\hat{r}_{d,i}^{\text{PFC}}$ with the observation, i.e. the bottom-up input $r_{d,i,\mathbf{x}}^{\text{TE}\uparrow}$. If the observation is similar to the expectation we increase the conspicuity. Such a mechanism enhances in parallel the conspicuity of all features in TE which are similar to the target template. The same procedure is performed in V4 to compute the conspicuity $r_{d,i,\mathbf{x}}^{\text{V4}}$ where the expected features are the ones encoded in TE.

In order to detect an object in space the conspicuities $r_{d,i,\mathbf{x}}^{\text{V4}}$ and $r_{d,i,\mathbf{x}}^{\text{TE}}$ are combined across all channels d and encoded in the frontal eye field visuomovement cells. The projection from the visuomovement cells to the movement cells generates an expectation in space $\hat{r}_{\mathbf{x}}^{\text{FEFm}}$. Thus, a location with high conspicuity in different channels d tends to have a high expectation in space $\hat{r}_{\mathbf{x}}^{\text{FEFm}}$. Analogous to the inference in feature space the expected location $\hat{r}_{\mathbf{x}}^{\text{FEFm}}$ is iteratively compared with the observation $r_{d,i,\mathbf{x}}^{\uparrow}$ in $\mathbf{x}$ and the conspicuity of a feature with a similarity between expectation and observation is enhanced. The conspicuity is normalized across each map by competitive interactions. Such interative mechanisms finally lead to a preferred encoding of the features and space of interest.

We now briefly explain the simulated areas in the model. A detailed description can be found in [9].

Early visual processing: Feature maps for Red-Green opponency (RG), Blue-Yellow opponency (BY), Intensity (I), Orientation (O), and Spatial Resolution (σ) are computed. The initital conspicuity is determined by center-surround operations [10]. Center-surround operations calculate the difference of feature values in maps with a fine scale and a coarse scale and thus, the obtained conspicuity value is a measure of stimulus-driven saliency. The feature information and the conspicuity are used to determine a population code, so that at each location the features and their related conspicuities are encoded.

V4: V4 has d channels which receive input from the feature conspicuity maps: $r_{\theta,i,\mathbf{x}}$ for orientation, $r_{I,i,\mathbf{x}}$ for intensity, $r_{RG,i,\mathbf{x}}$ for red-green opponency, $r_{BY,i,\mathbf{x}}$ for blue-yellow opponency and $r_{\sigma,i,\mathbf{x}}$ for spatial frequency (Fig. 2). The expectation of features

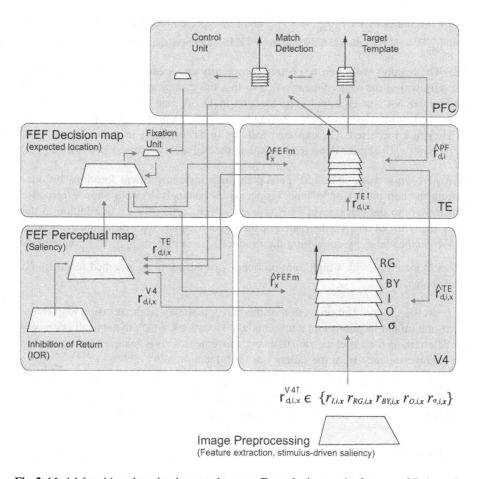

Fig. 2. Model for object detection in natural scenes. From the image, the features of 5 channels (RG, BY, I, O, σ) are obtained. For each feature we also compute its conspicuity as determined by the spatial arrangement of the stimuli in the scene and represent both aspects within a population code, so that at each location a feature and its related conspicuity is encoded. This initial, stimulus-driven conspicuity is now dynamically updated within a hierarchy of levels. From V4 to TE a pooling across space is performed to obtain a representation of features with a coarse coding of location. The target template encodes features of the target object by a population of sustained activated cells. It represents the expected features $\hat{r}^{PFC}_{d,i}$ which are used to compute the (posterior) conspicuity in TE. Similarly, TE represents the expectation for V4. As a result, the conspicuity of all features of interest is enhanced regardless of their location in the scene. In order to identify candidate objects by their saliency the activity across all 5 channels is integrated in the FEF perceptual map. The saliency is then used to compute the target location of an eye movement in the FEF decision map. The activity in this map $\hat{r}^{FEFm}_{x}$ is fed back, which in turn enhances the conspicuity of all features in V4 and TE at the activated areas in the FEF decision map. Thus, objects at expected locations are preferably represented. By comparing the conspicious features in TE with the target template in the match detection units it is possible to continuously track if the object of interest is encoded in TE. Visited locations are being tagged by an inhibition of return. This allows the model to make repeated fixations while searching for an object.

in V4 originates in TE $\hat{r}_{d,i,\mathbf{x}'}^{V4_F} = r_{d,i,\mathbf{x}}^{TE}$ and the expected location in the FEF decision map $\hat{r}_{\mathbf{x}'}^{V4_L} = r_{\mathbf{x}'}^{FEFm}$. Please note that even TE has a coarse dependency on location.

TE: The features with their respective conspicuity and location in V4 project to TE, but only within the same dimension d, so that the conspicuity of features at several locations in V4 converges onto one location in TE. A map containing 9 populations with overlapping receptive fields is simulated. The complexity of features from V4 to TE is not increased. The expected features in TE originate in the target template $r_{d,i,\mathbf{x}}^{TE_F} = w \cdot r_{d,i}^{PFC}$ and the expected location in the FEF decision map $\hat{r}_{\mathbf{x}}^{TE_L} = w \cdot r_{\mathbf{x}}^{FEFm}$.

FEF perceptual map: The FEF perceptual map indicates salient locations by integrating the conspicuity of V4 and TE across all channels. Its cells show a response which fits into the category of FEF visuomovement cells (FEFv). In addition to the conspicuity in V4 and TE the match of the target template with the features encoded in V4 is considered by computing the product $\prod_d \max_i r_{d,i}^{PFC} \cdot r_{d,i,\mathbf{x}}^{V4}$. This implements a bias to locations with a high joint probability of encoding all searched features in a certain area.

FEF decision map: The projection of the perceptual map to the decision map transforms the salient locations into a few candidate locations, which dynamically compete for determining the target location of an eye movement. This is achieved by subtracting the average saliency from the saliency at each location $w^{FEFv} r_{\mathbf{x}}^{FEFv} - w_{inh}^{FEFv} \sum_{\mathbf{x}} r_{\mathbf{x}}^{FEFv}$. Thus, the cells in the decision map show none or only little response to the onset of a stimulus, such that their response fits into the category of the FEF movement cells (FEFm). Their activity provides the expected location for V4 and TE units.

4   Results

An object is presented to the model for 100 ms and the model memorizes some of its features as a target template. We do not give the model any hints which feature to memorize. The model's task is to make an eye movement towards the target (Fig. 3A,B). When presenting the search scene, TE cells that match the target template quickly increase their activity to guide perception on the level of V4 cells. Thus, the features of the object of interest are enhanced prior to any spatial focus of attention. This feature-based attention effect allows for a goal-directed planning of a saccade in the FEF. The planning of an eye movement provides a spatially organized reentry signal, which enhances the gain of all cells around the target location of the intended eye movement. As a result of these inference operations, the high-level goal description in PFC is bound to an object in the visual world. Further simulation results are discussed in [9].

We now take a close view on the feature-based attention effects of the model. In this respect we compare two conditions: attend towards the visual properties of the lighter (Fig. 3A) and attend towards the cigarettes (Fig. 3B). Fig. 3C shows the difference activity of both conditions in V4 prior to any spatial selection as determined by a low FEFm activity ($\max_{\mathbf{x}} r_{\mathbf{x}}^{FEFm}(t) < 0.05$). Our analysis clearly shows that feature-based attention selectively modulates the activity according to the task at hand. Thus, the model

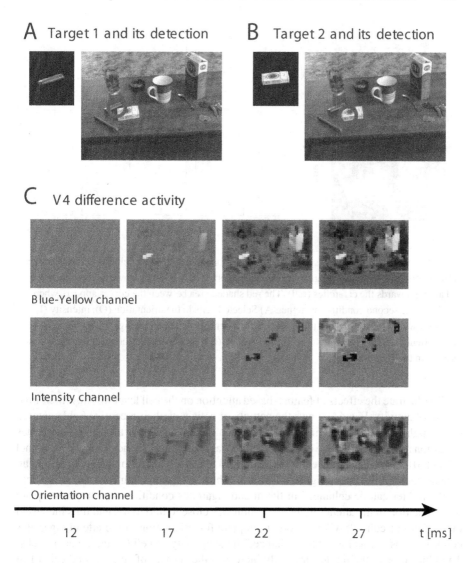

Fig. 3. Illustration of feature-based attention. A) Target object 1 and its detection in the visual scene. B) Target object 2 and its detection in the visual scene. C) Difference activity in V4 in three channels over time. For a comparison with cell recordings a latency of about 60 ms has to be added to the time axis. Only the difference of the maximal activity at each location is shown irrespective of the feature selectivity. Gray areas indicate equal (maximal) activity, light areas more activity in the first condition and dark areas more activity in the second condition. We can observe that parts of the scene are relatively enhanced or reduced according to the target template.

predicts feature-based attention effects independent of focused attention. Although the effect is global in space it can guide gaze towards the object of interest since it depends on the content encoded at each location.

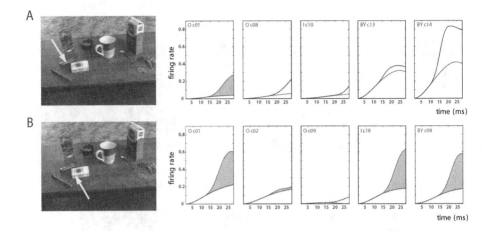

Fig. 4. Illustration of feature-based attention effects on the single cell level. The activity is shown in two conditions with time relative to search array onset (0 ms): attend towards the lighter (blue) and attend towards the cigarettes (red). The red shaded area between the curves appears when the activity in the second condition is higher. A) Selected cells in the orientation (O), intensity (I) and blue-yellow (BY) channel with the receptive field center located on the lighter. A) Selected cells in the orientation (O), intensity (I) and blue-yellow (BY) channel with the receptive field center located on the cigarette box.

To illustrate the effects of feature-based attention on the cell level we show their time course of activity. Fig. 4A shows the activity of cells with their receptive field centered on the lighter. A difference in activity between the attend lighter and attend cigarettes condition reflects the relative effect of feature-based attention. In the orientation channel (O) cell 01 shows an enhancement in the attend cigarettes condition whereas cell 08 an enhancement in the attend lighter condition. Thus, even cells with their receptive field on the lighter can be enhanced in the attend cigarettes condition. The target template for orientation in the attend lighter condition was close to horizontal and thus increased the activity of cell 08, whereas target template for orientation in the attend cigarettes condition was vertical and thus enhanced the sensitivity of cell 01 and adjacent cells. The blue color of the lighter primarily increased the activity of cells around cell 14 of the BY channel in the attend lighter condition. The white color of the cigarette box increased cell 18 of the intensity channel in the attend cigarettes condition. We observe also differences in the timing of the feature-based attention effect, which are based on recurrent interactions between V4 and TE as well as TE and PFC.

5   Discussion

We have introduced different models of attention and their implementation of feature-based attention. The classical approach, which defines attention solely by a selection of a location in the saliency map, predicts that target templates only guide the competition for spatial attention. Such guidance of spatial attention does also occur in the Selective

Tuning model as well as in our approach. These models use feature cues to enhance the activity of feature-sensitive cells. However, our approach seems to be closer to a neural correlate of feature-based attention, since we consider the temporal dynamics prior to any spatial selection. We predict that goal directed visual search first selectively modulates feature-sensitive cells prior to any spatial selection.

This prediction is consistent with cell recordings in visual search [2] and recent findings in which the learning of degraded natural scenes resulted in a selective enhancement of V4 cells [20]. According to this study V4 plays a crucial role in resolving an indeterminate level of visual processing by a coordinated interaction between bottom-up and top-down streams.

Our model further predicts that saliency is encoded as part of the variable itself through the dual coding property of a population code. Saliency is not encoded in a single map. Thus, attentional effects can be found throughout the visual system. The observation of an attentional modulation does therefore not allow to conclude that a stimulus has been selected by a spatially directed focus. For example, V4 also provides a spatially organized map encoding saliency (Fig. 3C), which is consistent with recent findings [15]. However, V4 cells are selective for location and specific features. Consistent with recordings in the FEF [23], the FEF visuomovement cells in our model are more related to the classical idea of a saliency map [11], since they solely encode location by integrating the activity across all channels and features. We assume that this information needs an additional, decisional stage of processing before it is feed back such that the saliency information is transformed into a dynamic, competitive representation of a few candidate regions.

Acknowledgements

Parts of this research had been supported by DFG HA2630/2-1 and the ERC Program of the NSF (EEC-9402726).

References

1. Ahmad, S. (1992) VISIT: a neural model of covert visual attention. In: J.E. Moody, et.al. (eds.) Advances in Neural Information Processing Systems, vol 4, 420-427, San Mateo, CA: Morgan Kaufmann.
2. Bichot, N.P., Rossi, A.F., Desimone, R. (2005) Parallel and serial neural mechanisms for visual search in macaque area V4. Science, 308:529-534.
3. Corchs, S., Deco, G. (2002) Large-scale neural model for visual attention: integration of experimental single-cell and fMRI data. Cereb. Cortex, 12:339-348.
4. Grossberg, S., Raizada, R. (2000) Contrast-sensitive perceptual grouping and object-based attention in the laminar circuits of primary visual cortex. Vis. Research, 40:1413-1432.
5. Hamker, F.H. (2004) Predictions of a model of spatial attention using sum- and max-pooling functions. Neurocomputing, 56C, 329-343.
6. Hamker, F.H. (2004) A dynamic model of how feature cues guide spatial attention. Vision Research, 44, 501-521.

7. Hamker, F. H. (2005a) Modeling Attention: From computational neuroscience to computer vision. In: L. Paletta et al. (eds.), Attention and Performance in Computational Vision. Second International workshop on attention and performance in computer vision (WAPCV 2004), LNCS 3368. Berlin, Heidelberg: Springer-Verlag, 118-132.

8. Hamker, F. H. (2005b) The Reentry Hypothesis: The Putative Interaction of the Frontal Eye Field, Ventrolateral Prefrontal Cortex, and Areas V4, IT for Attention and Eye Movement. Cerebral Cortex, 15:431-447.

9. Hamker, F. H. (in press) The emergence of attention by population-based inference and its role in distributed processing and cognitive control of vision. Journal for Computer Vision and Image Understanding.

10. Itti, L., Koch, C. (2000) A saliency-based search mechanism for overt and covert shifts of visual attention. Vision Res., 40:1489-1506.

11. Itti L, Koch C. (2001) Computational modelling of visual attention. Nat Rev Neurosci. 2:194-203

12. Kirkland, K. L., Gerstein, G. L. (1999) A feedback model of attention and context dependence in visual cortical networks. J. Comput. Neurosci., 7:255-267.

13. Koch C, Ullman S (1985) Shifts in selective visual attention: towards the underlying neural circuitry. Human Psychology 4:219-227.

14. Koechlin E., Burnod Y. (1996) Dual population coding in the neocortex: A model of interaction between representation and attention in the visual cortex. J. Cog. Neurosci., 8:353-370.

15. Mazer, J.A., Gallant ,J.L. (2003) Goal-related activity in V4 during free viewing visual search. Evidence for a ventral stream visual salience map. Neuron, 40:1241-1250.

16. Milanese, R., Gil, S., Pun, T. (1995) Attentive mechanisms for dynamic and static scene analysis, Optical Engineer., 34:2428-2434.

17. Motter, B.C. (1994) Neural correlates of feature selective memory and pop-out in extrastriate area V4. J. Neurosci., 14, 2190-2199.

18. Navalpakkam V, Itti L. (2005) Modeling the influence of task on attention. Vision Res., 45:205-31.

19. Olshausen, B., Anderson, C., van Essen, D. (1993) A neurobiological model of visual attention and invariant pattern recognition based on dynamic routing of information. J. Neurosci., 13:4700-4719.

20. Rainer G, Lee H, Logothetis NK. (2004) The effect of learning on the function of monkey extrastriate visual cortex. PLoS Biol., 2:275-283.

21. Roelfsema, P. R., Lammé, V. A., Spekreijse, H., Bosch, H. (2002) Figure-ground segregation in a recurrent network architecture. J. Cogn. Neurosci., 14:525-537.

22. Saenz M., Buracas G.T., Boynton G.M. (2002). Global effects of feature-based attention in human visual cortex. Nature Neuroscience. 5:631-632.

23. Schall, JD (2002) The neural selection and control of saccades by the frontal eye field. Phil Trans R Soc Lond B 357:1073-1082.

24. Treisman, A. (1988) Features and objects: The Fourteenth Bartlett Memorial Lecture. Quarterly Journal of Experimental Psychology, 40A:201-237.

25. Treue, S., Martínez Trujillo, J.C. (1999) Feature-based attention influences motion processing gain in macaque visual cortex. Nature, 399:575-579.

26. Tsotsos JK, Culhane SM, Wai W, Lai Y, Davis N, Nuflo F (1995) Modeling visual attention via selective tuning. Artificial Intelligence, 78:507-545.

27. van der Velde, F., de Kamps, M. (2001) From knowing what to knowing where: modeling object-based attention with feedback disinhibition of activation. J. Cogn. Neurosci., 13:479-491.

28. Wolfe, J. M. (1994) Guided search 2.0: A revised model of visual search. Psychonomic Bulletin & Review, 1, 202-238.

Multi-modal Primitives as Functional Models of Hyper-columns and Their Use for Contextual Integration

Norbert Krüger[1] and Florentin Wörgötter[2]

[1] Media Lab, Aalborg University Copenhagen
nk@cs.aue.auc.dk
[2] Computational Neuroscience, University of Stirling
worgott@cn.stir.ac.uk

Abstract. In this paper, we describe a biological motivated image representation in terms of local multi–modal primitives. These primitives are functional abstractions of hypercolumns in V1 [13]. The efficient and generic coding of visual information in terms of local symbolic descriptiones allows for a wide range of applications. For example, they have been used to investigate the multi–modal character of Gestalt laws in natural scenes [14], to code a multi–modal stereo matching and to investigate the role of different visual modalities for stereo [11], and to use a combination of stereo and grouping as well as Rigid Body Motion to acquire reliable 3D information as demonstrated in this publication.

1 Introduction

The aim of this work is to compute reliable feature maps from natural scenes. To establish artificial systems that perform reliable actions we need reliable features. These can only be computed through *integration across the spatial and temporal context and across visual modalities* since local feature extraction is necessarily ambiguous [1,15]. In this paper, we describe a new kind of image representation in terms of local multi–modal Primitives (see fig. 1) which can be understood as functional abstractions of hypercolumns in V1. These Primitives can be characterized by three properties:

Multi-modality: Different visual domains describing different structural properties of visual data are well established in human vision and computer vision. For example, a local edge can be analyzed by local feature attributes such as orientation or energy in certain frequency bands. In addition, we can distinguish between line and step–edge like structures (contrast transition). Furthermore, color can be associated to the edge. This image patch also changes in time due to ego-motion or object motion. Therefore time specific features such as a 2D velocity vector (optic flow) can be associated to this image patch. In addition the image patch has a certain source in 3D space and therefore also depth information can be associated. In this work we define local multi–modal Primitives that realize these multi-modal relations. These modalities are also processsed in so called hyper-columns in the first area of visual processing (V1) [7].

M. De Gregorio et al. (Eds.): BVAI 2005, LNCS 3704, pp. 157–166, 2005.
© Springer-Verlag Berlin Heidelberg 2005

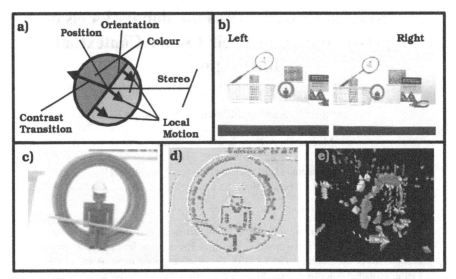

Fig. 1. Multi-modal Primitives **a)** One primitive covers different aspects of visual information in a condensed way. **b)** Stereo Image Pair. **c)** Frame taken from c). **d)** Representation of an image by multi-modal primitives (local motion and stereo information not shown for sake of understandability). **e)** 3D view of extracted stereo representation.

Adaptability: Since the interpretation of local image patches in terms of the above mentioned attributes as well as classifications such as 'edgeness' or 'junctionness' are necessarilly ambigious when based on local processing stable interpretations can only be achieved *through integration* by making use of contextual information [1]. Therefore, all attributes of our Primitives are equipped with confidences that are essentially *adaptable according to contextual information* expressing the reliability of this attribute. Adaptation occurs by means of recurrent processes (see, e.g., [21]) in which predictions based on statistical and deterministic regularities disambiguate the locally extracted and therefore neceassarily ambigious data.

Condensation: Integration of information requires *communication between Primitives* expressing spatial [14,11] and temporal dependencies [9]. This communication has necessarily to be paid for with a certain cost. This cost can be reduced by limiting the amount of information transferred from one place to the other, i.e., by reducing the bandwidth. Therefore we are after a *compression* of data. Essentially we only need less than 5% of the amount of the pixel data of a local image patch to code a Primitive that represents such a patch. However, condensation not only means a compression of data since communication and memorization not only require a reduction of information. Moreover, we want to reduce the amount of information within an image patch *while preserving perceptually relevant information*. This leads to *meaningful* descriptors such as our attributes position, orientation, contrast transition, color and optic flow. In [14], we have also shown that these descriptors (in particular when jointly applied) allow for strong mutual prediction that can be related to classical Gestalt laws.

In section 2, we describe the Primitive attributes and their extraction and in section 3 we describe the biological background. In section 4, we refer to applications of our Primitives for the modelling of disambiguation processes in mid-level vision.

2   Multi-modal Primitives

We compute the following semantic attributes and associate them to our Primitives (see also fig. 1).

Intrinsic Dimension: Local patches in natural images can be associated to specific local sub-structures, such as homogeneous patches, edges, corners, or textures. Over the last decades, sub-domains of Computer Vision have extracted and analysed such sub-structures.

The intrinsic dimension (see, e.g., [23]) has proven to be a suitable descriptor that distinguishes such sub-structures. Homogeneous image patches have an intrinsic dimension of zero (i0D); edge-like structures are intrinsically 1-dimensional (i1D) while junctions and most textures have an intrinsic dimension of two (i2D). In [10,4] it has been shown that the topological structure of intrinsic dimension essentially has the form of a triangle with the corners of the triangle representing 'ideal cases' of homogeneous structures, edges or corners (see figure 2b). This triangular structure can be used to associate 3 confidences $(c_{i0D}, c_{i1D}, c_{i2D})$ to homogenous-ness, edge–ness, or junction–ness according to the positioning of an image patch in the iD–triangle.

This association of confidences to visual attributes is a general design principle in our system. These confidences as well as the attributes themselves are subject to contextual integration via recurrent processes. Aspects with associated low confidences have a minor influence in the recurrent processes or can be disregarded.

Orientation: The local orientation associated to the image patch is described by θ. The computation of the orientation θ is based on a rotation invariant quadrature filter, which is derived from the concept of the *monogenic signal* [5]. Considered in polar coordinates, the monogenic signal performs a *split of identity* [5]: it decomposes an intrinsically one-dimensional signal into intensity information (amplitude), orientation information, and phase information (contrast transition). These features are pointwise mutually orthogonal. The intensity information can be interpreted as an indicator for the likelihood of the presence of a certain structure with a certain orientation and a certain contrast transition (see below).

Contrast Transition: The contrast transition is coded in the phase ϕ of the applied filter [5]. The phase codes the local symmetry, for example a bright line on a dark background has phase 0 while a bright/dark edge has phase $-\pi/2$ (see fig. 2a). There exists a whole continuum of i1D structures that can be coded in the phase by one parameter (see also [6,8]).

Color: Color (c^l, c^m, c^r) is processed by integrating over image patches in coincidence with their edge structure (i.e., integrating separately over the left and right side of the edge as well as a middle strip in case of a line structure). In case of a boundary edge of

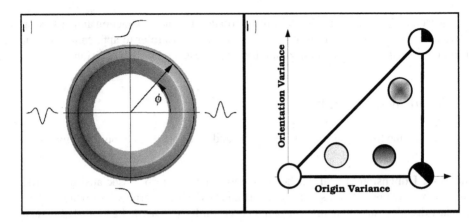

Fig. 2. a) The continuum of phases (indicated by ϕ) taking values between $-\pi$ and π correspond to a continuum of oriented grey-level structures as expressed in the changing circular manifold (sub–figure a) is based on a figure in [3]). **b)** The likelihood of a local image patch to be a homogenous image patch, an edge or a junction can be visualised as a triangle with corners representing ideal patterns. Points inside the triangle represent structures that are only with a certain likelihood categorizable as ideal homogenuous image patches, edges, or junctions. For example, there is a slight texture on the patch close to the lower left corner which produces a filter response with low contrast (origin variance) and low orientation variance or the structure close to the upper corner has some resemblance to a junction. In this triangular representation distances from the corners represent the likelihood of the structures being of the ideal type. This is used for the formulation of confidences indicating such likelihoods in [10]. Note that figure 2b is thought to be a schematic description. The exact positioning of patches in the triangle depends on two parameters (for details see [10]).

a moving object at least the color at one side of the edge is expected to be stable since (in contrast to the phase) it represents a description of the object.

Optic Flow: There exist a large variety of algorithms that compute the local displacement in image sequences. [2] have them devided into 4 classes: differential techniques, region-based matching, energy based methods and phase-based techniques. After some comparison we decided to use the well-known optic flow technique [16]. This allgorithm is a differential technique in which however (in addition to the standard gradient constraint equation) an anisotropic smoothing term leads to better flow estimation at edges (for details see [16]). The optic flow is coded in a vector **o**.

Stereo: By performing a matching between primitives in the left and right image and finding correspondences we can compute a 3D-primitive (see figure 1e). We code the correspondence by a link l to a primitive in the right image.

To determine the position **x** of the primitives we look for locations in the image where the magnitude of the response of a set of edge-detection filters [5] has local maxima. To avoid the occurrence of very close line–segments produced by the same image structure we also model a competition process between the primitives. Basically, for each primitive position it is checked whether another primitive exists with a position closer than a given threshold distance. If that is the case, the position with lower magnitude is dropped (for details see [12,13]). Finding of suitable positions is a sophisticated task and is also part of a cruicial transformation process from a signal–based to a symbol–based representation. Once the positions of the primitives are determined, the other attributes computed from the filter response at the found position is associated to the primitive.

Usually an image patch that is represented by our Primitives has a dimension of $3 \times 12 \times 12 = 432$ values (3 color values for each pixel in a 12×12 patch). However, the output of our Primitives has less than 20 parameters. Therefore, the Primitives condense the image information by more than 95%. This condensation is a crucial property of our Primitives that allows to represent meaningful information in a directly accessible and compressed way.

We end up with a parametric description of a Primitive as

$$\pi = (\mathbf{x}, \theta, \phi, (\mathbf{c}^l, \mathbf{c}^m, \mathbf{c}^r), \mathbf{o}, (c_{i0D}, c_{i1D}, c_{i2D}), l).$$

In addition, there exist confidences $c_i, i \in \{\phi, \mathbf{c}^l, \mathbf{c}^m, \mathbf{c}^r, \mathbf{o}\}$ that code the reliabilty of the specific sub–aspects that is also subject to contextual adaptation.

3   Multi-modal Primitives as Functional Abstractions of Hyper-columns

The above–mentioned visual modalities are processed at early stages of visual processing. Hubel and Wiesel [7] investigated the structure of the first stage of cortical processing that is located in an area called 'striate cortex' or V1 (see figure 3a). The striate cortex is organized like a continuous, but distorted map of the visual field (retinotopic map). This map contains a specific repetitively occurring pattern of substructures called hyper-columns. Thus, a hyper-column represents a small location of visual space and the neurons in such a hyper-column represent all important aspects of this spatial location; ideally all orientations, all colors, the complete distance-information (disparity), etc. To be able to achieve this in an orderly manner, hyper-columns themselves are subdivided into "columns" and "blobs". The blobs contain color sensitive cells, while the columns represent the continuum of orientations (see figure 3b). Here one observes that the orientation columns are organized in an ordered way such that neurons representing similar orientations tend to be adjacent to each other. However, it is not only orientation that is processed in an orientation column but the cells are sensitive to additional attributes such as disparity, contrast transition and the direction of local motion (see [22]). Even specific responses to junction–like structures have been measured [19]. Therefore, it is believed that in the striate cortex basic local feature descriptions are processed similar to the feature attributes coded in our primitives.

However, it is not only local image processing that is going on in early visual processing. As mentioned above, there occurs an extensive communication within visual brain areas as well as across these areas. The communication process leads to the binding of groups of local entities (see, e.g., [20]). In [14] we described a self–emergence

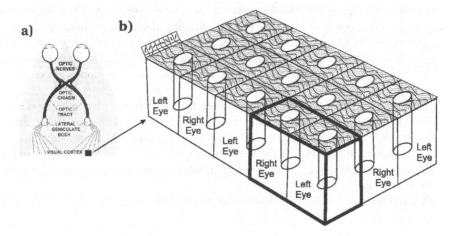

Fig. 3. a) Primary visual pathway and schematic location of a hyper-column (black box), which corresponds in reality to about 1 mm^2 of cortical surface. **b)** Schematic diagram of a hyper-column (thick lines) embedded in the visual cortex. Each hyper-column represents a small location in visual space. Vertically to the surface neurons share similar response properties, whereas their responses differ when moving horizontally on the surface. Information from both eyes is represented in adjacent slabs of the cortex. Each slab contains neurons that encode different orientations (depicted by tiny lines on the surface) but also all other important visual features such as local motion and stereo. In the cylinder-shaped part mainly color is processed. Note, the actual cortical structure is less crystalline than suggested by this diagram.

process in which groups organize themselves based on statistical regularities. Here we use grouping inthe context of improving stereo information.

4   Disambiguation in Recurrent Process Making Use of the Spatial-temporal Context

The processing of primitives is still based on local processes. Therefore, ambiguity can not be resolved at this level. However, using the richness of the image descriptors we can already decrease the amount of ambiguity by interaction of modalities on a local level (section 4.1). Global interdependencies realized in cross–modal recurrent processes based on perceptual organisation and rigid body motion can then further reduce the ambiguity and are described in section 4.2 and 4.3.

4.1   Multi-modal Stereo

To be able to reconstruct 3D primitives we require correspondences between image primitives π^l, π^r in the left and right image of a stereo system. For this we make use of a multi-modal similarity

$$sim(\pi^l, \pi^r) = \sum_{i \in \{o,p,c,f\}} \alpha_i d_i(\pi^l, \pi^r) \tag{1}$$

in which distance measures in the different modalities $d_i()$ are combined by a weighted average (see [11,17] for details). In table 1, we show the performance of the system on a sequence of images with known ground truth (see figure 4). The results for a stereo with only one modality (orientation), two modalities (orientation and phase) and three modalities (orientation, phase and colour) respectively are displayed in the first column of the left , middle and right block in table 1.

4.2   Stereo and Grouping

We formalized the spatial constraint indicated in figure 4.2a. Basically the constraint states that stereo correspondences must be consistent under collinear line structures. In [18], we have defined a multi-modal grouping process in which the likelihood of two primitives to be originated from a collinear image structure is coded in two link confidences $g(\pi_1^l, \pi_2^l)$ for the left and $g(\pi_1^r, \pi_2^r)$ for the right image. In combination with (1) we have defined an external similarity that is not based on a direct comparison of image patches but on the consistenny of the stereo with the grouping process only based on the two link confidences $g(\pi_1^l, \pi_2^l)$, $g(\pi_1^r, \pi_2^r)$ and the stereo matching similarity $c(\pi_2^l, \pi_2^r)$. We can use this external similarity to enhance stereo processing. Table 1

Fig. 4. Left and right image of one frame of the stereo image sequence (left) with 3D-ground truth (right)

Table 1. The number of false positives depending on four fixed numbers of trues is shown for stereo, grouping and accumulation. The results for uni-modal, two-modal and multi-modal representations are kept separately in the three blocks. n.a. stands for 'not applicable' which means that the number of trues as indicated in the left most column was not achieved.

Trues	Uni-modal (ori)			Two-modal (ori, pha)			Tri-modal (ori, pha, col)		
	Stereo	Group.	Accum	Stereo	Group.	Accum	Stereo	Group.	Accum
100	1479	1064	8	77	60	6	4	5	2
500	2126	1600	32	346	262	11	19	24	16
1000	2878	n.a.	102	832	586	25	85	78	19
2000	n.a	n.a.	1372	n.a.	n.a.	153	328	278	42

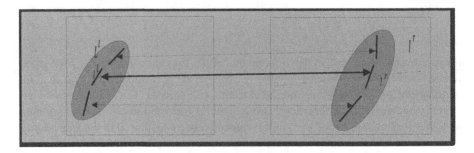

Fig. 5. Top: Stereo–Grouping Constraint

(second columns for each block) shows quantitative results. Performance usually incresaes by approximately 20–30 percent.

4.3 Accumulation Using a Spatial-temporal Context Based on Rigid Body Motion

A spatial–temporal constrained is based on rigid motion. Assuming the egomotion or the motion of objects between frames is known we can predict the occurence of spatial primitives $\pi(t + 1)$ in the next frame. This is possible since knowing the 3D structure underling the primitive (as coded in the link l) the spatial-temporal transformation of this primitive can be computed explicitly. The validation of such a correspondences is an indicator for a higher likelihood for the spatial primitive to be a correct one and the associated confidence becomes increased (see also [9]). Table 1 (third column in each block) gives quantitative results. As can be seen from the results even for quite unreliable stereo based on one modality only after only few iterations the number of false positives can be decreased significantly. Note that the scheme also allows for the integration of new hypothese generated in in new frames. In figure 6 the effect for an example sequence is shown.

5   Summary and Conclusion

We have introduced a functional model of hyper-columns in terms of multi-modal primitives representing local image information in a condensed way. This condensation leads to symbol-like descriptors of image information which allows the formalization of cross–modal processes and spatial-temporal integration.

Acknowledgement. We thank Nicolas Pugeault and Sinan Kalkan for their help. Furthermore, we gratefully acknowledge the support of Riegl Ltd. which provided the image data with 3D ground truth shown in figure 4 on which our quantitative evaluation is based.

Fig. 6. Top row: Left: Confidences of different hypothese are displayed by grey level values (white for high confidences and dark for low confidences) projected on the image. Right: Top view of the stereo of the first frame. Bottom row: Left: Image view of all hypothese with high confidence after 5 iterations of the accumulation. Right: Top view of all hypothese with high confidence after five iterations.

References

1. Y. Aloimonos and D. Shulman. *Integration of Visual Modules — An extension of the Marr Paradigm*. Academic Press, London, 1989.
2. J.L. Barron, D.J. Fleet, and S.S. Beauchemin. Performance of optical flow techniques. *International Journal of Computer Vision*, 12(1):43–77, 1994.
3. M. Felsberg. Optical flow estimation from monogenic phase. In B. Jähne, E. Barth, R. Mester, and H. Scharr, editors, *Complex Motion, Proceedings 1st Int. Workshop*, Günzburg, 12.-14.10. 2004.
4. M. Felsberg and N. Krüger. A probablistic definition of intrinsic dimensionality for images. *Pattern Recognition, 24th DAGM Symposium*, 2003.
5. M. Felsberg and G. Sommer. The monogenic signal. *IEEE Transactions on Signal Processing*, 49(12):3136–3144, December 2001.
6. G. H. Granlund and H. Knutsson. *Signal Processing for Computer Vision*. Kluwer Academic Publishers, Dordrecht, 1995.

7. D.H. Hubel and T.N. Wiesel. Anatomical demonstration of columns in the monkey striate cortex. *Nature*, 221:747–750, 1969.

8. P. Kovesi. Image features from phase congruency. *Videre: Journal of Computer Vision Research*, 1(3):1–26, 1999.

9. N. Krüger, M. Ackermann, and G. Sommer. Accumulation of object representations utilizing interaction of robot action and perception. *Knowledge Based Systems*, 15:111–118, 2002.

10. N. Krüger and M. Felsberg. A continuous formulation of intrinsic dimension. *Proceedings of the British Machine Vision Conference*, pages 261–270, 2003.

11. N. Krüger and M. Felsberg. An explicit and compact coding of geometric and structural information applied to stereo matching. *Pattern Recognition Letters*, 25(8):849–863, 2004.

12. N. Krüger, M. Felsberg, and F. Wörgötter. Processing multi-modal primitives from image sequences. *Fourth International ICSC Symposium on ENGINEERING OF INTELLIGENT SYSTEMS*, 2004.

13. N. Krüger, M. Lappe, and F. Wörgötter. Biologically motivated multi-modal processing of visual primitives. *The Interdisciplinary Journal of Artificial Intelligence and the Simulation of Behaviour*, 1(5):417–428, 2004.

14. N. Krüger and F. Wörgötter. Multi modal estimation of collinearity and parallelism in natural image sequences. *Network: Computation in Neural Systems*, 13:553–576, 2002.

15. N. Krüger and F. Wörgötter. Statistical and deterministic regularities: Utilisation of motion and grouping in biological and artificial visual systems. *Advances in Imaging and Electron Physics*, 131, 2004.

16. H.-H. Nagel and W. Enkelmann. An investigation of smoothness constraints for the estimation of displacement vector fields from image sequences. *IEEE Transactions on Pattern Analysis and Machine Intelligence*, 8:565–593, 1986.

17. N. Pugeault and N. Krüger. Multi–modal matching applied to stereo. *Proceedings of the BMVC 2003*, pages 271–280, 2003.

18. N. Pugeault, F. Wörgötter, , and N. Krüger. Stereo matching with a contextual confidence based on collinear groups. In *In U. Ilg et al. (eds.), Dynamic Perception, Infix Verlag, St. Augustin.*, 2004.

19. I.A. Shevelev, N.A. Lazareva, A.S. Tikhomirov, and G.A. Sharev. Sensitivity to cross–like figures in the cat striate neurons. *Neuroscience*, 61:965–973, 1995.

20. R.J. Watt and W.A. Phillips. The function of dynamic grouping in vision. *Trends in Cognitive Sciences*, 4(12):447–154, 2000.

21. F. Wörgötter, N. Krüger, N. Pugeault, D. Calow, M. Lappe, K. Pauwels, M. Van Hulle, S. Tan, and A. Johnston. Early cognitive vision: Using gestalt-laws for task-dependent, active image-processing. *Natural Computing*, 3(3):293–321, 2004.

22. R.H. Wurtz and E.R. Kandel. Perception of motion, depth and form. In E.R. Kandell, J.H. Schwartz, and T.M. Messel, editors, *Principles of Neural Science (4th edition)*, pages 548–571. 2000.

23. C. Zetzsche and E. Barth. Fundamental limits of linear filters in the visual processing of two dimensional signals. *Vision Research*, 30, 1990.

Three Dilemmas of Signal- and Symbol-Based Representations in Computer Vision

Norbert Krüger

Media Lab, Aalborg University Copenhagen
nk@media.aau.dk

Abstract. We discuss problems of signal– and symbol based representations in terms of three dilemmas which are faced in the design of each vision system. Signal- and symbol-based representations are opposite ends of a spectrum of conceivable design decisions caught at opposite sides of the dilemmas. We make inherent problems explicit and describe potential design decisions for artificial visual systems to deal with the dilemmas.

1 Introduction

Scientists in different fields such as speech processing or computer vision have been debating about signal- and symbol- based representations. This debate has been accompanied by research efforts in Artificial Intelligence (see, e.g., [5]) and Neural Networks (see, e.g., [24]). The argument underlying this debate has not been resolved until now, however many work does not fall sharply in one of the two categories and an increasing number of work emerges which attempts to bridge between the two sides (see, e.g., [11]).

In this paper the problems of signal- and symbol-based approaches are made explicit in terms of three dilemmas which are faced in the design of each vision system. The first dilemma (called the *interpretation/decision dilemma*) deals with the need of interpretation of the input signal which however requires decisions. These decisions constitute prejudices (in terms of assumptions about the input) that are difficult to justify. In the *completeness/feasibility dilemma* the need to condense information to make processing feasible interferes with the wish not to throw away information. The *non-learnable/non-formalisable dilemma* deals with the problem that on the one hand complex problems such as vision are not completely learnable but on the other hand neither completely formalisable.

Signal- and symbol-based representations are opposite ends of a spectrum of conceivable design decisions which are caught at opposite sides of the dilemmas. In this paper, we do not intend to take sides in the debate but to make inherent problems explicit and to describe design decisions interms of an existing artificial visual systems (also described in a contribution in this book, see [21]) to deal with the dilemmas.

M. De Gregorio et al. (Eds.): BVAI 2005, LNCS 3704, pp. 167–176, 2005.

2   Symbol and Signal-Based Representations

Before formalising the three dilemmas we give in the first subsection a brief general categorisation of signal- and symbol based representations. For a more detailed discussion we refer to (e.g., [11]).

The standard notion of symbols in a certain representational framework is that symbols are (1) semantic representatives for certain pieces of knowledge on which (2) operations can be performed that correspond to relevant functional relations in this framework (see also [12]).

> In general, a symbol serves as a surrogate for a body of knowledge that may be needed to be accessed and used in processing the symbol. And ultimately, this knowledge includes semantics or meanings of the symbol ... Symbolic processes are essentially transformations that operate on symbol structures to produce other symbol structures. [11]

Symbol-based representations have been successfully established in formalizable contexts such as chess computers or other expert systems. However, they have failed to solve 'easy tasks' such that to grasp a cup from a table, fill it with coffee and hand it over to Ann or Paul. It turned out that these 'easy' problems are apparently much harder to model than the 'hard' chess task.

There are two main problems symbol based representations ran into:

- The 'right symbols' and 'right rules' are either not exhaustively formalisable within a framework of reasonable complexity or, even more severely, might not exist at all (see, e.g., [2]).
- The meaning of symbols in perceptive systems comes from the environment and the body and purposes of the system itself (the so called symbol grounding problem, [10]).

Signal based representations (such as applied in neural networks or other statistical learning mechanisms) refrained from trying to formalise the functional relations but instead aim at *learning* starting with the (often preprocessed) signal as input. In this approach there is neither a problem of finding the right descriptors in terms of symbols nor their functional relations since these stages are supposed to be learned. There is also no grounding problem since meaning is not explicitly defined. However, it became clear that although statistical learning medthods have been successfully applied to a number of problems they were unable to solve more complex problems since they lack of inherent structure in form of bias (see the Bias/Variance dilemma [6]).

Signal-based (sometimes also referred to as sub-symbolic representations [25]) and symbol based representations in cmputer vision can be characterized by four key aspects:

Feature Maps: Signal-based representations are typically organized as dense feature maps, i.e., at every spatial coordinate a certain feature value is stored, whereas symbolic representations typically store a list or tree of feature vectors which include the spatial vectors.

Completeness: Signal-based representations are mostly complete in the sense that one can reconstruct the original image from the coefficients of the dense feature maps (e.g., a Laplace pyramid). In symbol-based representations information is essentially reduced and therefore incomplete in the sense that information judged as irrelevant for a certain purpose is dropped for the sake of a condensed representation.

Stability: Stability of the estimation can easily be guaranteed by using operators with finite operator norm. For instance, the response of a Laplace filter is stable, but the extraction of the zeros, i.e., the transition to a symbolic interpretation as an edge, leads to unstable estimates in terms of thresholding operations.

Transition to Higher Abstraction Levels: When it comes to the transition to higher levels in the system, the typical way a signal-based representation is used is to feed it into a neural network [26] or to use further deterministic processing steps which lead to higher-level signal-based representations [9]. In general, there is no mechanism taking discrete decisions, leading to a (spatial) selection of information. These mechanisms are however essential when it comes to symbol-based representations and allow for the incorporation of high level semantical knowledge.

3   Dilemma 1: Interpretation and Early Decisions

Dilemma 1 deals with the problem that the semantic information represented in single pixel values is limited. Feature extraction processes make such semantic more explicit but might lead to loss of information.

Scientists working with statistical approaches within the framework of signal-based representations usually do not apply their methods *directly to the the signal level* but introduce some kind of pre-processing (in terms of, e.g., filtering processes) beforehand. By this, the original problem is transferred to a more suitable feature space in which important aspects of the input are made more explicit. In vision, the feature maps carry in general 'meaning' in terms of attributes such as magnitude, orientation or phase that have higher semantic value than the original pixel value.

Independently which framework is used to estimate such attributes, the applied filters always impose some model assumption upon the signal. The filter response is not more than a matching of the data to the model. Thus, considering a single filter response in a particular point, information from the original signal is lost. However, in general the complete image information can be recovered from the filter responses (see, e.g., [8]). This is fundamentally good news, since the severeness of the prejudice applied in the interpretation by the filter operation is reduced since one can always go back to the original signal. However, it also leads to a larger feature space than the original image itself which leads to even more dramatic consequences when looking at the relational space (this will be discussed in detail in section 4).

However, the meaningfulness of interpretations in terms of filter operations leads to another problem that addresses the sampling of these features. The meaning of a 'feature' is based on information that covers a larger spatial area. For example, to estimate an orientation we need at least three samples which do not lie on a line. In general, depending on their bandwidth, filters cover much larger spatial areas. However, the extracted information is represented for each sample, leading to quantization errors if the features are (erroneously) considered at isolated samples. To apply e.g., phase as a feature, we need to take the exact position into account, i.e., we have to interpolate the phase information at the locus of maximum magnitude. Otherwise statements about the edge-ness or line-ness of the local structure become wrong for high frequencies. Another inherent problem is that the estimation of local local descriptors (such as orientation) from linear filters suffers from superposition of the true orientation and of values from structures in the vicinity of the measurement. Therefore, applying the straightforward and naive transition to a semantic interpretation in a point-wise way often leads to inaccurate of even false results, i.e., an ill-defined interpretation.

Seeing signal based representations caught in the problem of a too large features space in which semantic interpretations are partially ill-defined we now take a closer look at a representation that can be associated to the symbol-based approach. A straightforward solution that makes (1) use of and preserves the meaningfulness of the filter responses, (2) avoids the problem of ill-defined meaning, and (3) reduces the cost in terms of a large feature and unmanageable relational feature space is a sparsification of the signal in terms of position which is done in many artificial vision systems (see, e.g., [22]).

In this context, in [19] we have developed an new kind of image representation in terms of multi modal primitives (see figure 1 in [21]). In the primitives different aspects of visual information are coded in terms of visual sub-modalities known in human and computer vision. Primitives carry information about attributes such as local energy, orientation and phase in certain frequency bands. Colour is associated to the local patch in coincidence with the local orientation. Furthermore, time specific features such as a 2D velocity vector (optic flow) and also 3D information is associated to our Primitives.

The attributes such as orientation and phase are associated to the position of the structure such that the meaning (at least for edge-like structures) is clearly defined. Further processing is facilitated since information is coded in a *condensed way*. After a sparisfication process, a primitive represents a local image patch while the amount of information is reduced by 95% and relevant information is made explicit.

However, the sparsification does not come along without problems. The reconstructability of the complete signal (although we have a recognisable representation) is lost. Also, we are forced to do decisions about the positions as well as the features. These in general binary decisions are based on *thresholds* and transfer the continuous space of filter responses to a discrete space of symbol-like structures. However, such decisions can not be made at this level with full certainty since local visual information is necessarily ambiguous (see, e.g., [1,20]).

Interpretation/Decision Dilemma: Interpretation in terms of extraction of meaningful information is necessary to make relevant aspects available for higher levels of processing. However, this goes along with decisions about what aspects are relevant which constitutes a prejudice about the data.

Signal- and symbol-based representations differ in their willingness to apply assumption (in terms of decisions) to the signal. In signal based representations the consequences of interpretations are softened by avoiding to make use of explicit semantics and sparsification. In symbol-based representations sparsifications are performed that make explicit use of the semantic content of early filter operations.

Ways Out of the Interpretation/Decision Dilemma: To justify early filter operations successful biological systems can be taken as a model. In the ground breaking work [13] the functional organisation of the first stage of cortical processing could be explained. They could demonstrate that meaningful features such as orientation, colour, local motion, and stereo are processed in so called hyper-columns. Our primitives are functional abstractions pf these hypercolumns (see [21]).

In our examples, we have also seen that symbol based representations essentially need a good signal processing. Usually, the extraction of symbols is a step performed on top of filtering processes and therefore signal and symbol based representation can be seen as two levels of the processing hierarchy. Semantic meaning in the filter operations can be made explicit and representations sparsified by early hard decisions. There are two ways to soften the effect of the hard decision in the the sparsification: (1) Utilising of Confidences and (2) memorising of multiple hypotheses.

Both strategies are used in the visual primitives: to each parameter a confidence is associated that reflects the reliability of the feature attributes. In this sense the primitives are designed as first guesses with associated confidences that are not expected to deliver completely reliable information but become stabilised by the spatial and spatial-temporal context (see section 5 and [15,20]).

The meaningfulness of the orientation, phase and colour interpretation of the primitive depends essentially on the local structure. For example, orientation is ill defined for a homogeneous image patch or a corner. However, it makes perfect sense for an edge- or line-like structure. To associate a confidence to, e.g., the orientation we measure the 'edges-ness' of the local signal by a continuous concept for homogeneousness, edge-ness and corner-ness in terms of intrinsic dimensionality (see [16,4]).

Also the concept of position depends on the intrinsic structure. For example, for a corner like structure we want to have the position of the primitive to be placed on the intersection lines while for edges we want to have an aquidistal sampling along the line structure. Actually, for each local image patch (i.e., a local region represented by one primitive) three possible interpretation in terms of three positions corresponding to an interpretation as an homogeneous image patch, an edge or a corner is coded. In this way, multiple hypotheses preserve possible interpretations to be verified at later stages of processing.

4   Dilemma 2: Completeness and Feasibility

Dilemma 2 deals with the problem of the size of the space of relations. While signal-based representations face the problem of a complete but unmanageable relational space, symbol-based representations work in a manageable relational space which are however incomplete and difficult to justify. We will exemplify this on the problem of stereo processing. However, similar arguments hold for other relational problems such as grouping or motion estimation.

Important visual information is coded in the *relation* of visual events. A second order relation problem occurs for example in stereo processing. A straight forward signal based approach is to compute all possible correspondences by some kind of template matching resulting in a full disparity map. Even when using an epipolar constraint (see, e.g., [3]) this approach becomes quite costly and the full space of second order relations in the signal based approach becomes virtually unmanageable.

Sparsification reduces the size of the relational space. The primitives transfer the semantically weak defined pixel values to sparse symbol-like structures with strong semantics and by that condense the visual information. Because of the strong sparsification it is possible to deal with large disparities. Even multiple hypotheses can be kept now more easily and allow for better decisions at later stages of processing. Moreover, the result of the primitive representation is actually a dense disparity map. It is a representation in which the 'symbols' carry beside the depth information also information about other semantic aspects (see figure 1e and figure 6 in [21]).

However, the advantage of low computational complexity by concentration on semantically relevant information is accompanied by the drawback of a sparse disparity map. Moreover, errors in the feature extraction stage may lead to unrecoverable errors in the stereo matching. However, we will see in see section 5 that the inclusion of structural knowledge (based on the explicitness of symbol based representations) can overcome some of these problems. Similar arguments hold for other problems involving relations such as grouping or motion estimation (for details, see [20]). Summarising the discussions:

Completeness/Feasibility Dilemma: An efficient coding of this relational space is not feasible without a reduction of the visual events that become related. This reduction however requires a condensation of the local signal information and interferes with the wish to preserve the complete information.

The completeness/feasibility dilemma is related to the interpretation/ decision dilemma since a reduction in general also involves an interpretation and therefore a decision. The completeness/feasibility dilemma however, stresses the need of condensation and not the semantic aspect involved in the interpretation.

Ways Out of the Completeness/Feasibility Dilemma: There exist strategies within signal based representations to approach the relational space in a feasible way by, e.g., coarse to fine tracking mechanisms. If multiple hypotheses are tracked in these mechanisms, the computational effort scales not only with the image size, but also with the maximum disparity. Furthermore, there are certain restrictions which make these approaches unsuitable for (relative) wide baseline stereo.

The condensation process is problematic since throwing away relevant aspects of the data may weaken the overall performance. Therefore, the condensed local descriptors in [21] cover multiple aspects in terms of the relevant visual modalities. In [17], we showed that with the representation condensed by 95% we could achieve comparable performance to correlation based methods in which the full local image patch was used for matching.

There is also a strong potential to combine symbol- and signal-based representations. For example, if signal based and symbol based matching delivers the same result this can be used to increase local confidences in both approaches. However, if there is a disagreement then this indicates either an error in the feature (symbol) extraction or an error caused by the limitation of the signal-based approach. In any case, such incidences point to the need of a more detailed analysis of the specific local situation (for example by a shift of attention) and most likely also to an increase of importance of other non-local sources of information. In this sense we need to think about the signal-symbol relation not only as a feed-forward process but as a *signal-symbol loop* .

5   Dilemma 3: Neither Learnable nor Formalisable

Dilemma 3 deals with the problem that a vision system with similar complexity than the human system can not be fully pre-designed but that learning needs to be an essential part of such a system. However, successful learning already requires a quite significant amount of structural knowledge integrated into the system.

It is widely excepted that the formalisation of higher stages of visual processing requires a transition of the original signal to a more abstract level. This does not necessarily mean to switch directly to symbols. There are ways to follow a hybrid approach, which allows to directly feed signal-based representations into associative networks (see, ee.g., [7]).

The advantage of defining higher levels by statistical methods is a grounding of the mapping in the problem and the data. However, the reached level is only weakly defined in terms of semantic. This reduces the possibility to incorporate structural knowledge about the problem. In human vision structural knowledge can be embedded by *genetical coding* . Indeed, there is evidence that such prior structural knowledge is available at all stages of visual processing [14,20]. This

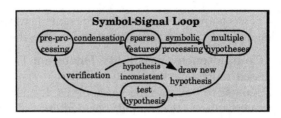

Fig. 1. Schematic description of a Signal-symbol loop

structural prior is necessary also in terms of the learning problem as such (see [6] and dilemma 1).

The symbol related representation of multi-modal primitives provides a clear structure for higher levels of visual processing which allow for the incorporation of structural knowledge. For example, using our visual primitives it is possible to define a non-local stereo constraint that makes use of a grouping process. This constraint is schematically displayed in figure 5 in [21]. It basically states that correspondences of entities in a group in the left image have to have correspondences in the only one group in the right image (for details, see [23]).

There occur even cases where correspondences can not be found by a local similarity derived from the local signal since the image patches in the left and right frame can become too dissimilar (e.g., in case of a large baseline and a small object distance). Signal based approaches are not able to deal with these situation. However, through integration of context information such cases can be handled. For example in [23], good reconstructions can be achieved by using a matching that did not take any local but only context information into account. Another example is the use of structural knowledge about rigid body motion for feature disambiguation (see figure 6 in [21]).

However, the incorporation of structure comes along with the problem of justifying this structure. In the signal based representation this was done through *learning*. In the symbol based representation we buy the incorporation of the structural constraints by heuristically defined rules working in a heuristically defined feature space (see dilemma 1). For example, in [23] the grouping is based on a set of standard criteria for good continuation of local line segments. Summarising the discussions above:

Non-learnable/non-formalizable Dilemma: A lack of inherent structure makes it difficult to formalise structural constraints that are however necessary to control the system and facilitate learning. Explicit structure allows for an incorporation of structural knowledge but is difficult to justify since it is in general not possible to formalise all aspects of the problem.

The non-learnable/non-formalizable dilemma is related to the other two dilemmas. First, the incooperation of structural knowledge constitute decisions that require justification as already postulated in dilemma 1. Since structural knowledge addresses essentially relations of visual events and can work only on condensed representations (as addressed in dilemma 2).

Ways Out of the Non-Learnable/Non-Formalizable Dilemma: There is justified doubt about the possibility to acquire representations by learning only as well about the possibility to fully formalize a vision system with similar complexity than the human visual system. It is more likely that a sufficient amount of structure has to be incorporated externally into the system probably at all stages of processing. This structure requires justification. In biological beings such structures are acquired by an learning mechanism, i.e., evolution, acting on a different time scale. This opens one possibility to justify such prior structure by looking at the hardwired components in human perception.

6   Summary and Conclusion

We have formulated three dilemmas that vision system face. Signal- and symbol-based representations are caught in opposite end of the dilemmas. We have also given examples to deal with these and by this we have experienced that the clear borders between signal- and symbol-based become diluted.

As the main result of the discussions above we conclude that the extremes of the signal- and symbol based approach is not feasable to design complex vision systems but that they represent different levels in a hierarchy that *should be deeply intertwined* . This is in analogy to the fact that an important factor for the success of human vision is the feedback from higher levels to lower levels. In this sense we argue that *symbol-signal loops* in which higher level structure feeds back to the signal to correct early decisions might be an important part also for a successful artificial system (see figure 1). In these loops, early interpretations that are not verified by the context can be disambiguated (see dilemma 1). The utilisation of contextual information is facilitated since the relational space is reduced by the condensation process (see dilemma 2). Such loops can be based on structural knowledge about properties of visual data that might be learned or hardwired (see dilemma 3).

Acknowgedgement. I thank Michael Felsberg for his contributions to this work. A related joint technical report can be found at [18]. I further thank Peter König and Florentin Wörgötter for many fruitful discussions about this topic.

References

1. Y. Aloimonos and D. Shulman. *Integration of Visual Modules — An extension of the Marr Paradigm.* Academic Press, London, 1989.
2. R.A. Brooks. Intelligence without reason. *International Joint Conference on Artificial Intelligence,* pages 569–595, 1991.
3. O.D. Faugeras. *Three–Dimensional Computer Vision.* MIT Press, 1993.
4. M. Felsberg and N. Krüger. A probablistic definition of intrinsic dimensionality for images. *Pattern Recognition, 24th DAGM Symposium,* 2003.
5. J. Fodor. *The language of thought.* Harvard University Press, Boston, 1976.

6. S. Geman, E. Bienenstock, and R. Doursat. Neural networks and the bias/variance dilemma. *Neural Computation*, 4:1–58, 1995.
7. G. H. Granlund. An Associative Perception-Action Structure Using a Localized Space Variant Information Representation. In *Proceedings of Algebraic Frames for the Perception-Action Cycle (AFPAC)*, Kiel, Germany, September 2000.
8. G. H. Granlund and H. Knutsson. *Signal Processing for Computer Vision*. Kluwer Academic Publishers, Dordrecht, 1995.
9. G.H. Granlund. In search of a general picture processing operator. *Computer Graphics and Image Processing*, 8:155–173, 1978.
10. S. Harnad. The symbol grounding problem. *Physica*, D(42):335–346, 1990.
11. V. Honavar and L. Uhr. Integrating symbol processing and connectionist networks, and beyond. *TR94-16 IOWA State University of Science and Technology, Department of Computer Science*, 1994.
12. V. Honavar and L. Uhr. Integrating symbol processing and connectionist networks, and beyond. In S. Goonatilake and S. Khebbal, editors, *Intelligent Hybrid Systems*. London, Wiley, 1995.
13. D.H. Hubel and T.N. Wiesel. Receptive fields, binocular interaction and functional architecture in the cat's visual cortex. *J. Phyiology*, 160:106–154, 1962.
14. P.J. Kellman and M.E. Arterberry, editors. *The Cradle of Knowledge*. MIT-Press, 1998.
15. N. Krüger, M. Ackermann, and G. Sommer. Accumulation of object representations utilizing interaction of robot action and perception. *Knowledge Based Systems*, 15:111–118, 2002.
16. N. Krüger and M. Felsberg. A continuous formulation of intrinsic dimension. *Proceedings of the British Machine Vision Conference*, pages 261–270, 2003.
17. N. Krüger and M. Felsberg. An explicit and compact coding of geometric and structural information applied to stereo matching. *Pattern Recognition Letters*, 25(8):849–863, 2004.
18. N. Krüger and M. Felsberg. Signal- and symbol-based representations in computer vision. *Technical Report 1, Aalborg University Copenhagen, Media Lab*, 2004.
19. N. Krüger, M. Lappe, and F. Wörgötter. Biologically motivated multi-modal processing of visual primitives. *The Interdisciplinary Journal of Artificial Intelligence and the Simulation of Behaviour*, 1(5):417–428, 2004.
20. N. Krüger and F. Wörgötter. Statistical and deterministic regularities: Utilisation of motion and grouping in biological and artificial visual systems. *Advances in Imaging and Electron Physics*, 131, 2004.
21. N. Krüger and F. Wörgötter. Multi-modal primitives as functional models of hyper-columns and their use for contextual integration. *Proceedings of the 1st International Symposium on Brain, Vision and Artificial Intelligence 19-21 October, 2005, Naples, Italy, Lecture Notes in Computer Science, Springer*, 2005.
22. H.-H. Nagel. Image sequence evaluation: 30 years and still going strong. *ICPR*, pages 149–158, 2000.
23. N. Pugeault, F. Wörgötter, , and N. Krüger. Stereo matching with a contextual confidence based on collinear groups. In *In U. Ilg et al. (eds.), Dynamic Perception, Infix Verlag, St. Augustin.*, 2004.
24. D. Rumelhart and J. McClelland. *Parallel Distributed Processing*. Cambridge: Bradford Books/MIT Press, 1986.
25. P. Smolensky. On the proper treatment of connectionism. *Behavioral and Brain Sciences*, 11:1–23, 1988.
26. M. Turk and A. Pentland. Eigenfaces for recognition. *Journal of Cognitive Neuroscience*, 3(1):71–86, 1991.

An LGN Inspired Detect/Transmit Framework for High Fidelity Relay of Visual Information with Limited Bandwidth

Nicholas A. Lesica and Garrett B. Stanley

Division of Engineering and Applied Sciences, Harvard University,
Cambridge MA 02138, USA
lesica@fas.harvard.edu

Abstract. The mammalian visual system has developed complex strategies to optimize the allocation of its limited attentional resources for the
relay of behaviorally relevant visual information. Here, we describe a framework for the relay of visual information that is based on the tonic and burst
properties of the LGN. The framework consists of a multi-sensor transmitter and receiver that are connected by a channel with limited total bandwidth. Each sensor in the transmitter has two states, tonic and burst, and
the current state depends on the salience of the recent visual input. In burst
mode, a sensor transmits only one bit of information corresponding to the
absence or presence of a salient stimulus, while in tonic mode, a sensor attempts to faithfully relay the input with as many bits as are available. By
comparing video reconstructed from the signals of detect/transmit sensors with that reconstructed from the signals of transmit only sensors, we
demonstrate that the detect/transmit framework can significantly improve
relay by dynamically allocating bandwidth to the most salient areas of the
visual field.

1 Introduction

The mammalian early visual pathway serves to relay information about the external world to higher brain areas where it can be analyzed to make decisions and
govern behavior. However, this relay is constrained by the availability of limited
attentional resources. Because mammals can only attend to a small fraction of
the visual field at any given time, the early visual pathway must carry out two
distinct tasks: the detection of salient input to direct the deployment of attentional resources and transmission of detailed features of those stimuli to higher
brain areas. Neurons in the lateral geniculate nucleus (LGN) of the thalamus
have two response modes known as tonic and burst, and there is evidence that
these response modes serve to facilitate the tasks of detection and transmission
(for review, see [1,2]).

The LGN relays the output of the visual system's peripheral sensors in the
retina, making both feedforward and feedback connections with the visual system's
computational center in the cortex. The response mode of an LGN neuron is determined by the state of a special set of low-threshold voltage-dependent channels

M. De Gregorio et al. (Eds.): BVAI 2005, LNCS 3704, pp. 177–186, 2005.

known as T channels [3]. When the membrane is depolarized and the neuron is firing frequently, the T channels are inactivated, and the neuron is in tonic mode. In tonic mode, the spontaneous firing rate is high, and modulations in the response are linearly related to modulations in the visual input, allowing the neuron to faithfully relay both excitatory and inhibitory features to the cortex. When the membrane is hyperpolarized for a prolonged period of time and the neuron is silent, the T channels are de-inactivated and the neuron enters burst mode. When the neuron is in burst mode, depolarization of the membrane opens the T channels, resulting in a wave of current which further depolarizes the membrane and causes a stereotyped burst of closely spaced action potentials. This allows the neuron to signal the appearance of a input with an amplified response.

During visual stimulation, the membrane potential (and thus, response mode) of an LGN neuron is controlled in part by feedback connections from the cortex [4]. Thus, the thalamocortical circuit is thought to perform both detection and transmission as follows: In the absence of a salient input, the membrane is hyperpolarized, the T channels are de-inactivated, and the neuron is in burst mode. Upon the appearance of a salient stimulus, the membrane is briefly depolarized and a burst is triggered. Cortical feedback then maintains the depolarization of the neuron, switching it to tonic mode and increasing the spontaneous firing rate. While the stimulus persists, tonic firing transmits detailed information about the stimulus. When the stimulus disappears, the neuron falls silent, cortical feedback hyperpolarizes the membrane, and the cycle repeats. This silence/burst/tonic/repeat response pattern has been observed in both anesthetized and awake animals, in the LGN responses to sinusoidal gratings [5,6] and natural scene movies, as objects moved in and out of the receptive field [7].

Here, we develop a detect/transmit framework for the relay of visual information based on the tonic and burst properties of the LGN. The framework consists of a multi-sensor transmitter (LGN) and receiver (cortex) that are connected by a channel with limited total bandwidth (attention). Each sensor in the transmitter has two states: tonic and burst. In burst mode, a sensor transmits only one bit of information corresponding to the absence or presence of a salient stimulus. In tonic mode, a sensor attempts to faithfully relay the visual input with as many bits as are available. The mode of each sensor is determined by the salience of the recent visual input. To evaluate the detect/transmit framework, we compare video reconstructed from the outputs of detect/transmit sensors with that reconstructed from the outputs of transmit only sensors. The results demonstrate that the detect/transmit framework can significantly increase the fidelity of relay by dynamically allocating bandwidth to the most salient areas of the visual field.

2   A Detect/Transmit Framework for the Relay of Visual Information

Based on the tonic and burst properties of the LGN that facilitate the detection and transmission of visual inputs, we have developed a framework for the high

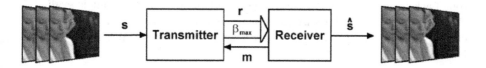

Fig. 1. An LGN inspired scheme for the relay of visual information

fidelity relay of visual information over a channel with limited bandwidth. The framework consists of a multi-sensor transmitter with tonic and burst modes, and a receiver that decodes the transmitted signal and controls the mode of each sensor in the transmitter, designed to mimic cortical feedback control of LGN response mode. A schematic diagram of the framework is shown in figure 1.

The intensity of the visual stimulus (s) is specified by P pixels per frame. The transmitter contains P sensors, each of which corresponds directly to one pixel of the visual input. The transmitter sends the output of each sensor to the receiver once per frame via a noise-free, lossless channel. The bandwidth limit on the channel (for all sensors combined) is specified as β_{max} bits/sec, which, for a frame rate of F frames/sec, corresponds to $\beta_{max}/F = \beta_{frame}$ bits/frame. Each sensor in the transmitter can operate in either tonic or burst mode. In tonic mode, the sensor will attempt to transmit detailed features of the visual stimulus with as many bits as are available. In burst mode, the sensor will signal either the absence or presence of a salient stimulus with only one bit. Following the relay of each frame, the receiver determines the mode (m) of each sensor for the next frame based on the salience of the recent visual input and sends the modes back to the transmitter (Note that the P bits/frame required to send the mode signal back to the transmitter is additional and is not included in constraint β_{max}).

We designed the detect/transmit framework to mimic the ability of the mammalian visual system to efficiently transmit visual information based on 'bottom-up' control of attention in response to changes in the external environment. However, 'bottom-up' control of attention is only one of many strategies that the visual system has developed to improve the transmission of visual information. Other strategies, such as spatial and temporal decorrelation, separate ON and OFF channels, and mechanisms for task dependent 'top-down' control of attention are not included in the model. Correspondingly, in evaluating the framework, we assumed that the goal of the transmitter is to send a representation of the visual stimulus with minimal mean-squared error (MSE). Thus, our model neglects any other features of the neural response that may be important, such as sparseness or redundancy [8]. Further discussion can be found in section 4.

2.1   Transmitter

The operation of the transmitter can be divided into three steps that must be repeated for each frame of the input. First, the total bandwidth β_{frame} is distributed among the P sensors in the transmitter based on the mode signal m

sent back from the receiver. Next, the recent history of the input is evaluated for comparison with the current input. Finally, the output of each sensor is calculated and sent to the receiver. Each of these steps is described in detail below.

Distribute bandwidth: Let the number of sensors in burst and tonic mode at a given time as determined by the mode signal m be denoted by n_{burst} and n_{tonic}. The total bandwidth β_{frame} must be distributed among the P sensors based on their modes. Each burst sensor is allotted one bit ($\beta_{burst} = 1$), and the remaining bits are distributed among the tonic sensors as follows:

$$\beta_{tonic} = floor \left\{ \frac{\beta_{frame} - n_{burst}}{n_{tonic}} \right\}$$

Thus, at time step t, the number of bits available to a given sensor, $\beta(p, t)$, is determined based on its mode $m(p, t)$ as follows:

$$\beta(p, t) = \begin{cases} \beta_{burst} & , \quad m(p, t) = 0 \\ \beta_{tonic} & , \quad m(p, t) = 1 \end{cases}$$

Evaluate input history: For each sensor, the recent input history must be evaluated to determine the salience of the current input. Typically, the salience of the input in a particular region of the visual field is evaluated across multiple dimensions (orientation, color, contrast, etc.) [9]. Here, salience is measured independently for each pixel by simply comparing the current intensity to previous intensities.

For a given sensor, the recent history of the input, H_{burst}, is specified by the average of the previous α intensities of the corresponding pixel:

$$H_{burst}(p, t) = \sum_{k=1}^{\alpha} s(p, t - k)$$

where α specifies the number of frames to be considered in the history of the input. If a sensor is in burst mode, it will signal a change in the input if the current input is significantly different from H_{burst}, alerting the receiver to switch the sensor to tonic mode. For all sensors that have just switched from tonic to burst mode at time t ($m(p, t - 1) = 1$ and $m(p, t) = 0$), the history term H_{burst} must be updated. For all sensors that remain in burst mode from the previous time step ($m(p, t - 1) = 0$ and $m(p, t) = 0$), H_{burst} remains the same ($H_{burst}(p, t) = H_{burst}(p, t - 1)$). For all sensors in tonic mode, the input history is evaluated at the receiver as described below.

Send signal: Once the mode, available bandwidth, and recent input history for each sensor have been set, the transmitter can relay its output to the receiver. The output of a sensor in burst mode depends on the salience of the current input relative to the recent history H_{burst}, with sensitivity determined by the parameter σ_{burst}. If the current input is significantly different from the recent history, then the sensor will indicate a change:

$$r(p,t) = \begin{cases} 1 & , & |s(p,t) - H_{burst}(p,t)| \geq \sigma_{burst} \\ 0 & , & \text{otherwise} \end{cases}$$

Sensors in tonic mode simply relay the visual input, quantized to available number of bits β_{tonic}:

$$r(p,t) = Q(s(p,t), \beta_{tonic})$$

where Q is the quantizer function.

2.2   Receiver

Receive signal: For sensors in burst mode, the receiver assumes that the input is unchanged, regardless of the transmitter output. Of course, if the sensor is in burst mode and the output $r(p,t) = 1$, the receiver will switch the sensor to tonic mode for the next frame (see below), but has received no new information about the input for the current frame. For sensors in tonic mode, the current value of the input has been relayed. Thus, the input s is reconstructed at the receiver as follows:

$$\hat{s}(p,t) = \begin{cases} \hat{s}(p,t-1) & , & m(p,t) = 0 \\ r(p,t) & , & m(p,t) = 1 \end{cases}$$

Evaluate input history: Just as the transmitter uses the recent input history to determine when the input changes significantly and signals the switch from burst to tonic mode, the receiver must determine when the input is no longer changing to control the switch back to burst mode. The switch from tonic to burst mode is controlled by comparing the current reconstruction to the recent history. At each time step, the history term for each tonic sensor is updated as follows:

$$H_{tonic}(p,t) = \sum_{k=1}^{\alpha} \hat{s}(p,t-k)$$

where α specifies the number of frames to be considered in the history of the reconstructed input.

Set mode: For each sensor, the mode for the next frame is determined by the current reconstruction and its recent history. Burst sensors that did not signal a change in the input at time t ($r(p,t) = 0$) remain in burst mode, while those that did ($r(p,t) = 1$) switch to tonic mode. The mode of each tonic sensor is determined by comparing the current reconstruction with H_{tonic} as follows:

$$m(p,t) = \begin{cases} 1 & , & |\hat{s}(p,t) - H_{tonic}| \geq \sigma_{tonic} \\ 0 & , & \text{otherwise} \end{cases}$$

The modes are sent back to the transmitter and the process is repeated for the next frame.

3   Examples of Video Relay with the Detect/Transmit Framework

To demonstrate the performance of the detect/transmit framework, we used it to relay and reconstruct a video movie. The video that we used contains footage of a vehicle traffic intersection in Karlsruhe, Germany, taken by a stationary camera. The video was provided by the Institut für Algorithmen und Kognitive Systeme, Universität Karlsruhe (http://i21www.ira.uka.de/image_ sequences). We used a section of the video consisting of 1000 frames, each of which contains 100 × 100 8-bit (0 - 255) grayscale pixels. In addition to reconstructing video from

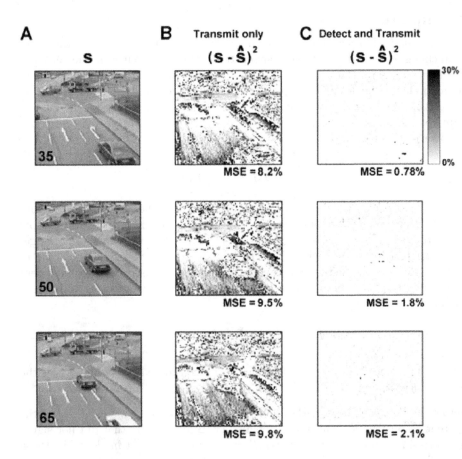

Fig. 2. Actual frames from the traffic video and the error in the reconstructions. Each frame consisted of 100 × 100 8-bit grayscale pixels. (A) Actual frames 35, 50, and 65. (B) Squared error in the reconstructed frames (% variance of intensity of actual frame) from TO sensors with $\beta_{frame}/P = 3$. The MSE of each reconstructed frame is shown. (C) Squared error in the reconstructed frames from D/T sensors with $\beta_{frame}/P = 3$ and $\sigma_{tonic} = \sigma_{burst} = 2$.

the signals of detect/transmit (D/T) sensors, we also reconstructed video from transmit only (TO) sensors as a baseline for comparison. To initialize the relay, all sensors were set to burst mode and the first α frames of the reconstructed input were set to the same value as the actual input. Because the frame rate of the video was 30 frames/sec, a value of $\alpha = 3$ was used so that the timescale of the history term was similar to the time constant of T channel de-inactivation in the LGN [3].

Example frames of the actual video and the error in the reconstructions are shown in figure 2. Figure 2A shows actual frames 35, 50, and 65 of the video. Figure 2B shows the squared error in the reconstructed frames (as a percent of the variance of the intensity of the actual frame) from relay with TO sensors

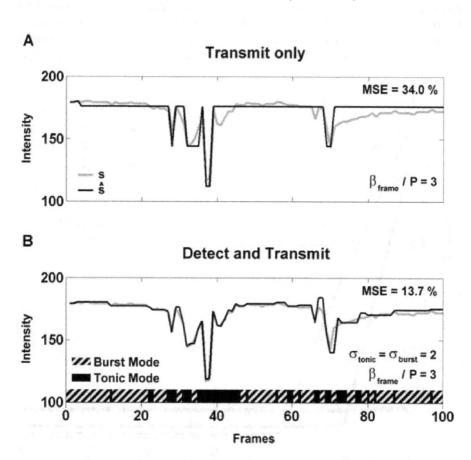

Fig. 3. Actual and reconstructed intensities of one pixel of the traffic video over 100 frames. (A) The actual (gray) and reconstructed (black) intensities from a TO sensor with $\beta_{frame}/P = 3$. The MSE of the reconstruction is shown (% variance of intensity of actual pixel). (B) The actual (gray) and reconstructed (black) intensities from a D/T sensor with $\beta_{frame}/P = 3$ and $\sigma_{tonic} = \sigma_{burst} = 2$.

with bandwidth limited to 3 bits/frame per sensor ($\beta_{frame}/P = 3$). The MSE of each reconstructed frame is also shown. Figure 2C shows the squared error in the reconstructed frames from relay with D/T sensors with $\beta_{frame}/P = 3$ and $\sigma_{tonic} = \sigma_{burst} = 2$. The reconstructions from the signals of the D/T sensors are superior to those from the TO sensors, as indicated by the decreased MSE.

Figure 3 shows actual and reconstructed intensities of one pixel of the video over 100 frames. Figure 3A shows the actual (gray) and reconstructed (black) intensities from a TO sensor with $\beta_{frame}/P = 3$, along with the corresponding MSE. Figure 3B shows the actual (gray) and reconstructed (black) intensities from a D/T sensor with $\beta_{frame}/P = 3$ and $\sigma_{tonic} = \sigma_{burst} = 2$. The mode of the sensor during the relay of each frame is indicated. During those times when the input is not changing, the sensor is in burst mode. Thus, it requires only 1 bit to transmit its signal, allowing the limited available bandwidth to be allocated to other sensors with more salient input. During those times when the input is varying, the sensor switches to tonic mode and transmits the value of the input

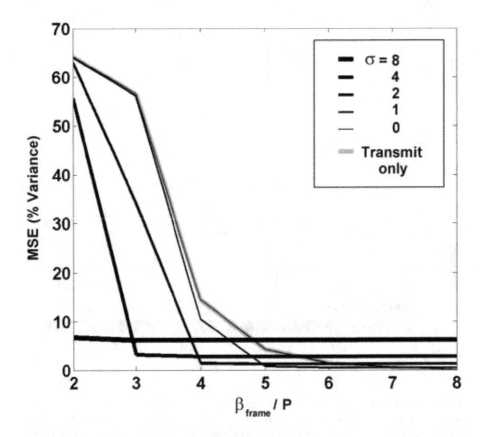

Fig. 4. Reconstruction error depends on β_{max} and σ. The MSE in the reconstruction from D/T sensors is shown for various values of β_{frame}/P and σ (see legend). For reference, the MSE in the reconstruction from TO sensors is shown in gray.

with all available bits. The dynamic allocation of bandwidth provided by the detect/transmit framework improves the reconstruction, as illustrated by the decreased MSE.

To investigate the effects of the salience sensitivity and the total available bandwidth on the fidelity of relay, we reconstructed the video from the signals of D/T and TO sensors with a range of values of β_{max} and $\sigma_{tonic} = \sigma_{burst} = \sigma$. The MSE of the reconstructions over all pixels and frames of the video are shown in figure 4. When a relatively small amount of total bandwidth is available, the lowest MSE is given by the reconstruction from the relay with the least sensitive sensors (thick black lines). This result indicates that, when bandwidth is severely limited, a better reconstruction is achieved by having fewer sensors in tonic mode with more available bits per sensor than by dividing the available bandwidth among many sensors. As more total bandwidth becomes available, the lowest MSE is given by the reconstruction from the relay with the most sensitive sensors (thin black lines). This result indicates that, when there is enough total bandwidth to encode all of the variations in the input, the best reconstruction is achieved when small fluctuations are detected.

4   Discussion

We have developed a detect/transmit framework based on the tonic and burst properties of LGN neurons to facilitate the high fidelity relay of visual information with limited bandwidth. The framework enables the dynamic allocation of bandwidth to those sensors which correspond to the most salient areas of the visual field. Each sensor in the transmitter operates in either tonic mode (signals input intensity with all available bits) or burst mode (signals the absence or presence of a salient input with only 1 bit), depending on the control signal sent by the receiver. We have demonstrated that video reconstructions from the signals of detect/transmit (D/T) sensors are superior to reconstructions from transmit only (TO) sensors and our results illustrate that the minimum MSE reconstructions are obtained when the sensitivity of the sensors (σ) is set to an appropriate value for the total available bandwidth (β_{max}).

We designed the detect/transmit framework to mimic the ability of the mammalian visual system to dynamically allocate attentional resources to behaviorally relevant areas of the visual field. However, our framework only includes mechanisms for 'bottom-up' control of attention based on changes in the external environment, and, correspondingly, control of transmitter mode was based solely on the salience of the input [10]. However, the mammalian visual system also contains mechanisms for 'top-down' control of attention that is dependent on the current behavioral task [11]. For example, if an animal is expecting something to appear in a certain area of the visual field, it may direct its attention to that area before anything actually appears. Modifications to the detect/transmit framework to incorporate 'top-down' attention would be made at the receiver, specifically to the method used to control the mode of the transmitter sensors.

In addition to attentional mechanisms, the mammalian visual system incorporates a number of other strategies to optimize the relay of visual information. While the sensors in our transmitter have a one-to-one correspondence with a pixel of the visual input, retinal ganglion cells, which transmit visual information from the retina to the LGN, are known to integrate the inputs of many photoreceptors over space and time to enhance contrast sensitivity and reduce the redundancy in their responses [12,13,14]. To incorporate these principles into our framework, each sensor would need to integrate multiple pixels of the visual input into its output and the reconstruction scheme in the receiver would have to be changed accordingly. The development of such modifications and the implementation of 'top-down' attention as described above are directions for future research.

Acknowledgments

This work was supported by National Geospatial-Intelligence Agency Grant HM1582-05-C-0009.

References

1. S. M. Sherman. Tonic and burst firing: dual modes of thalamocortical relay. *TINS*, 24:122–126, 2001.
2. R. Krahe and F. Gabbiani. Burst firing in sensory systems. *Nature Reviews: Neuroscience*, 5:13–23, 2004.
3. M. Steriade and R. R. Llinas. The functional states of the thalamus and the associated neuronal interplay. *Physiol. Rev.*, 68:649–742, 1988.
4. A. M. Sillito and H. E. Jones. Corticothalamic interaction in the transfer of visual information. *Phil. Trans. R. Soc. Lond. B*, 357:1739–1752, 2002.
5. W. Guido and T. Weyand. Burst responses in thalamic relay cells of the awake behaving cat. *J. Neurophysiol.*, 74:1782–1786, 1995.
6. T. G. Weyand, M. Boudreaux, and W. Guido. Burst and tonic response modes in thalamic neurons during sleep and wakefulness. *J. Neurophysiol.*, 85:1107–1118, 2001.
7. N. A. Lesica and G. B. Stanley. Encoding of natural scene movies by tonic and burst spikes in the lateral geniculate nucleus. *J. Neurosci.*, 24:10731–10740, 2004.
8. E. P. Simoncelli and B. A. Olshausen. Natural image statistics and neural representation. *Annu. Rev. Neurosci.*, 24:1193–1216, 2001.
9. L. Itti and C. Koch. A saliency-based search mechanism for overt and covert shifts of visual attention. *Vision Res.*, 40:1489–1506, 2000.
10. L. Itti and C. Koch. Computational modelling of visual attention. *Nature Rev. Neurosci.*, 2:194–203, 2001.
11. S. Shipp. The brain circuitry of attention. *TICS*, 8:223–230, 2004.
12. H. B. Barlow. Possible principles underlying the transformations of sensory messages. In W. A. Rosenblith, editor, *Sensory Communication*, pages 217–234. MIT Press, 1961.
13. M. V. Srinivasan, S. B. Laughlin, and A. Dubs. Predictive coding: A fresh view of inhibition in the retina. *Proc. R. Soc. Lond. B*, 216:427–459, 1982.
14. J. J. Atick and A. N. Redlich. What does the retina know about natural scenes? *Neural Computation*, 4:196–210, 1992.

On Cognitive Dynamic Map
and Its Use for Navigation in Space

Flavien Maingreaud[1,2], Edwige Pissaloux[2], and Ramiro Velazquez[2]

[1] CEA/LIST, BP 6, 92 265 Fontenay-aux-Roses, France
maingreaudf@zoe.cea.fr
[2] LRP, Univ. Paris 6, BP 61, 92 265 Fontenay-aux-Roses, France
{maingreaud, pissaloux, velazquez}@robot.jussieu.fr

Abstract. The paper addresses experimental results on peri-space geometry and topology perception with a touch sense. A dedicated "perception-action" platform, involving artificial vision and a hand tactile stimulation device as well as convenient touch-space perception experiments have been designed. The proposed gravitation representation of the space is based upon nearest object edge displays on tactile device, which dynamically modifies with subject navigating in the plate form. This representation has been evaluated on voluntary blindfolded healthy male and female subjects. The collected data show that it is possible to navigate in space using the touch stimulating device.

1 Introduction

The ability to move in 3D space, in safe and independent manner, is a basic and vital human activity, for which the space perception seems to be a fundamental element. Therefore, an adequate form of space internal (brain) representation is necessary. This latter is built only with our senses (vision, touch, hear, smell, kinesthesia, and so on); however, if the navigation task is considered, the space perception can be assisted via a map, a topographic representation of the space.

A (cognitive) map could be of assistance for space perception. Indeed, one of the map's functions is to provide data impossible to perceive with vision (because they are hidden or remote), data for objects' localization, data for distance to objects' estimation, data for displacement direction estimation, data for displacement (or journey) path elaboration, and so on.

The tactile map concept is used since 6000 years [8], but only very late the researchers have realized its importance for spatial information processing.

"Tactual map" can be used for evaluation of the influence of map's orientation and subject's orientation in the environment [15].

Some experimental environments, similar to tactile map [16], [9], [14], have been used for memory and inference tests performance evaluation during the haptic exploration of the spatial relationship between objects located in limited space.

A familiar environment reconstruction task via tabletop (map, gravitation) model construction allows to evaluate someone's ability for space integration [6-7].

A route construction model, in both small- and large- scale environment, can be supported by a map as well [13].

M. De Gregorio et al. (Eds.): BVAI 2005, LNCS 3704, pp. 187–194, 2005.
© Springer-Verlag Berlin Heidelberg 2005

Very simple static aligned maps encoding static beacons can be successfully used since the age of 4 for moving and for self localization in a peri-personal space [4], [11], [8], [15], [16]; the distance between 2 objects (affordance) can also be evaluated with an error less than 20% [18]. Visually impaired people can use these maps for navigation in unfamiliar indoor and outdoor environments [10].

Since its beginning a tactile map encompasses a cognitive (symbolic) 2D projection of a 3D real space, (quasi) global (such as a city map) or local (a peri-personal space, a few meters ahead of you).

The use of cognitive maps implies synergetic processes: space perception and space cognition. Perceptual processes require adaptation of a map provided knowledge representation to biosensors perceptual capabilities; line, geometric figures and global space configuration perception are the main challenges of this process. Cognitive processes are complex; they require 3D → 2D projection and its scale, map orientation (aligned, misaligned, etc.), map spatial localization, shift between spatial frames of referentials (allocentered <-> egocentered shift), inertial data processing, observed scene dynamics analysis, etc.

Concept of dynamic cognitive maps has been evaluated mainly in laboratories in the context of static tasks such as object recognition [12] on non-portable systems. However, recent physiology and technology progresses allow to implement portable dynamic cognitive maps, which content adapts to environment changes in real time. Moreover, such maps can display egocentered and allocentered scene representation (contrary to Bach-y-Rita's TVSS display unit which is egocentered only, [1]).

This paper presents an ego-allo- centered dynamic tactile map for 3D space binary representation structured by the navigation task, and its experimental evaluation.

Section 2 introduces the space binary representation, and sketches the main physiological basis justifying it. Section 3 briefly presents experimental plate-form Section 4 outlines experiments performed to validate the proposed space representation Section 5 summarizes the collected results and provides some future research directions.

2   Space Partition: Navigational Space Binary Representation

Figure 1 summarizes the main steps of cognitive map building process in 3D world perception task. Almost all senses, such as vision, touch, hearing, vestibule, proprioception (kinesthesia), etc., participate in space perception and its coherent representation coding (via data internal combination). Despite of some redundant information provided to the brain by different sensory channels, it seems that our senses ontogenesis requires/expects this redundancy [15].

Visual navigation action "naturally" partitions space into two subspaces: obstacles and obstacles-free zones, thus defines the *cognitive space binary   representation* (Figure 2).

This representation varies in time (with scene dynamic) and in space (changing of the observation point). Therefore navigation action can be efficiently executed if it is supported by space dynamic cognitive map supporting allo- and ego- centered space binary representations.

In the case of a sensory deficiency, it is necessary to provide the most appropriate representation of the space binary representation and to find the most appropriate sensory channel to make it participate in brain space cognitive map building. In the case of sightless, the touch sense has proven to be an efficient input data channel for static data (Braille code); moreover, the recent results on touch sense confirm [3] that the touch, as many other senses, reacts on the gradient of information.

Consequently, touch sense channel is a good candidate to (partly) replace visual channel and to receive data from the dynamic cognitive map of the space binary representation useful for navigation.

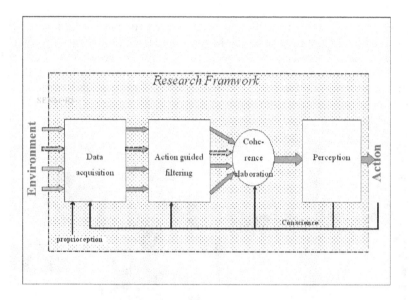

Fig. 1. Main steps of space cognitive map building

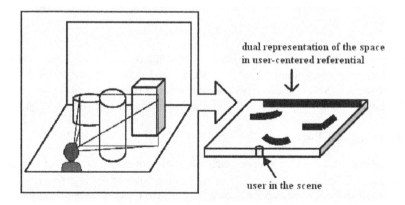

Fig. 2. Space binary representation for displacement task

3   Experimental Plate-Form

In order to validate our hypothesis on space for navigation binary representation an experimental plate-form has been designed. It encompasses two components: a tactile interface, which stimulates touch sense, and tracking plate-form, which allows to track subject's using the tactile device when moving in the space.

3.1   Tactile Interface

The tactile surface, a Braille surface, is realised as a two dimensional micro-actuators (taxels) matrix (Figure 3). The Shape Memory Alloy (SMA) technology (Figure 3a) has been chosen [19], because it is a good compromise between physical characteristics and tactile perception physiology. Indeed, physiological data allow to determine the most appropriate for touch sense stimulation taxel's dimensions (length, frequency contact force, inter taxel distance, etc.).

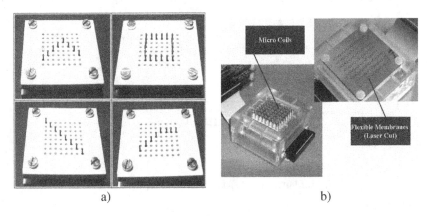

a)   b)

Fig. 3. Touch stimulating devices: a) SMA based, LRP/CEA designed; b) ViTAL, vibrating taxels, CEA designed

Moreover, the SMA technology makes possible the design of a system with a convenient energy consumption (wearable battery), good temporal performance and reliability. However, SMA tactile device being in prototype stage only, the vibrating VITAL device realised by the CEA, France has been used for experiments (Figure .3b)

3.2   Tracking Plat-Form

Figure 4 shows the built "perception-action" plat-form allowing subject tracking in limited space (7x7m^2), while Figure 5 shows its usage during the experiments.

This first version of "perception-action" plate-form encompasses three elements: a personal computer (PC), a wide angle color camera (webcam) located 6 m above the filmed (peri-personal) space and dedicated (original) tracking software.

The camera acquires images (every 10s), in allocentered referential, which are processed by the tracking software running on a PC. Acquired images encompass two information fundamental for the tracking system: direction of subject's head (gaze) navigating in the environment, and subject's seen part of the navigation space (its peri-personal space). The quite precise gaze direction is obtained via a bicolor pointer attached to the hat carried by subject during his navigation in the plate-form; indeed, the bicolor pointer direction corresponds to subject's gaze direction.

We display on the computer's screen three images for control: space "seen" by the camera (Figure 4, central part of the image), part of the space "seen" by the subject (Figure 4, to the left with respect to the central part of the image) and space representation on the touch stimulating device subject's carried during the navigation (Figure 4, to the right with respect to the central part of the image).

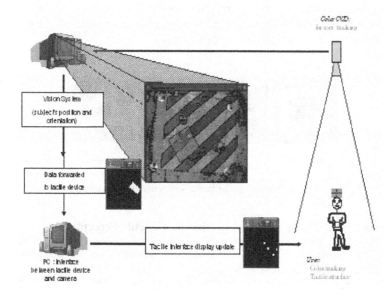

Fig. 4. Tracking plate-form

Fig. 5. Experimental data collection during the space exploration with VITAL interface

4   Experiments

Three experiments have been led with blindfolded voluntary subjects. In experiments 1 and 2 subjects have been seated in front of the VITAL device (stationary egocentered position), while they have carried the VITAL in place closed to their gravity center in the experiment 3 (almost stationary ego-centered position).

4.1   Experiment 1: Static Form Tactile Perception

The test of static forms displayed on the tactile surface perception has been the goal of this experiment. We wanted to identify if there are preferred geometric shapes in tactile perceptive modality (line, square, circle, arrow), and preferred tactile representation (wired-frame, as shown in Figure 6, or full); what is the best scale (out of three: large, medium and small) for the forms' perception.

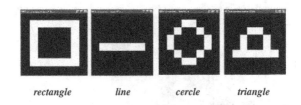

rectangle   line   cercle   triangle

Fig. 6. Static framed shapes for tactile recognition

4.2   Experiment 2: Form and Moving Direction Tactile Perception

This experiment collected data in order to know whether or not the displayed shape can induce the moving stimuli direction.

   In vision language, an arrow symbolizes the direction of the movement. This experiment aimed to determine if a "tactile" arrow could have the same effect: speed-up the direction recognition (Figure 7).

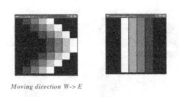

Moving direction W-> E

Fig. 7. Shapes for direction recognition

4.3   Experiment 3: Navigation in 3D Space with Tactile Interface

This experiment shown in Figure 5 has been defined in order to understand if and how it is possible to perceive the space by blindfolded people. After a very short period of learning how to the tactile device (2 minutes in the average) with the assistance of a supervisor, blindfolded subjects have been invited to navigate to navigate in the space using the tactile device. The whole experiments took 10 minutes.

5 Discussion

From data collected during the experiment 1 is it possible to conclude that there is a bad perception of filled forms. Moreover, many subjects have complained about tactile surface (8x8 taxels) too weak resolution.

Data collected during the experiment 2 shows that it is possible to recognize a direction, but the recognition process is shape insensitive (i,e., the arrow does not speed up the moving direction recognition).

From data collected during the experiment 3 it is possible to conclude that (1) it is possible to perceive the space organization via its tactile representation; (2) nearest obstacle edge representation can be appropriate for a space binary representation (obstacles – obstacle free space); (3) it is possible to integrate a space representation to a navigation tool.

Future experiments have to be performed on blind voluntary subjects.

All experiments have to be done on touch stimulating SMA based (not vibrating) tactile interface ; indeed, SMA device will involve in perception Meisner' biosensors, while vibrating interface will involve mainly Paccini's biosensors, so tactile information can be easier understood by subjects (blind people).

Furthermore, new experiments should provide additional data about space representation and representation precision.

Acknowledgement

We would like to thank Professor Alain Berthoz from Collège de France for his fruitfull discussions. We would also like to thank all Master Students from Robotics Laboratory of Paris 6 University for their voluntary participation in experiments. Finally, we would like to thank CONACYT, Mexico, for the partial financial support of this work.

References

1. Bach-y-Rita, P., Tyler, M. E., Kaczmarek, K., A., Seeing with the Brain, Int. J. Human-Computer Interaction, 2001
2. Bear, M. F., Connors, B., W., Paradiso, M. A., Neurosciences : A la découverte du cerveau, Editions Pradel, 2002
3. Berthoz, A., Le sens du mouvement, Odile Jacob, 1997.
4. Blades, Spencer, 1987
5. Bliss, J. , Dynamic Tactile Displays in Man-Machine Systems. IEEE Transactions on Man-Machine Systems. (Special issue: Tactile displays conference), Vol. 11, No 1 (1970).
6. Casey, S.M., Cognitive mapping by the blind, J. of Visual Impairment and Blindness, 72(297-301), 1978

7. Cierco, M., *Leçons de la mobilité*, INJA (Institut National des Jeunes Aveugles), Réunion de travail, 4 décembre 2002
8. Hatwell, Y., Streri, A., Gentaz, E., Toucher pour connaître : Psychologie cognitive de la perception tactile manuelle, PUF, 2000.
9. Herman, J.E., Herman, T.G., Chatman, S.P., Constructing cognitive maps from partial information : A demonstration study with congenitally blind and sighted children, Quaterly J. Experimental Psychology, 27(195-298), 1983
10. Jacobson, R.D., Lippa, Y., Golledge, R.G., Kitchin, R.M., and Blades, M. (2001) Rapid development of cognitive maps in people with visual impairments when exploring novel geographic spaces. IAPS Bulletin of People-Environment Studies 18, 3-6.
11. Landau, B., Early map use as an unlearned ability, Cognition, 22, pp. 201-223
12. Loose M. Maucher T., Schemmel J., Meier K., Keller M., « A Tactile Vision-Substitution System, Handbook of Computer Vsions and Applications », vol. 3, Academic Press, 1999, p. 531-541.
13. Ochaï ta, E., Huertas, J.A., Spatial representation by persons who are blind : A study of the effect of learning and development, J. of Visual Impairment and Blindnee, 87(37-41), 1993
14. Rieser, J.J., Hill, Hill, E.W., Sensitivity to perspective structure while walking without vision, Perception, 15(173-188)
15. Rossano, M.J., Warren, D.H., The importance of alignment in blind subjects' use of tactual map, Perception, 18 (215-229), 1989.
16. Rossano, M.J., Warren, D.H., Misaligned maps lead to predictable errors, Perception, 18 (215-299), 1989.
17. Shinohara, M., Shimizu, Y. Three-Dimensional Tactile Display for the Blind. IEEE Trans. Rehabilitation Engineering, Vol. 6, No. 3 (1998) 249-256.
18. Ungar, S., Blades, M. & Spencer, C. , The ability of visually impaired children to locate themselves on a tactile map, J. Visual Impairment and Blindness 90(6), 526-535,1997
19. Velázquez, F. Maingreaud and E. Pissaloux, "Intelligent Glasses: A New Man-Machine Interface Concept Integrating Computer Vision and Human Tactile Perception", in Proceedings of EuroHaptics 2003, Dublin, Ireland, 2003 pp 456-460.

Visual Selection in Human Frontal Eye Fields

Jacinta O'Shea[1], Neil G. Muggleton[2], Alan Cowey[1], and Vincent Walsh[2]

[1] Department of Experimental Psychology, South Parks Road, Oxford OX1 3UD, UK
[2] Department of Psychology and Institute of Cognitive Neuroscience,
University College London, Queen Square, London WC1N 3AR, UK

Abstract. Frontal eye field neurons discharge in response to behaviourally relevant stimuli that are potential targets for saccades. Distinct perceptual and oculomotor processes have been dissociated in the monkey FEFs, but little is known about the perceptual capacity of human FEFs. To explore this, transcranial magnetic stimulation (TMS) was applied over the FEFs while subjects carried out visual search. TMS impaired search performance (d') when applied between 40 and 80ms after search array onset. Unit recordings show that FEF signal during this time period predicts monkeys' behavioural reports on hit, miss, false alarm and correct rejection trials. Our data demonstrate that the human FEFs make a critical early contribution to search performance. We argue that this reflects the operation of a visuospatial selection process within the FEFs that is not reducible to saccade programs.

1 Introduction

The frontal eye fields (FEFs), in the arcuate sulcus of the monkey brain (BA8/6) [1], have an important role in converting the outcome of visual processing into eye movement commands. In classical anatomical models of the visual system [2], the FEFs are situated in the upper reaches of the visual hierarchy, several levels above sensory visual areas. However, recent findings have challenged the characterization of FEF function solely in terms of oculomotor control.

FEF neurons exhibit response latencies in the same 40-80ms range as early sensory visual areas V1, V2, MT and MST [3], whilst the discovery of feed-forward connectivity between FEF and V4 has re-defined the position of the FEFs within the visual hierarchy [4]. FEF damage can induce visual field defects which remain evident in raised detection thresholds after oculomotor deficits have recovered [5]. Using feature [6] and conjunction [7] search tasks, distinct processes have been dissociated in the FEFs: target selection by FEF visual neurons and saccade programming by FEF movement neurons. FEF visual neurons are not selective for particular physical visual attributes [8]. Instead, they respond to behaviourally relevant stimuli, and have been described as computing a saliency map which encodes targets for potential saccades [9]. The initial visual response (50ms post-stimulus) is non-selective, but by about 100-120ms the activity of FEF visual neurons distinguishes with 95% reliability targets from distractors in the receptive field [10]. Distractor-related activity is suppressed, while target-related activity evolves to signal the spatial location of the stimulus. FEF movement neurons do not respond to visual stimulation, but fire before

M. De Gregorio et al. (Eds.): BVAI 2005, LNCS 3704, pp. 195–204, 2005.

and during saccades, signalling whether and when to make a saccade [11]. Target selection occurs independently of saccade programming: the timing of selection does
not predict saccadic reaction times and selection occurs whether or not monkeys proceed to saccade to the target [12].

In neuroimaging studies, the FEFs are commonly activated in orienting paradigms,
whether or not an eye movement is required. In the latter case, FEF activation is attributed to the generation of saccade programs that are not overtly executed, rather
than to visual analytic processes in the FEFs. To date, only four published studies
have directly assessed the perceptual role of the human FEFs. These have reported
roles for the FEFs in contralateral visual stimulus analysis [13], preparatory vision
[14, 15], and target discrimination in conjunction visual search [16].

The present experiments used TMS to test the hypothesis that, as in the monkey
brain, human FEFs make a critical early (perceptual) contribution to visual search performance. To de-couple perceptual from oculomotor processes, a conjunction search
task was used in which eye movements were not required. Search arrays were presented briefly and fixation was monitored. Array duration was titrated so that each
subject performed at 75% accuracy. TMS effects were quantified using a measure of
perceptual sensitivity (d').

2   Methods

2.1   Subjects

Eight subjects (7 male, 1 female) participated in Experiment 1 (mean age = 27.6 +
4.3). Nine subjects (8 male, 1 female) participated in Experiment 2 (mean age = 27.7
+ 3.6). Of these, four had participated in Experiment 1. A further four subjects were
discarded for reasons given below (see Task Design). All subjects were right-handed
and had normal or corrected-to-normal vision. All gave informed written consent and
reported an absence of any neurological condition in their known family history. All
procedures were approved by the Oxford Research Ethics Committee (OxREC) and
the Institute of Neurology, University College London.

2.2   Visual Stimuli

Visual search arrays were displayed on a 16" VDU with 100 Hz vertical refresh rate
running E-Prime software (Psychology Software Tools, Pittsburgh). Subjects sat in a
dark room 57cm from of the screen and were restricted by a forehead and chin rest.
Each search array subtended 2 x 2 degrees of visual angle around a central fixation
cross. Each array contained 12 stimuli on a grey background ($35.8cd/m^2$). In Experiment 1, these were luminance-matched ($22 cd/m^2$) purple vertical (CIE: x = 0.217, y =
0.130) and green horizontal (CIE: x =0.282, y =0.589) lines, each subtending ca. 0.23
degrees of visual angle (DVA). The target was a purple horizontal and was present on
50% of trials. In Experiment 2, stimuli were luminance-matched ($23.3 cd/m^2$) pink
(CIE: x = 0.288, y = 0.149) and purple (CIE: x = 0.233, y = 0.203) diagonal lines in
opposite orientations. Each line subtended ca. 0.18 DVA. The target was a purple diagonal sharing the same orientation as the pink diagonals and was present on 50% of

trials. The background luminance of both arrays was uniform grey ($35.8cd/m^2$). In both experiments, the stimulus mask subtended 2 x 2 DVA and was composed of patches of the two stimulus colours used in that experiment.

2.3 Task Design

Task procedure replicated Muggleton, et al. (2003)(see Figure 1(a)). A trial began with a central fixation cross for 500ms, followed by a briefly presented search array, which was masked. Subjects had to make a target present/absent response using a key press. Accuracy was emphasized over speed. The inter-trial interval was 2 sec. Array duration was determined by a staircase procedure which varied presentation by one screen refresh (10ms) until subjects performed at 75% accuracy. Correct performance on 6/8 trials on two consecutive blocks (8 trials) determined a subject's viewing threshold. Subjects then ran one block of 60 trials (Experiment 1) or two blocks of 40 trials (Experiment 2) to confirm the validity of the threshold value. When subjects scored d' > 1.0, they began formal trials. If a subject failed to achieve this criterion, array duration was increased until the criterion was reached. Block order was counterbalanced. Procedures were identical in both experiments.

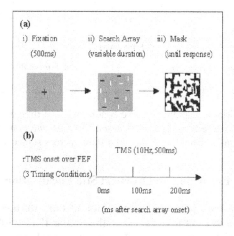

Fig. 1. (a) A trial began with central fixation (i), followed by the search array, for a duration determined individually for each subject (ii), and then a mask until the subject responded (iii). (b) TMS (10Hz, 500ms) was applied over the right FEFs at three times: (1) at search array onset (0ms), (2) 100ms after array onset (100ms), (3) 200ms after array onset.

In Experiment 1, subjects performed five blocks of 60 trials, one for each TMS condition: Vertex, V5, $FEF_{(0)}$, $FEF_{(100)}$ and $FEF_{(200)}$. In the first three conditions (Vertex, V5 and $FEF_{(0)}$), 10Hz TMS was applied for 500ms at search array onset (see Figure 1(b)). In the latter two conditions, TMS was applied 100ms ($FEF_{(100)}$) or 200ms ($FEF_{(200)}$) after array onset. By comparing $FEF_{(0)}$, $FEF_{(100)}$ and $FEF_{(200)}$ against Vertex, the aim was to test the effect of TMS over FEF during the first 100ms of visual processing ($FEF_{(0)}$); during visual processing, but after the first 100ms ($FEF_{(100)}$); and when subjects were no longer viewing the search array ($FEF_{(200)}$).

In Experiment 2, subjects ran two blocks (40 trials) in each of five timing conditions (0/40ms; 40/80ms; 80/120ms; "pre-threshold" and "post-threshold") for each TMS site (Vertex and right FEF). In the first three conditions, dual TMS pulses were applied at: 0/40ms; 40/80ms and 80/120ms after array onset; in the last two conditions, pulses were applied during the last 40ms below each subject's visual threshold ("pre-threshold") and during the first 40ms above threshold ("post- threshold"), (eg: for a threshold of 150ms, TMS was applied at 100/140 and 160/200ms, respectively) (Figure 2). Interspersed among these experimental blocks, subjects performed four blocks in which TMS was not applied. If d' was below 1.0 on any of these baseline blocks, the subject was excluded from the experiment. Four subjects were discounted on these grounds.

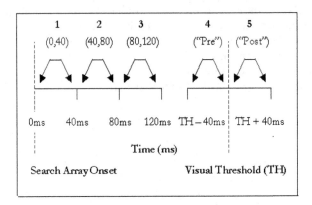

Fig. 2. Double-Pulse TMS was applied in five conditions. The timing of the first three conditions was determined relative to search array onset. The last two conditions were determined relative to each individual's visual threshold and differed across subjects.

2.4 Eye Movement Recording and Cortical Site Localization

To confirm that saccades or eye blinks could not account for the results, fixation was monitored using infrared light transducers in the Skalar IRIS 6500 system attached to the forehead rest. Signals were sampled at a rate of 1000 Hz by an A-D converter card and were recorded using DASYlab 5 software. Eye position traces were recorded for search array duration on every trial and the equipment was re-calibrated between blocks. Based on the results of a previous experiment [16], right FEF was chosen as the site of an expected TMS effect. FEF was localized using frameless stereotaxy (Brainsight, Rogue Research, Montreal, Canada) and anatomical landmarks. Stimulation was applied over the posterior middle frontal gyrus, at the junction of the precentral and superior frontal sulci [17] at coordinates that correspond well with other FEF TMS [18] and imaging studies [19]. Vertex was chosen as the principal control for somatosensory and acoustic TMS artefacts. V5 served as an additional control to demonstrate that FEF TMS effects were specific, and not a general consequence of interference with the visual system. V5 was functionally localized using the established method of moving phosphene elicitation [20].

2.5   Transcranial Magnetic Stimulation

A Magstim Super Rapid machine (Magstim Company, Dyfed, U.K.) was used to deliver repetitive- and double-pulse TMS through a series of small diameter (50mm) figure-of-eight TMS coils. Coils were cooled on ice before use to prevent overheating during a block. Over FEF and Vertex, the coil was oriented parallel to the floor with the handle running in an anterior-posterior direction. Over V5, the coil was oriented at a right angle to the floor. 10Hz TMS was applied at 65% of stimulator output over Vertex and FEF and at 110% of phosphene threshold over V5.

3   Results

3.1   Experiment 1: Repetitive-Pulse TMS

The d' data for all eight subjects in three of the five conditions (Vertex, V5, $FEF_{(0)}$) were submitted to a one-way repeated measures ANOVA to test whether TMS over the FEF degraded search performance. There was a main effect of TMS Site ($F(2,14)$ = 5.844, p = 0.014). Planned comparisons revealed a significant difference between Vertex and $FEF_{(0)}$ ($F(1,7)$ = 7.930, p = 0.026) but no difference between the two control sites, Vertex and V5 ($F(1,7)$ = 1.525, p = 0.257) (Figure 3). TMS reduced d' in the $FEF_{(0)}$ but not the Vertex block (mean $FEF_{(0)}$ = 1.124, SE = 0.263; mean vertex = 1.754, SE = 0.184). To test for a selective effect on hits or false alarms, the data were analysed by response type: ANOVA (TMS Site * Response Type (hits, false alarms)). The interaction was not significant ($F(6,42)$ = 1.984, p = 0.09). Bias scores (C) showed that subjects had a tendency towards "target absent" responses, but this was not affected by TMS ($F(2,14)$ = 0.512, p = 0.610; mean C values: vertex = 0.16 (SE = 0.2), $FEF_{(0)}$ = 0.356 (SE = 0.183), V5 = 0.417 (SE = 0.132)).

To test the hypothesis that earlier TMS application would produce greater interference, d' data from the $FEF_{(0)}$, $FEF_{(100)}$ and $FEF_{(200)}$ conditions were compared against

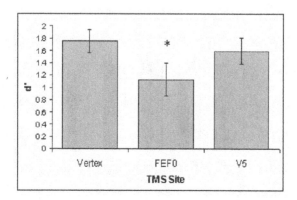

Fig. 3. Effect of rTMS over right FEF on Search Performance (Experiment 1). Search performance was impaired when TMS was applied over right FEF, but not over V5 or Vertex. TMS significantly reduced d' (* refers to planned comparison with Vertex, $p < 0.05$)(n = 8).

Vertex. It was expected that all subjects would have thresholds < 200ms, so that in the FEF$_{(200)}$ (control) condition TMS would be applied during the mask. Two subjects had longer thresholds (230/250ms, mean: 150ms), so their data were excluded. A repeated-measures ANOVA showed no main effect of TMS Condition (Vertex, FEF$_{(0)}$, FEF$_{(100)}$ and FEF$_{(200)}$)(F(3,15) = 2.249, p = 0.125). However, planned contrasts against Vertex revealed a significant reduction in d' in the FEF$_{(0)}$ condition only: (F(1,5) = 25.019, p = 0.004) (mean FEF$_{(0)}$ = 1.152, SE = 0.238; mean Vertex =1.585, SE = 0.198). There was a trend in the FEF$_{(100)}$ condition (F(1,5) = 4.904, p = 0.078), but the FEF$_{(200)}$ condition did not approach significance (F(1,5) = 1.513, p = 0.273). The results suggest that the earlier TMS was applied, the greater the reduction in d' (see Figure 4). Subjects tended towards "target absent" responses in all conditions. TMS did not affect this response bias (F(3,15) = 2.017, p = 0.215; mean C values: vertex = 0.376 (SE = 0.125), FEF$_{(0)}$ = 0.278 (SE = 0.199), FEF$_{(100)}$ = 0.296 (SE = .138), FEF$_{(200)}$ = 0.176 (SE = .214)).

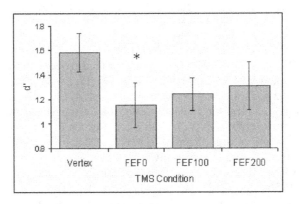

Fig. 4. Search performance (d') was impaired when TMS was applied over FEF at search array onset (* refers to planned comparison with Vertex, p < 0.05) (n = 6)

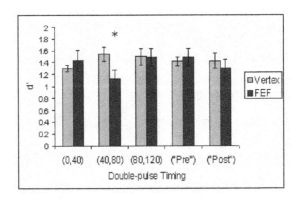

Fig. 5. Double-pulse TMS over right FEF at 40/80ms significantly reduced d' (* refers to MANOVA with "TMS Time" and "TMS Site" (Vertex, FEF) as factors, p < 0.05)(n = 9)

3.2 Experiment 2: Double-Pulse TMS

Experiment 2 was designed to sample discrete sub-sets of the first 200ms of array processing. A MANOVA tested whether TMS over the FEF differed significantly from Vertex (control) in any of the five time periods (0/40, 40/80, 80/120, 'Pre-Threshold', 'Post-Threshold'). TMS applied over FEF in the 40/80ms condition only significantly reduced perceptual sensitivity ($F(1,16) = 4.762$, $p = 0.044$) (FEF 40/80 mean d' = 1.132, SE = 0.133; Vertex 40/80 mean d' = 1.543, SE = 0.133) (Figure 5). There was no selective effect on hits or false alarms, nor did TMS affect subjects' baseline "target absent" response bias.

4 Discussion

These experiments aimed to test whether the human FEFs make a critical perceptual contribution to visual search. In Experiment 1, rTMS over right FEF reduced perceptual sensitivity (d'), compared to control TMS over Vertex or V5. Perceptual processing was de-coupled from saccade programming by using brief displays and by monitoring fixation. Saccades and blinks occurred on fewer than 3% of trials, which did not differ across conditions. The reduction in discriminability indicates that the human FEFs are critical for normal conjunction search performance when saccades are not required. This replicates the findings of Muggleton, et al (2003). Experiment 1 further suggested that the earlier TMS was applied, the greater the disruptive effect. Experiment 2 isolated disruption to within 40-80ms after search array onset. This temporal profile of interference coincides with neurophysiological data. Thompson & Schall (1999) showed that the amplitude of signal in FEF neurons 60-90ms after visual stimulus onset predicted monkeys' perceptual reports on hit, miss, false alarm and correct rejection trials. The early and discrete effect of TMS suggests disruption of visual selection processes in the FEFs rather than saccade programming.

Under normal circumstances, visual scenes are inspected by cycles of stimulus fixation and analysis, followed by saccades that direct gaze to subsequent targets in the visual scene. Minimum estimates of the time required to perform these operations suggest that perceptual processing requires approximately 100ms [21], while saccade programming requires 100-150ms [22]. The contention that early TMS interference reflects disruption of target selection, rather than saccade programming, seems to imply that there are temporally discrete stages processing. However, there is evidence that both processes occur in parallel [23]. Moreover, it has been shown that FEF movement neurons are modulated by distractor properties, suggesting a model of continuous information transfer between FEF visual and motor neurons [7]. Accordingly, disruption of visual analytic processes in FEF should produce a concomitant build-up of error in the signal that shapes the oculomotor response. Hence, despite no difference in saccade rates across conditions, one could argue that the TMS effects stem from disruption of latent saccade programming.

In Experiment 1, TMS reduced d' in the FEF$_{(0)}$ condition. This was attributed to disruption of target selection processes in FEF occurring during the first 100ms. However, TMS was applied for 500ms duration so may have disrupted both perceptual and oculomotor processes. It is beyond the scope of the rTMS design to evaluate this possibility. By contrast, the double-pulse design (Experiment 2) showed a discrete TMS effect that corresponds with the timing of target selection processes in monkey FEF. Interference occurred early (40-80ms), about 100ms earlier than the mean visual threshold (178ms). Since the effect of a TMS pulse on neural firing is immediate, if the effects were due to disruption of latent saccade programs then one would expect interference to occur later, closer to the time of saccade evolution (eg: in the 80/120 or 120/160 time bin). Significantly, there was no effect in any of the later time bins. Moreover, although it is clear that disrupting target selection should affect saccade programming, it is difficult to explain how disrupting saccade programs should affect visual discrimination (d'). In light of this, an account based on target selection is more parsimonious than one based on latent saccade programs.

The temporal correspondence between the TMS effect and FEF unit activity is not exact. Typically, target selection in FEF neurons evolves over 50-70ms after the onset of a search array and peaks at 100-120ms, by which time the neuronal response distinguishes targets from distractors with 95% reliability [10]. This peak has been shown to occur later as task difficulty is increased. The combination of conjunction search and an early TMS effect thus seems to pose an interpretative problem. The following observations are offered in an attempt to address this. First, FEF neurons can exhibit target selection during conjunction search that is as early as that recorded during feature search [10]. Second, our search arrays were foveal, whereas the monkey displays were peripheral, a factor which might contribute to the early timing of our effect. Third, repeated target/distractor combinations likely induced feature priming across the ten blocks of eighty trials in Experiment 2 [24]. Such priming has been shown to induce earlier target selection in the monkey FEFs [25]. Finally, species differences should not be dismissed in considering the lack of precise concordance between single unit and TMS interference times.

Based on the temporal correspondence between our TMS results and single-unit data, I have argued that our data reflect disruption of target selection processes within the FEFs. However, the target selection process manifested in FEF is likely to be closely related to selection processes observed in extrastriate areas, such as V4 [26]. FEF sends extensive feedback projections to extrastriate cortex [27], and has been proposed to exert "top-down control" on these areas, such as modulating the gain of visually driven signals [28]. A number of studies have shown that feedback connections are matched in conduction speed to feedforward connections [29], consistent with the notion that feedback modulation by FEF may occur simultaneous with feedforward driving input. Hence, the early timing of the TMS effect does not arbitrate between a feedforward or feedback interpretation.

The computational role of human FEF in vision remains to be established. Current functional sketches ascribe roles for FEF in covert orienting, search, saliency map formation and oculomotor responses [30]. Similar functions have been ascribed to posterior parietal cortex (PPC) [31]. FEF and PPC share strong reciprocal interconnections [32] and are both consistently activated nodes in imaging studies of these functions. Despite these similar profiles, imaging data are most commonly interpreted in terms of relative specialization of FEF for motor-exploratory and PPC for perceptual-representational aspects of attentional tasks [33]. A previous study applied TMS over the PPC and showed that interference times were yoked to subjects' responses: RT costs were induced 100ms after array onset on target present trials and at 160ms on target absent trials [34]. Although the search tasks used were not identical, taken together, the results suggest that the FEFs may contribute to search performance earlier than the PPC. These findings emphasize the need for future work to distinguish the relative contributions of the FEF and PPC to visual target selection.

References

1. Bruce, C.J. and M.E. Goldberg, *Primate frontal eye fields. I. Single neurons discharging before saccades.* Journal of Neurophysiology, 1985. 53(3): p. 603-635.
2. Felleman, D.J. and D.C. Van Essen, *Distributed hierarchical processing in the primate cerebral cortex.* Cereb Cortex, 1991. 1(1): p. 1-47.
3. Nowak, L.G. and J. Bullier, *The Timing of Information Transfer in the Visual System*, in *Cerebral Cortex*, e.a. Rockland, Editor. 1997, Plenum Press: New York. p. 205-241.
4. Barone, P., et al., *Laminar distribution of neurons in extrastriate areas projecting to visual areas V1 and V4 correlates with the hierarchical rank and indicates the operation of a distance rule.* Journal of Neuroscience, 2000. 20(9): p. 3263-81.
5. Latto, R. and A. Cowey, *Visual field defects after frontal eye-field lesions in monkeys.* Brain Res, 1971. 30(1): p. 1-24.
6. Thompson, K.G., et al., *Perceptual and motor processing stages identified in the activity of macaque frontal eye field neurons during visual search.* Journal of Neurophysiology, 1996. 76(6): p. 4040-55.
7. Bichot, N.P., S. Chenchal Rao, and J.D. Schall, *Continuous processing in macaque frontal cortex during visual search.* Neuropsychologia, 2001. 39(9): p. 972-82.
8. Mohler, C.W., M.E. Goldberg, and R.H. Wurtz, *Visual receptive fields of frontal eye field neurons.* Brain Research, 1973. 61: p. 385-389.
9. Schall, J.D. and N.P. Bichot, *Neural correlates of visual and motor decision processes.* Current Opinion in Neurobiology, 1998. 8(2): p. 211-7.
10. Bichot, N.P., et al., *Reliability of macaque frontal eye field neurons signalling saccade targets during visual search.* Journal of Neuroscience, 2001. 21(2): p. 713-25.
11. Hanes, D.P. and J.D. Schall, *Countermanding saccades in macaque.* Vis Neurosci, 1995. 12(5): p. 929-37.
12. Murthy, A., K.G. Thompson, and J.D. Schall, *Dynamic dissociation of visual selection from saccade programming in frontal eye field.* Journal of Neurophysiology, 2001. 86(5): p. 2634-7.
13. Blanke, O., et al., *Visual activity in the human frontal eye field.* Neuroreport, 1999. 10(5): p. 925-30.
14. Grosbras, M.H. and T. Paus, *Transcranial magnetic stimulation of the human frontal eye field facilitates visual awareness.* Eur J Neurosci, 2003. 18(11): p. 3121-6.
15. Grosbras, M.H. and T. Paus, *Transcranial magnetic stimulation of the human frontal eye field: effects on visual perception and attention.* Journal of Cognitive Neuroscience, 2002. 14(7): p. 1109-20.
16. Muggleton, N.G., et al., *Human Frontal Eye Fields and Visual Search.* Journal of Neurophysiology, 2003. 89(6): p. 3340-3343.
17. Blanke, O., et al., *Location of the human frontal eye field as defined by electrical cortical stimulation: anatomical, functional and electrophysiological characteristics.* Neuroreport, 2000. 11(9): p. 1907-13.
18. Muri, R.M., C.W. Hess, and O. Meienberg, *Transcranial stimulation of the human frontal eye field by magnetic pulses.* Experimental Brain Research, 1991. 86(1): p. 219-23.
19. Paus, T., *Location and function of the human frontal eye-field: a selective review.* Neuropsychologia, 1996. 34(6): p. 475-83.

20. Stewart, L., et al., *Motion perception and perceptual learning studied by magnetic stimulation.* Electroencephalogr Clin Neurophysiol Suppl, 1999. 51: p. 334-50.
21. Salthouse, T.A., et al., *Stimulus processing during eye fixations.* Journal of Experimental Psychology: Human Perception and Performance, 1981. 7: p. 611-23.
22. Lisberger, S.G., et al., *Effect of mean reaction time on saccadic responses to two-step stimuli with horizontal and vertical components.* Vision Research, 1975. 15: p. 1021-5.
23. McPeek, R.M. and E.L. Keller, *Superior Colliculus Activity Related to Concurrent Processing of Saccade Goals in a Visual Search Task.* J Neurophysiol, 2002. 87(4): p. 1805-1815.
24. Maljkovic, V. and K. Nakayama, *Priming of pop-out: I. Role of features.* Mem Cognit, 1994. 22(6): p. 657-72.
25. Bichot, N.P. and J.D. Schall, *Priming in macaque frontal cortex during popout visual search: feature-based facilitation and location-based inhibition of return.* J Neurosci, 2002. 22(11): p. 4675-85.
26. Luck, S.J., et al., *Neural mechanisms of spatial selective attention in areas V1, V2, and V4 of macaque visual cortex.* Journal of Neurophysiology, 1997. 77(1): p. 24-42.
27. Stanton, G.B., C.J. Bruce, and M.E. Goldberg, *Topography of projections to posterior cortical areas from the macaque frontal eye fields.* Journal of Computational Neurology, 1995. 353(2): p. 291-305.
28. Moore, T. and K.M. Armstrong, *Selective gating of visual signals by microstimulation of frontal cortex.* Nature, 2003. 421(6921): p. 370-3.
29. Hupe, J.M., et al., *Feedback connections act on the early part of the responses in monkey visual cortex.* Journal of Neurophysiology, 2001. 85(1): p. 134-45.
30. Corbetta, M. and G.L. Shulman, *Control of goal-directed and stimulus-driven attention in the brain.* Nature Reviews Neuroscience, 2002. 3(3): p. 201-215.
31. Colby, C.L. and M.E. Goldberg, *Space and attention in parietal cortex.* Annual Review of Neuroscience, 1999. 22: p. 319-49.
32. Cavada, C. and P.S. Goldman-Rakic, *Posterior parietal cortex in rhesus monkey: II. Evidence for segregated corticocortical networks linking sensory and limbic areas with the frontal lobe.* Journal of Computational Neurology, 1989. 287(4): p. 422-45.
33. Mesulam, M.M., *A cortical network for directed attention and unilateral neglect.* Annals of Neurology, 1981. 10(4): p. 309-25.
34. Ashbridge, E., V. Walsh, and A. Cowey, *Temporal aspects of visual search studied by transcranial magnetic stimulation.* Neuropsychologia, 1997. 35(8): p. 1121-31.

Multi-scale Keypoints in V1 and Face Detection

João Rodrigues[1] and J.M. Hans du Buf[2]

[1] University of Algarve – Escola Superior Tecnologia, Faro, Portugal
[2] University of Algarve – Vision Laboratory – FCT, Faro, Portugal

Abstract. End-stopped cells in cortical area V1, which combine outputs of complex cells tuned to different orientations, serve to detect line and edge crossings (junctions) and points with a large curvature. In this paper we study the importance of the multi-scale keypoint representation, i.e. retinotopic keypoint maps which are tuned to different spatial frequencies (scale or Level-of-Detail). We show that this representation provides important information for Focus-of-Attention (FoA) and object detection. In particular, we show that hierarchically-structured saliency maps for FoA can be obtained, and that combinations over scales in conjunction with spatial symmetries can lead to face detection through grouping operators that deal with keypoints at the eyes, nose and mouth, especially when non-classical receptive field inhibition is employed. Although a face detector can be based on feedforward and feedback loops within area V1, such an operator must be embedded into dorsal and ventral data streams to and from higher areas for obtaining translation-, rotation- and scale-invariant face (object) detection.

1 Introduction

Our visual system is still a huge puzzle with a lot of missing pieces. Even in the first processing layers in area V1 of the visual cortex there remain many open gaps, despite the amount of knowledge already compiled, e.g. [3,5,25]. Recently, models of cortical cells, i.e. simple, complex and end-stopped, have been developed, e.g. [7]. In addition, several inhibition models [2,17], keypoint detection [7,12,22] and line/edge detection schemes [2,12,14,15], including disparity models [6,11], have become available. On the basis of these models and possible processing schemes, it is now possible to create a cortical architecture for figure-background segregation [16] and visual attention or Focus-of-Attention (FoA), bottom-up and/or top-down [4,8,13], and even for object categorisation and recognition.

In this paper we will focus exclusively on keypoints, for which Heitger et al. [7] developed a single-scale basis model of single and double end-stopped cells. Würtz and Lourens [22] and Rodrigues and du Buf [12] presented a "multi-scale" approach: detection stabilisation is obtained by averaging keypoint positions over a few neighbouring micro-scales. In [13] we introduced a truly multi-scale analysis: if there are simple and complex cells tuned to different spatial frequencies, spanning an interval of multiple octaves, it can be expected that there are also

M. De Gregorio et al. (Eds.): BVAI 2005, LNCS 3704, pp. 205–214, 2005.
© Springer-Verlag Berlin Heidelberg 2005

end-stopped cells at all frequencies. We analysed the multi-scale keypoint representation, from very fine to very coarse scales, in order to study its importance and possibilities for developing a cortical architecture, with an emphasis on FoA. In addition, we included a new aspect, i.e. the application of non-classical receptive field (NCRF) inhibition to keypoint detection, in order to distinguish object structure from surface textures.

A difficult and still challenging application, even in machine vision, is face detection. Despite the impressive number of methods devised for faces and facial landmarks, which can be based on Gabor filters [18] or Gaussian derivative filters [26], colour [27], attention [19], morphology [9], behaviouristic AI [10], edges and keypoints [20], spiking neurons [1] and saliency maps [23], complicating factors that still remain are pose (frontal vs. profile), beards, moustaches and glasses, facial expression and image conditions (lighting, resolution). Despite these complications, in this paper we will study the multi-scale keypoint representation in the context of a possible cortical architecture. We add that (a) we will not employ the multi-scale line/edge representation that also exists in area V1, in order to emphasise the importance of the information provided by keypoints, and (b) we will not solve complications referred to above, because we will argue, in the Discussion, that low-level processing in area V1 needs to embedded in to a much wider context, including short-time memory, and this context is expected to solve many problems.

In Section 2 we present the models for end-stopped cells and non-classical receptive field inhibition, followed by keypoint detection with NCRF inhibition in Section 3, and the multi-scale keypoint representation with saliency maps in Section 4. In Section 5 we present facial landmark detection, and conclude with a discussion (Section 6).

2   End-Stopped Cells and NCRF Inhibition

Gabor quadrature filters provide a model of cortical simple cells [24]. In the spatial domain (x, y) they consist of a real cosine and an imaginary sine, both with a Gaussian envelope. A receptive field (RF) is denoted by (see e.g. [2]):

$$g_{\lambda,\sigma,\theta,\varphi}(x, y) = \exp\left(-\frac{\tilde{x}^2 + \gamma \tilde{y}^2}{2\sigma^2}\right) \cdot \cos(2\pi \frac{\tilde{x}}{\lambda} + \varphi),$$

$$\tilde{x} = x\cos\theta + y\sin\theta \ ; \ \tilde{y} = y\cos\theta - x\sin\theta,$$

where the aspect ratio $\gamma = 0.5$ and σ determines the size of the RF. The spatial frequency is $1/\lambda$, λ being the wavelength. For the bandwidth σ/λ we use 0.56, which yields a half-response width of one octave. The angle θ determines the orientation (we use 8 orientations), and φ the symmetry (0 or $\pi/2$). We apply a linear scaling between f_{min} and f_{max} with, at the moment, hundreds of contiguous scales.

Responses of even and odd simple cells, which correspond to real and imaginary parts of a Gabor filter, are obtained by convolving the input image with the

RF, and are denoted by $R_{s,i}^E(x,y)$ and $R_{s,i}^O(x,y)$, s being the scale, i the orientation ($\theta_i = i\pi/(N_\theta - 1)$) and N_θ the number of orientations. In order to simplify the notation, and because the same processing is done at all scales, we drop the subscript s. The responses of complex cells are modelled by the modulus

$$C_i(x,y) = [\{R_i^E(x,y)\}^2 + \{R_i^O(x,y)\}^2]^{1/2}.$$

There are two types of end-stopped cells [7,22], i.e. single (S) and double (D). If $[\cdot]^+$ denotes the suppression of negative values, and $\mathcal{C}_i = \cos\theta_i$ and $\mathcal{S}_i = \sin\theta_i$, then

$$S_i(x,y) = [C_i(x + d\mathcal{S}_i, y - d\mathcal{C}_i) - C_i(x - d\mathcal{S}_i, y + d\mathcal{C}_i)]^+ ;$$

$$D_i(x,y) = \left[C_i(x,y) - \frac{1}{2}C_i(x + 2d\mathcal{S}_i, y - 2d\mathcal{C}_i) - \frac{1}{2}C_i(x - 2d\mathcal{S}_i, y + 2d\mathcal{C}_i)\right]^+ .$$

The distance d is scaled linearly with the filter scale s, i.e. $d = 0.6s$. All end-stopped responses along straight lines and edges need to be suppressed, for which we use tangential (T) and radial (R) inhibition:

$$I^T(x,y) = \sum_{i=0}^{2N_\theta - 1} [-C_{i \bmod N_\theta}(x,y) + C_{i \bmod N_\theta}(x + d\mathcal{C}_i, y + d\mathcal{S}_i)]^+ ;$$

$$I^R(x,y) = \sum_{i=0}^{2N_\theta - 1} \left[C_{i \bmod N_\theta}(x,y) - 4 \cdot C_{(i+N_\theta/2) \bmod N_\theta}(x + \frac{d}{2}\mathcal{C}_i, y + \frac{d}{2}\mathcal{S}_i)\right]^+ ,$$

where $(i + N_\theta/2) \bmod N_\theta \perp i \bmod N_\theta$.

The model of non-classical receptive field (NCRF) inhibition is explained in more detail in [2]. We will use two types: (a) anisotropic, in which only responses obtained for the same preferred RF orientation contribute to the suppression, and (b) isotropic, in which all responses over all orientations equally contribute to the suppression.

The anisotropic NCRF (A-NCRF) model is computed by an inhibition term $t_{s,\sigma,i}^A$ for each orientation i, as a convolution of the complex cell responses C_i with the weighting function w_σ, with $w_\sigma(x,y) = [DoG_\sigma(x,y)]^+/\|[DoG_\sigma]^+\|_1$, $\|\cdot\|_1$ being the L_1 norm, and

$$DoG_\sigma(x,y) = \frac{1}{2\pi(4\sigma)^2}\exp(-\frac{x^2+y^2}{2(4\sigma)^2}) - \frac{1}{2\pi\sigma^2}\exp(-\frac{x^2+y^2}{2\sigma^2}).$$

The operator $b_{s,\sigma,i}^A$ corresponds to the inhibition of $C_{s,i}$, i.e. $b_{s,\sigma,i}^A = [C_{s,i} - \alpha t_{s,\sigma,i}^A]^+$, with α controlling the strength of the inhibition.

The isotropic NCRF (I-NCRF) model is obtained by computing the inhibition term $t_{s,\sigma}^I$ which does not dependent on orientation i. For this we construct the maximum response map of the complex cells $\tilde{C}_s = \max\{C_{s,i}\}$, with $i = 0, ...N_\theta - 1$. The isotropic inhibition term $t_{s,\sigma}^I$ is computed by the convolution of the maximum response map $\tilde{C}_s$ with the weighting function w_σ, and the isotropic operator is $b_{s,\sigma}^I = [\tilde{C}_s - \alpha t_{s,\sigma}^I]^+$.

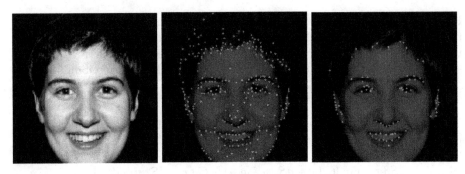

Fig. 1. Centre and right: keypoints without and with NCRF inhibition (face196)

3   Keypoint Detection with NCRF Inhibition

NCRF inhibition permits to suppress keypoints which are due to texture, i.e. textured parts of an object surface. We experimented with the two types of NCRF inhibition introduced above, but here we only present the best results which were obtained by I-NCRF at the finest scale.

All responses of the end-stopped cells $S(x,y) = \sum_{i=0}^{N_\theta-1} S_i(x,y)$ and $D(x,y)$ $= \sum_{i=0}^{N_\theta-1} D_i(x,y)$ are inhibited by $b_{s,\sigma}^I$, i.e. we use $\alpha = 1$, and obtain the responses $\tilde{S}$ and $\tilde{D}$ of S and D that are above a small threshold of $b_{s,\sigma}^I$. Then we apply $I = I^T + I^R$ for obtaining the keypoint maps $K^S(x,y) = \tilde{S}(x,y) - gI(x,y)$ and $K^D(x,y) = \tilde{D}(x,y) - gI(x,y)$, with $g \approx 1.0$, and the final keypoint map $K(x,y) = \max\{K^S(x,y),\, K^D(x,y)\}$.

Figure 1 shows, from left to right, an input image and keypoints detected (single, finest scale), before and after I-NCRF inhibition. After inhibition, only contour-related keypoints remain. Almost all texture keypoints have been suppressed, although some may still remain because of strong local contrast (see [13]).

4   Multiscale Keypoint Representation

Although NCRF inhibition can be applied at all scales, this will not be done for two reasons: (a) we want to illustrate keypoint behaviour in scale space for the application of FoA, and (b) at coarser scales, i.e. increased RF sizes, most detail (texture) keypoints will be eliminated automatically. In the multi-scale case, keypoints are detected the same way as done above, but now by using $K_s^S(x,y) = S_s(x,y) - gI_s(x,y)$ and $K_s^D(x,y) = D_s(x,y) - gI_s(x,y)$.

An important aspect of a face detection scheme is Focus-of-Attention by means of a saliency map, i.e. the possibility to draw attention to and to inspect, serially or in parallel, the most important parts of faces, objects or scenes. In terms of visual search, this includes overt attention and pop-out. If we assume that retinotopic projection is maintained throughout the visual cortex, the activities of all keypoint cells at the same position (x,y) can be easily summed over

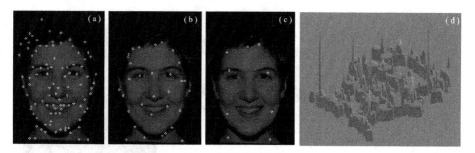

Fig. 2. Keypoints at fine (a), medium (b) and coarse (c) scales, with saliency map (d)

scale s, which leads to a very compact, single-layer map. At the positions where keypoints are stable over many scales, this summation map, which could replace or contribute to a saliency map [4], will show distinct peaks at centres of objects, important sub-structures and contour landmarks. The height of the peaks (summation cell activity) can provide information about the relative importance. In addition, this summation map, with some simple processing of the projected trajectories of unstable keypoints, like a dynamic lowpass filtering related to the scale and non-maximum suppression, might solve the segmentation problem: the object centre is linked to important sub-structures, and these are linked to contour landmarks. This is shown in Fig. 2(d) by means of a 3D perspective projection. Such a mapping or data stream is data-driven and bottom-up, and could be combined with top-down processing from inferior temporal cortex (IT) in order to actively probe the presence of certain objects in the visual field [8]. In addition, the summation map with links between the peaks might be available at higher brain areas where serial processing occurs for e.g. visual search.

In order to illustrate keypoint behaviour in the case of human faces we created an almost continuous, linear, scale space. Figure 2 ("face196"), shows three different scales from scale space: (a) fine scale with $\lambda = 4$, (b) medium scale with $\lambda = 20$, and (c) coarse scale with $\lambda = 40$. At even coarser scales there will remain only a single keypoint more or less in the centre of the face (not shown). Most if not all faces show a distinct keypoint the middle of the line that connects the two eyes, like in Fig. 2(b). Figure 2(d) shows the saliency map of the entire scale space ($\lambda = [4, 40]$) with 288 different scales. Important peaks are found at the eyes, nose and mouth, but also at the hairline and even the chin and neck. For a detailed analysis of keypoint behaviour and stability we refer to [13].

5   Detection of Facial Landmarks

In Fig. 2(d) we can see the regions where important features are located, but it is quite difficult to see which peaks correspond to important facial landmarks. On the other hand, looking at Fig. 2(b) it is easy to see that some keypoints correspond to landmarks that we pretend to find (in this study limited to eyes, nose and mouth), but (a) there are many more keypoints and (b) at other scales (e.g.

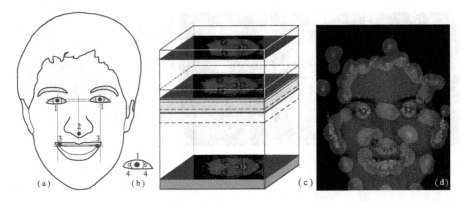

Fig. 3. Left to right: (a) facial landmarks, (b) eye landmarks, (c) impression of keypoint scale space, and (d) saliency map with single-scale keypoints and NCRF inhibition

Fig. 2(c)) they are located at other structures. Presumably, the visual system uses a "global" saliency map in combination with "partial" ones obtained by summing keypoints over smaller scale intervals, or even keypoints at individual scales, in order to optimise detection. This process can be "steered" by higher brain areas, which may contain prototype object maps with expected patterns (with approximate distances of eyes and nose and mouth), which is part of the fast "where path." The actual "steering" may consist of excitation and inhibition of pre-wired connections in keypoint scale space, i.e. grouping cells that combine end-stopped cells in approximate areas and at certain scales, which is part of the slower "what path."

In our simulations we explored one possible scenario. We assume the existence of very few layers of grouping cells, with dendritic fields in partial saliency maps that map keypoints in specific scale intervals. The top layer with "face" cells groups axons of "eyes" (plural!), "nose" and "mouth" grouping cells. The "eyes" cells group axons of pairs of "eye" cells. Only the "eye," "nose" and "mouth"

Fig. 4. Left: the saliency map of face196 ($\lambda = [13, 18]$); Right: result of face196

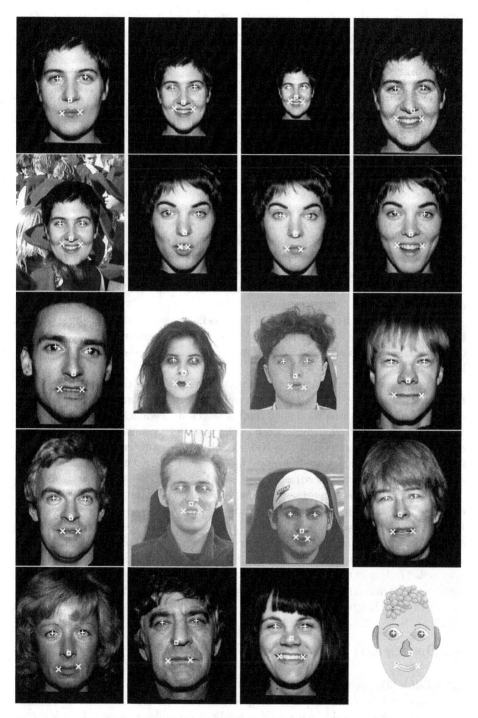

Fig. 5. Results obtained with different faces and expressions

cells connect to the saliency maps, the "face" and "eyes" cells do not. The scenario consists of detecting possible positions of eyes, linking two eyes, then two eyes plus nose, and two eyes plus nose plus mouth. This is done dynamically by activating synaptic connections in the partial saliency maps.

In our simulations, in which we experimented with faces of different sizes (Fig. 5), we used 7 partial saliency maps, each covering 40 scales distributed over $\Delta\lambda = 5$, but the scale intervals were overlapping 20 scales. The finest scale was at $\lambda = 4$. The search process starts at the coarsest scale interval, because there are much less candidate eye positions than there are at the finest scale interval. A feedback loop will activate connections to finer scale intervals, until at least one eye candidate is detected.

First, "eye" cells respond to significant peaks (non-maximum suppression and thresholding) in the selected saliency map (in the case of "face196" $\lambda = [13, 18]$, see Fig. 4 (left)), as indicated by Fig. 3(b)-1, but only if there are also two stable symmetric keypoints at the 40 finest scales (Fig. 3(b)-4). In order to reduce false positives, the latter is done after NCRF inhibition (Fig. 3(d)). If not a single eye cell responds, the scale interval of the saliency map is not appropriate and the feedback loop will step through all saliency maps (Fig. 3(c)), until at least one eye cell responds.

Second, "eyes" cells respond if two "eye" cells are active on an approximately horizontal line (Fig. 3(a)-1), each "eyes" cell being a grouping cell with two dendritic fields. If no eye pair is found, a new saliency map is selected (feedback loop).

Third, when two eyes can be grouped, a "nose" cell is activated, its dendritic field covering an area below the "eyes" cell in the saliency map (Fig. 3(a)-2). If no peak is detected, a new saliency map is selected (feedback loop).

Fourth, if both "eyes" and "nose" cells respond, a "mouth" cell with two dendritic fields at approximate positions of the two mouth corners (Fig. 3(a)-3) is activated. If keypoints are found, a "face" cell will be excited. If not, a new saliency map is selected (feedback loop).

The process stops when one face has been detected, but in reality it might continue at finer scale intervals (there may be more faces with different sizes in the visual field). However, see the Discussion section. The result obtained in the case of "face196" is shown in Fig. 4, where $+$, $\square$ and $\times$ symbols indicate detected and used keypoints at eyes, nose and mouth corners (actual positions of face and eyes cells are less important). More results are shown in Fig. 5, which includes a correctly detected (!) fake face. Obviously, more features must be used, including the multi-scale line/edge representation.

6   Discussion

As Rensink [21] pointed out, the detailed and rich impression of our visual surround may not be caused by a rich representation in our "visual memory," because the stable, physical surround already "acts" like memory. In addition, focused attention is likely to deal with only one object at a time. His triadic architecture therefore separates focused attention to coherent objects (System II) from nonattentional scene interpretation (Layout and Gist subsystems in System III), but both Systems are fed by low-level feature detectors, e.g. of edges, in System I.

In this paper we showed that keypoints detected by end-stopped operators, and in particular a few partial keypoint maps that cover overlapping scale intervals, may provide very important information for object detection. Exploring a very simple processing scheme, faces can be detected by grouping together axons of end-stopped cells at *approximate* retinotopic positions, and this leads to robust detection in the case of different facial expressions. However, the simple scheme explored only works if the eyes are open, if the view is frontal, and if the faces are approximately vertical. For pose-, rotation- and occlusion-invariant detection, the scheme must be fed by Rensink's short-term Layout and Gist subsystems, but also the long-term Scene Schema system that is supposed to build and store collections of object representations, for example non-frontal faces.

Owing to the impressive performance of current computers, it is now possible to test Rensink's [21] triadic architecture in terms of e.g. Deco and Rolls' [8] cortical architecture. The ventral WHAT data stream (V1, V2, V4, IT) is supposed to be involved in object recognition, independently of position and scaling. The dorsal WHERE stream (V1, V2, MT, PP) is responsible for maintaining a spatial map of an object's location and/or the spatial relationship of an object's parts as well as moving the spatial allocation of attention. Both data streams are bottom-up and top-down. Apart from input via V1, both streams receive top-down input from a *postulated* short-term memory for shape features or objects in prefrontal cortex area 46, i.e. the more ventral part PF46v generates an object-based attentional component, whereas the more dorsal part PF46d specifies the location. As for now, we do not know *how* PF46 works. It might be the neurophysiological equivalent of the cognitive Scene Schema system mentioned above, but apparently the WHAT and WHERE data streams are necessary for obtaining view-independent object detection through cells with receptive fields of 50 degrees or more [8]. However, instead of receiving input directly from simple cells, the data streams should receive input from feature extraction engines, including end-stopped cells.

Acknowledgments. The images used are from the Psychological Image Collection at Stirling University (http://pics.psych.stir.ac.uk/). Research is partly financed by PRODEP III Medida 5, Action 5.3, and by the FCT program POSI, framework QCA III.

References

1. A. Delorme and S.J. Thorpe. Face identification using one spike per neuron: resistance to image degradations. *Neur. Net.*, 14(6-7):795–804, 2001.
2. C. Grigorescu, N. Petkov and M.A. Westenberg. Contour detection based on non-classical receptive field inhibition. *IEEE Tr. Im. Proc.*, 12(7):729–739, 2003.
3. C. Rasche. *The making of a neuromorphic visual system.* Springer, 2005.

4. D. Parkhurst, K. Law and E. Niebur. Modelling the role of salience in the allocation of overt visual attention. *Vision Res.*, 42(1):107–123, 2002.
5. D.H. Hubel. *Eye, brain and vision.* Scientific American Library, 1995.
6. D.J. Fleet, A.D. Jepson and M.R.M. Jenkin. Phase-based disparity measurement. *CVGIP: Image Understanding*, 53(2):198–210, 1991.
7. F. Heitger et al. Simulation of neural contour mechanisms: from simple to end-stopped cells. *Vision Res.*, 32(5):963–981, 1992.
8. G. Deco and E.T. Rolls. A neurodynamical cortical model of visual attention and invariant object recognition. *Vision Res.*, (44):621–642, 2004.
9. H. Han, T. Kawaguchi and R. Nagata. Eye detection based on grayscale morphology. *Proc. IEEE Conf. Comp., Comm., Cont. Pow. Eng.*, 1:498–502, 2002.
10. J. Huang and Wechsler H. Visual routines for eye location using learning and evolution. *IEEE Trans. Evol. Comp.*, 4(1):73–82, 2000.
11. J. Rodrigues and J.M.H. du Buf. Vision frontend with a new disparity model. *Early Cogn. Vision Workshop, Isle of Skye, Scotland*, 28 May - 1 June 2004.
12. J. Rodrigues and J.M.H. du Buf. Visual cortex frontend: integrating lines, edges, keypoints and disparity. *Proc. Int. Conf. Image Anal. Recogn.*, Springer LNCS 3211(1):664–671, 2004.
13. J. Rodrigues and J.M.H. du Buf. Multi-scale cortical keypoint representation for attention and object detection. *2nd Iberian Conf. on Patt. Recogn. and Image Anal.*, Springer LNCS 3523:255–262, 2005.
14. J.H. Elder and A.J. Sachs. Psychophysical receptive fields of edge detection mechanisms. *Vision Research*, 44:795813, 2004.
15. J.H. van Deemter and J.M.H. du Buf. Simultaneous detection of lines and edges using compound Gabor filters. *Int. J. Patt. Rec. Artif. Intell.*, 14(6):757–777, 1996.
16. J.M. Hupe et al. Feedback connections act on the early part of the responses in monkey visual cortex. *J. Neurophysiol.*, 85(1):134–144, 2001.
17. N. Petkov, T. Lourens and P. Kruizinga. Lateral inhibition in cortical filters. *Proc. Int. Conf. Digital Signal Processing and Int. Conf. Computer Applications Engineering Systems*, Nicosa, Cyprus:122–129, July 14-16 1993.
18. P. Kruizinga and N. Petkov. Person identification based on multiscale matching of cortical images. *Proc. Int. Conf. and Exhib. High-Perf. Comp. Net.*, Springer LNCS 919:420–427, 1994.
19. R. Herpers and G. Sommer. An attentive processing strategy for the analysis of facial features. *Face Recog.: From Theory to Applications, H. Wechsler et al. (eds), NATO ASI Series F, Springer-Verlag*, 163:457–468, 1998.
20. R. Herpers et al. Edge and keypoint detection in facial regions. *Int. Conf. Automatic Face Gest. Recogn.*, pages 212–217, 1996.
21. R. Rensink. The dynamic representation of scenes. *Vis. Cog.*, 7(1-3):17–42, 2000.
22. R.P. Würtz and T. Lourens. Corner detection in color images by multiscale combination of end-stopped cortical cells. *Im. and Vis. Comp.*, 18(6-7):531–541, 2000.
23. S. Ban, J. Skin and M. Lee. Face detection using biologically motivated saliency map model. *Proc. Int. Joint Conf. Neural Netw.*, (1):119–124, 2003.
24. T.S. Lee. Image representation using 2D Gabor wavelets. *IEEE Tr. PAMI*, 18(10):pp. 13, 1996.
25. V. Bruce, P.R. Green and M.A. Geargeson. *Visual Perception Physiology, Psychology and Ecology.* Psychology Press Ltd, 2000.
26. W. Huang and R. Mariani. Face detection and precise eyes location. *Int. Conf. on Patt. Recogn.*, 4:722–727, 2000.
27. Z. Liu, Z. You and Y. Wang. Face detection and facial feature extraction in color image. *Proc. 5th Int. Conf. Comp. Intell. Mult. Appl.*, pages 126– 130, 2003.

Limitation of Maintenance of Feature-Bound Objects in Visual Working Memory

Jun Saiki and Hirofumi Miyatsuji

Department of Intelligence Science and Technology,
Graduate School of Informatics, Kyoto University,
Yoshida-Honmachi, Sakyo-ku, Kyoto, 606-8501, Japan
{saiki, miyatsuji}@cog.ist.i.kyoto-u.ac.jp
http://www.cog.ist.i.kyoto-u.ac.jp

Abstract. Studies on object visual working memory have claimed that we can maintain 3-5 objects. However, change detection tasks used in previous work have problems in evaluating feature-bound object representations in working memory. We devised a paradigm called multiple-object permanence tracking (MOPT) for more strict evaluation, where observers are required to identify the type of switch in feature combination between objects during an occlusion period, thus eliminating the use of feature memory or stimulus salience. We showed that capacity of feature-bound representations is more limited than previous estimates. To examine whether this limitation reflects memory retrieval or maintenance, we used a cueing version of MOPT. A flashing cue with 100 % validity was presented on a target object just before or after a feature-switch event. If memory-retrieval is the bottleneck, postcue will facilitate the task performance. A type identification task evaluating feature-bound representations failed to show any benefit of postcue, whereas a simple change detection task possibly reflecting saliency-based representations showed a significant benefit. This suggests that the previously reported capacity of 3-5 objects may reflect saliency-based representations. In contrast, feature-bound representations can be stored only for 1 or 2 objects.

1 Introduction

Our visual world contains numerous objects, and these objects have various different visual features. To perceive the world properly, correspondences must be made between feature values and multiple objects. This process of feature integration into coherent object representation has often been discussed under the name of "binding problems".

Feature binding has been studied empirically in the context of visual perception. Treisman and Schmidt [10] demonstrated that feature binding in visual perception is not automatic, and requires visual attention. The problem of feature binding in visual memory has only recently received attention from researchers, but the nature of feature binding in visual working memory is still poorly understood. As detailed below, we have devised an experimental paradigm called

M. De Gregorio et al. (Eds.): BVAI 2005, LNCS 3704, pp. 215–224, 2005.

multiple object permanence tracking (MOPT) [8,9] to address this issue, and have shown that our ability to hold feature binding in visual working memory is much more limited than previously revealed. This study extended this work to investigate whether the limitation in memory for feature binding is due to memory maintenance or memory retrieval.

1.1   MOPT and Memory for Feature Binding

Kahneman and colleagues proposed the notion of object file to account for how the visual system keeps track of object information in a visual scene [4]. Kahneman et al. [4] described an object file as "a temporary episodic representation, within which successive states of an object are linked and integrated", and claimed that the visual system can hold multiple object files simultaneously. Along this line, Luck and Vogel [6] showed that humans can hold about four object files simultaneously, using a change detection task with multidimensional objects. These studies suggest that the visual system binds object features by focused attention to form object files, and about four object files are maintained in the visual working memory (see [2] for a review).

However, these previous studies have problems in evaluating memory for feature binding at least in two respects. First, the stimulus design is not suitable for the issue of feature binding. As in the stimuli used in perceptual feature binding, we need to manipulate the combination of features while keeping the identities of component features constant. Most studies with change detection paradigm for visual memory have used a change of a feature to a new value, which can be detected without using conjunctions. Second, the task design of change detection may obscure the representations to be investigated. In the change detection task, any change can lead to correct detection. Thus, a change in feature combination may produce other kinds of changes in stimulus information. Consider the notion of saliency [3,5]. Many studies on visual cognition propose that objects' saliency determines deployment of visual attention. Saliency is assumed to be computed based on the summation of an object's features, thus saliency itself does not maintain the information about feature combination. To illustrate how saliency can be used in change detection, assume for simplicity that saliency of an object is a simple sum of component feature saliency values. Suppose that for an observer, saliency values of red, blue, circle, and square are 0.5, 0.3, 0.7, and 0.4, respectively. A change from a pair of red circle and blue square to a pair of red square and blue circle produces a saliency change from $(1.2, 0.7)$ to $(0.9, 1.0)$.

To overcome these problems, we devised a paradigm called multiple object permanence tracking (MOPT) to investigate whether humans can track multiple object files (Saiki, [8,9]). In the MOPT task, four to six objects defined by different colors and shapes are placed at equal eccentricity, then rotated behind a windmill-shaped occluder (Figure 1). In the middle of the rotation sequence, features of two objects may be switched during an occlusion. The task of the observer was to identify what kind of switch occurred. Because each object is defined by shape and color, there are four types: no switch, color switch, shape

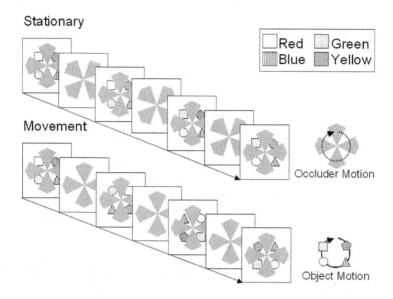

Fig. 1. Schematic illustration of MOPT paradigm. By manipulating relative motion of objects and an occluder, effects of object motion in memory for feature binding can be evaluated.

switch, and both switch. This task satisfies two requirements discussed above. First, stimuli have identical set of features and only their combination changes, and second, the type identification procedure requires access to feature binding representations, because it is almost impossible to identify the switch type just by stimulus salience. Speed of disk rotation was manipulated by relative motion of disks and occluder, to investigate the effect of motion in a parametric manner.

A series of experiments revealed that (1) even when objects are stationary, the task performance was quite poor compared with previous studies, and (2) object motion further impaired the performance, even if the motion speed was slow and easily trackable [11]. When memory capacity was estimated by a standard formula, it was only about 1.5 objects when stationary, and 1 object when moving.

1.2 Cueing Paradigm to Probe Memory Retrieval

The purpose of this study was to examine whether the severe limitation of memory for feature binding reflects limit in maintenance or in retrieval of visual working memory. One may be able to hold only 1 or 2 feature-bound object representations in visual working memory. Alternatively, memory can hold 4 to 5 objects simultaneously, but the difficulty resides in the process of retrieving memory representations in parallel in matching perceptual and memory representations. To discriminate these two alternatives, we added a new feature to the MOPT paradigm. New experiments used cues to indicate a changing object.

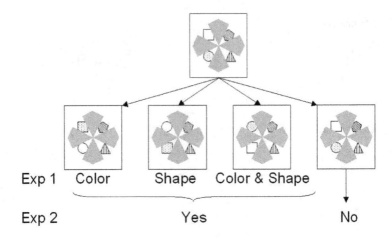

Fig. 2. Mapping between change types and responses in Experiments 1 and 2. Experiment 1 used type identification procedure, and Experiment 2 used a simple change detection.

Cues were 100% valid, and were presented either just before or after a change occurred, called precue or postcue condition, respectively. If a cue is effective, the precue condition is expected to show significantly better task performance compared with the no-cue control. This is because observers can maintain only cued object information to identify switch type. The critical condition was the postcue condition. If the difficulty in MOPT reflects memory retrieval, the postcue will facilitate performance, because it provides an effective retrieval cue. Wheeler and Treisman [12] showed that single probe condition, where only one probe object was used, improved performance compared with the whole probe condition, where observers had to retrieve memory for all objects. Alternatively, if the difficulty reflects memory maintenance, the postcue will not facilitate performance, because there are only one or two feature-bound object representations to be retrieved.

2   Experiment 1

2.1   Method

Participants. The experiment used six participants, including one author, and all displayed normal color vision.

Materials. Participants were shown a pattern of four colored objects and an occluder on top. Smooth rotation of the pattern and occluder at constant angular velocities resulted in alternating appearance and disappearance of the pattern. The four colored objects were configured in a diamond pattern, with each object placed at a visual angle of 2.9° from the center of the occluder. Objects were colored using four equiluminant colors ($20.85cd/m^2$, red [$CIEx = .56, y = .34$]; green [$x = .28, y = .60$]; blue [$x = .19, y = .14$]; and yellow [$x = .43, y = .49$]), and combinations of these colors were counterbalanced across trials. Shapes used for objects in the experiment were circle, square, hexagon and triangle. The colored pattern was occluded using a gray windmill-shaped occluder ($20.85cd/m^2$), and the background was black ($0.5cd/m^2$). The sequence was either regular clockwise or counterclockwise rotation throughout, containing one visible period in which locations of features of two objects were switched. A total of four events were possible: both-switch with simultaneous switch of color and shape; color-switch with color switch alone; shape-switch with shape switch alone; and no switch (Figure 2). In Experiment 1, no switch trials were not used. The occluder displayed four openings of $20°$, through which the colored pattern could be seen. A single trial contained seven occlusion periods, and a switch event occurred between the 3th and 5th occluded periods. Time and location of switches were unpredictable to the observers. Participants were asked to identify event types without feedback as to which was correct.

The main independent variables comprised object motion and cueing. To keep exposure duration of the pattern equivalent, object motion was manipulated by the relative motion of the pattern and occluder, as described by Saiki [9]. Object motion factor comprised of moving and stationary. In the moving condition, objects were rotating with the angular velocity of $84°/s$, whereas the occluder was stationary. In the stationary condition, the occluder was rotating with $84°/s$, whereas the objects were stationary. Note that both conditions had exactly the same duration of visible period ($518ms$) and occluded period ($518ms$). The cueing factor had three conditions: precue, postcue, and no-cue. The precue was presented at a period just prior to the switch to one of the to-be-switched objects as a flash. Cued object was selected randomly between the two. Flashing cue was presented for $12ms$ at the middle of a visible period of $518ms$. Thus, a cue was presented $259ms$ after an object appeared. The postcue was the same as the precue, except for being presented just after the switch. No-cue condition was the control condition, where no cue was presented (Figure 3). Experimental programs were written in MATLAB, using Psychophysics Toolbox extensions [1,7].

Procedure. Each experimental trial began with a keypress by a participant. After the beep, the initial display with objects and an occluder stationary for $500ms$. Then moving sequence began, followed by the appearance of three response boxes for event types (color, shape, and color-and-shape). Participants selected responses by clicking a response box. To avoid verbal encoding of color and shape, articulatory suppression was used by getting subjects to say "da, da, da". The entire experiment comprised three experimental sessions, each containing 216 trials. Participants performed one session a day. Within each session, cueing, and object motion conditions were randomly mixed from trial to trial. For each cueing condition, each object motion condition comprised 108 trials, with 36 trials for each event type, for a total of 648 experimental trials.

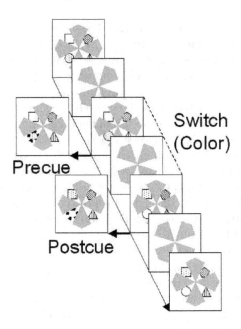

Fig. 3. Schematic illustration of cueing paradigm. Flashing cue with 100 % validity was presented either just before or after the switch. No-cue control condition was also used.

2.2 Results and Discussion

Figure 4 shows proportions of correct type identification as a function of object motion for three cueing conditions. First, the effect of precue was evaluated by comparing with no cue condition. There was a strong effect of precue in both stationary and moving conditions. An ANOVA with a 2 (cueing: precue and no-cue) x 2 (object motion: stationary and moving) x 3 (event type: color switch, shape switch, and both switch) design was conducted for the proportion of correct identification. The main effects of cueing ($F(1,5) = 139.01, p < .01$) and object motion ($F(1,5) = 71.78, p < .01$), and their interaction ($F(1,5) = 7.05, p < .05$) were statistically significant. Planned comparisons revealed that the stationary condition showed significantly higher correct identification than the moving condition in the no-cue condition, ($F(1,5) = 32.02, p < .01$). In the precue condition, both conditions showed no significant difference due to extremely high correct identification rates ($F(1,5) = 3.72, p > .1$). Thus, if one can focus attention in advance, one can maintain a feature-bound representation for the attended object, regardless of its motion. Second, the effect of postcue was evaluated. As shown in Figure 4, there was no effects of postcue at all. An ANOVA revealed the significant main effects of object motion ($F(1,5) = 27.27, p < .01$) and event type ($F(2,10) = 9.16, p < .01$). There was no advantage of postcue, and stationary condition showed better performance.

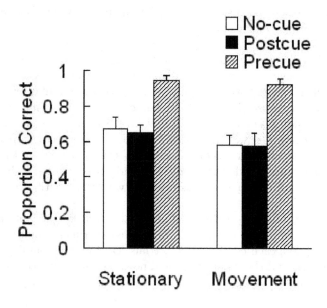

Fig. 4. Mean proportions correct in Experiment 1

Because Experiment 1 mixed precue and postcue in the same session, and precue was obviously quite effective, it may be the case that participants intentionally focused on precues and ignored postcues, though they were instructed that two kinds of cues were included. To test this possibility, we conducted an additional experiment where the precue condition was eliminated. The results were the same, revealing that only object motion had a significant main effect ($F(1,5) = 83.084, p < .01$). Clearly, the lack of postcue effect was not due to strategic ignorance by inclusion of precue. Even when participants knew that all cues were for memory retrieval, they could not utilize the postcues effectively.

The lack of postcue effects in this experiment is inconsistent with Wheeler and Treisman's findings [12]. One possible reason is that flashing cue used in this experiment was not strong enough to be an effective cue for memory retrieval. Although, flashing was quite effective as a precue, this does not necessarily mean that it is an effective retrieval cue. Alternatively, the discrepancy reflects difference in task design. A simple change detection task used in Wheeler and Treisman [12] could reflect representations other than feature binding, such as saliency. If this is the case, flashing cue with a simple change detection task will facilitate participants' performance.

3   Experiment 2

3.1   Method

Method was the same as in Experiment 1, except for the following changes.

Participants. The experiment used six participants, including one author, and all displayed normal color vision.

Materials. No change sequences were added. There were four event types: color change, shape change, both change, and no change. The task was a simple change detection, thus no change was mapped to no response, and all other types were mappied to yes response (Figure 2). Precue condition was eliminated, so that all cues were postcue. The cue was 100 % valid when there was a switch. In the no change sequence, cue was presented to a randomly selected object,and the cue timing was matched with sequences with a switch. To reduce the length of sequence, each sequence ended two occludion periods after the switch event. The length of the no change sequence was matched with those with switch events.

Procedure. The task was a simple change detection. Participants judged yes when they detect any type of switch. The entire experiment comprised two experimental sessions, each containing 144 trials. One session contained cues and the other did not, and the order of cue and no cue sessions was counterbalanced across participants.

3.2   Results and Discussion

Figures 5a and 5b show hit and false alarm rates, respectively, as a function of object motion and cueing. First, hit rates show that postcue had a facilitatory effect in the stationary condition, but not in the moving condition (Figure 5a). An ANOVA for hit rate data with a 2 (cueing) x 2 (object motion) design revealed a significant interaction ($F(1,5) = 8.167, p < .05$). Planned comparisons showed that postcue condition showed significantly higher hit rate in the stationary condition, ($F(1,5) = 107.758, p < .01$), whereas there was no significant effect in the moving condition. Second, as shown in Figure 5b, false alarms were in general low and there was no clear effects of object motion and cueing. ANOVA for false alarms with the same design revealed no main effects or interaction.

The results suggest that the lack of postcue effects in Experiment 1 is due to limits in maintenance capacity of feature-bound representations. A simple change detection task revealed a significant facilitation in the stationary condition. A retrieval cue facilitates judgment of whether there is any kind of change, but it does not help identifying the type of change. One interpretation of Experiments 1 and 2 in this study, and Wheeler and Treisman [12] is that we can hold multiple saliency-based representations in visual working memory, which are sensitive to retrieval bottleneck, whereas the capacity of feature-bound representations is more limited.

Another interesting result was the lack of postcue effects in moving condition, suggesting that even saliency-based representations are not stored simultaneously when objects are moving. This may reflect that saliency representations are location-based, so that motion with occlusion disrupts their continuity.

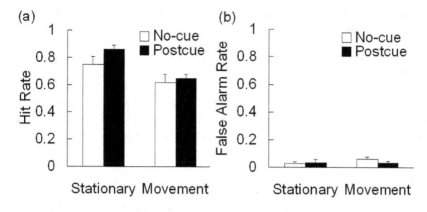

Fig. 5. Results in Experiment 2. (a) Mean hit rates. (b) Mean false alarm rates.

4   General Discussion

The present study investigated whether the limitation in feature-bound memory observed with MOPT tasks reflects limits in memory maintenance or memory retrieval, using a cueing version of MOPT. There was a significant effect of precue, but no effect of postcue, suggesting that helping memory retrieval does not facilitate the task performance. This result supports the hypothesis that limitation of feature-bound memory reflects memory maintenance, not memory retrieval. This was not due to peculiarity of MOPT paradigm itself, or the type of cue, because Experiment 2 with a simple change detection task showed results consistent with previous findings.

We interpret these data as different types of memory representations of objects. The type identification paradigm in Experiment 1 measures a function of feature-bound representation where component features of an object are bound together as a coherent whole. If such representations are formed, we should be able to identify the type of change, in addition to whether a change occured. On the other hand, a simple change detection task in Experiment 2 and many previous studies measures a function of less analytical representations such as object saliency, as well as feature-bound representations. Difference in postcue effects between Experiments 1 and 2 suggests that Experiment 2 and many previous works mainly measured saliency representations.

One limitation of this study is the use of explicit memory task. No facilitation by retrieval cue in an explicit type identification paradigm does not necessarily mean the lack of any type of feature-bound representations in our brain. Multiple feature-bound object representations may be used only in implicit ways. Although there are some studies on object working memory using implicit measures such as object review paradigm [4], it is unclear whether these previous works provide unequivocal evidence for the existence of feature-bound representations. For example, information which produced the object preview benefit [4] may be some type of saliency representations. Feature-bound representations in implicit memory is an important future direction, and new developments in experimental paradigm are necessary.

Acknowledgments

This work was supported by PRESTO "Intelligent cooperation and control" from Japanese Science and Technology Agency (JST) and the 21st Century COE Program from JMEXT (D-2 to Kyoto University).

References

1. Brainard, D. H. (1997) The psychophysics toolbox., *Spatial Vision*, *10*, 443-446.
2. Cowan, N. (2001). The magical number 4 in short-term memory: A reconsideration of mental storage capacity., *Behavioral & Brain Sciences*, *24*, 87-185.
3. Itti, L. and Koch, C. (2000). A saliency-based machanism for overt and covert shifts of visual attention., *Vision Research*, *40*, 1489-1506.
4. Kahneman, D., Treisman, A., & Gibbs, B. J. (1992). The reviewing of object files: Object specific integration of information., *Cognitive Psychology*,*24*, 175-219.
5. Koch, C. and Ullman, S. (1985). Shifts in selective visual attention: towards the underlying neural circuitry., *Human Neurobiology*, *4*, 219-227.
6. Luck, S. J., & Vogel. E. K. (1997). The capacity of visual working memory for features and conjunctions., *Nature*, *390*, 279-281.
7. Pelli, D. G. (1997) The videotoolbox software for visual psychophysics: Transforming numbers into movies., *Spatial Vision*, *10*, 443-446.
8. Saiki, J. (2003a). Feature binding in object-file representations of multiple moving items., *Journal of Vision*, *3*, 6-21.
9. Saiki, J. (2003b). Spatiotemporal characteristics of dynamic feature binding in visual working memory., *Vision Research*, *43*, 2107-2123.
10. Treisman, A., & Schmidt, H. (1982). Illusory conjunction in the perception of objects., *Cognitive Psychology*, *14*, 107-141.
11. Verstraten, F. J. A., Cavanagh, P., & Labianca, A. T. (2000). Limits of attentive tracking reveal temporal properties of attention., *Vision Research*, *40*, 3651-3664.
12. Wheeler, M. E., & Treisman, A. (2002). Binding in short-term visual memory., *Journal of Experimental Psychology: General*, *131*, 48-64.

Molecular and Functional Diversity of Visual Pigments: Clues from the Photosensitive Opsin–Like Proteins of the Animal Model *Hydra*

Silvia Santillo[1], Pierangelo Orlando[2], Luciano De Petrocellis[1],
Luigia Cristino[1], Vittorio Guglielmotti[1], and Carlo Musio[1]

[1] Istituto di Cibernetica "Eduardo Caianiello", CNR, Pozzuoli (NA), Italy
c.musio@cib.na.cnr.it
[2] Istituto di Biochimica delle Proteine, CNR, Napoli, Italy

Abstract. The primary event of vision is the absorption of photons by photosensitive pigments, which triggers the transduction process producing the visual excitation. Although animal eyes and eyeless photoreceptive systems developed along several levels of molecular, morphological and functional complexity, image–forming rhodopsin family appears ubiquous along visual systems. Moreover, all Metazoa have supplementary extraocular photoreceptors that regulate their temporal physiology. The investigation of novel non-visual photopigments exerting extraretinal photoreception is a challenging field in vision research. To study molecular and functional differences between these pigment families, we propose the cnidarian *Hydra*, the first metazoan owning a nervous system, as a powerful tool of investigation. *Hydra* shows only an extraocular photoreception lacking classic visual structures. Our findings provide the first evidence in a phylogenetically old species of both image– and non–image–forming opsins, giving new insights on the molecular biology of *Hydra* photoreception and on comparative physiology of visual pigments.

1 Introduction

Visual information, in the sense of what we catch and extract from the external world, represents the coding and the processing of a continuous image-forming mechanism. The primary step of the image construction is photoreception. It takes place in the photoreceptorial cellular structures of visual systems that respond directly to light, thanks to the presence of a visual pigment, absorbing its energy and converting it into an electrical signal. Following light excitation, all image component elements are elaborated by specialized peripheral neural circuits and then transmitted by visual pathways to higher brain visual structures for further processing which culminates with visual perception (for a complete treatment of neural and cognitive features of the visual stream see [1]).

Photoreception is phylogenetically one of the oldest sensorial systems due to the amazing ubiquity, in all animal phyla, of light–sensitive morphological, functional and molecular elements (from simple invertebrate light–sensitive cells to more complex vertebrate eyes) [2]. The photoreception process occurs within

M. De Gregorio et al. (Eds.): BVAI 2005, LNCS 3704, pp. 225–234, 2005.

highly specialized sensory cells, called photoreceptors, able to convert light into electrical signal. It is based on the scheme of a G–protein signal transduction cascade comprising three proteins, a G–protein–coupled receptor (GPCR), a G–protein (G) and an effector protein (E) [3]. Although the expression of the structure–function relationship in vertebrate and invertebrate visual cells leads to different cellular mechanisms underlying phototransduction, basically, photoreception starts with the photochemical isomerization of the retinal cromophore of the GPCR. This process is followed by the binding with a G–protein which leads an enzymatic visual cascade culminating in the production of a second messenger, the effector protein E, which gates light–sensitive ion channels in order to modulate and shape the electric signal toward the nervous system [3]. Nevertheless, the early steps of the transduction cascade are notably conserved in their principal GPCR and G–protein elements [4].

Both vertebrate and invertebrate photoresponses follow the above transduction scheme although remarkable differences concern the structure/function relationship of GPCR rhodopsin (Rh) and its photochemical reactions, the activation of distinct G–protein subtypes, the enzymatic processes occurring in the visual cascade and the electric signal of the visual excitation [3,4,5] (Fig. 1). Light–induced cascade produces a huge chemical amplification (*e.g.*, 1 photo–excited Rh activates 500 G* and finally 250 Na^+ channels are closed in vertebrate rods), proving the functional presence of a diffusible chemical effector [3].

The cyclic GMP (cGMP) is the final messenger that gates light–sensitive channels in vertebrates in response to light stimulation. As final result, a decreasing of cGMP level (caused by the enzymatic activity of a cGMP–phosphodi esterase, PDE) closes the light–dependent channels producing a hyperpolarizing receptor potential due to a reduction of the Na^+ influx [6]. In rhabdomeric photoreceptors mainly a phosphoinositide (PI) pathway signalling system rules the visual excitation cascade. Upon light stimulation, the G–protein activates a phospholipase C (PLC) generating a fast production of two intracellular messengers: inositol-1,4,5-trisphosphate (IP_3) and membrane lipid soluble diacylglycerol (DAG) which starts parallel signalling pathways acting on the intracellular Ca^{2+} concentration. The light–induced excitation terminates with the opening of light–sensitive channels that favour a cation influx and the increasing of mem-

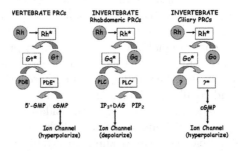

Fig. 1. Phototransduction pathways in vertebrate and invertebrate photoreceptors

brane conductance that leads to a depolarizing receptor potential [5]. Recently, ciliary photoreceptors hyperpolarizing to light stimulation have been found in scallop [5]. Their receptor potential, mediated by a cGMP–activated K^+ conductance, looks like that of vertebrate rods and cones [6] and their transduction behavior resembles that of some invertebrate extraocular photosensitive cells which have K^+ channels gated by cGMP [7]. The identification in invertebrates of multiple effector enzymes and their functional role are still debated.

In addition to classic ocular or retinal structures, vertebrates and invertebrates utilize supplementary extraocular photoreceptor (EOP) systems for non–image forming (non–visual) functions [8,9]. Photic information mediated by EOP integrates visual activity involved in temporal (time–of–day) and behavioral physiology of the animal (e.g., photoperiodism in locomotion and reproduction, timing and entrainment of circadian rhythms). Extraretinal or non–image forming photosensitive cells in invertebrates, and non–rod non–cone cells in vertebrates are mainly located within nervous system and share with retinal photoreceptors the same G–coupled phototransduction scheme but varying in some molecular and functional events [Gotow et al., this volume].

The searching for novel opsin–based photopigments triggering non image–forming photoreception is a new challenging field in vision research. Recently, these pigments have been identified in cells beyond the retinal photoreceptors [10] in several species. To deepen primary mechanisms of phototransduction, "simple" animal models, in which the homologues of the major signaling pathways can be better analyzed, have been proved as useful tools of investigation. Among those, we propose Hydra (Cnidaria, Hydrozoa), the first metazoan having a nervous system, in which photoreception is exerted only by EOP systems [11,12]. This paper reports main similarities and differences among visual and non–visual pigment families and their functional role in vertebrates and invertebrates. We also focus on the identification and the molecular characterization of presumably functional different opsin–based proteins in Hydra, outlining common strategies for light–detection and photo–signaling in Metazoa.

2 Rhodopsins for Seeing

As introduced above, the photoreceptors' light–detecting capability is due to the absorbing process of photons determined by the presence light–sensitive pigments. The luminous sensitivity (hence the ambient chromatic extracting features) of a visual cell is function of photopigment spectral properties that have evolved as function of the chemo–physical environmental characteristics.

In Metazoa the universal photosensitive protein for vision is rhodopsin (Rh), one of the GPCRs that constitutes the largest group of transmembrane receptor protein [13]. Rhodopsin (35-55 kDa) is constituted by a cromophore, 11-*cis* retinal (aldehyde of vitamin A1), covalently linked to a single polypeptide opsin by a Schiff–base [14] (Fig. 2). Exceptionally, insects use 3-,4-OH retinal cromophores [15]. The crystal structure of bovine Rh has confirmed that the cromophore is bound to Lys296 and Glu113 is the counter-ion in vertebrate Rh [16]. Opsin has 7

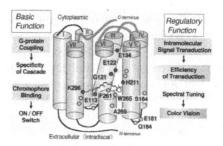

Fig. 2. Bovine Rh structural model. Amino acid residues responsible for chromophore binding, spectral tuning and signal transduction are shown. Cytoplasmic domains (III, IV, V, VI, VII helices' top) are involved in G–protein coupling. Modif. from [4].

membrane–embedded α–helical segments connected by 3 extracellular loops and 3 cytoplasmatic loops. Rhodopsin is located with the chromophore in the center of the membrane, the N–terminal is on the intradiscal side and the C–terminal with the phosphorylation sites is on the cytosolic side [14]. In rod photoreceptors Rh molecules perform rapid rotational and translational movements and diffuse laterally [14]. Conversely, in rhabdomeric photoreceptors, Rh is not mobile being anchored to microvilli membrane by cytoscheletric structures [15].

The visual cycle starts with the absorption of light by Rh, triggering the 11-*cis* to *all–trans* photoisomerization of the chromophore and formation of metarhodopsin (M), after the fast production of intermediates (photo–, batho–, lumi–rhodopsin), that is the transition state able to activate the G–protein signal transduction. Photochemical cycle is roughly common in vertebrates and invertebrates apart from the number of Ms and the regeneration mechanisms [14,15]. In vertebrates M, *all–trans* cromophore dissociates from opsin and must be re–isomerized by slow enzymatic isomerase produced by retinal pigment epithelium. In invertebrates, M is reconverted in Rh by light with λ in the range of its absorption: this fast photoregeneration is complementary to a slow renewal process similar to vertebrate Rh regeneration.

Vertebrate and invertebrate Rhs share the same cromophore but a different opsin: they differ in both molecular weight (higher in invertebrates, insects and vertebrates have the same MW) and spectral sensitivity. Invertebrate Rh ranges from λ_{max} 350 to 550 nm, while vertebrate Rh oscillates between λ_{max} 450-530 nm [15]. Humans have Rh (λ_{max} 496 nm) and 3 kinds of cone pigments, green–, blue– and red–sensitive pigments (λ_{max} 419, 531 and 558 nm), classified in 3 opsin groups, LWS (red– and green–sensitive), RH1 (rhodopsin) and SWS1 (blue–sensitive) [17]. *Drosophila* has 5 Rhs differently located in the photoreceptors constituting the ommatidium (R1-6 λ_{max} 480 nm, blu– and green–Rh5 λ_{max} 440 and 520 nm, ultraviolet Rh3 and Rh4 λ_{max} 345 and 375 nm) [15].

This fact gives reason of the great variability among all animal phyla to perceive, discriminate and integrate light information arising from natural environments with various chromatic and luminous contents. In other words, photoreceptors sample the visual environment and their spatial and spectral characteristics determine the optical information available to the brain. The molecular interactions between the opsins and chromophores define the spectral properties of a particular visual pigment. Differences in spectral shifts between pigments are due firstly to changes in the aminoacid composition of the opsins expressed within those photoreceptors.

In the bulk of our understanding of phototransduction, cutting–edge questions still need exhaustive answers. They concern the evolution of visual systems and the development of functional adaptations conserving molecular phylogenetic foundations from photosensitive ancestors. Multidisciplinary approaches greatly contributed to unravel the key–players involved in photosignaling. The powerful combination of electrophysiology and genetics has contributed to understand dynamical components (e.g., enzymatic mechanisms, ion channel gating) [18]. The most direct methods of structural analysis are X–ray crystallography, solution and solid–state NMR, atomic force microscopy (AFM), EM and image processing. They have enabled, to date, the molecular detail of more than ten distinct proteins of the phototransduction pathway (e.g., G protein transducin, cGMP–gated channels). Surely, the crystal structure of bovine rod Rh solved at 2.8 Å resolution has represented the turning point for a modern molecular depiction of the phototransduction components [16].

Comparative molecular strategies are addressed to reconstruct the opsin gene family pattern of duplication and functional diversification in vertebrates and invertebrates in order to outline the evolutionary history of visual pigments. This approach provides insights to the understanding of the molecular bases of spectral tuning of visual pigments as well as the evolutionary processes taken by different species to adapting to their photic environment. Despite inter– and intra–species functional differences, molecular genetics approaches have reported the sequence of vertebrate and invertebrate rhodopsins, showing the existence of similar regions of aminoacids conservation.

Phylogenetic trees of the vertebrate photosensitive proteins demonstrated that vertebrate opsin sequences (to date 113 classified) fall into five fundamental retinal subfamilies (RH1, RH2, SWS1, SWS2, LWS/MWS) and one non–retinal (P) [17]. Cones share isoforms that are different from those of rods. The difference in the molecular properties of these isoforms (and the switch of their expression) influences the light sensitivity between rods and cones [17].

Color vision evolved in vertebrates from the ancestral tetrachromatic system to the reduced dichromacy of mammals and the re–emergence of trichromacy in primates. The molecular basis of spectral tuning in red– and green–sensitive cone pigments have been studied by site–directed mutagenesis which demonstrates that the spectral shift is caused by 5-7 aminoacids additive in effect [17].

To date, in invertebrates 59 visual pigment sequences have been identified and assigned to 3 sub-classes following functional constraints: LW–green–, blue–, UV–absorbing pigments. Sequence alignment and comparison have revealed several structural features common to all visual pigments. Lowest similarities are function of the phylogenetic distances between the examined phyla. A phylogenetic tree has been constructed on the basis of the "rootless tree" model although the small number of sequences induces several doubts [15]. The tree is constituted by five limbs that group pigments according to their taxonomic relations and functional properties (limbs I, II V insect, III crayfishes, IV cephalopods).

Sequence comparison between invertebrate and vertebrate opsins has revealed more differences than degrees of similarity assigning respective pigments to two super–classes [15]. Hence, evolutionary analysis of visual pigments suggests that opsins utilize similar set of protein–protein interactions for signaling and main typology of sub–molecular structure is retained for that function.

3   Opsins for Timing

Vertebrates and invertebrates share other photosensory systems in addition to classical vision. Lower invertebrates lacking obvious eyed or optical structures use nervous or dermal cells (single or clustered) for light sensing. They do not form images but detect only irradiance. Any type of light sensing outside retinal/ocular systems is termed Extraocular Photoreception (EOP) [8,9].

Little more than a decade ago, apart the vital role in eyeless invertebrates, EOP was considered an unnecessary evolutive residue than a complementary component of visual function. Until recently, the EOP role has been recognized fundamental in the photoentrainment of circadian clocks, located in central brain and peripheral tissues, whose pacemaker activity provides endogenous timetable for vital expressions (development, reproduction, photoperiodism) [19].

Novel circadian photoreceptors do not depend upon the input of retinal photoreceptors. In fly *sine oculis* mutant the activity of extraocular H–B (Hofbauer–Buchner) eyelets and brain LNs neurons (lateral neurons) is necessary to generate circadian rhythms. Mice *rd/rd* (retinal degenerations) mutants show a massive degeneration of rods and cones but still retain circadian activity, pineal melatonin suppression, and pupil size modulation that all overlap those of mices with normal retinas. All circadian responses are abolished by the eye removal. Blind or retinal disease patients having lost conscious light perception show circadian responses and melatonin suppression. On the whole, these results indicate that in mice and humans eye image–forming and novel non–image forming photoreceptors co–exist [19].

Different experimental approaches in vertebrates have identified for these responses several photopigments all referred to as opsin–like proteins; insects provide exception using also the blue–light absorbing protein cryptochrome [20]. To date, since the first non–visual opsin, pinopsin, was identified in chicken pineal in 1994, novel opsins include: vertebrate ancient VA–opsin (expressed in a subset of amacrine and horizontal cells), parapinopsin (in catfish parapineal organ), exo–rhodopsin (in zebrafish pineal gland), encephalopsin (in amphibian deep brain regions), Opn5 neuropsin (in mice eye, brain and testis), Opn4 melanopsin (different tissue expression patterns in all vertebrates but constant in retinal ganglion cells), peropsin (in mouse retinal pigment epithelium, RPE) and RGR (RPE–retinal G protein–coupled receptor) [4, 9-10, 15, 17, 21-22].

Nowadays, a renewed molecular phylogenetic classification of known opsins comprises seven subfamilies: 1) vertebrate visual and non–visual opsins, 2) encephalopsins, 3) invertebrate Gq–coupled opsins and melanopsins, 4) invertebrate Go–coupled opsins, 5) neuropsins, 6) peropsins, 7) RGR isomerases [22].

Molecular and functional diversity of opsins indicate that higher percentages of these proteins deal with non–image forming systems. Indeed, in vertebrates, retinal photoreception is not restricted to the rod/cone pathways but is involved in non–image forming process [10]. So, the recent discovery of intrinsically photoresponsive retinal ganglion cells (ipRGCs) has provided the morphological correlate of non–visual phototransduction, namely non–rod non–cone photoreception [23], candidating melanopsin as the novel photopigment for this task (though a role of isomerase was not excluded). Recent papers collectively show that melanopsin is a photopigment more close to invertebrate opsins than a classical vertebrate rod–cone opsin [24]. Surprisingly, in primate Opn4–expressing RGC cells projecting to the lateral geniculate nuclei (the brain structure relaying image–forming information) send color and irradiance signals arising from different rod/cone inputs. Thus, image–forming and non–image–forming systems are merged and melanopsin may contribute to conscious visual perception [25]. These outstanding achievements notch our current opinions on vision and will influence future approaches to human light detection.

4 The Animal Model *Hydra* and Its Opsin–Based Pigments

The cnidarian *Hydra* shows EOP since it has no conventional visual structures; nevertheless single or clustered photosensitive cells have not yet been identified. Its photosensitivity can be measured electrophysiologically as modulation of a periodic behavior consisting of continuously alternating phases of body shortenings and elongations [12]. These movements are due to the agonist/antagonist actions of the myofibrils contained in the epitheliomuscular cells of both the ectodermal and endodermal layers. Our previous studies proved that different photic stimulation protocols are effective on the modulation of bioelectric correlates of the animal's periodic behavior [11]. *Hydra*'s behavioral action spectrum indicates red blindness and two peaks of response around 450 and 550 nm; corresponding respectively to an inhibitory and an excitatory effect on the occurrence of the cyclic behavioral sequence [11]. By polyclonal antibodies against squid rhodopsin, we identified an opsin–like protein (named by us HyRH) likely localized in sensory nervous cells of the ectodermal layer [26].

To isolate the HyRH gene, we have designed pairs of degenerated primers corresponding to the most conserved regions of known invertebrate Rhs. The BLAST suite at NCBI/NLM (www.ncbi.nlm.nhi.gov/BLAST) was used for bioinformatic screening of sequence data. Amplification of the target band of 250 bp was performed on *Hydra vulgaris* genomic DNA by conventional PCR (polymerase chain reaction) (Fig. 3). The correspondence between the size of the obtained fragment with that of the expected one will induce us to perform

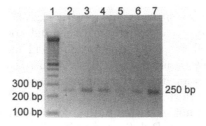

Fig. 3. PCR amplification on *Hydra vulgaris* genomic DNA by degenerated rhodopsin primers. Best amplifications (lanes 3-4) correspond to the better specificity/quantity ratio. Lane 1: 100 bp DNA ladder. Lane 2: MgSO$_4$ 2.5mM. Lane 3: MgSO$_4$ 3mM. Lane 4: MgSO$_4$ 3mM, DMSO 5%. Lane 5: MgSO$_4$ 3mM, DMSO 10%. Lane 6: MgSO$_4$ 3.5mM. Lane 7: MgSO$_4$ 4mM. Annealing temperature 51.5 °C.

the amplimer sequence and to design more specific probes to clone HyRH by RT–PCR (reverse transcription PCR) and RACE (rapid amplification cDNA ends).

Furtherly, our *Hydra* opsin(s) gene screening fits well the search for photopigments triggering EOP, ongoing in non–image forming photoreceptors. Among novel opsins, we focused on peropsin pigment (RRH), which is expressed in vertebrate RPE and it may act as direct light–sensor or as photoisomerase [21]. Possibly, *Hydra* ectodermal molecular and functional elements producing EOP processes could be phylogenetically close to those of vertebrate RPE.

The finding in *Hydra* genome of a sequence of 540 bp (GenBank CB073527), reported as similar to the mouse RRH, strengthened our aim. We designed pairs of RRH primers from this partial cDNA sequence, testing them on *Hydra vulgaris* genomic DNA and cDNA after RT–PCR of the total RNA. We obtained good evidence by a sharp amplification of the expected 312 bp fragment (Fig. 4).

This result has encouraged us to verify further light influences on the RRH expression as supported by the fact that circadian rhythms and light regulate mRNA expression of visual and non–visual photoisomerases [27]. Preliminary

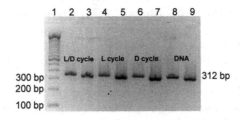

Fig. 4. RT–PCR expression analysis of peropsin–like sequence of *Hydra vulgaris* at different light adaptation settings (lanes 2,4,6) with RT β–actin, 344 bp, as endogenous reference (lanes 3,5,7). Same sequence amplification on genomic DNA (lanes 8-9). Annealing temperature 52 °C.

experiments have been performed with total RNA extracted by animals adapted for 3 days with different light cycles: L/D cycle (12:12 light–dark hours), L cycle (24h light–on), D cycle (24h light–off). At first, no marked differences were observed between the three groups with conventional PCR (Fig. 4). However, to screen significant differences in the RRH mRNA expression, a necessary real time quantitative PCR is in progress, also with animals adapted to normal and altered circadian light conditions.

5 Conclusions and Future Work

We propose the cnidarian *Hydra*, thanks to possible molecular and functional diversifications of its opsins, as a theoretical and experimental phylogenetic link to higher photoreceptive systems and as putative common animal ancestor having multiple opsin genes. The early identification in its EOP system of Rh and RRH belonging to ectodermal/neural epithelia could support the hypothesis of ancestor pigments bifurcating later into visual and non–visual functions.

Our findings call for molecular, anatomical and physiological investigations concerning the localization of *Hydra* novel photopigments and photosensitive cells, and their eventual correlations with invertebrate and vertebrate homologues/analogues visual photoreceptors, inner retina non–visual cells and RPE opsin–containing cells.[1] Firstly, we will refine the Rh and RRH characterization as well we will verify possible presence of melanopsin that is functionally closer to invertebrate opsins than to vertebrate ones. Moreover, as *Hydra* cells showing HyRh immunoreactivity seem to be of the ciliary type [5], we are aimed to search: 1) by patch–clamp recordings from single putative photosensitive cells, if cGMP and/or IP3 pathways mediate the visual cascade, 2) by immunohistology using anti–cGMP and –IP3 antibodies, the intracellular phototransductive players. Also, we plan to search NO–stimulated elements of the cGMP route by protocols for the NADPH–diaphorase activity [28].

An ultimate release [29] shows an invertebrate–like phototransduction cascade triggered by melanopsin. It emphasizes that the search for photosensory non–visual mechanisms in vertebrates and invertebrates, and their interactions with visual ones, is not matter of bizarre science but a new intriguing challenge.

References

1. Chalupa LM, Werner LS: The Visual Neurosciences. MIT Press (2003)
2. Fernald RD: Evolving eyes. Int. J. Dev. Biol. **48** (2004) 701–705
3. Arshavsky V, Lamb T, Pugh E: G proteins and phototransduction. Annu. Rev. Physiol. **64** (2002) 153–187
4. Shichida Y, Imai H: Visual pigment: G–protein–coupled receptor for light signals. Cell. Mol. Life Sci. **54** (1998) 1299–1315
5. Nasi E., Gomez M., Payne, R: Phototransduction mechanisms in microvillar and ciliary photoreceptors of invertebrates. In: Hoff AJ, Stavenga D, *et al.* (eds), Molecular Mechanisms in Visual Transduction. Elsevier, Amsterdam (2000) 389–448

---

[1] ICIB–CNR Project "Biophysical Processes of Non–Visual Photoreception".

6. Koutalos Y, Nakatani K, Xiong W–H, Yau K–W: Phototransduction in retinal rods and cones. In: Musio C (ed): Vision: The Approach of Biophysics and Neurosciences, World Scientific, Singapore (2001) 172–183

7. Gotow T, Nishi T: Light–dependent K$^+$ channels in the mollusc *Onchidium* simple photoreceptors are opened by cGMP. J. Gen. Physiol. **120** (2002) 581–97

8. Musio C: Extraocular photosensitivity in invertebrates. In: Taddei–Ferretti C (ed): Biophysics of Photoreception. World Scientific, Singapore (1997) 245–262

9. Foster RG, Grace M, Provencio I, et al.: Identification of vertebrate deep encephalic photoreceptors. Neurosci. Biobehav. Rev. **18** (1994) 541–46

10. Foster RG, Hankins MW: Non–rod, non–cone photoreception in the vertebrates. Prog. Ret. Eye Res. (PRER) **21** (2002) 507–527

11. Taddei–Ferretti C, Musio C: Photobehaviour of *Hydra* and correlated mechanisms: a case of extraocular photosensitivity. J Photochem Photobiol B **55** (2000) 88–101

12. Taddei–Ferretti C, Musio C, Santillo S, Cotugno A: The photobiology of *Hydra*'s periodic activity. Hydrobiologia **530/531** (2004) 129–134

13. Gualtieri P: Rhodopsin–like proteins: the universal and probably unique proteins for vision. See Ref. [6] 23–30

14. Filipek S, Stenkamp R, et al.: GPCR rhodopsin: a prospectus. Annu. Rev. Physiol **65** (2003) 851–879

15. Gärtner W: Invertebrate visual pigments. See Ref. [5] 297–388

16. Palczewski K, Kumasaka T, Hori T, et al.: Crystal structure of rhodopsin: a G protein-coupled receptor. Science **289** (2000) 739–745

17. Yokoyama S: Molecular evolution of vertebrate visual pigments. PRER **19** (2000) 385–419

18. Hardie RC: Phototransduction in *Drosophila*. J. Exp. Biol. **204** (2001) 3403–3409

19. Foster RG, Helfrich–Förster C: The regulation of circadian clocks by light in fruit-flies and mice. Phil. Trans. R. Soc. Lond. B **356** (2001) 1779–1789

20. Emery P, Stanewsky R, Helfrich–Förster C, et al.: *Drosophila* CRY is a deep brain circadian photoreceptor. Neuron **26** (2000) 493–504

21. Sun H, Gilbert D, Copeland N, et al.: Peropsin, a novel visual pigment–like protein located in the apical microvilli of the RPE. PNAS **94** (1997) 9893–9898

22. Terakita A: The opsins. Genome Biol. **6** (2005) 213 [Epub at GenomeBiology.com]

23. Berson DM, Dunn F, Takao M: Phototransduction by retinal ganglion cells that set the circadian clock. Science **295** (2002) 1070–1073

24. Foster RG: Bright blue times. Nature **433** (2005) 698–699

25. Dacey D, Liao HW, et al.: Melanopsin–expressing ganglion cells in primate retina signal colour and irradiance and project to the LGN. Nature **433** (2005) 749–754

26. Musio C, Santillo S, Taddei–Ferretti C, Robles LJ, et al.: First identification and localization of a visual pigment in *Hydra*. J. Comp. Physiol. **187A** (2001) 79–81

27. Bailey M, Cassone V: Opsin photoisomerases in the chick retina and pineal gland: characterization, localization, and circadian regulation. IOVS **45** (2004) 769–775

28. Florenzano F, Guglielmotti V: Selective NADPH–diaphorase histochemical labeling of Müller radial processes and photoreceptors in the earliest stages of retinal development in the tadpole. Neurosci. Lett. **292** (2000) 187–90

29. Isoldi MC, Rollag MD, et al.: Rhabdomeric phototransduction initiated by the vertebrate photopigment melanopsin. PNAS **102** (2005) 1217–1221

Learning Location Invariance for Object Recognition and Localization

Gwendid T. van der Voort van der Kleij[1], Frank van der Velde[1], and Marc de Kamps[2]

[1] Cognitive Psychology Unit, University of Leiden, Wassenaarseweg 52,
2333 AK Leiden, The Netherlands
{gvdvoort, vdvelde}@fsw.leidenuniv.nl
[2] Robotics and Embedded Systems, Department of Informatics,
Technische Universität München, Boltzmannstr. 3,
D-85748 Garching bei München, Germany
kamps@in.tum.de

Abstract. A visual system not only needs to recognize a stimulus, it also needs to find the location of the stimulus. In this paper, we present a neural network model that is able to generalize its ability to identify objects to new locations in its visual field. The model consists of a feedforward network for object identification and a feedback network for object location. The feedforward network first learns to identify simple features at all locations and therefore becomes selective for location invariant features. This network subsequently learns to identify objects partly by learning new conjunctions of these location invariant features. Once the feedforward network is able to identify an object at a new location, all conditions for supervised learning of additional, location dependent features for the object are set. The learning in the feedforward network can be transferred to the feedback network, which is needed to localize an object at a new location.

1 Introduction

Imagine yourself walking through the wilderness. It is very important that you recognize the company of a predator, wherever the predator appears in your visual field. Location invariant recognition enables us to associate meaningful information with what we see (here: danger), independent of where we see it. Hence location invariance is a very important feature of our visual system.

Nonetheless, location invariant recognition also implies a loss of location information about the object we have identified. Yet, information about where something is in our environment is also essential in order to react in a goal-directed manner upon what is out there.

We have previously proposed a neural network model of visual object-based attention, in which the identity of an object is used to select its location among other objects [1]. This model consists of a feedforward network that identifies (the shape of) objects that are present in its visual field. In addition, the model

M. De Gregorio et al. (Eds.): BVAI 2005, LNCS 3704, pp. 235–244, 2005.

also consists of a feedback network that has the same connection structure as the feedforward network, but with reciprocal connections. The feedback network is trained with the activation in the feedforward network as input [1]. By using a Hebbian learning procedure, the selectivity in the feedforward network is transferred to the feedback network. We argue that this is a very natural and simple way to keep the feedback network continuously up to date with ongoing learning in the feedforward network.

How does this architecture allow the step to go from implicitly knowing what to knowing where? Suppose the feedforward network identifies a circle in its visual field. The feedback network carries back information about the identity of this shape to the lower (retinotopic) areas of the model. In these areas, the feedback activation produced by the circle interacts with feedforward activation produced by the circle. The interaction between the feedforward network and the feedback network (in local microcircuits) results in a selective activation at locations in the retinotopic areas of the model that correspond to the location of the circle. This activation can be used to direct spatial attention to the location of the target [1].

Previous research has focused on location invariant recognition in feedforward neural networks [2,3]. Several models are proposed, in which information processing is routed in a bottom-up manner to a salient location rather than to other locations (e.g., see [4]). The goal of this paper is to explore the complementary task of finding, in a top-down manner, the location of what is recognized in a location invariant manner in the visual field. The model of Amit and Mascaro can perform this task [5]. They assume a replica module with multiple copies of the local feature input that gives (gated) input to a centralized module that learns to identify objects completely independent of location, and vice versa. We provide an alternative mechanism for location invariant object recognition, by which cells in the feedforward network not only become selective for location invariant features, but also for location dependent features. Next, we explore how learning such location invariant object recognition in the feedforward network transfers to location invariant learning in the feedback network in our neural network model. This transfer is necessary in order to find something at a new location.

We have built up learning in the feedforward network in such a way that it initially learns to identify simple features (e.g., oriented lines, edges) at all possible locations. After that, the feedforward network learns to identify objects at some possible locations. The rationale behind this learning procedure is that learning to recognize an object may then partly involve abstracting new conjunctions of known, location invariant features. This enables the feedforward network to generalize its ability to identify an object at trained locations to new locations. Simulations of the network confirmed this line of thought. These simulations are first presented in this paper.

The second simulations presented here investigated how the ability of the feedforward network to recognize an object at a new location relates to finding an object at a new location, given the fact that learning in the feedforward network is built up in successive stages. The simulations demonstrate that recognizing an object at a new location does not automatically lead to finding that new location of the object. However, we show that the recognition of an object at a new location facilitates efficient, supervised learning of additional location dependent features in the feedforward network. Once the improved selectivity for the object at that location in the feedforward network is transferred to the feedback network, the interaction between the feedforward network and the feedback network does enable the selection of the new location of the object.

2   Network Architecture

For the simulations we used a similar neural network model of (the ventral pathway in) the visual cortex that was used in the simulation of object-based attention in the visual cortex [1]. It basically consists of a feedforward network that includes the areas V1, V2, V4, the posterior inferotemporal cortex (PIT), the central inferotemporal cortex (CIT) and the anterior inferotemporal cortex (AIT), and of a feedback network that carries information about the identity of the object to the lower retinotopic areas in the visual cortex (V2 - PIT). The model shares the basic architecture and characteristics of the visual cortex. The receptive fields size of cells in an area increases, while climbing up the visual processing hierarchy. Secondly, the connections between cells in the network are determined so that the retinotopic organization is maintained throughout area V1 to area PIT. Differently, area CIT and AIT have input connections from all cells in the previous area. Cells in CIT and AIT receive information covering the whole visual field (all positions). Every two successive areas are interconnected. For example, area AIT only receives input from area CIT.

Figure 1 illustrates the architecture of the network schematically. From area V1 to area PIT, cells are arranged in a two-dimensional array that makes up the visual field. The number of layers in an area defines the number of cells per retinotopic position (e.g., two from area V2 to area PIT). Multiple layers within an area are not interconnected. Each layer in V1 codes for line segments of one of four possible orientations. The input is set in area V1 by activating cells in the four layers of cells. Area AIT functions as the output layer of the network.

3   Simulating Location Invariant Object Identification

The network was trained with backpropagation in three successive stages. In the first stage, the network learned to identify oriented line segments (having the length of two cells in the input layer) presented at any position within the networks visual field. In the second stage, the network was trained to identify edges consisting of various combinations of the oriented line segments (see figure 1) at any position within the networks visual field. In order to avoid (potential) catastrophic interference, the oriented line segments learned in the previous stage were also included in the training. Note that the nature of the

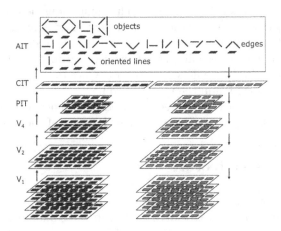

Fig. 1. The architecture of the network. The symbols above the cells in layer AIT show the features that the cells were trained to identify.

collection of edges (two different combinations of each identical set of line segments) forces the network to abstract local relation information at a low level in order to identify the edges correctly. Hence, throughout these two stages of supervised training, the network learned to identify features of increasing complexity. In the final stage, the network was trained to identify objects (see figure 1) consisting of line segments and of one or more trained edges. Importantly, the network was only exposed to the objects at four possible locations (see figure 2a). Again, the training set also incorporated features that were previously learned (at all locations).

The first two training stages were chosen to generate a network, in which cells in V4 and PIT are selective for a variety of simple and more complex features like the cells in comparable areas of the monkey brain [6]. The training in two successive stages offered the network an opportunity to draw on formerly constructed selectivity while encoding new, more complex information (i.e., bootstrapping). Note that the exact features that cells in the network learn to abstract are not set in advance, but develop as a result of learning. Furthermore, representation in the network is distributed, due to the connection structure of the network [1].

Cells in CIT have input connections that cover the whole visual field. In principle, during training these cells could become selective only for features that appear in a subset of the visual field. However, the number of cells in area CIT was not sufficient to allow such a specialization for location information. In order to identify the oriented lines and edges at all locations, the cells in CIT learned to abstract features largely independent of location information.

Interestingly, if cells in area CIT are selective for features largely independent of location information after the first two training stages, then the network may subsequently learn to identify the objects partly by learning new conjunctions of such location invariant features. In other words, the network could shape the selectivity of some cells by building upon the location invariant selectivity of cells that are already present. Such a mechanism would give the network the ability to generalize the identification of the objects to locations where the objects are never presented before.

4   Results of Location Invariant Object Identification

We trained the feedforward neural network according to the training scheme described above. This was done successfully five times, each time resulting in slightly different connection weights between the areas in the network.

Figure 2b shows the squared error of the networks output over the number of passes that the network has gone through the training set, both for the second and the third stage of training. The data for only one network are displayed in the graph, but these data are well representative for other instances of the network. As can be seen in the figure, the network very quickly learns to identify the objects in the third stage, once it has learned to identify the oriented lines and the edges in the previous stage.

After the training, the networks response was tested for each of the four objects presented at nine possible locations. Four of the locations were identical to the locations at which the objects appeared during training. In contrast, the objects were never presented before at the other five locations (see figure 2a). Given the connection structure of the network, more cells in the network receive input from an object when it is presented in the center of its visual field than when it is presented in a more peripheral location. Therefore, locations where objects appeared during training and new locations are chosen in such a way that on average the same number of cells in the network respond to an object at each kind of location (i.e., trained or new), apart from the center location.

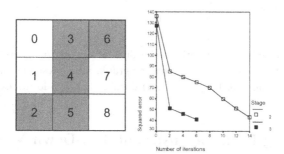

Fig. 2. (A) The nine possible locations in the visual field where objects were presented during testing. The network was exposed to objects at four locations during training (white). Before testing, the objects had never been presented at the five other (gray) locations. (B) Squared error of the networks output over the number of epochs during training, for the second (2) and third (3) learning stage.

Each panel in figure 3 shows the activation value of one cell in area AIT after the processing of its selective object and the other objects, at each location. Each cell clearly responds selectively to the object that it has been trained to identify. Moreover, each cell is optimally active when its preferred object appears at one of the trained locations, but it is also active, although to a lesser extend, when its preferred object appears at a new location. Particularly, the diamond and the square (object 1 and 2) are identified most strongly at new locations. The reduced response for a preferred object at new locations compared to trained locations shows that the network partly encodes location dependent features for the objects. This possibly takes place lower in the processing hierarchy of the network. However, the network is clearly able to generalize its identification of objects to new locations. This shows that the network also abstracts new conjunctions of known location invariant features in addition to location dependent features.

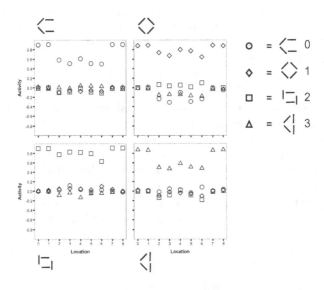

Fig. 3. Each panel shows the activation values of one cell in area AIT trained to identify the object drawn above or under the graph, after presentation of each of the 4 objects at both trained 0, 1, 7, 8 and untrained 2, 3, 4, 5, 6 locations

5   Simulating Location Invariant Top-Down Visual Search

Figure 4b illustrates how the (partly) location invariant object identification displayed by the feedforward network relates to the models ability to find the location of an object between other objects, when this object appears at new locations or trained locations in the visual field. In this second simulation the model performed a top-down visual search task. In this task, a cue is presented first. After that, the target object, matching the cue, appears in the visual field with three distracters (see figure 4a). The location of the cued object then has to be selected. The network was tested on this visual search task repeatedly with each of the four objects presented as the target. For each target object, 180 random search displays are presented (set as input) to the network. In the model the task is simulated as follows.

In the simulation, a cue selectively activates a cell in area AIT of the feedback network. Top-down activation in the feedback network results in the activation of all other cells in lower areas of the feedback network that are selective for features of that object. Next, the cued object and the other objects are set as input at random, non-overlapping locations in the visual field of the feedforward network. The feedforward network of the model processes all the objects simultaneously. After that, the interaction between the processing in the feedforward network and in the feedback network is simulated by computing the covariance between the activation of cells in the feedforward network and the activation of cells in the feedback network [1].

For each object, the covariance values of all the cells selective for the object in area PIT are summed up. To normalize the sum for each object, the sum of covariance values for an object is divided by the number of cells, which are selective for the object. The group of cells selective for one of the presented objects that has the highest level of normalized covariance indicates the location selected for the target. Note that area PIT still has a retinotopic organization and that cells in this area thus are also partly selective for location information.

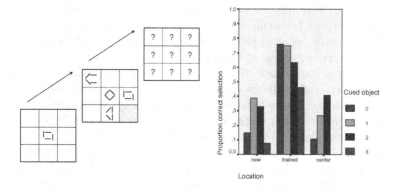

Fig. 4. (A) The top-down visual search task. A cue firstly indicates the target object (left) and after that the target object is presented between other objects (middle). The model then has to select the location of the target object (right). (B) The proportion of correct selections of the targets location for each of the objects as the target, when the target is presented at either the new locations, the trained locations or the center location.

6   Results of Location Invariant Top-Down Visual Search

Figure 4b illustrates the results of the simulation. For each of the four objects as the target, the proportion of correct selections of the targets location in the visual field is depicted separately for the trained locations, the new locations, and the (new) center location of the target. The data are averaged over five instances of the model. As can be seen in the figure, the network is better in finding the targets location when its location is one of the locations at which the network is trained to identify the target, than when its location is one of the locations at which the network is not trained to identify the target. Apparently, the networks ability to generalize its identification of an object to new locations does not transfer automatically to the task of finding the location of an object between other objects.

Part of the reason probably lies in the quality of the feedback connections that are the basis for top-down attentional selection in the model. The connections in the feedback network are trained in a Hebbian manner on all the activation patterns in the feedforward network during training [1]. As a result, cells in the feedback network that are selective for trained locations code more elaborate information about an object than cells that are selective for new locations (see figure 3). That is, at trained locations, cells in the feedback network are selective for both location invariant features and for location dependent features, just like cells in the feedforward network. Instead, at new locations, cells in the feedback network are at most selective for location invariant features.

Furthermore, to retrieve information about the location of an object at new locations, the reduced object selectivity in the feedback network has to interact with the activation in the feedforward network, which is also less selective for an object at new locations than for an object at trained locations. Hence, the limitations in the feedback encoding of an object at new locations and the limitations in the feedforward encoding of an object at new locations aggravate each other.

Despite this multiplicative effect of a less elaborated encoding of an object at new locations, we would still expect the network to select the location of the target in a visual search task somewhat above chance level. Figure 4b points out that this is, on average, not the case in our simulation. It is possible that cells in the network that respond to multiple objects present in the visual field (i.e., cells with large receptive fields), degrade the already basic, generalized feedforward encoding of the target at a new location too much for the model to put its top-down selection mechanism into effective use [7]. Nevertheless, the network selects object 1 and 2 at new locations between other objects above chance level. Note that these two objects are precisely the objects, which the feedforward network already identified most strongly at new locations (see figure 3).

7   Bridging the Gap Between Recognition and Localization

In summary, even when the network recognizes an object at a new location, this does not mean that it can immediately find the location of that object. Obviously, in real life it is very important that we rapidly learn to bridge this gap. What is the mechanism that may constitute that bridge?

Our simulations demonstrate that an object at a new location can be identified. All requirements for supervised learning are therefore present; an object is present at a new location and it is recognized. Figure 2b shows that, in supervised learning, the feedforward network can learn to abstract additional location dependent features of objects relatively fast. As a result the feedforward network becomes more selective for the object at that new location. This increased selectivity of the feedforward network transfers to the feedback network by means of the Hebbian learning in the feedback network [1]. After this, the interaction between the feedforward network and the feedback network will enable the localization of the object.

A similar result has emerged in a study, in which subjects had to search for a triangle of a particular orientation between triangles of another orientation [8]. The ability of the subjects to identify the target between the other objects improved dramatically over several days of training, but this learning was localized to a particular region of the visual field, namely the area used for training. This result might indicate that representations of the trained object are build separately for different positions across the cortical area [8].

It is crucial for the mechanism that we propose that the feedforward network learns in a build up manner, in which more complex features can partly be learned from more simple, location invariant, features. This allows the network to generalize its ability to identify an object to new locations and triggers more elaborated, location dependent learning that allows the network to find the object at new locations as well.

8   Discussion

Our neural network model predicts that the generalization to new locations by the visual system is more restricted when we have to find an object between other objects than when we have to recognize an object. In line with the second simulation, and with the study of Sigman and Gilbert [6], we hypothesize that when we search for an object between other objects, the abstraction of new location dependent features of an object may be essential to make the search more reliable. It might also speed up the search process.

We speculate that a visual system can rapidly abstract additional, location dependent features that are needed to reliably find an object at new locations, once it recognizes an object to some extent. Learning new, location dependent features proceeds in parallel to learning new conjunctions of known location invariant features. It possibly takes place mostly lower in the visual processing hierarchy. Our suggestions relate to Ahissar and Hochstein's Reverse Hierarchy Theory (RHT) [9], although RHT specifically focuses on perceptual learning, and asserts that visual perceptual learning *gradually* progresses backwards from high-level areas to the input levels of the visual system.

A visual system may generalize its recognition of an object to new locations, when it learns to identify the object partly by means of new conjunctions of location invariant features for which cells of the system are already selective. Simulations demonstrated this principle in our neural network model. Such learning may take place higher up the visual processing hierarchy. Our neural network model learned to recognize objects at multiple locations before testing its ability to generalize recognition to new locations. Yet, the neural network model may have shown comparable location invariant object recognition with fewer trained locations. Nevertheless, it is very likely that we learn to recognize an object at multiple locations, even during a single observation, due to movement of the object or ourselves (e.g., eye-movements, head movements, etcetera).

The neural network model localizes objects in disjoint windows, like some other models of visual search [5]. In the future, the selection of one of multiple, overlapping disjoint windows may be substituted by a WTA process, which localizes the location with the highest activation in the retinotopic areas of the model after the interaction between the feedforward and the feedback network.

The neural network model is not yet very robust to clutter. Scaling up its size and changing training to include a larger number of features and objects, will make its cells selective for a larger collection of both location dependent and location invariant features. In addition, providing multiple examples of an object with a realistic amount of within-object variability will strengthen the need to learn the most informative features for discriminating between that object and other objects [5]. Together these extensions could result in sparser object representations, helping the neural network model to cope with clutter.

References

1. Van der Velde, F., de Kamps, M.: From knowing what to knowing where: Modeling object-based attention with feedback disinhibition of activation, Journal of Cognitive Neuroscience **13** (4) (2001) 479-491
2. Fukushima, K.: Neocognitron capable of incremental learning, Neural Networks **17** (2004) 37-46
3. Riesenhuber, M., Poggio, T.: Models of object recognition, Nature Neuroscience **3** (2000) 1199-1204
4. Itti, L., Koch, C.: A saliency-based search mechanism for overt and covert shifts of visual attention, Vision Research **40** (2000) 1489-1506
5. Amit, Y., Mascaro, M.: An integrated network for invariant visual detection and recognition, Vision Research **43** (2003) 2073-2088
6. Tanaka, K.: Representation of visual features of objects in the inferotemporal cortex, Neural Networks **9** (1996) 1459-1475
7. Van der Voort van der Kleij, G.T., de Kamps, M., van der Velde, F.: A neural model of binding and capacity in visual working memory, Lecture Notes in Computer Science, Vol. **2714**. Springer, Berlin (2003) 771-778
8. Sigman, M., Gilbert, C.D.: Learning to find a shape, Nature Neuroscience **3** (2000) 264-269
9. Ahissar, M., Hochstein, S.: The reverse hierarchy theory of visual perceptual learning, Trends in Cognitive Sciences **8** (10) (2004) 457-464

Enacted Theories of Visual Awareness:
A Neuromodelling Analysis

Igor Aleksander[1] and Helen Morton[2]

[1]Imperial College, London SW7 2BT
i.aleksander@imperial.ac.uk
[2] Brunel University, Uxbridge UB8 3PH
helen.morton@brunel.ac.uk

Abstract. In recent years, issues of inattention blindness and change blindness have thrown doubt on theories of vision that assume that the visual signal is inwardly represented for further recognition and processing. The aim of this paper is to review so called enacted theories of vision and argue that they are too severe in terms of removing inner representations from the argument and removing the possibility of mental imagery. This is followed by an exposition of an axiomatic approach we have developed to explain issues of visual consciousness and show how this, while respecting enacted theories provides a new model of visual awareness which not only attempts to characterise the natural version, but may inspire the design of machinery.

1 Introduction

An often-seen film of an experiment by Simons and Chabris [1] shows a group of people bouncing a ball between them. The audience are asked to count the number of times a particular person bounces the ball. The astonishing event is that a person in a gorilla suit walks across the playing area, but only about 20% of the observers actually notice it. When shown the film again and released from the counting task, the audience laugh in disbelief. This is inattention blindness

Another film from the same laboratory shows Simons approaching an unsuspecting target individual on campus and asking him for directions. While the target is in full flow, a group of people carrying a door separate Simons from the target and stealthily replace Simons by Chabris. There is little physical similarity between the two. However the target carries on with his explanation unperturbed. When he is finished, Chabris asks the individual whether he had noticed anything odd. Yes, is the answer, he noticed being disturbed by people carrying a door. Then Simons makes his appearance and the target in some disarray suddenly realises what had gone on. This is change blindness.

Similar experiences involve the projection of still scenes, separated by a blank, in which vast areas of the scene are removed (New York skyline, the reflection of a building in a lake etc.) and this goes totally unnoticed by most of the audience. Strangely, if the separating blank is removed, the change becomes obvious. Then, without a blank, Kevin O'Regan of the Experimental Psychology Research Centre at the René Descartes University shows an image of a woman and a car in a busy street

M. De Gregorio et al. (Eds.): BVAI 2005, LNCS 3704, pp. 245–257, 2005.

and asks whether, over a two minute period, anything has changed. Most viewers do not notice that the colour of the car has slowly changed from bright red to bright blue under their very eyes. The car occupies about 30% of the screen.

Kevin O'Regan and Alva Noë based a theory of vision on the idea that change blindness and inattentional blindness should not be 'explained away' as aberrations due to careless attention in an otherwise rich and accurate perceptual system. They published a seminal paper which drew both criticism and support for proposing that 'the way we see' should undergo a radical revision [2]. This has become known as the enacted or sensorimotor theory of vision which is reviewed in this paper and attempts to understand better the role of attention which appears to be the thief that robs our vision of gorillas and other major changes in the world.

A major objection to this theory is that because it assumes an automatic link between visual input and motor responses it asserts that the world itself is the memory of the system which if not attended generates the blindnesses mentioned above. This makes it hard to explain visual imagery and imagination. Here I summarise our own axiomatic neuromodelling approach that includes visual consciousness and show that it provides an extention to enacted theory while removing the inadequacies.

2   Enacted Vision: A Summary

Specifically, O'Regan and Noë set out to address two puzzles [3]:

" ... how can we see at all if, in order to see we must first perceptually attend to that which we see? ..."

And

" ... if attention is required for perception, why does it seem to us as if we are perceptually aware of the whole detailed visual field when it is quite clear that we do not attend to the whole detail ..."

The first step in their argument is to distinguish between being perceptually sensitive to sensory input and attending to it so as to bring it into awareness. The example given is that we can drive a car without attending to all the details of the road. But should a child suddenly jump into the road, we may well slam on the brakes before actually becoming conscious of what has happened. Noë and O'Reagan call this kind of automatic link between perception and action *the rules of sensorimotor contingency*. These are rules that are built into living systems like the rules for homing in on a visual target might be in a guided missile. The organism is said to have *mastery* of the sensorimotor contingency rules if it can move itself or its sensory apparatus (e.g. eyes) to compensate for the peculiarities of the apparatus itself. For example, the superior colliculus that controls eye movement will cause the eyes to saccade exactly to the right spot in the world where a light might have just flicked on, despite the distortions and blind spots found on the retina.

Attention then, is the process of breaking into and controlling this sensorimotor activity. So one can be perceptually active without being aware, but one cannot be aware without being perceptually active. This solves the first puzzle: attention is a result of the sensorimotor contingency and perception is a kind of access of or 'breaking into' this process even though much of the detail of how 'breaking into' works, is missing. The second puzzle is well illustrated in pictures such as fig. 1.

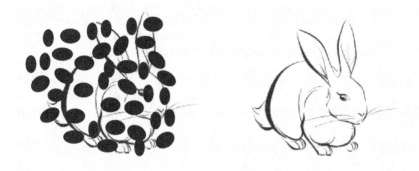

Fig. 1. The rabbit figure on the left feels almost as present as the one on the right despite being behind blobs

In looking at the left version of the picture, although we cannot see the detail, the rabbit appears as an entity. Noë and O'Reagan argue that it is the sensorimotor contingency that gives us the feeling that 'if only I could get out there and remove the spots, I would see the whole rabbit'. And this, they argue, happens when we look around at anytime. Although our fovea is tiny we *know* that once having seen bits of the world we can get back to them at any time. So the world provides us with all the short-term memory we need to achieve this sensation of rich detail. It never needs to be reconstructed in the head: we are just masters of a lot of sensorimotor contingencies which leads us to appreciate the richness that is out there in the world.

Now, is it the case therefore, that having a rich world in our head despite the inaccuracy of our sensory equipment is a 'grand illusion'? Not so, say O'Reagan and Noë. Most of us would not subscribe to the richness being in our heads (illusion) but realise that it's *only* out there (no illusion). The notion of a grand illusion is, therefore, wrong. In a sense it could be said that the world serves as the brain's short term memory. The sensation of richness comes from a sense of ability that if we want to access detail, it's out there for us to get it, no need to keep it in the head.

The major difficulty with this theory is that it does not allow for the occurrence of mental imagery. As this is an aspect of consciousness , I introduce below our axiomatic theory of consciousness particularly in the way that impinges on an understanding of visual awareness and imagination.

3   Axioms of Being Conscious

In this section I summarise the five primary pillars on which the design and functioning of a materially conscious machine can be based. I call these 'axioms' referring to assumed truths that may not be proven, but which is sufficiently evident to support a theory. These are the five primary elements of my sensation which I discover by looking inside myself, that is, by introspecting. The details of this approach are discussed at length in a recent book [4]. The use of introspection becomes justified as, when it comes to modelling inner sensation, behaviour becomes the untrustworthy parameter as the same behaviour can be due to various thoughts. Then 'thought' has to be addressed directly. The scientist therefore is stuck with his or her own inner sensation as the starting point for an enquiry.

3.1 A list of Axioms

The five axioms, the five different kinds of thought which are important to me and I feel need distinguishing are the following:

1.   I feel that I am a part of, but separate from an 'out there' world.
2.   I feel that my perception of the world mingles with feelings of past experience.
3.   My experience of the world is selective and purposeful.
4.   I am thinking ahead all the time in trying to decide what to do next.
5.   I have feelings, emotions and moods that determine what I do.

This is by no means an exhaustive or, indeed, an original list. It is just an initial one, that many others have identified and may be added to in the future. But this is enough for the time being.

3.2   Axiom 1 : The 'Self' in a Real World Out There

To make some headway, let me concentrate on one aspect of being conscious – the visual sensation of *me* being in the middle of an out-there world. Given that we believe in a neural activity which is identical to sensation, how could this happen? Why does the neural activity have this property of a sensation of me in an out-there world rather than some funny buzzes in my head or some sort of a headache?

I am staring at a vast white wall. Suddenly a little black fly lands on the wall, right in front of me. How do I know this? The tiny change in the world out there must have caused a tiny change in the Neural Activity, which is *identical* with my having the sensation of the little fly on the wall. It is possible that if the fly is tiny enough, the transmission across my visual apparatus is just inadequate to change Neural Activity at all. I would then not 'see' the fly on the wall at all. So, it is possible to think in terms of minimal visual events which call for minimal neural activity. That is a minimal visual event is that event which, were it to be smaller or less intense, it would not be sensed at all. Now imagine the fly shifting very rapidly slightly to the right. In slow-motion terms, the fly disappeared from where it was and reappeared somewhere nearby. I am conscious of this change. What this means is that the minimal neural activity for the new position of the fly must also be a new and unique neural activity.

Now, say, another fly, the same size as the last one lands next to the first one, but in the same position where the first one originally started. I now sense the two flies together as a separate visual event, but one which I sense as being composed of the first two. One way of achieving this is for the minimal events and the composed event just to be the firing of neurons in positions that faithfully reproduce the events in the world out there as would occur on a photosensitive surface. It would even mean that vast visual events, a waterfall, fireworks, my dog and the visitor who has just rung my doorbell could be uniquely represented in my neural system. But this would not be sufficient – what's missing is the 'out-thereness' of these neural representations of flies.

Out Thereness: Depiction in the Brain

Perceiving the flies on the wall or waterfalls is different from just seeing these things as if they were photographs. Somehow or other, the neural representations, to be identical to my perceptual sensation, must be identical to this feeling of space I have around me – a space in which I can move and influence things, a space which accommodates me in the centre of it and gives me what I call my point of view.

Looking closely at what happens in the brain gives us a good clue as to how this feeling of space might arise. First, the retina at the back of the eye is not like a photographic plate in one major respect. It only records *accurately* (by neural firing) a very small part of the world out there. There is an area in the centre of the retina called the *fovea* that has a high density of neural sensors (cells that fire in response to the intensity of the light falling on them). If you stretch out your arm in front of you and look at your thumb, the fovea records accurately an area about the size of your thumbnail. The rest of the retina records light patterns, in much less detail, both in colour and shape. This is called the perifovea.

Now, say I am fixating on a fly with my fovea, and another fly lands nearby, the event in the perifovea, will cause my eye to move to the new event to record it accurately. By this time the first event is no longer accurately recorded in the retina, but it is in my sensation. This means that neurons in my visual system beyond the retina must not only receive signals from the fovea, but also of where the fovea is and how it has moved. Without going into details of neuroanatomy here it is well known that such areas exist in the brain. That is, my neural activity for visual consciousness relies as much on what the fovea records as where the fovea is and how it moves.

Not only this, but when objects are closer or farther, this too is recorded as a result of the muscular mechanisms for eye convergence and focus. That is neurons responsible for giving me my sensation receive signals from muscles involve in eye positioning and shape. It is even known that neurons that drive muscles used in touching a seen object or are just preparing to move a finger to touch it broadcast firing signals that influence the firing of neurons that create sensation. No wonder that my visual sensation of the world out there is much richer than a photograph - its neural identity is extraordinarily rich. We have called this inner identity of neural activity a *depiction*. We chose *depiction* to get away from the word *representation* because of the richness that the neural activity implies. A photograph is a representation and, in computing, just symbols could be used to represent objects in the world (F for fly or F2 for another fly). Representations therefore have a functional character about them while I intend *depiction* to mean the full rich material quality that is required for being conscious.

Evidence: Locking

Is all this reliance on depiction just a theory or is there evidence that it actually happens in living conscious organisms? In fact, the evidence is overwhelming and continually being discovered. As I have suggested, depiction occurs because some cells are selected to fire only if muscles are being active in a particular way. In neurology, this selection process is called 'locking'.

Locking was first discovered as 'gaze locking' in an area of the brain called V3A which represents the form of visual stimuli   This was the pioneering work of Galletti and Battaglini from the University of Bologna [5]. They found that certain cells in monkeys would respond to small visual stimuli, but only if the eyes of the monkey were pointing in a particular direction. If the monkey would change its direction of gaze, different cells would respond to the same stimulus.

The same laboratory went on to discover even more evidence of locking. For example, neurons in visual area V6 (devoted to space representation) will only fire if certain arm muscles are engaged in moving the arm in a particular way . Other neurons in another part of the visual system are locked to neck muscle action. The fashion for looking for locked neurons has spread to other laboratories and such neurons have been found in profusion throughout the cerebral cortex (i.e. the part that is deeply implicated in making us conscious).

The Centrality of Axiom 1
The ability to internalise the out-there world is the central feature of consciousness: it is a kind of pivot on which all else depends. We should bear this in mind when considering the other axioms and their implied mechanisms.

3.3   Axiom 2: My Experience of the World Out There

Staying again with visual sensation, it is clear that, if I close my eyes, the visual world does not go away: I can imagine what things look like, that is, what they looked like at some time in the past. The sensation is not quite as vivid as when I am actually looking at something, but there nonetheless.

These 'visions' need not go away when I do open my eyes. Indeed they are part of my visual interaction with the world out there. I often loose my keys. When looking for them under cushions or behind the toaster I form a mental image of what they will look like when I do see them. Should I see a different bunch of keys, the differences between the depiction of these and the mental image are intensely, almost painfully, felt. When seeing a well known face, it is known that I can form a sufficiently appropriate mental image of the person even before my fovea has had a chance to look at every feature. That is, the mental image snaps in.

There is another aspect to these inner sensations: they can construct something we may never have seen or experienced.   Reading Shakespeare's Macbeth, the full impact of Birnam Wood descending on Dunsinane, is generated in our visual sensation even if we have never seen the play.   This is a case where visions are generated by words, but visions could be generated by any of the sensory modalities: the smell of freshly baked bread can trigger scenes from childhood, touching a slimy surface in the dark can create nightmarish visions of unpleasant gutters.

The material implication of these inner visions and memories is, in broad terms, quite simple. In detail it is fascinating and difficult. The broad principle is that of *feedback* or *re-entry* in depictive neural structures.   Having a mental image of something that has happened in the past has a strong material implication: closed information paths in depictive networks must exist which can *sustain* depictive firing patterns: the state of an automaton or state machine. So much for the mechanism of sustaining images, but where does what we imagine come from? How could it be that having seen examples of black dogs and white cats, we could imagine what a white dog or a black cat might look like even though we may never have seen one. The fact that we can do this implies that blackness and whiteness might be depicted and learned in different parts of the mechanism from, say, shape. Indeed, it is well known that, in the brain, different areas of the visual cortex become independently active for colour, shape and motion.

Then whiteness or any other colour-ness, is learned to be a stable depiction and associated with words in one part of the cortex while doggy-ness or catty-ness is learned in another. Then these learned features will be depicted independently if triggered by appropriate words even if the combination has never been seen before.

Finally, if depictions such as colour and shape happen in different parts of the brain, how is it that a black cat, say, *feels* like a single sensation? This is the celebrated *binding problem*.

Unwinding the Binding Problem

All sorts of solutions have been proposed to the binding problem. Crick and Koch, for example, first maintained that a signal with a firing rate of 40 pulses per second links any disparate activities that bind into one sensation [6]. They now prefer to talk of cell assemblies that 'coalesce' into single sensations through long-routed connections [7].

My colleague Barry Dunmall and I have suggested [8] that binding is a direct result of the muscular *locking* that I mentioned earlier in this paper. Going back to the fly on the white wall imagine that the fly could be red or blue. What happens when the fly is red? To simplify the rather complex way that colour and shape are represented in the visual cortex, I shall just call these two areas C and S. Whether the fly is red or blue, it will cause a group of cells to fire in S, and these cells are *locked* by the position of the fly on the wall. The fly, if only S were present, would feel like a blob in a particular out-there position. In C, however, two different groups of neurons would be activated one for the blue fly and the other for a red one. But whether blue or red they would all be locked by the position of the fly on the wall. The fact that this *feels* like a coloured blob in exactly the same place on the wall as the activity in S is due to the fact that, due to locking, the two activities are controlled by where in the world is the event that is causing them. This is the beauty and the cause of richness of the depictive process – the neurons causing a single sensation could be dispersed among different specialised parts of the brain.

Binding in Imagination

Of course, the binding problem applies to the basic depictive process of axiom 1. How does it affect axiom 2: imagination? The depictive areas in which I have suggested feedback creates the ability to reconstruct visual images (say) occur physically beyond the locking process. That is, what is remembered are 'out there' depictions. The only odd thing is that during a proper recall of an out-there events, many depictive areas are required to deliver their memories at once. This process is not perfect. It is quite possible to be in a situation where we remember the shape of, say, a hat that the Queen was wearing in a newsreel of Ascot last week but cannot remember its colour, or vice versa – remember the colour and not the shape.

3.4 Axiom 3: Attention: Out to Get Experience

So far, I have spoken of worlds out there as if the conscious organism just blunders around in them. Nothing is further from the truth. Selecting what we experience in the world and how we think about the world in our imagination, requires some selection mechanisms. This, in neurology and psychology, is called 'attention'.

In recent years attention has advanced in importance as a vital aspect of consciousness. Our tendency to attend to some things and not others determines what eventually enters our consciousness – the topic of this paper. There we shall see that, in vision in particular, specific brain areas such as the 'superior colliculus' are involved in the attentive selection of eye position for the most efficient extraction of meaning from complex images. Suffice it to say here that we have already noted that movement of the fovea contributes to depiction. Attention appears to call for important axiomatic mechanisms: it has been hailed by several investigators as the "Gateway to Consciousness". We return to this in the next section of the paper. For completeness, we now consider the remaining two axioms.

3.5 Axiom 4: Thinking Ahead

Thought is not just a process of having static depictions. It is a highly dynamic process. We are constantly thinking ahead, considering alternatives and, every now and then, deciding what to do next. What are the material implications of this possibility.

It is the simple property of a recursive net that it can remember sequences as well as the stationary patterns we have seen above. As before, the neurons repeat at the output axon the state of the input synapse. It helps to realise that there is always a slight delay between a change in input (say of duration t) and the corresponding change of output.

Say that I am looking at a pencil on my desk and deciding that I want to pick it up. This thought is a sensation of my actually doing it in my head, before I do it for real. My depictive areas are producing a kind of depicted movie in my head in anticipation of the real act. This comes from the fact that the depictive areas can learn appropriate depictive sequences as part of the build-up of experience as a sequence of depictive states. That is, as a child I learn to pick things up by trial and error. When I succeed reliably, my visual, tactile and muscular neurons have, together, learned to go from state to state by the same axiom 2 mechanism that allows them to remain stable in one state. There is very little technical difference between learning sequences and learning single stable states. So thinking ahead has to do with the system running through depictive sequences that are possible from the current state. But if there are many possibilities how are these controlled? What is it to *want* to execute one of the possible plans? This leads to axiom 5.

3.6 Axiom 5: Emotions – The Guardians of Thought

One of the criticisms levelled at those who speak of conscious machines is that there is one element of humanity that machines cannot have: feelings and emotions. I would argue that as these seem to be essential to being a conscious human being they must be essential to a model conscious machine. I would be very suspicious of the value of a machine model of being conscious were it not to have mechanisms that play the role of emotions in living organisms.

In the first instance emotions are related to the evaluation of depictive input. Children not more than a few hours old will show signs of fear (facial expression and a retreating action) if a large object moves towards them. The same occurs if the child is allowed to move freely over a glass surface that appears to stretch over a precipice. The child avoids the precipice and shows signs of fear. On the other hand the child shows contentment on being fed when hungry. So, basic emotions such as fear and pleasure, are neural activities that appear to be pre-wired at birth. They have obvious survival value. Other emotions in this innate group are anger, surprise, disgust and love.

Other emotions and feelings are developed during perceptual life. Feeling hurt after being rebuked or being jealous of the attention someone else is getting are examples of a vast group of such subtle phenomena. On the basis that every scrap of our sensation is due to some neural firing patterns, I would expect such patterns to have distinct characteristics that both adapt to be attached to perceptual depictive events as well as imagined events. As planning proceeds according to the mechanisms of axiom 4, predicted states of the world trigger emotional neural firing which determines which plans are preferred for execution and which might lead to unwanted consequences.

Volition and emotion are areas that have proved to be controversial. Not only does the question of free will have a theological and philosophical theory, but in modern neurology some doubts have arisen as to whether we are in wilful control of all our actions.

4   Axioms and Enacted Vision

The O'Regan and Noë enacted sensorimotor contingency is discovered in several ways in the axiomatic, depictive descriptions set out above. The most obvious place is the mechanism of eye movement that involves the superior colliculus mentioned earlier. It is known that this, in a totally unconscious way, moves the fovea of the eye to places where things are happening (changes, movements, edges and so on ...) which may be detected in the perifovea. But that is not all that causes the eye or, indeed, the head or body to move to bits of world that require attention: a sudden sound, the memory of having left the gas on in the kitchen, needing to check whether what is thought to be a familiar face, has correspondingly familiar features. Further, a strategy that involves memory and planning (axioms 2/4) can constrain foveal attention (e.g the ball rather than the gorilla). Note that here I speak of 'external' attention mechanisms that correspond to sensorimotor contingencies. Whatever this mechanism might be, the results of attending are left in axiom 1 depictive machinery *for a while*.

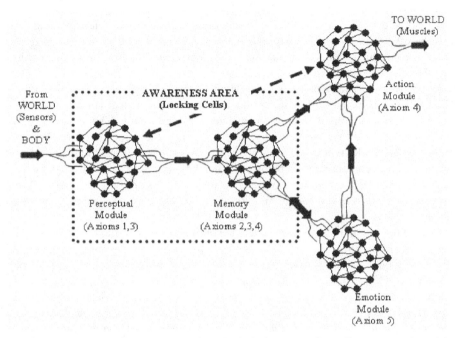

Fig. 2. A minimal architecture with axiomatic/depictive properties. The perceptual module directly depicts sensory input and can be influenced by bodily input such as pain and hunger. The memory module implements non-perceptual thought for planning and recall of experience. The memory and perceptual modules overlap in awareness as they are both locked to either current or remembered world events The emotion module evaluates the 'thoughts' in the memory module and the action module causes the best plan to reach the actions of the organism.

We recall that axiom 1 machinery is depictive by virtue of the fact that it 'knows' (i.e. encodes) the muscular effort that is being exerted in order to achieve a foveal position of the eyes. It is a mass of neurons that 'put things in place', but not for any length of time. It may be best to refer to fig. 2.   The perceptual module is active all the time and keeps a fading trace of experience which is accessible for a while, but does not necessarily lay down retrievable memories in the memory module.

It is possible then to interpret the 'breaking in' through attention as a facilitation of the transfer of depictions from the perceptual module (axiom 1) to the memory module (axiom 2) where it will be a much paler version of what may briefly have been accurately depicted in the perceptual module, but where it will have a much more enduring and accessible existence.   Then, according to axiom 3, the true function of attention is to control this facilitation. This requires a great deal more research and thought as to how such mechanisms work in the brain or even how they might work in a robot. However, it provides a basis for incorporating the ideas of sensorimotor contingencies into a broader framework that does not exclude the consciousness of mental imagery. This may be focussed as follows.

4.1   Axiomatic Puzzle Solving

The First Puzzle: Attention Without Seeing?
In this section we show how the axioms deal with the two puzzles outlined by O'Reagan and Noë. First one needs to address how it is that we can we see at all if, in order to see we must first perceptually attend to that which we see?

As stressed above, the key axiom here is 3 – attention. Attention is easily said but it is a complex concept and it may be found at many levels. First, as said above, the eye-moving superior colliculus can be influenced from a variety of sources some of which can be active ahead of depiction in axiom 1 and 2 mechanisms. It is quite true that in order to see, the basest mechanisms must be at work. As mentioned earlier, the effects of change, motion, edges are all automatic and pre-depictive. However, without them, according to axiom 1, depiction cannot happen. Second, deeper strategies for seeing are then triggered by the developing depiction. For example when a face is flashed suddenly on a previously blank screen, the foveal gaze will automatically be drawn to areas with much detail, such as an eye or the corner of a mouth. This will then be depicted causing the strategy of looking for base features to be switched to a higher level. Further saccades to where one might expect to find important   features, such as the other eye or the mouth become controlled from Axiom 2 mechanisms which are perceived even if the drive to find facial features may be somewhat automatic – like driving. There are even higher levels of search, for example, were a pair of twins distinguished by a little mole, having decided I am looking at one of the two, the search for the mole becomes a conscious affair driven strongly by the axiom 2 machinery.

Even ambiguous figures such as the well known "duck/rabbit", depend on hypothesis generation in Axiom 2 mechanisms (Fig. 3) . Hypothesis, 'it's a duck' causes the eyes to choose switching the gaze between the eye of the image and its beak with the occasional saccade to the wiggle at the back of the head. Should the hypothesis be, 'it's a rabbit' the saccades become more frequent from eye to wiggle (seen as a mouth now) with the odd glance at the 'ears'. The reason this is an ambiguous illusion is that the low level attention triggers a hypothesis for a higher level interpretation (duck or rabbit) which then controls the higher level attention to execute a defined set of saccades.

Fig. 3. Duck or Rabbit?

But a tiny perturbation can switch the whole system to settle into the alternative set of saccades. So the answer to the first puzzle is that *perceptual* (i.e. conscious) attention is *not* necessary to begin to build up a depiction: the process of base attention is innately automatic. Then as the depiction is being built, and perception is developing, perceptual attention sets in, which allows the developing depiction in axiom 1 mechanisms to allow hypotheses to emerge in axiom 2 memory mechanisms. I find it hard to describe this as a process of 'breaking in', more a question of the sensorimotor contingency stimulating depictive knowledge.

The Second Puzzle: Why Are We Unaware of Not Attending to Input?
The second peculiarity that is addressed by O'Regan and Noë is that if attention is required for perception, why does it seem to us as if we are perceptually aware of the whole detailed visual field when it is quite clear that we do not attend to the whole detail?

The second attentional mechanism mentioned above, where the depictive mechanism (ax. 2 machinery) drives attention to fill important gaps in depiction, clearly stops at some point where *sufficient* detail is present in the depiction. This is pretty rich and satisfying even if all the available detail may not be included. In fact this theory explains why we are not so bothered by the black blobs over the rabbit and why the 'presence' of the rabbit (fig. 1) is similar for the left and right images. The detail in each of the images causes very similar attention strategies to be unleashed, and these are due to the rabbit rather than the blobs. As indicated by the axiomatic/depictive theory it's the interplay between the mechanisms of the fist three axioms that give us the sense of a rich world. It may not be complete, but what is there is sufficient for our needs and therefore satisfying even if not all gorillas are accounted for or, helpfully, if blobs don't get in the way of what really draws our attention.

5 Current Research: The Necker Cube

A simple and well-known ambiguous figure is the Necker cube shown in fig. 4. The peculiarity of this figure is that the same sensory input gives rise to two sensations: one where X appears to be in front of Y and the other with Y in front of X. It turns out that this simple 'illusion' has a unique, 170-year history of attempts at explanation [9] which range over the psychophysical, the neurological and the cognitive. The significance of this in models that involve axiomatic approaches to enacted vision is that it points to an ambiguity in the unconscious, sensorimotor contigency mechanisms and provides cues as to how this enters conscious perception [10].

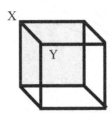

Fig. 4. The Necker cube looks like a wire frame that sometimes has point X in front and sometimes point Y

Experiments show that while fixing eye gaze on strategic corners of the cube has some effect on the periods spent in one of the two sensations it is impossible consciously to stop the reversals altogether. This indicates that it is necessary to elaborate the structure of fig. 4 to distinguish between dorsal and ventral processing streams and check hypotheses about how the dorsal, through having direct unconscious access to motor cortices (action module) that would drive a limb to touch the frame (sensorimotor contingency) also impacts on the ventral, conscious perception of the frame (perception and imagination modules). This is current work which should throw more light on enacted vision.

6   Conclusion: A New Generation of Computer Vision Systems?

Enacted vision ideas herald a new age in both the understanding of vision in living organisms and the design of artificial vision systems, particularly the design of visually competent robots. It is the contention of this paper that in its initial formulation by O'Regan and Noë, the existence of an independent sensorimotor contingency is too severe, and should be treated alongside models such as the depictive/axiomatic scheme summarised in this paper. In terms of visually driven robot design this is likely to improve the distinction between inbuilt or learned reactive mechanisms (the sensorimotor contingency) and acquired experience, that is the visual consciousness of the system.

References

1. Simons, D. J. and Chabris. C. F., Gorillas in our midst: sustained inattentional blindness for dynamic events. *Perception* 28(9) (1999) 1059-1074.
2. O'Reagan, J. K. and Noë, A., A sensorimotor account of vision and visual consciousness. *Brain and Behavioural Sciences,* 24(5) (2001).
3. Noë, A. and O'Reagan, J. K. (2000) Perception, Attention and the Grand Illusion, *Psyche,* 6(15).
4. Aleksander I.: *The World in my Mind, My Mind in the World,* Exeter, Imprint Academic (2005)
5. Galletti, C. and Battaglini, P.: Gaze-Dependent Visual Neurons in Area V3A of Monkey Prestriate Cortex. *Journal of Neuroscience,* **6**, (1989) 1112-1125.
6. Crick F and Koch C.: *Consciousness and Neuroscience.* Cereb Cortex. Mar;8(2): (1998) 97-107.
7. Crick F and Koch C.: A framework for consciousness. *Nature Neuroscience* 6, (2003) 119 – 126.
8. Aleksander, I and Dunmall, B.: An extension to the hypothesis of the asynchrony of visual consciousness. Proc Royal Soc, London, **267**, Jan 22, (2000) 197 – 200
9. Toppino. T. C. and Long, G. M.: Enduring Interest in Perceptual Ambiguity: Alternating Views of Reversible Figures, *Psy Bull,* **130**, 5, (2004)748 – 768.
10. Aleksander, I., Morton, H. B. and Witkowski, C. M.: Necker Flips in Time as an Indication of the Mechanisms of Visual Consciousness. *ASSC9,* Pasadena (2005)

Mind as an Anticipatory Device:
For a Theory of Expectations

Cristiano Castelfranchi

Institute for Cognitive Sciences and Technologies - CNR[*]

'More geometrico demonstrata'
Spinoza

Abstract. This work is about the central role of "expectations" in mental life and in purposive action. We will present a Cognitive Anatomy of expectations, their reduction in terms of more elementary ingredients: beliefs and goals. Moreover, those ingredients will be considered in their 'quantitative' dimension: the value of the Goal, the strength of the Beliefs. We will base several predictions on this analytical decomposition, and sketch a theory of hope, fear, frustration, disappointment, and relief, strictly derived from the analysis of expectations. Eventually, we will discuss how can we capture the global subjective character of such mental states that we have decomposed; how to account for their gestaltic nature.

1 Premise: The Anticipatory Nature of Mind

Basically mind is for "anticipation" [1], or – more precisely – for building and working upon "anticipatory representations" [2] [3] [4]. A real "mental" activity and representation starts to be there when the organism is able to endogenously (not as the output of current perceptual stimuli) produce an internal perceptual representation of the world (simulation of perception). Which is the origin and the use of such strange ability? There are several uses or functions but many (if not all) of them are anticipatory. For example, the organism can generate the internal "image" for matching it against perceptual inputs while actively searching for a given object or stimulus while exploring an environment; or can use it as prediction of the stimulus that will probably arrive, as in active 'recognition'. It can use the perceptual expectation like in Anticipatory Classifiers, for implicitly monitoring the 'success' of the rule-based, reactive behavior, and as criteria for reinforcing or not the rule. But it can also entertain a mental representation of the current word just for working on it, modifying this representation for virtually 'exploring' possible actions, events, results: "what will/would happens if…?".

This precisely is "intelligence": not just the capacity to exhibit complex adaptive behaviors (like in social insects or in spiders), nor the capacity to solve problems

---

[*] European Projects *MindRaces* N°511931- EC's 6th Framework Programme, IST priority-Unit: Cognitive Systems http://www.mindraces.org/; & European HUMAINE network http://emotion-research.net/.

(for example by stupid and blind trial and errors!), but the capacity to solve a problem by working on an internal representation of the problem, by acting upon 'images' with simulated actions, or on 'mental models' or 'symbolic representations' by mental actions, transformations ('reasoning'), before performing the actions in the world. The architect designs in her mind (and on a piece of paper) her building before building it; this is not the case of a spider although what it will build will be very complex (and - for us - beautiful).

Those mental representations that characterize the mind and the mental work are mainly for anticipation: before the stimulus to be matched (prediction), before the action to be executed (project), etc. This means that the ability that characterizes and defines a "mind" is that of building representations of the non-existent, of what is not currently (yet) "true", perceivable.

This clearly builds upon memory, that is the re-evocable traces of previously perceived scenes; usually is just past "experience" evoked and projected on the future. But this is only the origin. A fully developed mind is able to build never-seen scenes, new possible combinations of world elements never perceived; it is a real building and creation (by simulation) not just memory retrieval.

Moreover, the use of such internally and autonomously generated representations of the world is not only "epistemic", for knowledge of the past, the present, the future: that is memory, perception, prediction and expectations. Those representations can have a radically different function: they can have motivational, axiological, or deontic nature; saying us not how the world is, was, will be; but how the world should be, how the organism would like the world to be. That is these representations can be used as goals driving the behavior. While an adaptive organism tends to adjust its epistemic representations (knowledge; beliefs) to the "reality", to make their fidelity to the world as much as possible; on the opposite an effective goal-directed system try to adjust the "objective" external world to its endogenous representation! To change the world (through the "action" which in fact is goal-directed behavior) and make it the more close as possible to its internally creative mental picture (that could be a picture of something never already existing)! This really is a "mind": the presupposition for hallucinations, delirium, desires, and utopias.

Like "signs" are really signs when they can be used for deception and lie, not when they just are the non-autonomous index of reality, propagating from it; analogously, mental representations (that in fact - as any "representation" - are complex "signs") are really there were they can be false and independently generated from reality. The use of this is not only prediction (by definition the future is currently not-true) but also more importantly for the purposive character of the behavior, for internal explicit goal representation. [1]

---

[1] In this perspective the "homeostatic" view of goals and of their cybernetic, feed-back machinery is a bit misleading. "Homeo-stasys" gives the idea of maintaining and restoring an existing state that can be disturbed; but in fact the cybernetic model and the notion of goal refer also to the instauration of states that have never been there! This is why the notion of "purposive" behavior is much better, although definitely founded on the same model.

1.1 Steps in Anticipation: Anticipatory Behaviors vs. Anticipatory Representations

Any purposive behavior (in strict sense), any goal-directed system is necessarily anticipatory, since it is driven by the representation of the goal-state (set-point) and activated by its mismatch with the current state of the world [5] [6]. But not any anticipatory behavior, and even not necessarily any behavior based on anticipatory representations is goal-directed [2].

As for the claim relative to the fact that not any anticipatory behavior [7] is based on explicit cognitive representations of future relevant/concerning events, that is on expectations, one should consider many instances of 'implicit' or merely behavioral anticipation or preparation, where the agent simply 'reacts' to a stimulus with a behavioral response (conditioned/learned or unconditioned/inborn) but in fact the response is functional, apt to some incoming event. The stimulus is some sort of 'precursory sign' and the response in fact is preparatory to the 'announced' event:

Precursory stimulus $\Rightarrow$ **Preparatory behavior** $\Rightarrow$ **Event**
(e.g. noise)   (e.g. jump)   (e.g. approaching predator)

In this case there is no explicit 'mental' representation of the future event. It is just a case of what we propose to call 'merely anticipatory behavior'. A Stimulus St is exploited (thanks to selection or learning) as the precursor and the 'sign' of a following event Ev, and it is adaptive for the organism to respond immediately to St with a behavior which in fact is just the 'preparation' to the forthcoming Ev; the advantage is that the organism is 'ready', 'prepared to' Ev. But this does not require a 'mental' anticipated explicit representation of Ev, that is the prediction, or better the 'expectation' that Ev will occur.

1.1.1 Surprise

The first level of cognitive anticipation is the retrieval from memory of previous perceptual experience to be compared with the incoming perceptual input (some sort of procedural 'prediction'). The use of this perceptual anticipation is multiple.

On the one side it is applied not only to action but also to the processes of the world and it is for monitoring the course of the events. Its function seems to be detecting unusual events that might require additional epistemic processing (for example attention) or a fast reaction. One might claim that even before this clearly any form of pattern matching (where the pattern is either inborn or learned) is an *implicit* form of anticipation since it should be based on past experience and -more importantly- should fit some features of the environment, should be adapted to it, thus implicitly expecting and predicting given features in the environment [8]. Beyond this, there are true predictions activated by premonitory signs that 'announce' a given event.

The function of this systematic monitoring of the world is also of continuously updating and readjusting the world representation, to see whether predictions are correct and pertinent and the world can be 'assimilated' to current schemata or if it is the case to have some 'accommodation' of them (Piaget).

On the other side, the internal simulation of the next percept is fundamental for teleonomic behavior; during the action it is crucial to compare the perceptual feedback (both proprioceptive and external) with some representation of the expected state of the body and of the world. Indeed, we can argue that whenever an agent executes an action there is at least an automatic not intentional perceptive test on the success of the action. This idea is supported from empirical research and is a building block in neuro-psychology inspired computational models of action control (see [9] for a review): the importance of sensory feedback for the adjustment of the goal-directed motor behaviour in phase of action execution. Only this match or mismatch (after the test) can say to the agent if there is something wrong. [10]

This kinds of sensory-motor expectations already allows some form of 'surprise', the most peripheral one, just due to perceptual mismatch; a first-hand surprise. **'Surprise'** is the automatic reaction to a mismatch. It is:

- a (felt) reaction/response
- of alert and arousal
- due to an inconsistency (mismatch, non-assimilation, lack of integration) between incoming information and our previous knowledge, in particular an actual prediction or a potential prediction;
- invoking and mobilizing resources at disposal of an activity for a better epistemic processing of this 'strange' information (attention, search, belief revision, etc.),
- aimed at solving the inconsistency,
- and at preventing possible dangers (the reason for the alarm) due to a lack of predictability and to a wrong anticipation.

The deeper and slower forms of surprise are due to symbolic representations of expected events, and to the process of information integration with previous long-term knowledge. This is surprise due to *implausibility*, un-believability of the new information. [11]

In this work we mainly focus on true predictions (based on inference, reasoning, mental models) (although they can also be mental 'images' in sensory format), and on their combination with explicit goals to produce the specific mental object called 'Expectation'.

Low level 'predictions' are based on some form of 'statistical' learning, on frequency and regular sequences, on judgment of normality in direct perceptual experience, on the strength of associative links and on the probability of activation [12].

High level predictions have many different sources: from analogy ("The first time he was very elegant, I think that he will be well dressed") and, in general, inferences and reasoning ("He is Italian thus he will love pasta"), to natural laws, and – in social domain - to norms, roles, conventions, habits, scripts ("He will not do so; here it is prohibited"), or to "Theory of Mind" ("He hate John, so he will try to..."; "He decided to go in vacation, so he will not be here on Monday").

1.1.2 Proto-Expectations

As for anticipatory-representation-based behaviors that are not strictly goal-directed (intention like) let us briefly discuss also a weaker and more primitive form of 'expectation'; the anticipatory representation of the result of the action in 'Anticipatory Classifiers' (AC) [13] [7]. In our interpretation, they are not simply 'predictions'. They represent a forerunner of true Expectations because the agent is not unconcerned, but it actively checks whether the prediction is true, because the result is highly relevant, since it satisfies (or non-satisfies) a drive, and provides a reward. But on the other side, for us – in their basic form- they can (and should) be distinguished from true 'goal' in the classical 'purposive behavior' sense [5] [6].

As we just said Expectations should be distinguished from various forms of mere anticipation and of behavioral preparation. These are the implicit and procedural forerunners of true cognitive expectations. These are pseudo-expectations: the agent behaves "as if" it had an expectation. Consider for example unconditioned salivation in Pavlov experiments. This is just a preparatory reaction for eating. It is based on a current stimulus eliciting a response that is useful (a condition) for a future behavior: preparation. Consider automatic coordination (either inborn or learned) in swallowing or walking, or in dodging a flying rock. Finally, consider our implicit and procedural trust that the ground will not sink under our feet, or that water is liquid, and snow cold, etc. In some case there is no representation at all; but simply a default behavior or procedure: the expectation is the lack of special control (ex, of the ground).

However, in other cases there is the *anticipatory representation* internally generated, simulated, of a sensation (perceptual input) which will be compared with the actual one. This is very close to an Expectation (at least to its Prediction component); however, there is no necessarily an explicit real Goal initiating the process, searching for the action, and a purposive-behavior feedback, for monitoring and adjusting the action. A simple AC is enough. An AC can just remain a production rule, a classifier, something close to a stimulus-response link, that has also (in the right part) some representation of the predicted/learned result.

Cond ==> Act + ExpResult

This representation is compared against the actual result: if it matches (correct expectation) the links (between Cond and Act and between Act and ExpResult) will be reinforced; if it does not match (wrong prediction) the rule will be weakened.

We assume that this (which for us too is the device underlying Skinner's 'instrumental learning' [1]) in not necessarily yet 'purposive behavior' and that the expected result (ExpResult) is not really a Goal (like in the TOTE model). The behavior is data/input driven, rule-based, not explicitly 'purposive', not top-down elicited and guided by the representation of its Goal, and cannot be creative and new, cannot start a problem-solving activity [2].

In this paper we will model only explicit anticipatory representations, and in particular Expectations in strong sense, and their role in a goal-directed mind and intentional behavior. We will present a *Cognitive Anatomy* of Expectations, their reduction in terms of more elementary ingredients: beliefs and goals; and their 'strength'. We will base several predictions on this analytical decomposition. We will present a theory of hope, worries, frustration, disappointment, relief, ready for artificial creature: could robots and software agents move from low level form of anticipation, surprise, etc. to explicit expectations and related mental states?

Let us start by disentangling simple predictions from true expectations.

2 Cognitive Anatomy of Expectations

2.1 Prediction vs. Expectation

'Expectation' is not synonymous of 'prediction' or 'forecast'; they have a common semantic core (a belief – more or less certain [2]– about the future [3]) and thus a partially overlapping extension. We consider a forecast [3] [4] as a mere belief about a future state of the world and we distinguish it from a simple 'hypothesis'. The difference is in term of degree of certainty: a hypothesis may involve the belief that future p is possible while in a forecast the belief that future p is probable. A forecast implies that the chance threshold has been exceeded (domain of probability). According to the agent's past experience or knowledge of physical or social rules and laws p should happen (in an epistemic sense). [4]

Putting aside the degree of confidence (we need a general term covering weak and strong predictions), one might say that EXPECTATION ➔ PREDICTION, or better that both of them imply a representation of a possible future: a possible Belief about the future. But they also have different features. The primary difference is that in 'expectation' (but not necessarily and conceptually in 'prediction') there is also a motivational component; some Goal of the subject X is involved. X is 'concerned': she didn't just 'predict' and be indifferent to the event or mindless. Let's carefully analyze this motivational and active component.

2.1.1 Epistemic Goals and Activity

First of all, X has the Goal to know whether the predicted event or state really happens (epistemic goal). She is 'waiting for' this; at least for curiosity. This concept of 'waiting for' and of 'looking for' is necessarily related to the notion of expecting and expectation, but not to the notion of prediction.

Either X is actively monitoring what is happening and comparing the incoming information (for example perception) to the internal mental representation; or X is doing this cyclically and regularly; or X will in any case at the moment of the future event or state compare what happens with her prediction (epistemic actions) [14] [15]. Because in any case she has the Goal to know whether the world actually is as anticipated, and if the prediction was correct. Schematically [5]:

---

[2] In some Dictionary 'Expectation' is defined as: "1. a *confident* belief or *strong hope* that a particular event will happen" (Encarta® World English Dictionary © 1999 Microsoft Corporation). Notice also the positive connotation of the expected event (hope), while in fact also 'negative or bad' expectations are possible (worries). Notice also the second definition: "2. a mental image of something expected, often compared to its reality" where both the nature of an explicit mental representation, and the monitoring/epistemic activity are correctly identified.

[3] Also predictions and expectations about the past are possible but only in the sense that one will come in the future to know something about the past and has some hypothesis and wish on that.

[4] Consider for example the definition of 'forecasting': "to predict or work out something that is likely to happen…" (Encarta® World English Dictionary © 1999 Microsoft Corporation.)

[5] We will not use here a logical formalization; we will just use a self-explanatory and synthetic notation, useful for a schematic characterization of different combinations of beliefs and goals. For a real formalization of some of these mental attitudes see [4].

Expectation x p →

Bel x at t' that p at t'' (where t'' > t')

Goal x from t' to t''' KnowWhether x p or Not p at t'' (t''' ≥ t'')

This really is 'expecting' and the true 'expectation'.

2.1.2 Content Goals

This Epistemic/monitoring Goal is combined with Goals about p: the agent's need, desire, or 'intention that' the world should realize. The Goal that p is true (that is the Goal that p) or the Goal that Not p. This is really why and in which sense X is 'concerned' and not indifferent, and also why she is monitoring the world. She is an agent with interests, desires, needs, objectives on the world, not just a predictor. This is also why computers, that already make predictions, do not have expectations[6].

When the agent has a goal opposite to her prediction, she has a 'negative expectation'; when the agent has a goal equal to her prediction she has a 'positive expectation' (see § 3.1). To be true a Goal equal to the prediction in Expectation is always there, although frequently quite weak and secondary relatively to the main concern. In fact, when X predicts that p and monitors the world to know whether actually p, she has also the Goal that p, just in order to not disconfirm her prediction, and to confirm to be a good predictor, to feel that the world is predictable and have a sense of 'control'. (see § 3.2). We are referring to *predictability*, that is, the cognitive component of self-efficacy [16]: the need to anticipate future events and the consequent need to find such anticipation validated by facts. This need for prediction is functional in humans in order to avoid anxiety, disorientation and distress. Cooper and Fazio [17] have experimentally proved that people act in order to find their forecasts (predictions) validated by facts and feel distressed by invalidation.

3   Defining Expectations

In sum, Expectations are axiological anticipatory mental representations, endowed with Valence: they are positive or negative or ambivalent or neutral; but in any case they are *evaluated against some concern, drive, motive, goal of the agent*.

In expectations we have to distinguish two components:

- On the one side, there is a mental anticipatory representation, the belief about a future state or event, the "mental anticipation" of the fact, what we might also call the pre-vision (to for-see).

The format of this belief or pre-vision can be either propositional or imagery (or mental model of); this does not matter. Here just the function is pertinent.

- On the other side, as we just argued, there is a co-referent Goal (wish, desire, intention, or any other motivational explicit representation).

---

[6] For example, computers make weather 'forecasts' but it would be strange to say that they 'have expectations' about the weather. Currently they are 'unconcerned'.

Given the resulting *amalgam* these representations of the future are charged of value, their intention or content has a 'valence': it is positive, or negative, and so on.

- Either, the expectation entails a cognitive evaluation [18].

  In fact, since the realization of p is coinciding with a goal, it is "good"; while if the belief is the opposite of the goal, it implies a belief that the outcome of the world will be 'bad'.

- Or the expectation produces an implicit, intuitive appraisal, simply by activating associated affective responses or somatic markers [18]; or both;
- Or the expected result will produce a *reward* for the agent, and – although not strictly driving its behavior, it is positive for it since it will satisfy a drive and reinforce the behavior.[7]

We analyze here only the Expectations in a strong sense, with an explicit Goal; but we mentioned Expectations in those forms of reactive, rule-based behaviors, first in order to stress how the notion of Expectation always involves the idea of a *valence* and of the agent being concerned and monitoring the world; second, to give an idea of more elementary and forerunner forms of this construct.

3.1 Positive and Negative Expectations

Expectation can be:

- **positive** (goal conformable): $(\text{Bel } x \, p^{t'})^{t<t'}$ & $(\text{Goal } x \, p^{t'})$
- **negative** (goal opposite): $(\text{Bel } x \, p^{t'})^{t<t'}$ & $(\text{Goal } x \, \neg p^{t'})$
- **neutral:** $(\text{Bel } x \, p^{t'})^{t<t'}$ & $\neg(\text{Goal } x \, p^{t'})$ & $\neg(\text{Goal } x \, \neg p^{t'})$
- **ambivalent:** $(\text{Bel } x \, p^{t'})^{t<t'}$ & $(\text{Goal } x \, p^{t'})$ & $(\text{Goal } x \, \neg p^{t'})$

3.2 To Be Happy or to Be a Good Predictor?

To be more subtle, given the Epistemic Goal that we have postulated in any true Expectation, one might say that in negative expectations always there is a minor conflict, since X on the one side desires, wishes that p [G1: (Goal x p)], but since she is induced (by some evidence or experience) to forecast that Not p, she also has the opposite goal [G2: (Goal x ¬p)]. However, this goal usually is not so relevant as the first objective, since it is just in order to confirm X to be a good predictor or that the world is predictable enough; it is just a by-product of control mechanisms and meta-goals. If the negative expectations result to be wrong, X is happy as for G1, but G2 is frustrated. Vice versa, if the negative expectation has been right, X is unhappy as for G1, but can have some 'comfort' because at least she is a good predictor, expert of the world. In positive expectations, since the G1 and G2 converge (that is X has the Goal that p both for intrinsic reasons, and for confirming her prediction and competence), when the prediction is wrong the frustration is appraised without compensation.

---

[7] We mention this because it is the case of proto-expectations or expectations in 'Anticipatory-Classifiers' based behaviors, strictly conceived as reactive (not really goal-driven) behaviors, but based on anticipatory representation of the outcomes.

4 Expectations and Intentional (Goal-Driven) Behavior

Intentional and in general goal-driven action requires and implies Expectations in strict sense, but not the other way around. Expectations are broader that intentional (or goal-directed) actions, they are not necessarily related to action; since even goals are not necessarily related to action.[8] First of all, there are Expectations also for goals we are not actively pursuing. Second, not all goals imply expectations. Inactive goals, or already realized goals, or discarded goals do not bring any expectation.

4.1 Expectation Without Intention and Pragmatic Action

Only active and non-realized goals build Expectations. This covers two kinds of goals:

A) Active achievement goals [9]: goals to be achieved by the subject's action; to be brought about; it is not simply a matter of waiting for them.

B) Self-realizing achievement goals; the agent has nothing to do for achieving them (X has just to wait) since they are realized by other agents and she can just delegate [19] this realization to them. The delegated 'agent' can either be "nature" and some natural process, and usually X can do nothing at all because the desired state only depends on the world ("tomorrow be a sunny day"; "to grow and become a woman"); or can be a social agent Y like X, acting in a common world. For example, Y stops the bus as desired by X, and X relies on this.

Having such a goal may perfectly produce an Expectation (positive or negative) when there also is a prediction about the desired event. X is just expecting, while doing nothing for realizing the Goal, but doing something for monitoring the world. If I wish that tomorrow will be sunny (since I plan for a trip in the country) and I believe it (positive expectation: hope), I can do nothing for it being sunny, but when I wake up in the morning I check whether it is sunny or not. Let's call these 'passive expectation' while calling 'active expectations' those related to intentional pragmatic actions and active pursuit of the Goal. Obviously a passive expectation can become an active one during the evolution of the events.

4.2 Expectations in Intentions

As we said, no Intention is possible without Expectation, but this is not a new irreducible primitive, to be added for example in the BDI (Beliefs, Desires, Intentions) framework [20] [21]. It can and must be recollected to beliefs and goals. And it is a molecule, not a set of atoms; a *mixed* attitude: in part epistemic, in part

---

[8] Although we are pushed – especially in English – to conceive 'goals' as 'objectives', 'targets' of some *action*.

[9] For a complete analysis we should also take into account the distinction between *achievement* and *maintenance* goals (see [19]).

motivational.[10] In fact in order to deliberate to act and to commit to a given course of action [23] one should believe a lot of things (that it is to be preferred, that is not self-realizing or already realized, to have a plan, to be able and in condition for executing the actions, etc.). Among those beliefs supporting intentions [24] some crucial ones are the beliefs about the expected effects of the actions (that motivated its choice) and the expected achievement. One cannot intend to do action α in order to achieve p if she does not believe that after action α is executed p will be true. Thus any Intention presupposes and entails a 'positive' Expectation.

More precisely, also a *weak* positive expectation is compatible with intentional behavior. At least one has not to believe that $\neg$p; otherwise her act would be completely irrational (subjectively useless). Thus there is a Weak Expectation, when X has the Goal (and in this case the Intention) that p and does not believes that not p in the future: $\neg \, (\text{Bel } x \neg (p^{t'}))^{t<t'}$ & $(\text{Goal } x \, p^{t'})$;

X is 'attempting', intentionally trying to realize p.

In any case in intentional action it is excluded a negative certain expectation

$$(\text{Bel } x \neg (p^{t'}))^{t<t'} \, \& \, (\text{Goal } x \, p^{t'})$$

We mean: acting with the certainty to fail. It would be fully irrational.

5   The Quantitative Aspects of Mental Attitudes and of Their Emergent Configurations

As we have just seen, decomposing in terms of beliefs and goals is not enough. We need 'quantitative' parameters. Frustration and pain have an *intensity*, can be more or less severe; the same holds for surprise, disappointment, relief, hope, joy, ... Since they are clearly related with what the agent believes, expects, likes, pursues, can we account for those dimensions on the basis of our (de)composition of those mental states, and of the basic epistemic and motivational representations? We claim so.

Given the two basic ingredients of any Expectation (as we defined it as different from simple forecast or prediction) Beliefs + Goals, we postulate that:

P1: Beliefs & Goals have specific quantitative dimensions; that are basically independent from each other.

Beliefs have strength, a degree of subjective certainty; the subject is more or less sure and committed about their content [25].

Goals have a value, a subjective importance for the agent.

This gives us four extreme conditions (but in fact those variations are continuous and one should model precisely this continuity):

---

[10] In AI there have been other attempt to insert Expectations among the necessary mental ingredients of a BDI like agent [22]. The difference is not only that we derive several "psychological" assumptions and consequences from our model, but also that we do not introduce Expectations as an additional primitive. We prefer to build these mental states on former ingredients (beliefs and goals/intentions) in order to have mental states that preserve both properties, epistemic and conative. Expectations have a specific functional role in practical reasoning that is better understood when those mental states are defined in a compositional fashion.

		BELIEF	
		high credibility (pretty sure)	**low credibility** (perhaps)
GOAL	**high value** (very important)	**1**	**2**
	low value (marginal)	**3**	**4**

To simplify, we may have very important goals combined with uncertain predictions; pretty sure forecasts for not very relevant objectives; etc.

Thus, we should explicitly represent these dimensions of Goals and Beliefs:

$$\text{Bel}^{\%} \; x\, p^t; \qquad \text{Goal}^{\%} \; x\, p^t$$

Where % in Goals represents their subjective importance or value; while in Beliefs % represents their subjective credibility, their certainty.

An Expectation (putting aside the Epistemic Goal) will be like this:

$$\boxed{\text{Bel}^{\%} \; x\, p^t \;\&\; \text{Goal}^{\%} \; x\, [\neg]\, p^t}$$

The subjective *quality* of those "configurations" or macro-attitudes will be very different precisely depending on those parameters. Also the effects of the invalidation of an expectation are very different depending on:

a) the positive or negative character of the expectation;
b) the strengths of the components. (See § 6.)

We also postulate that:

> **P2:** The dynamics and the degree of the emergent configuration, of the Macro-attitude are strictly function of the dynamics and strength of its micro-components.

For example anxiety will probably be greater in box 2 than in 1, inferior in 4, nothing in 3. Box 2 (when the expectation is 'positive') produces an intense hope; and so on. Let us characterize a bit some of these emergent macro-attitudes.

5.1 Hope and Fear

'Hope' is in our account [3] [4] a peculiar kind of 'positive expectation' *where the goal is rather relevant for the subject while the expectation (more precisely the prediction) is not sure at all but rather weak and uncertain.*

$$\boxed{\text{Bel}^{\textbf{low}} \; x\, p^t \;\&\; \text{Goal}^{\textbf{high}} \; x\, p^t}$$

We may also have – it is true - 'strong hope' but we explicitly call it 'strong' precisely because usually 'hope' implies *low* confidence and some anxiety and worry. In any case, 'hope' (like explicit 'trust') can never really be subjectively 'certain' and absolutely confident. Hope implies uncertainty.

Correspondingly one might characterize being afraid, 'fear', as an expectation of something bad, i.e. against our wishes:

$$\text{Bel}^{\%} \times p^t \,\&\, \text{Goal}^{\%} \times \neg p^t$$

but it seems that there can be 'fear' at any degree of certainty and of importance.[11]

Of course, these representations are seriously incomplete. We are ignoring their 'affective' and 'felt' component, which is definitely crucial. We are just providing their cognitive skeleton [26].

5.2 Expecting Artificial-Agents

One reason for such a quite abstract, essential (and also incomplete) analysis is that this can be formalized and implemented for artificial creatures. Computers and robots can have different kinds of Expectations: low level perceptual expectations for monitoring the world; proto-intentions for monitoring the action and reinforcing it by learning; and high level explicit expectations. They are in fact able of making predictions on the physical world and on the other (also human) agents. They can do this on various bases (from inference and analogy to statistical learning, from laws and norms to mind reading and plan recognition) as we do; and they can have true 'purposive' behavior, intentional actions guided by pre-represented goals. Thus, they can entertain true Expectations. It would be necessary to also represent and use the strength and credibility of Beliefs (based on sources and evidences) [24] and the value of the Goals (on which preferences and choices should be based). Given this and various kinds of Epistemic actions, one might model surprise, disappointment, relief, hope, fear, etc. in robots and software agents.

Which should be the advantage of having machines anxious like us?

Seriously speaking, we believe that these reactions (although unfelt and incomplete) would be very adaptive and useful for learning, for reacting, for interacting with the user and with other agents. (See § 8.)

5.3 Analytical Decomposition and the Gestalt Character of Mental Attitudes

Moreover, a hard problem for symbolic (and analytic) cognitive science deserves to be underlined: *the mental Gestalt problem*. Disappointment, expectation, relief, etc.

---

[11] To characterize *fear* another component would be very relevant: the goal of avoiding the foreseen danger; that is, the goal of Doing something such that Not p. This is a goal activated while feeling fear; fear 'conative' and 'impulsive' aspect. But it is also a component of a complete fear mental state, not just a follower or a consequence of fear. This goal can be a quite specified action (motor reaction) (a cry; the impulse to escape; etc.); or a generic goal 'doing something' ("my God!! What can I do?!") [27]. The more intense the felt fear, the more important the activate goal of avoidance [26].

seem to be unitary subjective experiences, typical and recognizable "mental states"; they have a global character; although made up of (more) atomic components they form a *gestalt*. To use again the metaphor of molecules vs. atoms, the molecule (like 'water') has emergent and specific properties that its atoms (H & O) do not have. How can we account for this gestalt property in our analytic, symbolic, (de)composition framework? We have implicitly pointed out some possible solution to this problem. For example:

- A higher-level predicate exists (like 'EXPECT') and one can assume that although decomposable in and implying specific beliefs and goals, this molecular predicate is used by mental operations and rules.
- Or one might assume that the left part of a given rule for the activation of a specific goal is just the combined pattern: belief + goal; for example, an avoidance goal and behavior would be elicited by a serious negative *expectation* (and the associated 'fear'), not by the simple prediction of an event.
- One might assume that we "recognize" - or better "individuate" (and "construct")- our own mental state (thanks to this complex predicate or some complex rule) and that this "awareness" is part of the mental state: since we have a complex category or pattern of "expectation" or of "disappointment" we recognize and *have* (and feel) this complex mental state.

This would create some sort of "molecular" causal level. However, this might seem not enough in order to account for the gestaltic subjective experience, and reasonably something additional should be found in the direction of some typical "feeling" related to those cognitive configurations. Here we deal with the limits of any disembodied mind (and model) (See § 8.).

6   The Dynamic Consequences of Expectations

As we said, also the effects of the *invalidation* of an expectation are very different depending on: a) the positive or negative character of the expectation; b) the strengths of the components. Given the fact that X has previous expectations, how this changes her evaluation of and reaction to a given event?

Invalidated Expectations
We call invalidated expectation, an expectation that results to be wrong: i.e. while expecting that p at time t', X now beliefs that NOT p at time t'.

$$(\text{Bel } x \; p^{t'})^{t<t'} <==> (\text{Bel } x \; \neg p^{t'})^{t''>t}$$

This crucial belief is *the 'invalidating' belief*.

- Relative to the goal component it represents "frustration", "goal-failure" (is the *frustrating* belief): I desire, wish, want that p but I know that not p.

    FRUSTRATION: $(\text{Goal } x \; p^{t'}) \; \& \; (\text{Bel } x \; \neg p^{t'})$
- Relative to the prediction belief, it represents 'falsification', 'prediction-failure':

    INVALIDATION: $(\text{Bel } x \; p^{t'})^{t<t'} \; \& \; (\text{Bel } x \; \neg p^{t'})^{t''>t}$

(Bel x p$^{t'}$)$^{t<t'}$ represents the former illusion or delusion (X illusorily believed at time t that at t' p would be true).

This configuration provides also the cognitive basis and the components of **"surprise"**: *the more certain the prediction the more intense the surprise.* Given positive and negative Expectations and the answer of the world, that is the *frustrating* or *gratifying* belief, we have:

	P	**¬P**
Bel x p & Goal x p	no surprise + achievement	*surprise + frustration* *disappointment*
Bel x ¬p & Goal x p	*surprise + non-frustration* *relief*	no surprise + frustration

6.1 Disappointment

Relative to the whole mental state of "positively expecting" that p, the *invalidating&frustrating* belief produces "disappointment" that is based on this basic configuration (plus the affective and cognitive reaction to it):

DISAPPOINTMENT: (Goal$^{\%}$ x p$^{t'}$)$^{t\,\&t'}$ & (Bel$^{\%}$ x p$^{t'}$)^{t} & (Bel$^{\%}$ x ¬p$^{t'}$)$^{t'}$

At t X believes that at t' (later) p will be true; but now – at t' – she knows that Not p, while she continues to want that p. Disappointment contains goal-frustration and forecast failure, surprise. It entails a greater *sufferance* than simple frustration [28] for several reasons: (i) for the additional failure; (ii) for the fact that this impact also on the self-esteem as epistemic agent (Badura's "predictability" and related "controllability") and is disorienting; (iii) for the fact that losses of a pre-existing fortune are worst than missed gains (see below), and long expected and surely expected desired situation are so familiar and "sure" that we feel a sense of loss.

The stronger and well grounded the belief the more disorienting and restructuring is the *surprise* (and the stronger the consequences on our sense of predictability). The more important the goal the more *frustrated* the subject.

In Disappointment these effects are combined: *the more sure the subject is about the outcome & the more important the outcome is for her, the more disappointed the subject will be.*

- The degree of disappointment seems to be function of both dimensions and components [12]. It seems to be felt as a unitary effect.
    "How much are you disappointed?" "I'm very disappointed: I was sure to succeed"
    "How much are you disappointed?" "I'm very disappointed: it was very important for me"
    "How much are you disappointed?" "Not at all: it was not important for me"
    "How much are you disappointed?" "Not at all: I have just tried; I was expecting a failure".

---

[12] As a first approximation of the degree of Disappointment one might assume some sort of multiplication of the two factors: Goal-value * Belief-certainty. Similarly to 'Subjective Expected Utility': the greater the SEU the more intense the Disappointment.

Obviously, worst disappointments are those with great value of the goal and high degree of certainty. However, the *surprise* component and the *frustration* component remain perceivable and function of their specific variables.

6.2 Relief

Relief is based on a 'negative' expectation that results to be wrong. The prediction is invalidated but the goal is realized. There is no frustration but surprise. In a sense relief is the opposite of disappointment: the subject was "down" while expecting something bad, and now feel much better because this expectation was wrong.

$$\text{RELIEF: (Goal } x \neg p^{t'}) \ \& \ (\text{Bel } x \ p^{t'}) \ \& \ (\text{Bel } x \ \neg p^{t'})^{13}$$

- *The harder the expected harm and the more sure the expectation (i.e. the more serious the subjective threat) the more intense the 'relief'.*

More precisely: the higher the worry, the treat, and the stronger the relief. The worry is already function of the value of the harm and its certainty.

Analogously, **joy** seems to be more intense depending on the value of the goal, but also on how *unexpected* it is.

A more systematic analysis should distinguish between different kinds of surprise (based on different monitoring activities and on explicit vs. implicit beliefs), and different kinds of disappointment and relief due to the distinction between 'maintenance' situations and 'change/achievement' situations. In fact expecting that a good state will continue is different from expecting that a good state (that currently is not real) becomes true; and it is different worrying about the cessation of a good state vs. worrying about the instauration of a bad event. Consequently, the Relief for the cessation of a painful state that X expected to continue, is different from the Relief for the non-instauration of an expected bad situation. Analogously: the Disappointment for the unexpected non-prosecution of a welfare state (*loss*) is psychologically rather different from the non-achievement of an expected goal.

		FORECAST that P	
		currently P *(expected continuation)*	currently Not P *(expected instauration)*
ACTUALLY Not P	**GOAL P**	Disappointment *loss* *1*	Disappointment *missed gain 2*
	GOAL Not P	Relief *3* *cessation, alleviation*	Relief *4* *escaped danger*

---

[13] Or – obviously - (Goal x pt') & (Bel x ¬pt') & (Bel x pt').

More precisely (making constant the value of the Goal) the case of loss (1) is usually worst than (2), while (3) is better than (4). This is coherent with the theory of psychic suffering [28] that claims that pain is greater when there is not only frustration but disappointment (that is a previous Expectation), and when there is 'loss' (1), not just 'missed gains' (2), that is when the frustrated goal is a maintenance goal not an achievement goal.

7 The Implicit Counterpart of Expectations

Since we introduce a quantification of the degree of subjective certainty and reliability of Belief about the future (the forecast) we get a hidden, strange but nice consequence. There are other implicit opposite beliefs and thus implicit Expectations.

For "implicit" beliefs we mean here a belief that is not 'written', contained in any 'data base' (short term, working, or long term memory) but is only potentially known by the subject since it can be simply derived from actual beliefs. For example, while my knowledge that Buenos Aires is the capital city of Argentina is an explicit belief that I have in some memory and I have just to retrieve it, on the contrary my knowledge that Buenos Aires is not the capital city of Greece (or of Italy, or of India, or of ...) is not in any memory, but can just be derived (when needed) from what I explicitly know. Until it remains implicit, merely potential, until is not derived, it has *no effect* in my mind; for example, I cannot perceive possible contradictions: my mind is only potentially contradictory if I believe that p, I believe that q, and p implies Not q, but I didn't derive that Not q.

Now, a belief that "70% it is the case that p", implies a belief that "30% it is the case that Not p"[14]. This has interesting consequences on Expectations and related emotions. The Positive Expectation that p entails an implicit (but sometime even explicit and compatible) Negative Expectation:

$$
\boxed{\begin{array}{l} \text{Bel}^{\%}\ x\ p^{t} \\ \& \\ \text{Goal}^{\%}\ x\ p^{t} \end{array}} \rightarrow \boxed{\begin{array}{l} \text{Bel}^{\%}\ x\ \neg p^{t} \\ \& \\ \text{Goal}^{\%}\ x\ p^{t} \end{array}}
$$

This means that any hope implicitly contains some fear, and that any worry implicitly preserves some hope. But also means that when one get a 'relief' because a serious threat strongly expected is not arrived and the world is conforming to her desires, she also get (or can get) some exultance. It depends of her focus of attention and framing: is she focused on her worry and evanished treat, or on the unexpected achievement? Vice versa when one is satisfied for the actual expected realization of an important goal, she also can get some measure of relief while focusing on the implicit previous worry.

---

[14] We are simplifying the argument. In fact it is possible that there is an interval of ignorance, some lack of evidences; that is that I 45% evaluate that p and 30% that Not p, having a gap of 25% neither in favor of p nor of Not p [29] [30].

Not necessarily at the very moment that one feels a given emotion (for example fear) she also feels the complementary emotion (hope) in a sort of oscillation or ambivalence and affective mixture. Only when the belief is explicitly represented and one can focus – at least for a moment – her attention on it, it can generate the corresponding emotion.

8 Concluding Remarks

This analysis obviously is very simplistic, and reductionist. It misses a lot of important psychological aspects. As we mentioned, an important missed point is the fact that those mental states (especially when 'affective') are usually joined with bodily activation and feeling components, and these components –with their *intensity*- shape the whole subjective state and determine the nature of future reactions. Moreover, other cognitive aspects are elicited by and combined with those configurations. For example, in worrying the activity of monitoring, waiting, be more or less anxious. Now the degree of relief also depends on the presence and intensity of those somatic components and of those activities (Was the subject very stressed, feeling her stomach contracted? ... Was she continuously checking and checking?) .

We also did not consider the important interaction between the two basic components and their strength. For example, there might be an influence of the goal on the belief. In 'motivated reasoning' [31], in wishful thinking we tend to believe more agreeable (goal conformable) beliefs and we defend ourselves from bad (goal opposite) beliefs. In Expectations we precisely have goal-related beliefs, thus – with an important value of the goal – we might be prone to go against the independent sources and evidences of our beliefs and change their credibility in conformity with their desirability. In other words, our predictions might be influenced by the value of the expected outcome. Vice versa, in some psychological attitude or personality one might reduce the concern, the value of the goal just in order to not feel so bad in case of failure, since she mainly focuses such an eventuality.

However, this simplification is just a necessary, preliminary step: nothing prevents AI and ALIfe from enriching this skeleton with more mussels and blood. This anatomy is necessary for identifying basic structural relationships between mental states, and – in this case- the crucial (sometimes hidden) role of expectations in mind.

Notice that –even with such a simplification - several nice predictions follow from this cognitive anatomy. For example, we predict that Disappointment implies Surprise, but not the other way around; or that Hope implies a Prediction, but not vice versa. We can predict that there is a contradiction between 'to be frightened of' something and be disappointed if it does not happen; or between forecasting that p and be surprised when it actually happens; or between 'hoping' that p and feeling down if it happens. We predict that a strong hope, when the prediction is realized, entails satisfaction, realization; while in the opposite case entails frustration, disappointment, and pain.

Will we have the satisfaction of surprising our artificial Agent, our computer or our domestic robot? And possibly even of disappointing them (as they frequently disappoint us)? We think so, and – as we said – this objective has been an additional reason for being schematic. Computers and robot can have Expectations and one might model robotic surprise, disappointment, relief, hope, fear, etc.

Of course, to really having artificial fear or hope one should reproduce or simulate also the 'affective' component, that is the 'feeling', by providing to computers, artificial agents, and robots a 'body' not simply a hardware. This means introducing some form of proprioception and enteroception, pain and pleasure, feeling what happens to the body and its internal states and events, its automatic reactions to the world; and modeling the impact of these signals (*motions*) on the 'mental' representations and activity [26]. This is still quite far to be achieved. This is why we can have for the moment only the 'cold' counterpart of those affective states, just reduced to the mental representations on which they are based.

However, the objective remains that of building some (useless?) anxious machine.

Acknowledgments

I would like to thank Maria Miceli and Emiliano Lorini that have been working with me on these topics for several years, and all the *MindRaces* ISTC group for precious discussions.

References

1. Butz, M.V., Hoffman, J. Anticipations control behavior: Animal behavior in an anticipatory learning classifier system. *Adaptive Behavior*, 10, (2002) 75-96.
2. Castelfranchi, C., Tummolini, L., Pezzulo, G. Proto-Intentions Theory: From Classifiers to Purposive Behavior, and Back In Proceedings of *From Reactive to Anticipatory Cognitive Embodied Systems*, AAAI Fall Symposium Series Technical Report (2005).
3. Miceli, M., Castelfranchi, C.. The Mind and the Future. The (Negative) Power of Expectations. *Theory & Psychology*, 12(3), (2002) pp. 335-366.
4. Castelfranchi, C., Lorini, E. Cognitive Anatomy and Functions of Expectations. In *Proceedings of IJCAI'03 Workshop on Cognitive Modeling of Agents and Multi-Agent Interactions*, Acapulco, Mexico, August 9-11, (2003).
5. Rosenblueth, A., Wiener, N., Bigelow, J. Behavior, Purpose, and Teleology. In W. Buckley (ed.), *Modern Systems Research for the Behavioral Scientist*, Aldine, Chicago (1960).
6. Miller, G., Galanter, E., Pribram, K. H. *Plans and the structure of the behavior*. Rinehart & Winston, New York (1960).
7. Butz, M.V. *Anticipatory learning classifier system* Boston, MA: Kluwer Academic Publisher, (2002).
8. Bickhard, Mark H. Anticipation and Representation. In Proceedings of *From Reactive to Anticipatory Cognitive Embodied Systems*, AAAI Fall Symposium Series Technical Report (2005).
9. Jordan, M. I., Wolpert, D. M. Computational Motor Control. In M. Gazzaniga (Ed.), *The Cognitive Neuroscience*, Cambridge, MA: MIT Press. (1999).
10. Ortony, A., Partridge, O. Surprisingness and expectation failure: What's the difference? In *Proceedings of the 10th International Joint Conference on Artificial Intelligence*, (1987) pp. 106-108, Los Altos, CA: Morgan Kaufmann.
11. Lorini, E., Castelfranchi, C.(in preparation). *Towards a cognitive model of Surprise*.
12. Kahneman, D., Miller, D. T., Norm Theory: Comparing reality to its alternatives. *Psychological Review*, 93, (1986) pag. 136-153, 1986.
13. Drescher, G. *Made-up minds: A constructivist approach to artificial intelligence*. MIT Pres (1991).

14. Lorini, E., Castelfranchi, C., The role of epistemic actions in expectations. In *Proceedings of Second Workshop of Anticipatory Behavior in Adaptive Learning Systems (ABIALS 2004)*, Los Angeles, 17 July 2004. (2004).

15. D., Kirsh, P., Maglio. On distinguishing epistemic from pragmatic action. *Cognitive Science, 18*, (1994) pp. 513-549.

16. Bandura A., Self-efficacy mechanism in human agency. *American Psychologist, 37*, (1990) pp. 122-147, 1990.

17. Cooper, J., Fazio, R. H., A new look at dissonance theory. In L. Berkovitz (Ed.), *Advances in experimental social psychology, Vol. 17*, (1984) pp. 229-266, San Diego, CA: Academic Press.

18. Miceli, M. e Castelfranchi, C. The role of evaluation in cognition and social interaction. In K. Dautenhahn (Ed.), *Human cognition and agent technology*. Amsterdam: Benjamins, 225-61, (2000).

19. Castelfranchi, C., Individual social action. In G. Holmstrom-Hintikka and R. Tuomela (eds.), *Contemporary theory of action*, vol.II, Kluwer, Dordrecht, pp. 163-192 (1997).

20. Cohen, P. R., Levesque, H. J., Intention is choice with commitment. *Artificial Intelligence, 42*, (1990) pp. 213-261.

21. Rao, A. S., Georgeff, M. P., An abstract architecture for rational agents. In Proceedings of the *Third International Conference on Principles of Knowledge Representation and Reasoning*, C. Rich, W. Swartout, and B. Nebel (Eds.), pp. 439-449, Morgan Kaufmann Publishers, San Mateo, CA, (1992).

22. Corrêa, M., Coelho, E. Agent's programming from a mental states framework. In Proceedings of the *14th Brazilian Symposium on Artificial Intelligence (SBIA98)*, Lecture Notes in AI 1515, pp. 31-39, Springer-Verlag, (1998).

23. Bratman, M. E., *Intentions, plans, and practical reason*, Cambridge, MA: Harvard University Press, (1988).

24. Castelfranchi, C., Reasons: Belief Support and Goal Dynamics. *Mathware & Soft Computing, 3*. (1996). pp. 233-47.

25. Galliers, J.R. Modelling Autonomous Belief Revision in Dialogue, In *Decentralized AI-2*, Y. Demazeau, J.P. Mueller (eds), (1991) pp. 231-43. Armsterdam: Elsevier.

26. Castelfranchi, C. *Ri-emboding 'hope' and 'fear'* T.R. European Project HUMAINE, (2005).

27. Miceli, M., Castelfranchi,, C. For a Cognitive Theory of Anxiety. *British Medical Journal: Anxiety disorder* (in press).

28. Miceli, M., ,Castelfranchi, C. Basic principles of psychic suffering: A preliminary account. *Theory & Psychology, 7*, (1997) pp. 769-798.

29. Shafer, G. *A mathematical theory of evidence*. Princeton University Press, Cambridge, (1976).

30. Pezzulo, G., Lorini, E., Calvi G., How do I know how much I don't know? A cognitive approach about Uncertainty and Ignorance. In *Proceedings of 26th Annual Meeting of the Cognitive Science Society (CogSci 2004)*, Chicago, USA, 5-7 August, (2004).

31. Kunda, Z., The case of motivated reasoning. Psychological Bullettin, 108, (1990) pp. 480-498.

A Cognitive Model for Autonomous Agents Based on Bayesian Programming⋆

F. Aznar, M. Sempere, M. Pujol, and R. Rizo

Department of Computer Science and Artificial Intelligence,
University of Alicante
{fidel, mireia, mar, rizo}@dccia.ua.es

Abstract. This paper presents a cognitive model for an autonomous agent based on emotional psychology and Bayesian programming. A robot with emotional responses allows us to plan behaviour in a different way than present robotic architectures and provides us with a method of generating a new interface for human/robot interaction. The use of emotional modules means that the emotional state of the robot can be obtained directly and, therefore, it is relatively simple to obtain a virtual face that represents these emotions. An autonomous agent could have a model of the environment to be able to interact with the real universe where it is working. It is necessary to consider that any model of a real phenomenon will be incomplete due to the existence of uncertain, unknown variables that influence the phenomenon. Two example arquitectures are proposed here. Using these architectures some experimental data, to verify the correctness of this approach, is provided.

Keywords: Cognitive Models, Autonomous Agents, Bayesian Programming, Bayesian Units.

1 Introduction

Humanizing computer interfaces has long been a major goal of both computer users and programmers [1]. Humanizing has at two main advantages, firstly that of making interfaces easier and more comfortable to use and secondly of giving interfaces a more human appearance [2]. The human face is one of the most compelling components of a human-like interface. Facial expressions are an important channel of nonverbal communication. Emotional expressions over time may make people's faces descriptive of their personalities and their state of mind. There are some papers that study the importance of the face in the interaction and communication between people [3] [4].

On the other hand, an autonomous agent could have a model of the environment to be able to interact with the real universe where it is working. Nevertheless, it is necessary to consider that any model of a real phenomenon will be incomplete due to the existence of uncertain, unknown variables that

---

⋆ This work has been financed by the Generalitat Valenciana project GV04B685.

M. De Gregorio et al. (Eds.): BVAI 2005, LNCS 3704, pp. 277–287, 2005.

influence the phenomenon. The effect of these variables is to cause the model and the phenomenon to never have the same behaviour. Although reasoning with incomplete information continues to be a challenge for autonomous agents, learning and probabilistic inference tries to solve this problem using a formal base. Bayesian programming [5] [6] [7] is a formalism, based on the principle of the Bayesian theory of probability and is proposed as a solution when dealing with problems relating to uncertainty and incompleteness.

Certain parallelisms exist between this kind of programming and the structure of living organisms, as shown in a theoretical way in [6]. In this way, natural evolution provided living beings with both the pertinent variables, and the adequate decomposition and parametric forms.

2   Fusing with Bayesian Programming

As commented above, it is necessary to bear in mind that any model of a real phenomenon will always be incomplete due to the permanent existence of unknown, hidden variables that will influence the phenomenon. These variables cause the model and the phenomenon to adopt different behaviour. An artificial system must perceive, infer, decide and act using an incomplete model of the environment. Bayesian inference and learning try to solve this problem using a formal theory. Bayesian programming is a new formalism, and it is proposed as a solution when dealing with problems relating to uncertainty and incompleteness.

A Bayesian program is defined as a means of specifying a family of probability distributions. It is made up of different components (see figure 1).

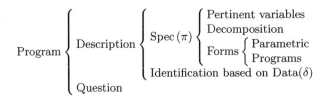

Fig. 1. Structure of a Bayesian program

The first is a declarative component where the user defines a description. The purpose of a description is to specify a method to compute a joint distribution on a set of variables given a set of experimental data (δ) and preliminary knowledge (π). The second component is of a procedural nature and consists of using a previously defined description with a question. A question is obtained by partitioning the variables into three groups: *Searched*, *Known* and *Unknown*, computing a probability distribution of the form $P(Searched|Known)$. Answering this question consists in deciding a value for the variable *Searched* according to $P(Searched|Known)$ using the Bayesian inference rule:

$$P(Searched|Known \otimes \delta \otimes \pi) = \frac{1}{\Sigma} \times \sum_{Unknown} P(Searched \otimes Unknown \otimes Known|\delta \otimes \pi) \tag{1}$$

Considering both the system decomposition in modules and the fusion of information a definition of Bayesian processing Unit is proposed, based on the Bayesian programming formalism. A processing unit u is a description that defines this probabilistic distribution: $P(I \otimes S \otimes O \otimes |u)$, where I is an input variable that specifies the information to be processed, S is a state variable that represents the situation of the processing unit and O is an output variable that specifies the newly generated information.

The variables I, S and O are allowed to be atomic and can be made up of some random variables that will be assumed as discrete. The decomposition of this probabilistic distribution and its form is not limited. In this way, the decomposition of the variable or input variables can be defined using queries to other processing units. Specific learning is not specified in order to allow the system designer to use the method that he considers to be more appropriate. The variable state S represents the situation in a processing unit. For example, in reactive behaviours, where the input information directly provides the output information, the shape of the probability of this variable will tend to be uniform. In more complex behaviours S can take more complex shapes depending on the information to be processed and the desired output.

3   Proposed Architectures

An emotion is an affective state, a subjective reaction to the environment that shows internal feelings, motivations, wishes, needs and objectives. Emotions and the actions linked to them are an essential part of an organism's relation with its environment. They can be the means by which a person appraises the significance of stimuli and prepares the body for an appropriate response [8]. The core of an emotion is readiness to act in a certain way [9]. In this way, emotions can interrupt ongoing action; they also prioritise certain kinds of social interaction.

3.1   Complementary Architecture to Obtain a Human/Robot Interface

In the model proposed here an autonomous agent, which can have a traditional management system, is able to plan a set of objectives. With this system and using the principles of the emotional bases previously commented, a subconscious model that combines the emotions provided by the robot, is defined. These emotions depend on the condition of all variables (sensors, laser, batteries...) and the previous knowledge of the environment. An emotion can make the robot change its behaviour in a reactive or deliberate way.

In our case we have a previous navigation system that is able to deliver correspondence under petition [10]. This system will be expanded with four emotional modules to help achieve the tasks and provide an effective mechanism for building an interface with the characteristics outlined above.

Emotional Modules. An emotional module is a Bayesian processing unit that interacts with other emotional modules, with the traditional system for the resolution of objectives or with the robot using an interface connected directly to the robot. An emotional module usually has a corresponding human emotion. It is advisable to combine all the emotional modules using a Bayesian unit that we call subconscious. This unit is responsible for collecting all the *emotional charge* of the robot in a given moment.

As previously stated, an emotional module can act directly with the robot actuators. However, the conscious system must be connected to the robot to execute tasks. A Bayesian execution unit is proposed to be in charge of controlling the robot. This unit will carry out the tasks depending on the emotional values of the robot and the present piece of work to be completed.

Most emotional modules have a reactive base, this is the reason why they will not need a state variable. In our system (see figure 2a) we use the following modules: a dissatisfaction module (defined to show the probability that the robot has a problem in the execution of its task), a tiredness module (defined as a protection system), a depression module that determines when work conditions are not suitable (for example, when sensor readings provide low reliability or tiredness levels are excessively high). It can produce a decrease in movement intensity or even halt the robot. And finally a fear module (to maintain the integrity of the robot and to take reactive action to avoid collisions and obstacles). This modules are grouped using a subconscious module (that determines the state of the robot and is used in the interface development). In order to execute an action we require an execution module. This is a system that determines which actions are more probable to execute. This probability depends on the outputs of the emotions that interact with the system as well as the actions proposed by the traditional system. We briefly will describe some of them:

Fear. The main function of this module is to maintain the integrity of the robot and to take reactive action to avoid collisions and obstacles. Input variables are the action to be executed in this moment (Ac) (it must be provided by the conscious module, it is made up of variables that describe robot actuators, in this case $Vrot$ for rotational velocity and $Vtrans$ for transactional velocity) and the readings from sensors (Ps). Starting from these variables, the module obtains an indication of the robot's degree of fear $(Vmie)$ and the action to be executed $(Amie)$ in order to avoid any actions that could damage the robot.

In this way, the following decomposition is defined with these variables:

$P(Ps \otimes Ac \otimes Vmie \otimes Amie|\pi) =$
$P(Ps|\pi) \times P(Ac|Ps \otimes \pi) \times P(Vmie|Ac \otimes Ps \otimes \pi) \times P(Amie|Vmie \otimes Ac \otimes Ps \otimes \pi) =$
$P(Ps|\pi) \times P(Ac|\pi) \times P(Vmie|Ac \otimes Ps \otimes \pi) \times P(Amie|Vmie \otimes \pi)$

Initially the distribution of the sonar readings $P(Ps|\pi)$ and the distribution of the actions to be executed $P(Ac|\pi)$ are unknown. These terms are uniform distributions. $P(Vmie|Ac \otimes Ps \otimes \pi)$ is specified as a table that defines the fear degree of the robot from the sensor values and the action developed. Finally, $P(Amie|Vmie \otimes \pi)$ is a table that represents the action to be taken depending on the fear degree obtained.

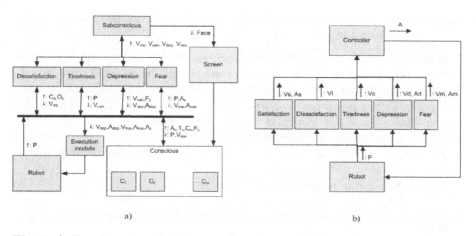

a)   b)

Fig. 2. a) *Complementary Architecture.* Conscious module is a classic system for the interaction of the robot with the world. Subconscious module combines the emotional system modules determining the present state of the robot. A dissatisfaction module is defined to show the probability $(Vins)$ that the robot has a problem in the execution of its task. There are two input variables that establish this probability: completed task rate (Cc) and task completion problems (Oc). Tiredness is defined as a protection system. In this way, the function of this unit is to calculate the condition of the robot from the time of continuous execution (Pt) and the state of the batteries $(Pbat)$. The unit shows if the robot needs to return to the charge station in order to recharge its batteries or if the robot must restrict its movements $(Vcan)$. The depression module determines when work conditions are not suitable, for example, when sensor readings provide low reliability or tiredness levels are excessively high. Knowing the system reliability (Fc) and tiredness level $(Vcan)$ the robot will calculate the degree of depression $(Vdep)$ and the action to be taken $(Adep)$. A fear module is used to maintain the integrity of the robot and to take reactive action to avoid collisions and obstacles. Input variables are the action to be executed in this moment (Ac) and the readings from sensors (Ps). Starting from these variables, the module obtains an indication of the robot's degree of fear $(Vmie)$ and the action to be executed $(Amie)$ in order to avoid any actions that could damage the robot. Finally, we use an execution module in order to determine which actions are more probable to be execute. b) *Architecture for an Autonomous System.* The Dissatisfaction, Tiredness, Depression and Fear modules work in the same way as the previous architecture. The Satisfaction module includes all objectives that the robot must perform. The Controller module manage the robot from the emotional modules, it indicates the actions to execute (A) from the results of the emotional modules and the previous an current state of the robot.

The specification of tables for some terms of the module decomposition provides some advantages. These advantages are obtained when we specify the problem to solve in an inverse way than usual. Given an output, any possible input that generated it, is reasoned. Inverse programming has two main advantages: it is robust in unexpected situations (an output will always be obtained even in not considered cases) and taking into account conditional independence the number of cases increases in a lineal way with the number of variables. More details can be found in [5].

Execution Module. As commented above, emotional modules and the traditional system can interact with the robot actuators. Therefore, it is necessary to define a system that determines which actions are more probable to execute. This probability depends on the outputs of the emotions that interact with the system $Vmie$, $Amie$ (for fear) and $Vdep$, $Adep$ (for depression) as well as the actions proposed by the traditional system A_c.

In this way, this joint distribution is defined with the following decomposition:

$$P(Vdep \otimes Adep \otimes Vmie \otimes Amie \otimes A_C \otimes \pi) =$$
$$P(Vdep|\pi) \times P(Adep|Vdep \otimes \pi) \times P(Vmie|Adep \otimes Vdep \otimes \pi) \times$$
$$P(Amie|Vmie \otimes Adep \otimes Vdep \otimes \pi) \times P(A_c|Amie \otimes Vmie \otimes Adep \otimes Vdep \otimes \pi) \times$$
$$= P(Vdep|\pi) \times P(Adep|Vdep \otimes \pi) \times P(Amie|Vmie \otimes \pi) \times P(A_c|\pi) = \tfrac{1}{\Sigma} \prod_i P(A_i|\pi)$$

It is specified as the product of each term of the actions that form it. The distribution $P(Vdep|\pi)$ is supposed to be uniform for execution task and it is included in the normalization term $\frac{1}{\Sigma}$. $P(A_c|\pi)$ is defined starting from two terms. The first term is the actions to be executed by the conscious system obtained assigning probabilities to the set of actions to be executed. The second is the subconscious module that usually will have more execution priority than the conscious module. The rest of terms of the previous equation must be obtained from the remaining modules (tiredness and depression).

Subconscious. The subconscious module determines the state of the robot and is used in the interface development. This state is represented using a human face that expresses the emotions of the robot in a given moment. In this way, the input variables are the probability of the different emotions ($Vins,Vcan$, $Vdep,Vmie$). Starting from these variables the system will obtain the face ($Face$) that best represents these emotions. In this way, the following decomposition is defined:

$$P(V_i \otimes V_c \otimes V_d \otimes V_m \otimes Face \otimes \pi) = \prod P(V|Face \otimes \pi)$$

Conditional independence is therefore assumed for all emotions. This can seem a strong hypothesis, for example, in the emotions tiredness and depression, where both are related. Nevertheless, given a face it can be assumed that the probability that it represents an emotion is independent from the rest. This hypothesis provides some advantages [5]. On the other hand, it is defined:

$$P(V|Face \otimes \pi) = G(\mu(V, Face), \sigma(V, Face))$$

Where G specifies a discrete Gaussian. The parameters of this Gaussian can be learned by asking the robot users. Everybody that interacts with the robot will, when given a face $Face$, say how it represents an emotion V. In this module, a set of 17 representative faces have been designed.

3.2   Architecture for an Autonomous System

In the previous section we presented an architecture that complements a classical robotic system. This architecture provides a human/machine interface. One of the benefits of using this architecture is that we can obtain the emotional state of the robot. Nevertheless, it requires an external system to control the robot.

In this section another architecture, that has been designed specifically to carry out a task (concretely a navigation task), is proposed. This architecture contains a Controller module that decides the action for the robot to take. The Controller module is the only one that controls the robot. Using this architecture (see figure 2b) we develop an autonomous behaviour from the state of a set of emotions.

The Dissatisfaction, Tiredness, Depression and Fear modules work in the same way as the previous architecture. The Satisfaction module includes all of the tasks to be executed by the robot. The main objective of the robot is to move to a defined point, avoiding the obstacles in the environment. Although not described in this paper, any navigation method between two points in a known environment could be used, as long as the distance between the current position and the final point is known. This distance will be used to establish the V_s probability.

The Controller module manage the robot from the emotional modules. The function of this unit is to give orders for the robot to carry out (A) taken from the results of the emotional modules (V_s, A_s, V_i, V_c, V_d, A_d, V_m and A_m), the current state (S) and previous state (S').

In this way, the following joint distribution is defined:

$$P(A \otimes S \otimes S' \otimes V_s \otimes A_s \otimes V_i \otimes V_c \otimes V_d \otimes A_d \otimes V_m \otimes A_m \otimes \pi) =$$
$$P(V_s|\pi) \times P(A_s|V_s \otimes \pi) \times P(V_i|\pi) \times P(V_c|\pi) \times P(V_d|V_c \otimes \pi) \times P(A_d|V_d \otimes \pi) \times$$
$$P(V_m|\pi) \times P(A_m|V_m \otimes \pi) \times P(S'|\pi) \times$$
$$P(S|S' \otimes A_m \otimes V_m \otimes A_d \otimes V_d \otimes V_c \otimes V_i \otimes A_s \otimes V_s \otimes \pi) \times$$
$$P(A|S \otimes S' \otimes A_m \otimes V_m \otimes A_d \otimes V_d \otimes V_c \otimes V_i \otimes A_s \otimes V_s \otimes \pi) =$$
$$\tfrac{1}{\Sigma} \times P(A_s|V_s \otimes \pi) \times P(V_d|V_c \otimes \pi) \times P(A_d|V_d \otimes \pi) \times P(A_m|V_m \otimes \pi) \times$$
$$P(S|S' \otimes V_m \otimes V_d \otimes V_c \otimes V_i \otimes V_s \otimes \pi) \times$$
$$P(A|S \otimes S' \otimes A_m \otimes A_d \otimes A_s \otimes \pi)$$

The First equation is obtained assuming conditional independences between modules. $\frac{1}{\Sigma}$ is a normalization term that groups the uniform distributions ($P(V_s|\pi)$, $P(V_i|\pi)$, $P(V_c|\pi)$ and $P(S'|\pi)$). Probabilities $P(A_s|V_s \otimes \pi)$, $P(V_d|V_c \otimes \pi)$, $P(A_d|V_d \otimes \pi)$ and $P(A_m|V_m \otimes \pi)$ are defined in the emotional modules previously presented. The probability of a global state S depends on the probability of a previous global state S' and the state of the emotional units. In the same way, an action A depends on the current state S, the previous state S' and on the actions of the emotional modules. Both distributions can be defined with a table. This table can be specified by the programmer or be learned as is shown in [11].

4   Experimental Validation

4.1   Complementary Architecture to Obtain a Human/Robot Interface

The architecture proposed here has been designed for a correspondence delivery system presented in [10] and developed by the robot PeopleBot (http://www.activmedia.com). This robot provides a good platform for the development of human/robot interfaces because of its upright shape and its touch screen. The emotional interface presented here has been implemented on this robot and shown on its screen. This interface is based on the probability distribution $P(V_i \otimes V_c \otimes V_d \otimes V_m \otimes Face)$ and concretely in one of the questions that can be asked to this unit applying equation 1: $P(Face|V_i \otimes V_c \otimes V_d \otimes V_m)$.

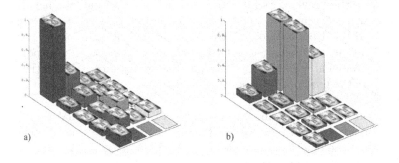

Fig. 3. Graphical representation of the probability $P(Face|V_i \otimes V_c \otimes V_d \otimes V_m)$. a) $(V_i, V_c, V_d, V_m) = (0, 0, 0, 0)$ b)$(V_i, V_c, V_d, V_m) = (0.2, 0.23, 0.21, 0.19)$.

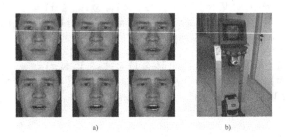

Fig. 4. a) Example of a fear sequence. The images show the transition from neutral face to the base face of fear. b) PeopleBot in its working environment.

When a face is obtained from this distribution, this face is one of the 17 base faces designed for the system, where a base face represents a set of emotions. From this base face a transition to a neutral face is generated, a neutral face is a face devoid of emotion (see figure 4a). This process continuously provides uniformity and realism to the facial movements. In figure 3 the value of the distribution $P(Face|V_i \otimes V_c \otimes V_d \otimes V_m)$ in two specific moments is shown.

When the user wants to interact with the robot he has two options at his disposal. The first is to use a verbal command (using the speech recognition module integrated in PeopleBot) and the second is to use the touch screen where the face is shown. When the user clicks the screen, all the information needed for the management of the robot is shown. On the other hand, the use of emotions provides the same versatility and operation as traditional systems, with the difference that the separation between modules makes integration and reusability easier. The use of emotional modules provides the robot with an emotional state. This state can be used for planning, for the development of tasks and for building an interface like that proposed in this paper.

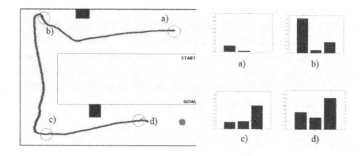

Fig. 5. A robot trajectory. The graphs show the level of fear V_m (left column), tiredness V_c (center column) and satisfaction V_s (right column) in four different positions of the robot.

4.2   Architecture for an Autonomous System

The second architecture has been designed to develop a concrete navigation task. This architecture fuses emotional modules in order to complete the tasks using a Markovian point of view, taking into acount the present and the previous robot state. The Satisfaction module contains the main tasks to be executed by the robot, in this case the robot will try to reach a goal point. These behaviours will be affected by the other modules of the system. The Fear module will reduce the velocity and rotational angle when it considers that the robot is near to an obstacle and therefore, it is possible that the robot collides with them. In this way, the Tiredness module also will modify the main behaviour, trying to reduce the robot motor overload in order to save the batteries level. In figure 5 the robot is shown in four different positions in an environment. The graphs show, for each position, the level of fear (left column), tiredness (center column), and satisfaction (right column), taken from the respective modules.

5 Conclusions

In this paper a model to imitate human emotional behaviour has been proposed. This model is based on Bayesian programming, and specifically Bayesian processing Units. The main purpose of this paper is to provide a cognitive model for an autonomous agent. A visual communication interface, simple to use and whose interpretation is not restricted by language, are developed. A human face capable of showing different emotions has been integrated into a robot. An association between human emotions and the tasks to be executed by the robot has been produced. In this way the robot has been provided with emotional modules. In addition an autonomous architecture and example of its use have been provided.

An emotional state of the robot is obtained from the information received from the emotional modules presented in this paper. Using this state, a representative face that defines this condition is obtained and shown as an indication of its present *feeling*. Some experimental data, to verify the correctness of the model and the interface, have been provided.

In an uncertain world it is necessary to work taking this uncertainty into consideration. The model proposed here contains the uncertainty within itself because it is rigorously based on Bayes Theorem. Future studies will try different applications of this architecture in autonomous robots.

References

1. Breazeal, C.: Affective Interaction between Humans and Robots. In: Advances in Artificial Life : 6th European Conference, ECAL 2001. Proceedings. Springer-Verlag GmbH (2001) 582
2. Walker, J.H., Sproull, L., Subramani, R.: Using a human face in an interface. In ACM Press New York, NY, U., ed.: Proceedings of the SIGCHI conference on Human factors in computing systems: celebrating interdependence ISBN:0-89791-650-6. (1994) 85 – 91
3. P., E., T., H., T., S., J., H.: Final report to nsf of the planning workshop on facial expression understanding. Technical report, National Science Foundation, Human Interaction Lab., UCSF, CA 94143 (1993)
4. Schmidt, K. L., .C.J.F.: Human facial expressions as adaptations: Evolutionary questions in facial expression research. Yearbook of Physical Anthropology **44** (2001) 3–24
5. Lebeltel, O., Bessière, P., Diard, J., Mazer, E.: Bayesian robots programming. Autonomous Robots **16** (2004) 49–79
6. Bessière, P., Group, I.R.: Survei: Probabilistic methodology and tecniques for artefact conception and development. INRIA (2003)
7. Diard, J., Lebeltel, O.: Bayesian programming and hierarchical learning in robotics. SAB2000 Proceedings Supplement Book; Publication of the International Society for Adaptive Behavior, Honolulu (2000)
8. MIT Institute of Technology, M.: The MIT encyclopedia of the cognitive sciences. The MIT Press (1999)
9. Frijda, N.: The emotions. Cambridge University Press, UK (1986)

10. Aznar, F., Pujol, M., Rizo, R.: Obtaining a bayesian map for data fusion and failure detection under uncertainty. In the Proceedings of the 18th International Conference on Industrial & Engineering Applications of Artificial Intelligence & Expert Systems (2005)
11. Le Hy, R., Arrigoni, A., Bessière, P., Lebetel, O.: Teaching bayesian behaviours to video game characters. Robotics and Autonomous Systems **47** (2004) 177–185

A Structural Learning Algorithm and Its Application to Predictive Toxicology Evaluation

Pasquale Foggia[2], Michele Petretta[1], Francesco Tufano[1], and Mario Vento[1]

[1] Dipartimento di Ingegneria dell'Informazione ed Ingegneria Elettrica,
Università di Salerno Via P.te Don Melillo 1 I-84084 Fisciano (SA), Italy
{mpetretta, ftufano, mvento}@unisa.it
[2] Dipartimento di Informatica e Sistemistica, Università di Napoli "Federico II"
Via Claudio 21 I-80125 Napoli, Italy
foggiapa@unina.it

Abstract. A common problem encountered in structural pattern recognition is the difficulty of constructing classification models or rules from a set of examples, due to the complexity of the structures needed to represent the patterns. In this paper we present an extension of a method for structural learning applied to predictive toxicology evaluation.

1 Introduction

Structured information is widely used in many areas of computer science and in other relevant scientific disciplines as robotics, chemistry, medicine, linguistics etc. Usually, structured information is represented by means of data structures able to express a set of primitives and the relations existing among them. To this aim graphs are used in this contest in a variety of forms; the most expressive ones are the Attributed Relational Graphs (ARG) [1] because they enrich the base structure with a set of attributes associated to nodes and edges. Despite their attractiveness in terms of representational power, structural methods (i.e., methods dealing with structured information) imply complex procedures both in the recognition and in the learning processes.

Namely, a common problem with this kind of representation is the difficulty of constructing, from a suitably chosen collection of examples, the models or the rules that are needed to perform the classification task. In fact, the well known learning methodologies available when the patterns are represented by means of vectors, like the Statistical Learning theory or the Artificial Neural Networks, cannot be applied to the more complex structures which encode the structural descriptions. These reasons determined, in the scientific community, the birth of two different approaches to the problem. One of the first paper introducing the first approach is [2]; the rational of it relies upon the conviction that structured information can be suitably encoded in order to obtain a representation in terms of a vector, thus making possible the adoption of well-known statistical/neural paradigms. The main disadvantage deriving from the use of these techniques is the impossibility of accessing the knowledge built by the system. The second approach, pioneered by [3], faces the learning problem directly in the representation space of the structured data, instead of converting graphs into

M. De Gregorio et al. (Eds.): BVAI 2005, LNCS 3704, pp. 288–297, 2005.
© Springer-Verlag Berlin Heidelberg 2005

vectors and using vector-based learning paradigms. The approach considers the determination of the class prototypes as a symbolic machine learning problem: given a suitably chosen training set, the goal of the system is to derive, by means of an inductive process, a description of each class which is more general than the bare enumeration of the training examples. In particular the description has also to cover instances of the class which are not present in the training set, but still to preserve the ability of discriminating the objects belonging to other classes. Furthermore, these descriptions must be explicit and easily interpretable by humans (in contrast, for instance, with the ones produced by neural networks), allowing an expert to validate or to improve them, or to understand what has gone wrong in case of errors. First-order logic predicates constitute a powerful representation means for this kind of knowledge, since they are expressive enough to encode both structural descriptions and complex classification rules, and can be directly employed to build a classification system by means of a logic programming language such as Prolog. For this reason the learning task has been performed using an Inductive Logic Programming method [5], based on the FOIL algorithm [6], which, given a set of positive and negative examples represented by means of logical relations, produces for each class a classification rule expressed as a Prolog program. This representation, although very expressive, results hard to be managed due to the computational cost of the prototypation phase. In our approach, that is an extention of [4], we formulate the prototypation problem directly in the graphs space avoiding to need the expressive power of the first order logic programming. This property allows to reduce considerably the complexity of the algorithm.

Our application domain is that of predictive toxicology evaluation that is the characterization of the cancerogenic characteristics of chemical compounds. Due to the countless number of chemical compounds it would be preferable to avoid the use of biological tests because of the time needed to obtain the results. To this aim it has been proposed to solve the problem of the predictive toxicology evaluation identifying Structure Activity Relationships (SARs) that are models of the relationship between the structural information of chemical compounds and their cancerogenic characteristics. In the last years different works about the classification of cancerogenic compounds were published: [7,8] presented systems based on logic programming. However interesting, their approaches do not try to recognize always the SARs because they used, for the classification, also the results of toxicity or mutagenesis tests. The Department of Computer Science and Engineering of the University of Texas at Arlington presented in 1994 a system, SUBDUE [9], for logic inductive learning based on the graphs. The algorithm tries to describe the training-set characterizing it with the substructures that more frequently occurs. The prototypes are validated by means of an inexact matching algorithm. Afterwards in 2001 Gonzales et al. [10] modified the learning process of the algorithm. The learning process computes the prototypes considering the ability of covering the samples of the same class. The weak point of these approaches is the representation of the database: it results too complex for chemical compounds (Fig 1.) because using simple graph representation, the nodes represents the objects (atoms, bonds and structural groups) and edges represents the relations between the objects. The complexity of the representation determines a considerable increase of the computational time for the prototypes calculation.

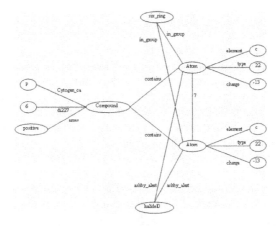

Fig. 1. Representation of a part of a compound by the SUBDUE-CL system

2   The Proposed Symbolic Learning Method

The rationale of our approach is that of devising a method which, inspired to basic machine learning methodologies, particularizes the inference operations to the case of graphs. To this aim we consider descriptions given in terms of Attributed Relational Graphs (ARG) and we introduce a new kind of Attributed Relational Graph, devoted to represent prototypes of a set of ARGs. For this reason these graphs, called Generalized Attributed Relational Graphs (GARGs), have to contain generalized nodes, edges, and attributes. Then, we formulate a learning algorithm which builds such prototypes by means of a set of operations directly defined on graphs. The algorithm preserves the generality of the prototypes generated by classical machine learning algorithms and moreover, similarly to most of machine learning systems [11, 12,13, 14], the prototypes obtained by our system are consistent, i.e., each prototype covers samples of a same class.

2.1   Graph-Based Representations of Objects and Prototypes

We assume that the objects are described in terms of Attributed Relational Graphs (ARG). An ARG can be defined as a 6-tuple $(N, E, A_N, A_E, a_N, a_E)$, where N and $E \subset N \times N$ are, respectively, the sets of the nodes and the edges of the ARG, A_N and A_E the sets of nodes and edge attributes and, finally, a_N and a_E the functions which associate to each node or edge of the graph the corresponding attributes.

We will assume that the attributes of a node or an edge are expressed in the form $t(p_1,...,p_{k_t})$, where t is a type chosen over a finite alphabet T of possible types and $(p_1,...,p_{k_t})$ are a tuple of parameters, also from finite sets $P_1^t,...,P_{k_t}^t$. Both the number of parameters (k_t, the *arity* associated to type t) and the sets they belong to depend on the type of attribute; for some type k_t may be equal to zero, so meaning that the corresponding attribute has no parameters. It is worth noting that the introduction of the

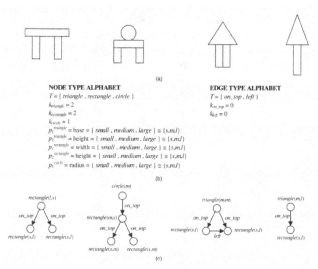

Fig. 2. An example of the use of the type information: (a) A set of objects made of three different kinds of parts (circles, triangles, rectangles). (b) The description scheme introduces three types of nodes, each associated to a different part. Each type contains a set of parameters suitable for describing each part. Similarly, edges of the graph, describing topological relations among the parts, are associated to two different types. (c) The graphs corresponding to the objects in (a).

type permits us to differentiate between the description of the different kinds of nodes (or edges); in this way, each parameter associated to a node (or an edge) assumes a meaning depending on the type of the node itself. For example, we could use the nodes to represent different parts of an object, by associating a node type to each kind of part (Fig. 2).

A GARG is used for representing a prototype of a set of ARGs. In order to allow a GARG (i.e., the prototype it represents) to match a set of possibly different ARGs (the samples covered by the considered prototype), we extend the attribute definition. First of all, the set of types of node and edge attributes is extended with the special type ϕ, carrying no parameter and allowed to match any attribute type, ignoring the attribute parameters. For the other attribute types, if the sample has a parameter whose value is within the set P_i^t, the corresponding parameter of the prototype belongs to the set

$$P_i^{*t} = \wp(P_i^t),$$ where $\wp(X)$ is the power set of X, i.e., the set of all the subsets of X. Referring to the previous example of the geometric objects, a node of the prototype could have the attribute rectangle({s,m},{m}), meaning a rectangle whose width is small or medium and whose height is medium.

We say that a GARG $G^*=(N, E, A_N, A_E, a_N, a_E)$ covers a sample G and we use the notation $G^* \models G$ (the symbol $\models$ denotes the relation called covering) if there is a mapping $\mu: N^* \rightarrow N$ such that μ is a *monomorphism* and the attributes of the nodes and of the edges of G^* are *compatible* with the corresponding ones of G. The first condition requires that each primitive and each relation in the prototype is present also in the sample; note that the converse condition does not hold, i.e., the sample can have additional primitives/relations not considered by the prototype. This allows the prototype to specify only the features which are strictly required for discriminating among the various classes, neglecting the irrelevant ones. The latter condition constrains the *monomorphism* to be consistent with the attributes of the prototype and of the sample in the sense that the type of the attribute of the prototype must be either equal to the special type ϕ or to the type of the corresponding attribute of the sample. In the latter case, all the parameters of the attribute, which are actually sets of values, must contain the value of the corresponding parameter of the sample.

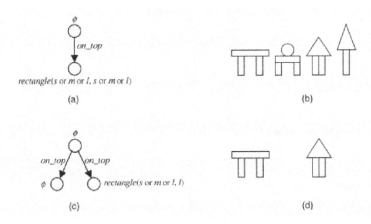

Fig. 3. (a) A GARG representing the set of the four different ARGs associated to objects presented in (b), whose ARGs are given in Fig. 1c. Note that, for the sake of clarity, we have used the disjunction (or) instead of the usual set-theoretic notation. Informally, the GARG represents "any object made of a part on the top of a rectangle of any width and height." (c) A specialization of the GARG given in (a), obtained by adding a node and an edge, and (d) the objects covered by it. Informally, the latter GARG represents "any object made of a part on the top of two other parts, that are a rectangle with a large height and any width and another unspecified part."

3   The Proposed Learning Algorithm

The goal of the learning algorithm can be stated as follows: there is a (possibly infinite) set S^* of all the patterns that may occur, partitioned into C different classes $S_1^*,.....,S_C^*$, with $S_i^* \cap S_j^* = \varnothing$; for i $\neq$ j; to the algorithm is given a finite subset $S \subset S^*$ (training set) of labeled patterns ($S = S_1 \cup ... \cup S_C$ with $S_i = S \cap S_i^*$), from which it tries to find a sequence of prototype graphs $G_1^*, G_2^*, ..., G_p^*$, each labeled with a class identifier, such that:

$$\forall G \in S^* \exists i : G_i^* \models G \quad (\textit{completeness of prototype set}) \tag{1}$$

$$\forall G \in S^*, G^* \models G \Rightarrow class(G) = classG_i^* \; (\textit{consistency of the prototype set}) \tag{2}$$

where class(G) and class(G*) refer to the class associated with sample G and proto-type G*, respectively.

Of course, this is an ideal goal since only a finite subset of S* is available to the al-gorithm; in practice, the algorithm can only demonstrate that completeness and con-sistency hold for the samples in S. On the other hand, (1) dictates that, in order to get as close as possible to the ideal case, the prototypes generated should be able to model samples also not found in S, that is, they must be more general than the enumeration of the samples in the training set. However, they should not be too general otherwise (2) will not be satisfied. The achievement of the optimal trade-off between complete-ness and consistency makes the prototypation a really hard problem.

A description of the learning algorithm is presented in the following: the algorithm starts with an empty list L of prototypes and tries to cover the training set by succes-sively adding consistent prototypes. When a new prototype is found, the samples covered by it are eliminated and the process continues on the remaining samples of the training set. Then a sample is compared sequentially against the prototypes in the same order in which they have been generated, and it is attributed to the class of the first prototype that covers it. In this way, each prototype implicitly entails the condi-tion that the sample is not covered by any previous prototype. Thus, with a careful choice of the order in which the prototypes are generated, the problems arising when the samples of a class are subpatterns of another class are avoided.

The algorithm fails if no consistent prototype covering the remaining samples can be found. It is worth noting that the test of consistency in the algorithm actually checks whether the prototype is almost consistent, i.e., almost all the samples covered by G* belongs to the same class:

$$Consistent(G^*) \Leftrightarrow \max_i \frac{|S_i(G^*)|}{|S(G^*)|} \geq \theta \tag{3}$$

where $S(G^*)$ denotes the sets of all the samples of the training set covered by a pro-totype G^*, and $S_i(G^*)$ the samples of the class i covered by G^* and θ is a threshold close to 1. Note that the assignment of a prototype to a class is done after the proto-type has been found, meaning that the prototype is not constructed in relation to an a priori determined class. The most important part of the algorithm is the construction of a prototype, starting from a trivial prototype with one node whose attribute is ϕ (i.e., a prototype which covers any nonempty graph), and refining it by successive specializations until either it becomes consistent or it covers no samples at all. An important step of this step is the construction of a set Q of specializations of the tenta-tive prototype G*. The adopted definition of the heuristic function H, guiding the search of the current optimal prototype, will be examined later.

To obtain Q, we have defined a set of specialization operators which, given a pro-totype graph G* produce a new prototype $\overline{G^*}$ such that $\overline{G^*}$ specializes G*. The con-sidered specialization operators are:

1. **Node addition:** G^* is augmented with a new node n whose attribute is ϕ.

2. **Edge addition:** A new edge (n_1^*, n_2^*) is added to the edges of G^*, where n_1^* and n_2^* are nodes of G^* and G^* does not contain already an edge between them. The edge attribute is ϕ.

3. **Attribute specialization:** The attribute of a node or an edge is specialized according to the following rule:

   - If the attribute is ϕ, then a type t is chosen and the attribute is replaced with $t\left(P_1^t, ..., P_{k_t}^t\right)$. This means that only the type is fixed, while the type parameters can match any value of the corresponding type.

   - Else, the attribute takes the form $t\left(p_1^*, ... p_{k_t}^*\right)$, where each p_i^* is a (nonnecessarily proper) subset of P_i^t. One of the p_i^* such that $\left|p_i^*\right| > 1$ is replaced with $p_i^* - \{p_i\}$ with $p_i \in p_i^*$. In other words, one of the possible values of a parameter is excluded from the prototype.

The heuristic function H is introduced for evaluating how promising the provisional prototype is. It is based on the estimation of the consistency and completeness of the prototype (see (4), (5) and (6)).

$$H = H_{cons} \bullet H_{compl} \tag{4}$$

To evaluate the consistency degree of a provisional prototype G^*, we have used an entropy based measure:

$$H_{cons}\left(S, G^*\right) = -\sum_i \frac{|S_i|}{|S|} \log_2 \frac{|S_i|}{|S|} - \left(-\sum_i \frac{|S_i(G^*)|}{|S(G^*)|} \log_2 \frac{|S_i(G^*)|}{|S(G^*)|} \right) \tag{5}$$

It follows that the larger the value of $H_{cons}\left(S, G^*\right)$ is, the more consistent G^* is. The completeness of a provisional prototype is taken into account by a second term of the heuristic function:

$$H_{compl}\left(S, G^*\right) = \left|S(G^*)\right| \tag{6}$$

4   Application to Predictive Toxicology Evaluation

The experimental phase has been carried out using the database NIEHS of molecular chemical compounds. The database includes a training-set of 298 chemical compounds (162 of them are cancerogenic and 136 non-cancerogenic) and two test sets PTE1 e PTE2 respectively of 39 and 23 chemical compounds (Fig. 4). The com pounds are described in terms of atoms and bonds, structural groups included in the compound and results of toxicity tests. In our approach, like in [9,10], only structural information is used because we are interested in the *Structure Activity Relationships*. It is manifest that ARGs are able to describe completely the structures of atoms, bonds and structural groups. In our work we use the following representation:

- **Atoms** are represented by "*atom*" nodes whose parameters are: element and charge;
- **Bonds** are represented by a couple of edges (for representing bidirectional bonds) of type "*bond*";
- **Structural groups** are described by "*group*" nodes whose single parameter is the group name. These groups are connected to the atoms whose they are constituted by an edge "*part of*";

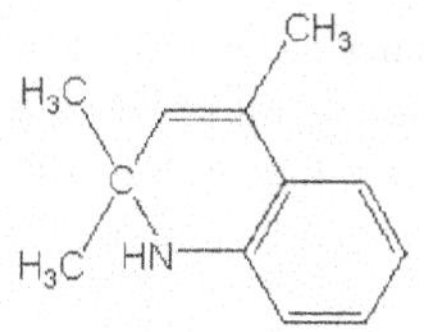

Fig. 4. Bidimensional chemical structure of 1,2-Dyhydro-2,2,4-Trimethylquinoline

Besides, because of in molecular structures, isolated atoms or structural groups do not exists, the specialization operator *Node addition* was replaced by the operator:

- **ConnectedNodeAddition**: G^* is augmented with a new node and it is connected to one of the n pre-existent nodes of G^*; both node and edge attributes are ϕ

The algorithm was implemented in Python/C++. The training of the system produced 86 prototypes spending about one week on a P4 512 RAM. The test on PTE datasets showed the following results:

- On PTE1: 64% accuracy
- On PTE2: 69% accuracy

In the following we report a comparative table of results obtained on PTE1 dataset (because of the lack of results on PTE2 dataset) by different approaches. It is worth noticing that [8] used also information deriving from mutagenesis tests; [7], instead, used the results of in-vivo short term biochemical tests.

We can compare our system with the results obtained by [9,10] because they are the only systems that used exclusively structural information for characterizing Structure Activity Relationships (SARs). The analysis of the results table induce to the conclusion that, using the same input data, the proposed method produces the best performances of accuracy for the database NIEHS.

Table 1. Results of different algorithms on PTE1 dataset

Algorithm	Type	Accuracy (%)
TIPT [7]	Logic Programming	67%
This Work	Inductive Learning on Graphs	64%
Progol [8]	Logic Programming	64%
SUBDUE-CL [10]	Inductive Learning on Graphs	62%
SUBDUE [9]	Inductive Learning on Graphs	46%

5 Conclusions

In this work we presented an extension of a method for the structure learning and its application to the automatic identification of Structure-Activity Relationships. The algorithm was tested on the dataset of the Predictive Toxicology Evaluation Challenge. The results were compared with the other approaches and they showed the effectiveness of our method. Besides it is worth noticing that the proposed approach produces interpretable prototypes that permit the user to interpret the results of the learning process and to identify errors due to a poor representativeness of the training set.

References

1. M. A. Eshera, K.S. Fu: An image understanding system using attributed symbolic representation and inexact graph matching, IEEE Trans. Pattern Analysis and Machine Intelligence, vol. PAMI-8, n. 5 (1986) 604-617.
2. G.E. Hinton: Mapping Part-Whole Hierarchies into Connectionist Networks, Artificial Intelligence, vol. 46 (1990) 47-75.
3. P.H. Winston: Learning Structural Descriptions from Examples, Technical Report MAC-TR-76, Dept. of Electrical Engineering and Computer Science, MIT (1970).
4. P. Foggia, R. Genna, M. Vento: Symbolic vs Connectionist Learning: an Experimental Comparison in a Structured Domain, IEEE Transactions on Knowledge and Data Engineering, IEEE Computer Society Press, Washington, USA. Vol. 13 – 2 (2001) 176-195.
5. S. Muggleton: Inductive Logic Programming, New Generation Computing, vol. 8, n. 4 (1991) 295-318.
6. J. R. Quinlan: Learning logical definitions from relations, Machine Learning, vol. 5, n. 3 (1990) 239-266.
7. D. Bahler and D. Bristol: The induction of rules for predicting chemical cancirogenesis, Proceedings of 26th Hawaii International Conference on System Science, Los Alamitos, IEEE Computer Society Press (1993).
8. S. Muggleton: Inverse Entailment and Progol, New Generation Computing Journal, Vol. 13 (1995) 245-286.
9. D. Cook, L. B. Holder: Substructure Discovery Using Minimum Description Length and Background Knowledge, Journal of Artificial Intelligence Research, Vol. 1 (1994) 231-255.
10. J. Gonzales, L. Holder, D. Cook: Application of Graph-Based Concept Learning to the Predictive Toxicology Domain, Proceedings of the Florida Artificial Intelligence Research Symposium (2001) 377-381.

11. L.P. Cordella, P. Foggia, R. Genna, and M. Vento: Prototyping Structural Descriptions: An Inductive Learning Approach, Advances in Pattern Recognition, Lecture Notes in Computer Science, n°. 1451 (1998) 339-348.
12. R.S. Michalski: Pattern Recognition as Rule-Guided Inductive Inference, IEEE Trans. Pattern Analysis and Machine Intelligence, vol. 2, n°. 4 (1980) 349-361.
13. R.S. Michalski: A Theory and Methodology of Inductive Learning, Machine Learning: An Artificial Intelligence Approach, R.S. Michalski, J.S. Carbonell, and T.M. Mitchell, eds., vol. 1, chapter 4 (1983) 83-133.
14. T.G. Dietterich, R.S. Michalski: A Comparative Review of Selected Methods for Learning from Examples, Machine Learning: An Artificial Intelligence Approach, R.S. Michalski, J.S. Carbonell, and T.M. Mitchell, eds., vol. 1, chapter 3 (1983) 41-82.

Combining Rule-Based and Sample-Based Classifiers - Probabilistic Approach

Marek Kurzynski[1,2]

[1] Wroclaw University of Technology, Faculty of Electronics,
Chair of Systems and Computer Networks, Wyb. Wyspianskiego 27,
50-370 Wroclaw, Poland
marek.kurzynski@pwr.wroc.pl
[2] The Witelon University of Applied Sciences, Ul. Sejmowa 5A,
59-220 Legnica, Poland

Abstract. The present paper is devoted to the pattern recognition methods for combining heterogeneous sets of learning data: set of training examples and the set of expert rules with unprecisely formulated weights understood as conditional probabilities. Adopting the probabilistic model two concepts of recognition learning are proposed. In the first approach two classifiers trained on homogeneous data set are generated and next their decisions are combined using local weighted voting combination rule. In the second method however, one set of data is transformed into the second one and next only one classifier trained on homogeneous set of data is used. Furthermore, the important problem of consistency of expert rules and the learning set is discussed and the method for checking it is proposed.

1 Introduction

The design of the classifier in statistical pattern recognition generally depends on what kind of information is available about the probability distribution of classes and features. If this information is complete, then the Bayes decision scheme can be used. If such information is unknown or incompletely defined, a possible approach is to design a system which will acquire the pertinent information from the actually available data for constructing a decision rule. Usually it is assumed that available information on the probability characteristics is contained in a learning set consisting of a sequence of observed features of patterns and their correct classification. In such a case many learning procedures are known within empirical Bayes decision theory, which lead to the different sample-based pattern recognition algorithms (e.g. [3], [5]).

Another approach, interesting from both theoretical and practical point of view, supposes that appropriate information is contained in expert knowledge. A typical knowledge representation consists of rules of the form IF A THEN B with the weight (uncertainty measure) α. These rules are obtained from the expert as his/her conditional beliefs: if A is known with certainty then the expert's belief into B is α. In this case numerous inference procedures are proposed and

M. De Gregorio et al. (Eds.): BVAI 2005, LNCS 3704, pp. 298–307, 2005.
© Springer-Verlag Berlin Heidelberg 2005

very well investigated for different formal interpretations of the weight α ([4], [6], [14]).

In this paper we shall focus our attention on decision algorithms for the case in which both the learning set and expert rules are available. Additionally, adopting the probabilistic interpretation of weight coefficients, we suppose that expert rules are not provided with exact value of α (i.e. conditional probability), but only an interval is specified (by its upper and lower bounds), into which this probability belongs.

We may expect that the quality of the recognition algorithm will improve when both kinds of information are concurrently utilized. The concept of pattern recognition for considered case requires that both kinds of information have unified formal interpretation. In this paper the probabilistic model is adopted and hence we assign probabilistic meaning to both the information obtained from experts and the numerical data. According to general principles of this model we assume that the classes and features are observed values of appropriate random variables for which the joint probability distribution exists but is unknown. We treat expert-acquired information (rules) and numerical data as a source of knowledge about the unknown probability characteristics.

This paper is a sequel to the author's earlier publications ([10], [11], [12], [13]) and it yields an essential extension of the results included therein.

The contents of the work are as follows. Section 2 introduces necessary background and provides the problem statement. In section 3 the important problem of consistency of expert rules and the learning set is discussed and furthermore the algorithm for evaluating it is proposed. In section 4 we present two different concepts of pattern recognition algorithms for the problem in question. In the first approach two classifiers trained on homogeneous data set are generated and next their decisions are combined using local voting and linear combination rules. In the second method however, one set of data is transformed into the second one and next only one classifier trained on homogeneous set of data is used.

2   Preliminaries and the Problem Statement

Let us consider the pattern recognition problem with probabilistic model. This means that vector of features describing recognized pattern $x \in \mathcal{X} \subseteq \mathcal{R}^d$ and its class number $j \in \mathcal{M} = \{1, 2, ..., M\}$ are observed values of a couple of random variables $(\mathbf{X}, \mathbf{J})$, respectively. Its probability distribution is given by *a priori* probabilities of classes

$$p_j = P(\mathbf{J} = j), \ j \in \mathcal{M} \tag{1}$$

and class-conditional probability density function (CPDFs) of $\mathbf{X}$

$$f_j(x) = f(x/j), \ x \in \mathcal{X}, \ j \in \mathcal{M}. \tag{2}$$

Pattern recognition algorithm Ψ maps the feature space $\mathcal{X}$ to the set of class numbers $\mathcal{M}$, viz.

$$\Psi : \mathcal{X} \rightarrow \mathcal{M}, \tag{3}$$

or equivalently, partitions $\mathcal{X}$ into decision regions:

$$C_x^{(i)} = \{x \in \mathcal{X} : \Psi(x) = i\}, \quad i \in \mathcal{M}. \tag{4}$$

If probabilities (1) and CPDFs (2) are known, i.e. in the case of complete probabilistic information, the optimal (Bayes) recognition algorithm Ψ^*, minimizing the probability of misclassification, makes decision according to the following rule:

$$\Psi^*(x) = i \text{ if } p_i(x) = \max_{k \in \mathcal{M}} p_k(x), \tag{5}$$

where *a posteriori* probabilities $p_j(x)$ can be calculated from the Bayes formula.

Let us now consider the interesting from practical point of view concept of recognition. We assume that *a priori* probabilities (1) and CPDFs (2) are not know, whereas the only information on the probability distribution of $\mathbf{J}$ and $\mathbf{X}$ is contained in the two qualitatively different kinds of data.

1. Learning Set:

$$S = \{(x_1, j_1), (x_2, j_2), ..., (x_N, j_N)\}, \tag{6}$$

where x_i denotes the feature vector of the i-th learning pattern and j_i is its correct classification.

Additionally, let S_i denotes the set of learning patterns from the i-th class.

2. Expert Rules:

$$R = \{R_1, R_2, ..., R_M\}, \tag{7}$$

where

$$R_i = \{r_i^{(1)}, r_i^{(2)}, ..., r_i^{(L_i)}\}, \quad i \in \mathcal{M}, \quad \sum L_i = L \tag{8}$$

denotes the set of rules connected with the i-th class. The rule $r_i^{(k)}$ has the following general form:

IF $w_i^{(k)}(x)$ **THEN J** $= i$ **WITH** probability greater than $\underline{p}_i^{(k)}$ and less than $\overline{p}_i^{(k)}$,

where $w_i^{(k)}(x)$ denotes a predicate depending on the values of the features x.

These rules obtained from an expert are a consequence of his experience and competence and furthermore, they reflect the common regularities resulting from the general knowledge. Experiences have proved that an expert is very frequently not able to formulate the logical rules describing the dependences between the observed and internal values of the system and he cannot describe his way of reasoning. What is relatively easy to obtain is a kind of input-output description of the expert decision making process.

We will continue to adopt the following equivalent form of the rule $r_i^{(k)}$:

$$\underline{p}_i^{(k)} \le p_i^{(k)} \le \overline{p}_i^{(k)} \text{ for } x \in D_i^{(k)}, \tag{9}$$

where

$$D_i^{(k)} = \{x \in \mathcal{X} : w_i^{(k)}(x) = true\} \tag{10}$$

will be called rule-defined region and

$$p_i^{(k)} = \frac{\int_{D_i^{(k)}} p_i(x)dx}{\int_{D_i^{(k)}} dx} \tag{11}$$

is the mean *a posteriori* probability of the i-th class in the set $D_i^{(k)}$.

We suppose that rules R are not contradictory ([13]).

Let $\mathcal{D}_i = \{D_i^{(k)}, k = 1, 2, ..., L_i\}$, $i \in \mathcal{M}$ and $\mathcal{D} = \{D_i^{(k)}, k = 1, 2, ..., L_i, i \in \mathcal{M}\}$ denote appropriate families of rule-defined regions and let additionally

$$\mathcal{X}_R = \cup \mathcal{D} \quad \text{and} \quad \mathcal{X}_R^{(i)} = \cup \mathcal{D}_i \tag{12}$$

denote feature subspaces covered by families $\mathcal{D}$ and , $\mathcal{D}_i$ respectively.

Now our purpose is to construct the recognition algorithm

$$\Psi(S, R, x) = \Psi_{SR}(x) = i, \tag{13}$$

which using information contained in the learning set S and the set of expert rules R recognizes a pattern on the basis of its features x. Some propositions of the rule (13) will be presented in section 4, first however, let discuss the problem of consistency of rule set R and sample set S.

3   Consistency of the Expert Rules Set and the Learning Set

In logical reasoning systems the problem of consistency of the gathered knowledge is usually considered and the consistency is verified by proving that the set of collected facts is consistent in the two-valued logic. As far as knowledge representation with uncertainty characteristics is considered, the notion of consistency is based on the assumed properties of uncertainty measure. In the case of the approach being considered the gathered knowledge concerns the probabilistic properties of the population and therefore the consistency conditions should be considered in the probabilistic bearing. Generally, consistency conditions lead to the following question: are probability characteristics resulting from the rules R and learning set S consistent, i.e. does the learning set come from the population with the probability distribution determined by the expert rules?

Since consistency of sets S and R should be treated as consistency of probabilistic information contained in the both sets, hence we accept the hypothesis that the set of rules and the learning set are consistent if probability of observations from the set S, under restrictions resulting from the set R, is over a some adopted level.

Let introduce first families of sets $\mathcal{B}_i = \{B_i^{(1)}, B_i^{(2)}, ...B_i^{(l_i)}\}$, $i \in \mathcal{M}$ and $\mathcal{B} = \{B^{(1)}, B^{(2)}, ...B^{(l)}\}$, where $B_i^{(m)}$ and $B^{(m)}$ denote not empty constituents of families of sets $\mathcal{D}_i$ and $\mathcal{D}$, respectively. It is clear, that sets from every family are disjoint and furthermore $\mathcal{X}_R = \cup \mathcal{B}$ and $\mathcal{X}_R^{(i)} = \cup \mathcal{B}_i$, i.e. families $\mathcal{B}$ and $\mathcal{B}_i$ form partitions of feature subspaces $\mathcal{X}_R$ and $\mathcal{X}_R^{(i)}$, respectively ([15]).

Let next $I_i^{(m)}$ $(\widehat{I}_i^{(m)})$ be the set of indices of rules from R_i fulfilling the conditions $w_i^{(k)}(x)$ for $x \in B_i^{(m)}$ (for $x \in B^{(m)}$), or equivalently

$$I_i^{(m)} = \{k : B_i^{(m)} \subseteq D_i^{(k)}\}, \quad \widehat{I}_i^{(m)} = \{k : B^{(m)} \subseteq D_i^{(k)}\}. \tag{14}$$

From (10) it results that in expert opinion

$$P(\underline{p}_i^{(m)} \leq p_i^{(m)} \leq \overline{\overline{p}}_i^{(m)}) = 1, \tag{15}$$

where

$$\underline{p}_i^{(m)} = \min_{k \in I_i^{(m)}} \underline{p}_i^{(k)}, \quad \overline{\overline{p}}_i^{(m)} = \max_{k \in I_i^{(m)}} \overline{p}_i^{(k)}. \tag{16}$$

$p_i^{(m)}$ denotes mean *a posteriori* probability (see (12)) of the i-th class in the set $B_i^{(m)}$. Let $N_i^{(m)}$ and $N^{(m)}$ denote the number of learning patterns belonging to the set $B_i^{(m)}$ from sets S_i and S, respectively. Class numbers of learning patterns from $B_i^{(m)}$ will be treated as observed values of Bernoulli random variable $\mathbf{Y}_i^{(m)}$:

$$\mathbf{Y}_i^{(m)} = \begin{cases} 1 \text{ if } x \in B_i^{(m)} \text{ is from } i\text{th class,} \\ 0 \text{ if } x \in B_i^{(m)} \text{ is not from } i\text{th class.} \end{cases} \tag{17}$$

with probability $P(\mathbf{Y}_i^{(m)} = 1) = p_i^{(m)}$.

Let now introduce two definitions.

Definition 1. If

$$P(\underline{p}_i^{(m)} \leq p_i^{(m)} \leq \overline{\overline{p}}_i^{(m)}) \geq \alpha_i^{(m)}, \tag{18}$$

where the confidence level is determined on the base of observations $\mathbf{Y}_i^{(m)}$, then we say that the sets S and R are locally (in the set $B_i^{(m)}$) consistent on the level $\alpha_i^{(m)}$.

Definition 2. Sets R and S are said to be α consistent, where

$$\alpha = \frac{\sum_{i=1}^{M} \sum_{m=1}^{l_i} \alpha_i^{(m)} V(B_i^{(m)})}{\sum_{i=1}^{M} V(\mathcal{X}_R^{(i)})}. \tag{19}$$

In order to calculate $\alpha_i^{(m)}$ in (19) let note that for Bernoulli distribution on the base of observation k successes in n trials, we can determine the confidence interval

$$P(p_1(\underline{\beta}, k, n) \leq p \leq p_2(\overline{\beta}, k, n)) = 1 - (\underline{\beta} + \overline{\beta}). \tag{20}$$

The endpoints in (21) (confidence limits) are equal ([16]):

$$p_1(\underline{\beta}, k, n) = \frac{k}{k + (n - k + 1)F(\underline{\beta}, 2(n - k + 1), 2k)}, \tag{21}$$

$$p_2(\overline{\beta}, k, n) = \frac{(k + 1)F(\overline{\beta}, 2(k + 1), 2(n - k))}{n - k + (k + 1)F(\overline{\beta}, 2(k + 1), 2(n - k))}, \tag{22}$$

where $F(\beta, k, n)$ is quantile in the range of β of a Snedecor's F distribution with k and n degrees of freedom.

Hence and from (19) and (21) we first find significance levels $\underline{\beta}_i^{(m)}$ and $\overline{\beta}_i^{(m)}$ as solutions of the following equations:

$$\underline{\underline{p}}_i^{(m)} = p_1(\underline{\beta}_i^{(m)}, N_i^{(m)}, N^{(m)}), \quad \overline{\overline{p}}_i^{(m)} = p_2(\overline{\beta}_i^{(m)}, N_i^{(m)}, N^{(m)}), \qquad (23)$$

and next we simply get

$$\alpha_i^{(m)} = 1 - (\underline{\beta}_i^{(m)} + \overline{\beta}_i^{(m)}). \qquad (24)$$

It should be emphasised that generally, proposed evaluation (19) of consistency between two sets of data is not a measure of quality of set of expert rules (and in consequence a measure of expert quality [1], [7]). There are many reasons which can lead to the relatively small value of α, e.g. not sufficently numerous learning set, noises in feature measurements or errors of learning set source. The index α may be considered as a measure of expert rules quality in the case if we suppose that learning set is noise-free and furthermore for every set $B_i^{(m)}$ the number $N^{(m)}$ satisfies inequality ([16]):

$$N^{(m)} \geq \frac{(u_\alpha)^2}{2(\underline{\underline{p}}_i^{(m)} + \overline{\overline{p}}_i^{(m)})^2}, \qquad (25)$$

where u_α is critical value of the Gaussian random variable for acceptable confidence level α.

4   Pattern Recognition Algorithms

In the sample-based classification, i.e. when the only learning set S is given, one obvious and conceptually simple method is to estimate *a priori* probabilities and CPDFs and then to use these estimators to calculate *a posteriori* probabilities (let say $p_i^{(S)}(x)$), i.e. discriminant functions of the optimal (Bayes) classifier (5).

On the other hand, using this concept in the case when only the set of rules R is given, we obtain the so-called GAP (the Greatest Approximated *a posteriori* Probability) rule-based algorithm, which originally was introduced in [10]:

$$\Psi_R(x) = i \quad \text{if} \quad p_i^{(R)}(x) = \max_{k \in \mathcal{M}} p_k^{(R)}(x). \qquad (26)$$

$p_i^{(R)}(x)$ denotes approximated *a posteriori* probability of i-th class, which - for $x \in B^{(m)}$ - is calculated from the set R according to the following formulas:

– for $i \in \mathcal{M}^{(m)} = \{I : \hat{I}_i^{(m)} \neq \varnothing\}$:

$$\hat{p}_i(x) = \frac{\hat{\underline{p}}_i^{(m)} + \overline{\hat{p}}_i^{(m)}}{2}, \quad \overline{\hat{p}}_i^{(m)} = \min_{k \in \hat{I}_i^m} \overline{p}_i^{(k)}, \quad \hat{\underline{p}}_i^{(m)} = \min_{k \in \hat{I}_i^m} \underline{p}_i^{(k)}, \qquad (27)$$

– for $i \in \mathcal{M} - \mathcal{M}^{(m)}$:

$$\hat{p}_i(x) = [1 - \sum_{j \in \mathcal{M}^{(m)}} \hat{p}_j]/[M - \mid \mathcal{M}^{(m)} \mid]. \tag{28}$$

The final value of $p_i^{(R)}(x)$ should be normalized to 1, i.e.

$$p_i^{(R)}(x) = \hat{p}_i(x)/ \sum_{i \in \mathcal{M}} \hat{p}_i(x). \tag{29}$$

When both sets S and R are given we propose two concepts of recognition algorithms, which are presented in next subsections. In our propositions information included in sets S and R is submitted to processing and fusion. Difference consists in order of both activities.

4.1   Mixed Algorithm

In so-called mixed algorithm decision is made according to the following rule:

$$\Psi_S R(x) = i \quad \text{if} \quad p_i^{(SR)}(x) = \max_{k \in \mathcal{M}} p_k^{(SR)}(x), \tag{30}$$

where

$$p_i^{(SR)}(x) = \gamma(x)\, p_i^{(R)}(x) + [1 - \gamma(x)]\, p_i^{(S)}, \quad 0 \le \gamma(x) \le 1. \tag{31}$$

It means, that first we calculate approximated (estimated) values of *a posteriori* probabilities separately from both sets, and next we use their weighted sum in the Bayes algorithm (5).

In the mixed algorithm (30) a mixing coefficient $\gamma(x)$ plays the crucial role. Assuming that $\gamma(x)$ is constant in set $B^{(m)}$ and equal to $\gamma^{(m)}$, $m = 1, 2, ..., l$, we propose three methods of calculating it.

1. The first method takes into account intuitively obvious character of dependence between $\gamma^{(m)}$ and the number of learning patterns in $B^{(m)}$ (let say $N^{(m)}$) and the accuracy of determining *a posteriori* probabilities $p_i(x)$ in rules R for $x \in B^{(m)}$ (let say $\Delta^{(m)}$). Namely, $\gamma^{(m)}$ should be a decreasing function of $N^{(m)}$ and $\Delta^{(m)}$, for example:

$$\gamma^{(m)} = \frac{1 - \Delta^{(m)}}{(1 - \Delta^{(m)}) + (1 - e^{-N^{(m)}})}. \tag{32}$$

2. In the second approach, for a particular $B^{(m)}$ such value $\gamma^{(m)} \in [0,1]$ is applied which maximizes the number of correctly classified learning patterns from $B^{(m)}$.

3. As previously, but now $\gamma^{(m)} \in \{0, 1\}$. It means that we always use a simple algorithm Ψ_R or Ψ_S, which for each set $B^{(m)}$ is selected independently to obtain the better local result of recognition.

4.2   Unified Algorithms

Now, in order to find (13) we will transform one set of data into the second set and next, having the homogeneous form of information, we can simply use either the GAP algorithm (for transformation $S \rightarrow R'$) or recognition algorithm with learning (e.g. NN - nearest neighbour decision rule [3], [5]) for transformation $R \rightarrow S'$.

Our proposition of procedures for "the unification of information" leads to the following algorithms.

Algorithm $R \rightarrow S'$

```
Input data: N'_i^(m)-the number of generated patterns for region B_i^(m)
for i = 1 to M
      for m = 1 to l_i
            for k = 1 to N'_i^(m)
                  generate random class number j ∈ M with probabilities
                  if j = i
                  then
                        (variant 1) p(j) = (p_i^(m) + p̄̄_i^(m))/2
                        (variant 2) p(j) randomly (uniformly) selected
                        from the interval [p_i^(m), p̄̄_i^(m)]
                  else
                        p(j) = [1 - p(i)]/(M - 1)
                  fi
                  generate random feature vector x uniformly distributed
                  in B_i^(m)
            endfor
      endfor
endfor
```

Algorithm $S \rightarrow R'$

```
Input data: α - confidence level for created rules
            L'_i - number of rules for i-th class (i ∈ M)
            D'_i^(k) - feature regions for rules k = 1, 2, ..., L'_i
for i = 1 to M
      for k = 1 to L'_i
            find N^(k) - number of learning patterns belonging to D'_i^(k)
            find N_i^(k) - number of learning patterns belonging to D'_i^(k)
            calculate p'_i^(k)(1-α/2, N_i^(k), N^(k)) and p̄'_i^(k)(1-α/2, N_i^(k), N^(k))
            according to (21) and (22), respectively
      endfor
endfor
```

In order to determine regions $D'_i{}^{(k)}$ we can use methods known in procedures of generating fuzzy rules from numerical data, e.g. based on cluster analysis, graph theory or decomposition of CPDFs ([2]).

5   Conclusions

During the past decade the fusion of various sources of knowledge was firmly established as a practical and effective solution for difficult pattern recognition tasks ([1], [7], [8]). This idea is established using classifier combination approach, which in the literature is known under many names: hybrid methods, decision combinations, classifier fusion, mixture of experts, modular systems, to name only a few ([9]).

Most of the research on classifier ensambles is concerned with generating ensambles by using a single learning model. Different classifiers are received by manipulating the training set, or the input features, and next their decisions are combined in some way (typically by voting) to classify new patterns. Another approach is to generate classifiers by applying different learning algorithms to a single data set ([17]).

The present paper is devoted to the methods for combining heterogeneous sets of learning data: set of training examples and the set of expert rules with unprecisely formulated weights. Adopting the probabilistic model of classification, we discuss two different concepts of pattern recognition algorithms in which the both sets of data are treated as a source of information about the probability distribution of features and classes. In the first approach two classifiers trained on homogeneous data set are generated and next their decisions are combined using local weighted voting combination rules. In the second method however, one set of data is transformed into the second one. This procedure of unification of information allows to generate only one classifier trained on homogeneous set of data.

References

1. Chen D., Cheng X. (2001) An asymptotic analysis of some expert fusion methods, Pattern Recognition Letters, vol. 22 : 901 - 904
2. Czabanski R. (2002) Self-generating fuzzy rules from numerical data, Techn. Report Silesian Technical Univ. Gliwice (PhD Thesis) (in Polish)
3. Devroye L., Gyorfi P., Lugossi G. (1996) A Probabilistic Theory of Pattern Recognition, Springer Verlag, New York
4. Dubois D., Lang J. (1994) Possibilistic logic, [in:] Handbook of Logic in Artificial Intelligence and Logic Programming, Oxford Univ. Press : 439-513
5. Duda R., Hart P., Stork D. (2001) Pattern Classification, John Wiley and Sons
6. Halpern J. (2003) Reasoning about Uncertainty, MIT Press
7. Jacobs R. (1995) Methods for combining experts probability assessments, Neural Computation, vol 7 : 867-888
8. Kittler J., Duin R., Matas J. (1998) On combining classifiers, IEEE Trans. on PAMI, vol. 20 : 226-239
9. Kuncheva L. (2001) Combining classifiers: Soft computing solutions, [in.] Pattern Recognition: from Classical to Modern Approaches, Pal S., Pal A. [eds.], World Scientific: 427-451
10. Kurzynski M., Sas J., Blinowska A. (1993) Rule-Based Medical Decision-Making with Learning, Proc. 12th World IFAC Congress, Vol. 4, Sydney : 319-322

11. Kurzynski M., Wozniak M. (2000) Rule-Based Algorithms with Learning for Sequential Recognition Problem, Proc. 3rd Int. Conf. Fusion 2000, Paris : 10-13
12. Kurzynski M., Puchala E. (2001) Hybrid Pattern Recognition Algorithms Applied to the Computer-Aided Medical Diagnosis, Medical Data Analysis, LNCS 2199, Springer Verlag : 133-139
13. Kurzynski M. (2004) Consistency Conditions of the Expert Rule Set in the Probabilistic Pattern Recognition, Computer Information Systems, Springer Verlag, LNCS 3314 : 831-836
14. Mitchell T. (1997), Machine Learning, McGraw-Hill Science
15. Kuratowski K., Mostowski A. (1986) Set Theory, Nort-Holland Publishing Co, Amsterdam
16. Sachs L. (1982), Applied Statistics. A Handbook of Techniques, Springer Verlag, New York, Berlin, Tokyo
17. Woods K., Kegelmeyer W. (1997), Combination of multiple classifiers using local accuracy estimates, IEEE Trans. on PAMI, vol. 19 :405-410

Mapping and Combining Combinatorial Problems into Energy Landscapes via Pseudo-Boolean Constraints

Priscila M.V. Lima[1], Glaucia C. Pereira[2],
M. Mariela M. Morveli-Espinoza[2], and Felipe M.G. França[2]

[1] NCE/Instituto de Matemática, UFRJ, Rio de Janeiro, Brazil
priscila@nce.ufrj.br
http://www.geti.dcc.ufrj.br/
[2] COPPE – Sistemas e Computação, UFRJ, Rio de Janeiro, Brazil
{gpereira, mme, felipe}@cos.ufrj.br
http://www.cos.ufrj.br/~felipe

Abstract. This paper introduces a novel approach to the specification of hard combinatorial problems as pseudo-Boolean constraints. It is shown (i) how this set of constraints defines an energy landscape representing the space state of solutions of the target problem, and (ii) how easy is to combine different problems into new ones mostly via the union of the corresponding constraints. Graph colouring and Traveling Salesperson Problem (TSP) were chosen as the basic problems from which new combinations were investigated. Higher-order Hopfield networks of stochastic neurons were adopted as search engines in order to solve the mapped problems.

Keywords: Higher-order Networks; Graph Colouring; Pseudo-Boolean Constraints; Satisfiability; Simulated Annealing; TSP.

1 Introduction

The ability to learn associative behaviour through examples is a desirable feature in an adaptive system. Nevertheless, it would not be practical to acquire, through examples, certain pieces of knowledge that had already been learnt by other systems. Besides, sometimes it is easier to describe a problem via its constraints to an artificial neural network (ANN) such that the set of its global energy minima corresponds to the set of solutions to the problem in question. For example, an explanation of how the Traveling Salesperson Problem (TSP) can be defined as a set of mathematical constraints that are solvable by an ANN can be found in [6] and [5].

Alternatively, constraints may be essentially logical, constituting a kind of description or specification of a suitable solution for a problem being modeled. A problem that apparently does not involve optimizing a cost function is that of finding a *model* for a logical sentence. In propositional logic, that would consist

M. De Gregorio et al. (Eds.): BVAI 2005, LNCS 3704, pp. 308–317, 2005.

of the assertion of truth-values to the propositional symbols that appear in the formula in question, in such a way that the formula as a whole becomes true. That mapping of truth-values to propositions constitutes, for propositional formulae, an interpretation of it [9]. A formula that has no models is said to be *unsatisfiable* or *inconsistent* . Some problems may be better described as a combination of logical and mathematical constraints. A subset of this combination could be seen as a sum of weighted products of boolean variables, pseudo-Boolean constraints [2].

This paper introduces a novel approach to the specification of hard combinatorial problems as pseudo-Boolean constraints defining an energy landscape representing the space state of solutions of the target problem. It is shown how easy is to map and combine different problems into new ones mostly via the union of the corresponding constraints. Graph colouring and Traveling Salesperson Problem (TSP) were chosen as the basic problems from which new combinations were investigated. Among other possible computational intelligence models that could have been used, (e.g., genetic algorithms, artificial immune systems, etc) this work adopted higher-order Hopfield networks of stochastic neurons in order to solve all the mapped problems.

2   Higher-Order Hopfield Networks

A notable step towards understanding the collective properties of artificial neural networks (ANNs) was taken by J. Hopfield [4] when he saw an analogy between the evolution of a spin-glass system towards minimizing its energy function and the evolution of the activity function of a so-called *Hopfield network* . For a function to be called an *energy function* it is necessary that its value decreases monotonically until the (or one of the) stable state(s) of the system is reached. The direct consequence of such interpretation is the proof of *convergence to energy minima* of artificial neural networks (ANNs) composed of symmetrically connected (i. e., $w_{ij} = w_{ji}$) McCulloch-Pitts' neurons $(i, j, \ldots)$ acting as energy minimization (EM) systems. The proof required the observation of a constraint: that nodes operate *asynchronously* , i.e., that no two nodes operate at the same time step. This restriction can be weakened to one where asynchronous operation is only required for *neighbouring nodes* , i.e., it is guaranteed that non-neighbouring nodes can operate at the same time and energy will still decrease monotonically [1]. Two nodes i and j are said to be *neighbours* if they are linked by a connection with weight $w_{ij} \neq 0$.

Sometimes it is convenient to express not only the mutual influence between two neurons, but also the influence of concurrent activation of three or more neurons. Such connections are known as multiplicative or *higher-order* and the number of units pertaining to a connection is called the *arity* of the connection. Only one value (positive or negative) is associated to each higher-order connection and networks containing one or more multiplicative connections are called *higher-order networks* . Notice that higher-order connections are still considered symmetric, i.e., they take part in the activation function of all nodes involved in the connection, and have the same weight value.

Unfortunately, a Hopfield network, even of higher-order, is only capable of finding local minima. In this sense, an improvement consists of incorporating an stochastic component to the neurons behavior such that the resulting network could find global minima through a mechanism known as *simulated annealing* [7]. In this way, consider a random variable d_i associated to each binary node $v_i \in V$, V denoting the set of random variables $v_1, v_2, \ldots, v_n$, $n = | V |$. The values of these random variables are taken from a common finite domain $D = \{0, 1\}$, so that v_i represents the state of neuron i and each element of D^n is a possible network state. Each $v_i \in V$ define a set of neighbours $Q(v_i)$ in such a way that a homogenous neighbourhood is obtained, i.e., for any two $v_i, v_j \in V$, if $v_j \in Q(v_i)$, then $v_i \in Q(v_j)$. The result of this incorporation can be described by the following equations:

$$
\begin{cases}
p(v_i = 1 | v_j = d_j; v_j \in Q(v_i)) = \frac{1}{1+e^{(-net_i)/T}} \\[2ex]
p(v_i = 0 | v_j = d_j; v_j \in Q(v_i)) = \frac{e^{(-net_i)/T}}{1+e^{-net_i/T}}
\end{cases}
$$

Where $net_i = (\sum w_{ij} v_j(t)) - \theta_i$, θ_i is the threshold of neuron i, and T is the parameter known as *temperature* $(T \geq 0)$.

3   Mapping Satisfiability to Energy Minimization

In order to convert satisfiability (SAT) to energy minimization (EM), consider the following mapping of logical formulae to the set $\{0, 1\}$:

$H(true) = 1$
$H(false) = 0$
$H(\neg p) = 1 - H(p)$
$H(p \wedge q) = H(p) \times H(q)$
$H(p \vee q) = H(p) + H(q) - H(p \wedge q)$

If a logical formula is converted to an equivalent in clausal form, the result being a conjunction φ of disjunctions φ_i, it is possible to associate energy to $H(\neg \varphi)$. Nevertheless, energy calculated in this way would only have two possible values: *one*, meaning solution not found (if the network has not reached global minimum), and *zero* when a model has been found. Intuitively, it would be better to have more "clues", or degrees of "non-satisfibililty", on whether the network is close to a solution or not.

Let $\varphi = \wedge_i \varphi_i$ where $\varphi_i = \vee_j p_{ij}$, and p_{ij} is a literal. Therefore $\varphi = \vee_i \varphi_i$ where $\varphi_i = \wedge_j \neg p_{ij}$. Instead of making $E = H(\neg \varphi)$, consider $E = H^*(\neg \varphi) = \sum_i H(\neg \varphi_i)$. So, $E = \sum_i H(\wedge_j \neg p_{ij}) = \sum_i \prod_j H(\neg p_{ij})$, where $H(p)$ will be referred to as p. Informally, E counts the number of clauses that are *not satisfied* by the interpretation represented by the network's state.

An issue to point out is that the resulting network of the above mapping may have higher-order connections, i.e., connections involving more than two neurons. That does not constitute a hindrance as has been demonstrated that, with higher-order connections, Boltzmann Machines still converge to energy minima [3]. Remarks on a learning mechanics for this network are made in [6]. Parallel and distributed simulation of network with higher-order connections can be done by substituting each higher-order connection by a completely-connected subgraph. Alternatively, [10] converts the higher-order network to a binarily connected one that preserves the order of energy values of the different network states. A simple example demonstrates how SAT can be mapped to EM. Let φ be the formula, expressed as a conjunction of clauses:

$$\varphi = (p \lor \neg q) \land (p \lor \neg r) \land (r).$$

SAT(φ) can be translated to the minimum of the following energy function:

$$
\begin{aligned}
E &= H(\neg(p \lor \neg q)) + H(\neg(p \lor \neg r)) + H(\neg r) \\
&= H(\neg p \land q) + H(\neg p \land r) + H(\neg r) \\
&= (1 - p) * q + (1 - p) * r + (1 - r) = q - pq - pr + 1
\end{aligned}
$$

where $H(prop) = prop$.

4 Combinatorial Problems as Pseudo-Boolean Constraints

So far, the problem of mapping SAT to EM, by associating energy to "amount of non-satisfiability" and minimizing it, has been presented. This, together with the fact that the language of logic can be used to define a set of constraints, may lead to a technique for mapping and combining optimization problems into energy minimization. The mapping of three problems into constraint satisfiability are introduced next: TSP, Graph Colouring and a third problem resulting from the combination of the first two problems.

4.1 Mapping TSP

Let $G = (V, A)$ be an undirected graph, where V is the graph's vertex set, A the set of G's edges, being each edge an unordered pair of G's vertices. Associating each vertex $i \in V$ to a city and each edge $(i, j) \in A$ to a path between i and j, if $|V| = n \geq 3$ and $dist_{ij}$ is the cost associated to the edge $(i, j) \in A$ where $\{i, j\} \in V$, then, the Travelling Salesperson Problem (TSP) consists on determining the minimum cost Hamiltonian cycle of G. In order to enable the tour to end at an initial city a, a twin name a' is given so that it will be clamped as the least city of the tour (with all traveling costs repeated), in the same way that a is clamped as the first city of the tour. In this way, a problem with m cities has to use an augmented $n \times n$ matrix, where $n = m + 1$, so that all conditions may be applied to a round tour.

Mapping to Constraint Satisfiability. The network is composed by an $n \times n$ matrix of binary neurons v_{ij}, where i represents a city in V and j represents the position of i in the tour. The repetition of propositional clauses, which differ only by the value of indices, is represented in a compact form by the symbol of universal quantification. However, it should be stressed that the use of universal quantifiers to compress the representation of the propositional constraints does not mean that the language of logic used to describe such constraints has become first order logic. The network's behavior is specified by the following constraints:

Integrity Constraints:

> **(i)** All n cities must take part in the tour:
> $\forall i, \forall j | 1 \leq i \leq n, 1 \leq j \leq n : \vee_j(v_{ij})$. So, let $\varphi_1 = \wedge_i(\vee_j(v_{ij}))$.

> **(ii)** Two cities cannot occupy the same position in the tour:
> $\forall i, \forall j, \forall i' | 1 \leq i \leq n, 1 \leq j \leq n, 1 \leq i' \leq n, i \neq i' : \neg(v_{ij} \wedge v_{i'j})$.
> So, let $\varphi_2 = \wedge_i \wedge_{i' \neq i} \wedge_j \neg(v_{ij} \wedge v_{i'j})$.

> **(iii)** A city cannot occupy more than one position in the tour:
> $\forall i, \forall j, \forall j' | 1 \leq i \leq n, 1 \leq j \leq n, 1 \leq j' \leq n, j \neq j' : \neg(v_{ij} \wedge v_{ij'})$.
> So, let $\varphi_3 = \wedge_i \wedge_j \wedge_{j' \neq j} \neg(v_{ij} \wedge v_{ij'})$.

Optimality Constraints:

> **(iv)** The cost between two consecutive cities in the tour:
> $\forall i, \forall j, \forall i' | 1 \leq i \leq n, 1 \leq j \leq n - 1, 1 \leq i' \leq n, i \neq i' : dist_{ii'}(v_{ij} \wedge v_{i'(j+1)})$
> So, let $\varphi_4 = \vee_i \vee_{i' \neq i} \vee_{j < n} dist_{ii'}(v_{ij} \wedge v_{i'(j+1)})$.

Constraints **(ii)** and **(iii)** are Winner-Takes-All (WTA) constraints. They can be used to justify the conversion of disjunctions in the middle of constraints to a conjunction of disjuncts. All the constraints above are associated to a penalty strength that is expressed through multiplicative constants. The highest multiplicative constant, represented by β, is applied to the WTA constraints. The other integrity constraints (type **(i)**) are weighetd by α. The lowest penalty strength is given to optimality constraints (type **(iv)**), which are weighted by constant 1. So,

$$\begin{cases} dist = \max\{dist_{ij}\} \\ \alpha = ((n^3 - 2n^2 + n) * dist) + h \\ \beta = ((n^2 + 1) * \alpha) + h \end{cases}$$

Mapping SAT into EM. We will use the method described in [10] to map logical propositional formulae into the set $\{0, 1\}$. The H operator will be employed in all three problems approached by this work. The energy equation relative to the integrity constraints is presented next followed by the detailing of its components:

$$E_i = \alpha H^*_{WTA}(\neg\varphi_1) + \beta H^*(\neg\varphi_2) + \beta H^*(\neg\varphi_3)$$

As $\varphi_1 = \wedge_i(\vee_j(v_{ij})), \neg\varphi_1 = \vee_i(\wedge_j(\neg v_{ij}))$.

$$H^*(\neg\varphi_1) = \sum_{i=1}^n H(\wedge_j(\neg v_{ij})) = \sum_{i=1}^n \prod_{j=1}^n H(\neg v_{ij}) = \sum_{i=1}^n \prod_{j=1}^n (1 - v_{ij})$$

However, due to WTA constraints, the actual mapping of $\neg\varphi_1$ is

$$H^*_{WTA}(\neg\varphi_1) = \sum_{i=1}^n \sum_{j=1}^n (1 - v_{ij})$$

As $\neg\varphi_2 = \vee_i \vee_{i' \neq i} \vee_j (v_{ij} \wedge v_{i'j})$,

$$H^*(\neg\varphi_2) = \sum_{i=1}^n \sum_{i'=1, i' \neq i}^n \sum_{j=1}^n H(v_{ij} \wedge v_{i'j}) = \sum_{i=1}^n \sum_{i'=1, i' \neq i}^n \sum_{j=1}^n v_{ij} v_{i'j}$$

As $\neg\varphi_3 = \vee_i \vee_j \vee_{j' \neq j} (v_{ij} \wedge v_{ij'})$,

$$H^*(\neg\varphi_3) = \sum_{i=1}^n \sum_{j=1}^n \sum_{j'=1, j' \neq j}^n H(v_{ij} \wedge v_{ij'}) = \sum_{i=1}^n \sum_{j=1}^n \sum_{j'=1, j' \neq j}^n v_{ij} v_{ij'}$$

Next, the term of the energy equation relative to the tour's cost (optimality constraints) is introduced: $E_o = \sum_s H^*(\varphi_4)$.

$$H^*(\varphi_4) = \sum_{i=1}^n \sum_{i'=1, i' \neq i}^n \sum_{j=1}^{n-1} dist_{ii'} H(v_{ij} \wedge v_{i'(j+1)}) =$$
$$= \sum_{i=1}^n \sum_{i'=1, i' \neq i}^n \sum_{j=1}^{n-1} dist_{ii'} v_{ij} v_{i'(j+1)}$$

The complete energy equation becomes: $E = E_i + E_o$.

4.2   Graph Colouring Mapping

Let $G = (V, A)$ be an undirected graph, where V is the graph's vertex set, A the set of G's edges, being each edge an unordered pair of G's vertices. The Graph Colouring Problem consists in determining the minimum assignment of colours (positive integers) to the vertices such that each vertex has only one colour and no two neighbouring vertices have the same colour.

Mapping to Constraint Satisfiability. The network is mainly composed by a matrix V_{colour} having $n \times n$ binary neurons vc_{ik} and a matrix C_{olour} having $1 \times n$ binary neurons c_k, where i is a vertex in V and k represents the colour associated to vertex i. Addicionally, a matrix $neigh_{ii'}$ is used to indicate the neighbouring relationship between vertices:

Integrity Constraints:

(**v**) Every vertex must have one colour assigned to it:
$\forall i, \forall_k | 1 \leq i \leq n, 1 \leq k \leq n : \vee(vc_{ik})$. So, let $\varphi_5 = \wedge_i(\vee_k vc_{ik})$.

(**vi**) Two neighbouring vertices cannot have the same colour:
$\forall i, \forall i', \forall_k | 1 \leq i \leq n, 1 \leq i' \leq n, 1 \leq k \leq n, i \neq i' :$
$\neg(neigh_{ii'}) \vee \neg(vc_{ik} \wedge vc_{i'k})$.
So, let $\varphi_6 = \wedge_i \wedge_{i' \neq i} \wedge_k (\neg(neigh_{ii'}) \vee \neg(vc_{ik} \wedge vc_{i'k}))$.

(vii) A vertex cannot have more than one colour:

$\forall i, \forall_k, \forall_{k'}|1 \leq i \leq n, 1 \leq k \leq n, 1 \leq k' \leq n, k \neq k' : \neg(vc_{ik} \wedge vc_{ik'})$.

So, let $\varphi_7 = \wedge_i \wedge_k \wedge_{k' \neq k} \neg(vc_{ik} \wedge vc_{ik'})$.

(viii) If a colour k is assigned to a vertex in matrix V_{colour}, then the corresponding unit in matrix C_{olour} must be activated:

$\forall i, \forall k|1 \leq i \leq n, 1 \leq k \leq n : \neg vc_{ik} \vee c_k$. So, let $\varphi_8 = \wedge_i \wedge_k (\neg vc_{ik} \vee c_k)$.

Optimality Constraints:

(ix) The number of activated elements in matrix C_{olour}:

$\forall k|1 \leq k \leq n : c_k$. So, let $\varphi_9 = \vee_k c_k$.

Similarly to the case of TSP, multiplicative constants α and β are used to indicate the penalty strength:

$$\begin{cases} \alpha = (n * 1) + h \\ \beta = ((n^3 + n^2 + 1) * \alpha) + h \end{cases}$$

Mapping SAT into EM. Let's generate the energy equation relative to the integrity constraints: $E_i = \beta[H^*(\neg\varphi_7)] + \alpha[H^*_{WTA}(\neg\varphi_5) + H^*(\neg\varphi_6) + H^*(\neg\varphi_8)]$. Since $E_o = \sum_s H^*(\varphi_9)$, then

$$E = E_i + E_o = \beta[\sum_{i=1}^{n}\sum_{k=1}^{n}\sum_{k'=1,k'\neq k}^{n} vc_{ik}vc_{ik'}] + \alpha[\sum_{i=1}^{n}\sum_{k=1}^{n}(1 - vc_{ik})] +$$
$$\alpha[\sum_{i=1}^{n}\sum_{i'=1,i'\neq i}^{n}\sum_{k=1}^{n} vc_{ik}vc_{i'k}neigh_{ii'}] + \alpha[\sum_{i=1}^{n}\sum_{k=1}^{n} vc_{ik}(1-c_k)] + \sum_{k=1}^{n} c_k$$

4.3   Map Colouring-TSP Mapping

A combination of two different problems is tackled here: Map Colouring and TSP. This hybrid problem is based on a set of cities, which are organised in contiguous regions. The TSP restrictions are maintained and the neighbourhood among adjacent regions is represented by different colours. The cost functions of the original problems, i.e., number of colours and tour cost, are part of the new cost function to be minimized. Interesting solutions would be tradeoffs between solutions of the two problems and this could be obtained by minimizing the change of colours between consecutive cities in the tour.

Let $M = (V, A_1, A_2)$ be an undirected multigraph, where V is the graph's vertex set, being each vertex $i \in V$ associated to a city. A_1 is the set of M's edges so that an edge $(i, j) \in A_1$ exists iff i and j belong to different adjacent regions. A_2 is the set of M's edges associated to all possible direct paths between any pair of cities i and j. Each edge $(i, j) \in A_2$ has an associated distance cost $dist_{ij}$. The resulting Map Colouring-Travelling Salesperson Problem (MC-TSP) consists of determining (i) a tour and (ii) a colour assignment to the different regions (by assigning colours to the visited cities).

Mapping to Constraint Satisfiability. The resulting network is composed by the matrices devised for (a) Graph Colouring and (b) TSP:

(a) A matrix V_{colour} having $n \times n$ binary neurons vc_{ik} and a matrix C_{olour} having $1 \times n$ binary neurons c_k, where i is a vertex in V and k represents the colour associated to vertex i. Addicionally, an $n \times n$ matrix $neigh$ is used to indicate the neighbouring relationship between vertices;

(b) An $n \times n$ matrix of binary neurons v_{ij},
where i represents a city in V and j represents the position of i in the tour.

Integrity Constraints:

The set of integrity constraints is the union of TSP's integrity constraints **(i)**, **(ii)**, **(iii)** and graph colouring's integrity constraints **(v)**, **(vi)**, **(vii)**, **(viii)**.

Optimality Constraints:

The set of optimality constraints is the union of TSP's and Graph Colouring's optimality constraints **(iv)**, **(ix)** and constraints of type **(x)** below:

(x) The change of colours between consecutive cities in the tour:
$\forall i, \forall j, \forall i', \forall k, \forall k' | 1 \le i \le n, 1 \le j \le (n-1), 1 \le i' \le n, 1 \le k \le n, 1 \le k' \le n, i \ne i', k \ne k' : (v_{ij} \wedge v_{i'(j+1)} \wedge vc_{ik} \wedge vc_{i'k'})$.
So, let $\varphi_{10} = \bigvee_i \bigvee_{j<n} \bigvee_{i' \ne i} \bigvee_k \bigvee_{k' \ne k}(v_{ij} \wedge v_{i'(j+1)} \wedge vc_{ik} \wedge vc_{i'k'})$.

Multiplicative constants γ and δ are added to the multiplicative constants of TSP and Graph Colouring in order to indicate the new penalty strengths:

$$\begin{cases} dist = \max\{dist_{ij}\} \\ \alpha = ((n^3 - 2n^2 + n) * dist) + h \\ \beta = ((n^5 - n^4 - n^3 + n^2 + 1) * \alpha) + h \\ \gamma = ((n+1) * \beta) + h \\ \delta = ((2n^3 - n^2 + n + 1) * \gamma) + h \end{cases}$$

Mapping SAT into EM. The energy equation relative to the integrity and optimality constraints are:

$$E_i = \delta[H^*(\neg\varphi_2) + H^*(\neg\varphi_3) + H^*(\neg\varphi_7)] + \gamma[H^*_{WTA}(\neg\varphi_1) + H^*_{WTA}(\neg\varphi_5) + H^*(\neg\varphi_6) + H^*(\neg\varphi_8)], \text{ and}$$

$$E_o = \beta[H^*(\varphi_9)] + \alpha[H^*(\varphi_{10})] + H^*(\varphi_4).$$

Finally, $E = E_i + E_o$. Notice that E_o above corresponds to a possible way of combining the two original problems. In this case, minimizing the number of colours has been prioritized over the other two components of E_o, namely φ_{10} and φ_4. Similarly, φ_{10} has been prioritized over φ_4. Different priority orders could be explored originating the specification of new problems. In fact, the possibility of combining a multitude of problems,is quite an interesting feature

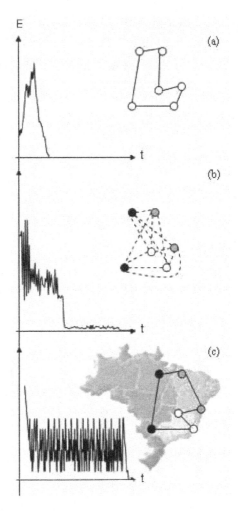

Fig. 1. Samples of the energy (E) behaviour and global minima found in (a) TSP, after 560 steps (t); (b) Graph Colouring, after 9967 steps (t), and (c) Map Colouring–TSP, after 38277 steps (t). Geometrical cooling (0.99) was used in (a), (b) and (c).

of our modeling, since real practical problems requiring optimization treatment are often not reducible to a single combinatorial problem. Figure 1 illustrates experimental results from the mapping of the three problems over simple six nodes graphs into stochastic high-order networks.

5   Conclusion

Although there are already language proposals oriented to the specification of problems via sets of constraints, e.g., Z notation [11], the possibility of combining different sets of such constraints in order to specify a new target problem is the main contribution of this work. Moreover, our approach profits from the intermediate definition of an energy function, which can be minimized by any available solver, not only higher-order Hopfield networks of stochastic neurons, as considered in this work. The development of a compiler which translates constraints into high-order networks and the mapping of molecular modeling via pseudo-boolean constraints are ongoing work. Among the most interesting investigations for future work, we intend to develop an integration of first-order logic inferencing [8] with pseudo-boolean constraints as an alternative and natural way of processing constraint logic programming.

References

1. Barbosa, V.C, Lima P.M.V.: On the distributed parallel simulation of Hopfield's neural networks. Software-Practice and Experience **20**(10) (1990) 967–983.
2. Dixon, H.E., Ginsberg, M.L., Parkes, A.J.: Generalizing Boolean Satisfiability I: Background and Survey of Existing Work. Journal of Artificial Intelligence Research **21** (2004) 193–243.
3. Geman S., Geman D. : Stochastic relaxation, Gibbs distribution, and the Bayesian restoration of images IEEE Transactions on Pattern Analysis and Machine Intelligence **PAMI-6** (1984) 721–741.
4. Hopfield, J.J.: Neural networks and physical systems with emergent collective computational abilities. Proc. of the National Academy of Sciences USA **79** (1982) 2554–2558.
5. Hopfield, J.J., Tank D.W.: Neural computation of decisions in optimization problems. Biological Cybernetics **52** (1985) 141–152.
6. Jones, A.J.: Models of Living Systems: Evolution and Neurology. Lecture Notes. Department of Computing. Imperial College of Science, Technology and Medicine, London, UK (1994).
7. Kirkpatrick, S., Gellat Jr., C.D., Vecchi, M.P.: Optimization via Simulated Annealing. Science **220** (1983) 671–680.
8. Lima P.M.V.: Resolution-Based Inference on Artificial Neural Networks. Ph.D. Thesis, Department of Computing. Imperial College of Science, Technology and Medicine, London, UK (2000).
9. Lima P.M.V.: A Goal-Driven Neural Propositional Interpreter. International Journal of Neural Systems **11** (2001) 311–322.
10. Pinkas, G.: Logical Inference in Symmetric Neural Networks. D.Sc. Thesis, Sever Institute of Technology, Washington University, Saint Louis, USA (1992).
11. Mike Spivey: The Z Notation: A Reference Manual. 2nd edition, Prentice Hall International Series in Computer Science (1992).

Robust Ellipse-Specific Fitting
for Real-Time Machine Vision

Eliseo Stefano Maini

ARTS Lab - Scuola Superiore Sant'Anna, Polo Sant'Anna Valdera,
Viale R. Piaggio, 34 - 56025 Pontedera, Italy
es.maini@ieee.org

Abstract. This paper presents a robust and non-iterative algorithm for
the least-square fitting of ellipses to scattered data. In this work, we
undertake a critical analysis of a previous reported work [1] and we propose a novel approach that preserves the advantages while overcomes the
major limitations and drawbacks. The modest increase of the computational burden introduced by this method is justified by the achievement
of an excellent numerical stability. Furthermore the method is simple
and accurate and can be implemented with fixed time of computation.
These characteristics coupled to its robustness and specificity makes the
algorithm well-suited for applications requiring real-time machine vision.

1   Introduction

One of the basic tasks in pattern recognition and computer vision is the fitting of
geometric primitives to a set of data points that are supposed to pertain to the
same token [2]. The compact representation obtained after fitting (i.e. estimating
the parameters of the geometric model) plays a fundamental role in decreasing
the computational burden to be charged on higher levels of processing when
scene-interpretation or object-tracking might be performed. A wide recognized
geometric primitive is the ellipse which owes its popularity to the property of
being the perspective projection of a circle. Elliptic patterns are commonly found
both in natural and in manmade environments, hence, applications requiring the
fitting of elliptic primitives are wide-spread over several fields such as astronomy,
physics, biology, medical imaging, industrial inspection, robotics etc.

Over recent decades, the increasing demand for machine vision resulted in
many different methods that were proposed for solving fitting problems. Broadly
speaking, these methods follow two major approaches: the clustering/voting
(CV) techniques and the least square (LS) techniques. The former approach
makes use of different algorithms such as RANSAC, Hough transform and fuzzy
clustering whereas the latter approach is based on optimization criteria in which
different objective functions are minimized with respect to a specific set of data
points [3]. The choice among these two approaches is usually performed by evaluating the trade-off between the computational burden and the robustness that
is required by the application. In fact the CV techniques are extremely robust
but their visiting characteristics are time-demanding and memory-consuming

M. De Gregorio et al. (Eds.): BVAI 2005, LNCS 3704, pp. 318–327, 2005.

notably if the adopted geometric model is other than the straight-line. In those cases, the computational load may become overwhelming for applications requiring real-time performances, such as object-tracking or visual-servoing, which are frequently investigated in mobile-robotics [4][5]. Moreover, the classical Hough Transform suffers from limitations of the sensitivity that are due to the possible presence of spurious and blurred peaks in the accumulators [6]. Compared with the CV approach, usually the approach based on LS techniques is less resource-demanding even if the latter algorithms work on a single primitive at time. Furthermore, the LS techniques have a low breakdown point; this means that they perform poorly in presence of severe non-Gaussian outliers although some variants (such as the Theil-Sen approach, the least median of squares, the Hilbert curve and the minimum volume estimator) are reported to improve the robustness of the results especially on specific conic sections [7]. Despite these limitations the LS techniques are often preferred for applications requiring real-time machine vision especially when the geometric primitive is a conic. There are two main reasons for this: first, the already mentioned computational costs. As an example, consider the problem of using a traditional Hough transform for the identification of an ellipse. In this case each pixel of the image can generate a surface in a five-dimensional space then the parameters are recovered by searching the intersections of all the generated surfaces. With increasing levels of resolution this process tends to require high computational performances and huge amounts of memory for the accumulator [6]. Although many efforts were made to reduce the computational cost, the Hough transform algorithms seem still excessively resource consuming for real time machine vision [8]. The second objection to be considered is that the iterative algorithms do not have fixed time of computation therefore they are not suited for real time applications. Unfortunately, the latter consideration affects both the CV and some of the LS techniques that are often iterative. In short: if an ellipse fitting is required one has to rely on generic conic fitting or, otherwise, on iterative methods that tend to push the estimation toward ellipticity by iterating, hence spoiling the opportunity to use them in a real-time application.

An interesting breakthrough in this field was the one proposed in [1]. In that paper the authors indicated a strategy to overcome the limitations of previous methods that were either iterative or not ellipse-specific. As illustrated by the authors, the method offers several remarkable advantages. First, by incorporating the ellipticity constraint into the normalization factor, the algorithm yields to unique elliptical solutions even in presence of noisy-data thereby improving one of the most notable limitations of the LS techniques (i.e. the low breakdown point). Furthermore, the low eccentricity bias, the invariance to an affine transformation and the non-iterative characteristic represent three relevant properties introduced by this method. On the other hand, the proposed approach suffers from some important drawbacks which are not described in the paper. Despite the claimed robustness, in some circumstance the method turns out to be numerically instable and produces non optimal or completely wrong results such as infinite or complex solutions.

In this paper we analyze the original approach, we characterize its drawbacks and we purpose an improved method that seems to solve the numerical instabilities with a reasonable growth of the computational load. The paper is organized as follows: in Section 2 we describe the original approach and we discuss the situations where it fails or produces non-optimal results, in Section 3 we purpose our improved method. Finally, in Section 4, we present and discuss a comparative evaluation and the experimental results.

2   Original Approach and Limitations

2.1   Analytical Background

A central conic can be expressed by an implicit second order polynomial such as:

$$F(x, y) = ax^2 + bxy + cy^2 + dx + ey + f = 0 \tag{1}$$

or, in vectorial form:

$$F_{\mathbf{a}}(\mathbf{x}) = \mathbf{x} \cdot \mathbf{a} = \mathbf{0} \tag{2}$$

where $\mathbf{a} = [a, b, c, d, e, f]^T$ and $\mathbf{x} = [x^2, xy, y^2, x, y, 1]$ are the vectors of the coefficients and the coordinates of the points on the conic section respectively. Given the set of data points:

$$T = \{(x_i, y_i) : i = 1 \ldots N\} \tag{3}$$

and assuming that $F(\mathbf{a}; \mathbf{p}_i)$ represents the *algebraic distance* of the point $\mathbf{p}_i = (x_i, y_i)$ from (2), the problem of fitting a conic section to (3) may be tackled by minimizing the sum of the squared distances of the curve to the given points [4]. The solution of the resulting non-linear minimization problem:

$$\min_{\mathbf{a}}(\sum_{i=1}^{N} F(\mathbf{a}; \mathbf{p}_i)) = \min_{\mathbf{a}}(\sum_{i=1}^{N} (\mathbf{p}_i \cdot \mathbf{a})^2) \tag{4}$$

may be found making use of the classical iterative least squares approach after having introduced an appropriate constraint to discard the trivial solution $\mathbf{a} = \mathbf{0}_6$. To this aim, several authors suggested many different equations to express the constraint but a review of their methods is out of the objectives of this paper. Conversely, we recall that the solution of (4) will be a general conic and not necessarily an ellipse. In order to guarantee the ellipse-specificity of the fitting, the well-known discriminant-constraint (i.e. $b^2 - 4ac < 0$) has to be considered when solving the problem (4). As pointed out in [1], the resulting constrained minimization problem is hard to solve for the presence of the non-convex inequality, hence some authors concluded that, for its basically nonlinear characteristics, an ellipse-specific fitting must always require iterative methods [9]. In [1] authors tackled this matter observing that for any real number $\alpha \neq 0$ the conic $\alpha \cdot F_{\mathbf{a}}(\mathbf{x}) = \alpha \cdot \mathbf{xa} = 0$ is the same conic as the one reported in (2).

Therefore, by arbitrary scaling the coefficients of the conics the constraint becomes $b^2 - 4ac = 1$, or, in vectorial form:

$$\mathbf{a}^T \cdot \mathbf{C} \cdot \mathbf{a} = 1 \tag{5}$$

where $\mathbf{C}$ indicates the following *constraint matrix* :

$$\mathbf{C} = \begin{pmatrix} 0 & 0 & +2 & 0 & 0 & 0 \\ 0 & -1 & 0 & 0 & 0 & 0 \\ +2 & 0 & 0 & 0 & 0 & 0 \\ 0 & 0 & 0 & 0 & 0 & 0 \\ 0 & 0 & 0 & 0 & 0 & 0 \\ 0 & 0 & 0 & 0 & 0 & 0 \end{pmatrix} \tag{6}$$

Now, coming back to (4) and following [10] the ellipse-specific problem reduces to find the solution of the minimization problem:

$$\begin{cases} \min \|\mathbf{D} \cdot \mathbf{a}\|^2 \\ \mathbf{a}^T \cdot \mathbf{C} \cdot \mathbf{a} = 1 \end{cases} \tag{7}$$

where the *design matrix* $\mathbf{D}$ is a $N \times 6$ real matrix representing the least square minimization (4). In extenso:

$$\mathbf{D} = \begin{pmatrix} x_1^2 & x_1 y_1 & y_1^2 & x_1 & y_1 & 1 \\ \vdots & \vdots & \vdots & \vdots & \vdots & \vdots \\ x_N^2 & x_N y_N & y_N^2 & x_N & y_N & 1 \end{pmatrix} \tag{8}$$

The optimal solution of (7) may be found using the Lagrange multiplier λ:

$$\begin{cases} 2\mathbf{D}^T \mathbf{D} \mathbf{a} - 2\lambda \mathbf{C} \mathbf{a} = 0 \\ \mathbf{a}^T \cdot \mathbf{C} \cdot \mathbf{a} = 1 \end{cases} \tag{9}$$

This may be rewritten in the form:

$$\begin{cases} \mathbf{S} \mathbf{a} = \lambda \mathbf{C} \mathbf{a} \\ \mathbf{a}^T \cdot \mathbf{C} \cdot \mathbf{a} = 1 \\ \mathbf{S} = \mathbf{D}^T \mathbf{D} \end{cases} \tag{10}$$

where $\mathbf{S}$ is the *scatter matrix* of size 6×6. The system (10) is solved by considering the generalized eigenvectors of the first equation and by observing that, for any non-zero scalar μ, if $(\lambda_k, \mathbf{u}_k)$ solves the generalized eigenvector problem evenly $(\lambda_k, \mu \mathbf{u}_k)$ does it. Hence, making use of the second equation of (10), we may calculate:

$$\mu_k^2 \mathbf{u}_k^T \mathbf{C} \mathbf{u}_k = 1 \quad \Rightarrow \quad \mu_k = \sqrt{\frac{1}{\mathbf{u}_k^T \mathbf{C} \mathbf{u}_k}} = \sqrt{\frac{\lambda_k}{\mathbf{u}_k^T \mathbf{S} \mathbf{u}_k}} \tag{11}$$

therefore the solutions are found by setting $\tilde{\mathbf{a}}_k = \mu_k \mathbf{u}_k$. Based on this derivation the authors demonstrated in [1] that the solution of the conic-fitting problem (4) subject to the constraint (5) admits exactly one elliptical solution corresponding to the single positive generalized eigenvalue of (10).

2.2   Advantages and Limitations

As remarked, the method proposed in [1] (i.e. B2AC) offers several relevant advantages but, on the other hand, the algorithm suffers from some important drawbacks that are not properly addressed in the original paper and that are likely to cause severe numerical instabilities or even wrong results. The major limitations of the algorithm are two. First: the scatter matrix is severely ill-conditioned and this may seriously affect the following eigenvector problem. If calculating the ratio of the largest to smallest singular value of the matrix $\mathbf{S}$ in (10) (i.e. the 2-norm condition number) it may be noticed that the reported values are extremely high, giving evidence of the potential numerical instabilities arising from the finite-precision representation. This problem is clearly unveiled if the software implementation is carried out using compilers such as ANSI C that admits a smaller representation for floating-point numbers compared to the MATLAB tools used by authors (roughly 10^{37} vs 10^{380}).

Secondly, in some circumstance, the localization of the fitting's optimal solution may result ambiguous or even impossible. In [1] authors stated that there exist exactly one elliptical solution of the problem (8) corresponding to vector associated to the *single positive* generalized eigenvalue of (10) and that, this solution, is optimal in the least square sense. Unfortunately, this statement is not always true. Because of the numerical instabilities, it is often impossible to find a positive eigenvalue or, in other cases, the reported numerical solutions may be misleading and the optimal solution may be associated with a small negative eigenvalue. Furthermore, from a theoretical point of view, it has to be remarked that the algorithm has a *specific* source of errors that is not mentioned in paper [1]. In fact, if the data points lie *exactly* on the ellipse the eigenvalue corresponding to the optimal solution is zero and the original algorithm does not lead to any solution. Once more, because of the numerical calculation, this circumstance may happen even if the data points are "close" to the ideal ellipse; this means that the algorithm may perform poorly when noise is absent or even in presence of a small amount of noise in the data. In order to overcome the limitations of the B2AC meanwhile preserving the advantages offered from the approach we propose an enhanced algorithm for direct least square fitting of ellipses. The algorithm is based on re-centering and scaling data points and on the use of a simple re-sampling technique and offers the advantage of finding a good solution even in those cases in which B2AC fails.

3   Enhanced Direct Least Square Fitting of Ellipses

The enhanced direct least-square fitting of ellipses (EDFE) is based on the analytical background previously discussed. In this section we will shortly describe the techniques adopted to insure an adequate robustness to the method. Even since now, we introduce the operator $\Theta_{x_i y_j} = \sum_{k=1}^{N} x_k^i y_k^j$ that will be used to have a compact representation for the scatter matrix.

3.1 Re-centering and Scaling

It is worth noticing that the scatter matrix $\mathbf{S}$ has the following structure:

$$\mathbf{S} = \begin{pmatrix}
\Theta_{x^4} & \Theta_{x^3 y} & \Theta_{x^2 y^2} & \Theta_{x^3} & \Theta_{x^2 y} & \Theta_{x^2} \\
\Theta_{x^3 y} & \Theta_{x^2 y^2} & \Theta_{xy^3} & \Theta_{x^2 y} & \Theta_{xy^2} & \Theta_{xy} \\
\Theta_{x^2 y^2} & \Theta_{xy^3} & \Theta_{y^4} & \Theta_{xy^2} & \Theta_{y^3} & \Theta_{y^2} \\
\Theta_{x^3} & \Theta_{x^2 y} & \Theta_{y^2} & \Theta_{x^2} & \Theta_{xy} & \Theta_x \\
\Theta_{x^2 y} & \Theta_{xy^2} & \Theta_{y^3} & \Theta_{xy} & \Theta_{y^2} & \Theta_y \\
\Theta_{x^2} & \Theta_{xy} & \Theta_{y^2} & \Theta_x & \Theta_y & N
\end{pmatrix} \tag{12}$$

In this expression the coordinates of each point $\mathbf{p}_i = (x_i, y_i)$ may assume values in the interval between zero and the maximal resolution of the frame grabber. In modern devices, these resolutions can easily reach values of 10^3, hence the maximum values appearing in $\mathbf{S}$ may reach values in the order of $N(10^3)^4$ while $\mathbf{S}_{6,6} = N$. In these circumstance, $\mathbf{S}$ is *intrinsically* ill-conditioned therefore the eigenvector problem may yield to erratic results. To overcome this source of errors a simple re-centring and scaling procedure may be performed on the data-points before constructing the scatter matrix. Introducing the centring factors :

$$x_m = \min_{i=1}^{N}\{x_i\} \qquad y_m = \min_{i=1}^{N}\{y_i\} \tag{13}$$

and the scale factors:

$$s_x = \frac{\max_{i=1}^{N}\{x_i\} - \min_{i=1}^{N}\{x_i\}}{2} \qquad s_y = \frac{\max_{i=1}^{N}\{y_i\} - \min_{i=1}^{N}\{y_i\}}{2} \tag{14}$$

the normalized ellipse is obtained by applying the following affine transformation:

$$\hat{x} = \frac{x - x_m}{s_x} - 1 \qquad \hat{y} = \frac{y - y_m}{s_y} - 1 \tag{15}$$

Recalling expression (2) the resulting ellipse may be written in the form:

$$F_{\hat{\mathbf{a}}} = \hat{\mathbf{x}} \cdot \hat{\mathbf{a}} = 0 \tag{16}$$

With these positions equation (16) represents an ellipse similar to (2) but normalized to be enclosed in a square, (side length=2, center=$(0,0)$). Therefore, after solving the eigenvector-problem the reported parameters have to be de-normalized. From (16) the calculation of the de-normalizing coefficients is straightforward. By imposing the equality $F_{\hat{\mathbf{a}}} = \hat{\mathbf{x}} \cdot \hat{\mathbf{a}} = \mathbf{x} \cdot \mathbf{a} = F_{\mathbf{a}}$ and executing the dot products results:

$$\begin{aligned}
a &= \hat{a} s_y^2; & d &= \hat{d} s_x s_y^2 - \hat{b} s_x s_y K_y - 2\hat{a} s_y^2 K_x \\
b &= \hat{b} s_x s_y; & e &= \hat{e} s_x^2 s_y - \hat{b} s_x s_y K_x - 2\hat{c} s_x^2 K_y \\
c &= \hat{c} s_x^2; & f &= \hat{a} s_y^2 K_x^2 + \hat{b} s_x s_y K_x K_y + \hat{c} s_x^2 K_y^2 - \hat{d} s_x s_y^2 K_x - \hat{e} s_x^2 s_y K_y + \hat{f} s_x^2 s_y^2.
\end{aligned} \tag{17}$$

Therefore, the coefficients of the original conic may be calculated from those of the normalized ellipse using (17) where $K_x = (x_m + s_x)$ and $K_y = (y_m + s_y)$. After this affine transformation, the data points assume values in $[-1, 1]$ thereby the maximum values in the scatter matrix may reach values in the order of N. As reported in Section 4 the normalization of the data points reduce of several orders the 2-norm condition number hence improving the robustness of the solution.

3.2   Resampling with Perturbations

Recalling that if the data points lie exactly on the ellipse or "close" to it the algorithm does not converge, one should conclude that the method purposed in [1] must be rejected as useless since it may not insure the retrieval of the solution. In order to overcome this limitation we propose a simple "perturb-and-resample" strategy to be performed when the localization of the eigenvalue is impossible. The basic idea of the strategy is quite simple. Given that B2AC does not converge in absence of noise and that it is, instead, robust when the noise tends to increase it is feasible to modify the data points by adding a known Gaussian noise and, after that, perform the fitting. The robustness of the method is insured by applying this procedure an adequate number of times. After M iterations there will be created a family of M ellipses each one fitting the original data points previously perturbed by a controlled level of noise. The searched ellipse is then found by averaging the parameters obtained over replications. Moreover, given that the noise distribution is known to be Gaussian, it is straightforward to compute the confidence level of the parameters. Using this approach, it is also possible to control both the level of noise and the number of replications in order to achieve the desired level of accuracy. On the other hand this method increases the computational burden therefore we purpose to apply this strategy only in those cases in which the localization of the solution turns out to be impossible or numerically unstable. The EDFE algorithm is depicted in Fig. 1.

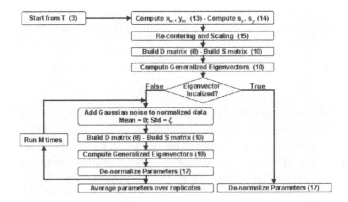

Fig. 1. Schematic representation of the EDFE algorithm

4   Experimental Results

The algorithm was tested on synthetic data obtained during simulations. The parameters controlled by the simulator were: 1) the number of points on the curve (N), 2) the standard deviation of noise in original data (σ), 3) the portion of elliptic arc from which data points were extracted (g), 4) the horizontal (h_{res}) and the vertical (v_{res}) resolution, 5) the number of replicates in the resampling procedure (M), 6) the standard deviation of the perturbing noise (ζ).

Table 1. *Varying resolution*: B2AC average percentage of *FAIL* and comparative analysis of the CN values of **S**. (Parameters $N=50$, $\sigma=0.01$, $g=2\pi$, $M=100$, $\zeta=0.01$).

$h_{res} \times v_{res}$	320×240	640×480	1024×768	1280×1024	1600×1200
F (%)	4.5	24.9	50.0	64.2	72.2
CNB	$0.5 \cdot 10^{23}$	$0.3 \cdot 10^{25}$	$1.0 \cdot 10^{26}$	$0.2 \cdot 10^{27}$	$0.2 \cdot 10^{28}$
CNE	$1.0 \cdot 10^{10}$	$0.9 \cdot 10^{10}$	$1.0 \cdot 10^{10}$	$0.3 \cdot 10^{10}$	$0.4 \cdot 10^{10}$

Table 2. *Varying std. of noise*: B2AC average percentage of *FAIL* and comparative analysis of the CN values of **S**. ($N=50$, $g=2\pi$, $M=100$, $\zeta=0.01$, $h_{res}=640$, $v_{res}=480$).

σ	0	0.001	0.002	0.005	0.01	0.02	0.05	0.1	0.2	0.5	0.75	1
F(%)	48.3	32.5	30.3	26.7	23.8	20.3	15.8	14.2	13.0	11.5	11.1	9.9
CNB	$2 \cdot 10^{26}$	$4 \cdot 10^{25}$	$3 \cdot 10^{25}$	$7 \cdot 10^{24}$	$3 \cdot 10^{24}$	$2 \cdot 10^{24}$	$6 \cdot 10^{23}$	$2 \cdot 10^{23}$	$2 \cdot 10^{22}$	$2 \cdot 10^{21}$	$3 \cdot 10^{20}$	$2 \cdot 10^{20}$
CNE	$3 \cdot 10^{12}$	$2 \cdot 10^{12}$	$2 \cdot 10^{11}$	$4 \cdot 10^{10}$	$9 \cdot 10^{9}$	$2 \cdot 10^{9}$	$2 \cdot 10^{8}$	$9 \cdot 10^{6}$	$2 \cdot 10^{6}$	$2 \cdot 10^{5}$	$3 \cdot 10^{4}$	$2 \cdot 10^{4}$

The simulator generated synthetic data points by randomly extracting uniformly distributed values for the five ellipse's parameters. (i.e.: coordinates of the center (x_c, y_c), length of the major (a_M) and minor axes (a_m) and angle of rotation (ϕ)). For comparative purposes, the fitting procedures were carried out both for the EDFE algorithm and for the B2AC as described in [1]. The results of the fitting procedures were evaluated by calculating the root mean square error (RMSE) of the parameters obtained from fitting. The numerical stability of the eigenvector problem was assessed by computing the 2-norm condition number (CN) both for the B2AC (CNB) and the EDFE (CNE) algorithms. Those cases in which the original algorithm was not capable to provide a solution were marked as *FAIL* either if the error was originated by numerical instability or by impossible localization of the eigenvalue. The trials marked as *FAIL* were counted (F(%)) and excluded from further examinations. The same criterion was applied to the EDFE. Each case was investigated by averaging results obtained over 10 simulation runs, each one generating 1000 ellipses. The effects of increasing resolution on the numerical stability are reported in Table 1. As expected, to increasing values of resolution corresponds increasing CN for the B2AC that compromise the numerical stability of the method. This evidence is furthermore confirmed by the increasing percentage of *FAIL* marks reported for B2AC. The EDFE algorithm always found the solution therefore we do not report the EDFE *FAIL* percentage on the tables. Thanks to the re-centering and scaling, the EDFE shows lower CN that reflect an improved robustness of the method. Moreover, the CN values are not affected by changing the resolution hence the EDFE seems to provide a proper insurances of device-independency. The effects of varying the standard deviation of noise in the input data are reported in Table 2. Even if the CN of B2AC is several orders higher than EDFE, Table 2 shows that both algorithms tends to increase the CN when the noise level tends to zero. As already remarked, this evidence may be explained considering that there is a theoretical reason for having ill-conditioned problems when the noise is absent. The reported rates of failure suggest that the B2AC algorithm performs poorly even

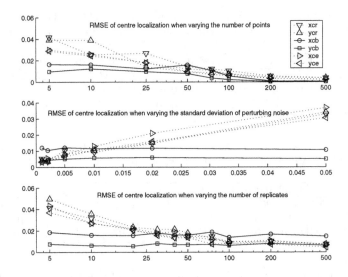

Fig. 2. *Accuracy of centre localization when varying N, ζ, M*: Averages, over 10 runs of the RMSE of fitting. (x_{cb}, y_{cb}) obtained using B2AC, (x_{ce}, y_{ce}) obtained using EDFE, (x_{cr}, y_{cr}) obtained using EDFE only on those ellipses for which re-sampling was applied.

if small a amount of noise is present. On contrary, the re-sampling procedure of the EDFE always yields to a robust estimation of the ellipse even when the noise level is set to zero (i.e. theoretical instability). The accuracy of (x_c, y_c) estimation is reported in Fig. 2 both for EDFE and B2AC. The estimation of a_M, a_m and ϕ are not reported because of space restrictions but they follow similar trends. For assessing the accuracy of the method we studied the effects of varying: 1) N (with $M=100$, $\zeta=0.01$), 2)ζ (with $N=50$, $M=100$) and 3)M (with $N=50$, $\zeta=0.01$). All the simulations presented here were conducted with the following setting of parameters: $\sigma=0$, $g=2\pi$, $h_{res}=640$, $v_{res}=480$. It is worth noticing that, in Fig. 2, those curves that are referred to B2AC are calculated only in the cases in which the method converged (roughly the 50% of the whole). Obviously, the accuracy of estimations increases when the number of data points increase. From Fig. 2 it may be noticed that, when the data points are few (i.e. $5 \leq N \leq 15$) the RMSE of fitting tends to be higher when using the EDFE; particularly on those solutions obtained using re-sampling with perturbation. This is well explained considering that even small perturbation may have noticeable effects on ellipses geometry if the number of points tends to its minimum of five. Conversely, when the number of points increases, roughly above 25, the EDFE shows a quality of fitting that is numerically equivalent to the one obtained on the non failing trials of B2AC. With respect to the effect induced by increasing the level of perturbing noise we observe that, as expected, it has no effect on the B2AC since the RMSE of fitting is rather constant whereas it affects the EDFE that shows an increasing trend roughly linear. The latter evidence confirms what already observed in [1]. Furthermore, when perturbing noise is small ($\zeta \leq 0.015$) the EDFE performs the fitting better than the best results obtained by B2AC without reporting any *FAIL* mark. When varying the number of replicates the EDFE behaves similarly. In fact, when the number of replicates is low (M≤15) the algorithm tends to estimate the parameters with an higher error with respect to the best results of B2AC. Conversely, when increasing the number of replicates the EDFE reaches the accuracy of the B2AC even with a moderate number of repetitions (i.e. 50≤ M ≤100). As depicted in Fig. 2, the re-sampling strategy does not affect the accuracy of the B2AC that is, in fact, approximately constant. On contrary, to further increasing of M corresponds further improvement of the estimation and, beyond 200 repetitions, the EDFE shows better performances in comparison to B2AC.

5   Conclusions

Our experiments give evidence of the superior robustness of the EDFE which was always capable to compute the best fitting in the least-square sense while preserving the advantages offered by the B2AC. Furthermore, the accuracy of the estimates may be tuned by operating on the number of replicates and on the magnitude of the perturbing noise therefore offering the flexibility that different applications may require. The increased computational load introduced by the centering and scaling coupled to the re-sampling procedures may be justified by the numerical stability of the method and by considering that, even if increased, the computational time are fixed therefore making the EDFE a suitable algorithm for real-time machine vision.

References

[1] Fitzgibbon, A., Pilu, M., Fisher, R.: Direct least square fitting of ellipses. IEEE Trans. PAMI **21** (1999) 476–480

[2] D.A.Forsyth, J.Ponce: Computer vision: a modern approach. P. Hall, NJ (2002)

[3] Gander, W., Golub, G., Strebel, R.: Least-square fitting of circles and ellipses. BIT **34** (1994) 558–578

[4] Desouza, G., Kak, A.: Vision for mobile robot navigation: a survey. IEEE Trans. PAMI **24** (2002) 237–267

[5] Sabatini, A., Genovese, V., Maini, E.: Low-cost vision-based 2D localization systems for application in rehabilitation robotics. IEEE Proc. IROS (2002) 1355–60

[6] Grimson, W., Huttenlocher, D.: On the sensitivity of the hough transform for object recognition. IEEE Trans. PAMI **12** (1990) 2555–74

[7] Rosin, P.: Further five-point fit ellipse fitting. Graph. Models and Image Process **61** (1999) 245–59

[8] Bennet, N., Burridge, R., Saoki, N.: A method to detect and characterize ellipses using the hough transform. IEEE Trans. PAMI **21** (1999) 652–657

[9] Rosin, P., West, G.: Nonparametric segmentation of curves into various representations. IEEE Trans. PAMI **17** (1995) 140–53

[10] Bookstein, F.: Fitting conic sections to scattered data. Computer Graphics and Image Processing **9** (1979) 56–71

A Feature-Based Model of Semantic Memory: The Importance of Being Chaotic

A. Morelli[1], R. Lauro Grotto[2], and F.T. Arecchi[3]

[1] Departement of Engineering, University of Florence, Italy
morelli@ino.it
[2] Departement of Psychology, University of Florence, Italy
[3] Departement of Physics, University of Florence, Italy

Abstract. Semantic memory representations have often be modeled in terms of a collection of semantic features. Although feature-based models show a great explanatory power with respect to cognitive and neuropsychological phenomena, they appear to be underspecified if interpreted from a neuro-computational perspective. Here we investigate the retrieval dynamics in a feature-based semantic memory model, in which the features are represented by neurons of the Hindmarsh-Rose type in the chaotic regime. We study the state of synchronization among features coding for the same or different representations and compare the correlation patterns obtained by analyzing the whole neural signal and a manipulated signal in which the sub-threshold component is ruled out. In all cases we find stronger correlations among features belonging to the same representations. We apply a formal method in order to represent the state of synchronization of features which are simultaneously coding for different representations. In this case, the synchronization and de-synchronization pattern that allows for a shared feature to participate in multiple memory representations appears to be better defined when the whole signal is considered. We interpret the simulation results as suggestive of a role for chaotic dynamics in allowing for flexible composition of elementary meaningful units in memory representations.

1 Introduction

Semantic memory can be defined as our relatively permanent memory store for world knowledge: it comprises information about words meaning and allows for the recognition of meaningful perceptual stimuli. The featural description of memory representations produced accounts for a large part of the experimental phenomena described in semantic memory literature, such as basic level naming [1], typicality effects [2], context effects [3], priming [4] and category structure [5]. The existence of subgroups of shared features is at the base of the explanatory account of the models in both cases. The main problem with the feature-based account is that it appears to have a great deal of explanatory power at a general level, but it is extremely underspecified in the details. There is a remarkable lack of consensus about what could be reasonably conceived as

M. De Gregorio et al. (Eds.): BVAI 2005, LNCS 3704, pp. 328–337, 2005.

a semantic feature for different classes of stimuli [6], such as percepts and words belonging to different semantic and morpho-syntactic classes (concrete words, abstract words, verbs etc.), although recent explicit proposals in this sense have appeared in the literature [7]. Here we will approach the problem of modeling semantic memory representations with shared features starting from some assumptions on the dynamic process of memory retrieval. First of all we assume that a semantic feature is a cognitive component of the semantic representation that is encoded in the collective activity of a segregated population of neurons [8] with chaotic dynamics. In fact, although memory processes and their neural correlates have been extensively modeled in terms of Attractor Neural Networks [9] and recent approaches emphasize the role that dynamic "latching" between attractors might have in unleashing the computational capabilities of fixed point dynamics [10], simultaneous retrieval of overlapping patterns still remain very difficult to implement with more "sedate" dynamical systems. Second, recent approaches have emphasized the need to shift to dynamic paradigms in which memory representations are built 'on the fly' according to the specificity of the task demands and of the behavioral goals the subject is engaged in [11]. Chaotic dynamics might be a preferential tool in this framework due to low cost and fast transition between attractor states.

Building on some ideas that were first proposed in the case of perceptual features [12] [13] [14], we explore the possibility to resort to chaotic dynamics in order to implement a toy model of a multimodular semantic memory system in which shared features can be dynamically allocated to different semantic representations in order to allow for the co-occurring retrieval of two or more related patterns, as it is possibly needed for the memorization and retrieval of complex scenes or concepts. Taking as a starting point the multimodular structure defined in [15], we propose a richer quantitative analysis of the network behavior by applying different types of synchronicity measures. We also contrast the results obtained by the different signal manipulations in an attempt to disclose the characteristics of the neural signal that appears to be more relevant for the emergency of the hierarchical structure of memory representations.

2   The Model

We study an associative neural network characterized by a *multimodular architecture*, which represents the functional segregation observed in some cortical areas (V1 and beyond [16]). The modular architecture of the network, depicted in Fig.1, is given by a set of M *feature modules*, each representing a specific dimension, or domain, in the memory pattern (e.g. color, dimension, shape, etc.). Each module includes F neurons coding for different *features* of the pattern (features are encoded by a single neuron), along the dimension specified by the module (e.g. red in color module, sphere in shape module, etc.). For the sake of computational simplicity we choose to substitute the population dynamics at the featural level with single unit dynamics. Although this is clearly a limit of the present simulations it is nevertheless known that single neuron spiking

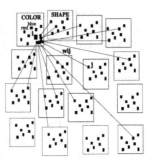

Fig. 1. Representation of the multimodular architecture. The network includes M (M=16) feature modules, represented here as boxes. Each module contains F (F=8) neurons, depicted as squares. Each single neuron i is connected to all neurons j in the other modules, through excitatory coupling (w_{ij}).

activity shares many relevant properties with network activity in terms of temporal statistics [17]. A memory pattern is defined by a vector of M features, each from a different module. In order to obtain all possible patterns, every neuron is connected via excitatory coupling to all neurons of the other modules (*cooperation*). Since neurons belonging to the same module code for mutually exclusive features (e.g. either red or yellow), we also introduce a *competitive* mechanism between them which take into account the average intra-modular activity. We use Hindmarsh-Rose model-neurons, which exhibit realistic response properties such as the presence of long interspike intervals between action potentials. Those models are characterize by a periodic or chaotic (irregular bursting) dynamic behavior, depending on a single parameter [18]. The network consists of N HR neurons ($N = 128$), belonging to M different modules ($M = 16$). In each module we have F feature neurons ($F = 8$)(i is the index for neurons in the network, j is the index identifying neurons belonging to different modules from the module of i, k identifies neurons inside the same module as i). Each HR neuron in the network is described by the first-order differential equations

$$\dot{X}_i = Y_i - aX_i^3 + bX_i^2 - Z_i + I_i + \sum_{j=1}^{F(M-1)} w_{ij}S_j(t) - \frac{1}{F-1}\sum_{k=1}^{F-1} S_k^{(i)}(t) \quad (1)$$

$$\dot{Y}_i = c - dX_i^2 - Y_i \quad (2)$$

$$\dot{Z}_i = r[s(X_i - x_0) - Z_i]. \quad (3)$$

The state of neuron i is described by three time-dependent variables, namely, the membrane potential X_i, the recovery variable Y_i, and a slow adaptation current Z_i. The external input I_i, for the standard choice of parameters ($a = 1.0, b = 3.0, c = 1.0, d = 5.0, s = 4.0, r = 0.006$, and $x_0 = -1.6$), is set such that the single neuron dynamics is chaotic. The synaptic input given by the firing activity of the j-th neuron on the i-th neuron is modeled in Eq.(1) by the impulse current to the i-th neuron, proportional to the synaptic strength w_{ij}, generated when the

j-th neuron is active. A neuron is here considered active whenever its membrane potential exceeds a threshold value X^* ($X^* = 0$ in our study) and its activity is coded by the variable $S_j = \Theta(X_j(t) - X^*)$, where $\Theta(x) = 1$ if $x \geq 0$ and $\Theta(x) = 0$ if $x < 0$. A local inhibition mechanism, active on the i-th neuron, is modeled in Eq.(1) by a negative impulse current to the i-th neuron, generated when the k-th neuron, belonging to the same module as i, is active. S_i here represents the activity variables of the neurons in the module (i).

Our memory patterns are defined by sets of 16 features, coded by 16 active neurons. Given two memory patterns, we distinguish between *Patterns which do not share features* (NSF) and *Patterns which share features* (SF). In the first case, vectors coding for the two patterns are orthogonal: they do not share any features. In this case, all active neurons are coding for a pattern only. In the second case, vectors are not orthogonal, so some neurons are coding for more than one pattern. We implement a *learning stage*, during which input memory patterns are stored, and a *retrieval stage*, in which the network activates some memory patterns out of the stored ones. A variable number of memory patterns is randomly generated and stored in long-term memory via updating of connection weights by a one-shot Hebbian mechanism: if two connected neurons i and j (belonging to different modules) are active at the same time, the synaptic efficacy of their connection (w_{ij}) is increased. In this work w_{ij} is defined as

$$w_{ij} = \frac{1}{M}\frac{1}{F}(1 - exp\,(-(\frac{1}{P}\sum_{p=1}^{P} S_i(p)S_j(p))))), \tag{4}$$

where $S_l(p)$=1 if neuron l is active for pattern p, $S_l(p)$=0 otherwise; P is the number of stored patterns. The learned connection weights are kept costant during memory retrieval and successive simulations. In the later section, we report results concerning the multiple retrieval dynamics of the network. We are interested on the retrieval of patterns which share features and which do not. The numerical integration was done by using a fixed-step fourth-order Runge-Kutta method. The integration step-size was chosen equal to 0.05 ms to compare our results with experiments.

3   Results and Discussion

3.1   Retrieval Dynamics: Results and Discussion

In order to investigate the retrieval dynamics of the network, we study the temporal firing state of the neurons which are activated by input patterns (working-memory [19]). We activate those neurons coding for the 16 features of a given pattern, by setting the external input current I_i in a chaotic regime, randomly between 3.0 and 3.1 (I_i is equal to 0 for inactive neurons). We are interested on what happens when the retrieved patterns are more than one, and when they share some features (SF) or not (NSF). Simulations were run with a variable number of stored patterns, retrieved patterns and shared features. Here, for the sake of simplicity, we report the results concerning two simulation conditions: the retrieval of two NSF patterns and that of two SF patterns with three shared features. In both conditions the number of stored patterns P is equal to 15. In order to characterize the degree of correlation within and between patterns, we analyze the normalized correlation functions with variable lag τ, between the time series $x(t), y(t)$ generated by the membrane potential X of the active neurons. In Figs.2-3 the maxima of correlation functions defined as $C_{xy} = \max_{(\tau)}\{\frac{\langle x(t-\tau)y(t)\rangle_t - \langle x\rangle\langle y\rangle}{\sigma_x \sigma_y}\}$ are plotted, where $\langle.\rangle$ and σ denote time averages and standard deviations respectively. As the binarization is a standard type of manipulation of the neural signals, we use the same correlation analysis with the binarized time series of the membrane potential. We define a threshold (taken here as $thr = 0$) to encode the membrane potential $X(t)$ of the neurons as a string of 0's and 1's ($X(t) = 1$ when $X(t) > thr$ and $X(t) = 0$ otherwise). This analysis is done in order to determine if this different format encodes the same information as non binarized signals, and if this information is sufficient to describe the correlation structure of the retrieved patterns. We expect that this structure does not change dramatically for the binarized time series, due to the fact that the temporal informations about the spikes (their temporal position, length and separation from other spikes) are maintained in binarized time series.

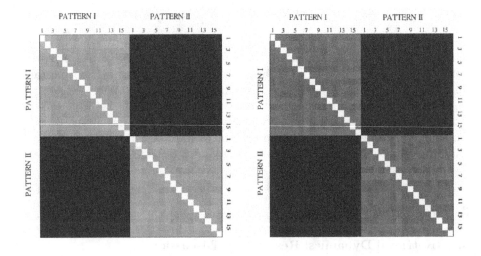

Fig. 2. Retrieval of two patterns with Not Shared Features. Maxima of correlation functions between time series (left) and binarized time series (right) of the membrane potential of active neurons (16 for Pattern I and 16 for Pattern II). Within each matrix: the maxima values for the 16 pairs of neurons belonging to Pattern I and Pattern I (top-left), Pattern I and Pattern II (top-right), Pattern II and Pattern I (bottom-left), Pattern II and Pattern II (bottom-right). Values are represented using grayscales, from 0 (black) to 1 (white).

Retrieval of Patterns with Not Shared Features (NSF). In this simulation condition, we activate two NSF patterns (Pattern I and Pattern II) out of the P stored patterns. We have 32 active neurons, each one coding for one pattern only. By analyzing the structure of correlation functions for the binarized and non binarized time series, we find stronger correlations between neurons coding for the same pattern, and weaker correlations between neurons coding for different patterns (Fig.2). The maxima of correlation functions are greater for non binarized time series compared to binarized time series, but the structure of the matrix is similar.

Retrieval of Patterns with Shared Features (SF). In this second condition, the network retrieves two SF patterns which share three features (there are three neurons which are coding for both Pattern I and Pattern II). By evaluating maxima of correlation functions for the binarized and non binarized time series (Fig.3), we observe stronger correlations between neurons coding for the same pattern and weaker correlations between neurons coding for different patterns, except for those neurons coding for shared features: they are correlated with neurons coding for both Pattern I and Pattern II. As in NSF condition, the maxima of correlation functions are greater for non binarized time series compared to binarized time series, but the structure of the matrix is similar. The neuronscoding for shared features are correlated with neurons coding for

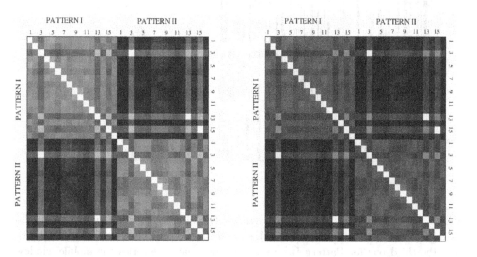

Fig. 3. Retrieval of two patterns with three Shared Features. Maxima of correlation functions between time series (left) and binarized time series (right) of the membrane potential of active neurons (16 for Pattern I and 16 for Pattern II). Within each matrix: the maxima values for the 16 pairs of neurons belonging to Pattern I and Pattern I (top-left), Pattern I and Pattern II (top-right), Pattern II and Pattern I (bottom-left), Pattern II and Pattern II (bottom-right). Values are represented using grayscales, from 0 (black) to 1 (white).

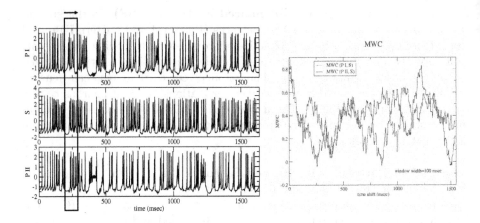

Fig. 4. Left: from top, the first time series is the membrane potential of a neuron coding for Pattern I only (PI), second one for Pattern I and Pattern II (S), and the third one for Pattern II only (PII). Over the time series the mobile window ($w = 100$ msec) for MWC is depicted. Right: the MWC between the shared neuron S and the two neurons coding for one pattern only (PI and PII), are plotted, as a function of time shift.

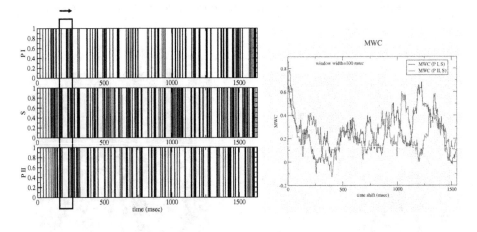

Fig. 5. Left: from top, the first time series is the binarized membrane potential of a neuron coding for Pattern I only (PI), second one for Pattern I and Pattern II (S), and the third one for Pattern II only (PII). Over the time series the mobile window ($w = 100$ msec) for MWC is depicted. Right: the MWC between the shared neuron S and the two neurons coding for one pattern only (PI and PII), are plotted, as a function of time shift.

Pattern I and Pattern II in a nonstationary way. In order to investigate this non-stationarity, we introduce the Mobile Window Correlation (MWC) (see next section).

Fig. 6. The maximum of correlation functions between time series of neurons coding for the three shared features in SF simulation condition (neurons 3, 13 and 15 from Fig.3)

Mobile Window Correlation (MWC). The Mobile Window Correlation is defined as $MWC(\theta) = \frac{\langle xy \rangle - \langle x \rangle \langle y \rangle}{\sigma_x \sigma_y}$, where the averages and the standard deviations are evaluated in the mobile (synchronous) window $[\theta - w/2, \theta + w/2]$. We analyze the MWC, as a function of the time shift, for the time series of a neuron coding for both patterns (indicated with 'S', in Fig.4 for non binarized time series and in Fig.5 for binarized) and two neurons, the first coding for Pattern I (MWC(PI,S)) and the second for Pattern II (MWC(PII,S)) only. As shown in Fig.4 and Fig.5, the shared neuron S is *alternatively* correlated with the neurons coding for the two patterns (PI and PII).

3.2   Hierarchical Organization in Neural Representation

Overall, the results of the correlation analysis show that units that are coding for shared features tend to be more strongly correlated among them than units that are coding for item specific features belonging to the same pattern (Fig.6). In the model it is therefore possible to disclose the emergence of pools of units coding for shared features. We suggest that these pools of units are representative of super-ordinate information with respect to what is coded at the level of Shared Features. In the semantic memory system, the stronger correlation between shared features could be at the base of the hierarchical structure of the memory representations.

4   Discussion

Previous connectionist models of semantic memory assuming feature-based representations [5] and point attractor dynamics [20] have proven to be a suitable tools to investigate and explain a great deal of cognitive and neuropshychological data. What is therefore the main advantage obtained by shifting to a chaotic dynamic regime? Our results enhance the role of chaotic dynamics in allowing much greater flexibility of semantic representations during memory retrieval. In fact, in our model the same semantic features can be dynamically allocated to different memory representations by alternating their synchronization state with different pools of units. Furthermore the same mechanism is able to sustain the separation and concurrent retrieval of partially overlapping memory representations, and avoids spurious synchronization of unrelated semantic features. Neither attractor networks with Hopfield dynamics [20] nor models resorting to static synchronization of neural activities [21] are able to solve this computational problem. We would like to speculate that this mechanisms could play a relevant role in other cognitive domains, possibly linked to frontal lobes functions, such as conflict resolution and coherence assessment [11]. In an attempt to provide a formal description of dynamic synchronicity, we introduce the Mobile Window Correlation Analysis. In the present set of simulations dynamic synchronization shows up even when we take into account the spiking signals alone and leave out the contribution of sub-threshold neural activity (Fig.5). Nevertheless, it appears that the alternate synchronization to different pools of features is more neatly defined when the whole signal is considered (Fig.4), e.g. when the sub-threshold activity of the units is also taken into account.

5   Conclusions

In the present work we presented a toy model of the semantic memory system in which semantic features are coded by Hindmarsh-Rose neurons in the chaotic regime. We devised a formal method to quantify the level of synchronous and asynchronous activity among units coding for Shared and Not Shared Features, and we applied it to the whole signal and to different manipulated neural signals, in which the contribution of sub-threshold activity was ruled out. Although the emergence of a hierarchical structure is evident in all cases, the synchronization shifts that allow for the same feature to participate in the retrieval of multiple semantic memory representations appears to be better defined when the sub-threshold activity is also taken into account. Based on our results, we suggest that the structure of correlations typical of groups of Shared Features would be more robust with respect to damage when compared to the one of Not Shared Features. Further simulations will empirically address this issue. Overall, our results suggest that chaotic dynamics might play a relevant role in allowing for flexible composition of elementary representational states in cognition.

References

1. Rosch, E., Mervis, C., Gray, W., Johnson, D., Boyes-Braem, P.: Basic objects in natural categories. Cognitive Psychology **8** (1976) 382–439
2. Rosch, E.: On the internal structure of perceptual and semantic categories. In: Moore, T. (Ed.) Cognitive Development and the Acquisition of Language. Academic Press, New York (1973)
3. Barsalou, L.: Context-independent and context-dependent information in concepts. Memory and Cognition **10** (1982) 82–93
4. Plaut, D.: Semantic and associative priming in a distributed attractor network. In: Proceedings of the 17th Annual Conference of the Cognitive Science Society (pp. 37–42). Hillsdale, NJ: Lawrence Erlbaum Associates (1995)

5. Rumelhart, D. E.: Brain style computation: Learning and generalization. In: Zornetzer, S. F., Davis, J. L., Lau, C. (Eds), An introduction to neural and electronic networks. Academic Press, San Diego pp 405–420 (1990)
6. Malt, B.: Water is not H20. Cognitive Psychology **27** (1994) 41–70
7. Landauer, T. K., Dumais, S. T.: A solution to Plato's problem: the Latent Semantic Analysis theory of the acquisition, induction, and representation of knowledge. Psychological Review **104** (1997) 211–240
8. Schyns, P. G., Goldstone, R. L., Thibaut, J.: The development of features in object concepts. Behavioral and Brain Science **21** (1998) 1–54
9. Amit, D.: Modeling brain function. Cambridge University Press, Cambridge UK (1998)
10. Treves, A.: Frontal latching networks: a possible neural basis for infinite recursion. Cognitive Neuropsychology **22** (2005) 276–291
11. Shallice, T.: Fractionation of the Supervisory System. In: Stuss, T. S., Knight, R. (Eds). Principles of Frontal Lobe Function. Oxford University Press, Oxford UK (2002)
12. Von der Malsburg, C.: The what and why of binding: The modeler's perspective. Neuron **24** (1999) 95–104
13. Engel, A. K., König, P., Kreiter, A. K., Schillen, T. B., Singer, W.: Temporal coding in the visual cortex: New vistas on integration in the nervous system. Trends Neurosci. **15** (1992) 218–226
14. Gray, C. M.: The temporal correlation hypothesis of visual feature integration: Still alive and well. Neuron **24** (1999) 31–47
15. Raffone, A. and van Leeuwen, C.: Dynamic synchronization and chaos in associative neural network with multiple active memories. Chaos **13** (2003) 1090–1104
16. Felleman, D.J., van Essen, D. C. V.: Distributed hierarchical processing in the primate visual cortex. Cereb.Cortex **1** (1991) 1–47
17. Segev, R. et al.: Long term behavior of lithographically prepared *in vitro* neuronal networks. Phys. Rev. Lett. **11** (2002) 118102–1
18. Hindmarsh, J. L., Rose, R. M.: A model of neuronal bursting using three coupled first order differential equations. In: Proc. R. Soc. London B **221** (1984) 87–102
19. Baddeley, A. D.: Working memory. Science **255** (1992) 556–559
20. LauroGrotto, R., Reich, S., Virasoro, M. A.: The computational role of conscious processing in a model of semantic memory. In: Miyashita, M., Ito, M., Rolls, E. (Eds), Cognition,Computation and Consciousness, Oxford University Press, Oxford UK pp 248–263 (1997)
21. Fujii, H., Hito, H., Aihara, K., Ichinose, N., Tsukada, M.: Dynamical cell assembly hypothesis: theoretical possibility of spatiotemporal coding in the cortex. Neural Networks **9** (1996) 1303–1350

Semantic Web Services with SOUL

Mladen Stanojević and Sanja Vraneš

The Mihailo Pupin Institute, Volgina 15,
11060 Belgrade, Serbia and Montenegro
{Mladen, Sanja}@lab200.imp.bg.ac.yu

Abstract. Semantic Web Services should make it easier for a user to find the
needed information on Web by using natural language queries, instead of simple keywords like in search engines. It has been widely recognized that the
main problem in the implementation of this idea is the problem of semantic representation, the same problem that AI researchers were trying to solve for a
long time. Various ontology and schema languages are used in Semantic Web
to represent the semantics of Web pages, but they require an extensive effort to
translate the existing Web pages. We propose a new knowledge representation
technique, so called Hierarchical Semantic Form, together with a supporting
SOUL algorithm, which should provide a rudimentary understanding of existing, non-annotated Web pages, thus eliminating the need for their laborious
translation. As an example we have implemented a prototype Semantic Web
Service that gives information about flights stored in an ordinary Web page.

1 Introduction

Nowadays, Internet represents a very useful medium for information retrieval, because it stores a vast quantity of data. However, at the same time this vast quantity of
information introduces a limit for even wider use of Internet, because it becomes
difficult for a human to find the relevant Web site [1]. As a response, many search
engines were introduced, but the problem still exists; when you get thousands of hits,
it is not easy to locate the right one.

Web community recognized the importance of the problem and launched Semantic
Web [2] in an attempt to allow computer programs (esp. intelligent agents) to search
the Web (using semantic categories instead of keywords) and find the needed information for a user. However, computers are not able to extract semantic categories
from Web pages in their current form (HTML), hence new knowledge representation
techniques have been proposed to represent the meaning of Web pages.

Although the problem of semantic representation emerged again in Semantic Web,
this is not a new problem. The same problem was recognized by researchers in the
field of Artificial Intelligence, and since then, many knowledge representation techniques have been proposed [3], [4]: logic formalism, semantic nets, conceptual dependencies, frames (schemas), scripts, rules, etc. In Semantic Web different ontology
and schema languages such as XOL [5], SHOE [6], OML [7], RDFS [8],
DAML+OIL[9], OWL [10], are used to represent the semantics.

M. De Gregorio et al. (Eds.): BVAI 2005, LNCS 3704, pp. 338–346, 2005.

These techniques can be used to represent semantics and proved useful in many applications, although they have some drawbacks. All these languages and formalisms represent a kind of meta-language in which knowledge should be represented. However, these meta-languages have a form different from natural language. As a consequence, after meta knowledge (definitions of semantic categories and relations), has been defined, objects from the domain of application must be translated from natural language form using the selected representation. In case of Semantic Web this means translation of billions of existing Web pages, which is hard to imagine.

Unlike ontology and schema languages which are used to represent semantics only, Hierarchical Semantic Form (HSF) [11] can be used to represent semantics, but also grammar rules, which are used by Space Of Universal Links (SOUL) algorithm to parse natural language input and recognize semantic categories. This way HSF with SOUL provides the necessary base for rudimentary understanding of natural language content.

In this paper we will describe first, on an example of flight search, how semantics and grammar rules are represented using HSF, and then we will briefly describe the capabilities of a flight search prototype implemented as a Semantic Web Service.

2 Hierarchical Semantic Form

The Hierarchical Semantic Form (HSF) can be used to represent various kinds of syntax and semantic categories as well as relationships between these syntax and semantic categories. The automatic extraction of semantic categories and relations between them is provided by the SOUL (Space Of Universal Links) algorithm, which gives support to the Hierarchical Semantic Form. HSF uses two data types, *groups* and *links*, to build the hierarchy of categories.

The group data type (Fig. 1.a) designates characters, a group of characters, words, a group of words, sentences, etc. Except at the lowest level, where groups represent single characters, this data abstraction is used to represent sequences at different levels of hierarchy (a group points to the first link of a sequence). One group can appear in different contexts, so it can have many associated links (for each context – one link). This way a unique representation of category is provided.

The link data type (Fig. 1.b) enables the creation of sequences at different hierarchy levels (sequences of characters, words, group of words, sentences, etc.). The main role of links is to represent categories (groups) in different contexts. For each new context where category appears, we need a new link. A link points to group it represents within the sequence, but also to predecessing link and all successive links (defining the context of the category). If a link is the last in the sequence of links, instead to successive links it points to a group that represents this sequence.

When we read a sentence:

"There is an AlItalia flight AZ423/AZ1019 from Berlin to Rome departing at 06:50 and arriving at 11:30 on Sunday."

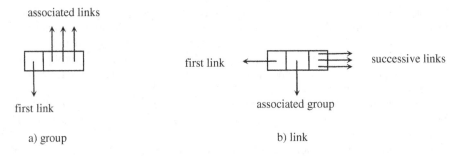

Fig. 1. Basic data types

Our brain could recognize the following semantic categories:

```
<airline-flight> = "AlItalia flight"
<flight-number> = "AZ423/AZ1019"
<from-phrase> = "from Berlin"
<to-phrase> = "to Rome"
<departure-time> = "departing at 06:50"
<arrival-time> = "arriving at 11:30"
<day-of-week> = "Sunday"
```

These semantic categories represent our understanding of the sentence. Using SOUL Commander, a kind of Natural Language Processing shell, we can define various semantic categories. The <flight-number> semantic category can be defined using the following commands:

```
Definition: "AZ" is a "<airline-code>"
Definition: "AZ423" is a "<flight-number>"
Definition: "AZ423/AZ1019" is a "<flight-number>"
```

thus producing the following grammar rules:

```
<airline-code> ::= AZ
<flight-number> = <airline-code><number>
<flight-number> = <flight-number>/<flight-number>
```

In the same way we can define other semantic categories. Finally, using SOUL Commander we can define that only the sentences containing <flight-number>, <from-phrase>, <to-phrase>, <departure-time>, <arrival-time> and <day-of-week> semantic categories will be understood as flight definitions. Using these definitions, SOUL Commander will be able to recognize the following flight definitions although it will not understand all the words:

"On Saturday, the Italian national airline, AlItalia, has a flight from Rome to Berlin, AZ1020/AZ422, arriving at 11:30 and departing at 07:05."
"AlItalia has a new flight, AZ429/AZ1043, on Sunday departing at 17:10 from Berlin and arriving at 21:35 to Rome."

After recognizing the flight definition, SOUL Commander creates its representation using the Hierarchical Semantic Form (Fig. 2).

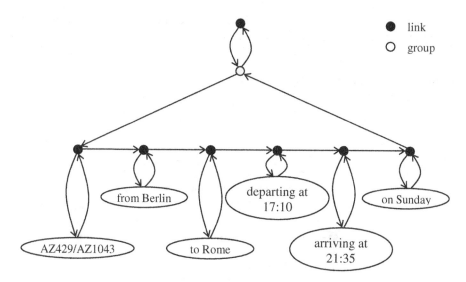

Fig. 2. Flight definition in HSF

Notice that "AZ" group is represented only once within "AZ429/AZ1043" group (Fig. 3).

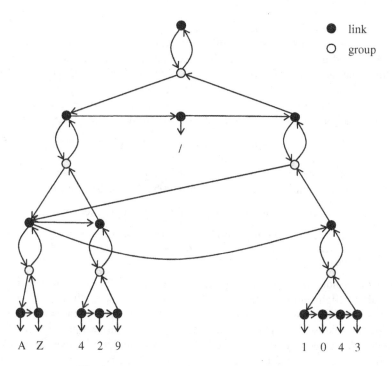

Fig. 3. HSF representation of "AZ429/AZ1043" group

Grammar rules are represented in HSF using the keyword, <is-a>. As an example, a grammar rule:

```
<flight-number> = <airline-code><number>
```

will be represented in HSF like in Fig. 4.

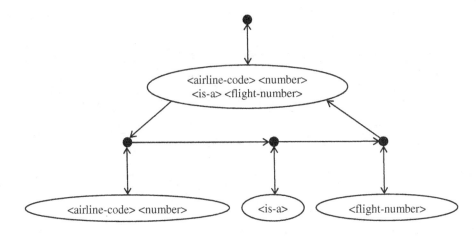

Fig. 4. Complex grammar rule in HSF

With the semantic categories defined so far SOUL Commander will show a poor performance. It will be able to process only AlItalia flights between Berlin and Rome with a very limited understanding capability. However, it is easy to define codes for other airlines and new towns to be able to process more flights. Similarly, by adding few new semantic categories like <departure-phrase>, <arrival-phrase>, <from-to>, <time-phrase> and <part-of-day>, SOUL Commander understanding capabilities will be enhanced, and it will now be able to process the flight definitions like:

"Welcome aboard on a Lufthansa Berlin-Paris flight LH4310 departing at 5:25 in the afternoon and arriving at 7:05 PM each Sunday."

"Air France announces promotional prices for a flight AF1604 leaving Paris at 11 o' clock in the morning and arriving at Rome at 13:05 on Saturday and Sunday."

The final form of a flight definition will contain the following semantic categories:

```
<flight-number> <from-phrase> <to-phrase> <from-to>
<departure-phrase> <arrival-phrase> <departure-time>
<arrival-time> <day-of-week>
```

SOUL Commander will process a sentence as a flight definition if it contains information about flight number, departure town (<from-phrase>, <from-to>, <departure-phrase>), arrival town (<to-phrase>, <from-to>, <arrival-phrase>), departure time (<departure-phrase>, <departure-time>), arrival time (<arrival-phrase>, <arrival-time>), and at least one day of week. Of course, this form doesn't cover all possible cases for flight definitions, but as we already saw, by adding new semantic categories, understanding capabilities can be enhanced.

In a similar way, by adding some new semantic categories (<flight-time-list>, <flight-list>, <airline>, <flight>, <date>, <relative-date>), we can define a general form of a query:

```
<flight-time-list> <flight-list> <airline> <flight>
<from-phrase> <to-phrase> <from-to> <departure-phrase>
<arrival-phrase> <departure-time> <arrival-time> <time-
phrase> <time> <part-of-day> <day-of-week> <date>
<relative-date>
```

When processing a query, SOUL algorithm performs partial parsing and recognizes some of the semantic categories from query definition. Code underlying this query request checks first if the query contains the semantic category <flight> (either directly, or within more complex semantic categories <flight-time-list> and <flight-list>), departure town (<from-phrase>, <from-to> <departure-phrase>), arrival town (<to-phrase> <from-to> <arrival-phrase>) and date of flight (<day-of-week> <date> <relative-date>). If these basic semantic categories have been found, query will be executed.

The semantic categories (<from-town>, <to-town>, <day-of-week>) from the query are matched with the same semantic categories from flight definitions and then missing information is found (e.g. flight number, departure time, arrival time and airline).

The flight query can contain some constraints on time or on the number of flights that should be presented. The time constraints can be set on departure or arrival time, or both:

"I need flights from Berlin to Rome arriving at 5 o'clock in the afternoon next Sunday."

"Please, find me a flight from Berlin to Rome departing in the morning and arriving before 1 PM on 10th of April."

"What flights are there from Rome to Berlin departing after 6:00 and arriving between 1 PM and 14:00 on 10/04?"

If the exact time constraint is set (e.g. at 5 o'clock in the afternoon), then the flights between 16:30 and 17:30 will be searched.

If the query matches many flights, then the list length can be constrained by requiring only "first flight", "first three flights" or "last five flights".

Flight definitions in the flight base contain days of week, so if the query contains a date (month and day), it will be converted to day of week.

3 Flight Search Example

ARPA launched Spoken Language Systems program in 1988, a five-year program centered around a pseudo-application called the Air Travel Information Service (ATIS). An idea was to develop an interactive system for querying the ATIS database and essentially going through all the steps it would take to book a real flight. Although the emphasis was on speech recognition, due attention was also paid to Natural Language Processing. A number of well-functioning prototypes of the ATIS application was developed, however neither of them reached the status of a product. One can come to the conclusion that the technology was not mature enough to provide a satisfactory solution.

Inspired with ATIS project, we have developed a prototype Flight Information Service (FIS), a Semantic Web Service, which should provide information about airline timetables. We have defined first meta knowledge, i.e. the definitions of semantic categories and relations used in this domain, and then we defined a flight base (using an ordinary HTML file) in natural language for major European airlines.

FIS incorporates SOUL Commander, all grammar rules and stores the context of dialog with user. FIS is storing the context which is deep enough to find all basic information required for a flight query, departure and arrival city and day (date) of flight. One possible conversation between user and FIS is represented in Fig. 5.

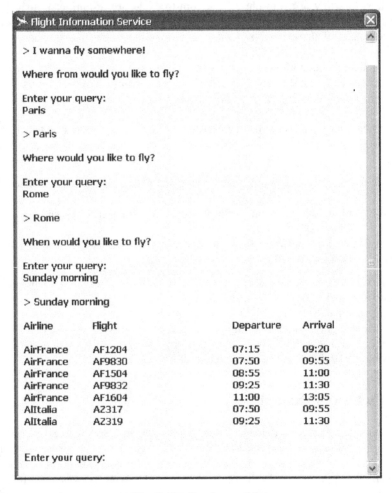

Fig. 5. Simple conversation

However, FIS is also able to process complex queries such as:

"What flights are there from Rome to Berlin departing before 10:00 o'clock in the morning and arriving between 1 PM and 14:00 on April the 10th?"

FIS will find only one flight matching all these constraints, a Lufthansa flight, LH3853/LH180, departing at 7:00 and arriving at 13:30.

If we would like to see some more flights, we could relax a bit constraint on departure and arrival time by typing:

"Departing after 10:00 and arriving between 2 PM and 18:00"

and FIS will now present 7 flights (Fig. 6), taking into account new constraints and context information about departure city (Berlin), arrival city (Rome) and flight date (April the 10th).

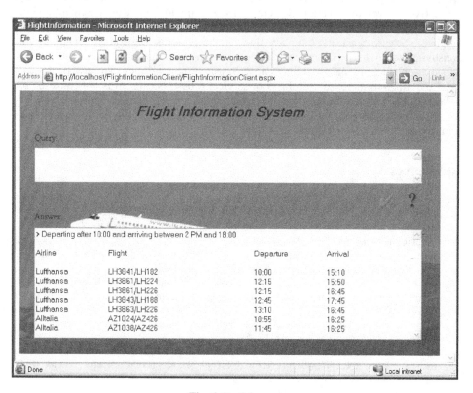

Fig. 6. Partial query

If we need some additional (or more restricted) information, we need not repeat the whole query. It is enough that we type only the changed parts, and FIS will find the missing information from the context.

Notice that FIS could be relatively easy upgraded to TIS (Travel Information Service) by defining few semantic categories, four new commands and timetables for bus and train trips.

4 Conclusions

The main obstacle in broader use of Semantic Web lies in the necessity for translation of existing Web pages into one of ontology or schema languages. However, this laborious job of translating existing Web pages could be avoided if some kind of rudimentary understanding of natural language is provided.

In this paper we have proposed a Hierarchic Semantic Form (HSF), which is a hierarchical equivalent of plain text form, where all semantic categories are explicitly represented and hierarchically organized. HSF and SOUL (Space of Universal Links) algorithm can be used to learn sequences representing natural language input, which easies a lot the definition of semantic categories and relations, and eliminates the need for manual translation of existing Web pages.

To validate the ideas of HSF and SOUL we have developed a flight search prototype, Flight Information Service (FIS), which was inspired by the ARPA project ATIS (Air Travel Information System). FIS was implemented as a Semantic Web Service, which uses an ordinary HTML file with flight timetables defined in natural language, processes natural language queries and presents the flights that satisfy the constraints set by user. FIS is scalable, because new semantic categories can be easily added to enhance its understanding capabilities and new airlines and new flights can be also defined to increase usefulness of service, robust, because it is not confused by unknown words and phrases or by syntactically incorrect queries, and portable, because semantic categories used in FIS, could be reused, for example, in an information service about bus or railway timetables.

References

1. Cercone, N., Hou, L., Keselj, V., An, A., Naruedomkul, K., Hu, X.: From Computational Intelligence to Web Intelligence. COMPUTER, Vol. 35. 11 (2002) 72-76
2. Berners-Lee, T., Hendler, J., Lassila, O.: The Semantic Web. Scientific American. Vol. 284. 5 (2001) 34-43
3. Sowa, J.: Knowledge Representation: Logical, Philosophical, and Computational Foundations. Brooks/Cole Publishing Co., Pacific Grove, CA, (2000)
4. Vraneš, S., Stanojević, M.: Prolog/Rex - A Way to Extend Prolog for Better Knowledge Representation , IEEE Transactions on Knowledge and Data Engineering. Vol. 6. 1 (1994) 22-37.
5. Karp, R. et al: XOL: An XML-Based Ontology Exchange Language (version 0.4). www.ai.sri.com/pkarp/xol/. (March 29, 2005)
6. Heflin, J. et al: SHOE: A Knowledge Representation Language for Internet Applications. Technical Report. CS-TR-4078 (UMIACS TR-99-71), Dept. of Computer Science, University of Maryland. (1999)
7. Kent, R.: Ontology Markup LanguageVersion 0.3. www.ontologos.org/OML/OML%200.3.htm. (March 29, 2005)
8. Brickley D., Guha, R.V. (Eds.): RDF Vocabulary Description Language 1.0: RDF Schema. W3C Recommendation. www.w3.org/TR/rdf-schema/. (March 29, 2005)
9. McGuinness, D., Fikes, R., Handler, J., Stein, L.: DAML+OIL: An Ontology Language for the Semantic Web. IEEE Intelligent Systems., Vol. 17. 5 (2002) 72-80
10. McGuinness, D., van Harmelen, F. (Eds.): OWL Web Ontology Language – Overview. W3C Recommendation. www.w3.org/TR/owl-features/. (March 29, 2005)
11. Stanojević, M., Vraneš, S.: Semantic Web with SOUL, In Proceedings of the IADIS International Conference e-commerce 2004. Lisbon, Portugal. (2004) 123-130

Modeling the Brain's Operating System

Dana Ballard[1] and Nathan Sprague[2]

[1] University of Rochester
[2] Kalamazoo College

Abstract. To make progess in understanding human brain functionality, we will need to understand its basic functions at an abstract level. One way of accomplishing such an integration is to create a model of a human that has a useful amount of complexity. Essentially, one is faced with proposing an embodied "operating system" model that can be tested against human performance. Recently technological advances have been made that allow progress to be made in this direction. Graphics models that simulate extensive human capabilities can be used as platforms from which to develop synthetic models of visuo-motor behavior. Currently such models can capture only a small portion of a full behavioral repertoire, but for the behaviors that they do model, they can describe complete visuo-motor subsystems at a level of detail that can be tested against human performance in realistic environments. This paper outlines one such model and shows both that it can produce interesting new hypotheses as to the role of vision and also that it can enhance our understanding of visual attention.

1   Introduction

All brain operations are situated in the body [1]. Even when the operations are purely mental, they reflect a developmental path through symbols that are grounded in concrete interactions in the world. The genesis of this view is attributed to the philosopher Merleau-Ponty [2], but more recently it has been taken as a tenet of research programs for the reason that tremendous computational economies result. Essentially the body does a large part of the necessary computation, leaving the brain with much less to do.

Research programs that focus on embodiment have been facilitated by the development of virtual reality (VR) graphics environments. These VR environments can now run in real time on standard computing platforms. The value of VR environments is that they allow the creation of virtual agents that implement complete visuo-motor control loops. Visual input can be captured from the rendered virtual scene, and motor commands can be used to direct the graphical representation of the virtual agent's body. Terzoupolous and Rabie [3] pioneered the use virtual reality as a platform for the study of visually guided control. Embodied control has been studied for many years in the robotics domain, but virtual agents have enormous advantages over physical robots in the areas of experimental reproducibility, hardware requirements, flexibility, and ease of programming.

M. De Gregorio et al. (Eds.): BVAI 2005, LNCS 3704, pp. 347–366, 2005.

Embodied models can now be tested using new instrumentation. Linking mental processing to visually-guided body movements at a millisecond timescale would have been impractical just a decade ago, but recently a wealth of high resolution monitoring equipment has been developed for tracking body movements in the course of everyday behavior, particularly head, hand and eye movements (e.g. [4]). This allows for research into everyday tasks that typically have relatively elementary cognitive demands but require elaborate and comprehensive physical monitoring. In these tasks, overt body signals provide a direct indication of mental processing.

During the course of normal behavior humans engage in a wide variety of tasks, each of which requires certain perceptual and motor resources. Thus there must be mechanisms that allocate resources to tasks. Understanding this resource allocation requires an understanding of the ongoing demands of behavior, as well as the nature of the resources available to the human sensori-motor system. The interaction of these factors is complex, and that is where the virtual human platform can be of value. It allows us to imbue our artificial human with a particular set of resource constraints. We may then design a control architecture that allocates those resources in response to task demands. The result is a model of human behavior in temporally extended tasks that may be tested against human performance.

We refer to our own virtual human model as 'Walter.' Walter has physical extent and programmable kinematic degrees of freedom that closely mimic those of real humans. His graphical representation and kinematics are provided by the DI-guy package developed by Boston Dynamics. This is augmented by the Vortex package developed by CMLabs for modeling the physics of collisions. The crux of the model is a control architecture for managing the extraction of information from visual input that is in turn mapped onto a library of motor commands. The model is illustrated on a simple sidewalk navigation task that requires the virtual human to walk down a sidewalk and cross a street while avoiding obstacles and collecting litter. The movie frame in Figure 1 shows Walter in the act of negotiating the sidewalk which is strewn with obstacles (blue objects) and litter (purple objects) on the way to crossing a street.

2   Behavior Based Control

As pointed out by Newell [5], any system that must operate in a complex and changing environment must be compositional, that is It has to have elemental pieces that can be composed to create its more complex structures. Figure 2 illustrates two broad compositional approaches that have been pursued in theories of cognition, as well as in robotics. The first decomposition works on the assumption that the agent has a central repository of symbolic knowledge. The purpose of perception is to translate sensory information into symbolic form. Actions are selected that result in symbolic transformations that bring the agent closer to goal states. This sense-plan-act approach is typified in the robotics community by early work on Shakey the robot [6], and in the cognitive science community

Fig. 1. The Walter simulation. The insets show the use of vision to guide the humanoid through a complex environment. The upper inset shows the particular visual routine that is running at any instant. The lower insert shows the visual field in a head-centered frame.

by the theories of David Marr [7]. In principle, the symbolic planning approach is very attractive, since it suggests that sensation, cognition and action can be studied independently, but in practice each step of the process turns out to be difficult to characterize in isolation. It is hard to convert sensory information into general purpose symbolic knowledge, it is hard to use symbolic knowledge to plan sequences of actions, and it is hard to maintain a consistent and up to date knowledge base.

The difficulties with the symbolic planning approach have led to alternate proposals. In the robotics community Brooks [8] has attempted to overcome these difficulties by suggesting a radically different decomposition, illustrated in Figure 2B. Brooks' alternate approach is to attempt to describe whole visuo-motor behaviors that have very specific goals. Behavior-based control involves a different approach to composition than planning-based architectures: simple microbehaviors are sequenced and combined to solve arbitrarily complex problems. The best approach to attaining this sort of behavioral composition is an active area of research. Brooks' own *subsumption* architecture worked by organizing behaviors into fixed hierarchies, where higher level behaviors influenced lower level behaviors by over-writing their inputs. Subsumption works spectacularly well for trophic, low-level tasks, but generally fails to scale to handle more complex problems [9]. For that reason we have chosen a more flexible control architecture.

Our version of Brooks' behavior-based control centers around primitives that we term *microbehaviors* . A microbehavior is a complete sensory/motor routine that incorporates mechanisms for measuring the environment and acting on it to achieve specific goals. For example a collision avoidance microbehavior would have the goal of steering the agent to avoid collisions with objects in the environment. A microbehavior has the property that it cannot be usefully split

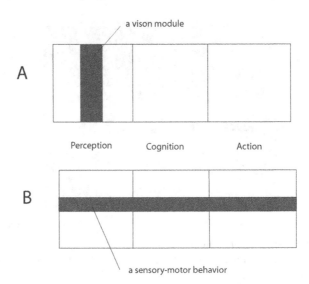

Fig. 2. Two approaches to behavioral research contrasted. A) In the Marr paradigm individual components of vision are understood as units. B) In the Brooks paradigm the primitive unit is an entire behavior.

into smaller subunits. Walter's microbehavior control architecture follows more recent work on behavior based control (e.g. [10,11]) that allows the agent to address changing goals and environmental conditions by dynamically activating a small set of appropriate behaviors. Each microbehavior is triggered by a template that has a pattern of internal and environmental conditions. The pattern-directed activation of microbehaviors provides a flexibility not found in the fixed subsumption architecture.

3   The Human Operating System Model

We think of the control structure in terms of an operating system as the basic functions are needed to implement it are similar as shown in Figure 3. The behaviors themselves, when they are running, each have distinct jobs to do. Each one interrogates the sensorium with the objective of computing the current state of the process. Once the state of each process is computed then the action recommended by that process is available. Such actions typically involve the use of the body. Thus an intermediate task is the mapping of those action recommendations onto the body's resources. Finally the behavioral composition of the microbehavior set itself must be chosen. We contend that, similar to multiprocessing limitations on silicon computers, that the brain has a multiprocessing constraint that allows only a few microbehaviors to be simultaneously active. This constraint, we believe, is the same as that for working memory.

Addressing the issues associated with this vantage point leads directly to an abstract computational hierarchy. The issues in modeling vision are different at

Three Levels of a Human "Operating System"

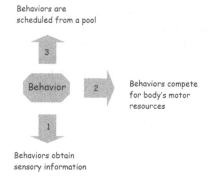

Behaviors are
scheduled from a pool

Behaviors compete
for body's motor
resources

Behaviors obtain
sensory information

Fig. 3. The venue of the behavioral model defines computations at three distinct levels.
1) At the most basic level sensory routines define the state of a behavior. 2) At an
intermediate level, behaviors compete with each other for the body's resources. 3) At
the most abstract level the composition of behaviors must be continually adjusted.

Table 1. The organization of human visual computation from the perspective of the
microbehavior model

Abstraction Level	Problem Being Addressed	Role of Vision
Behavior	Need to get state information	Provide State Estimation
	The current state needs to be updated to reflect the actions of the body	None
Arbitration	Active behaviors may have competing demands for body, legs, eyes. Conflicts have to be resolved	Move gaze to the location that will minimize risk
Context	Current set of behaviors B is inadequate for the task. Have to find a new set	Test for off-agenda exigencies

each level of this hierarchy. Table 1 shows the basic elements of our hierarchy
highlighting the different roles of vision at each level.

The behavior level of the hierarchy addresses the issues in running a microbehavior. These are each engaged in maintaining relevant state information
and generating appropriate control signals. Microbehaviors are represented as
state/action tables, so the main issue is that of computing state information
needed to index the table. The arbitration level addresses the issue of managing
competing behaviors. Since the set of active microbehaviors must share perceptual and motor resources, there must be some mechanism to arbitrate their

needs when they make conflicting demands. The context level of the hierarchy maintains an appropriate set of active behaviors from a much larger library of possible behaviors, given the agents current goals and environmental conditions.

The central tenet of Walter's control architecture is that, although a large library of microbehaviors is available to address the goals of the agent, at any one time, only a small subset of those are actively engaged as shown in Figure 4. The composition of this set is evaluated at every simulation interval, which we take to be 300 milliseconds commensurate with the eyes' average fixation time.

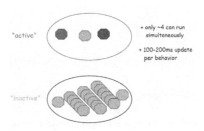

Fig. 4. The model assumes that humans have an enormous library of behaviors that can be composed in small sets to meet behavioral demands. When an additional behavior is deemed necessary it is activated by the 'operating system.' When a running behavior is no longer necessary, it is deactivated.

The issues that arise for vision are very different at the different levels of the hierarchy. Moving up the levels:

1. At the level of individual behaviors, vision provides its essential role of computing state information. The issue at this level is understanding how vision can be used to compute state information necessary for meeting behavioral goals. Almost invariably, the visual computation needed in a task context is vastly simpler than that required general purpose vision and, as a consequence, can be done very quickly.
2. At the arbitration level, the principal issue for vision is that the center of gaze is not easily shared and instead generally must be allocated sequentially to different locations. Eye tracking research increasingly is showing that all gaze allocations are purposeful and directed toward computing a specific result [12,13,14]. Our own model [15] shows how gaze allocations may be selected to minimize the risk of losing reward in the set of running behaviors.
3. At the context level, the focus is to maintain an appropriate set of microbehaviors to deal with internally generated goals. One of these goals is that the set of running behaviors be response to rapid environmental changes. Thus the issue for vision at this level is understanding the interplay between agenda-driven and environmentally-driven visual processing demands.

This hierarchy immediately presents us with a related set of questions: How do the microbehaviors get perceptual information? How is contention managed?

How are sets of microbehaviors selected? In subsequent sections, we use the hierarchical structure to address each of these in turn, emphasizing implications for vision.

4 State Estimation Using Visual Routines

The first question that must be addressed is how individual microbehaviors map from sensory information to internal state descriptions. The position we adopt is that this information is gathered by deploying visual routines. These are a small library of special-purposed functions that can be composed. The arguments for visual routines have be made by [16,17,18]. The main one is that the representations of vision such as color and form, are problem-neutral in that they do not contain explicitly the data upon which control decisions are made.[1] and thus an additional processing step must be employed to make decisions. The number of potential decisions that must be made is too large to pre-code them all. Visual routines address this problem in two ways: 1) routines are composable and 2) routines process visual data in an as-needed fashion.

To illustrate the use of visual routines, we describe the ones that create the state information for three of Walter's microbehaviors: collision avoidance, sidewalk navigation and litter collection. Each of these requires specialized processing. This processing is distinct from that used to obtain the feature images of early vision even though it may use such images as data. The specific processing steps are visualized in Figure 5.

- Litter collection is based on color matching. Litter is signaled in our simulation by purple objects, so that potential litter must be isolated as being of the right color and also nearby. This requires combining and processing the hue image with depth information. The result of this processing is illustrated in Figure 5b.
- Sidewalk navigation uses color information to label pixels that border both sidewalk and grass regions. A line is fit to the resulting set of pixels which indicates the estimated edge of the sidewalk. The result of this processing is illustrated in Figure 5c.
- The collision detector uses a depth image. A depth image may be created by any of a number of cues, (stereo, kinetic depth, parallax depth, etc.) but for collisions, it must be processed to isolate potential colliders. The result of this processing is illustrated in Figure 5d. A study with human subjects shows that they are very good at this, integrating motion cues with depth to ignore close objects that are not on a collision course [19].

Regardless of the specific methods of individual routines, each one outputs information in the same abstract form: the state needed to guide its encompassing microbehavior. The next section describes how Walter can learn to use this information to guide its parent microbehavior.

---

[1] Marr recognized this difficulty of processing visual data prior to knowing what it will be needed for implicitly in his 'principle of least commitment' [7].

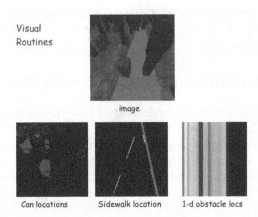

Visual
Routines

image

Can locations   Sidewalk location   1-d obstacle locs

Fig. 5. The Visual Routines that compute state information. a) Input image from Walter's viewpoint. b) Regions that fit the litter color profile. Probable litter locations are marked with circles. c) Processed image for sidewalk following. Pixels are labeled in white if they border both sidewalk and grass color regions. The red line is the most prominent resulting line. b) One dimensional depth map used from obstacle avoidance (not computed directly from the rendered image).

5   Learning Microbehaviors

Once state information has been computed, the next step is to find an appropriate action. Each microbehavior stores actions in a state/action table. Such tables can be learned by reward maximization algorithms: Walter tries out different actions in the course of behaving and remembers the ones that worked best in the table. The reward-based approach is are motivated by studies of human behavior that show that the extent to which humans make such trade-offs is very refined [20] as well as studies using monkeys that reveal the use of reinforcement signals in a way that is consistent with reinforcement learning algorithms [21].

Formally, the task of each microbehavior is to map from an estimate of the relevant environmental state s, to one of a discrete set of actions, $a \in A$, so as to maximize the amount of reward received. For example the the obstacle avoidance behavior maps the distance and heading to the nearest obstacle $s = (d, \theta)$ to one of three possible turn angles, that is, $A = \{-15^\circ, 0^\circ, 15^\circ\}$. The *policy* is the action so prescribed for each state. The coarse action space simplifies the learning problem.

Our approach to computing the optimal policy for a particular behavior is based on a standard reinforcement learning algorithm, termed Q-learning[22]. This algorithm learns a value function $Q(s, a)$ for all the state-action combinations in each microbehavior. The Q function denotes the expected discounted return if action a is taken in state s and the optimal policy is followed thereafter. If $Q(s, a)$ is known then the learning agent can behave optimally by always choosing $\arg\max_a Q(s, a)$(See Appendix for details). Figure 6 shows the table used by the litter collection microbehavior, as indexed by its state information.

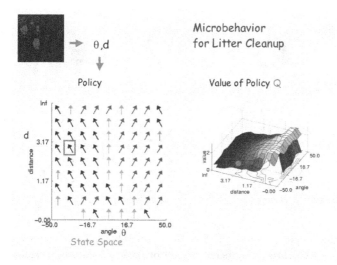

Fig. 6. The central portion of the litter cleanup microbehavior after it has been learned. The color image is used to identify the heading to the nearest litter object as a heading angle θ and distance d. Using this state information to index the table allows the recovery of the policy, in this case $heading = -45°$, and its associated value. The fact that the model is embodied means that there is we can assume there is neural circuitry to translate this abstract heading into complex walking movements. This is true for the graphics figure that has a 'walk' command that takes a heading parameter.

Table 2. Walter's reward schedule

Outcome	Immediate Reward
Picked up a litter can	2
On sidewalk	1
Collision free	4

Each of the three microbehaviors has a two-dimensional state space. The litter collection behavior uses the same parameterization as obstacle avoidance: $s = (d, \theta)$ where d is the distance to the nearest litter item, and θ is the angle. For the sidewalk following behavior the state space is $s = (\rho, \theta)$. Here θ is the angle of the center-line of the sidewalk relative to the agent, and ρ is the signed distance to the center of the sidewalk, where positive values indicate that the agent is to the left of the center, and negative values indicate that the agent is to the right. All microbehaviors use the logarithm of distance in order to devote more of the state representation to areas near the agent. All these microbehaviors use the same three-heading action space described above. Table 2 shows Walter's reward contingencies. These are used to generate the Q-tables that serve as a basis for encoding a policy. Figure 7 shows a representation of the Q-functions and policies for the three microbehaviors.

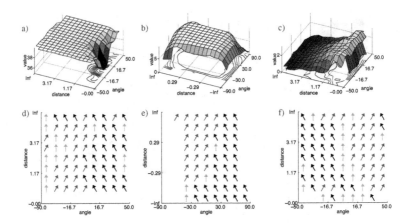

Fig. 7. Q-values and policies for the three microbehaviors. Figures a)-c) show $\max_a Q(s, a)$ for the three microbehaviors: a) obstacle avoidance, b) sidewalk following and c) litter collection. Figures d)-f) show the corresponding policies for the three microbehaviors. The obstacle avoidance value function shows a penalty for nearby obstacles and a policy of avoiding them. The sidewalk policy shows a benefit for staying in the center of the sidewalk $\theta = 0, \rho = 0$. The litter policy shows a benefit for picking up cans that decreases as the cans become more distant. The policy is to head toward them.

When running the Walter simulation, the Q-table associated with each behavior is indexed every 300 milliseconds. The action that is the policy is selected and submitted for arbitration. The action chosen by the arbitration process is executed by Walter. This in turn results in a new Q-table index for each microbehavior and the process is repeated. The path through a Q-table thus evolves in time and can the visualized as a thread of control analogous to the use of the term thread in computer science.

6   Microbehavior Arbitration

A central complication with the microbehavior approach is that concurrently active microbehaviors may prefer incompatible actions. Therefore an arbitration mechanism is required to map from the demands of the individual microbehaviors to final action choices. The arbitration problem arises in directing the physical control of the agent, as well as in handling gaze control and each of these requires a different solution. This is because in Walter's environment, his heading can be a compromise between the demands of different microbehaviors but his gaze location is not readily shared by them. A benefit of knowing the value function for each behavior is that the Q-values can be used to handle the physical arbitration problem in each of these cases.

Heading Arbitration. Since in the walking environment each behavior shares the same action space Walter's heading arbitration is handled by making the assumption that the Q-function for the composite task is approximately equal to the sum of the Q-functions for the component microbehaviors:

$$Q(s,a) \approx \sum_{i=1}^{n} Q_i(s_i, a), \tag{1}$$

where $Q_i(s_i, a)$ represents the Q-function for the ith active behavior. Thus the action that is chosen is a compromise that attempts to maximize reward across the set of active microbehaviors. The idea of using Q-values for multiple goal arbitration was independently introduced in [23] and [24].

In order to simulate the fact that only one area of the visual field may be foveated at a time, only one microbehavior is allowed access to perceptual information during each 300ms simulation time step. That behavior is allowed to update its state information with a measurement, while the others propagate their estimates and suffer an increase in uncertainty. The mechanics of maintaining state estimates and tracking uncertainty are handled using Kalman filters - one for each microbehavior. In order to simulate noise in the estimators, the state estimates are corrupted with zero-mean normally distributed random noise at each time step. The noise has a standard deviation of .2m in both the x and y dimensions. When a behavior's state has just been updated by its visual routine's measurement, the variance of the state distribution will be small, but as we will demonstrate in simulation, in the absence of such a measurement the variance can grow significantly.

Since Walter may not have perfectly up to date state information, he must select the best action given his current estimates of the state. A reasonable way of selecting an action under uncertainty is to select the action with the highest expected return. Building on Equation (1) we have the following: $a_E = \arg\max_a E[\sum_{i=1}^{n} Q_i(s_i, a)]$, where the expectation is computed over the state variables for the microbehaviors. By distributing the expectation, and making a slight change to the notation we can write this as:

$$a_E = \arg\max_a \sum_{i=1}^{n} Q_i^E(s_i, a), \tag{2}$$

where Q_i^E refers to the expected Q-value of the ith behavior. In practice we estimate these expectations by sampling from the distributions provided by the Kalman filter.

Gaze Arbitration. Arbitrating gaze requires a different approach than arbitrating control of the body. Reinforcement learning algorithms are best suited to handling actions that have direct consequences for a task. Actions such as eye movements are difficult to put in this framework because they have only indirect consequences: they do not change the physical state of the agent or the environment; they serve only to obtain information.

A much better strategy is to choose to use gaze to update the behavior that has *the most to lose* by not being updated. Thus, the approach taken here is to try to estimate the value of that information. Simply put, as time evolves the uncertainty of the state of a behavior grows, introducing the possibility of low rewards. Deploying gaze to measure that state reduces this risk. Estimating the cost of uncertainty is equivalent to estimating the expected cost of incorrect action choices that result from uncertainty. Given that the Q functions are known, and that the Kalman filters provide the necessary distributions over the state variables, it is straightforward to estimate, this factor, $loss_b$, for each behavior b by sampling (See Appendix). The maximum of these values is then used to select which behavior should be given control of gaze.

Figure 8 gives an example of seven consecutive steps of the sidewalk navigation task, the associated eye movements, and the corresponding state estimates.

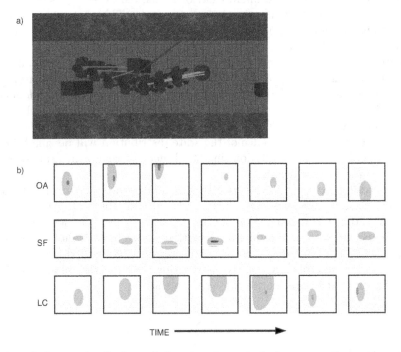

Fig. 8. a) An overhead view of the virtual agent during seven time steps of the sidewalk navigation task. The blue cubes are obstacles, and the purple cylinder is litter. The rays projecting from the agent represent eye movements; red correspond to obstacle avoidance, blue correspond to sidewalk following, and green correspond to litter collection. b) Corresponding state estimates. The top row shows the agent's estimates of the obstacle location. The axes here are the same as those presented in Figure 7. The beige regions correspond to the 90% confidence bounds before any perception has taken place. The red regions show the 90% confidence bounds after an eye movement has been made. The second and third rows show the corresponding information for sidewalk following and litter collection.

The eye movements are allocated to reduce the uncertainty where it has the greatest potential negative consequences for reward. For example, the agent fixates the obstacle as he draws close to it, and shifts perception to the other two microbehaviors when the obstacle has been safely passed. Note that the regions corresponding to state estimates are not ellipsoidal because they are being projected from world-space into the agents non-linear state space.

One possible objection to this model of eye movements is that it ignores the contribution of extra-foveal vision. One might assume that the pertinent question is not which microbehavior should direct the eye, but which location in the visual field should be targeted to best meet the perceptual needs of the whole ensemble of active microbehaviors. There are a number of reasons that we choose to emphasize foveal vision. First, eye tracking studies in natural tasks show little evidence of "compromise" fixations. That is, nearly all fixations are clearly directed to a particular item that is task relevant. Second, results in [25] suggest that simple visual operations such as local search and line tracing require a minimum of 100-150ms to complete. This time scale roughly corresponds to the time required to make a fixation. This suggests that there is little to be gained by sharing fixations among multiple visual operations.

7 Microbehavior Selection

The successful progress of Walter is based on having a running set of microbehaviors $B_i, i = 0, .., N$ that are appropriate for the current environmental and task context. The view that visual processing is mediated by a small set of microbehaviors immediately raises two questions: 1) What is the exact nature of the context switching mechanism? and 2) What should the limit on N be to realistically model the limitations of human visual processing?

Answering the first question requires considering to what extent visual processing is driven in a top down fashion by internal goals, versus being driven by bottom up signals originating in the environment. Somewhat optimistically, some researchers have assumed that interrupts from dynamic scene cues can effortlessly and automatically attract the brain's "attentional system" in order to make the correct context switch e.g [26]. However, a strategy of predominantly bottom-up interrupts seems unlikely in light of the fact that what constitutes a relevant cue is highly dependent on the current situation. On the other hand, there is a strong argument for some bottom up component: humans are clearly capable of responding appropriately to cues that are off the current agenda.

Our model of the switching mechanism is that it works as a state machine as shown in Figure 9. For planned tasks, certain microbehaviors keep track of the progress through the task and trigger new sets of behaviors at predefined junctures. Thus the microbehavior "Look for Crosswalk" triggers the state NEAR-CROSSWALK which contains three microbehaviors: "FollowSidewalk", "Avoid Obstacles", and "Approach Crosswalk."

Figure 9B shows when the different states were triggered on three separate trials.

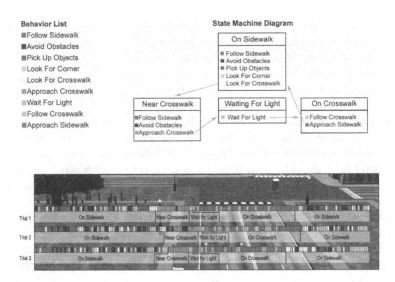

Fig. 9. (Top left) A list of microbehaviors used in Walter's overall navigation task. (Top right) The diagram for the programmable context switcher showing different states. These states are indicated in the bands underneath the colored bars below. Bottom) Context switching behavior in the sidewalk navigation simulation for three separate instances of Walter's stroll. The different colored bars denote different microbehaviors that are in control of the gaze at any instant.

This model reflects our view that vision is predominantly a top-down process. The model is sufficient for handling simple planned tasks, but it does not provide a straightforward way of responding to off-plan contingencies. To be more realistic, the model requires some additions. First, microbehaviors should be designed to error-check their sensory input. In other words, if a microbehavior's inputs do not match expectations, it should be capable of passing control to a higher level procedure for resolution. Second, there should be a low latency mechanism for responding to certain unambiguously important signals such as rapid looming.

Regarding the second question of the possible number of active microbehaviors, there are at least two reasons to suspect that the maximum number that are simultaneously running might be modest. The first reason is the ubiquitous observation of the limitations of spatial working memory (SWM). The original capacity estimate by Miller was seven items plus or minus two [27], but current estimates favor the lower bound [28]. We hypothesize that this limitation is tied to the number of independently running microbehaviors which we have termed threads. The identification of the referents of SWM has always been problematic, since the size of the referent can be arbitrary. This has lead to the denotation of the referent as a 'chunk,' a jargon word that postpones dealing with the issue of not being able to quantify the referents. The thread concept is clearer and more specific as it denotes exactly the state necessary to maintain a microbehavior.

The second factor limiting the number of running microbehaviors is that large numbers of active microbehaviors may not be possible given that they have to be implemented in a neural substrate. Cortical memory is organized into distinct areas that have a two-dimensional topography. Furthermore spatial information is usually segregated from feature based information so that the neurons representing the colors of two objects are typically segregated from the neurons representing their location. As a consequence there is no simple way of simultaneously associating one object's color with its location together with another object's association of similar properties (This difficulty is the so-called "binding problem" [29]). Some proposals for resolving the binding problem hypothesize that the number of active microbehaviors is limited to one, but this seems very unlikely. However the demands of a binding mechanism may limit the number of simultaneous bindings that can be active. Thus it is possible that such a neural constraint may be the basis for the behavioral observation.

Although the number of active microbehaviors is limited there is reason to believe that it is greater than one. Consider the task of walking on a crowded sidewalk. Two fast walkers approaching each other close at the rate of 6 meters/second. Given that the main source of advanced warning for collisions is visual and that eye fixations typically need 0.3 seconds and that cortical processing typically needs 0.2-0.4 seconds, during the time needed to recognize an impending collision, the colliders have traveled about 3 meters, or about one and a half body lengths. In a crowded situation, this is insufficient advance warning for successful avoidance. What this means is that for successful evasions, the collision detection calculation has to be ongoing. But that in turn means that it has to share processing with the other tasks that an agent has to do. Remember that by sharing we mean that the microbehavior has to be simultaneously active over a considerable period, perhaps minutes. Several elegant experiments have shown that there can be severe interference when multiple tasks have to be done simultaneously, but these either restrict the input presentation time or the output response time [30]. The crucial issue is what happens to the internal state when it has to be maintained for an extended period.

8 Conclusions

The focus of this paper was to introduce the issues associated with using a graphical agent as a proto-theory of human visuo-motor behavior. One criticism of such a project is that, even though the system is vastly reduced from that needed to capture a substantial fraction of human behavior, the model as it stands is complicated and has enough free parameters so that any data from real human performance would be easy to fit. Although the system is complex, most of the constraints follow from the top-level assumption of composable microbehaviors. Once one decides to have a set of running microbehaviors, the questions of how many and when are they running are immediate. Furthermore they have ready answers in observations of human behavior in the classic observations of working memory and eye movements: Working memory suggests the number of

Table 3. The relationships between attention and working memory and the microbehavior model

Abstraction Level	Attention	Working Memory
Behavior	YES	The *contents* of working memory
Arbitration	YES	The referents of working memory or "chunks"
Context	YES	

simultaneous microbehaviors is small; eye movements suggest when a behavior is running as each fixation is an indication of the brain's instantaneous problem being updated. Table 3 summarizes the relationships between the hierarchy used by the model and the notions of attention and working memory.

The restricted number of active microbehaviors means that there must be a mechanism for making sure that a good behavioral subset has been chosen. Such a mechanism must interrogate the environment and 1) add needed microbehaviors as well as 2) drop microbehaviors if needed to meet the capacity constraint.

The essential description of microbehaviors is captured by reinforcement learning's Q-tables that relate the states determined by vision to actions for the motor system. Indeed the commands are in coded form, taking advantage of known structure in the body that carries them out. Assuming the existence of a table as is done at the reinforcement learning level finesses important details. Thus a more detailed model is necessary to account for how the table index is created.

The reinforcement learning venue provides a different perspective on gaze allocation. One of the original ideas was a bottom-up view that gaze should be drawn to the most salient locations in the scene as represented in the image, where salience was defined in terms of the spatial conjunction of many feature points. However recent measurements have shown that eye movements are much more agenda driven than that predicted by bottom-up saliency models. For example Henderson has shown that subjects examining urban scenes for people examine place where people might be even though these can have very low feature saliency [19]. Walter's use of Q-tables suggest that to interpret gaze allocation, an additional level of indirection may be required. For example, the controller for sidewalk navigation uses gaze to update the estimate of the location of the sidewalk. In order to predict when gaze might be allocated to do this, in our model, requires knowing the uncertainty in the current estimate of the sidewalk location.

The most important benefit of the kind of model presented in this paper is that it encourages the modeler to frame experimental questions in the context of integrated natural behavior. There are dramatic differences between this perspective and traditional approaches to studying vision:

1. The desired schedule of interrupts under normal behavior has a temporal distribution that is very different than worst-case laboratory situations. In the lab, subjects are typically in extremis with respect to reaction times, whereas natural behaviors typically allow flexibility in responding.
2. In a multiple task situation, the most important task facing the deployment of gaze is to choose the behavior being serviced. This problem is hardly considered in the search literature which concentrates on within-task saliency of individual targets.
3. The natural timescale for studying microbehavior components is on the order of 100 to 200 milliseconds, the time to estimate state information. Below that one is studying the process of state formation, a level of detail is interesting in its own right but is below the central issues in human behavioral modeling.
4. The context for the deployment of visual routines is reversed from a laboratory situation. In that situation the typical structure of a task forces a bottom-up description. The image is most often presented on a previously blank CRT screen. In a natural task, the particular test needed in a gaze deployment is known. Furthermore this test is known before the saccade is made. Thus in the natural case the situation is reversed, the test can be in place before the data is available. This has the result of making the test go as fast as possible. The speed of tests may account for the fact that fixation times in natural situations can be very short. Dwell times of 100 milliseconds are normal, less than half those observed in many laboratory studies.

All of these observations underline the importance of graphic simulation as a new tool in the study of human vision. While the model has extensive structure, each component of the structure serves a specific purpose and the whole combine to direct the performance of human behaviors. A competing performance model might look very different but would have to address these issues.

Perhaps the most important theme in recent vision research, is that no component of the visual system can be properly understood in isolation from the behavioral goals of the organism. Therefore, properly understanding vision will ultimately require modeling complete sensori-motor systems in behaving agents. The model presented in this paper is certainly not true in all of its particulars, and it leaves many details unspecified. However, it does provide a framework for thinking about action-oriented human vision. The fact that developing complete and correct models of human vision is such a difficult task should not stop us from trying to put as many of the pieces together as possible.

References

1. Clark, A.: Being There: Putting Brain, Body, and World Together Again. Cambridge, MA: MIT Press (1997)
2. Merleau-Ponty, M.: Phenomenology of Perception. Routledge & Kegan Paul (1962)

3. Terzopoulos, D., Rabie, T.F.: Animat vision: Active vision in artificial animals. Videre: Journal of Computer Vision Research 1 (1997) 2-19
4. Pelz, J., Hayhoe, M., Loeber, R.: The coordination of eye, head, and hand movements in a natural task. Experimental Brain Research 139 (2001) 166-177
5. Newell, A.: Unified Theories of Cognition. Harvard University Press (1990)
6. Nilsson, N.: Shakey the robot. Technical Report 223, SRI International, (1984)
7. Marr, D.: Vision. W.H. Freeman and Co., Oxford (1982)
8. Brooks, R.A.: A robust layered control system for a mobile robot. IEEE Journal of Robotics and Automation RA-2 (1986) 14-23
9. Hartley, R., Pipitone, F.: Experiments with the subsumption architecture. In: Proceedings of the International Converence on Robotics and Automation. (1991)
10. Firby, R.J., Kahn, R.E., Prokopowicz, P.N., Swain, M.J.: An architecture for vision and action. (1995) 72-79
11. Bryson, J.J., Stein, L.A.: Modularity and design in reactive intelligence. In: International Joint Conference on Artificial Intelligence, Seattle, Washington (2001)
12. Land, M.F., Mennie, N., Rusted, J.: Eye movements and the roles of vision in activities of daily living: making a cup of tea. J. Neuroscience 21 (2001) 6917-6932
13. Hayhoe, M.M., Bensinger, D., Ballard, D.H.: Task constraints in visual working memory. Vision Research 38 (1998) 125-137
14. Johansson, R., Westling, G., Backstrom, A., Flanagan, J.R.: Eye-hand coordination in object manipulation. Perception 28 (1999) 1311-1328 21
15. Sprague, N., Ballard, D.: Eye movements for reward maximization. In: Advances in Neural Information Processing Systems 15. (2003)
16. Ullman, S.: Visual routines. Cognition 18 (1985) 97-159
17. Roelfsema, P., Lamme, V., Spekreijse, H.: The implementation of visual routines. Vision Research 40 (2000) 1385-1411
18. Ballard, D., Hayhoe, M., Pook, P.: Deictic codes for the embodiment of cognition. Behavioral and Brain Sciences 20 (1997) 723-767
19. Ballard, D., Sprague, N.: Attentional resource allocation in extended natural tasks [abstract]. Journal of Vision 2 (2002) 568a
20. Maloney, L., Landy, M.: When uncertainty matters: the selection of rapid goaldirected movements [abstract]. Journal of Vision ((to appear))
21. Suri, R.E., Schultz, W.: Temporal difference model reproduces anticipatory neural activity. Neural Computation 13 (2001) 841-862
22. H., C.J.C., Dayan, P.: Technical note: Q-learning. Machine Computation 8 (1992) 279-292
23. Humphrys, M.: Action selection methods using reinforcement learning. In: Proceedings of the Fourth International Conference on Simulation of Adaptive Behavior. (1996)
24. Karlsson, J.: Learning to Solve Multiple Goals. PhD thesis, University of Rochester (1997)
25. Roelfsema, P.R., P.S., K., Spekreijse, H.: Subtask sequencing in the primary visual cortex. Proceedings of the National Academy of Sciences USA 100 (2003) 5467-5472
26. Itti, L., Koch, C.: A saliency-based search mechanism for overt and covert shifts of visual attention. Vision Research 40 (2000) 1489-1506
27. Miller, G.: The magic number seven plus or minus two: Some limits on your capacity for processing information. Psychological Review 63 (1956) 81-96
28. Luck, S.J., Vogel, E.K.: The capacity of visual working memory for features and conjunctions. Nature 390 (1997) 279-281
29. von der Malsburg, C.: The what and why of binding: the modelers perspective. Neuron 24 (1999) 95-104

30. Pashler, H.: The Psychology of Attention. Cambridge, MA: MIT Press (1998)
31. Kaelbling, L.P., Littman, M.L., Moore, A.W.: Reinforcement learning: A survey. Journal of Artificial Intelligence Research 4 (1996) 237-285
32. Sutton, R., Barto, A.: Reinforcement Learning: An Introduction. MIT Press (1998)
33. Watkins, C.J.C.H.: Learning from Delayed Rewards. PhD thesis, Kings College, Oxford (1989)
34. Sutton, R.: Generalization in reinforcement learning: Successful examples using sparse coarse coding. In: Advances in Neural Information Processing Systems. Volume 8. (1996)
35. Sprague, N., Ballard, D.: Multiple goal learning for a virtual human. (in preparation)
36. Sprague, N., Ballard, D.: Multiple-goal reinforcement learning with modular sarsa(0). In: International Joint Conference on Artificial Intelligence. (2003)

Appendix: Reinforcement Learning Details

Learning behaviors There are a number of algorithms for learning $Q(s, a)$ [31,32] the simplest is to take random actions in the environment and use the Q-learning update rule [33]:

$$Q(s, a) \leftarrow (1 - \alpha)Q(s, a) + \alpha(r + \gamma \max_{a'} Q(s', a'))$$

Here $\alpha \in (0, 1)$ is a learning rate parameter, $\gamma \in (0, 1)$ is a term that determines how much to discount future reward, and s' is the state that is reached after action a. As long as each state-action pair is visited infinitely often in the limit, this update rule is guaranteed to converge to the optimal value function. The Q-learning algorithm is guaranteed to converge only for discrete case tasks with Markovian transitions between states. Walter's tasks are more naturally described using continuous state variables. The theoretical foundations of continuous state reinforcement learning are not as well established as for the discrete state case. However empirical results suggest that good results can be obtained by using a function approximator such as a CMAC along with the Sarsa(0) learning rule: [34]

$$Q(s, a) \leftarrow (1 - \alpha)Q(s, a) + \alpha(r + \gamma Q(s', a'))$$

This rule is nearly identical to the Q-learning rule, except that the max action is replaced by the action that is actually observed on the next step. The Q-functions used throughout this paper are learned using this approach. A more detailed account of the learning procedure can be found in [35] and [36].

Choosing behaviors for a state update Whenever Walter chooses an action that is sub-optimal for the true state of the environment, he can expect to lose some return. We can estimate the expected loss as follows:

$$loss = E[\max_a \sum Q_i(s_i, a)] - E[\sum Q_i(s_i, a_E)]. \qquad (3)$$

The term on the left-hand side of the minus sign expresses the expected return that Walter would receive if he were able to act with knowledge of the true state of the environment. The term on the right expresses the expected return if he is forced to choose an action based on his state estimate. The difference between the two can be thought of as the cost of the agent's current uncertainty. This value is guaranteed to be positive, and may be zero if all possible states would result in the same action choice.

The total expected loss does not help to select *which* of the microbehaviors should be given access to perception. To make this selection, the loss value can be broken down into the losses associated with the uncertainty for each particular behavior b:

$$loss_b = E\left[\max_a \left(Q_b(s_b, a) + \sum_{i \in B, i \neq b} Q_i^E(s_i, a)\right)\right] - \sum_i Q_i^E(s_i, a_E). \quad (4)$$

Here the expectation on the left is computed only over s_b. The value on the left is the expected return if s_b were known, but the other state variables were not. The value on the right is the expected return if none of the state variables are known. The difference is interpreted as the cost of the uncertainty associated with s_b.

A Bayesian Approach to Situated Vision

Giuseppe Boccignone[1], Vittorio Caggiano[1], Gianluca Di Fiore[2],
Angelo Marcelli[1], and Paolo Napoletano[1]

[1] Natural Computation Lab, DIIIE - Universitá diSalerno,
via Ponte Don Melillo, 1 Fisciano (SA), Italy
{boccig, amarcelli, pnapoletano}@unisa.it
[2] Co.Ri.Tel. Labs, via Ponte Don Melillo, 1, Fisciano (SA), Italy
gdifiore@coritel.it

Abstract. How visual attention is shared between objects moving in an observed scene is a key issue to situate vision in the world. In this note, we discuss how a computational model taking into account such issue, can be designed in a bayesian framework. To validate the model, experiments with eye-tracked human subjects are presented and discussed.

1 Introduction

One of the main concerns in modeling active organisms or agents such as humans and robots is how to "situate" vision in the world. It has been argued that what is needed to navigate the world is a way of directing attention to individual objects; then, additional information can be encoded as needed [1], [2]. Attention not only restricts various types of visual processing to certain spatial areas of the visual field but also accounts for object-based information, so that attentional limitations are characterized in terms of the number of discrete objects which can be simultaneously processed.

Several theories have been concerned with how these visual objects are individuated accessed and used. In particular Pylyshyn's FINST (FINgers of INSTantiation) theory has complemented such theories by postulating a mechanism by which object-based individuation, tracking and access is realized [2]. The model is based on a finite number of visual indexes (fingers, inner pointers) which can be assigned to various items and serve as means of access to such items for higher level process that allocates focal attention. The visual indexes bestow a processing priority to the indexed items, insofar as they allow focal attention to be shifted to indexed, possibly moving, items without first searching for them by spatial scanning. In this note, we discuss how such mechanism may find its computational counterpart in the bayesian framework of multiple hypotheses tracking, and how it may be embodied in a general model of visual attention.

2 Background and a Foreword on Visual Inference

The model presented here grounds its rationale in the functional architecture of biological vision [3], [4], [5]. A simplified outline of the neural pathways for

M. De Gregorio et al. (Eds.): BVAI 2005, LNCS 3704, pp. 367–376, 2005.

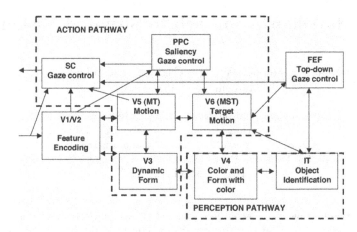

Fig. 1. Main neural pathways and modules for vision and gaze control [3], [4], [5]

gaze control is shown in Fig. 1. Early visual neurons in V1 and V2 are generally seen as spatiotemporal filters that extract local features and feed them to two information pathways. These two pathways, rather than being characterized by classic"what" (object-based) and "where" (spatial-based) type of processing, can be more generally viewed, according to Goodale and Humprey [4], as the *action* and *perception* pathways. The former processes visual information in order to accomplish some action in the world; it is mainly spatial-based, but yet can handle object-based information in visuomotor tasks, even in the presence of lesions within the perception pathway [4]. The latter is basically concerned with object identification/recognition and is the main route to visual perception. The action pathway principally involves middle temporal (MT) areas which perform motion analysis, area V3 dealing with the analysis of dynamic form [3] and medial superior temporal (MST) areas involved, for instance, in target pursuit. The perception pathway involves area V4 involved in the analysis of form in association with color, and infero-temporal cortex (IT) areas, that can be defined the highest-order areas for the visual perception of objects (e.g., faces).

Clearly, the two pathways are not segregated but cooperate to provide a coherent picture of the world. Overt visual attention, and thus gaze control, is one critical facet of the cooperation between these two pathways. It is possible to roughly distinguish three levels of control. At the highest level, frontal eye fields (FEF) are involved in target selection and regulate the decision of when to initiate or cancel a gaze-shift, and its related neurons respond more strongly when the stimulus in their response field is a target relevant from a behavioral standpoint. At an intermediate level, posterior parietal cortex (PPC) provides some form of saliency encoding [6],[5]. The lowest stage is represented by the superior colliculus (SC), which provides the necessary target-position signals to premotor circuitry in the brainstem; its eye movements-related neurons are likely to encode the probability that the stimulus in the response field is the target from a priori information or from a posteriori analysis of the sensory cue to target information [5]. Note that PPC and FEF can be considered as modules of the action pathway.

Summing up, in each visual module, information is processed by considering input signals fed by lower levels together with contextual information, such as backward signals from higher level modules in the same pathway and sideward signals from different pathway. This fact raises the issue of how to account for such complexity in designing computational models. It has been argued [7] that a Bayesian approach could be an appropriate model to deal with cross-processing of information among modules. To summarize the rationale of such approach, consider a module M_1 receiving an input signal z_{obs} (observation) from a lower level module and contextual information z_{cont}, then the task of the module is to infer (hidden) information z_1, given z_{cont} and z_{obs}, namely to compute the posterior probability $P(z_1|z_{obs}, z_{cont}) = \frac{P(z_{obs}|z_1, z_{cont})P(z_1|z_{cont})}{P(z_{obs}|z_{cont})}$, where $P(z_{obs}|z_1, z_{cont})$ represents the likelihood weighted by prior information $P(z_1|z_{cont})$, and $P(z_{obs}|z_{cont})$ is a normalizing factor. Note that if markovianity is assumed, then $P(z_1|z_{obs}, z_{cont}) \simeq P(z_{obs}|z_1)P(z_1|z_{cont})$.

3   Overview of the Model

The model presented here is summarized at a glance in Fig. 2. In the following for sake of simplicity, with a slight abuse of notation, we will indicate with z_t^{feat} either a scalar feature or a feature vector measured at time t, and input frames are denoted z_t, z_{t-1}; also O_k is used to label either a generic region or a specific object. In the proposed system the pair (z_t, z_{t-1}) is represented in color opponent space and undergoes a pyramidal transformation. On such representation, probability density functions (pdf) are computed relative to contrast,

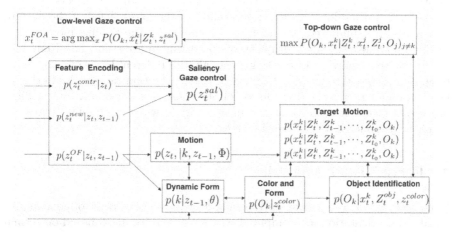

Fig. 2. Bayesian modeling of visual modules and their interactions. Inputs from the left are provided by a pair of frames and related pyramidal representations.

$p(z_t^{contr}|z_t)$, novel events occurring in the scene, $p(z_t^{new}|z_t, z_{t-1})$, and optical flow, $p(z_t^{OF}|z_t, z_{t-1})$. Contrast and novelties are straightforwardly combined in a local saliency density, $p(z_t^{sal})$.

In the perceptual pathway a preliminary object segmentation based on color features, $p(O_k|z_t^{color})$, is performed, and this in turn is used to initialize the dynamic form segmentation module, which computes the probability $p(k|z_{t-1}, \theta_k)$ that a point is labelled with label k, and thus assigned to object O_k described by segmentation parameters θ_k. Dynamic form segmentation is jointly performed together with object motion estimation, which derives affine motion parameters Φ of motion likelihood $p(z_t|k, z_{t-1}, \Phi)$. The preliminary region segmentation previously introduced is also forwarded to higher identification modules that compute the joint probability $p(O_k|x_t^k, Z_t^{obj}, z_t^{color})$ of having, at time t an object of class k in a state x_t^k given low-level features like color and a set Z^{obj} of object or model dependent features - e.g., eye and mouth position for face detection.

In this context Pylyshyn's conjecture of fingers of instantiation is acknowledged in terms of multiple hypotheses instantiation. Object and state information (for instance, position and dimension at time t) together with motion parameters Φ are used along multiple object tracking which is performed as a Bayesian recursive filtering of multiple hypotheses, $p(x_t^k|Z_t^k, Z_{t-1}^k, \cdots, Z_{t_0}^k, O_k)$, Z_t^k denoting the set of features observed on object O_k. The decision of tracking object O_k among other objects $O_j, j \neq k$ is contextually performed by jointly taking into account features and priority of the object with respect to a specified task via the MAP rule, namely $\max p(O_k, x_t^k|Z_t^k, x_t^j, Z_t^j, O_j)_{j \neq k}$. Such top-down focus of attention (FOA) is used to modulate, with local saliency, the final decision (motor command) of setting the FOA at location $x_t^{FOA} = \arg\max_x p(O_k, x_t^k|Z_t^k, z_t^{sal})$. In this respect, the model allows to control the gaze at three levels of complexity: at the highest level, attention is focused on the base of prior information (motivations, task, behavior); if this is not available tracking of objects may still be performed using local saliency; eventually at the lowest level, if the perception pathway is inhibited, point of gaze is chosen by the SC-like module only relying upon novelties and abrupt events occurring in the scene, according to a purely reactive behavior. Interestingly enough, this different levels of complexity, roughly correspond to the development of visual attention capabilities in the infant, or, on a larger scale, to evolution of biological vision systems. Intermediate processing results are shown at a glance in Fig. 3, where probability maps are graphically rendered as grey-level images.

4 Early Visual Analysis

From a color video sequence, early visual features such as color opponents, intensity and orientation are computed in a set of feature maps based on retinal input and represented using pyramids. Then, center-surround operations, are implemented as differences between a fine and a coarse scale for a given feature [6]. One feature type encodes for on/off image intensity contrast, two encode for

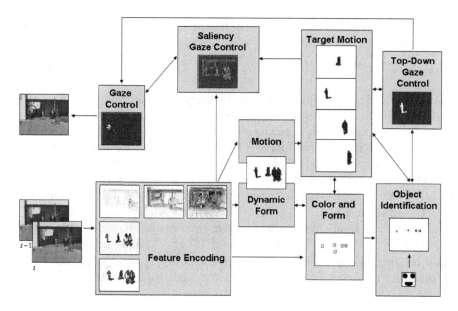

Fig. 3. Results obtained by different modules visualized as grey-level maps. Bottom, from left to right: the frame at time t; feature encoding providing three contrast maps, novelty and raw optical flow; motion segmentation and estimation map; skin map and model -based face detection maps. Top, from right to left: top-down saliency map; tracked objects maps; mid-level saliency map; final gaze control map; FOA drawn as a circle on the original frame. Due to space limitations, pyramidal representation is not shown.

red/green and blue/yellow double-opponent channels and four encode for local orientation contrast.

The contrast pyramids for intensity, color, and orientation are summed across scales into three separate conspicuity maps [6], obtaining a vector of contrast features z_t^{contr} (cfr. Fig. 3). Novelty features z_t^{new} are obtained on a lower level l of the image intensity Gaussian pyramid as the difference between two subsequent frames, smoothed via anisotropic filtering.

Contrast and novelty features are mapped to likelihoods by fitting a gaussian to their distribution in the image, e.g., $p(z_t^{contr}) = \frac{exp(-\frac{1}{2}(z_t^{contr}-\mu)^T \Sigma^{-1}(z_t^{contr}-\mu_k)}{(2\pi)^{(D/2)}|\Sigma_k|^{1/2}}$. In this way the saliency of a point is proportional to $p(z_t^{contr})^{-1}$, being large when the feature is unexpected. Motion analysis is performed on Gaussian pyramids of pairs of frames using Anandan's algorithm [8] in order to obtain optical flow pdf $p(z_t^{OF}|z_t, z_{t-1})$.

5   The Perception Pathway

The perception pathway deals with object-based information that, in the current implementation of the system, is represented by faces and other generic moving objects, $\mathcal{O} = \{\mathcal{F}, \mathcal{M}\}$. The ultimate goal here is to identify objects $O_k \in \mathcal{O}$, that is to compute

$$p(O_k|x_t^k, Z_t^{obj}, z_t^{color}) \simeq p(Z_t^{obj}|x_t^k, O_k, z_t^{color})p(x_t^k|O_k, z_t^{color})p(O_k|z_t^{color})P(O_k). \tag{1}$$

The term $p(O_k|z_t^{color})$ represents a preliminary segmentation, and is approximated as the likelihood $p(z_t^{color}|O_k)$ computed by using a spatially sensitive variant of the Expectation-Maximization (EM) algorithm [9].

For instance, in the case of faces ($O_k = F_k$), $p(F_k|z_t^{color})$ represents in Eq.1 a skin map, while $p(x_t^k|F_k, z_t^{color})$ is the probability of detecting a face in state x_t^k and is basically derived through eye detection via Discrete Symmetry transform, x_t^k being represented through center and dimensions of a face bounding box [10]. The likelihood $p(Z_t^{face}|x_t^k, F_k, z_t^{color})$ models face specific features Z_t^{face}, for instance "low level" distributions of skin texture and shape features, namely $p(z_t^{skin}|x_t^k, F_k z_t^{color})$, $p(z_t^{tex}|x_t^k, F_k)$ and $p(z_t^{shape}|x_t^k, F_k)$ and "high level" model-based information, such as facial shape likelihood $p(z_t^{shape}|x_t^k, F_k)$, accounting for similarity to a model template (cfr. Fig. 3, and [10] for details).

6   The Action Pathway

The goal of motion processing modules is to compute motion features related to objects O_k, so that, if the case, gaze can focus and track a specific object with respect to some given task.

The problem of object motion estimation and prediction can be formulated in Bayesian terms as by the recursive Bayesian filter which solves the problem in two step. The objective of tracking an object O_k is to estimate the state x_t^k given all the measurements $\mathcal{Z}_t = \{Z_1, \cdots, Z_t\}$ up to that moment, or equivalently to construct the posterior pdf $p(x_t^k|\mathcal{Z}_t, O_k)$. In our case the state accounts for position, height and width of a bounding box, and rotation, $x_t^k = \{x, y, wX, wY, \theta\}$. The *prediction* step uses the dynamic equation and the already computed pdf of the state at time $t-1$, $p(x_{t-1}|\mathcal{Z}_{t-1}, O_k)$, to derive the prior pdf of the current state, $p(x_t^k|\mathcal{Z}_{t-1}, O_k)$. Then, the *update* step employs the likelihood function $p(Z_t|x_t^k, O_k)$ of the current measurement to compute the posterior pdf $p(x_t^k|\mathcal{Z}_t, O_k)$. Formally:

$$p(x_t^k|\mathcal{Z}_t^k, O_k) \propto p(Z_t^k|x_t^k, O_k) \int p(x_t^k|x_{t-1}^k, O_k)p(x_{t-1}^k|\mathcal{Z}_{t-1}^k, O_k)dx_{t-1}^k. \tag{2}$$

The likelihood is provided by a specific measurement on object features (color, velocity and dimension). The term $p(x_t^k|x_{t-1}^k, O_k)$ represents our knowledge about how the object might evolve from time $t-1$ to t. Here we assume that the dynamics $p(x_t^k|x_{t-1}^k, O_k)$ of each object is described by a parametric (affine) model:

$$z^{motion} = \begin{pmatrix} 1 & x & y & 0 & 0 & 0 \\ 0 & 0 & 0 & 1 & x & y \end{pmatrix} \phi_k, \tag{3}$$

where $\phi_k = (\alpha_1, \cdots, \alpha_6)^T$ are the motion parameters of such region/object.

The motion model is derived using the information fed through contextually by modules that, on the basis of raw motion vectors z_t^{OF} and by cooperating with object segmentation modules, compute the complete data likelihood $p(z_t, k | z_{t-1}, \phi_k, \theta_k)$, where $k = (k_1, \cdots, k_N)^T$ is a "hidden" vector of binary indicator labels that assign each pixel to a unique region/object O_k and θ_k are the parameters describing region k. The cooperation among different modules, that is the computation of the complete data (z_t, k) (Fig. 3) is obtained by maximizing   via   the   EM   algorithm   the   complete   likelihood $p(z_t, k | z_{t-1}, \Phi, \theta) = \prod_r p(z_t, | k, z_{t-1}, \Phi) p(k | z_{t-1}, \theta)$, where r indexes all sites of the frame lattice and $\Phi = (\phi_1, \cdots, \phi_N)^T$ is the vector of all motion parameters. To this end we experimented both with algorithms described in [11] and [12], and opted for the latter because more efficient. Initialization of motion vectors is performed by using optical flow vectors, and the initial segmentation/labelling is obtained by combining rough information obtained by the novelty detector with a preliminary segmentation performed on frame z_{t-1} again via the EM algorithm [9].

In order to model multiple object tracking, in the vein of Pylyshyn, we must account for the fact that human observers can perform smooth pursuit of one object, while keeping inner "pointers" to other objects moving in the scene $(k \simeq 4, 5)$, so that they are able to rapidly switch to one such background object, either under volitional control or due to habituation factors [2]. From a computational point of view, a viable solution is to consider on the one hand objects to track as a multiple hypotheses process, while on the other hand the selection of one among these is performed by taking into account prior information related to the task the agent should perform. For what concerns the first problem, one such tool is particle filtering (PF) [13]. The main idea of PF relies upon approximating the pdf by means of a set of weighted samples $S = \{(s^{(n)}, \pi^{(n)})\}, n = 1 \ldots N$. Every sample s represents the current object status to which is associated a discrete sampled probability π, where $\sum_{n=1}^{N} \pi^{(n)} = 1$. The goal is to compute by sampling the posterior pdf $p(s_t | \mathcal{Z}_t, O_k)$ in place of $p(x_t^k | \mathcal{Z}_t, O_k)$. Here, $s_t = \{x, y, wX, wY, \theta\}$ and $\pi_t^{(n)} = p(Z_t | x_t^k = s_t^{(n)}, O_k)$. Thus, filtering is performed by using Eq. 2 and substituting $x_t^k = s_t$.

To generate S_t, after having selected N samples from the set S_{t-1} with probability $\pi_{t-1}^{(n)}$, prediction $p(s_t | s_{t-1}, O_k)$ is obtained by propagating each sample of an object by the motion affine model of the tracked region. Then, data observation is accomplished and the likelihood $p(Z_t^k | s_t, O_k)$ evaluated. Each particle is then weighted in terms of the observation with probability $\pi^{(n)}$. Eventually, the mean state of O_k is estimated at each time step from $\mu_s = E[s] = \sum_{n=1}^{N} \pi^{(n)} s^{(n)}$, and this determines the position of the object. At time t, the sample selection from the sample set S_{t-1}, performed before the propagation step, is accomplished as described in [13]. For computational efficiency (lower number of samples) we use multiple PFs to track the different objects, represented in Fig. 3 as a stack of tracking maps.

7   Gaze Control

High level gaze control is obtained by estimating the posterior probability of gazing, at time t, object O_k and its state x_t^k while observing object features Z^j and other moving objects $\{O_j\}_{j \neq k}$, $p(O_k, x_t^k | Z_t^k, x_t^j, Z_t^j, O_j)_{j \neq k}$. By using Bayes rule:

$$p(O_k, x_t^k | Z_t^k, x_t^j, Z_t^j, O_j)_{j \neq k} = \frac{p(Z^k, x^k | O_k, Z^k, x^j, Z^j, O_j)_{j \neq k} P(O_k)}{\sum_l p(Z_t^l, x_t^l | O_l, x_t^j, Z_t^j, O_j)_{j \neq l} P(O_l)}. \tag{4}$$

The object to be focused is selected via a MAP criterion, $\max p(O_k, x_t^k | Z_t^k, x_t^j, Z_t^j, O_j)_{j \neq k}$. In Eq. 4, $P(O_k)$ denotes the prior probability of observing object O_k, and captures the relevance of the object with respect to a task pursued by the agent. It can be modeled as the product of two independent components, $P(O_k) = P_{task}(O_k) p_{hab}(O_k)$, where $P_{task}(O_k)$ is the prior knowledge on task, while $p_{hab}(O_k)$ accounts for habituation, loss of interest effects, namely $p_{hab} = \exp(-\lambda t)$. By assuming weak coupling between features, the likelihood in Eq. 4 can be estimated as

$$\prod_{z_i \in Z} p(z_{i,t}^k, x_t^k | O_k, z_{i,t}^k, x_t^j, z_{i,t}^j, O_j)_{j \neq k} = \prod_{z_i \in Z} \frac{1}{1 + \exp(-\beta(z_{i,t}^k - \langle z_{i,t}^j \rangle))}, \tag{5}$$

where $\langle z_{i,t}^j \rangle = \frac{1}{n-1} \sum_{j \neq k} z_{i,t}^j$. The rationale behind Eq.5 is to grant higher probability to an object that is more salient with respect to others surrounding it. Interestingly enough, the use of a sigmoid function to model the likelihood term in Eq.4 together with the MAP selection rule, implements a winner-take-all strategy, which Pylyshyn [2] conjectured as a plausible neural implementation of FINST dynamics.

For what concerns mid level gaze control, the probability of focusing on a region of space on the basis of its saliency $p(z_t^{sal})$ takes into account static and dynamic features through the mixture $p(z_t^{sal}) = \alpha_c p(z_t^{contr} | z_t) + \alpha_n p(z_t^{new} | z_t, z_{t-1}) - \alpha_h p(z_t^{hist} | z_{t-1}^{sal}, x_t^{FOA})$, where $p(z_t^{hist} | z_{t-1}^{sal}, x_t^{FOA})$ is a "history" term which accounts for recently focused regions and implements the inhibition of return mechanism.

Eventually in the SC-like module the point of fixation can be obtained as

$$x_t^{FOA} = \arg \max_x p(O_k, x_t^k | Z_t^k, z_t^{sal}) \simeq \frac{p(O_k, x_t^k | Z_t^k)}{p(z_t^{sal})}, \tag{6}$$

thus combining high and mid-level focusing probabilities. The chosen FOA position x_t^{FOA} is also fed backward to PPC-like module, in order to compute $p(z_t^{hist} | z_{t-1}^{sal}, x^{FOA})$ in the next frame.

8   Experimental Work

Different clips produced to simulate different conditions have been used to compare model-generated scanpaths with those of human observers, either syntheti-

Fig. 4. Gaze control results (left to right, top to bottom): the FOA of the average observer is drawn as a black circle; the white circle is the FOA set by the system

cally generated or representing fixed-camera outdoor sequences. The subjects involved in the experiments were 39 students, from 19 to 26 years old; all subjects had normal or corrected-to-normal vision, and were naive with respect to the purpose of the experiment. Each of them was sitting in front of the display of the eye-tracking system at a distance of 60 cm, and was asked to look at the video clip, so as to be able to answer a few questions about the content of the video that would have been asked immediately after. Scanpath capture and recording was performed using an ASL 5000 eye-tracking device. Results eye-tracked from 5 subjects have been preliminary used to train the model, and derive prior probabilities (estimated as fixation frequencies of specific objects, e.g., faces, moving persons, etc.); the other 34 subjects where eye-tracked in order to compute a "reference" scanpath to include fixations which are common to many observers (average observer), while leaving out fixations that are observer-specific. Due to space limitations, we present here results obtained on a clip where three people are walking at different distances from the camera, with different speeds and directions, then a new person enters the scene running towards the camera. In this case, the "reference" scanpath was generated in free-viewing conditions (no task), and turned to be the most critical to compare with our system. Fig. 4 shows a summarization of results. Note that the FOAs set by the system match with a short time delay the scanpath of the average observer; clearly, in the absence of a specified task (uniform $P_{task}(O_k)$, Eq.4), the system deploys attention to walkers near to the camera (frames 7 and 8, mid row), while interestingly human observers keep on focusing the face of the popped-in runner, trying to perform identification.

9   Final Remarks

The model integrates different visual modules and levels of gaze control in a Bayesian framework, and in particular allows attentive multiple object tracking [2]. Also, gaze control via saccade and pursuit is shared among modules [5]; for instance, pure saccadic behavior may take place in the absence of objects in motion or top-down inhibition of tracking. Preliminary results give evidence of reasonable performance in comparison with human visual behavior. Experiments have shown that the system increases performance when visual tasks are specifically committed, which is not surprising, since human attentive behavior is known to be subjectively biased and idiosyncratic along unconstrained viewing. Future research will consider tighter integration of modules via nonparametric generalized belief propagation techniques [7].

References

1. Hayhoe, M.M., Ballard, D.H., Bensinger, D.: Task constraints in visual working memory. Vision Research **38** (1998) 125–137
2. Pylyshyn, Z.: Situating vision in the world. Trends in Cognitive Sciences **4** (2000) 197–207
3. Zeki, S.: A Vision of the Brain. Backwell Science, Oxford,UK (1993)
4. Goodale, M., Humphrey, G.: The objects of action and perception. Cognition **67** (1998) 181–207
5. Krauzlis, R., Stone, L.: Tracking with the minds eye. Trends Neuroscience **22** (1999) 544–550
6. Itti, L., Koch, C.: Computational modelling of visual attention. Nature Reviews - Neuroscience **2** (2001) 1–11
7. Lee, T.S., Mumford, D.: Hierarchical bayesian inference in the visual cortex. J. Opt. Soc. Am. A **20** (2003) 1434–1448
8. Anandan, P.: A computational framework and an algorithm for the measurment of visual motion. Int. Journal of Computer Vision **2** (1989) 283–310
9. Boccignone, G., Ferraro, M., Napoletano, P.: Diffused expectation maximisation for image segmentation. Electronics Letters **40** (2004) 1107–1108
10. Boccignone, G., Caggiano, V., Di Fiore, G., Marcelli, A., Napoletano, P.: Attentive video analysis using spatial-based and object-based cues. In: Proceedings CAMP 05, IEEE Computer Soc. Press (2005)
11. Vasconcelos, N., Lippman, A.: Empirical bayesian motion segmentation. IEEE Trans. on Pattern Analysis and Machine Intelligence **23** (2001) 217–220
12. Weiss, Y., Adelson, E.: A unified mixture framework for motion segmentation: incorporating spatial coherence and estimating the number of models. In: Proc. IEEE Conf. CVPR '96, IEEE Computer Soc. Press (1996) 321–326
13. Isard, M., Blake, A.: Condensation-conditional density propagation for visual tracking. International Journal of Computer Vision **29** (1998) 5–28

A Fuzzy Scale-Space Approach to Feature-Based Image Representation and Retrieval

M. Ceccarelli[1], F. Musacchia[3], and A. Petrosino[2,3]

[1] RCOST, University of Sannio, Benevento, Italy
[2] DSA, University of Naples "Parthenope", Naples, Italy
[3] ICAR-CNR, Italy

Abstract. We propose an image indexing and retrieval method which is based on the multiscale image analysis theory in conjunction with fuzzy image feature extraction. The main idea is based on the assumption that the fundamental cues for image description such as shape and textures should be considered together within a unified model. Here the multiscale analysis is modeled by a differential morphological filter, and the feature are extracted by a multiscale fuzzy gradient operation applied to the detail images, which are the differences between images at successive scales. Experiments with large image databased and comparisons with classical methods are reported .

1 Introduction

The recent explosion of availability of digital media together with the even increasing communication bandwidth has made possible the distribution and storage of digital images and videos for a wide variety of purposes, from the protection of cultural patrimony to the use of advanced watermarking techniques for copyright, to the development of large on line image and video databases. Large scale image repositories are pervasive in several domains such as medical image management, multimedia libraries, document archives, art collections, geographical information systems, law enforcement agencies, and journalism. In all these fields the need of advanced content-based image retrieval (CBIR) systems is even increasing due to the wide availability of high definition sensors and scanners, therefore the development of CBIR methodologies has been an active research area in the recent years [20].

CBIR systems commonly use a set of features for image representation in addition to some meta information that is stored as keywords. Most systems use color features in the form of color histograms to compare images [17,21]. The ability to retrieve images when color features are similar across the database is achieved by using texture features [14,13]. Shape is also an important attribute that is employed in comparing similarity of regions in images [6,15,12]. In CBIR systems, the queries that are used to retrieve images can be broadly classified as primitive, logical, and abstract. A query is said to be a primitive query if it is based on features extracted from the images. A query is said to be logical if it employs the identities of the objects in the image. Abstract queries are typically

M. De Gregorio et al. (Eds.): BVAI 2005, LNCS 3704, pp. 377–385, 2005.

based on a notion of similarity which is a concept that cannot be easily captured in a mathematical model. Here we focus on the use of fuzzy scale-space primitive features for the efficient realization of a image retrieval algorithm. In particular we show how the algorithm reported in [5] can be extended to be used for image representation and retrieval. In order to build advanced CBIR the theory of fuzzy logic has been already applied in several forms which are essentially related with the way the user performs or expresses a query, see for example [9]. Here we adopt a different approach, showing that the primitive feature extraction can strongly benefit from the combined adoption of non-linear scale space analysis with the fuzzy information fusion relating local to wide support features.

Most feature based approaches share as common factor the concept of *scale* which is related to the unknown mean size objects or texture primitive ("texels"). The use of multiple scales can be of aid when facing complex pattern recognition problems such those involved in image indexing and retrieval. Indeed a scale-space analysis of an image is a family of smoothed images derived on the basis of a continuous scale parameter [11,10] As the scale increases the image get coarser and fine details are gradually suppressed. The meaningful features in the original signal, which persist at higher scales, can be then identified by following their path in the resulting scale-space. Although early works on scale-space were essentially based on linear filtering using the Gaussian function as smoothing kernel (known as Gaussian Pyramid), it is now recognized that even non-linear filters such as multiscale dilation and erosion can posses the monotonic property for signal extrema which is the fundamental requirement of continuous scale-space analysis [3,11]. The morphological approach to image analysis has been shown to be an efficient tool for textural feature extraction and description [5].

The paper is organized as follows. The next Section reports the adopted model consisting into the multiscale representation and the textural gradient features which we use for image indexing. In the last Section we present the experimental results and comparisons on a large data image database.

2   The Proposed Approach

Here we focus on a feature based approach for image indexing and retrieval. As in every image vision system, the choice of the kind of feature to select for the classification ad description of pictorial information influences the performance and complexity of the system being developed. As already pointed out, shape, color and texture play a fundamental role within this context. Several works have been developed trying a unified approach at shape and texture segmentation [22] as they represent the main computational cues for three-dimensional object description. Textural gradient [5] are one of such integrated approaches for unifying shape and texture. Here we report the application of this kind cues to the development of a CBIR system. In the sequel we describe the main computational steps of our algorithm implemented within a framework of image indexing ad retrieval[7].

2.1   Non-linear Scale Space Filtering

A morphological *scale–space* representation of an image $u_0(\mathbf{x})$, $\mathbf{x} \in \Re^2$, is defined as a family of smoothed images, derived on the basis of a scale parameter t, *i.e.* given $u_0(\mathbf{x})$, $u(\mathbf{x}, t)$ means the "image u_0 analyzed at scale t". The *Ane Morphological Scale Space* (AMSS) model, introduced in [1], is defined as the solution of the following second order non linear partial differential equation

$$\frac{\partial u}{\partial t} = |\nabla u|(\mathrm{curv}(u))^{\frac{1}{3}} \quad u(\mathbf{x}, 0) = u_0(\mathbf{x}) \tag{1}$$

where $curv(u)$ represents a second order differential operator corresponding to the curvature of level curves of $u(\mathbf{x}, t)$, *i.e.* $curv(u) = \frac{u_{xx}u_y^2 - 2u_{xy}u_x u_y + u_{yy}u_x^2}{(u_x^2 + u_y^2)^{3/2}}$. Here the notation u_x represents the partial derivative of u with respect to the variable x and analogously for the other differential operators.

This kind of smoothing possesses invariance properties; specifically, the model (1) is the unique multi-scale analysis which has the properties of:

- *Contrast Invariance* . We perceive textures on the basis of relative spatial relationships between pixels, rather than the luminosity itself. This means that a filtering process aimed at analyzing textures should be invariant to changes which preserve the relative order of luminance values. In particular, a *contrast change* of an image $u(\mathbf{x})$ is the application to u of any increasing function, eventually non linear; a contrast invariant filter operates just on the level curves of the image.
- *Rotation and Translation Invariance* , as we perceive textures independently of position and orientation.
- *Ane Stretching Invariance* , as our perception of textures is influenced by stretching, *i.e.* discrimination of textures can be reduced by stretching the individual textons. Therefore, the invariance to this operation can preserve the perception of the original texture. Unfortunately, the invariance to general stretching is difficult to be formally imposed. However, linear stretching corresponds to an affine transformation and the model expressed by equation (1) has been shown by Alvarez *et al.* (1993) to be invariant under affine transformations.

These properties allow the model (1) to preserve the structure of the textural patterns even at coarser scales; this is due to its geometrical behavior, which moves the level curves of the image with a speed proportional to their curvature.

Starting from a textured image, a multichannel image can be built by using its smoothed versions generated through the iterative application of model (1). Indeed, the anisotropy of the filtering process tends to smooth out the level curves of the image, which eventually collapse into larger groups, but the shape of the curves which embeds the preferred orientation of the textures is maintained.

2.2   Detail Images

The *detail images* provide information about how the level curves move during the evolution of equation (1) and represent the structure of the textural patterns in terms of differences between the level curves at different "times". The detail images are obtained as differences between the images analyzed at successive scales

$$d_i(\mathbf{x}) = u(\mathbf{x}, t_i) - u(\mathbf{x}, t_{i-1}) \qquad (2)$$

with the scale parameter t discretized at increasing values $t_0 = 0, t_1, t_2, ..., t_n$. Since the filtering process is influenced by the orientations of the textural patterns, *i.e.* the model expressed by equation (1) is anisotropic, we do not need to perform orientation selective smoothing.

The sequence of detail images corresponds to a representation of the motion of the level curves through time. The discrimination between textural patterns is performed by applying a multi-scale fuzzy gradient operation to each detail image followed by a hierarchical clustering algorithm as shown in the next section.

2.3   Morphological Gradient Images and Segmentation

Here, we face the problem of analyzing the detail images in order to extract textural gradients which indicate the local change of structural relationships between neighboring pixels. To this purpose, we will use elements of the rough set theory [16] which is an extension of the set theory dealing with coarse information. Here we briefly introduce the main concepts of this theory referring to [2,5] for the details.

Let $X = \{x_1/\mu(x_1), ..., x_n/\mu(x_n)\}$ be a fuzzy set F on X defined by adding to each element of X the degree of its membership to the set through a mapping $\mu : X \rightarrow [0,1]$. A C-set, [2] is defined as a triple $C = (\mathcal{X}, m, M)$, where $\mathcal{X} = \{X_1, ..., X_p\}$ is a partition of X into p disjoint subsets $X_1, ..., X_p$, and m and M are mappings defined by

$$m_k = \inf\{\mu(x)|x \in X_k\}$$

and

$$M_k = \sup\{\mu(x)|x \in X_k\}$$

$\mathcal{X}$ and μ uniquely define a composite set and

$$m(X) \leq \mu(X) \leq M(X)$$

In addition to usual operations on fuzzy sets, like union and intersection, a basic operation is valid over these sets, called *C-product*. The operation C-product between couple of C-sets is defined as follows. Given two sets C and C', both related to different partitions of the same set X, the C-product, denoted as $\otimes$, is defined as the new C-set C'':

$$C'' = C \otimes C' = (\mathcal{X}'', m'', M'')$$

where $\mathcal{X}''$ is a new partition whose elements are

$$\mathcal{X}''_{k,l} = X_k \cap X_l$$

and $m''_{k,l} = \max\{m_k, m'_l\}$, $M''_{k,l} = \min\{M_k, M'_l\}$. The C-product satisfies:

$$m(X) \leq m''(X) \leq \mu(X) \leq M''(X) \leq M(X)$$

and

$$m'(X) \leq m''(X) \leq \mu(X) \leq M''(X) \leq M'(X)$$

It has been also demonstrated in [2] that recursive application of the previous operation provides a refinement of the original sets, realizing a powerful tool for measurement and a basic signal processing technique. Edge detection, gray-level image segmentation and image coding have been performed by combining the low-level analysis provided by these operations together with fuzzy classification [4].

Returning to the problem of image analysis, let us explain how we apply the above theory to the extraction of textural gradient. Our starting point is the set of detail images computed according to (2). Let X be the set of pixel positions, *i.e.* X is the Cartesian product $\{0, ..., N-1\} \times \{0, ..., M-1\}$. Let us define as fuzzy membership function μ over X the singleton membership function according to which

$$\mu(\mathbf{x}) = d(\mathbf{x})$$

i.e., μ measures just the luminance value of the detail image d. Local properties can be extracted by a multiresolution mechanism based on C-sets [18]. In particular, let us consider four different partitions $\mathcal{X}^i$, $i = 1, 2, 3, 4$, of the set-image X, such that each element of $\mathcal{X}^i$ is a subimage of dimension $w \times w$ and $\mathcal{X}^2, \mathcal{X}^3, \mathcal{X}^4$ are taken as shifted versions of $\mathcal{X}^1$ in the directions of 0°, 90° and 45° of $w-1$ pixels. In such a case each pixel of the image can be seen as the intersection of four corresponding elements of the partitions $\mathcal{X}^1, \mathcal{X}^2, \mathcal{X}^3, \mathcal{X}^4$. Since for each partition a C-set may be defined, each pixel can be seen as belonging to the partition obtained by C-producting the original four C-sets:

$$\mathcal{C} = \mathcal{C}^1 \otimes \mathcal{C}^2 \otimes \mathcal{C}^3 \otimes \mathcal{C}^4 \tag{3}$$

where $\mathcal{C}^i$ is the composite set corresponding to partition $\mathcal{X}^i$. In this case the *scale* is represented by the size w of each partition element. Let us introduce the *multiscale gradient* definition based on the previous operations.

Definition 1. Given the maxima and minima images (respectively M and m) generated by the application of the operation 3 over four different partition of an image with a scale w the *multiscale gradient* at the position (i, j) is

$$G^w_{i,j} = M^w_{i,j} - m^w_{i,j}, \tag{4}$$

Therefore, this operation corresponds to the difference between the lower and upper approximation of a fuzzy set. To extract texton gradient information at different scales, the gradient operation (4) has to be applied to all the detail images obtained from (2), by using increasing values of w and generating a multichannel image to be segmented. This means that we first perform a nonlinear smoothing depending on the parameter t, which at the first stage represents the scale of the smoothed image, and then apply the fuzzy gradient operation to all the images d_i which are the differences between images at successive scales. This last fuzzy gradient operation also depends on another scale parameter: the window size w.

3   Implementation and Results

The fuzzy multiscale image gradients are selected as indexing feature for a textured image indexing and retrieval system. Here we want to report the obtained result over a large image database, the Stanford10K Database, consisting of about 10000 images. The first indexing phase required about 20 hours of running time over a Linux personal computer. In order to evaluate the system of a set of queries over the whole database, we adopt as measure of performance the model reported in [8]. Indeed, the recall precision should depend on the similarity degree between the relevant images and their position over the query results. Let us define the following parameters:

– R, the number of relevant entries in the database
– E_r the number of returned image from the query
– R_r the number of relevant imaged returned from the query
– M_r the number of misses ($M_r = R - R_r$)

In order to consider the position of the relevant images within the query result, let us consider the parameter $SumR$ defined as the the sum of the positions of the relevant images in the results. The normalized effectivenes (EFF) is defined as

$$EFF = \frac{\frac{2*SumR}{R-1} - \frac{R-1}{2*E_r+R-1}}{1 - \frac{R-1}{2*E_R+R-1}}$$

In addition, we also use the Relative Weighted Displacement (RWD) measure from [19]. Let the user label each image in the retrieved set as "a", "b" or "c", where "a" denotes an image that is similar to the query as perceived by the user, "b" one that is somewhat similar, and "c" one that is dissimilar. Then, RWD is defined as follows:

$$RWD = \frac{\sum_{i=1}^{m} w_i \|r_i - h_i\|}{\sum_{i=1}^{m} w_i}$$

where w_i is 0.8, 0.5 and 0.05 for the cases when the image is labeled "a", "b" and "c", respectively. The weights used in the case of RWD do not punish the measure if nonsimilar images are ranked high. We therefore modify w_i to be 0.8 for the case when the image is labeled "c".

The testing database contains color JPEG images of size 128×85, 85×128, 128×96, or 96×128, etc. The database images have the same dimensions, but not necessarily the same orientation. Our well-balanced large-scale testbed is very realistic and helps us to reach a fair evaluation of different methods. The content of the database images ranges from animals, people, scenery, and architecture,

Table 1. Risults with the Stanford10K database of the two variants of the algorithm compared with those obtained by using Gabor features and co-occurence matrces

Algoritmo	RWD	EFF
Gabor Features	0.982	0.30419
SS1	1.013	0.27863
SSN	0.977	0.30876
Co-Occurence Matrices	0.876	0.18653

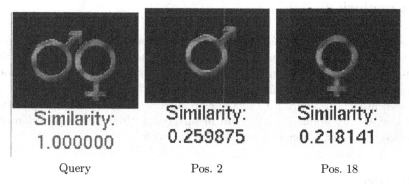

Fig. 1. Some query results with the proposed algorithms; the query correctly returns the searched image and the other two images in position 2 and 18 respectively

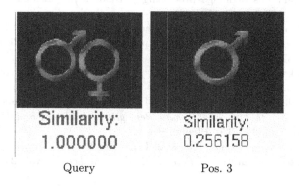

Fig. 2. Some query results with Gabor features; the query returns the searched image and just one image in position 3

etc. We tested two different variants of the model reported in [5], the first, called SS1, uses the sequence of multiscale gradients over the detailed images, whereas the second, referred as SSN, performs a further reduction by combining into a single datum all the N detail images and then the fuzzy gradient is applied.

Our tests, obtained by averaging the measures over 100 test runs, show that the the fuzzy mulsiscale feature extraction scheme attains results comparable or even better than those obtained by using other standard approaches such as

Gabor features or co-occurence matrices. As a visual example of application of the proposed method the figure 1 reports the result poduces by a simple query over the whole database. Our approach returns three images over five relevant images in the database. Whereas, the Gabor feature approach, implemented in the GIFT package, returns just two images. Moreover the position and similarity of the relevant images within the query results are significantly better for our approach.

4   Conclusions

We have reported an image indexing and retrieval based on a nonlinear multiscale representation of the input image. The main idea is based on the assumption that the fundamental cues for image description such as shape and textures should be considered together within a unified model. We have demonstrated that the proposed model, in addition to serve as an efficient tool for texture separation, can be efficiently applied in the field of image indexing. The reported results show positive comparison with standard approaches.

References

1. L. Alvarez, F. Guichard, P. L. Lions, and J. M. Morel 1993, "Axioms and fundamental equations of image processing", *Archives for Rational Mechanics and Analysis*, vol. 123 n. 3, pp. 199-257.
2. A. Apostolico, E. R. Caianiello, E. Fischetti and S. Vitulano, "C-Calculus: an elementary approach to some problems in pattern recognition", *Pattern Recognition*, vol. 19, pp. 375 387, 1878.
3. R. W. Brockett and P. Maragos 1994, "Evolution equations for continuous-scale morphological filtering" *IEEE Trans. Signal Processing*, vol. 42, pp. 3377-3386.
4. E. R. Caianiello and A. Petrosino 1994, "Neural networks, fuzziness and image processing", in *Machine and Human Perception: Analogies and Divergences*, V. Cantoni (ed.), pp. 355–370, Plenum Press.
5. M. Ceccarelli, A. Petrosino, "A parallel fuzzy scale-space approach to the unsupervised texture separation", *Pattern Recognition Letters*, vol. 23, pp. 557 567, 2002.
6. A. Del Bimbo and P. Pala, "Visual Image Retrieval by Elastic Matching of User Sketches", *IEEE Trans. Pattern Analysis and Machine Intelligence*, vol. 19, no. 2, pp. 121-132, Feb. 1997.
7. Gnu   Fundation,   "The   GNU   Image-Finding   Tool", http://www.gnu.org/software/gift/gift.html.
8. D. A. Keim, M. Heczko, A. Hinneburg, "Multi-Resolution Similarity Search in Image Databases", *ACM/Springer Multimedia Systems Journal*, 2003.
9. R. Krishnapuram, S. Medasani, S-H Jung, Y-S Choi, R. Balasubramaniam, "Content-Based Image Retrieval Based on a Fuzzy Approach", *IEEE Trans. on Knowledge and Data Engineering*, vol. 16(10) 2004.
10. J. Koenderink 1984, "The structure of images", *Biological Cybernetics*, vol. 5, pp. 363-370.

11. P. T. Jackway and M. Deriche 1996, "Scale-Space properties of the Multiscale Morphological Dilation-Erosion", *IEEE Trans. Pattern Analysis and Machine Intelligence*, vol. 18, n. 1, pp. 38-51.
12. A. Jain and A. Vailaya, "Image Retrieval Using Color and Shape", *Pattern Recognition*, vol. 29, no. 8, pp. 1233-1244, 1996.
13. F. Liu and R.W. Picard, "Periodicity, Directionality, and Randomness: Wold Features for Image Modeling and Retrieval", *IEEE Trans. Pattern Analysis and Machine Intelligence*, vol. 18, no. 7, pp. 722-733, July 1996.
14. B.S. Manjunath and W.Y. Ma, "Texture Features for Browsing and Retrieval of Image Data", *IEEE Trans. Pattern Analysis and Machine Intelligence*, vol. 18, no. 8, pp. 837-842, Aug. 1996.
15. R. Mehrotra and J.E. Gary, "Similar-Shape Retrieval in Shape Data Management", *Computer*, vol. 28, no. 9, pp. 57-62,Sept. 1995.
16. Z. Pawlak, "Rough Sets", *Int. Journal on Inform. Comput. Sci.*, vol. 11, no. 5, pp. 341-356, 1982.
17. M.J. Swain and D.H. Ballard, 'Color Indexing', *Int J. Computer Vision*, vol. 7, no. 1, pp. 11-32, 1991.
18. A. Petrosino, "Rough fuzzy sets and unsupervised neural learning: applications in computer vision", in *New trends in Fuzzy Logic* A. Bonarini, D. Mancini, F. Masulli and A. Petrosino (eds), pp. 166–176, World Scientific, 1996.
19. S. Santini and R. Jain, "Similarity Measures", *IEEE Trans. Pattern Analysis and Machine Intelligence*, vol. 21, no. 9, pp. 871-883, Sept. 1999.
20. A.W.M. Smeulders, M. Worring, S. Santini, A. Gupta, and R. Jain, "Content-Based Image Retrieval at the End of the Early Years", *IEEE Trans. Pattern Analysis and Machine Intelligence*, vol. 22, no. 12, pp. 1349-1380, Dec. 2000.
21. M. Stricker and M. Orengo, Similarity of Color Images, *Proc. SPIE Conf. on Storage and Retrieval for Image and Video Databases III*, W.R. Niblack and R.C. Jain, eds., pp. 381-392, 1995.
22. S. C. Zhu and A.L Yuille, "Unifying Snake/balloon, Region Growing and Bayes/MDL/Energy for multi-band Image Segmentation", *IEEE Trans. Pattern Analysis and Machine Intelligence*, vol.18(9), pp.884-900, Sept. 1996.

Active Acquisition of 3D Map in Robot Brain by Combining Motion and Perceived Images

Koichiro Deguchi and Tomohiro Nakagawa

Graduate School of Information Sciences, Tohoku University,
Aoba 01, Aramaki, Aoba-ku, Sendai, Miyagi, Japan

Abstract. In this paper, we propose an active vision strategy for the construction of a 3D map in a robot brain from its stereo eye images. We show that, by the direct combination of its action and image change caused by the action, the robot can acquires a 3D accurate map in his brain. If the robot stereo cameras and his motion parameters have been calibrated, the obtained reconstruction of the static scene stays stationary. But, if not, the reconstructed scene changes according to the robot action. We utilise this change to modify the robot parameters so as to obtain stationary scene in his 3D map under the action. We show the feasibility of this idea as an auto-calibration of robot vision with some simulation experiments and implementation on actual robots.

1   Introduction

Robots must acquire the 3D map of our environment to act in the real world. One of the conventional approaches is the CAD based map building, and many strategies have been proposed in the literatures[1]. However, a complete design data of the 3D environment of his work space can seldom be prepared beforehand. The most feasible strategy for the robot will be to construct a 3D map of an unknown environment by itself using its own eyes (cameras) and its own intentional actions. This idea is common to the techniques of the self(or auto)-calibration[2][3][4]. Those techniques have been proposed as the calibration of the camera parameters. Usually, then, the motion parameters are calibrated.

These two calibrations and the following construction of the 3D map have been considered separately in the self-calibration. Here we combine them to achieve totally efficient and accurate calibration and the construction of the map. The objective of this paper is to introduce a straight-forward strategy for the robot 3D space perception. In this paper, we do not use any 3D calibration objects, and only rely on the consistency in the calibration results. We introduce the fact that "stationary object both in the real environment and on the robot's 3D map never moves even when the robot moves around". This means that we accept some types of the geometric distortion of the constructed 3D map. We consider that the most important for the 3D map is the consistency between the intended motion of the robot and the perceived image by the robot.

M. De Gregorio et al. (Eds.): BVAI 2005, LNCS 3704, pp. 386–395, 2005.

2 Robot's Space Recognition by Combining the Motion and Perceived Images

2.1 Stereo Camera System

We consider a robot mounting a stereo camera system. We set two cameras parallel, but the arrangement cannot be accurate and it has small error. The real arrangement of the stereo cameras is shown in Fig.1(a), for example.

Many techniques have been proposed to calibrate this stereo camera system and also to calculate 3D reconstructions from uncalibrated stereo cameras [5][6]. The first step of these techniques is to calculate the internal and external parameters of the cameras. The internal parameters consist of focal length, aspect ratio, image center and lens skew, and the external parameters consist of the positions and postures of the cameras. But, here, we claim that we need not to calculate those individual parameters to directly combine the motion and perceived images.

2.2 Direct Construction of the Robot's 3D Map

Although the real arrangement of the parallel stereo camera has error, we assume that it is accurately parallel(Fig.1(b)). That is, the robot constructs its 3D map based on the parallel stereo geometry, even though the error between the real arrangement and the assumed arrangement exists in the external parameters. As the result, the map may have distortions against the real world.

For example, consider that we are given a point in 3D space and it images on the stereo image planes as shown in Fig.1(a). Fig.2 shows the stereo image forming and the map construction by the robot under above assumptions. Fig.2(a) is the real space, where an object point is projected onto the left and right camera image planes. Fig.2(b) is the 3D map, on which the robot back-projects these point images with the arrangement of Fig.1(b). The point at the position marked as "real object" will be believed by the robot to position at "imaginary object", because the robot believes that its cameras are arranged parallel as Fig.2(b).

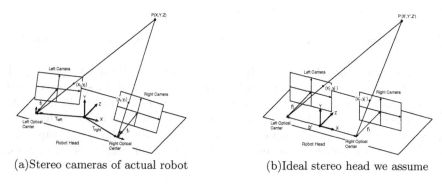

(a)Stereo cameras of actual robot   (b)Ideal stereo head we assume

Fig. 1. Actual and ideal stereo heads

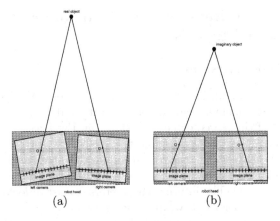

Fig. 2. Real space and robot's 3D map when the robot's assumption has the error of the camera arrangement. ((a) shows that the object is projected onto the left and right camera planes with the arrangement of Fig.1(a), and (b) shows that the robot back-projects these images with the arrangement of Fig.1(b).)

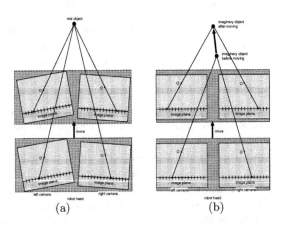

Fig. 3. Change of real space and robot's 3D map when the robot moves advance by one step

The robot cannot notice that it just is making misunderstanding only from this situation.

Now, imagine that the robot walks ahead by one step. Then, the spatial position of the "imaginary object" changes as shown in Fig.3. If the stereo geometry model is correct, spatial absolute positions of stationary points will not move even if the robot moves. This concludes that, if the robot has the idea that "stationary object both on the real environment and on the robot's 3D map never moves even if the robot moves around", it notices incorrectness of own system parameters.

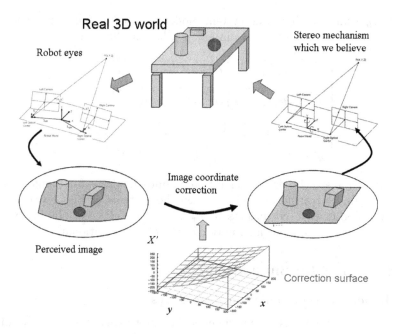

Fig. 4. Flow of the model modification process

Of course, when the robot also has incorrect internal parameters or robot's motion parameters, the similar unexpected motions of the "imaginary object" will occur.

In this paper, we introduce a system model which converts the set of obtained image coordinates of the stereo cameras into a new set of image coordinates. Then, we modify the parameters of the system models so that the reconstructed stationary objects do not move in space. If they are modified correctly, the robot acquires a consistent geometric model to construct the exact 3D map. This concept to modify the robot's system models is summarised in Fig.4. In this concept, the acquisition of the correct 3D map consists of iterations of the next three steps as,

I. The robot constructs 3D map according with its system models,
II. The robot moves in the space according with the 3D map, and
III. The robot modifies the system model to reduce the inconsistency of the successively constructed 3D maps.

2.3 Description of the Robot's System Model

We introduce the robot's system model to modify all the camera parameters simultaneously. Now, we denote the input image coordinates with (x_l, y_l) and (x_r, y_r) for left and right cameras, respectively, and their modified coordinates with (x'_l, y'_l) and (x'_r, y'_r). The system model is a set of functions generating (x'_l, y'_l) and (x'_r, y'_r) from (x_l, y_l) and (x_r, y_r), having the forms of

$$
\begin{cases}
x'_l = \dfrac{(P_{x_l 0}+P_{x_l 1}x_l)\cdot(P_{x_l 2}+P_{x_l 3}x_r)\cdot(P_{x_l 4}+P_{x_l 5}y_l)}{(P_{x_l 6}+P_{x_l 7}x_l)\cdot(P_{x_l 8}+P_{x_l 9}x_r)\cdot(P_{x_l 10}+P_{x_l 11}y_l)} \\[2mm]
y'_l = \dfrac{(P_{y_l 0}+P_{y_l 1}x_l)\cdot(P_{y_l 2}+P_{y_l 3}x_r)\cdot(P_{y_l 4}+P_{y_l 5}y_l)}{(P_{y_l 6}+P_{y_l 7}x_l)\cdot(P_{y_l 8}+P_{y_l 9}x_r)\cdot(P_{y_l 10}+P_{y_l 11}y_l)} \\[2mm]
x'_r = \dfrac{(P_{x_r 0}+P_{x_r 1}x_l)\cdot(P_{x_r 2}+P_{x_r 3}x_r)\cdot(P_{x_r 4}+P_{x_r 5}y_l)}{(P_{x_r 6}+P_{x_r 7}x_l)\cdot(P_{x_r 8}+P_{x_r 9}x_r)\cdot(P_{x_r 10}+P_{x_r 11}y_l)} \\[2mm]
y'_r = \dfrac{(P_{y_r 0}+P_{y_r 1}x_l)\cdot(P_{y_r 2}+P_{y_r 3}x_r)\cdot(P_{y_r 4}+P_{y_r 5}y_l)}{(P_{y_r 6}+P_{y_l 7}x_l)\cdot(P_{y_l 8}+P_{y_l 9}x_r)\cdot(P_{y_l 10}+P_{y_l 11}y_l)}
\end{cases}
\tag{1}
$$

These forms are the first order rational approximations for the geometrical image coordinate transformations between the systems of Figs.1 (a) and (b). Then, we modify each coefficients of $P_{x_l i}$, $P_{y_l i}$, and $P_{x_r i}$ to obtain the ideal system models by using our assumption of the object's stationarity.

3   Experimental Simulation

3.1   Experimental Simulation Procedures

We carried out two kinds of experiments. The first experiment is: A set of 100 object points were arranged in the coordinate system centering at the robot's head and within the ranges of [-1000,1000] in X-axis, [-1000,1000] in Y-axis, and [1000,2000] in Z-axis. These points were projected onto the left and right camera planes according with their internal and external parameters listed on Table 1. Then, the robot back-projected those images into its front space and identified their spatial positions based on the stereo geometry which the robot assumed. Those assumed parameters are also listed on the table.

The robot moved by a step forward and rotated. It was also assumed not to know correct values of its step lengths and rotation angles. Table 2 shows the real and assumed motion values. The real parameter values were different from those the robot believed, and as the result, the spatial points moved, which the robot constructed with its parameters, although they must be stationary. Then, we modified the values of the coefficients in Eqs.(1) so as to reduce the motions of the reconstructed spatial points. We iterate this process starting with the initial system functions below.

$$
x'_l = x_l, \quad y'_l = y_l, \text{ and } x'_r = x_r
\tag{2}
$$

Next, the second experiment is: The robot moved toward the object by using its position on the robot's 3D map. Then, we examined how much were the differences between the robot position and the object position on the real space before and after modification.

3.2   Setting-Up of Each Parameter Values

The values set-up in the experimental simulations are also listed in Table 1, where the unit for lengths is *mm* and that for angles is *degree*. In the experimental

Table 1. Set-up values of the internal and external parameters ((a) is the list of values of actual robot system, and (b) is the list of the values we assumed.)

external parameters		(a)	(b)
left camera			
position	X-axis	-107.5	-100.0
	Y-axis	-10.0	0.0
	Z-axis	-3.0	0.0
posture around X-axis		0.2	0.0
around Y-axis		1.0	0.0
around Z-axis		0.0	0.0
right camera			
position	X-axis	97.5	100.0
	Y-axis	-10.0	0.0
	Z-axis	-3.0	0.0
posture around X-axis		0.2	0.0
around Y-axis		-2.2	0.0
around Z-axis		0.0	0.0

internal parameters		(a)	(b)
focal length			
	left camera	235.0	250.0
	right camera	240.0	250.0
other parameters		×	×

Table 2. Set-up values of robot's motion value (X of second row, Y of third row, and Z of fourth row mean "X-axis", "Y-axis", and "Z-axis", respectively. And X of fifth row, Y of sixth row, and Z of seventh row mean "around X-axis", "around Y-axis", and "around Z-axis", respectively.)

(a)Set-up values of actual motion.

experiment number	translation motion			rotation motion		
	X	Y	Z	X	Y	Z
1	368.8	462.3	269.3	0.0	0.0	0.0
2	0.0	0.0	0.0	5.7	3.9	1.3
3	368.8	462.3	269.3	5.7	3.9	1.3

(b)Set-up values which the robot believed.

experiment number	translation motion			rotation motion		
	X	Y	Z	X	Y	Z
1	300.0	300.0	300.0	0.0	0.0	0.0
2	0.0	0.0	0.0	5.0	5.0	0.0
3	300.0	300.0	300.0	5.0	5.0	0.0

simulations, we carried out three types of the robot motions. The actual motion values are listed in Table 2 (a), and the corresponding motion values which the robot believed are listed in (b).

3.3 Results of Experimental Simulations and Discussions

In the first experiments, we modified the coefficients of the system models with three motions. The 3D map in the Experiment 3 is shown in Fig.5. Fig.5(a) shows the changes of the object positions by moving before modification, and Fig.5(b) shows those after modification. "+"s in this figure show the positions before moving, and "□"s show those after moving. Fig.5 totally shows that the robot's 3D map became more correct by the modification of the system model. Table 3 shows that the motions of the spatial object positions before and after the modification. These show that the modifications satisfied our assumption.

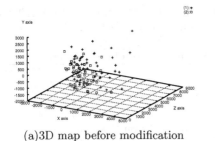 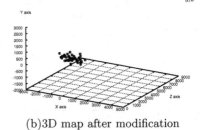

(a)3D map before modification   (b)3D map after modification

Fig. 5. The change of 3D map by moving (mm)

Table 3. The change values of the objects on 3D map between before and after moving (mm)

experiment	Modification	
number	Before	After
1	1.73×10^3	1.20×10^{-1}
2	2.29×10^2	1.01
3	1.74×10^3	1.04×10

Table 4. The accuracy of robot's action (mm). ((a) is the experiment number. (b) is the disparity between robot's position and objects before modification, and (c) is the disparity after modification. And (d) is the difference between (a) and (b).)

(a)	(b)	(c)	(d)
1	2.91×10^3	9.25×10^2	1.99×10^3
2	2.79×10^3	1.52×10^3	1.27×10^3
3	2.95×10^3	8.14×10^2	2.13×10^3

Next, we show the second experimental result. Fig.6 shows the 3D map that consists of the modified robot's 3D map and the real 3D map. "×"s in this figure show the real object positions, "•"s show the constructed object positions before moving and "o"s show those after moving. Table 4 shows the improvement of the accuracy of robot's action between before modification and after modification. The values of (b) are the differences on the real world between the robot's position and the object position before modification. Those values must be zero if the system model is modified accurately. The values of (c) are the differences after modification. (d) shows the differences between above two. We tried the second experiment with 100 object points. In this experiment, the robot's action were improved by the modification with all object points.

Table 3 shows that we could modify the robot's system model so that the object positions on the robot's 3D map between before and after motion might not change. Table 4 shows that the robot motion in the Experiment 2 was less accurate than those in the Experiments 1 and 3. Additionally, the improvement of the motion accuracy in Experiment 2 is smaller than those in the Experiments 1 and 3. These results suggest that we cannot modify the system model with the rotation only, and that the motion of the translation is important to obtain the useful 3D map. Next, the robot's motion in the Experiment 3 was slightly more accurate than that in the Experiment 1, and the improvement of the motion accuracy in Experiment 3 is also slightly larger than that in the Experiment 1. Therefore, the motion that consists of both rotation and translation is better than the rotation only or the translation only.

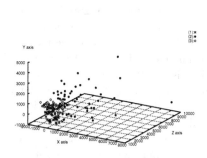

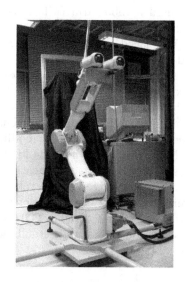

Fig. 6. Robot's 3D maps we adjust to real world before and after modification, and real 3D map (*mm*)

Fig. 7. Robot system

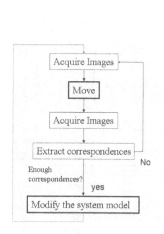

Fig. 8. Iteration of the image acquisition and model modification processes

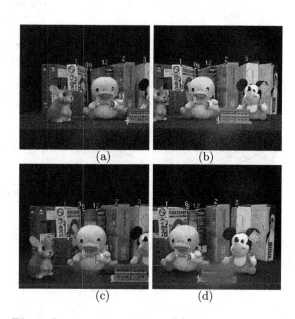

Fig. 9. Stereo camera images. (a) left image at $t = k$. (b) right image at $t = k$. (c) left image at $t = k + 1$, (d) right image at $t = k + 1$.

4   Experiments by Actual Robot

4.1   Experiment Procedures

We used a robot arm (MITSUBISHI PA-10) mounting two cameras (SONY EVI-G20) (Fig.7).

We placed objects in the range of [-300,300] in X-axis, [-100,200] in Y-axis, and [800,1400] in Z-axis in front of the robot (the unit for lengths is mm).

As shown in Fig.8, the robot took the images by both cameras while moving. Next, it extracted corresponding points between images before and after motions. If the total numbers of the corresponding points is less than 100, the above step is tried again. Then, the robot constructed its 3D map using the parallel stereo geometry. Finally, the robot modified its system model using our assumption.

Next, we verified how the 3D map changed by the translational motion between before and after modification of the system models. The coordinate systems were always centered at the robot's head. In the experiment, the robot moved translationally by 100.0mm along X-axis in Experiment 1, by 50.0mm along Y-axis in Experiment 2 and by 200.0mm along Z-axis in Experiment 3. We assumed these motion values, and actually we did not know the true motion values.

Table 5. Results of experiment by actual robots. ((a) experiment numbers. (b) indexes either before correction or after correction. (c) directions of its motion. (d) averages of the disparity of object positions between before motion and after motion.)

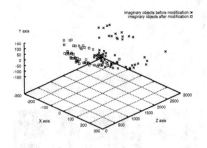

Fig. 10. Robot's 3D map before and after modification in the experiment by using actual robot

(a)	(b)	(c)	(d)
1	before correction	X-axis	−114.81
		Y-axis	−0.55
		Z-axis	40.27
	after correction	X-axis	−100.03
		Y-axis	−0.10
		Z-axis	1.41
2	before correction	X-axis	0.59
		Y-axis	−108.66
		Z-axis	−13.69
	after correction	X-axis	0.65
		Y-axis	−40.99
		Z-axis	−5.70
3	before correction	X-axis	−0.66
		Y-axis	13.94
		Z-axis	−462.60
	after correction	X-axis	4.36
		Y-axis	−5.65
		Z-axis	−199.33

4.2   Experimental Results and Discussions

Fig.9 shows the images on which the corresponding points between k-th images and $(k+1)$-th images were numbered. The robot constructed its 3D map by using the coordinates of these corresponding points. The system model was modified using our assumption of the stationarity. Before the modification, the positions of the points on its 3D map changed by 2.24×10^3. But after the modification, those positions changed by 1.28×10^3. So the change of its 3D map after the modification became smaller. (Here, these values were the average of the disparity of the 100 object positions between before motion and after motion.) Fig.10 shows the change of the 3D map before and after the modification. (Here, we show the half of the object points used in this experiment.)

Table 5 shows how much the object motions changed between before and after robot's moving in each experiment. If the objects on its 3D map move by $-100.0mm$ along X-axis when the robot moves by $100.0mm$ along X-axis, we conclude that the robot can recognize the space accurately. Fig.10 shows that the robot recognized the object positions around actual positions after robot modified its system model using our assumption. Table 5 shows that robot was able to move more accurately after the modification than before modification.

5   Conclusion

In this paper, we proposed a strategy to build up the 3D map in robot through its stereo vision system combined with its active motions. Then, we showed some simulation experiments and implementation on actual robots with our idea. Still our experiments were not enough to verify the feasibility of our idea. In order to improve the robot's system models and the modification algorithm into more sophisticated ones is the next problem.

References

1. G.DeSouza and A.Kak, Vision for Mobile Robot Navigation: A Survey, IEEE Trans. PAMI, Vol.24, No.2, pp.237-267, 2002.
2. O.D.Faugeras and Q.T.Luong and S.J.Maybank, Camera self-calibration: Theory and experiments, ECCV, pp.321-334, 1992
3. M.J.Brooks and L.de Agapito and D.Q.Huynh and L.Baumela, Direct methods for self-calibration of a moving stereo head, In Proc. 4th ECCV, pp.415-426, April 1996.
4. Richard I.Hartley, Estimation of Relative Camera Positions for Uncalibrated Cameras, In Proc. ECCV, pp.579-587, 1992
5. Paul A.Beardsley, Philip H.S.Torr and Andrew Zisserman, 3D Model Acquisition from Extended Image Sequences, ECCV(2), pp.683-695, 1996
6. M.Pollefeys, R.Koch and L.Van Gool, Self calibration and metric reconstruction in spite of varying and unknown internal camera parameters, In Proc. ICCV, pp90-96, 1998

Lateral Interaction in Accumulative Computation: Motion-Based Grouping Method

Antonio Fernández-Caballero[1], Jose Mira[2], Ana E. Delgado[2],
Miguel A. Fernández[1], and Maria T. López[1]

[1] Universidad de Castilla-La Mancha, E.P.S.A., 02071 - Albacete, Spain
{caballer, miki, mlopez}@info-ab.uclm.es
[2] Universidad Nacional de Educación a Distancia,
E.T.S.I. Informática, 28040 - Madrid, Spain
{jmira, adelgado}@dia.uned.es

Abstract. To be able to understand the motion of non-rigid objects, techniques in image processing and computer vision are essential for motion analysis. Lateral interaction in accumulative computation for extracting non-rigid blobs and shapes from an image sequence has recently been presented, as well as its application to segmentation from motion. In this paper we show an architecture consisting of five layers based on spatial and temporal coherence in visual motion analysis with application to visual surveillance. The LIAC method used in general task "spatio-temporal coherent shape building" consists in (a) spatial coherence for brightness-based image segmentation, (b) temporal coherence for motion-based pixel charge computation, (c) spatial coherence for charge-based pixel charge computation, (d) spatial coherence for charge-based blob fusion, and, (e) spatial coherence for charge-based shape fusion. In our case, temporal coherence (in accumulative computation) is understood as a measure of frame to frame motion persistency on a pixel, whilst spatial coherence (in lateral interaction) is a measure of pixel to neighbouring pixels accumulative charge comparison.

1 Introduction

There has been a great deal of research interest in motion tracking [1],[2],[3] because of its great applicability in a wide variety of applications. Vision is probable the most powerful source of information used by man to represent a monitored scene. Visual information is composed of a great deal of redundant sets of spatial and temporal data robustly and quickly processed by the brain. There has also been much work carried out on the extraction of non-rigid shapes from image sequences. In general, all papers take advantage of the fact that the image flow of a moving figure varies both spatially and temporally.

Little and Boyd [4] found it reasonable to suggest that variations in gaits are recoverable from variations in image sequences. There have been several attempts to recover characteristics of gait from image sequences. Polana and Nelson [5] characterize the temporal texture of a moving figure by summing the

M. De Gregorio et al. (Eds.): BVAI 2005, LNCS 3704, pp. 396–405, 2005.
© Springer-Verlag Berlin Heidelberg 2005

energy of the highest amplitude frequency and its multiples. Their more recent work [6] emphasizes the spatial distribution of energies around the moving figure. Bobick and Davis [7] introduced the Motion Energy Image (MEI), a smoothed description of the cumulative spatial distribution of motion energy in a motion sequence. Yang and Ahuja [8] segment an image frame into regions with similar motion. The algorithm identifies regions in each frame comprising the multiscale intraframe structure. Regions at all scales are then matched across frames. Affine transforms are computed for each matched region pair. The affine transform parameters for region at all scales are then used to derive a single motion field that is then segmented to identify the differently moving regions between two frames. Olson and Brill [9] propose a general purpose system for moving object detection and event recognition where moving objects are detected using change detection and tracked using first-order prediction and nearest neighbour matching.

Behind all of these papers one can guess the idea of grouping spatially andf temporally coherent image pixels into regions based on a common set of features. Coherence is defined as logical and orderly and consistent relation of parts. Spatial coherence describes the correlation between a set of features at different points in space. Temporal coherence describes the correlation or predictable relationship between those (or other) features observed at different moments in time. Spatial coherence is described as a function of distance (a measure or a metric), and is often presented as a function of correlation versus absolute distance between observation points. The same operation can be performed in time. It is well known that temporal and spatial coherence are involved in the promotion of perceptual binding.

The goal of this paper is to present our method for spatio-temporally shape building taking advantage of the inherent motion present in image sequences. In an indefinite succession of images, our motion-based algorithms allow to obtain the shape of the moving elements. Somehow, the method is bound to the generic behaviour of the permanency memories [10]. Specifically, we will say that the observer is unable to discern any object unless it starts moving. In other words, the system only acts on those image pixels where some change in the grey level is detected between two consecutive frames.

2   Lateral Interaction in Accumulative Computation (LIAC)

Lateral interaction in accumulative computation has recently been introduced [11],[12], as well as its application to segmentation from motion [13]. For it, a generic model based on a neural architecture was presented. We shall now remind of the most important characteristics of this model. The proposed model is based on accumulative computation function followed by a set of cooperating lateral interaction processes. These are performed on a functional receptive field organised as centre-periphery over non-linear and temporal expansions of their input spaces. A lateral interaction model consists of a layer of modules of the same type with local connectivity, such that the response of a given module does not only depend on its own inputs, but also on the inputs and outputs of the module's neighbors. From a computational point of view, the aim of the lateral interaction nets is to partition the input space into three regions: centre, periphery and excluded. The following steps have to be done: (a) processing over the central region, (b) processing over the feedback of the periphery zone, (c) comparison of the results of these operations and a local decision generation, and, (d) distribution over the output space.

We also incorporate the notion of double time scale present at sub-cellular microcomputation. So, the following properties are applicable to the model. (a) Local convergent process around each element, (b) semiautonomous functioning, with each element capable of spatio-temporal accumulation of local inputs in time scale T, and conditional discharge, and, (c) attenuated transmission of these accumulations of persistent coincidences towards the periphery that integrates at global time scale t. Therefore we are in front of two different time scales: (1) the local time T, and, (2) the global time t, $(t = n \cdot T)$. Global time is applicable to steps (a) and (d) of our neuronal lateral interaction model, whereas steps (b) and (c) use local time scale T.

3   LIAC for Spatio-Temporal Coherent Shape Building

In first place, and in the following figure, the complete structure chosen as the modular computational solution to apply the model to spatio-temporal shape building is presented.

In Figure 1, five layers can be appreciated that form the architecture of the lateral interaction in accumulative computation method.

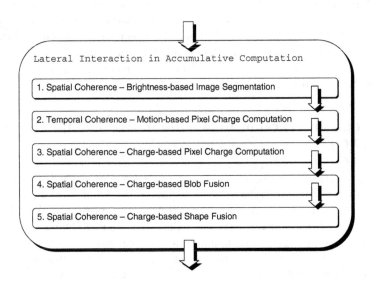

Fig. 1. LIAC architecture for coherent shape building

Now we are going to explain the role of each of these five layers devoted to shape building. As it will be easy to appreciate, in each of these layers seeking for coherence is the main objective. In effect, layers 1, 3, 4 and 5 are based on spatial coherence, whereas layer 2 is a typical application of temporal coherence. The consistency of the LIAC method for spatio-temporal coherent shape building lays on motion-based grouping of pixels and blobs.

3.1   Spatial Coherence – Brightness-Based Segmentation

This layer covers the possibility to segment the image into a predefined group of n grey level bands just from the brightness of each input image pixel. This layer enables to smoothening the transitions among neighbouring pixels of the input image. This may be considered a first step that contributes to spatial coherence.

Let $GL(x, y, t)$ be the input grey level value at element (x, y) at time t, and let $GLS(k, x, y, t)$ be the presence or absence of grey level k at element (x, y) at time t. Then

$$GLS(k, x, y, t) = \begin{cases} 1, & \text{if } \frac{GL[x,y,t]}{GL_{max} - GL_{min} + 1} + 1 = k, \forall k \in [0, n-1] \\ -1, & \text{otherwise} \end{cases} \quad (1)$$

where n is the *number of grey level bands*, and, k is a particular grey level band.

In other words, we are determining in which grey level band a certain pixel falls. So, we are not evaluating, at this level, if there is motion in a grey level band for a given pixel, but a brightness-based spatially coherent segmentation is performed. Coherence, in this case, has to be understood as the relation of belonging to a same grey level band.

It must be clear that one, and only one, of the outputs of all the detecting modules of the grey level bands can be activated at a given instant. This fact, although obvious, is of a great interest at the higher layers of the architecture, since it will avoid possible conflicts among the values offered by the different grey level bands. Indeed, only one grey level band will contain valid values.

3.2   Temporal Coherence – Motion-Based Pixel Charge Computation

This layer has been designed to obtain the permanence value $PM(k, x, y, t)$ [10], [11] on a decomposition in grey level bands basis. We will have n sub-layers and each one of them will memorise the value of the accumulative computation present at global time scale t for each element. Lateral interaction in this layer is thought to reactivate the permanence charge of those elements partially loaded and that are directly or indirectly connected to maximally charged elements. The permanence charge of each element will be offered as the input of the following layer.

Firstly, at global time scale t, permanence memory charge or discharge due to motion detection is performed. This information, given as input from the previous layer, is associated to sub-layer k of layer 1 (grey level band k). The accumulative computation equation may be formulated as

$$PM(k,x,y,t) = \begin{cases} l_{dis}, \text{if } GLS(k,x,y,t) = -1 \\ l_{sat}, \text{ if } GLS(k,x,y,t) = 1 and GLS(k,x,y,t - \triangle t) = -1 \\ \max(PM(k,x,y,t - \triangle t) - d_v, l_{dis}), \\ \quad \text{if } GLS(k,x,y,t) = 1 and GLS(k,x,y,t - \triangle t) = 1 \end{cases} \quad (2)$$

where l_{dis} is the discharge or *Minimum permanence value*, l_{sat} is the saturation or *Maximum permanence value*, and, d_v is the *Discharge value due to motion detection*.

Note that t determines the sequence frame rate and is given by the capacity of the model's implementation to process one input image. At each element (x, y) we are in front of three possibilities: (1) The sub-layer does not correspond to the grey level band of the image pixel. The permanence value is discharged down to value l_{dis}. (2) The sub-layer corresponds to the grey level band of the image pixel at time instant t, and it didn't correspond to the grey level band at the previous instant $t - \triangle t$. The permanence value is loaded to the maximum of saturation l_{sat}. (3) The sub-layer corresponds to the grey level band of the image pixel at time instant t, and it also corresponded to the grey level band at the instant $t - \triangle t$. The permanence value is discharged by a value d_v (discharge value due to motion detection); of course, the permanence value cannot get off a minimum value l_{dis}. The discharge of a pixel by a quantity of d_v is the way to stop maintaining attention to a pixel of the image that had captured our interest in the past. Notice that we really are in front of a temporal coherence mechanism, where coherence depends on the comparison between the grey level bands of each pixel at two consecutive time instants (two sucessive frames).

3.3   Spatial Coherence – Charge-Based Pixel Charge Computation

Obviously, if a pixel is not directly or indirectly bound by means of lateral interaction mechanisms to a maximally charged pixel (l_{sat}), it goes down to the total discharge with time. That is why, secondly, an extra charge r_v (*Recharge value due to neighbouring*) is added to the permanence memory in those image pixels that receive a stimulus from a maximally charged element almost l_1 pixels far away in any of four directions. This recharge can only happen one time, and provided that none neighbour element up to the maximally charged element is discharged. l_1 is called *Number of neighbours in accumulative computation*. This recharge mechanism allows maintaining attention on those pixels directly or indirectly connected to maximally charge pixels. This mechanism is even able to reinforce the permanence memory value if the $r_v > d_v$.

$$PM(k,x,y,t) = min(PM(k,x,y,t) + \epsilon \cdot r_v, l_{sat}) \quad (3)$$

where

$$\epsilon = \begin{cases} 1, & \text{if } \exists(i \leq l_1)|\forall(1 \leq j \leq i) \\ & ((PM(k, x+i, y, t)) = l_{sat} \bigcap (PM(k, x+j, y, t)) \neq l_{dis} \bigcup \\ & (PM(k, x-i, y, t)) = l_{sat} \bigcap (PM(k, x-j, y, t)) \neq l_{dis} \bigcup \\ & (PM(k, x, y+i, t)) = l_{sat} \bigcap (PM(k, x, y+j, t)) \neq l_{dis} \bigcup \\ & (PM(k, x, y-i, t)) = l_{sat} \bigcap (PM(k, x, y-j, t)) \neq l_{dis}) \\ \\ 0, & \text{otherwise} \end{cases} \quad (4)$$

Lastly, back at global time scale t, the permanence value at each pixel (x, y) is threshold (θ_1) and sent to the next layer.

$$PM(k, x, y, t) = \begin{cases} PM(k, x, y, t), & \text{if } PM(k, x, y, t) > \theta_1 \\ \theta_1, & \text{otherwise} \end{cases} \quad (5)$$

In order to explain the central idea of this layer, we will say that the activation toward the lateral modular structures (up, down, right and left) is again based on coherence, this time spatial coherence. Spatial coherence is related to the permanence memory values of neighbouring pixels up to a distance of l_1. The algorithm looks for coherent permanency value paths.

Now here are the basic ideas underlying lateral interaction at this layer. (1) All modular structures with maximum permanence value l_{sat} (saturated) output the charge toward the neighbours. (2) All modular structures with a not saturated charge value, and that have been activated from some neighbour, allow passing this information through them (they behave as transparent structures to the charge passing). (3) The modular structures with minimum permanence value l_{dis} (discharged) stop the passing of the charge information toward the neighbours (they behave as opaque structures). Therefore, we are in front of an explosion of lateral activation beginning at the structures with permanence memory set at l_{sat}, and that spreads lineally toward all the addresses, until a structure appears in the pathway with a discharged permanence memory.

3.4   Spatial Coherence – Charge-Based Blob Fusion

Layer 4 is also formed of n sub-layers, where, by means of lateral interaction, charge redistribution among all connected neighbours in a surrounding window of $l_2 * l_2$ pixels that hold a minimum charge, is performed. Besides distributing the charge $C(k, x, y, t)$ in grey level bands, at this level, the charge due to the motion of the background is also diluted. The new charge obtained in this layer is offered as an output toward layer 5. Starting from the values of the permanence memory in each pixel on a grey level band basis, we will see how it is possible to obtain all the parts of an object (blobs) in movement. A blob concretely means the union of pixels that are together and in a same grey level band. The discrimination of each one of the blobs is equally obtained by lateral co-operation mechanisms. In case of layer 4, the charge will be homogenised among all the pixels that pertain to the same grey level band and that are directly or indirectly united to each other, providing a means towards spatial coherence.

This way, a double objective will be obtained: (1) Diluting the charge due to the false image background motion along the other pixels of the background. This way, there should be no presence of motion characteristic of the background, but we will rather keep motion of the objects present in the scene. (2) Obtaining a parameter common to all the pixels of the blobs in a surrounding window of $l_2 * l_2$ pixels with a same grey level band. Initially, at global time scale t, the charge value at each pixel (x, y) and at each sub-layer k is given the value of the permanence value from the previous layer. After-wards, at local time scale T, provided that the neighbour input charge values are high enough, the centre element (x, y) calculates the mean of its value and the partially charged neighbours in a surrounding window of $l_2 * l_2$ pixels. l_2 is denominated *Number of neighbours in charge redistribution*.

$$C(x, y, T) = \frac{C(k, x, y, T - \triangle T) + \sum\limits_{i=-l_2}^{l_2} \sum\limits_{i=-l_2}^{l_2} \delta_{x+i,y+j} \cdot C(k, x + i, y + j, T - \triangle T)}{1 + \sum\limits_{i=-l_3}^{l_3} \delta_{x+i,y+j}},$$

$$\forall (i, j) \neq (0, 0) \tag{6}$$

where

$$\delta_{\alpha,\beta} = \begin{cases} 1, & \text{if } C(k, \alpha, \beta, T - \triangle T) > l_{dis} \\ 0, & otherwise \end{cases} \tag{7}$$

Again at global time scale t, the charge value at each pixel (x, y) is threshold (θ_2) and sent to the next layer.

$$C(k, x, y, t) = \begin{cases} C(k, x, y, t), & \text{if } C(k, x, y, t) > \theta_2 \\ \theta_2, & otherwise \end{cases} \tag{8}$$

3.5   Spatial Coherence – Charge-Based Shape Fusion

In each element of layer 5, we have an input from each corresponding element of the n sub-layers of layer 4. This layer has as purpose the fusion into uniform shapes of the objects in a surrounding window of $l_3 * l_3$ pixels. That is why it takes the input charges of each one of the grey level bands and performs a fusion of these values, obtaining uniform parts of all the moving objects of the original image. Its output is a set of shapes $S(x, y, t)$. Up to now attention has been captured on any moving objects in the scene by means of co-operative calculation mechanisms in all grey level bands. Motion due to background has also been eliminated. It is now necessary to fix as a new objective to clearly distinguish the motion of the different objects. This discrimination is obtained equally by lateral cooperation mechanisms. Nevertheless, now we will no longer work with sub-layers, but rather all information of the n sub-layers of layer 4 end up in a single layer. In layer 5, we will homogenise the charge values among all the pixels that contain some charge value superior to a minimum threshold and that are physically connected to each other in a radius of l_3 pixels. This is again the criteria used for spatial coherence. Firstly, the shape charge value at each pixel (x, y) is given the charge value of the maximally charged sub-layer k from the previous layer.

$$S(x, y, t) = max(C(k, x, y, t)), \forall k \in [0, 255] \tag{9}$$

At local time scale, provided that the neighbour input charge values are high enough, the centre element (x, y) calculates the mean of its value and the partially charged neighbours in a surrounding window of $l_3 * l_3$ pixels. l_3 is denominated *Number of neighbours in object fusion*.

$$S(x, y, T) = \frac{S(x, y, T - \triangle T) + \sum_{i=-l_3}^{l_3} \sum_{i=-l_3}^{l_3} \delta_{x+i, y+j} \cdot S(x + i, y + j, T - \triangle T)}{1 + \sum_{i=-l_3}^{l_3} \delta_{x+i, y+j}},$$

$$\forall (i, j) \neq (0, 0) \tag{10}$$

where

$$\delta_{\alpha, \beta} = \begin{cases} 1, & \text{if } S(k, \alpha, \beta, T - \triangle T) > l_{dis} \\ 0, & otherwise \end{cases} \tag{11}$$

Back to global time scale t, the shape charge value at each pixel (x, y) is again threshold (θ_3).

$$S(x, y, t) = \begin{cases} S(x, y, t), & \text{if } S(k, x, y, t) > \theta_3 \\ \theta_3, & otherwise \end{cases} \tag{12}$$

4   Data and Results

In this section we offer some results of applying our LIAC method in visual surveillance to the traffic intersection sequence recorded at the Ettlinger-Tor in Karlsruhe by a stationary camera, copyright 1998 by H.-H. Nagel, Institut für Algorithmen und Kognitive Systeme, Fakultät für Informatik, Universität Karlsruhe (TH), Postfach 6980, D - 76128 Karlsruhe, Germany.

Figure 2 shows two images of the sequence. You may observe the existence of ten cars and one bus driving in three different directions. At the bottom of the image there is another car, but this one is still. The parameter values for this experiment are $\triangle t = 0.42$ seconds, $\triangle t = 64 * T$, l_{dis}=0, l_{sat}=255 and d_v=32. Only three frames are needed to obtain accurate segmentation results. Figure 2c shows the result of applying our model to some images of the traffic intersection sequence. As you may observe, the system is perfectly capable of segmenting all the moving elements present on Figure 2. Note that the grey levels of the output image are consistent with the charge values common to the shapes obtained.

(a)   (b)   (c)

Fig. 2. Two images of the traffic intersection sequence. (a) Image number 1. (b) Image number 26. (c) Result of applying the lateral interaction mechanisms [13].

5   Conclusions

A simple algorithm of lateral interaction in accumulative computation, which is capable of segmenting all rigid and non-rigid objects in an indefinite sequence of images in a robust and coherent manner, with application to visual surveillance, has been proposed in this paper. Our method may be compared to background subtraction or frame difference algorithms in the way motion is detected. But, the main difference is that we look for spatial coherence through segmentation in grey level bands. Then, a region growing technique, based on spatio-temporal coherence of charge values assigned to image pixels, is performed to define moving objects. In contrast to similar approaches, no complex image preprocessing has to be performed, no reference image has to be offered to our model, and, no high-level knowledge has to be inferred to obtain accurate results. Our model is a 2-D approach to motion estimation. In these kinds of approaches, motion estimates are obtained from 2-D motion of intensity patterns. In these methods there is a general restriction: the intensity of the image along the motion trajectory must be constant, that is to say, any change through time in the intensity of a pixel is only due to motion. This restriction does not affect our model at all. This way, our algorithms are prepared to work with lots of situations of the real visual surveillance world, where changes in illumination are of a real importance.

The gradient-based estimates have become the main approach in the applications of computer vision. These methods are computationally efficient and satisfactory motion estimates of the motion field are obtained. The disadvantages common to all methods based on the gradient also arise from the logical changes in illumination.

Obviously, a way of solving the former limitations of gradient-based methods is to consider image regions instead of pixels. In general, these methods are less sensitive to noise than gradient-based methods. Our particular approach takes advantage of this fact and uses all available neighbourhood state information as well as the proper motion information. On the other hand, our method is not affected by the greatest disadvantage of region-based methods. Our model does not depend on the pattern of translation motion. In effect, in region-based methods, regions have to remain quite small so that the translation pattern remains valid. We also have to highlight that our proposed model has no limitation in the number of non-rigid objects to differentiate. Our system facilitates object classification by taking advantage of the object charge value, common to all pixels of a same moving element. This way, all moving objects are clearly segmented. Thanks to this fact, any higher-level operation will decrease in difficulty.

Acknowledgements

Traffic intersection sequence at the Ettlinger-Tor in Karlsruhe, courtesy of Universität Karlsruhe, Fakultät für Informatik, Institut für Algorithmen und Kognitive Systeme. This work is supported in part by the Spanish CICYT TIN2004-07661-C02-01 and TIN2004-07661-C02-02 grants.

References

1. Huang, T.S.: Image Sequence Analysis. Springer-Verlag (1983)
2. Aggarwal, J.K., Nandhakumar, N.: On the computation of motion from sequences of images - A review. Proceedings of the IEEE **76**:8 (1988)
3. Wang, J., Huang, T.S., Ahuja, N.: Motion and Structure from Image Sequences. Springer-Verlag (1993)
4. Little, J.J., Boyd, J.E.: Recognizing people by their gait: The shape of motion. Videre: Journal of Computer Vision Research **1**:2 (1998) 2-32
5. Polana, R., Nelson, R.: Detecting activities. Proceedings of the IEEE Conference on Com-puter Vision and Pattern Recognition (1993) 2-7
6. Polana, R., Nelson, R.: Recognition of nonrigid motion. Proceedings DARPA Image Understanding Workshop (1994) 1219-1224
7. Bobick, A.F., Davis, J.W.: An appearance-based representation of action. Proceedings 13th International Conference on Pattern Recognition (1996) 307-312
8. Yang, M.-H., Ahuja, N.: Extracting gestural motion trajectories. Proceedings 2nd International Conference on Automatic Face and Gesture Recognition (1998) 10-15
9. Olson, T., Brill, F.: Moving object detection and event recognition algorithms for smart cameras. Proceedings DARPA Image Understanding Workshop (1997) 159-175
10. Fernández, M.A., Fernández-Caballero, A., López, M.T., Mira, J.: Length-speed ratio (LSR) as a characteristic for moving elements real-time classification. Real-Time Imaging **9** (2003) 49-59
11. Fernández-Caballero, A., Fernández, M.A., Mira, J., Delgado, A.E.: Spatio-temporal shape building from image sequences using lateral interaction in accumulative computation. Pattern Recognition **36**:5 (2003) 1131-1142
12. Mira,J.,Delgado, A.E., Fernández-Caballero, A.,Fernández, M.A.: Knowledge modelling for the motion detection task: The algorithmic lateral inhibition method. Expert Systems with Applications **27**:2 (2004)169-185
13. Fernández-Caballero, A., Mira, J., Fernández, M.A., López, M.T.: Segmentation from motion of non-rigid objects by neuronal lateral interaction. Pattern Recognition Letters **22**:14 (2001) 1517-1524

Detecting and Ranking Foreground Regions in Gray-Level Images

Maria Frucci, Carlo Arcelli, and Gabriella Sanniti di Baja

Institute of Cybernetics "E.Caianiello", CNR, Pozzuoli, Italy
{mfr, car, gsdb}@imagm.cib.na.cnr.it

Abstract. Starting from a gray-level image partitioned into regions by watershed segmentation, we introduce a method to assign the regions to the foreground and the background, respectively. The method is inspired by visual perception and identifies the border between foreground and background in correspondence with the locally maximal changes in gray-level. The obtained image representation is hierarchical, both due to the articulation of the assignment process into three steps, aimed at the identification of components of the foreground with decreasing perceptual relevance, and due to a parameter taking into account the distance of each foreground region from the most relevant part in the same foreground component. Foreground components are detected by resorting to both global and local processes. Global assignment, cheaper from a computational point of view, is accomplished as far as this can be safely done. Local assignment takes place in the presence of conflictual decisions.

1 Introduction

Image segmentation is the first, and possibly the most important, step in any image analysis task. The procedure adopted to distinguish from the background and individually identify the foreground components depends on the specific image domain as well as on the successive processing to be accomplished on the segmented image.

In the majority of cases, segmentation cannot be achieved by simply thresholding the image, i.e., by assigning all pixels with gray-level lower than a given threshold to the background and all remaining pixels to the foreground. Different thresholding methods can be found in [1-3]. Foreground pixels are all assigned one of two possible values (generally 1 for the foreground and 0 for the background), or keep their original gray-level values, depending on the successive analysis task. For example, in the case of shape analysis, the information derivable from the silhouette of the objects in the image is generally sufficient, and hence a binarized segmented image is adequate. However, in more complex tasks such as recognition, also information from texture or gray-level can be crucial, so that in the segmented image foreground components should be distinguished from the background, while keeping gray-level information.

Segmentation done by thresholding is generally used when the original images are perceived as naturally binary, e.g., written documents where there are only two perceived gray-levels that characterize the text and the background. Indeed, after acquisition and digitization, even a written document image is characterized by a number of different gray-levels. However, the gray-level distribution for this kind of images is

M. De Gregorio et al. (Eds.): BVAI 2005, LNCS 3704, pp. 406–415, 2005.
© Springer-Verlag Berlin Heidelberg 2005

expected to be such that two peaks, well separated by an evident valley, constitute the gray-level histogram and, hence, a threshold value selected in correspondence with the valley should be adequate to binarize the document.

When the original image is not naturally binary, its segmentation becomes more complex and methods based on thresholding become ineffective. Often, the threshold should assume different values in different parts of the image, to allow correct identification of foreground components since gray-level values that in a part of the image characterize background pixels, in other portions of the image are associated with pixels constituting foreground components. This is the case, for example, in images of biomedical nature. The digitized version of an histological specimen presents a number of regions that are characterized by a different gray-level since they correspond to regions actually having different intensity, or to portions of the specimen placed at a different depth in the slide and so resulting as having different intensity. Also the way in which the specimen has been cut has an influence on the light intensity transmitted through different portions of the specimen during its acquisition. Segmentation techniques more sophisticated than thresholding, e.g., based on watershed transformation, generally produce better result in these cases. See [4,5] for early papers on watershed segmentation. These techniques originate a partition of a gray-level image into regions characterized by a common property. This common property can be the almost homogeneous gray-level distribution, or a more specific geometrical/morphological property to be selected depending on the specific image domain. However, once the partition is obtained the problem of correctly assigning the various regions to either the foreground or the background still remains to be solved. In this communication, we face this problem.

Starting from a partition of a gray-level image obtained by using watershed based segmentation, we introduce a procedure to identify the foreground components. Different solutions are suggested for the same image, depending on the desired detail of information to be preserved. The case study is a section of layers of neurons of frog's brain. The gray-level values are in the range [0, 255].

The paper is organized as follows. In Section 2, we briefly discuss the method proposed in [6] to obtain a gray-level image partitioned into a set of regions. In Section 3, we introduce a graph structure that will be used to accomplish in an efficient manner the remaining computation; in Section 4, we describe the method to identify foreground components and show the obtained results on a test image. Finally, some conclusions are given in Section 5.

2   Gray-Level Image Partition

We start with a 2D gray-level image. This image is interpreted as a 3D landscape, where for every pixel in position (x,y), its gray-level plays the role of the z-coordinate in the landscape. This interpretation is useful to illustrate in a simple manner the paradigm on which watershed based segmentation is founded. High gray-levels correspond in the landscape to mountains and hills, while low gray-levels correspond to valleys. If the bottom of each valley is pierced and the landscape is immersed in water, then valleys are filled in by water. Filling starts from the deepest valleys and then continues through less and less deep valleys. These begin to be filled as soon as the water level reaches their bottom. A dam (watershed) is built wherever different basins are going to meet, to prevent water to spread from a basin into the close ones. When the whole landscape has been covered by water, the basins are interpreted as the parts into which the landscape is partitioned.

Watershed segmentation can be used in different contexts. In general, the gradient image is used instead of the image itself, to enhance the differences in gray-level. Gray-level information is used to identify the regional minima, and the watershed transformation generates a partition of the (gradient) image into regions characterized by some common property regarding gray-levels.

A problem common to all methods based on watershed transformation is the excessive fragmentation of the image, which, in turn, is caused by the presence of a too large number of regional minima, many of which are not significant in the problem domain. Although any algorithm producing a watershed based image partition would be fine for our purposes, we prefer the algorithm presented in [6], since this includes a careful selection of the regional minima. In fact, the quality of the partition strongly conditions the quality of the results concerned with foreground and background detection. We briefly illustrate the two techniques (flooding and digging) used to select among the regional minima only those regarded as significant. To this purpose, a new criterion was introduced to evaluate the significance of the basins, and perform merging of a non-significant basin only with selected adjacent basins. In this way, non-significant basins could be removed, while avoiding that non-significant basins were grouped to form a new, unexpected, significant basin, or a basin whose shape was altered with respect to the foreseen shape. Merging was obtained by applying again the watershed transformation on a suitably modified gradient image, which included a smaller number of regional minima with respect to the original landscape.

In [6], the significance of a basin X is defined in terms of some of its morphological properties, and by evaluating the interaction of X with the adjacent basins. The basin X is significant with respect to an adjacent basin Y if a given condition holds. The measurements involved in the significance condition are i) the maximal depth of X when the water reaches the pixel (local overflow pixel) having the minimal height along the watershed line separating X from Y, and ii) the absolute value of the difference of altitude between the regional minima in X and Y. Three types of significance for X are possible and, correspondingly, decision on merging is taken and different procedures are applied, when merging has to be performed.

1. The significance condition is verified for X in correspondence of every adjacent basin Y. Then, X is meaningful and cannot be merged with any adjacent basin.
2. The significance condition is never verified for X in correspondence of any adjacent basin Y. Then, X is not meaningful and should be absorbed by (some) adjacent basin(s). The regional minimum of X has to be removed before applying again the watershed transformation. A suitable process (flooding) is accomplished to this purpose. The lowest local overflow value q is identified, and all pixels of X with gray-level lower than q are set to this value.
3. The significance condition is verified for X only in correspondence of some adjacent basins. Then, X has to be merged with selected neighboring basins, with respect to which X is not significant. Any such a basin Y shares with X a watershed line with a local overflow pixel, which is not necessarily the lowest local overflow pixel. A canal connecting X with Y is opened by a process (digging) which

will allow Y to absorb X. This canal is the minimal length path linking the regional minima of X and Y, and passing through the local overflow pixel common to X and Y. The gray-level of all the pixels in the path is set to the lower value between those of the regional minima of X and Y. Thus, when the watershed transformation is newly applied, the water can flow through the canal from X to Y, and the desired merging is obtained. The basin resulting after merging is such that the watershed lines of X, which were already detected as separating significant basins, are still present.

The process is iterated until all basins are found as significant. The performance of the segmentation algorithm can be seen in Fig. 1 on the test image, initially including 1729 regional minima, which results to be partitioned into 497 regions.

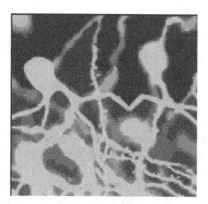 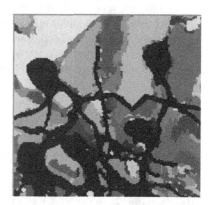

Fig. 1. Test image, left. Image resulting after segmentation produced by algorithm [6], right. The regions of the partition are colored in different gray-tones.

3 Graph Representation

Starting from the image partitioned into, say, N regions, we build a graph with N nodes. Each node R_i, i=1,2,...,N, corresponds to a region of the partitioned image and the arcs describe the adjacency relations among nodes. In the following, the two terms node and region will be used interchangeably. At this stage of the process, background and foreground nodes are undistinguishable. Of course, it should be *a priori* known which parts of the image, the darker or the lighter, constitute the foreground. Here we assume that the foreground be constituted by the lighter parts, i.e., by those characterized by locally higher intensity.

Two parameters are assigned to each node R_i. The first parameter, r_i, identifies a representative gray-level value for the whole region corresponding to R_i. This value is used, in the proposed method, to assign regions to one of the two categories (foreground and background). The second parameter, s_i, is used to hierarchically rank regions, depending on their perceptual relevance. Ranking can be done for regions of both the foreground and the background. We limit ourselves to ranking only foreground regions. Thus, s_i will remain set to its initial value 0 for background regions.

It will assume increasing values $s_i=1,2,3,...$ for foreground regions, value 1 indicating the maximal relevance.

To compute r_i, we must take into account that any region of the partition is union of image subsets, each including pixels with the same gray-level. Which among all gray-levels in a region is the most representative one depends on problem domain. We have investigated alternative criteria to compute r_i and have found the best results with the following two criteria, which can be used individually or in combination.

1. r_i is the average of the gray-levels with the maximal occurrence in the region.
2. r_i is the average of the gray-levels of all pixels in the region.

A possible way to combine the above criteria is to use the first one provided that the computed maximal occurrence is at least 30% of the total number of pixels in the region, and use the second criterion otherwise.

Note that two adjacent nodes may result to be characterized by the same value of r_i. When this is the case, the two nodes are interpreted as constituting a single node.

When the gray-levels in the original image are replaced by the r_i values representing the regions, a smoothed image is obtained.

4   Foreground Detection

The partition has created a mosaic image where regions are distinguished from each other, but their membership to either the foreground or the background has not yet been established. The model we follow to ascribe regions to the background or to the foreground is inspired by visual perception. In a gray-level image one of the two sets, say the foreground, is perceived as characterized by locally higher intensity. If all nodes characterized by representative gray-level values greater (smaller) than the representative values of all their adjacent nodes are ascribed to the foreground (background) two problems occur. Not all nodes are assigned to a category, and the regions ascribed to the foreground are scattered through the image and do not account for the perceived foreground. Indeed, to have a better result, other regions taken from the still undecided ones should be ascribed to the foreground.

Since the border between foreground and background is perceived as placed wherever strong differences in gray-level occur, two adjacent nodes R_i and R_j are, hence, more likely to belong to distinct categories if the difference $\Delta=|r_i-r_j|$ is large. We use this feature to devise a method to discriminate foreground and background. The method is based on both global and local processes. We use a global process as far as region assignment can be done safely guided by the maximal Δ value in the image. In all other cases, we resort to a local process.

4.1   Step 1

The first step of the process is the identification of the nodes certainly corresponding to regions of the foreground and of the background. These are respectively the nodes characterized by locally maximal and locally minimal representative gray-level values. Values of maxima (i.e., peaks in the landscape representation) and minima (i.e., valleys) are not taken into account to decide on region assignment, which is done globally on the whole image.

The value of the parameter s_i is also determined for each node ascribed to the foreground as follows. Let us call r_{Fi} and r_{Bi} the representative gray-level value of a node, depending on whether the node has been ascribed to the foreground or to the background. Let *max* denote the largest r_{Bi}. We set $s_i=2$ for each node such that $r_{Fi} \leq max$, and $s_i=1$ otherwise. This allows us to assess the different perceptual relevance of the nodes in the foreground. In fact, a node with $s_i=2$ is a peak, in the landscape description, and as such is worth to belong to the foreground. On the other hand, it results to have a gray-level smaller than that characterizing a valley, clearly assigned to the background, and as such has a perceptual relevance smaller than that pertaining peaks higher than any valley.

In Fig. 2, the regions ascribed to the foreground at the end of Step 1 are shown in two dark gray-tones.

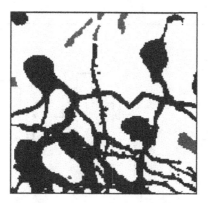

Fig. 2. Foreground regions detected after Step 1. Two different gray-tones denote the different relevance values of foreground regions.

4.2 Step 2

The second step includes both global and local processes to assign not yet decided nodes to one of the two categories. Already decided nodes do not change category. The process is an iterated one guided by the maximal Δ value, determined at each iteration. It is concerned with the assignment to the foreground and to the background of regions placed along slopes in the landscape. Only pairs of adjacent nodes out of which at least one is still undecided are considered. The process terminates when no more undecided nodes exist. For each node R_i assigned to the foreground during each iteration, the parameter s_i is set to $n_{i,j}+s_j+1$, where $n_{i,j}$ is the number of nodes separating R_i from the closest node, say R_j, assigned to the foreground during previous iterations or during Step 1, and s_j is the perceptual relevance of R_j.

At each iteration, two cases are possible depending on whether only one pair of adjacent nodes has maximal Δ value, or more than one such a pair exists.

In the first case, Case I, let R_i and R_j constitute the unique pair of nodes and let $r_i<r_j$. Since in correspondence with these two adjacent nodes Δ has assumed the maximal value, a transition from background to foreground occurs between R_i and R_j. We interpret this event as the fact that R_j belongs to the foreground and R_i to the

background. Moreover, we assume that if the values of the gray-level representatives of R_i and R_j have been sufficient for us to ascribe the two regions to the two categories, the same should hold at any other place in the image. Thus, we assign all regions characterized by a representative gray-level value not smaller than r_j to the foreground and all regions with representative value not larger than r_i to the background.

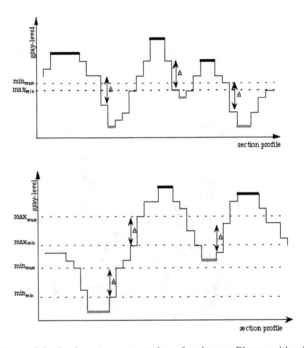

Fig. 3. Sections of the landscape representation of an image. Plateaux identify regions.

In the second case, Case II, when the maximal value of Δ is found in correspondence of more than one pair of adjacent nodes, assignment will be global or local depending on the distribution of representative gray-level values of the pairs of such nodes. Fig.3 can help to understand the two cases. There, two sections of the landscape representation of an image are shown. Both in Fig.3 top and Fig.3 bottom, three pairs of adjacent nodes are characterized by the maximal Δ value. In particular, in Fig.3 top, the three pairs of nodes are such that the maximum, max_{min}, among the three minimal values in the three pairs is smaller than the minimum, min_{max}, among the three maximal values in the three pairs. In this case, the process will be a global one. In Fig.3 bottom, this condition does not hold and a local process is necessary.

When the case exemplified in Fig.3 top occurs, the global process already described in Case I is accomplished. This time, however, instead of considering the two representative gray-level values r_i and r_j of two adjacent nodes, the two values max_{min} and min_{max} are employed, which do not correspond to adjacent nodes. All nodes with associated representative gray-level value not greater than max_{min} are ascribed to the background and all nodes with representative gray-level not smaller than min_{max} to the foreground. Note that the same result would have been obtained by processing, in a more lengthy way, one after the other all the pairs of nodes with the maximal Δ value.

When the case of Fig.3 bottom occurs, conflictual assignments could be accomplished for the same nodes. For example, the node characterized by min_{max} could be assigned to the foreground, by taking into account the gray-level values in the pair of adjacent nodes including it; on the contrary, it could be assigned to the background, by taking into account the relation between the gray-level values of the node itself and of the node characterized by max_{min}. To avoid this conflict, the process cannot be done completely in a global way. All nodes with representative gray-level value not smaller (not larger) than the maximum max_{max} (minimum min_{min}) among the maximal (minimal) values in the pairs of nodes with the maximal Δ are assigned to the foreground (background). For all other nodes, the following local investigation is done.

For each pair of nodes with maximal Δ, all ascending (descending) paths, consisting of nodes with increasing (decreasing) representative gray-level values, are traced until a decided node is met. The so traced surface of the slope includes all the undecided nodes that will be assigned to a category by the local process. Along the slope, more than one single pair of adjacent nodes having the maximal Δ can be found. Since according to our model, the separation between the foreground and the background is expected where the maximal difference in gray-level occurs, and more than one pair of nodes is likely to satisfy this requirement, a decision should be taken. We select the pair of nodes with the maximal Δ, and such that the minimal value in the pair is the smallest possible minimal value among all pairs of adjacent nodes with the maximal Δ along the slope.

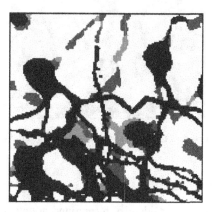

Fig. 4. Foreground components found at the end of Step 2. Different gray-tones account for different values of the parameter s_i.

Our local process favors assignment of most of the slope to the foreground. Note, however, that the parameter s_i allows us to hierarchically rank foreground nodes in terms of their distance, measured in number of nodes, from the most relevant foreground regions they are linked to. Thus, even if most of the slope is ascribed to the foreground, the nodes constituting it are less and less significant when their distance from the most important part of the component increases.

In Fig.4, the foreground components found at the end of Step 2 are shown. Again, gray-tones denote different values of the parameter s_i.

4.3 Step 3

Though all nodes have been already assigned to either the foreground or the background, a final local process is accomplished aimed at possibly changing the status of some background nodes placed at the border with respect to foreground components along the slopes treated during Step 2.

Background nodes that are adjacent to foreground nodes and have maximal representative gray-level with respect to their neighboring background nodes are candidate to change their status and become foreground nodes. This status change is done only if it causes a topology change. Namely, a background region that acts as a connecting link between two foreground components, or as a bridge linking two distinct parts of the same foreground component is assigned to the foreground. The corresponding parameter s_i is set to $n_{i,j}+s_j+1$, where s_j and $n_{i,j}$ respectively denote the parameter set for the closest foreground node R_j and the number of nodes between R_i and R_j.

The final result of the process is illustrated in Fig.5.

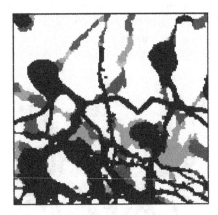

Fig. 5. Final result of the process to identify foreground components

5 Conclusion

We have introduced a method to identify foreground components in a partition of a gray-level image obtained by using watershed segmentation. In fact, the partitioned image includes regions whose membership to the foreground or the background is unknown. Our method is based both on global and local assignment. Since a process active on the whole image is computationally more efficient, we use global assignment, based on the maximal difference in gray-level between adjacent regions, as far as this can be done with high degree of confidence. We resort to local assignment when different decisions should be taken in different parts of the image, though characterized by the same maximal gray-level difference.

The performance of the method has been shown on a sample image only, but we have tested our procedure on a set of biological images and the obtained results are promising. The computational cost of the procedure is modest since all computations are actually accomplished on a graph whose nodes correspond to the regions of the partitioned image.

An interesting feature of the method is the fact that foreground regions are hierarchically ranked. We can see two different kinds of hierarchy. The first hierarchy ranks the regions of the foreground components in at most three levels, since three are the steps of the process. Foreground regions detected at Step 1 are the most perceptually relevant as they correspond to peaks of mountains and hills in the landscape representation; regions detected at Step 2 have smaller relevance, since they correspond to nodes placed along the slopes of mountains and hills; finally, regions detected at Step 3 are the less significant ones, as they were actually assigned to the background during Step 2 and changed their status only for topological reasons. The second hierarchy is driven by the parameter s_i and by the relative positions of the nodes within a component. The two kinds of hierarchies allow us to provide alternative representations of the original image to a potential user of the proposed method.

References

1. P.K. Sahoo, S. Soltani, A.K.C. Wong, Y.C. Chen, 'A survey of thresholding techniques', *Computer Vision, Graphics and Image Processing*, 41, pp. 233-260, 1988.
2. D-M. Tsai, Y-H. Chen, 'A fast histogram-clustering approach for multi-level thresholding', *Pattern Recognition Letters* 13, pp 245-252, 1992.
3. J-C. Yen, F-J. Chang, S. Chang, "A new criterion for automatic multilevel thresholding", *IEEE Trans. on Image Processing*, 4-3, pp. 370-378, 1995.
4. S. Beucher, C. Lantuejoul, "Use of watersheds in contour detection", *Proc. Int. Workshop on Image Processing ,Real-Time Edge and Motion Detection/Estimation*, Rennes, France, 1979.
5. S. Beucher, F. Meyer, 'The morphological approach of segmentation: the watershed transformation', In Dougherty E. (Editor) *Mathematical Morphology in Image Processing*, Marcel Dekker, New York, pp. 433-481, 1993.
6. M. Frucci, "A novel merging method in watershed segmentation", *Proc. 4th Indian Conf. on Computer Vision, Graphics, and Image Processing*, Applied Publishing Private Ltd, Kolkata, India, pp. 532-537, 2004.

Incomplete Contour Representations and Shape Descriptors: ICR Test Studies

Anarta Ghosh and Nicolai Petkov

Institute of Mathematics and Computing Science, University of Groningen,
P.O.Box. 800, 9700 AV Groningen, The Netherlands
{anarta, petkov}@cs.rug.nl

Abstract. Inspired by psychophysical studies of the human cognitive abilities we propose a novel aspect and a method for performance evaluation of contour based shape recognition algorithms regarding their robustness to incompleteness of contours. We use complete contour representations of objects as a reference (training) set. Incomplete contour representations of the same objects are used as a test set. The performance of an algorithm is reported using the recognition rate as a function of the percentage of contour retained. We call this evaluation procedure the ICR test. We consider three types of contour incompleteness, viz. segment-wise contour deletion, occlusion and random pixel depletion. We illustrate the test procedure using two shape recognition algorithms. These algorithms use a shape context and a distance multiset as local shape descriptors. Both algorithms qualitatively mimic human visual perception in the sense that the recognition performance monotonously increases with the degree of completeness and that they perform best in the case of random depletion and worst in the case of occluded contours. The distance multiset method performs better than the shape context method in this evaluation framework.

1 Introduction

We can easily recognize the butterflies depicted in Fig. 1, even though 50% of the contour is removed segment-wise in the left image, the right half of the contour is not visible in the middle image, and 80% of the contour points have been removed (randomly) in the right image. Psychologist E. S. Gollin [6] investigated this human ability to recognize objects from incomplete contour representations. The main objective of his study was to investigate the performance of humans in recognizing objects with incomplete contours as a function of developmental characteristics, such as mental and chronological age and intelligence quotient. As subjects of his experiments he chose children of different age groups and a group of adults. In his experiments Gollin used sets of contour images with different degrees of incompleteness (Fig. 2) and addressed the following questions: (1) In order to be recognized, how complete the contours of common objects need to be? (2) How does training affect the recognition performance in case of incomplete representations? Through his experiments he found that human

M. De Gregorio et al. (Eds.): BVAI 2005, LNCS 3704, pp. 416–425, 2005.

ability to recognize objects with incomplete contours (a) depends on intelligence quotient and (b) is improved by training.

This aspect of recognition of objects with incomplete contours is also very important in the context of processing visual information using computers. A natural image and two edge images, obtained from it are shown in Fig. 3. The middle image was obtained by applying a bank of Gabor energy filters [8]. It contains the contours of the object of interest, viz. a gazelle, but it also contains a large number of texture edges in the background that are not related in any way to the shape of the gazelle. There would be a devastating effect of these texture edges on any currently known contour based shape recognition algorithm. Advanced contour detection methods based on surround suppression [8,9] succeed in separating the essential object contours from the texture edges, as illustrated

(a)   (b)   (c)

Fig. 1. A butterfly can be recognized even though (a) 50% of its contour has been removed segment-wise, (b) one of its wings is not fully visible (occluded), (c) 80% of the contour pixels have been randomly removed

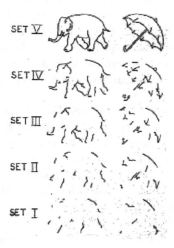

Fig. 2. Example of image sets used in Gollin's original test [1]. The images in set V are complete contour representations and the other sets are derived from set V by removing segment-wise an increasing fraction of the contour. Reproduced with the permission from the author and the publisher of: E. S. Gollin, Developmental studies of visual recognition of incomplete objects. Perceptual and Motor Skills, Vol. 11 pp. 289-298, 1960, copyright Southern University Press.

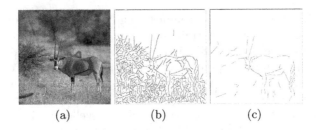

(a)   (b)   (c)

Fig. 3. (a) Image of a gazelle in its natural habitat. (b) Result of edge detection with a bank of Gabor energy filters. (c) Result of contour detection by a bank of Gabor energy filters augmented with a biologically motivated surround suppression of texture edges.

by the right-most image in Fig. 3, but at the same time these methods have a certain negative side effect of depleting the contours of the objects of interest. Hence in practical situations the robustness of shape recognition methods to contour incompleteness is also an issue of importance.

Inspired by Gollin's study we put forward a novel attribute, viz. *robustness to incomplete contour representations*, that any contour based object recognition system/algorithm should have. We choose an idealized situation where: (a) complete contour representations of the objects to be recognized form the reference (training) set or "memory" of the system/algorithm, (b) incomplete contour representations of the same objects are derived from the afore mentioned complete representations and are used as a test set, (c) the performance of the system/algorithm in recognizing the objects from these incomplete representations is evaluated. The main reason behind evaluating the performance of object recognition algorithms in such an ideal situation is the rational logic that in order to perform well in a real world scenario (natural images) any recognition system should first perform well in such idealized (simple) situations.

We investigate the performance of two contour based shape recognition methods, which use a shape context [1] and a distance multiset [7] as shape descriptors, by comparing an object represented by incomplete contours with all objects in a reference set represented by complete contours and determining the nearest neighbor. If the nearest neighbor is the object from which the incomplete contour representation is derived we consider the recognition to be correct, otherwise incorrect. As incomplete contour representations of an object, in addition to Gollin's method of segment-wise contour deletion (Fig. 2) we also consider other types of incompleteness, viz. occlusion and random pixel depletion. We name the corresponding studies segment-wise deletion test, occlusion test, and depletion test and collectively call these tests in short *Incomplete Contour Representation (ICR) tests*.

In Section 2 we describe the shape recognition methods which we use for illustration. The experimental design and the achieved results are discussed in Section 3. A summary and conclusions are presented in Section 4.

2   Shape Recognition Methods

The recognition of objects in the methods studied below is done by computing dissimilarity between the contour representations of two objects by using a point correspondence paradigm. Shape descriptors associated with the points are used to find the point correspondences. To maintain brevity and focus on the illustration of the ICR test framework we use simpler versions of the algorithms described in [7] and [1].

2.1   Distance Multiset

The *distance multiset* for a point p in the contour of an object $\mathcal{O}$ of N points, is formally defined as the following vector [7]: $D_N^{\mathcal{O}}(p) = (ln(d_1(p)), ln(d_2(p)), \ldots, ln(d_{N-1}(p)))$ where $d_j(p)$ is the Euclidean distance between p and its jth nearest neighbor in $\mathcal{O}$. In this approach the shape of an object $\mathcal{O} \equiv \{p_1 \ldots p_N\}$ defined by a set of contour points is described by the set of distance multisets in the following way: $S_{\mathcal{O}}^{DM} \equiv \{D_N^{\mathcal{O}}(p) | p \in \mathcal{O}\}$. Next, a cost $c(X, Y)$ of matching two distance multisets X and Y is defined and computed by using the algorithm described in [13]. Let $c_{i,j}^{DM}$ be the cost of matching a point p_i in an object $\mathcal{O}_1$ represented by M contour points to a point q_j in an object $\mathcal{O}_2$ represented by N contour points, $M \leq N$: $c_{i,j}^{DM} \equiv c(D_N^{\mathcal{O}_1}(p_i), D_M^{\mathcal{O}_2}(q_j))$. Then the dissimilarity between the shapes $S_{\mathcal{O}_1}^{DM}$ and $S_{\mathcal{O}_2}^{DM}$ is defined as follows: $d^{DM}(S_{\mathcal{O}_1}^{DM}, S_{\mathcal{O}_2}^{DM}) \equiv \sum_{i=1}^{M} min\{c_{i,j}^{DM} | j = 1 \ldots N\}$.

2.2   Shape Context

The *shape context* [1] of a point p belonging to the contour of an object is a bivariate histogram in a log-polar coordinate system that gives the distribution of contour points in the surroundings of p. Let an object $\mathcal{O}$ be represented by a set of contour points, $\mathcal{O} \equiv \{p_1 \ldots p_N\}$. Formally, the authors of this method define the shape context of a point $p \in \mathcal{O}$ as a vector in the following way: $H_K^{\mathcal{O}}(p) = (h_1(p), h_2(p), \ldots, h_K(p))$, where $h_k(p) = card\{q \neq p | q \in \mathcal{O}, (q - p) \in bin(k)\}$ is the number of contour points in the kth bin $bin(k)$ and K is the total number of histogram bins. The bins are constructed by dividing the image plane into K partitions (in a log-polar coordinate system) with p as the origin. In this study we use 5 intervals for the log distance r, and 12 intervals for the polar angle θ, so $K = 60$. As suggested in [1], we randomly choose 100 points (if available) from the contour of an object and calculate their shape contexts. The shape of the object is described using the set of shape contexts associated with the contour points in the following way: $S_{\mathcal{O}}^{SC} \equiv \{H_K^{\mathcal{O}}(p) | p \in \mathcal{O}\}$. The cost of matching a point p_i that belongs to the contour of an object $\mathcal{O}_1$ of M points, to a point q_j from the contour of an object $\mathcal{O}_2$ of N points is defined as follows: $c_{i,j}^{SC} \equiv \frac{1}{2} \sum_{k=1}^{K} \frac{[h_k(p_i) - h_k(q_j)]^2}{h_k(p_i) + h_k(q_j)}$, which yields an $M \times N$ cost matrix of point-wise dissimilarities. Next we compute the dissimilarity between the shapes $S_{\mathcal{O}_1}^{SC}$ and $S_{\mathcal{O}_2}^{SC}$ of the objects in the following way: $d^{SC}(S_{\mathcal{O}_1}^{SC}, S_{\mathcal{O}_2}^{SC}) \equiv \sum_{i=1}^{M} min\{c_{i,j}^{SC} | j = 1, \ldots, N\}$.

3   Experiments and Results

3.1   Image Set

We choose the silhoutte images from the MPEG-7 database [10] as our dataset. In this dataset there are 1400 images divided into 70 classes, each of 20 similar objects (eg. apple, bird, bat, etc). One object from each class is chosen and the contours of the objects are extracted using Gabor filters [8]. These 70 contour images are rescaled in such a way that the diameter (maximum Euclidean distance between contour pixels) is approximately the same (76 pixels) for all objects (Fig. 4). These 70 rescaled contour images are used as the reference ("memory" of the recognition system) images in our experiments. These images are analogous to the complete representations, set V of Fig. 2, used in Gollin's original study.

Incomplete contour representations of objects for the *segment-wise deletion test* are constructed by randomly removing continuous segments of the contours and retaining a given percentage of contour pixels from the above mentioned complete contour representations. For c percent of retained pixels approximately $\lceil log_2(\frac{100-c}{8}) \rceil$ segments are deleted. Incomplete representations for the *occlusion test* are created by removing a given percentage of consecutive contour pixels starting from the leftmost (Fig. 5(b)) or the rightmost pixel (Fig. 5(c)) of an object. The left and right occlusion are deliberately chosen due to the fact that in case of natural images the object of interest is most commonly occluded either from the left or from the right. A rondom pixel deletion is performed to construct the incomplete representations for the *depletion test* (Fig. 5(d)). The percentages of retained pixels are chosen in the following way: from 2% to 4% in steps of 1%, from 5% to 85% in steps of 5%, and 100% for the depletion test; from 5% to 85% in steps of 5%, and 100% for the segment-wise deletion and the occlusion tests. For each type (segment-wise deletion, occlusion and depletion) and degree of contour degradation 70 test images are created. In the web-site *www.cs.rug.nl/ ~petkov* the complete dataset for the proposed ICR test is available.

3.2   Methodology

A test image (incomplete contour representation of an object) obtained from one of the 70 reference images is compared with all 70 reference images using a given

Fig. 4. Rescaled contour images obtained from samples of MPEG-7 silhoutte database. These images are considered as complete representations that comprise the memory of the recognition system.

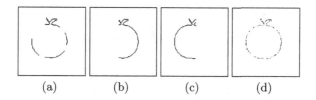

Fig. 5. Incomplete contour representations: (a) Segment-wise deleted contour representaion (this type of incompleteness corresponds to incomplete representations of Gollin's original study, set I to IV of Fig. 2). (b) Left-occluded contour representation. (c) Right-occluded contour representation. (d) Depleted contour representation.

shape comparison algorithm, described in Section 2 and a decision is taken about which reference image the degraded image is most similar to (nearest neighbor search). If the nearest neighbor is the reference image from which the degraded image was obtained, the recognition is considered correct, otherwise incorrect. If the nearest neighbor is found to be not unique then the recognition is also considered incorrect. For each of the three tests (segment-wise deletion, occlusion, depletion) and for each degree (c percentage of retained contour pixels) of contour image degradation, the corresponding 70 test images are compared with each of the 70 reference images and the percentage of correct recognition $P(c)$ is determined. An average of the recognition rates with left and right occluded images for a given percentage of retained contour is computed to evaluate the performance of the algorithms in the occlusion test.

3.3   Results and Discussions

The results of our experiments are illsutrated in Fig. 6. The recognition rate is a monotonic increasing function of the percentage of contour retainment in all three tests. In this respect the considered algorithms resemble the human visual system [3,4,14]. Both methods perform worst in the occlusion test and best in the depletion test, which also conforms with the recognition performance of humans, as occluded contour images carry the least amount of shape information and depleted contour images carry maximum shape information in the context of human visual perception.

The performance of the distance multiset method is appreciably better than that of the shape context method for any percentage of retained contour pixels in the case of the segment-wise deletion test (Fig. 6(top left)) and the occlusion test (Fig. 6(top right)). From the results of the depletion test (Fig. 6(bottom)) we see that both the shape context method and the distance multiset method perform very well in recognizing objects with depleted contour representations, if more than 40% and 5%, respectively, of the contour points are retained. For higher degree of depletion ($c \leq 40$) the distance multiset method outperforms the shape context method.

The better performance of the distance multiset method in general can be explained by the fact that the proposed ICR tests give advantage to the algorithms

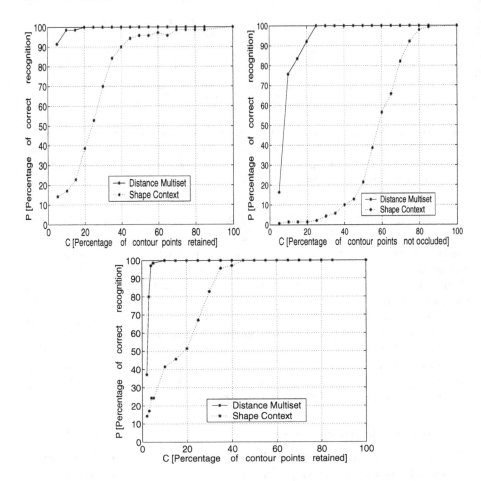

Fig. 6. Results of the ICR tests with a subset of MPEG-7 dataset: (top left) Segment-wise deletion test; (top right) Occlusion test; (bottom) Depletion test

which yield zero dissimilarity in a comparison of two objects represented by two sets of points where one is a subset of the other. This property of the distance multiset algorithm is explained in more detail below. Let two sets $A, B, \subset \mathbf{R}^2$ be such that $B = \{f(\mathbf{x}) : \mathbf{x} \in A\}$, where $f : \mathbf{R}^2 \to \mathbf{R}^2$ is an isometry.

Lemma 1. *If $B = f(A)$, $C \subset B$ and $card\,(C) \geq 2$. then $d^{DM}(S_C^{DM}, S_A^{DM}) = 0$ where S_C^{DM} and S_A^{DM} are the shapes, described by distance multisets, corresponding to C and A, respectively.*

For the proof of the lemma refer to [5]. In our study A corresponds to the set of contour points of a reference object, f is the identity transformation (i.e. $B = A$) and C is the set of contour points of an incomplete representation.

The implication of the lemma is two-fold: (1) The recognition will be incorrect by the distance mutliset method only when the nearest neighbor of a test object in the reference set is not unique. (2) The distance multiset method should perform exactly the same way when f is not the identity transformation [5].

The above lemma does not hold for the shape context method, but this method can be modified in such a way that the relation $d^{SC}(S_{\mathcal{O}}^{SC}, S_{\mathcal{O}'}^{SC}) = 0$ can be approximately fulfilled if $\mathcal{O}'$ is an incomplete representation (of modest degree) derived from $\mathcal{O}$. Specifically, we normalize the shape context $H_K^{\mathcal{O}}(p)$ by dividing its elements by the total number of points $card(\mathcal{O})$ in the corresponding object $\mathcal{O}$. If $\mathcal{O}' \subset \mathcal{O}$ is an incomplete representation derived from $\mathcal{O}$ and if $H_K^{\mathcal{O}'}(p)$ is the normalized (by $card(\mathcal{O}')$) shape context of a point p ($p \in \mathcal{O}'$) in this incomplete representation, the relation $H_K^{\mathcal{O}'}(p) \approx H_K^{\mathcal{O}}(p)$ will hold for modest degrees of contour deletion because the ratio of the number of contour points in each bin to the total number of points will be approximately the same for the complete and the incomplete contour representations and hence we have $d^{SC}(S_{\mathcal{O}}^{SC}, S_{\mathcal{O}'}^{SC}) \approx 0$ for normalized shape context. In our experiments we found that the performance of the shape context method is greatly imporved due to this normalization in the segment-wise deletion and the depletion test [5].

As the scope of this paper is to introduce a new test, it is important to check if the conclusions drawn from the ICR test are consistent across *datasets*. We carried out experiments using a second set of images, the Columbia University Image Library (COIL-20) dataset and (compared to the MPEG-7 dataset) no qualitative difference in the performances of the algorithms was observed, c.f [5].

The *object size* can have effect on the results of an ICR test through (a) the resolution of the reference objects and (b) a possible mismatch between the size of a reference object and a test object. Regarding the resolution of the reference objects, in our experiments we found that for a given percentage of contour degradation (by any method) the performance of the algorithms grows with the diameter of the reference objects. To eliminate this effect and to standardize the test procedure we rescaled the reference contour images to a fixed diameter (76 pixel units). For more detailed discussion on the effect of the object size on the proposed ICR test refer to [5]. The problem of a possible mismatch between the sizes of reference and test objects can be dealt with either by using scale invariance procedures prescribed in [1], [7] or by using a multiscale apporach.

The performance curves obtained in the ICR tests can be used to compare algorithms as illustrated in Fig. 6. To define a *criterion for acceptable performance* of an algorithm in the ICR test, the performance of humans in similar experimental [3,4,14] setup can be used as a reference [5].

A good performance in the original ICR test does not guarantee good performance in other respects, e.g. robustness to shape or size variation. Hence, a good performance in the ICR test should be considered as a *necessary condition* for object recognition methods to perform well in a real world scenario but not as a sufficient one. We are not aware of any evaluation procedure for shape recognition methods which is sufficient in such respect. The basic framework of the ICR test proposed in this paper can easily be extended to test robustness of algorithms to more than one criterion, e.g. a *bull's eye* ICR test for evaluating robustness to shape variations along with robustness to incomplete contour representations. We present results of such a bull's eye ICR test in [5].

4   Summary and Conclusion

Shape descriptor based object recognition methods have been evaluated and compared using various characteristics like invariance, uniqueness and stability [12]. Marr and Nishihara [11] proposed three criteria for judging the effectiveness of a shape descriptor, viz. accessibility, scope and uniqueness, stability and sensitivity. Brady [2] put forward a set of criteria for representation of shape, viz. rich local support, smooth extension and propagation. In the current work, motivated by characteristics of the human visual system [6], we propose an additional new criterion, viz. robustness to contour incompleteness to compare and characterize contour based shape recognition algorithms using their performance in recognizing objects with incomplete contours. We are not aware of any such comparison and characterization in the present literature.

We put forward the following procedure which we call the ICR test: (1) Take a set of images of objects and extract contours. Rescale all contour images to the same object diameter. (2) Train the recognition system with these complete contour representations. (3) Construct different sets of incomplete representations from the complete contour representations; quantify the level of incompleteness using the percentage of contour pixels retained. (4) Using the incomplete representations as a test set evaluate the recognition rate as a function of the percentage of contour pixels retained.

To illsutrate the framework we use two shape recognition methods based on the shape context and the distance multiset. The two methods tested were chosen merely for illustrative purposes and we did not aim to prove superiority of any method. A complete comparative study of the two methods is out of the scope of this work. In our illustrative experiments we found that: (1) The distance multiset shape recognition method outperforms the shape context method. (2) Both methods perform similar to the human visual system in the sense that their performances are increasing functions of the degree of contour completeness and are best in the case of the depletion test and worst in the case of the occlusion test.

References

1. S. Belongie, J. Malik, and J. Puzicha. Shape matching and object recognition using shape contexts. *IEEE Transaction on Pattern Analysis and Machine Intelligence, Vol. 24, No. 24*, pages 509–522, 2002.
2. M. Brady. Criteria for representations of shape. *In J. Beck, B. Hope and A. Rosenfeld, editors, Human and Machine Vision, Academic Press*, pages 39–84, 1983.
3. V. Chihman, V. Bondarko, Y. Shelpin, and M. Danilova. Fragmental figure perception. *Perception. Vol. 33 Supplement*, page 76a, 2004.

4. N. P. Foreman and R. Hemmings. The Gollin incomplete figures test: A flexible, computerised version. *Perception. Vol. 16*, pages 543–548, 1987.
5. A. Ghosh and N. Petkov. Robustness of shape descriptors to incomplete contour representations. *IEEE Transactions on Pattern Analysis and Machine Intelligence, In press*, 2005.
6. E.S. Gollin. Developmental studies of visual recognition of incomplete objects. *Perceptual and Motor Skills. Vol. 11*, pages 289–298, 1960.
7. C. Grigorescu and N. Petkov. Distance sets for shape filters and shape recognition. *IEEE Transactions on Image Processing, Vol. 12, No. 10*, pages 1274–1286, 2003.
8. C. Grigorescu, N. Petkov, and M. Westenberg. Contour detection based on non-classical receptive field inhibition. *IEEE Transactions on Image Processing, Vol. 12, July*, pages 729–739, 2003.
9. C. Grigorescu, N. Petkov, and M. A. Westenberg. Contour and boundary detection improved by surround suppression of texture edges. *Image Vision and Computing, Vol. 22*, pages 609–622, 2004.
10. L.J. Latecki, R. Lakämper, and U. Eckhardt. Shape descriptors for non-rigid shapes with single closed contour. *In Proc. of IEEE Conf. on Computer Vision and Pattern Recognition*, pages 424–429, 1998.
11. D. Marr and H.K. Nishihara. Representation and recognition of the spatial organization of three dimensional shapes. *In Proc. Roy. Soc. London, B., Vol. 200*, pages 269–294, 1978.
12. F. Mokhtarian and A.K. Mackworth. A theory of multiscale, curvature-based shape representation for planar curves. *IEEE Transactions on Pattern Analysis and Machine Intelligence, Vol. 14, No. 8*, pages 789–805, 1992.
13. N. Petkov. Algorithm for the cost of an optimal assignment of two sets of real numbers. *Technical report, 2003-9-07, Institute of Mathematics and Computing Science, University of Groningen*, 2003.
14. Y. Shelepin, O. Vahromeeva, A. Harauzov, S. Pronin, N. Foreman, and V. Chihman. Recognition of incomplete contour and half-tone figures. *Perception. Vol. 33 Supplement*, page 85c, 2004.

Rotation and Scale Invariant Shape Description Using the Contour Segment Curvature

Min-Ki Kim

Research Institute of Computer and Information Communication,
Dept. of Computer Science Education, Gyeongsang National University,
900, Gajwa-dong, Jinju, 660-701, Korea
mkkim@gsnu.ac.kr

Abstract. This paper presents a shape description method based on contour segment curvature (CSC). The CSC is defined as the ratio of the line length connecting two endpoints of a contour segment to its curve length. To extract consistent contour segment, the concept of overlapped contour segment is introduced. The rotation and scale invariant CSC can be extracted through the use of the overlapped contour segment. The proposed method describes the shape of objects with feature vectors that represents the distribution of the CSC, and measures the similarity by comparing the feature vector acquired from the corresponding unit-length segment. The experimental results show that the proposed method is not only invariant to rotation and scale but also superior to the NCCH and the TRP method in clustering power. Furthermore, the performance improvement is expected by adding the distance information to the CSC.

1 Introduction

Content-based image retrieval requires various pattern recognition techniques. In particular, shape description techniques are essential for successful content-based image retrieval [1, 2, 3]. Various shape description methods have been studied. These methods are classified according to many different criteria [4]. The first criterion is the part of use in shape description: boundary vs. region. The second is the result of shape description: the numeric (scalar transform) vs. the nonnumeric (space domain). The third is information preservation: accurate reconstruction vs. partial reconstruction.

In the field of content-based image retrieval, rotation and scale invariant shape description features are also required. Fourier descriptor and moments are representative features in the scalar transformation method. These features can effectively represent the global shape. However, they are required to improve the local shape description power and to reduce time complexity [5, 6]. Chain code, polygonal approximation, and medial axis transformation are typical features in the space domain method. Iivarinen [7] proposed a feature of normalized chain code histogram (NCCH). Gaussian filter was used to reduce the contour distortion and each chain code direction on contour was counted and normalized by the contour length. Chang [8] used a function of distance from the centroid to a feature point on the contour. The feature points are extracted based on curvature information. In the case where a contour is approximated by a polygon, the vertexes are used as feature points. Tang [9] presented the feature of

M. De Gregorio et al. (Eds.): BVAI 2005, LNCS 3704, pp. 426–435, 2005.
© Springer-Verlag Berlin Heidelberg 2005

transformation ring projection (TRP). Unlike Chang's [8] method, Tang used all the points in the region to compute the distance, and the frequency in each distance range was counted.

This paper presents a rotation and scale invariant shape description method using contour segment curvature (CSC). Like the NCCH method, the proposed method is a scalar transformation method using contour information. The basic concept of the CSC is described in section 2. In section 3, the shape description method using the CSC is explained. In the two final sections that follow, the experimental results and conclusion are presented.

2   Contour Segment Curvature

The contour segment curvature (CSC) is defined as the ratio of the line length connecting two endpoints of a contour segment to its curve length. A circle has a unique CSC regardless of the location of contour segment. However other shapes have different CSC according to the location of contour segment. For a contour segment S of length L that has two endpoints A and B, the CSC(S) is defined by

$$CSC(S) = \frac{length(\overline{AB})}{L} .$$ (1)

When the topmost left pixel A_0 is determined as the base point for segmenting contour into unit-length segments, S_i is defined as the i-th segment that has two endpoints A_i and B_i. A straight segment like S_6 has a CSC close to 1. In contrast, curved segment like S_5 has a CSC close to 0.5. The range of the CSC is 0 to 1. The CSC(S_i) describes the feature of a contour segment S_i. So the feature of the entire contour can be described by combining the CSCs acquired from all the segments composing the contour.

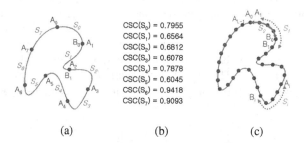

$$CSC(S_0) = 0.7955$$
$$CSC(S_1) = 0.6564$$
$$CSC(S_2) = 0.6812$$
$$CSC(S_3) = 0.6078$$
$$CSC(S_4) = 0.7878$$
$$CSC(S_5) = 0.6045$$
$$CSC(S_6) = 0.9418$$
$$CSC(S_7) = 0.9093$$

(a)   (b)   (c)

Fig. 1. (a) Contour segments; (b) CSCs; (c) Overlapped contour segments

It is necessary to extract contour segments that are invariant to rotation and scale to acquire stable CSCs regardless of these variations. In literature [8], it first extracts the special feature points in order to obtain these contour segments. However, it is difficult to extract stable feature points. The proposed method divides the contour into unit-length segments. The unit-length is set in proportion to the entire contour length to cope with scale variation. It also defines overlapped contour segment corresponding to each point on a contour. Therefore, a contour consisting of L points has overlapped contour segment S_0, S_1, …, and S_{L-1} as described in Fig. 1-(c).

3   Shape Description Using CSC

3.1   Preprocessing

To acquire stable contour segments, preprocessing methods such as binarization and contour smoothing is needed. A fixed threshold was used to emphasize the silhouette of the image and the outer boundary contour was extracted based on the 8-neighbor connectivity. Image variation and noise partially disrupt contour shape. In particular, the proposed CSC feature is sensitive to the minute fluctuation of a contour. Hence contour smoothing was performed. The 1-D Gaussian convolution mask was used for contour smoothing, where r is plus or minus 13 for σ=5. The r argument gives the distance in pixels from the centre of the mask, and σ specifies the 'width' of the mask. Fig. 2 shows the sequential process and corresponding result of each preprocessing step.

Fig. 2. (a) An input image; (b) Binarized image; (c) Outer contour; (d) Smoothed contour

3.2   Feature Vector Generating and Matching

The unit-length of a contour segment should be set to compute the CSC. To extract scale invariant features, the unit-length was set as the quotient of dividing the entire contour length L by d. If d increases, the unit-length is shortened and the CSC represents local feature of a contour. On the contrary if d decreases, the unit-length is enlarged and the CSC represents the global feature of a contour. Therefore, extracting the local or global feature of a contour shape using the CSC becomes viable through the means of changing d. In equation (2), the CSC(l, S_i) represents the curvature of i-th segment of unit-length l. The digital curve length l is computed by the sum of the product of each weighted pixel direction's frequency. The weight of vertical or horizontal direction is 1.0 and the others are 1.414.

$$CSC(l, S_i) = \frac{length(\overline{A_i B_i})}{l} \qquad (2)$$

Fig. 3 shows the CSC graphs when d is 3, 7, and 11. The graphs show the curvature variation as the base point is moved around the contour. In Fig. 3-(a), the contour segment with the base point located at $2L/3$ has a CSC smaller than 0.5 because the segment is curved in a '<' shape. Although the base points located at $2L/3$, $5L/7$, and $8L/11$ do not coincide with each other, the figure shows that as the unit-length becomes shorter its corresponding curvatures-the CSC($L/3$, $S_{2L/3}$), CSC($L/7$, $S_{5L/7}$), and CSC($L/11$, $S_{8L/11}$) become larger. These are displayed in the CSC graphs. In the CSC

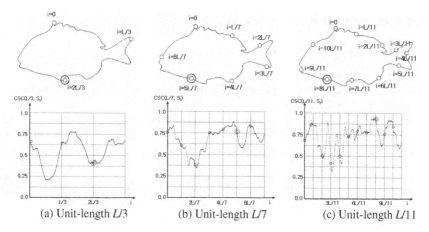

Fig. 3. Contour segments and their corresponding CSC graphs

graph, moving upward means that corresponding contour segment becomes close to being a straight line.

The CSC(l, S_i) is converted into n-dimensional contour segment feature vector $V_l(S_i)$ according to the equation (3). As shown in equation (4), the entire contour's feature vector is defined as the sum of each feature vector $V_l(S_i)$. It means that the entire contour shape is described by the frequency count accumulated according to the range of the CSC. The sum of each element's value in feature vector V_l equals to the entire contour length L. Hence, it is necessary to normalize the feature vector with the length L to cope with scale variation.

$$V_l(S_i) = [v_0, v_1, v_2, ..., v_k, ..., v_{n-1}]$$
$$v_k = \begin{cases} 1, & \text{if } CSC(S_i) \times n = k \\ 0, & \text{otherwise} \end{cases} \tag{3}$$

$$V_l = \sum_{i=0}^{L} V_l(S_i) \tag{4}$$

A similarity measure is needed to search for a similar-shaped image from an image database. The similarity measure is described in equation (5), where QV_l and TV_l refer to the normalized feature vectors of query image and target image in the database respectively.

$$D_l = \sum_{i=0}^{n-1} \left| QV_l(v_i) - TV_l(v_i) \right| \tag{5}$$

The final feature vector is acquired by using multiple length contour segments as the short and long segments effectively represent local and global features. The final feature distance is defined as the average distance between corresponding feature vectors.

4   Experimental Results and Discussion

4.1   Experimental Environment

The proposed method was implemented at Pentium4 PC using Visual C++ 6.0, and the performance was evaluated using fish images. Two types of experiments were performed: one to test the performance and the other to examine the applicability to the content-based image retrieval. The fish images selected from a web site (http://www.kunsan.ac.kr/fishes/ menu.html) were used for performance testing. Five groups of fish images, a total 15 images, were selected according to the boundary shape as shown in Fig. 4. To test the robustness for similarity variation, additional 150 images were generated by rotation (15°, 30°, 45°, 90°, 180°) and scale (50%, 80%, 110%, 120%, 150%). Fig. 5 shows some sample images among the objects of content-based image retrieval. A database consisting of 1,100 marine creature images were used for the experiment of image retrieval. They were provided at the CVSSP site (http://www.ee.surrey.ac.uk/Research/VSSP/imagedb/demo.html).

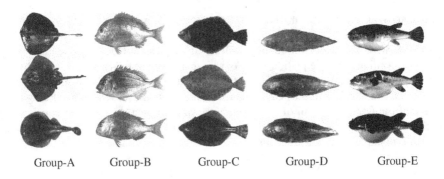

Group-A   Group-B   Group-C   Group-D   Group-E

Fig. 4. Fish images: Group-A(A1, A2, A3), Group-B(B1, B2, B3), Group-C(C1, C2, C3), Group-D(D1, D2, D3), Group-E(E1, E2, E3)

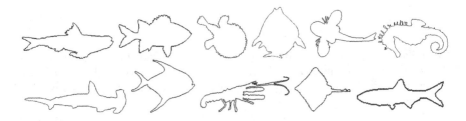

Fig. 5. Samples of the database consisting of 1,100 marine creature images

4.2   Experimental Results and Analysis

The performance evaluation was performed with two aspects in consideration: clustering power and invariance to rotation and scale variation. The clustering power means the ability to make similar shapes locate closely and different shapes locate far away in a feature space. The invariance refers to the degree of closeness between original and rotated or scaled image at feature space.

As explained earlier, the unit-length was determined as the quotient of dividing the entire contour length L by d, and multiple unit-length contour segments were used to extract local and global features. To reduce the redundant information, prime numbers were selected as d values. In this experiment, 3, 7, and 11 were used. The comparison with two other methods was performed: the normalized chain code histogram (NCCH)[7] and the transformation ring projection (TRP)[9]. For comparison, the two methods were implemented. Table 1 shows the absolute feature distance between each pair of groups. It is difficult to compare the clustering power with the absolute distance shown in table 1, because each method has different feature distance measures. Therefore it is necessary to introduce a relative distance defined by the ratio of average inter-group distance to average intra-group distance. For example, the relative distance of group A, $RD(A)$, is computed by equation (6), where $D(A,X)$ is the distance between group A and X, and A_i is a feature vector of i-th image in group A.

Table 1. Feature distance at each pair of groups

	Method	Group A	Group B	Group C	Group D	Group E
Group A	NCCH	109	146	153	469	207
	TRP	298	502	615	431	447
	CSC	306	1002	495	856	729
Group B	NCCH	146	128	182	396	147
	TRP	502	236	315	374	359
	CSC	1002	384	845	1246	612
Group C	NCCH	153	182	138	485	218
	TRP	615	315	166	604	588
	CSC	495	845	269	770	562
Group D	NCCH	469	396	485	80	289
	TRP	431	374	604	46	267
	CSC	856	1246	770	74	914
Group E	NCCH	207	147	218	289	123
	TRP	447	359	588	267	206
	CSC	729	612	562	914	192

$$RD(A) = \frac{Average(D(A,B)+D(A,C)+D(A,D)+D(A,E))}{Average(D(A,A))},$$

$$D(A,X) = \sum_{i=1}^{3}(\sum_{j=1}^{3}|A_i - X_j|)$$

(6)

To compare the clustering power using relative distance is a feasible option. Fig. 6 shows the relative distance of each group when three different methods were applied. The images at group D were clearly discriminated from the other groups' images in all the three methods. The proposed CSC method demonstrates superior clustering power than the NCCH and the TRP method with the exception of group C.

The rotated or scaled images were used in the experiment to test the invariance against these variations. Table 2 shows the absolute feature distance between the original image and rotated or scaled image. It is necessary to introduce another rela-

tive distance to compare the three methods. It is defined by the ratio of average variation distance to average inter-group distance. The variation distance is the distance
between the feature vector of the original image and the feature vector of a rotated or
scaled image. The relative distance of i-th image in group X, $RD(X_i)$, is computed by
equation (7), where X_i' is a rotated or scaled image of X_i.

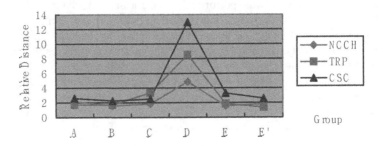

Fig. 6. A comparison of clustering power

Table 2. The absolute features distance according to the variation of rotation or scale

	Method	Rotation angle					Scale (%)				
		15	30	45	90	180	50	80	110	120	150
Group A	NCCH	173	182	164	25	31	48	45	71	91	176
	TRP	64	228	333	60	85	77	42	38	50	107
	CSC	162	236	178	140	96	290	60	112	200	397
Group B	NCCH	186	238	176	35	41	69	63	74	107	124
	TRP	84	114	114	32	50	161	37	38	67	58
	CSC	164	170	184	165	184	486	151	167	205	372
Group C	NCCH	156	188	150	47	57	67	54	69	126	169
	TRP	78	153	202	64	73	210	134	101	70	73
	CSC	133	186	99	78	116	157	43	111	203	349
Group D	NCCH	369	421	225	15	18	53	36	69	122	192
	TRP	17	23	49	14	19	21	11	23	21	27
	CSC	28	61	75	34	34	23	19	15	24	44
Group E	NCCH	237	246	155	17	14	37	34	67	106	135
	TRP	43	62	85	56	66	86	30	34	57	44
	CSC	76	103	108	41	35	296	54	62	106	188

$$RD(X_i) = \frac{Average(D(X_i, X_i'))}{Average(D(X, X))} \qquad (7)$$

A relative distance greater than 1.0 means that the feature distance to the rotated or
scaled images is greater than the distance out of the different images in the same
group. Therefore, the relative distance less than 1.0 indicates robustness in rotation or
scale variation. Fig. 7 shows that the CSC and the TRP feature have superior rotation
invariance than the NCCH feature. However, as shown in Fig. 8, any one does not
show distinctive superiority in scale invariance.

An experiment to diagnose the applicability of content-based image retrieval was
performed. The retrieval results shown in Fig. 9 show five candidates per query

image. The topmost images (*A1, B1, C1, D1*, and *E1*) in each group shown in Fig. 4. were used as query images. Like the results of the performance test, the retrieval results show that the CSC and the TRP methods are superior to the NCCH method. However, there is no clear distinction in superiority between the CSC and the TRP method. The CSC method shows better result than the TRP method for the *A1* query image, whereas the TRP method shows better than the CSC method for the *E1* query image. The CSC2 is a refined feature of the CSC combining the TRP feature. The CSC features are refined according to the distance between a centroid and the midpoint of contour segment. It shows better result than any other three methods.

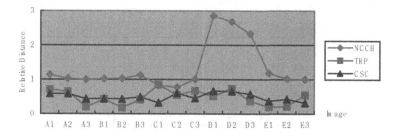

Fig. 7. Relative distance to the rotation variation

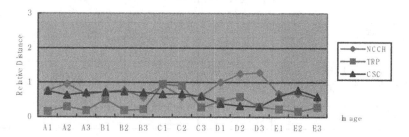

Fig. 8. Relative distance to the scale variation

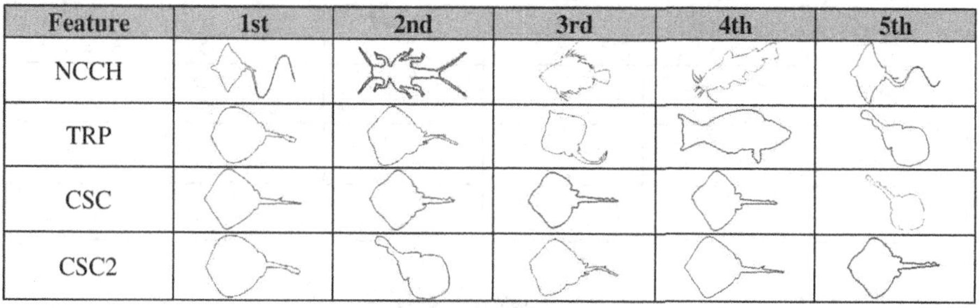

Feature	1st	2nd	3rd	4th	5th
NCCH					
TRP					
CSC					
CSC2					

(a) Query image: A1

Fig. 9. Image retrieval results for the marine creatures database

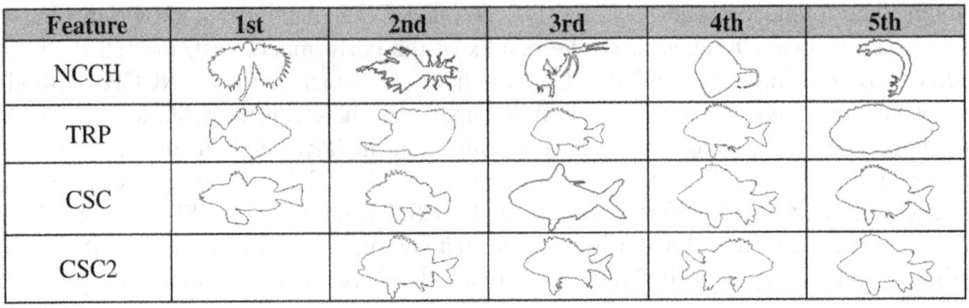

Feature	1st	2nd	3rd	4th	5th
NCCH					
TRP					
CSC					
CSC2					

(b) Query Image: B1

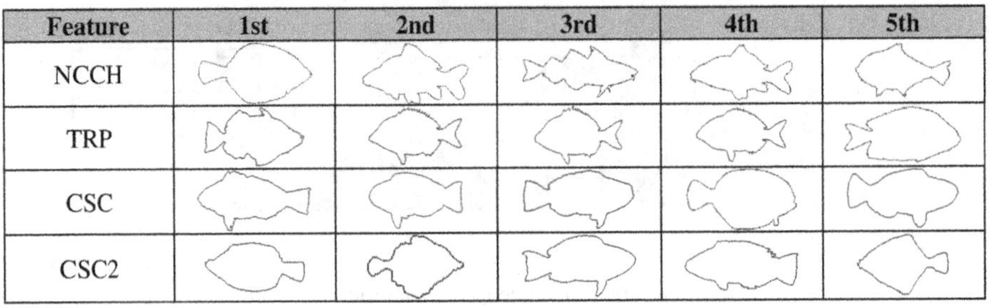

Feature	1st	2nd	3rd	4th	5th
NCCH					
TRP					
CSC					
CSC2					

(c) Query Image: C1

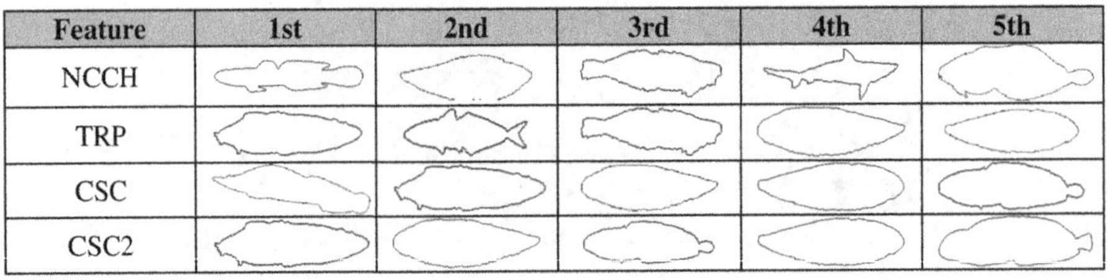

Feature	1st	2nd	3rd	4th	5th
NCCH					
TRP					
CSC					
CSC2					

(d) Query Image: D1

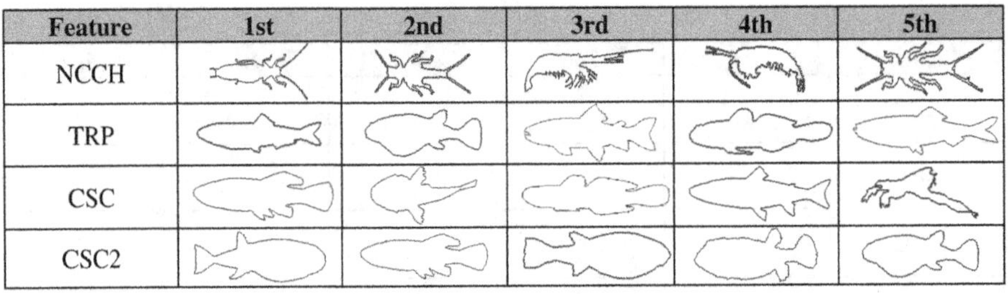

Feature	1st	2nd	3rd	4th	5th
NCCH					
TRP					
CSC					
CSC2					

(e) Query Image: E1

Fig. 9. Image retrieval results for the marine creatures database (cont.)

5 Conclusion

In conclusion, this paper has proposed a rotation and scale invariant shape description method. The proposed method has defined the overlapped contour segment in which length is in proportion to the entire contour length. The CSC can describe the feature of local or global shape according to the unit-length of the segment. For this reason, multiple unit-length segments were used to calculate the CSC. The experimental results show that the proposed method is superior to the NCCH and the TRP methods in clustering power. Furthermore, the refined CSC feature shows improved retrieval results. This study has focused on the shape description method only, thus a simple similarity measure and the nearest neighbor classifier were used. Future work will be to refine the CSC feature and to develop an appropriate classifier.

Acknowledgement

I would like to thank F. Mokhtarian (CVSSP, University of Surrey) for providing the marine creature images used in the experiments.

References

1. Rui, Y., Huang, T.S., and Chang, S.: Image Retrieval: Past, Present, and Future, Journal of Visual Communication and Image Representation, Vol. 10 (1999) 1-23
2. Safar, M., Shahabi, C., and Sun, X.: Image Retrieval by Shape: A Comparative Study, Proc. Of the IEEE International Conference on Multimedia and Expo (I) (2000) 141-154
3. Zhang, D. and Lu, G.: Review of shape representation and description techniques. Pattern Recognition, Vol. 37 (2004) 1-19
4. Loncaric, S.: A Survey of Shape Analysis Techniques. Pattern Recognition, Vol. 31, No. 8 (1998) 983-1001
5. Rui, Y., She, A.C., and Huang, T.S.: A Modified Fourier Descriptors for Shape Matching in MARS, Image Databases and Multimedia Search, Series on Software Engineering and Knowledge Engineering, Vol. 8., World scientific Publishing, Singapore (1998) 165-180
6. Flusser, J.: Fast calculation of geometric moments of binary images. Proc. Of 22nd OAGM'98 Workshop Pattern Recognition Medical Computer Vision, Illmitz, Austria (1998) 265-274
7. Iivarinen, J. and Visa, A.:Shape Recognition of Irregular Objects. Proc. of SPIE, Vol. 2904 (1996) 25-32
8. Chang, C.C., Hwang, S.M., and Buehrer, D.J.:A Shape Recognition Scheme Based on Relative Distances of Feature Points form the Centroid. Pattern Recognition Vol. 24, No. 11 (1991) 1053-1063
9. Tang, Y.Y., Cheng, H.D., and Suen, C.Y.: Transformation-Ring-Projection(TRP) Algorithm and Its VLSI Implementation. In Character & Handwriting Recognition, Editor: PSP Wang, World Scientific Series in Computer Science. Vol. 30 (1991) 25-56

A Study on Enhanced Dynamic Signature Verification for the Embedded System

Jin Whan Kim[1], Hyuk Gyu Cho[2], and Eui Young Cha[3]

[1] School of Computer, Youngsan University, Korea
kjw@ysu.ac.kr
[2] School of Computer, Youngsan University, Korea
hgcho3@ysu.ac.kr
[3] Dept. of Computer Science, Pusan National University, Korea
eycha@pnu.edu

Abstract. This paper is a research on the dynamic signature verification of error rate which are false rejection rate and false acceptance rate, the size of signature verification engine, the size of the characteristic vectors of a signature, the ability to distinguish similar signatures, and so on. We suggest feature extraction and comparison method of the signature verification. Also, we have implemented our system with Java technology for more efficient user interfaces and various OS Platforms and embedded system.

1   Introduction

The need to be able to identify other individual human beings is fundamental to the security of the family unit and has been true since the beginning of human history. Members of a tribe needed to be able to identify other members of the tribe quickly, easily and usually from a distance. Using the remembered physical or behavioral characteristics of each member achieved this. How a person looked, what they were wearing, how they moved or combinations of these were used to authenticate the person as a member. The biometric technology allows for a greater reliability of authentication as compared with badges, card readers or password systems.

The chances of an individual losing his/her biometric information are far less the forgetting a password or losing a card. Through these types of verification, comes an increased role of responsibility, and security.

Dynamic signature verification technology is to verify the signer by calculating his writing manner, speed, angle, and the number of strokes, order, the down/up movement of pen when the signer input his signature with an electronic pen for his authentication.

Verifying yourself to a machine is the first step of most automated transaction. The desire for increasing convenience and security motivates the development of biometric techniques in order to replace keys, passwords, and smart cards. Signature verification presents four advantages unlike over other physiological biometric techniques from the point of view of adoption in the market place. First, it is a socially accepted identification method already in use in bank and credit card transaction; second, most of the new generation of portable computer, personal digital

M. De Gregorio et al. (Eds.): BVAI 2005, LNCS 3704, pp. 436–446, 2005.

assistants (PDAs) and especially smart phone use handwriting as the main input channel; third, a signature may be changed by the user, similarly to a password, while it is not possible to change fingerprints, iris or retina patterns; fourth, group users can share signature key with very simple pattern of signature unlike physiological biometric technology. That is, physiological biometric technology cannot be shared for group users.

All biometric techniques have false accepts generated by the imperfections of the classification method or by errors in the acquisition device. However, dynamic signature verification using behavioral biometric technique, compared with physiological biometric techniques such as fingerprint, face, iris or retina, have additional advantage that a forger with not-enough information about the true signature could not deceive the verification algorithm because multi-dimensional feature information of dynamic signature, that is, speed of stroke, size of signature, pressure, variable shape, pen down/up information and so on decrease the risk of accepting skilled forgeries since they are not available to the forger.

2 Dynamic Signature Verification System

DSVS, like all other biometric verification systems, involves two processing modes: registering and verifying. In the registering mode include three phases: training, testing and saving. In the training, the user provides signature samples that are used to construct a template (or prototype feature vector) representing some distinctive characteristic of his signature. In the testing, the user provides a new signature to judge authenticity of the presented sample and choose his own threshold security level for him. The performance of a verification system is generally evaluated with equal error rate (EER).

The errors of verification can be classified in two categories; False rejection rate (FRR) indicates the rate of genuine signatures rejected that is, evaluates the number of false signatures classified as real one False acceptance rate (FAR) indicates the rate of accepted forgeries that is, measures the number of genuine signatures classified as forgeries. The Equal Error Rate (EER) corresponds to the error value for which FAR is equal to FRR. These rates determine the quality of an authentication system, but the acceptable values depend on the level of security desired for a specific application.

Anyway, EER provides an estimate of the statistical performance of the algorithm, i.e., it provides an estimate of its generalization error.

3 Feature Extraction

We introduce useful feature points in our on-line signature verification system. Finding out the best method to calculate the degree of similarity is very important. The previous approach for that is to select and arrange distinctive points. For the best signature verification, it is important to reduce the range of variation of the true signature and to extend distinctiveness between the true and forgeries. Assigning the adequate weight for each feature is another important point.

The useful feature points are below:

- Speed, velocity, acceleration, pressure information
- Shape of coordinates, direction and slope between two points
- Number of pen down/up points
- Information of pen down/up movement (Fig. 1)
- Total time taken in signing
- Pen down/up time between strokes
- Number of strokes
- Total number of coordinates

Our system primarily uses directions and absolute distances (in Fig. 2) between two points for the pen down/up strokes. We know that these two features include many information of the signature that is, the shape and speed, information of strokes, elapsed time and so on with our experiment and experience.

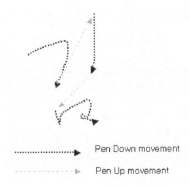

Pen Down movement

Pen Up movement

Fig. 1. Pen Up/Down movement

The feature vectors of pen down movement have values of 1 to 36 directions. And the feature vectors of pen up movement have values of 91 to 126 directions. But, distances have absolute length of value between two points as Fig. 2. All distances are defined less than 128. So, these directions and distances can be stored as byte strings in small memory.

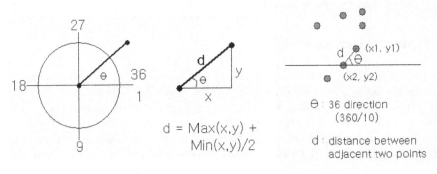

Fig. 2. Signature features of direction and distance

4 Comparison Method

One of the most important difficulties in authentication using on-line signatures is the choice of the comparison method. On-line signatures are given by a sequence of points sorted with respect to acquisition time. Since two signatures of the same person cannot be completely identical, we must make use of a measure that takes into account this variability. Indeed, two signatures cannot have exactly the same timing, besides these timing differences are not linear. Dynamic Time Warping is an interesting tool; it is a method that realizes a point-to-point correspondence. It is insensitive to small differences in the timing. Calculation distances between signatures with DTW allows to achieve a verification system more flexible, more efficient and more adaptive than the systems based on neural networks or Hidden Markov Models, as the training phase can be incremental. This aspect is very important when we must enroll our new signature along the years or new environment.

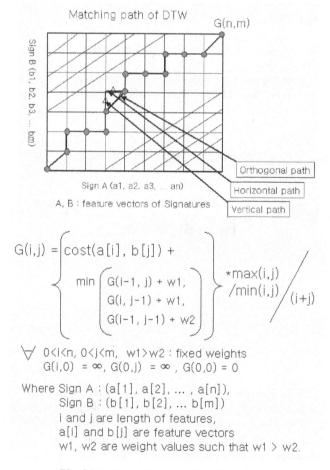

$$G(i,j) = \left\{ cost(a[i], b[j]) + \min \begin{pmatrix} G(i-1, j) + w1, \\ G(i, j-1) + w1, \\ G(i-1, j-1) + w2 \end{pmatrix} \right\} {}^{*max(i,j)} \Big/_{min(i,j)} \Big/_{(i+j)}$$

∀ 0<i<n, 0<j<m, w1>w2 : fixed weights
$G(i,0) = \infty$, $G(0,j) = \infty$, $G(0,0) = 0$

Where Sign A : (a[1], a[2], ... , a[n]),
Sign B : (b[1], b[2], ... b[m])
i and j are length of features,
a[i] and b[j] are feature vectors
w1, w2 are weight values such that w1 > w2.

Fig. 3. Method of Dynamic Time Warping

W1 is a weight value adopted in case horizontal path or vertical path, and w2 is a weight value adopted in case orthogonal path. Given two sequences $A = (a1, a2, ...,$ $an)$ and $B = (b1, b2, ..., bm)$, the distance DTW(A,B) is similar to edit distance. To calculate the DTW distance G(A,B), we can first construct an n-by-m matrix, as shown in Fig. 3. Then, we find a *path* in the matrix which starts from cell (1, 1) to cell (n,m) so that the average cumulative cost along the path is minimized. If the path passes cell (i, j), then the cell (i,j) contributes *cost*(ai, bj) to the cumulative cost. The *cost* function can be defined flexibly depending on the application, for example, *cost*(ai, bj) = $|ai-bj|$*weight. This path can be determined using dynamic programming, because the recursive equation holds: $G(i, j) = [cost(ai, bj) + min\{G(i - 1, j)+w1, G(i -1, j -1)+w2, G(i, j -1)+w1\}]*max(i,j)/min(,j)/(i+j)$. The path may goes several cells horizontally along A or vertically along B, which makes the matching between the two sequences not strictly one-one but one-many and many-one. This is the robustness that DTW provides to align sequences. Also we suggest that w1 and w2 are very important weight value for the measure of similarity in DTW.

5   Java Implementation

We provide two windows (Fig. 4 and Fig. 6) for the dynamic signature verification system. Fig. 4 is a window to save signer's signature feature vectors in remote database. First step: Signer writes his signature on the white rectangle area and then click 'Register' button. Second step: Signer writes his same signature again and then clicks 'Test&Verify' button to see recommended security level and degree of similarity in Fig. 5 between two signatures. According to the results of several times trial, the signer can choose his security level. If the signer clicks 'Save' button finally, his signature's feature vectors, security level, ResidentID and password are saved in remote sign database.

Fig. 4. Signature register   **Fig. 5.** Signature testing   **Fig. 6.** Signature verification

Above Fig. 6 is user interface window to verify the signer's authentication and 'SignView' check button is a function to display or disappear the writing signature. These interface windows for the DSVS are implemented with JAVA to support various OS platforms and anyone can test the DSVS at our web site:

(http://www.mmigroup.net/en/mmi_products_signq.php)

6 Application Fields

This technology is applicable to various areas as a more enhanced user authentication security system than existing methods such as PIN numbers, passwords, simple keys and card keys for entrance. Nowadays, mobile electronic payments and transactions are increased as well as wired Internet transactions. Personal privacy of **ubiquitous sensor network** is hot issue all over the world. Especially, **RFID (Radio Frequency Identification)** system is used widely and must be considered about the use of "selective blocking" by "blocker tags" as a way of protecting consumers from unwanted scanning of RFID tags attached to items they may be carrying or wearing. In the **ubiquitous world**, the DSVS technology for user authentication will be one of very important things.

The various application fields are as follows:

Internet (Wired / Wireless / Mobile)
-VPN (Virtual Private Network)
-Internet Banking
-Internet HTS (Home Trading System)
-Virtual University LOGIN
-EC (Electronic Commerce)
-Client/Server
-Electronic Approval
Electronic Money Transaction
-ATM (Automated Teller Machine)
-Electronic Money
-Credit Card Reader
Computer (PC, PDA, Smart-Phone, WebPad, Tablet PC, Panel PC)
-Data, Program, File Access.
-LOGIN
Business
-Safer Security
-Admittance for Building Entrance
Health Care
-Electronic Prescription
Combination with other security technology for more reliable, flexible security system
-Password, Signature, Voice, Fingerprint, Iris, Palm, Vein, DNA, Brain Wave, etc.

7 Conclusions

In conclusion, it is quite evident that biometrics is here to say as the most valuable form of not only computer-related security, but in a plethora of other forms also. Markets to be penetrated include using biometrics for passports, birth certificates, forensics, banking, ticket-less air travel, computer log-in, driving licenses, automobile ignition and unlocking, anti-terrorism, anti-theft, and to replace the archaic use of PIN and passwords. As the technologies become increasingly produced and the market fully embraces the newest forms of biometric security, biometric solutions will inevitably become cheaper and more abundant in the information systems market and therefore available to almost anybody with a need for enhanced security measures.

We have implemented the DSVS with Java based various technologies such as Java applet, Java servlet, JSP, HTML, servlet container of Resin and MySQL database. The importance of security is emphasized more and more at present, this system is applicable to the security of a computer, important document, the access restriction of network server, on-line shopping, credit card, military secret, national administrative security, internet banking, cyber trading, admittance to building, personal approval and so on. Government owes people to protect from an unsafe transaction in Internet. Also we have to pay attention to adopting the verification approval system teenagers to protect from the numerous immoral adult sites. This dynamic signature verification technology has been realized as one of the highly valued, useful and efficient technology for the security all over the world.

Descending with years, a useful bibliography is also provided for interested readers.

References

(2000 ~ 2004)

[1] J.W. Kim, H.G. Cho, E.Y. Cha, "A Study on the Dynamic Signature Verification System", *International Journal of Fuzzy Logic and Intelligent System*, vol. 4, no. 3, Dec 2004 pp. 271-276

[2] J.W. Kim, H.G. Cho, E.Y. Cha, "A Study on the Evaluation of Dynamic Signature Verification System", *IT SoC Conference 2004* pp. 583-587, Korea

[3] H. Lei, V. Govindaraju, "A Study on the Consistency of Features for On-line Signature Verification", *Joint IAPR International Workshops on Syntactical and Structural Pattern Recognition (SSPR 2004) and Statistical Pattern Recognition (SPR 2004).*

[4] M. Wirotius, J.-Y. Ramel, N. Vincent, "Selection of Points for On-Line Signature Comparison", *Ninth International Workshop on Frontiers in Handwriting Recognition (IWFHR'04)*, October 2004 pp. 503-508

[5] G. Dimauro, S. Impedovo, M. G. Lucchese, R. Modugno, G. Pirlo, "Recent Advancements in Automatic Signature Verification", *Ninth International Workshop on Frontiers in Handwriting Recognition (IWFHR'04)*, October 2004 pp. 179-184

[6] Hansheng Lei, Srinivas Palla, Venu Govindaraju, "ER²: An Intuitive Similarity Measure for On-Line Signature Verification", *Ninth International Workshop on Frontiers in Handwriting Recognition (IWFHR'04)*, October 2004 pp. 191-195

[7] Sascha Schimke, Claus Vielhauer, Jana Dittmann, "Using Adapted Levenshtein Distance for On-Line Signature Authentication", *Pattern Recognition, 17th International Conference on (ICPR'04) Volume 2*, August 2004 pp. 931-934

[8] Flor Ramirez Rioja, Mariko Nakano Miyatake, Hector Perez Meana, Karina Toscano, "Dynamics features Extraction for on-Line Signature verification", *14th International Conference on Electronics, Communications and Computers*, February 2004 pp. 156

[9] M. Munich, P. Perona, "Visual identification by signature tracking", *IEEE Trans. on Pattern Analysis and Machine Intelligence*, 2003.

[10] Alessandro Zimmer, Lee Luan Ling, "A Hybrid On/Off Line Handwritten Signature Verification System", *Seventh International Conference on Document Analysis and Recognition Volume I*, August 2003 pp. 424

[11] Mingfu Zou, Jianjun Tong, Changping Liu, Zhengliang Lou, "On-line Signature Verification Using Local Shape Analysis", *Seventh International Conference on Document Analysis and Recognition Volume I*, August 2003 pp. 314

[12] Mohammad M. Shafiei, Hamid R. Rabiee, "A New On-Line Signature Verification Algorithm Using Variable Length Segmentation and Hidden Markov Models", *Seventh International Conference on Document Analysis and Recognition Volume I*, August 2003 pp. 443

[13] A.K. Jain, F. D.Griess, S.D. Connell "On-line signature verification", *Pattern Recognition*, Vol. 35, 2002, pp.2963-2972.

[14] C. Quek, R.W. Zhou, "Antiforgery: a novel pseudo-outer product based fuzzy neural network driver signature verification system", *Pattern Recognition*, Vol. 23 , 2002, pp.1795-1816.

[15] M. Fuentes, S. Garci-Salicetti, B. Dorizzi, "On line Signature Verification: Fusion of a Hidden Markov Model and a Neural Network via a Support Machine", *Proc. of IWFHR-8*, Canada, 2002, pp.253-258.

[16] G. Dimauro, S. Impedovo, R. Modugno, G. Pirlo, L. Sarcinella, "Analysis of Stability in Hand-Written Dynamic Signatures", *Proc. IWFHR-8*, Canada, 2002, pp. 259-263.

[17] Masahiro Tanaka, Yumi Ishino, Hironori Shimada, Takashi Inoue, "DP Matching Using Kalman Filter as Pre-Processing in On-Line Signature Verification", *Eighth International Workshop on Frontiers in Handwriting Recognition (IWFHR'02)*, August 2002 pp. 502

[18] Marc Fuentes, Sonia Garcia-Salicetti, Bernadette Dorizzi, "On-Line Signature Verification: Fusion of a Hidden Markov Model and a Neural Network via a Support Vector Machine", *Eighth International Workshop on Frontiers in Handwriting Recognition (IWFHR'02)*, August 2002 pp. 253

[19] Andrea Vergara da Silva, Daniel Santana de Freitas, "Wavelet-Based Compared to Function-Based On-Line Signature Verification", *XV Brazilian Symposium on Computer Graphics and Image Processing (SIBGRAPI'02)*, October 2002 pp. 218

[20] H. S. Yoon, J. Y. Lee, H. S. Yang, "An On-Line Signature Verification System Using Hidden Markov Model in Polar Space", *Eighth International Workshop on Frontiers in Handwriting Recognition (IWFHR'02)*, August 2002 pp. 329

[21] Claus Vielhauer, Ralf Steinmetz, Astrid Mayerhofer, "Biometric Hash based on Statistical Features of Online Signatures", *16th International Conference on Pattern Recognition (ICPR'02)* Volume 1, August 2002 pp. 10123

[22] D.Sakomoto,H.Morita, T.Ohishi,Y.Komiya,T.Matsumoto, "On-line Signature Verification Algorithm Incorporating, Pen position, Pen pressure and Pen inclination trajectories", *Proc. of. 2001 IEEE international conf. Acoustics, Speed and signal processing*, Vol. 2. Page. 993-996, 2001.

[23] Taik H.Rhee,Sung J. Cho , Jin H. Kim "On-line Signature Verification Using Model-Guided Segmentation and Discriminative feature Selection for Skilled Forgeries", *Proc. Of. Sixth International conf. On Document Analysis and recognition*, page. 645-649, 2001.

[24] D. Letjman and S. George , "On-line handwritten signature verification using wavelets and back-propagation neural networks", *Proc. of ICDAR '01*, Seattle, 2001, pp. 596-598.

[25] H. Baltzakis, N. Papamarkos, "A new signature verification technique based on a two-stage neural network classifier", *Engineering Application of AI*, Vol. 14 , 2001, pp. 95-103.

[26] C. Vielhauer, R. Steinmetz, "Transitivity Based Enrollment Strategy for Signature Verification", *International Conference on Document Analysis and Recognition (ICDAR)*, 1:1263-1266, 2001

[27] K. Tanabe, M. Yoshihara, H. Kameya, S. Mori, S. Omata, T. Ito, "Automatic Signature Verification Based on the Dynamic Feature of Pressure", *Sixth International Conference on Document Analysis and Recognition (ICDAR '01)*, September 2001 pp. 1045

[28] Ma Mingming, W. S. Wijesoma and Eric Sung, "An automatic on-line signature verification system based on tree models", in *Proc of Canadian Conference on Elect and Comp. Eng.*, pp.890-894, 2000.

[29] Yue,K.W.;Wijesoma,W.S. Wijesoma, "Improved segmentation and segment association for on-line signature verification", *Systems ,Man ,and Cybernetics , 2000 IEEE International Conference on*, Volume : 4, 2000

[30] T. Ohishi, Y. Komiya, T. Matsumoto, "On-line Signature Verification using Pen-Position, Pen-Pressure and Pen Inclination trajectories", *ICPR'00*-volume 4, September 03-08,2000

[31] S. Hangai, S. Yamanaka, T. Hamanoto, "On-line signature verification based on altitude and direction of pen movement", *International Conference on Multimedia (ICME)*, 1:489-492, 2000

[32] K.W.Yue and W.S.Wijesuma, "Improved Sementation and segment Association for On-line Signature Verification", *Proc. Of. 2000 IEEE International conf. On Systems Man and Cybernetics*, Vol. 4, page. 2752-2756, 2000.

[33] R. Plamondon, Sargur N. Srihari, "On-line and Off-line Handwriting Recognition A comprehensive Survey", *IEEE transaction on patter analysis and machine intelligence*, Vol. 22,No.1, page. 63-78, January 2000

[34] L.P. Cordella, P. Foggia, C. Sansone, F. Tortorella , M. Vento, "A Cascaded Multiple Expert System for Verification", in *Multiple Classifier Systems, ed. J.Kittler and F.Roli, LNCS, Springer 2000*, pp. 330-339.

[35] V. Di Lecce, G. Dimauro, A. Guerriero, S. Impedovo, G. Pirlo, A. Salzo, "A Multi-Expert System for Dynamic Signature Verification", in *Multiple Classifier Systems, eds.J.Kittler and F.Roli, LNCS, Springer 2000*, pp.320-329.

[36] E. Newham, "Survey: Signature Verification Technologies", *Bit (2000), 8--10.*

[37] F. D. Griess, "On-line Signature Verification", *Projet Report, Michigan State University, Department of Computer Science and Engineering, 2000.*

[38] T. Wessels and C. Omlin, "A Hybrid System for Signature Verification," *Proc. South African Telecommunications Networks and Applications Conf.*, pp. 5509-5514, 2000.

(1990 ~ 1999)

[39] V. Di Lecce, A. Guerriero, G. Dimauro, S. Impedovo, G. Pirlo, A. Salzo, L. Sarcinella, "Selection of Reference Signatures for Automatic Signature Verification", *Fifth International Conference on Document Analysis and Recognition*, September 1999 pp. 597

[40] X.H. Xiao, G. Leedham, "Signature Verification by Neural Networks with Selective Attention", *Applied Intelligence*, Vol .11, 1999, pp. 213-223.

[41] M. E. Munich, P. Perona, "Continuous Dynamic Time Warping for Translation Invariant Curve Alignment with Applications to Signature Verification", *(1999), Available at: http://citeseer.nj.nec.com/munich99continuous.html.*

[42] J.G.A. Dolfing, E.H.L. Aarts and J.J.G. M., "On-line signature verification with hidden markov models",In *Proceedings of the International Conference on Pattern Recognition*, pages 1309, August 1998.

[43] Nai-Jen Cheng ; Chi-Jain Wen ; Hon-Fai Yau ; David Hwang Liu; Kuei Liu ; Kun-Chi Cheng ,Bor-Shenn Jeng, "Online Chinese signature verification with mixture of experts, Security Technology", *Proceeding . ,32nd Annual 1998 International Carnahan Conference* on ,1998.

[44] T. Ruggles, "Comparison of Biometric Techniques", *Technical Report for The Biometric Consulting Group (1998), Available at: http://biometricconsulting.com/bio.htm*

[45] V. DiLecce, G. Dimauro, A. Guerriero, S. Impedovo, G. Pirlo, A. Salzo, L. Sarcinella, "Selection of Reference Signatures for Automatic Signature Verification", *Proc.ICDAR'99*,India, 1999, pp. 597-600.

[46] R. Kashi, J. Hu, W.L. Nelson, W. Turin, "A Hidden Markov Model approach to on-line handwritten signature verification", *IJDAR*, Vol. 1, 1998, pp. 102-109.

[47] Q.-Z.Wu, S.-Y.Lee, I.-C.Jou, "On-line signature verification based on logarithmic spectrum", *Pattern Recognition*, Vol. 31, No. 12, 1998, pp. 1865-1871.

[48] B. Wirtz, "Technical Evaluation of Biometric Systems", *Proc. of ACCU '98*, Hong Kong, 1998.

[49] C. Schmidt, K.-F. Kraiss, "Establishment of personalized templates for automatic signature verification", *Proc. ICDAR '97*, IEEE Press, pp. 263-267.

[50] Q.Z. Wu, S.-Y. Lee, I-C. Jou, "On-line signature verification based on split-and-merge matching mechanism", *Pattern Recognition Letters*, Vol. 18, 1997, pp. 665-673.

[51] V.S. Nalwa., "Automatic on-line signature verification", *Proceedings of the IEEE*, 85(2), pp. 213-239, 1997.

[52] R. Plamondon, "A Kinematic Theory of Rapid Human Movements: Part III: Kinetic Outcomes", *Biological Cybernetics*, Jan. 1997.

[53] R. Bajaj, S.Chaudhury, "Signature Verification using multiple neural classifiers", *Pattern Recogn.*, Vol.30, No.1, 1997, pp.1-7.

[54] B. Wirtz, "Average Prototypes for Stroke-Based Signature Verification", *Proc. ICDAR '97*, IEEE Press, pp. 268-272.

[55] R. Sabourin, G. Genesi, F. Preteux, "Off-line Signature Verification by Local Granulometric Size Distributions", *IEEE TPAMI*, Vol. 19, n. 9, 1997, pp. 976-988.

[56] K. Huang and H. Yan, "Off-line signature verification based on geometric feature extraction and neural network classification", *Pattern Recognition*,Vol. 30, No.1, 1997, pp.9-17.

[57] G. Dimauro, S. Impedovo, G. Pirlo, A. Salzo, "A multi-expert signature verification system for bankcheck processing", *IJPRAI*, Vol. 11, n. 5, 1997, pp. 827-844.

[58] L.L.Lee, T.Berger, E. Aviczer, "Reliable On-Line Human Signature Verification Systems", *IEEE T-PAMI*, Vol. 18, n. 6, 1996, pp. 643-647.

[59] R. Martens, L. Claesen., "On-line signature verification by dynamic time-warping", *The 13th International Conference on Pattern Recognition*, pp. 38-42, 1996.

[60] L. Lee, T. Berger, E. Aviczer, "Reliable On-Line Human Signature Verification Systems", *IEEE Trans. on Pattern Analysis and Machine Intelligence*, pp. 643-647, 1996.

[61] J. Kim, J.R. Yu, S.H. Kim, "Learning of prototypes and decision boundaries for a verification problem having only positive samples", *Pattern Recognition*, Vol.17,1996, pp.691-697.

[62] Y.Xuhua, T. Furuhashi, K.Obata, Y. Uchikawa, "Selection of features for signature verification using the genetic algorithm", *Computers ind. Eng.*, Vol. 30, No. 4, 1996, pp. 1037-1045.

[63] Y. Qi, B.R. Hunt, "A multiresolution approach to computer verification of handwritten signatures", *IEEE Trans. Image Processing*, Vol. 4, n. 6, 1995, pp. 870-874.

[64] R. Plamondon, "A Kinematic Theory of Rapid Human Movements: Part I: Movement Representation and generation", *Biological Cybernetics*, vol. 72, 4, 1995, pp. 295-307.

[65] R. Plamondon, "A Kinematic Theory of Rapid Human Movements: Part II: Movement Time and Control", *Biological Cybernetics*, vol. 72, 4, 1995, pp. 309-320.

[66] Wirtz B., "Stroke-based Time Warping for Signature Verification",*Proc.ICDAR* 1995,IEEE Press, pp. 179-182.

[67] L. Yang, B. K. Widjaja, R. Prasad, "Application of hidden Markov models for signature verification", *Pattern Recognition*, Vol.28, No. 2, pp.161-170, 1995.

[68] W. Nelson, W. Turin and T. Hastie, "Statistical methods for online signature verification",*IJPRAI*,v.8,n.3,1994, pp.749-770.

[69] R. Sabourin, R. Plamondon, L. Beaumier, "Structural interpretation of handwritten signature images", *IJPRAI*, Vol. 8, 3, 1994, pp.709-748.

[70] H. Cardot, M. Revenu, B. Victorri, M.-J. Revillet, "A Static Signature Verification System based on a cooperative Neural Networks Architecture", *IJPRAI*, Vol. 8, n. 3, 1994, pp. 679-692.

[71] G. Pirlo, "Algorithms for Signature Verification", in *Fundamentals in Handwriting Recognition*, ed. S. Impedovo, Springer Verlag, Berlin, 1994, pp. 433-454.

[72] R. Plamondon (ed.), "Progress in Automatic Signature Verification", *World Scientific Publ.*, Singapore, 1994.

[73] F. Leclerc, R.Plamondon, "Automatic signature verification: The state of the art ..1989-1993",*IJPRAI*, V.8, n.3, 1994,pp. 643-660.

[74] G. Dimauro, S. Impedovo, G. Pirlo, "Component-oriented algorithms for signature verification", *IJPRAI*, Vol. 8, n. 3, 1994, pp. 771-794.

[75] G. Dimauro, S. Impedovo, G. Pirlo, "Off-line Signature Verification through Fundamental Strokes Analysis", in *Progress in Image Analysis and Processing III*, ed. S.Impedovo, World Scientific Publ., 1994, pp.331-337.

[76] Q.Z. Wu, I-C. Jou, B.-S. Jeng, N.-J. Cheng, S.-S. Huang, P.-Y. Ting, D.-M. Shieh, C.-J. Wen, "On the Distorsion Measurement of On-Line Signature verification", *Proc. of IWFHR IV*, Taipei, Taiwan, Dec. 7-9, 1994, pp. 347-353.

[77] G. Congedo, G. Dimauro, S. Impedovo, G. Pirlo, "A new methodology for the measurement of local stability in dynamic signatures", *Proc. IWFHR IV*, Taiwan, 1994, pp. 135- 144.

[78] J.J. Brault, R. Plamondon, "A complexity Measure of Handwritten Curves: Modeling of Dynamic Signature Forgery", *IEEE T-SMC*, Vol. 23, no. 2, 1993, pp. 400-413.

[79] L.Yang, B.K.Widjaja, R.Prasad, "On-line signature verification applying hidden Markov models", in *Proc. of 8th Scandinavian Conf. Image Analysis*, Tromso, 1993, pp. 1311-1316.

[80] J.J. Brault and R. Plamondon, "Segmenting handwritten signatures at their perceptually important points", *IEEE T-PAMI*, Vol. 15, n. 9, 1993, pp. 953-957.

[81] G.Dimauro, S.Impedovo and G.Pirlo, "On-line Signature Verification by a Dynamic Segmentation Technique", in *Proc. 3th IWFHR*, Buffalo, May 1993, pp. 262-271.

[82] G.Dimauro, S.Impedovo, G.Pirlo, "A stroke-oriented approach to signature verification", in From *Pixels to Features III - Frontiers in Handwriting Recognition*, S. Impedovo and J.C.Simon eds., Elsevier Publ., 1992, pp. 371-384.

[83] R. Sabourin and J.P. Drouhard, "Off-line signature verification using directional PDF and neural networks", in *Proc. of 11th ICPR*, 1992, pp.321-325.

[84] L.Y. Tseng and T.H. Huang, "An on-line Chinese signature verification scheme based on the ART1 neural network", *Proc. of Int. J. Conf. on NN*, Maryland, 1992, pp. 624-630.

Spatio-temporal Attention Mechanism for More Complex Analysis to Track Multiple Objects

Heungkyu Lee[1] and Hanseok Ko[2]

[1] Dept. of Visual Information Processing
[2] Dept. of Electronics and Computer Engineering,
Korea University, Seoul, Korea
hklee@ispl.korea.ac.kr, hsko@korea.ac.kr

Abstract. This paper proposes the spatio-temporal attentive mechanism to track multiple objects, even occluded objects. The proposed system provides an efficient method for more complex analysis using data association in spatially attentive window and predicted temporal location. When multiple objects are moving or occluded between them in areas of visual field, a simultaneous tracking of multiple objects tends to fail. This is due to the fact that incompletely estimated feature vectors such as location, color, velocity, and acceleration of a target provide ambiguous and missing information. In addition, partial information cannot render the complete information unless temporal consistency is considered when objects are occluded between them or they are hidden in obstacles. Thus, the spatially and temporally considered mechanism using occlusion activity detection and object association with partial probability model is proposed. For an experimental evaluation, the proposed algorithms are applied to real image sequences. Experimental results in a natural environment demonstrate the usefulness of the proposed method.

1 Introduction

Automatic visual tracking has a challenging problem to track multiple objects reliably. A disadvantage is derived from complex scene and bad noise conditions for enhancing an image or representing a scene. To resolve this problem, the human visual system (HVS) shows different color perception sensitivity according to the color distribution and attention to a particular location in the scene [1][2]. The HVS assumes that perceptual description produces a structured representation of the visual field at several levels of spatial scale, and the selection process access the visual short-term memory (VSTM) on the basis of the matching between perceived descriptions and internal template. This assumption provides the factors and possibility to handle and describe the composite scene using recently captured information and predictable information of near future. For example, in the monitoring and visual surveillance of human activity, this requires complex tracking algorithms because of the unpredictable situations which occur whenever multiple peoples are moving, stopping, hiding behind obstacles and interacting with each other [3][5].

Thus, we propose to address these issues by exploiting spatio-temporal attentive mechanism in terms of the human visual system [1]. In pre-attentive mode, motion

M. De Gregorio et al. (Eds.): BVAI 2005, LNCS 3704, pp. 447–456, 2005.

detection is performed using time difference method between background model and currently captured image. And then, in attentive mode, selective attention mechanism that performs the local feature analysis (LFA) is applied to an attention window that includes complex scenes such as occluded moving objects, obstacles, and partial object information of interests. In previous work [5], the limitation of some multi-target tracking algorithm using the JPDA is not specified in occlusion time because they does not refer necessary condition for constructing the validation matrix in JPDA filter. This assumes that a moving blob can have only one source, and no more than one moving blob can originate from one person [6]. Thus, accurate position of each object even in the occlusion time should be recomputed. To do this, our proposed occlusion predictor using temporal attention enables to re-compute the semi-accurate position at the predicted position. In addition, general Kalman tracking algorithm has only an iterative innovation and prediction procedure to pursue a target trajectory, while we perform the occlusion reasoning procedure by comparing region occupancy in predicted position as an extra task with iterative innovation and prediction. To identify and associate an occluded target for occlusion reasoning, partial information of moving object can be used to search the overlapping region of occluded object in attention window. Thus, we propose the occlusion activity detection algorithm and object association method using successive elimination algorithm (SEA) [4] with partial probability model in spatio-temporal attentive mechanism.

The content of this paper is as follows. In Section 2, we propose the spatio-temporal attention mechanism to track multi-targets reliably. In Section 3, we show the result and analysis of multi-target tracking using the proposed method. Finally, concluding remarks are presented in Section 4.

2   Spatio-temporal Attention for Multi-target Tracking

We assume that the moving blobs from image sequences is computed in the stage of pre-attentive mode using time difference between adaptive background model and currently captured image, and data alignment is applied to image coordinates. Then, spatially sensed region is labeled with attention windows that describes a set of minimum bounding rectangles (MBR) employing "object range" and "validation region", as a means to represent the position, size and region of a target for describing the accuracy bound and range. From this, feature selection is followed.

2.1   Feature Selection

Each feature sets describing multiple objects is integrated into a set of feature map. This feature map is used for visual search process to associate each blob with a real target. In this paper, color, location, velocity, and acceleration are used to describe object shape and model the kinematics of moving objects [6].

Let $o = [o_1, o_2, ..., o_M]$ denote the set of objects to track, φ denotes the movement directions for object o_i and $x=[x_i , y_i]^T$ denote the vector of points of center corresponding to o_i , with $v=[\dot{x}_i, \dot{y}_i]^T$,where $\dot{x}_i$ and $\dot{y}_i$ denote the derivative of x_i and y_i

with respect to t, respectively. First, center points of moving objects are computed, and then movement directions are computed using motion vectors extracted by the optical flow method [7]. To obtain the movement directions of objects, we compute the direction of motion vector for each pixel. The direction φ of the vector is defined and computed using the Lucas-Kanade tracking equation [8] as follows:

$$\varphi(rad) = angle(\frac{v_y}{v_x}) \qquad 0 \le \varphi < 2\pi \tag{1}$$

$$= \{\varphi \mid \sin\varphi = v_y/\| v \|\} \cap \{\varphi \mid \cos\varphi = v_x/\| v \|\} \cap \{\varphi \mid \tan\varphi = v_y/v_x\}$$

where v_x and v_y are motion vectors for x and y direction respectively, and $\| v \| = \sqrt{v_x^2 + v_y^2}$. From Equation (1), we know $\dot{x} = \|v\|\cos\varphi$ and $\dot{y} = \|v\|\sin\varphi$. The equations are differentiated with respect to t as follows.

$$\frac{d}{dt}\varphi = -\frac{1}{\| v \| \sin\varphi}\ddot{x} = \frac{1}{\| v \| \cos\varphi}\ddot{y} = \frac{1}{2\| v \|}(\frac{1}{\cos\varphi}\ddot{y} - \frac{1}{\sin\varphi}\ddot{x}) \tag{2}$$

Using Equations (1) and (2), the proposed system model is given by

$$\dot{s} = \Psi s + \Pi u^e + v \qquad v \sim N(0,Q) \tag{3}$$

$$\Psi = \begin{bmatrix} O_{2\times2} & I_2 & O_{2\times2} & O_{2\times1} \\ O_{2\times2} & -G^{-1}\Sigma & O_{2\times2} & O_{2\times1} \\ O_{2\times2} & O_{2\times2} & O_{2\times2} & O_{2\times1} \\ O_{1\times2} & O_{1\times2} & \frac{1}{2\| v \|}[-\csc\varphi \quad \sec\varphi] & 0 \end{bmatrix}, \Pi = \begin{bmatrix} O_{2\times2} \\ -G^{-1}I_2 \\ O_{2\times2} \\ O_{1\times2} \end{bmatrix} \tag{4}$$

where O_{mxn} is an m x n zero matrix, I_m is an m x m identity matrix and $s = [x^T, v^T, a^T \varphi]^T$ denote the system state, which is composed of center points, velocity, acceleration and direction of moving object. In the proposed method, the acceleration component in state vector is included to cope with maneuvering of object. The model assumes random acceleration with covariance Q, which accounts for changes in image velocity. As the eigenvalues of Q become larger, old measurements are given relatively low weight in the adjustment of state. This allows the system to adapt to changes in the object velocity. Since time interval Δt between one frame and next is very small, it is assumed that F is constant over the (t_k, t_{k+1}) interval of interest. The state transition matrix is simply given by

$$F_k = e^{\Psi\Delta t} = \begin{bmatrix} I_2 & I_2\Delta t & \frac{\Delta t^2}{2}I_2 & O_{2\times1} \\ O_{2\times2} & I_2 - G^{-1}\Sigma\Delta t & O_{2\times2} & O_{2\times1} \\ O_{2\times2} & O_{2\times2} & I_2 & O_{2\times1} \\ O_{1\times2} & O_{1\times2} & \frac{\Delta t}{2\| v \|}[-\csc\varphi \quad \sec\varphi] & 1 \end{bmatrix} \tag{5}$$

Let $z = [z_1, z_2, ..., z_M]$ and z_i denote the measurement vector for object o_i. In the proposed model, center points and movement directions for each object are treated as system measurements. The measurement vector satisfies:

$$z_i = Hs + w \qquad w \sim N(0,R) \tag{6}$$

$$H = \begin{bmatrix} 1 & 0 & 0 & 0 & 0 & 0 & 0 \\ 0 & 1 & 0 & 0 & 0 & 0 & 0 \\ 0 & 0 & 0 & 0 & 0 & 0 & 1 \end{bmatrix}$$

where matrix H connects the relationship between z_i and s. After all, the object kinematics model is determined by setting the appropriate parameters.

2.2 Temporal Attention Using Occlusion Activity Detection

Temporal information gives the time difference information such as time difference energy and motion. If the modeling of object movement is applied, we can predict the object movement from the LTM. Thus, we can utilize the predicted information when the multiple objects are occluded between them or hidden back to obstacles even if it is an inaccurate estimation. For doing this, occlusion activity detection algorithm is proposed. This method predicts the occlusion status of next step employing kinematics model of moving objects, and notify it for next complex analysis. Thus, this describes the temporal attention model. Then, the occlusion status is updated in current time of captured image after comparing the MBR of each object in attention window. Proposed occlusion activity detection algorithm has two-stage strategies as follows.

- STEP 1: Occlusion Prediction Stage
As shown in Figure 1, this step predicts the next center points of blobs employing the Kalman prediction [6] using equation (3) as follows:

$$\hat{S}(k+1/k) = F(k)\hat{S}(k/k) + u(k) \tag{7}$$

$$\hat{Z}(k+1/k) = H(k+1)\hat{S}(k+1/k) \tag{8}$$

where $S(k+1/k)$ is the state vector at time $k+1$ given cumulative measurements to time k, $F(k)$ is a transition matrix, and $u(k)$ is a sequence of zero-mean, white Gaussian process noise. Using the predicted center points, we can determine the redundancy of

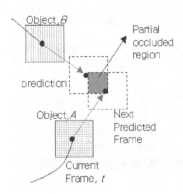

Fig. 1. Occlusion prediction method using predicted position information

objects using the intersection measure in attention window. The occlusion activity is computed by comparing if or not there is an overlapping region between MBR_i of each object in the predicted center points as follows.

$$Fg = \begin{cases} 1 & \text{if } (MBR_i \cap MBR_j) \neq \phi \\ 0 & \text{otherwise} \end{cases}, \text{where } i, j = 1,...,m \qquad (9)$$

where Fg is an occlusion alarm flag, the subscript i and j are the index of the detected target at the previous frame, and m is a number of a target. If a redundant region has occurred at the predicted position, the probability of occlusion occurrence in the next step will be increased. Therefore, the occlusion activity status is notified for next complex analysis.

- STEP 2: Update Stage of Occlusion Status
The occlusion activity status can be updated in the current frame. The first, the size of the labeled blobs is verified whether they are contained within the validation region or not. If the shape of labeled blobs is contained within the validation region, the occlusion status flag is disabled. Otherwise, we conclude that the occlusion has occurred at the region, and the occlusion status is enabled. At this time, we apply the predicted center points of the previous step to the system model and the predicted MBR is recomputed as in Figure 2. Then, the Kalman gain is computed and the measurement equation is updated.

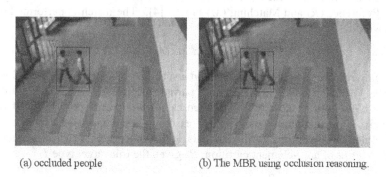

(a) occluded people   (b) The MBR using occlusion reasoning.

Fig. 2. Validation region using occlusion reasoning

2.3 Spatial Attention for Object Association

Spatial attention mechanism for more complex analysis can be applied in attention window. When the occlusion status is maintained during some periods, tracking system causes a tracking failure due to miss-association or loss of trajectories if there is no track association. For doing this, an object association using partial information in spatial attentive mode can be applied for not only decision of the position in the occlusion state, but also for the decision of the identity of a target between frames. Thus, the spatial attention mechanism considering previous object color model from LTM can be described as the process of combining a position and color information incorporating the data from a prior target model, a target dynamic model, and a feature measurement model. In addition, for the identity of the occluded blobs, the object association technique using only partial information provides the partial possibility through the association a measured object with a real target when the occlusion status is enabled.

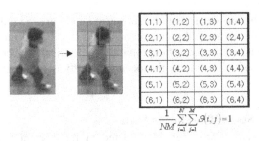

$$\frac{1}{NM}\sum_{i=1}^{N}\sum_{j=1}^{M}\vartheta(i,j)=1$$

Fig. 3. Partial probability model for object association using local feature analysis

To do this, we applied the SEA [4] for an object association between a priori target model and a feature measurement model. The object color data from LTM for the prior target model is searched. This calculates the matching relationship between the buffered data in LTM and a candidate block. If the size of a blob is $N \times N$ pixels, the search window is of size $(2N+1) \times (2N+1)$ pixels in a basis of the predicted position. The mean absolute difference (MAD) is used to measure the match between two blocks: Reference (R) and Matching (M) blocks [4]. The match is performed on attention window as follows:

$$R(x, y) - M(x, y) \le MAD(x, y) \tag{10}$$

Matching result of a hidden object behind a specific object may result in a false acceptance. A hidden object provides only partial information. Thus, we divide the reference block into N sub-blocks, and then calculate a partial probability of candidate blocks. It is an alternative evidential reasoning based approach for identity reasoning under the partial probability models. The concept of a typical sequence is defined in terms of a i, j-element partition, P_i, given the true target type T_i.

$$P_i = \{a_{11}, \dots, a_{ij} / T_i\} \tag{11}$$

We consider it as a target if the sum of probability values of a sub-window is greater than and equal to a given threshold value as follows.

$$p(P_i) = \frac{1}{NM}\sum_{i=1}^{N}\sum_{j=1}^{M}\vartheta(a_{ij}) \ge Th \tag{12}$$

The matching probability of an occluded object is computed using an equation (13) after dividing into $i \times j$ partition window as in Figure 3.

$$\vartheta(i, j) = \begin{cases} 1 & \text{if } MAD(x, y) \ge R - M(x, y) \\ 0 & \text{oterwise} \end{cases} \tag{13}$$

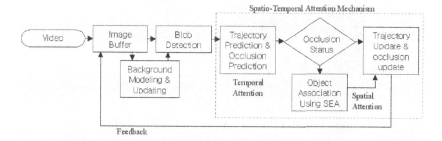

Fig. 4. Proposed system flow for multi-target tracking

Thus, we can estimate the occupancy region of the occluded objects. By using this information, the center point of an individual object is calculated again.

2.4 Multi-target Tracking Using Data Association

For multi-target tracking, the joint probabilistic data association filter (JPDA) is applied. Similarly to the PDA algorithm, the JPDA computes the probabilities of association of only the latest set of measurements $Z(k)$ to the various targets [6]. The key to the JPDA algorithm is the evaluation of the conditional probabilities of the following joint association events pertaining to the current time k.

$$\Theta = \bigcap_{j=1}^{m_k} \theta_{jt_j} \tag{14}$$

where θ_{jt} is measurement j originated from target t $(j=1,...,M_k,\ t=0,...,T)$ and m is a number of a target and subscript k is the current time. In this filter, we employ the process state transition model to differently cope with occlusion status according to the state transition mode. Seven transition modes are applied as follows. (1) A specific target enters into the scene. (2) Multiple targets enter into the scene. (3) A specific target is moving and forms a group with other targets, or just moves beside other targets or obstacles. (4) A specific target within the group leaves a group. (5) A specific target continues to move alone, or stops moving and then starts to move again. (6) Multiple targets in a group continue to move and interact between them, or stop interacting and then start to move again. (7) (8) A specific target or a group leaves a scene. The events of (1), (4), (5), and (7) can be tracked using general Kalman tracking. In addition, the events of (2), (3), (6) and (8) can be tracked reliably using predictive estimation method. Figure 4 describes the overall proposed system flow.

3   Experimental Results

The proposed scheme was tested on real image sequences to assess its capabilities for tracking multiple moving targets using spatio-temporal attention mechanism in complex road scenes. Two different road scenes with increasing complexity were considered. This system addresses the problem of occlusions in tracking multi-targets

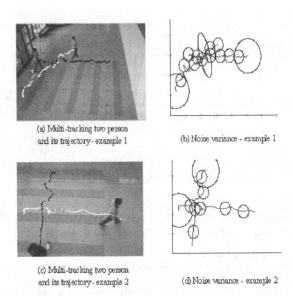

(a) Multi-tracking two person
and its trajectory- example 1

(b) Noise variance - example 1

(c) Multi-tracking two person
and its trajectory- example 2

(d) Noise variance - example 2

Fig. 5. Multi-target tracking of two persons using JPDAF: (a) and (c) show the trajectories of tracking two people. (b) and (d) show ellipses to represent noise variance.

in a known environment by employing spatio-temporal attention such as occlusion prediction and object association. The proposed system showed efficiency to multiple tracking under problems of tracking adjacent, overlapped targets and crossing targets.

Obtained images were sampled at video rate: example 1 (total 640 frames, 15 frames per seconds, and its size is 240×320) and example 2 (total 570 frames, 15 frames per seconds, and its size is 240×320) which is processed in a gray level image. In the initial value of the JPDA algorithm to track multi-targets in Figure 5, the process noise variance = 10 and the measurement noise variance = 25 are used. An occlusion state is maintained for 34, 24 frames respectively. We assumed that we know the size of a target to track within field of view. Assumed size of target is set with the following parameters: validation region is (100 pixel, 60~150 pixel) in example 1. In example 2, validation region is (100~120 pixel, 60~170 pixel). First, pre-attentive mode is performed to obtain the adaptive background model, and time difference image. An obtained image is globally thresholded, and particular region of interests is focused. At this time, attentive mode is performed. Thus, local threshold is applied to the focused region of interests, and then MBR is computed. Using obtained MBR, feature selection procedure is computed. Finally, spatio-temporal attention mechanism for multi-target tracking is applied using occlusion prediction in temporal attention mode, and object association in spatial attention mode. If the spatio-temporal mechanism is not applied to the JPDA filter, tracking failure is notified in occlusion times because the necessary condition for constructing the validation matrix is not satisfied in the JPDA filter. In addition, if we apply the general Kanman tracking filter, tracking failure or missing association is obtained in occlusion times. Thus, these general approaches cannot track multiple objects reliably.

Robustness has been evaluated mainly in terms of location accuracy and error rate of feature extraction and capability to track under occlusion in complex load scenes. The table 1 is an error rate that extracted blobs are not targets within field of view. It is computed as

$$\varepsilon = \frac{1}{N}\sum_{k=1}^{N} \frac{|N_f - N_0|}{N_0} \qquad (15)$$

where N is number of frames, N_f is number of extracted feature sets at frame k, and N_0 is number of moving objects at frame k.

In addition, we can evaluate the robustness of the object association algorithm using the RMS (Root Mean Square) error of the computed position values as in Figure 6. In example 1, the RMS error is high. This is due to the fact that the overlapping region is large. Meanwhile, Figure 6 (b) shows that the RMS error is similar with that of the non-occlusion frames. This is due to the fact that it has a small overlapping region between targets.

Table 1. Simulation results of test image sequences

	Error Rate of Feature Extraction		
Error Rate(ε)	Spatial attention is only applied.	Temporal Attention is only applied	Spatio-temporal attention is applied.
Example 1	22.341	15.8805	0.796
Example 2	7.421	6.5621	0.341

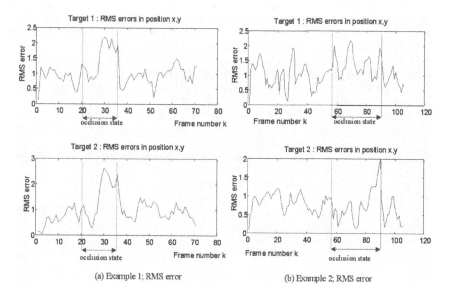

(a) Example 1; RMS error   (b) Example 2; RMS error

Fig. 6. RMS errors of test image sequences

The result of blob decision through gating and occlusion reasoning has a smallest error rate. When occlusion activity is enabled, coupled objects are isolated using predictive estimation and each of the position of the two objects is re-computed. The computed position value is inputted to the state measurement equation within a JPDA algorithm, and then proposed system tracked two people reliably.

4 Conclusions

In this paper, we proposed the spatio-temporal attention mechanism using occlusion activity detection and object association and the JPDA filter is applied to associate the relationship between moving blobs and real targets. When using the JPDA filter for multi-target tracking, the necessary condition for constructing the validation matrix should be satisfied. This filter assumes that a moving blob can have only one source, and no more than one moving blob can originate from one person. Thus, accurate position of each object even in the occlusion time should be recomputed. To do this, our proposed methods enabled to re-compute the semi-accurate position at the predicted position. Thus, the proposed method tracked multiple objects even in occlusion time, while general Kalman tracking filter resulted in a tracking failure.

Acknowledgements

This work was supported by grant No. 10012805 from the Korea Institute of Industrial Technology Evaluation & Planning Foundation.

References

[1] Virginio Cantoni, Stefano Levialdi, and Vito Roberto, "*Artificial Vision:Image description, Recognition and Communication,*" pp3-64, Academic Press, 1997.

[2] O. Stasse, Y. Kuniyoshi, G. Cheng, "Development of a Biologically inspired Real-Time Visual Attention System," LNCS, Vol .1811, pp 150-159, May 2000.

[3] S. J. McKenna, S. jabri and Z. Duric, A. Rosenfeld, H. Wechsler "Tracking Groups of people", Computer Vision and Image Understanding, pp42-56, 2000.

[4] W. Li and E. Salari, "Successive elimination algorithm for motion estimation, "IEEE Trans. Image processing. Vol 4, pp. 105-107, Jan. 1995.

[5] Rasmussen, C, Hager, G.D, "Joint probabilistic techniques for tracking multi-part objects", Computer Vision and Pattern Recognition, Proceedings. IEEE Computer Society Conference on, pp 16 -21, June 1998.

[6] Y. Bar-Shalom and X. R. Li, Multitarget-multisensor tracking: principles and techniques, YBS Press, 1995.

[7] Kollnig, Nagel, Otte, "Association of Motion Verbs with Vehicle Movements Extracted from Dense Optical Flow Fields," proc. of ECCV94, pp. 338-350, 1994.

[8] Tomasi, C. and Kanade, T., "Detection and tracking of point features," Tech. Rept. CMUCS- 91132, Pittsburgh:Carnegie Mellon University, School of Computer Science.

Stereovision Disparity Analysis by Two-Dimensional Motion Charge Map Inspired in Neurobiology

José M. López-Valles[1], Miguel A. Fernández[2], Antonio Fernández-Caballero[2], and Francisco J. Gómez[2]

[1] Universidad de Castilla-La Mancha,
Escuela Universitaria Politécnica de Cuenca, 13071 - Cuenca, Spain
JoseMaria.Lopez@uclm.es
[2] Universidad de Castilla-La Mancha,
Escuela Politécnica Superior de Albacete, 02071 - Albacete, Spain
{miki, caballer, fgomez}@info-ab.uclm.es

Abstract. Up to date several strategies of how to retrieve depth information from a sequence of images have been described. In this paper a method that is inspired in Neurobiology and that turns around the symbiosis existing between stereovision and motion is introduced. A motion representation in form of a two-dimensional motion charge map, based in the so-called permanency memories mechanism is presented. For each pair of frame of a video stereovision sequence, the method displaces the left permanency stereo-memory on the epipolar restriction basis over the right one, in order to analyze the disparities of the motion trails calculated.

1 Introduction

In general there are several strategies of how to retrieve depth information from a sequence of images, like depth from motion, depth from shading and depth from stereovision. In this paper we introduce a new method to retrieve depth based on motion and stereovision. So far, many algorithms have been developed to analyze the depth in a scene. Brown et al. [1] describe a good approximation to all of them in their survey article. In many previous works, a series of restrictions are used to approach the correspondence problem. The most usual restriction is the disparity restriction, which considers that is not probable that there exist objects very close to the camera. The scene uses to be limited to a medium distance. According to the correspondence techniques used, we may classify methods into correlation-based [2], relaxation-based [3], gradient-based [4], and feature-based [5].

In this paper a method that is inspired in Neurobiology and that turns around the symbiosis existing between stereovision and motion is introduced; motion minimizes correspondence ambiguities, and stereovision enhances motion information. This symbiosis, evident in biological systems, has been studied to get a

M. De Gregorio et al. (Eds.): BVAI 2005, LNCS 3704, pp. 457–466, 2005.

major performance in our artificial three-dimensional disparity analysis of moving non-rigid objects through stereovision. Most methods have as a common denominator that they work with static images and not with motion information, although some approaches have been introduced so far [6],[7],[8]. In this paper, we have chosen as an alternative not to use direct information from the image, but rather the one derived from motion analysis. The system proposed uses as input the motion information of the objects present in the stereo-scene, and uses this information to perform a depth analysis of the scene, through the use of a two-dimensional motion charge map.

2   Neurobiological Inspiration

When looking for inspiration in Biology for stereoscopic disparity analysis, some questions hit our attention. As explained next we have based our method in motion perception -due to micro-saccadic eye movements and ego-motion of the targets-, luminescence perception -perception of brightness rather than colour perception-, and binocular perception, present in most superior primates.

2.1   Motion Perception

The first important question is that all living beings with the capacity of seeing, only perceive objects that move relatively with respect to their retinas. This characteristic, which is evident in most mammals, is present also in superior primates and humans; but this is not as evident in this case. This is due to an illusion that we are fixing our look in a static object. Nonetheless, the perception of static objects respect to the retina is only possible thanks to the micro-saccadic movements of our eyes [9].

On the other hand, these micro-saccadic eye movements only affect in a sufficient manner the fovea region. That is why it is usual that we do not detect objects in the periphery of the visual field, if the objects have no ego-motion. The perception of a moving object in the periphery produces a reflex movement, so that the object is instantaneously centred in the visual field to be observed in a correct and detailed way [10],[11]. Motion is really a top cue in our proposal.

2.2   Luminescence Perception

Motion and stereovision perception are closely related as largely demonstrated in isoluminance experiments [12]. Isoluminant stimuli are stimuli whose luminance does not change over time; only their wavelength (colour) changes. The magnocellular pathway, which relates motion perception with the depth, is practically insensible to colours and only distinguishes among stimuli whose brightness levels are different. Experiments performed with isoluminant stimuli show that the isoluminance is a difficulty for the perception of motion and of the depth of the scene [13],[14]. In our approach motion from brightness difference is calculated, and colour is not used at all.

2.3   Binocular Perception

In relation to stereoscopic visual perception, the ocular dominance columns and the near cells and far cells are a fundamental reference [15]. But it seems that these are not the only responsible for the complete three-dimensional perception [16]. Indeed, in humans and superior primates there is no total three-dimensional perception. There is only a little margin centred on the fixation point. Outside of this margin there is double vision. Both eyes travel along the tracked object, converging and diverging in order to fuse into a single image the couple of instantaneous perspectives gotten from the object. In our proposal, for each pair of frame of a video stereovision sequence, the method displaces the left image on the epipolar restriction basis over the right one.

3   Disparity Analysis from Motion Charge Map

Starting from these neurobiological evidences, our system for the analysis of the depth of a scene integrates stereovision and motion. Our proposal is to analyze motion in the original sequences by means of the so-called permanency effect [17], and from the resulting charge maps to analyze the disparities. This is an important contribution to the traditional disparity analysis, where disparity is gotten from the image luminescence. In our approach, disparity is studied from a persistency charge measure.

3.1   Motion Charge Map

The input to our system is a pair of stereo image sequences. These sequences have been acquired by means of two cameras arranged in a parallel configuration. The central idea behind our approach is to transpose the spatially-defined problem of disparity estimation into the temporal domain and compute the disparity simultaneously with the incoming data. This can be achieved realizing that in a well-calibrated fronto-parallel camera arrangement the epipolar lines are horizontal and thereby identical to the camera scan-lines. Thus, they will capture two similar, although not exactly equal, scenes. In case the images have been acquired in a convergent configuration, horizontal epipolar lines can be obtained by image-rectification techniques [18].

The motion analysis algorithm used in this work has already been tested in applications such as moving object shape recognition in noisy environments [19],[20], moving objects classification by motion features such as velocity or acceleration [17], and in applications related to selective visual attention [21]. Motion analysis performs separately on both stereovision sequences in two phases. The first analysis phase is based in grouping neighbouring pixels that have similar grey levels in closed and connected regions in an image frame. The method used is segmentation in grey level bands. This method consists in reducing the resolution of illumination levels of the image, obtaining this way a lower number of image regions, which potentially belong to a single object in motion. Let

$B(x, y, t)$ be the grey level band associated to pixel (x, y) at time instant t, $GL(x, y, t)$ the grey level, n the number of grey level bands, and N the number of grey levels, then:

$$B(x, y, t) = \lfloor \frac{B(x, y, t - 1) \cdot n}{N} + 0.5 \rfloor \tag{1}$$

A detailed analysis of the features and performances of this segmentation method is described in [22]. Obviously, segmentation in grey level bands performs in parallel on each couple of images of the stereo sequence.

Once the objects present in the scene are approximated in a broad way, the second phase has to detect possible motions of the segmented regions. Again, motion information of both video sequences that form the stereo pair is extracted. Motion detection is obtained from image pixels change in luminosity as the video sequence goes on through time. Motion in an image segmented in grey level bands is detected through the variation of the grey level band of the pixels. Notice that it is not that important that regions neither completely adjusts to the shape of the objects, nor that at a given moment two different objects appear overlapped in a same region. Consider that the proper relative motion of the objects will force those regions belonging to a same object to move in a uniform way, and those regions that hold different objects separate in the future.

From motion detection, we now introduce a representation that may help to establish further correspondences between different motion information. This representation finds its basis in the permanency memories mechanism. Precisely, this mechanism considers the jumps of pixels between bands, and it consists in a matrix of charge accumulators. The matrix, also called motion charge map, is composed of as many units in horizontal and vertical direction as pixels there are in an image frame. This way, a position (x, y) of the image is associated to a permanency memory charge unit. Initially all accumulators are empty; that is to say, their charge is minimal. The charge in the permanency memory depends on the difference between the current and the previous images grey level band value. An accumulator detects differences $diff(x, y, t)$ between the grey level bands of a pixel in the current and the previous frame:

$$diff(x, y, t) = \begin{cases} 0, \text{ if } B(x, y, t) = B(x, y, t - 1) \\ 1, \text{ if } B(x, y, t) \neq B(x, y, t - 1) \end{cases} \tag{2}$$

When a jump between grey level bands occurs at a pixel, the charge unit (accumulator) of the permanency memory at the pixel's position - $Ch(x, y, t)$ - is completely charged (charged to the maximum charge value max). This is the way to record that motion has just been detected at this pixel. This complete charge is produced when there is a jump to superior bands as well as to inferior bands. Thus, charge units of the permanency memory are able to inform on the presence of motion of the associated pixels. After the complete charge, each unit of the permanency memory goes decrementing with time (in a frame by frame basis) down to reaching the minimum charge value min, while no motion is detected, or it is completely recharged, if motion is detected again.

This behaviour is described by means of the following formula, where again $B(x, y, t)$ is the grey level band associated to pixel (x, y) at time instant t. dec is a fixed application-dependent quantity, which is decremented to the instantaneous charge of each charge unit each time that a frame is analyzed and no motion is detected. Thus, this quantity shows the discharge velocity of the permanency memory.

$$Ch(x, y, t) = \begin{cases} max, \\ \qquad \text{if } diff(x, y, t) = 1 \\ max[Ch(x, y, t - 1) - dec, min], \\ \qquad \text{if } diff(x, y, t) = 0 \end{cases} \qquad (3)$$

Values of parameters dec, max and min have to be fixed according to the applications characteristics. Concretely, values max and min have to be chosen by taking into account that charge values will always be between them. dec defines the charge decrement interval between time instants $t - 1$ and t. Thus, notice that the two-dimensional motion charge map stores motion information as a quantified value, which may be used for several classification purposes.

Thus, obviously, the evolution of charge in space depends on the velocity of the mobile in a direction. A slow mobile causes a short charge slope, as the object's advance from pixel to pixel may last various frames. During this time elapsed all affected units are discharging. In this case, between the charge and discharge of a unit, the mobile covers a short distance. On the other hand, a quick mobile causes that various memory units charge at the same time, such that there will be many more units affected by this motion. Thus, in this second case, between the total charge and discharge of a unit of the memory the mobile covers many pixels.

Fig. 1 shows all these issues. Fig. 1a and Fig. 1b show two images of a monocular sequence. The advance of a car may be appreciated, as well as a more slight movement of a pedestrian. In Fig. 1c you may observe the effect of these moving objects on the permanence memory.

The difference between a quick object as the car, which is leaving a very long motion trail (from dark grey to white), and a pedestrian whose velocity is clearly slower and whose motion trail is nearly unappreciable with respect to the cars one, is presented. Thus, permanency memories enable representing the motion history of the frames that form the image sequence, that is to say, there is segmentation from the motion of the objects present in the scene.

Fig. 1. Motion charge map: (a) one image of a sequence, (b) same perspective after some seconds, (c) motion trails as represented on the bidimensional motion charge map

However, the dependency of the permanency memories from the segmentation in grey level bands imposes a restriction. The diminishment of the resolution in illumination levels produced by the segmentation in grey level bands does not exactly imply segmentation into objects. Some of the objects of the images are segmented into various regions, and physically distinct objects may be overlapped into a same region. Nevertheless, this issue is not that important when taking into account that our aim is to characterize motion of the objects and not their shape.

3.2   Stereovision Disparity Analysis

Motion-based segmentation into a two-dimensional motion charge map, as explained in the previous section, facilitates the correspondence analysis. Indeed, motion trails obtained through the permanency memories charge units are used to analyze the disparity between the objects in the stereo pair in a more easy and precise way. The set of all disparities between two images of a stereo pair is called the disparity map.

The retrieval of disparity information is usually a very early step in image analysis. It requires stereotyped processing where each single pixel enters the computation. In stereovision, methods based on local primitives as pixels and contours may be very efficient, but they are too much sensitive to locally ambiguous regions, such as occlusions or uniform texture regions. Methods based on areas are less sensitive to these problems, as they offer an additional support to obtain correspondences of difficult regions in a more easy and robust way, or they discard false disparities. Although methods based on areas use to be computationally very expensive, we introduce a simple area-based method with a low computational cost.

In order to explain our disparity analysis method, it is sufficient to analyze the process at the level of epipolar lines. The key idea is that a moving object causes two identical trails to appear in epipolar lines of the permanency stereo-memories. The only difference relies in their relative positions, affected by the disparity of the object at each moment.

In Fig. 2, the charge values in two corresponding superimposed epipolar lines of the memories are represented. In a parallel configuration as the one we have chosen, there will be no disparity in right and left image for objects that are in a great depth - imagine in the infinite. Nevertheless, when an object approaches to the central point of the base line, that is to say, between the two cameras, the object goes appearing more to the right on the left image and more to the left on the right image. This is precisely the disparity concept; the more close objects have a greater disparity than the more distant ones. Looking at Fig. 2 it is possible to analyze the motion of each one of the three objects present in the permanency memories from their motion trails. This initial analysis is independent of the epipolar constraint studied. You may observe that object "a", which has a long trail and has his maximum charge towards the left, is advancing to the left at a high speed. Object "b", with a shorter trail, is also

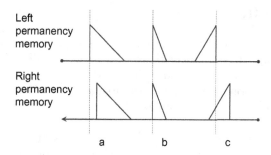

Fig. 2. Disparity by permanency memories

advancing towards the same direction but at a slower velocity. Finally, object "c", whose trail is inverted in horizontal, is moving to the right at a medium velocity, as shown by its trail.

Also from Fig. 2, but now comparing between the motion trails in both epipolar lines, disparity is analyzed. Motion trail of object "b" presents a null disparity. Therefore, we can conclude that this trail corresponds to an object that is far away from the cameras. Remember that due to our parallel cameras configuration, pixels with a null disparity are located in the infinite. Object "a" has a little greater disparity. Finally, object "c" offers the greatest disparity.

This simple example draws three main conclusions. Firstly, in order to consider two motion trails to be correspondent, it must only be checked that both are equal enough in length and in discharge direction in epipolar lines of the permanency stereo-memories. Secondly, we may affirm that, in order to analyze disparities, one possibility is to displace one epipolar line over the other one, until we get the exact point where both lines are completely superimposed. In other words, an epipolar line has to be displaced over the other until motion trails coincide. Of course, the right epipolar line can be displaced over the left or the left epipolar line over the right. When the motion trails coincide, the displacement value applied to the epipolar line is the disparity value. In third place, if we consider the representation of a mobile with a high velocity, various charge units of the permanence memories may charge simultaneously. This way, an object may correspond to various disparities. This is the reason why one single memory unit is not able to establish the disparity of an object. It is necessary to analyze the correspondence from the values of various units. The decision of all units has to validate the overall disparity value. The more efficient way to manage this is that each pixel chooses its disparity in such a way that the maximum of its neighbouring units confirm the disparity.

All these considerations tell us that the disparity analysis at epipolar line level consists in superimposing both epipolar lines with different relative displacements and in analyzing the correspondences produced in the neighbourhood of each unit. The one displacement, which produces that a maximum number of surrounding elements confirm its correspondence, demonstrates to be the more trustful disparity value.

4   Data and Results

In order to test our algorithms, a real stereo sequence is shown. We show the results of applying our algorithms to a scenario called "OutdoorZoom", downloaded from labvisione.deis.unibo.it/ smattoccia/stereo.htm. The whole sequence is 30 seconds long and has been acquired at a rate of 10 images per second. The values of the main parameters used in our test series were: $dec = 128; n = 8; min = 0; max = 255$.

Fig. 3 shows the result for some of the more representative results of applying our algorithms to the "OutdoorZoom" scenario. In row (a) the segmentation in grey level bands may be appreciated, in row (b) motion information as represented in the right permanency memory is offered, and in row (c) the final output, that is to say, the scene depth as detected by the cameras, is presented.

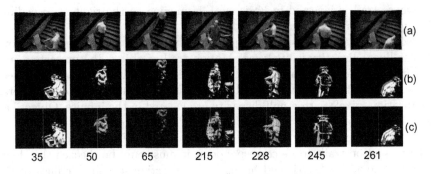

35   50   65   215   228   245   261

Fig. 3. Results for "OutdoorZoom" scenario

You may observe on Fig. 3 that light colours in row (c) means that persons are closer to the cameras. Black means there is no motion detected. The main information is available in columns (b) and (c). We may observe some details, as, for example, the following ones:

- In frame 35, a person is entering the scene on the right side, very close to the cameras. This is why, in column (c), the final output, very light grey levels appear.
- This person progressively is moving away from the cameras, in such a way that on frame 50 it is represented by intermediate grey levels.
- In frame 65, the person is now far away from the cameras. Its shape appears in dark grey values.
- Let us now focus on frame 215. A person is walking down the steps and at the same time an object is appearing on the right side of the image. It may be appreciated at the output of the system that the object is a bit lighter than the person. Thus, the object has to be closer to the cameras than the walking person.
- From frame 215 to frame 228, the pedestrian is walking horizontally (to the left). Thus, we appreciate no difference in the grey levels present in these frames.

- In frame 245, the person turns around, but there is still no difference appreciated in its depth in the scene.
- Lastly, in frame 261, we may observe the person leaving the scene on the right side, and at the output very light grey levels. This obviously means that the man is very close to the cameras.

5   Conclusions

In this paper we have introduced a new method to retrieve depth based on motion and stereovision with a clear inspiration in Neurobiology. A motion detection representation helps establishing further correspondences between different motion information. This representation bases in the permanency memories mechanism, where jumps of pixels between grey level bands are computed in a matrix of charge accumulators. Thus, for the purpose to analyze scene depth from stereo images, we have chosen the alternative not to use direct information from the image, but rather the one derived from motion analysis.

The biologically-motivated symbiosis between motion and stereovision enables getting two concrete aims. Firstly, it is possible to eliminate all static information in artificial vision systems. This is really important in dynamic systems (e.g. robotic vision), where the real important thing is the motion information in the environment. In second place, it is easier to correlate the motion information from both stereoscopic views, as motion is much more robust in eliminating ambiguities in the correspondence process.

Biological systems use simple cells to detect motion, by tuning characteristic stimuli; charging and discharging provide relative information of position and motion. In our case, the permanency effect permits to maintain the history of each movement of the scene. This effect is really simple and its results have been successfully explored [19],[20],[21],[22]. Finally, biological systems use the convergence of the eyes as a means to explore the individual's environment and to fuse the information coming from the two perspectives into the ocular dominance columns. In approach introduced, the inspiration leads to the mechanism of displacing one image over the other looking for the maximum number of corresponding elements, which provides an idea of the correspondence confidence.

Acknowledgements

This work is supported in part by the Spanish CICYT TIN2004-07661-C02-02 grant.

References

1. M.Z. Brown, D. Burschka, G.D. Hager: Advances in computational stereo. IEEE Transactions on Pattern Analysis and Machine Intelligence 25:8 (2003) 993–1008
2. R. Zabih, J. Woodfill: Non parametric local transforms for computing visual correspondence. Third European Conference on Computer Vision (1994) 150–158

3. W.E.L. Grimson: Computational experiments with a feature based stereo algorithm. IEEE Transactions on Pattern Analysis and Machine Intelligence **7** (1985) 17–34

4. I. Choi, J.-G. Yoon, Y.-B. Lee, S.I. Chien: Stereo system for tracking moving object using log-polar transformation and zero disparity filtering. 10th International Conference on Computer Analysis of Images and Patterns (2003) 182–189

5. V. Venkateswar, R. Chellappa: Hierarchical stereo and motion correspondence using feature groupings. International Journal of Computer Vision **15** (1995) 245–269

6. A.Y.K. Ho, T.C. Pong: Cooperative fusion of stereo and motion. Pattern Recognition **29**:1 (1996) 121–130

7. J. Liu, R. Skerjane: Stereo and motion correspondence in a sequence of stereo images. Signal Processing: Image Communication **5**:4 (1993) 305–318

8. G. Xu. Unification of stereo, motion and object recognition via epipolar geometry. 2nd Asian Conference on Computer Vision **I** (1995) 287–291

9. D.H. Hubel: Eye, Brain, and Vision. Scientific American Library (1995)

10. E.R. Kandel, J.H. Schwartz, T.M. Jessel: Principles of Neural Science. McGraw Hill (2000)

11. J.H. Martin: Neuroanatomy: Text and Atlas. Elsevier (1989)

12. Z.-L. Lu, L.A. Lesmes, G. Sperlingdagger: The mechanism of isoluminant chromatic motion perception. Proceedings of the National Academy of Sciences of the United States of America **96**:14 (1999) 8289–8294

13. W.H. Merigan, J.H.R. Maunsell: How parallel are the primate visual pathways? Annual Review of Neuroscience **16** (1993) 369–402

14. P.H. Schiller, N.K. Logothetis, E.R. Charles: Functions of the colour-opponent and broad-band channels of the visual system. Nature **343**:4 (1990) 68–70

15. G.F. Poggio, B. Fischer: Binocular interaction and depth sensitivity in striate and prestriate cortex of behaving rhesus monkey. Journal of Neurophysiology **40** (1977) 1392–1405

16. H.A. Mallot, H. Bideau: Binocular vergence influences the assignment of stereo correspondences. Vision Research **30** (1990) 1521–1523

17. M.A. Fernández, A. Fernández-Caballero, M.T. López, J. Mira: Length-speed ratio (LSR) as a characteristic for moving elements real-time classification. Real-Time Imaging **9** (2003) 49–59

18. O. Faugeras: Three-Dimensional Computer Vision, A Geometric Viewpoint. The MIT Press (1993)

19. A. Fernández-Caballero, M.A. Fernández, J. Mira, A.E. Delgado: Spatio-temporal shape building from image sequences using lateral interaction in accumulative computation. Pattern Recognition **36**:5 (2003) 1131–1142

20. A. Fernández-Caballero, J. Mira, M.A. Férnandez, A.E. Delgado: On motion detection through a multi-layer neural network architecture. Neural Networks **16**:2 (2003) 205–222

21. A. Fernández-Caballero, J. Mira, A.E. Delgado, M.A. Fernández: Lateral interaction in accumulative computation: A model for motion detection. Neurocomputing **50** (2003) 341–364

22. A. Fernández-Caballero, M.T. López, M.A. Fernández, J. Mira, A.E., Delgado, J.M. López-Valles: Accumulative computation method for motion features extraction in dynamic selective visual attention. 2nd International Workshop on Attention and Performance in Computational Vision, Lecture Notes in Computer Science **3368** (2004) 206–215

Image Analysis and Automatic Surface Identification by a Bi-level Multi-classifier

J.M. Martínez-Otzeta, B. Sierra, and E. Lazkano

Dept. of Computer Science and Artificial Intelligence,
University of the Basque Country, P. Manuel Lardizabal,
s/n. 20009. San Sebastián, Spain
ccbmaotj@si.ehu.es
http://www.sc.ehu.es/ccwrobot

Abstract. Combining the predictions of a set of classifiers has shown to be an effective way of creating composite classifiers that are more accurate than any of the component classifiers; we have performed a research work consisting of the design, development and experimental use of a multi-classifier system for image analysis and surface classification of the different segments that might appear on a given picture in order to help a Mobile Robot in its navigation task. The presented approach combines a number of component classifiers which are standard *machine learning* classification algorithms, using a second layer paradigm to obtain a better classification accuracy. Experimental results have been obtained using a datafile of cases that contains information about surfaces, extracted from images obtained by the robot. The classification problem consists of recognizing to which of the surfaces belongs a $n \times n$ size subimage. The accuracy obtained using the presented new approach statistically improves those obtained using standard *machine learning* methods.

Keywords: Supervised Classification, Image Analysis, Image Segmentation, Machine Learning, Stacked Generalization, Classifier Combination.

1   Introduction

Huge research has been carried out in the field of image segmentation (see [17] for a detailed introduction); more specifically, some authors have dealt with the problem of using color and texture information from images to obtain a good classification of the underlying surface [3]. Supervised image segmentation is a particular kind of supervised classification, in which the objective is to classify each image pixel in order to be able to distinct the different surface segments of the scene in the image. The information obtained from the segmentation process can be used as a first step towards a high-level processing of visual information [18,15].

But visual information is complex and it is hard to extract useful data in real-time in order to, for example, navigate in the robotics area [7]. Some attempts use optic flow techniques [4] to navigate in semi-structured environments, under the assumption that the environment has enough features to get good flow vectors.

M. De Gregorio et al. (Eds.): BVAI 2005, LNCS 3704, pp. 467–476, 2005.
© Springer-Verlag Berlin Heidelberg 2005

But flat colored surfaces with few textures are dominant in actual office-like indoor environments.

Image segmentation is a basic step to extract useful information from the global scene and the segmentation process is very dependent on the task to be performed [12].

In this paper, we present a new multi-classifier construction methodology based on the well-known stacked generalization paradigm [21,19]. Combining the predictions of a set of component classifiers has shown to yield higher accuracy than the most accurate component on a long variety of supervised classification problems [6,22]. A good review of the state of the art can be found in [5,16].

Classifier combination falls within the *supervised learning* paradigm. This task orientation assumes that we have been given a set of training examples, which are customarily represented by feature vectors. Each training example is labeled with a class target, which is a member of a finite, and usually small, set of class labels. The goal of supervised learning is to predict the class labels of examples that have not previously been seen.

We have designed a two layer classification system in which we use a set of six standard *machine learning* algorithms as first layer single classifiers, and we induce, over the predictions they made, a new model. To build this model eight different approaches have been tested at the second layer. Once the multi-classifier is constructed, and given a new case to be classified, we run every single classifier with the new case as input, and take the prediction given by the second layer paradigm as the multi-classifier predicted class. Empirical results show that this multi-classifier outperforms each of the single classifiers used independent on the classifier used in the second step.

The final objective is to obtain a reliable segmentation method for being used for robot localization. Therefore, the data used in this study has been obtained by a Pioneer 3 robot, provided with a Cannon VCC4 camera. In the datafiles used, the class corresponds to four different surfaces predominant in the environment the robot moves in: wooden doors, brick walls, blue pladour panels and tiled floor; Figure 1 shows an image of each of the surfaces.

The rest of the paper is organized as follows: The multi-classifier schemata and the process of its construction is shown in Section 2. It follows Section 3, presenting the experimental methodology used, while Section 4 is devoted to experimental results obtained applying the previous methodology to a collection

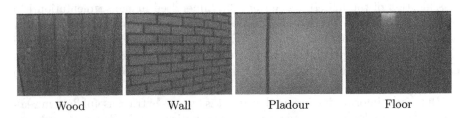

Wood   Wall   Pladour   Floor

Fig. 1. Surfaces to classify

of thirty databases of cases extracted from captured images. Finally, conclusions are presented in Section 5.

2   Multi-classifier Schemata

Stacked generalization is a framework for classifier combination in which each layer of classifiers is used to combine the predictions of the classifiers in its preceding layer [21]. At the top-most layer, a single classifier outputs the ultimate prediction. In our approach, we use a two-layer system that uses one among eight different machine learning methods as this final single classifier. The choice is based on the idea that we can assume we are making a *consensus vote system* over the predictions of the first layer single classifiers. Therefore, from the datafile obtained with the *machine learning* classifier predictions, we induce a new model according to each of the eight machine learning inducers.

Test datafile results from the first layer are used to build the training database for the second layer from which the final model for vote combination is obtained. This process is depicted in Figure 2(a). We have used six classifiers (*Table majority* [8], *Ib* [1], *C4.5* [14], *Cn2* [2], *Naive Bayes* [11] and *Oc1* [13]) for the first layer and seven classifiers (the previous six and *NBTree* [9]) for the second layer. The experiments were made using $\mathcal{MLC}$++ [10]. We have also experimented with a new method for combining the first layer models: a special voting approach presented in subsection 2.1 here below has been used as second layer eighth paradigm. Figure 2(b) draws the schemata of our stacked generalization classifier and also shows the operation mode of the multi-classifier: first the new case to be classified is analyzed by each of the single classifiers belonging to the initial layer, and then all the six predictions made are considered as predictor variables by the classification model used in the second layer; this final classifier gives the output of the whole classification system.

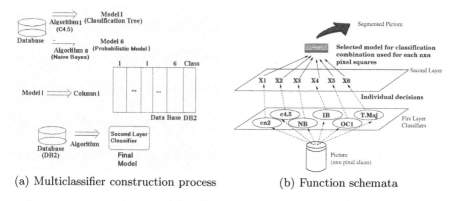

(a) Multiclassifier construction process   (b) Function schemata

Fig. 2. Multi-classifier construction process and function schemata

2.1   Voting Schema for Classifier Weighting

To obtain the final decision, we use a voting schema where each classifier's vote (decision) is weighted inversely proportional to its error rate (as obtained from the thirty experiments done). Let Er_i be the error rate of the i-th classifier; then, its weight in the decision combination is defined as:

$$W_i = 1/Er_i$$

Thereby, this schema returns as the predicted class the most voted one,

$$C = argmax_j(O_j), \text{ j in } \{floor, wall, bricks, pladour\}$$

where

$$O_j = \sum_{i=1}^{6} \begin{cases} W_i \text{ if } (C_i = j) \\ 0 \quad \text{otherwise} \end{cases}$$

In other words, given a new pattern, each first layer classifier gives a vote, function of its classification power, to its predicted class.

2.2   Multi-classifier Construction

We collected a database containing more than three million of labeled cases ($n \times n$ square pixels). In order to obtain a training datafile to be used for the machine learning inducers in the second layer, we made a random subsampling of 20,000 cases from our database and split them into three sets: A, B and C (see Figure 3). Set A is composed by 16,000 cases and set B and C by 2,000 each.

Our system builds a set of six models using six different inducers (*Table majority*, *Ib*, *C4.5*, *Cn2*, *Naive Bayes* and *Oc1*), taking A as training set. Then set B is tested against those six models, and their predictions along with the right

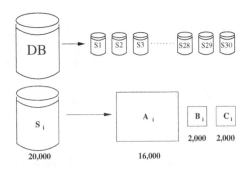

Fig. 3. Extraction of random subsamples from the global database and its decomposition into A, B and C

class are combined to form a new database. Each case in this new database has seven attributes, the first six corresponding to the predictions given by the classifiers, and the seventh element is the real class. Over this database, consisting of 2,000 cases, another machine learning inducer is run, in order to build the second layer model. Set C is then passed through the classifier to obtain the error rate, i.e. C is used for testing the new classifier. This process is made 30 times to obtain a honest validation of the proposed approach. In that way, we obtain $s_1, s_2, \cdots , s_{30}$ datafiles, and their corresponding accuracies in order to be able to draw statistically significant conclusions.

3   Experimental Methodology

We worked with a Pioneer 3 dual drive holonomous robot from ActivMedia Robotics provided with a Cannon VCC4 camera. We collected images inside the building of the Faculty of Computer Sciences, in three different zones: hall, laboratory and corridor. There was sunlight through the windows as well as light from the bulbs on the ceiling. These light conditions lead to a wide range of different values for the pixels in the image, making difficult to recognize a surface just by RGB, HSI or other color representation values.

We defined four classes, corresponding to four surfaces dominant in the environment: tiled floor, brick wall, wooden door and blue panel. The goal is to be able to discriminate among these four surfaces, so the robot could distinguish them and use this information for localization purposes (landmarks). The kind of surfaces we want to recognize are not of a uniform color, making the task difficult. The ideal situation would be to be able to label each pixel with one of the four classes we previously defined. But with just that granularity it is not possible to achieve great accuracy. Thus, our approach consists of labelling a square of $n \times n$ pixels, covering a bigger portion of the image.

To obtain the raw data we worked with, we cut slices of the images, so that just one of the four categories (tiled floor, brick wall, wooden door and blue panel) was present in each slice.

We chose square sizes of *2×2*, *3×3*, *4×4* and *5×5*. We got all the possible squares, so from a subimage of width w and height h, we obtain a total amount of $w - (k - 1) * h - (k - 1)$ squares, where k is the size of the square side. Characteristics of resulting databases are depicted in Table 1. As it can be seen, the amount and distribution of the cases into the four classes roughly maintain

Table 1. Surface distribution

Surfaces	Floor (41%)	Wall (25%)	Wooden door (23%)	Blue panel (11%)	Total (100%)
2 × 2	1,311,335	805,007	730,440	339,254	**3,186,036**
3 × 3	1,272,792	785,873	715,480	330,813	**3,104,958**
4 × 4	1,242,509	766,947	700,680	323,646	**3,033,782**
5 × 5	1,212,570	748,229	686,040	316,553	**2,963,392**

the distribution of the slices we previously chose. Notice also the huge size of the databases.

As the size of the square increases, the number of cases in the database decreases. The relative percentage of each class in each database varies slightly because of non-uniformity of slices.

4   Experimental Results

Tables 2, 3 and 4 show the average error rates of the thirty times we built the multiclassifier according to our algorithm.

Table 2 depicts the error rate of each classifier of the first layer when using set A to learn the inducer and set C to test it. In boldface is shown the minimum error rate for each square size. Here, sets A, B and C refer to the sets obtained after the random subsampling described in subsection 2.2 (Figure 3). With regard to the obtained accuracies, $Oc1$ achieves the best performance for 2×2 and 3×3 sized blocks, while for 4×4 and 5×5 square sizes, Ib outperforms any other classifier.

Table 3 is equivalent to Table 2, but here, instead of using set A to train the inducer and set C to test it, set $A \cup B$ is used for training. This is done in order to provide a fair comparison, because $A \cup B$ would be the training set used if only the first layer classifiers would be used to choose the best one. Relative results among classifiers are equal to those in Table 2, but the error rate is somewhat lower, as it would be expected, given that more cases are used to

Table 2. Error rates obtained by each individual classifier using A as training set and C as test set for each of the considered n ✗ square sizes

Classifiers	Tab-maj	Ib	C4.5	Cn2	Naive	Oc1
2 × 2	59.03 ± 1.18	15.30 ± 0.73	16.11 ± 0.81	28.63 ± 2.78	47.80 ± 1.24	**13.96 ± 0.93**
3 × 3	58.69 ± 1.08	14.37 ± 1.20	16.82 ± 1.11	30.02 ± 1.90	47.62 ± 1.06	**14.11 ± 0.80**
4 × 4	58.65 ± 1.18	**13.75 ± 0.83**	17.05 ± 0.94	30.63 ± 1.97	47.73 ± 1.14	14.24 ± 0.80
5 × 5	58.77 ± 1.26	**12.85 ± 0.53**	16.93 ± 0.94	30.65 ± 2.24	47.74 ± 1.10	14.23 ± 0.80

Table 3. Error rates obtained using $A \cup B$ as training set and C as test set

Classifiers	Tab-maj	Ib	C4.5	Cn2	Naive	Oc1
2 × 2	59.01 ± 1.19	15.13 ± 0.75	15.70 ± 0.74	28.30 ± 2.58	47.81 ± 1.23	**13.72 ± 0.77**
3 × 3	58.69 ± 1.08	14.13 ± 1.17	16.30 ± 0.96	29.86 ± 2.36	47.61 ± 1.06	**13.99 ± 0.80**
4 × 4	58.65 ± 1.18	**13.44 ± 0.81**	16.80 ± 0.68	29.92 ± 2.27	47.75 ± 1.21	13.94 ± 0.75
5 × 5	58.76 ± 1.26	**12.62 ± 0.51**	16.74 ± 0.91	30.64 ± 1.88	47.83 ± 1.06	13.89 ± 0.84

Table 4. Bi-layer classifier. Error rates obtained using A to learn the first layer, B to construct the database used for the second layer model induction, and C as test set.

Classif	Tab-maj	Ib	C4.5	Cn2	Naive	Nbtree	Oc1	Voting
2 × 2	14.54 ± 0.96	13.53 ± 0.95	13.71 ± 0.97	13.27 ± 1.04	13.02 ± 0.89	**12.97 ± 0.90**	13.58 ± 1.12	13.01 ± 0.83
3 × 3	14.47 ± 1.43	13.31 ± 1.28	13.46 ± 1.28	13.16 ± 1.20	12.93 ± 1.04	12.90 ± 1.04	13.47 ± 1.28	**12.71 ± 1.11**
4 × 4	14.15 ± 1.00	13.09 ± 0.91	13.24 ± 0.94	12.79 ± 0.91	12.58 ± 0.61	12.52 ± 0.62	13.26 ± 0.93	**12.50 ± 0.71**
5 × 5	13.59 ± 0.82	12.43 ± 0.83	12.58 ± 0.76	12.33 ± 0.93	12.14 ± 0.86	**12.07 ± 0.85**	12.49 ± 0.81	12.10 ± 0.88

train the inducers. As the size of square grows, the error rate becomes smaller, with just one exception in Table 2, where the error rate associated to the 3×3 case is bigger than in the 2×2 case.

Experiments show how classifiers induced using $Oc1$ and Ib algorithms perform the best in the first layer. For bigger values of the square size, Ib outperforms $Oc1$.

Table 4 shows the performance of the bi-layer classifier described in the previous section. We use the sets A and B to learn the two layers (A to learn the first layer and B to learn the second layer) and C as test set. $Nbtree$ performs the best in the databases generated using 2×2 and 5×5 square sizes, and $Voting$ in the databases corresponding to 3×3 and 4×4 square sizes. Error rates of this bi-layer classifier are smaller than first layer classifiers' ones.

We carried out a Wilcoxon signed rank test [20] to check the significance of differences among performances of one layer classifiers and two layers classifiers, with a significance level of 95%.

Table 5 shows the results of the Wilcoxon test. Each cell represents the result of the test confronting two classifiers. There, a plus sign means that the classifier labelling that row outperforms the classifier labelling the corresponding column. A minus sign means the opposite case and a equal sign means there is no significant difference at this level (95%).

The classifiers are divided into two groups: the six in the first group correspond to the case where A is used as training set (Table 2) and the six in the second group to the case where $A \cup B$ is used as training set (Table 3).

The classifiers heading rows are the classifiers used in the second layer. As we can see, every classifier in the second layer outperforms almost every classifiers in the first layer, with very few exceptions. Only *Table majority* loses against $Oc1$, while *C4.5*, *Naive*, *Nbtree* and *Voting* outperform every classifier in the first layer.

We carried out the same statistical test (Wilcoxon signed rank) to measure the relative performance of the classifiers in the second layer among themselves. *Voting* and *Nbtree* seem to be the best ones, not losing against any other one, and performing significatively better than the rest.

Table 5. Second layer vs. first layer

	\multicolumn{6}{}{(2 × 2) case}											\multicolumn{6}{}{(3 × 3) case}										
	A as training set						A ∪ B as training set						A as training set						A ∪ B as training set					
Classif	Tbm	Ib	C4.5	Cn2	Nb	Oc1	Tbm	Ib	C4.5	Cn2	Nb	Oc1	Tbm	Ib	C4.5	Cn2	Nb	Oc1	Tbm	Ib	C4.5	Cn2	Nb	Oc1
Tbm	+	+	+	+	+	-	+	+	+	+	+	-	+	=	+	+	+	-	+	=	+	+	+	-
Ib	+	+	+	+	+	+	+	+	+	+	+	+	+	+	+	+	+	+	+	+	+	+	+	+
Cn2	+	+	+	+	+	=	+	+	+	+	+	=	+	+	+	+	+	+	+	+	+	+	+	+
C4.5	+	+	+	+	+	+	+	+	+	+	+	+	+	+	+	+	+	+	+	+	+	+	+	+
Nb	+	+	+	+	+	+	+	+	+	+	+	+	+	+	+	+	+	+	+	+	+	+	+	+
Oc1	+	+	+	+	+	+	+	+	+	+	+	=	+	+	+	+	+	+	+	+	+	+	+	+
Nbtree	+	+	+	+	+	+	+	+	+	+	+	+	+	+	+	+	+	+	+	+	+	+	+	+
Voting	+	+	+	+	+	+	+	+	+	+	+	+	+	+	+	+	+	+	+	+	+	+	+	+

	\multicolumn{6}{}{(4 × 4) case}											\multicolumn{6}{}{(5 × 5) case}										
	A as training set						A ∪ B as training set						A as training set						A ∪ B as training set					
Classif	Tbm	Ib	C4.5	Cn2	Nb	Oc1	Tbm	Ib	C4.5	Cn2	Nb	Oc1	Tbm	Ib	C4.5	Cn2	Nb	Oc1	Tbm	Ib	C4.5	Cn2	Nb	Oc1
Tbm	+	-	+	+	+	=	+	-	+	+	+	+	+	-	+	+	+	+	+	-	+	+	+	+
Ib	+	+	+	+	+	+	+	+	+	+	+	+	+	+	+	+	+	+	+	=	+	+	+	+
Cn2	+	+	+	+	+	+	+	+	=	+	+	+	+	+	+	+	+	+	+	=	+	+	+	+
C4.5	+	+	+	+	+	+	+	+	+	+	+	+	+	+	+	+	+	+	+	+	+	+	+	+
Nb	+	+	+	+	+	+	+	+	+	+	+	+	+	+	+	+	+	+	+	+	+	+	+	+
Oc1	+	+	+	+	+	+	+	=	+	+	+	+	+	+	+	+	+	+	+	=	+	+	+	+
Nbtree	+	+	+	+	+	+	+	+	+	+	+	+	+	+	+	+	+	+	+	+	+	+	+	+
Voting	+	+	+	+	+	+	+	+	+	+	+	+	+	+	+	+	+	+	+	+	+	+	+	+

Table 6. Experimental results of the relative performance of second layer classifiers among themselves

Size	2 × 2			3 × 3			4 × 4			5 × 5		
Classifiers	+	-	=	+	-	=	+	-	=	+	-	=
Tab-maj	0	7	0	0	7	0	0	7	0	0	7	0
Ib	2	4	1	3	4	0	3	4	0	2	3	2
Cn2	1	5	1	1	5	1	1	5	1	1	5	1
C4.5	4	3	0	4	3	0	4	3	0	2	1	4
Nb	5	1	1	5	2	0	5	1	1	4	1	2
Nbtree	6	0	1	6	0	1	6	0	1	5	0	2
Oc1	1	4	2	1	5	1	1	5	1	1	3	3
Voting	5	0	2	6	0	1	5	0	2	5	0	2

Fig. 4. Original and segmented images

In Table 6 the results for the four databases are shown. As we can see, there is little change among these databases. In the case of *2×2* and *4×4* square sizes, *Nbtree* defeats six out of seven other classifiers, tying with the remaining (*Voting*), while *Voting* defeats five out of seven, tying with the remaining two. In the case of *3×3* and *5×5* square sizes, both classifiers (*Nbtree* and *Voting*) make the same global results: in the case of *3×3*, six wins out of seven tests and one tie; in the case of *4×4*, five wins out of seven tests and two ties. As it is obvious from this data, *Nbtree* and *Voting* tie in their particular 'match'.

Looking to the numerical results, it has to be said that the best results are obtained for the *5 × 5* pixel squares, both by *Nbtree* (12.07±0.85) and for *Voting* (12.10 ± 0.88) as showed in Table 4.

Figure 4 shows some real examples of the segmentation obtained by this procedure using a square size of *5×5* and *Voting* as second layer classifier. It has to be said that bricks and floor tiles have very similar color and therefore, the multiclassifier has problems to discriminate between those surfaces. Fortunately, other surfaces and specially wooden doors are very well segmented.

5   Conclusions and Further Work

In this paper, we develop and test a new bi-level classifier to segment indoor surfaces. Improvements over first layer classifiers are achieved, even in the case of using a very simple method to combine the predictions of the compound of classifiers: a weighted vote inversely proportional to the error rate.

A different line of research involves taking less squares from a given subimage, so that one pixel would be present in just one square. This would reduce the amount of squares to $w/k * h/k$, where w and h are the width and the height of the subimage, respectively, and k the size of the square side, speeding up the whole segmentation process. Balance between amount of squares, computation time and accuracy could be subject of further work.

We also pretend to divide a $n \times n$ square into smallest squares, so that the class assigned to the $n \times n$ square would be computed according to the classes assigned to the smaller ones.

The final goal is to integrate this multiclassifier in the robotic control architecture and test its performance under real-time constraints, to be able to use the surface recognition behavior for robot localization during navigation.

Acknowledgments

This work has been supported by the University of the Basque Country under grant 1/UPV00140.226-E-15412/2003 and by the Gipuzkoako Foru Aldundia OF-838/2004.

References

1. D. Aha, D. Kibler, and M. K. Albert. Instance-based learning algorithms. *Machine Learning*, 6:37–66, 1991.
2. P. Clark and T. Niblett. The CN2 induction algorithm. *Machine Learning*, 3:261–284, 1988.
3. Y. Deng, B. S. Manjunath, C. Kenney, M. S. Moore, and H. Shin. An efficient color representation for image retrieval. *IEEE Transactions on Image Processing*, 10(1):140–147, 2001.
4. A. Dev, B. J. A. Kröse, and F. C. A. Groen. Navigation of a mobile robot on the temporal development of the optic flow. In *Proceedings IROS'97, IEEE*, pages 558–563, 1997.
5. V. Gunes, M. Ménard, P. Loonis, and S. Petit-Renaud. Combination, cooperation and selection of classifiers: A state of the art. *International Journal of Pattern Recognition*, 17:1303–1324, 2003.
6. T. K. Ho, J. J. Hull, and S. N. Srihari. Decision combination in multiple classifier systems. *IEEE Transactions on Pattern Analysis and Machine Intelligence*, 16(1):66–75, 1994.
7. I. Horswill. *Specialization of Perceptual Processes*. PhD thesis, Massachusetts Institute of Technology, 1993.
8. R. Kohavi. The power of decision tables. In *Proceedings of the 8th European Conference on Machine Learning*, volume 912 of *LNAI*, pages 174–189, Berlin, 1995. Springer.
9. R. Kohavi. Scaling up the accuracy of Naive-Bayes classifiers: a decision-tree hybrid. In *Proceedings of the Second International Conference on Knowledge Discovery and Data Mining (KDD-96)*, pages 202–207. AAAI Press, 1996.
10. R. Kohavi, D. Sommerfield, and J. Dougherty. Data mining using $\mathcal{MLC}$++ : A machine learning library in $\mathcal{C}$++ . *International Journal on Artificial Intelligence Tools*, 6(4):537–566, 1997.

11. M. Minsky. Steps towards artificial intelligence. *Proceedings of the IRE*, 49:8–30, 1961.

12. I. Monasterio, E. Lazkano, I. Rañó, and B. Sierra. Learning to traverse doors using visual information. *Mathematics and Computers in Simulation*, 60:347–356, 2002.

13. S. K. Murthy, S. Kasif, and S. Salzberg. A system for induction of oblique decision trees. *Journal of Artificial Intelligence Research*, 2:1–32, 1994.

14. J. R. Quinlan. *C4.5: Programs for Machine Learning*. Morgan Kaufmann, 1993.

15. I. Rañó, E. Lazkano, I. Zarautz, I. Monasterio, and B. Sierra. Mobile robot navigation using color image segmentation. *Systems Science*, 4(27):97–108, 2001.

16. Fabio Roli, Josef Kittler, and Terry Windeatt, editors. *Multiple Classifier Systems, 5th International Workshop, MCS 2004, Cagliari, Italy, June 9-11, 2004, Proceedings*, volume 3077 of *Lecture Notes in Computer Science*. Springer, 2004.

17. J. C. Russ. *The Image Processing Handbook*. CRC Press, Boca Raton, FL, 2nd edition, 1995.

18. B. Sierra, I. Rañó, E. Lazkano, and U. Gisasola. Machine learning approaches for image analysis: Recognition of hand orders by a mobile robot. In *Proceedings of the Third International Conference on Enterprise Information Systems*, volume I, pages 330–335, 2001.

19. B. Sierra, N. Serrano, P. Larrañaga, E. J. Plasencia, I. Inza, J. J. Jiménez, P. Revuelta, and M. L. Mora. Using bayesian networks in the construction of a bi-level multi-classifier. A case study using intensive care unit patients data. *Artificial Intelligence in Medicine*, 22(3):233–248, 2001.

20. F. Wilcoxon. Individual comparisons by ranking methods. *Biometrics*, 1:80–83, 1945.

21. D. H. Wolpert. Stacked generalization. *Neural Networks*, 5:241–259, 1992.

22. L. Xu, A. Kryzak, and C. Y. Suen. Methods for combining multiple classifiers and their applications to handwriting recognition. *IEEE Transactions on SMC*, 22:418–435, 1992.

Real Time Virtualized Real Object Manipulation in an Augmented Reality Environment

Brahim Nini and Mohamed Batouche

Faculty of Engineering, LIRE laboratory, Vision and Computer Graphics Group,
Mentouri University, 25000 Constantine, Algeria
Tel & Fax: 213 31 61 43 46 / 63 90 10
Brahim_nini@yahoo.fr

Abstract. Graphical libraries are used usually in augmentation process in order to merge together virtual and real objects. This paper focuses on a new type of virtual objects and their visual manipulation by a user. They are the captured real objects' images and are not graphically generated. We call them virtualized real objects (VRO). They are important for cases where real objects' 3D models are not available. They are also useful to test heavy or big real objects adaptation to some places. The paper presents one foundation of an augmentation that uses VRO and a camera's auto-calibration related on a 2D pattern. In the occurrence, how real objects' images can be inserted in a sequence and how to allow their manipulation for an operation of a visual disposition.

1 Introduction

The augmentation of a scene is the addition, in real time, to the related video sequence one or several virtual objects. The objects are assumed virtual because they are visual computer generated entities added to the video flow. Their accurate registration is an important objective for the major works in this research area. This relates to the respect of some aspects in order to keep the apparent realism of the generated scene.

Scene's marks are always used for the alignment of virtual objects. They can be introduced explicitly in the scene and then used in augmentation process. In contrast, some natural characteristics of a mark-less scene can be deduced in order to serve the purposes of the application, especially for outdoor environments. The foremost solutions used without explicit marks suffer from computation time-consuming and do not allow a real time augmentation [2]. However, most solutions using an explicit mark are typical patterns constrained despite the reached real time augmentation [13].

Accurate registration of real and virtual objects is a difficult process, and to reach such augmentation, a set of problems must be solved. There are ones of algorithmic type, related to static and dynamic parameters errors cited by Azuma [11], and others related to semantic nature of the scene. Our most important objectives are to maintain the scene real aspect once augmented.

The reached realism can be improved by a possible user manipulation of inserted objects. It would differ from the objects' natural manipulation by the absence of their feeling. Virtual manipulation must preserve all physical real aspects of real objects [7].

M. De Gregorio et al. (Eds.): BVAI 2005, LNCS 3704, pp. 477–486, 2005.

It allows the user to improve the meaning of expressed ideas by a visual manner and facilitates the achievement of any particular task.

Several areas are invested by researchers [11], [12]. Medicine, maintenance [14], repairs, historical sites reconstruction [6], conception, orientation of a user in meticulous environments and many other areas are largely covered by works. The objective for the totality of these areas is to provide new means of communication and to allow the improvement of tasks achievement.

Our work can be inserted in the framework of virtual objects manipulation in a collaborative environment. According to user's objectives, she/he may be able to adjust them into a scene. These objects can be either constructed using any graphical library [1], [10] or used directly as captured real object's images related to different views and merged into captured frames. We call the former 'virtualized real objects'. To do so, we use a monitor-based display augmentation system implemented by using a video-based approach. This consists of 2D patterns added in the scene in order to serve as a reference for the registration of virtual elements. Initially, the virtual object is projected onto the pattern's detected region so as to appear in the augmented scene nearby it [13]. After that, the user will be able to move it anywhere in the scene and to orientate it according to some objectives. The used algorithm allows an acceptable visual approximation of the scene's 3D features. These last allow the projection of 3D objects in different dispositions. Although, virtualized real objects are projected as 2D images and do not need 3D characteristics. This is because of the 3D aspect is deducted visually by objects' images related to their different views.

This work's objective is to show an object anywhere without having to displace it really. For example, a commercial organization should develop a database of images related to its products and allow its customers to visualise them at target places. In that way, we have developed a platform allowing the handling of virtual objects in a network. It summarises in three translations following the pattern's coordinate system and three rotations following the object's coordinate system centred on its gravity centre. A central module provides the augmentation of the scene. It allows the sharing of virtual objects by two users. The objects' manipulation follows a simple principle of mutual exclusion. This means that processed events getting from one user's module inhibit those getting at the same time from the other. The user can handle virtual objects by using only the mouse and the keyboard. The advantage of this approach is its simplicity and the affordability of its required means [10].

To present this approach and our obtained results, the paper is divided into four more sections. The next one presents a state of the art of the augmented reality and states our work relatively to current works. The third section conveys the theoretical framework used for virtualized real objects augmentation. It presents a realized prototype through its advantages and limits. The fourth section brings out the solution used for the manipulation of virtual objects and particularly virtualised real ones in implemented platform. The last section, as conclusion, presents points not yet covered, insufficiencies and future work orientations.

2 Vision-Based Techniques Related Works

Two technologies are used to accomplish augmentation: optic and video [11]. Optical technology uses a see-through HMD device with transparent glasses. They let the user see the real world above which virtual objects are superimposed. The video technology is either an ordinary screen or a closed-view HMD which totally occludes user's eyes and in which a small screen exists. The filmed scene by HMD's cameras or independent ones is projected on the screen after having been augmented by virtual objects.

A video augmentation begins by analyzing the generated numerical scene to find its correspondence with the real world and to augment it. Several techniques are used following that the environment is prepared or not [2], [6], [11]. A prepared environment is a scene containing some known properties added explicitly. They are used in augmentation process. Our work is concerned by a prepared environment because of its simplicity, affordability and accuracy. More aver, it allows real time augmentation. It consists of adding explicitly indices or markers (2D patterns) whose form and size are known. The augmentation process loops in searching for them in each frame of the generated sequence. Once found, they will allow to auto calibrate the camera [13], to deduce the geometry of the scene and to proceed with augmentation.

Camera calibration procedure determines its intrinsic and extrinsic parameters. They allow the establishment of the relationship between what is generated in images and its position in the real environment. Intrinsic parameters represent a camera's features. Extrinsic parameters are concerned with the position and orientation information of a camera in the real world's system coordinates.

A perspective transformation is required in order to determine analytic relations allowing the projection of virtual elements. Some cameras' models are used, and the simplest and the mostly used one is the pinhole camera model (Fig. 1). It allows finding different transformations (T_o, T_c, T_i) which can convert a 3D point into 2D image space. The disadvantage of this approach is the loss of the realistic perspective.

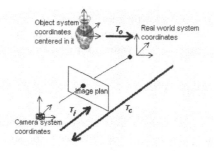

Fig. 1. Correspondence model used in augmentation

Fig. 2. Binarisation using dynamic threshold and corners detection: (from the left to the right) despite the darkness of the original image, it is possible to binarize it correctly and to detect pattern and its corners successfully

More over, virtual objects are distorted when they are observed close-by the camera video. However, other models can be used for refine cameras [9].

Extrinsic parameters constitute the transformation 'T_o'. It reflects a rotation R and a translation T to apply to each point $p_o(x_o, y_o, z_o)$ of any real or virtual object. It is called camera viewpoint. The transformation 'T_i' defines a projection from each 3D point $p(x, y, z)$ in the camera coordinates into image coordinates, such as a projection $p'(x', y', d)$, where 'd' is the focal length. Then, a transformation between world coordinates and image coordinates is possible to compute in homogeneous matrix form by using the relationship (1). M_{int} and M_{ext} are respectively intrinsic and extrinsic matrices and the matrix $M = M_{int} \cdot M_{ext}$ is called the perspective projection matrix. It is used for projection of a 3D object in a desired position in the real world [13].

$$\begin{bmatrix} x_1 \\ x_2 \\ x_3 \end{bmatrix} = M_{int} M_{ext} \begin{bmatrix} x_o \\ y_o \\ z_o \\ 1 \end{bmatrix} \quad where \quad x_1/x_3 = x' \quad and \quad x_2/x_3 = y' \tag{1}$$

The application of these concepts begins by searching for the pattern in the sequence. The process thresholds the captured frame into binary image. Dynamic thresholding method is used based on lighting scene conditions. It uses the middle value of the minimum and maximum intensity peaks of the greyscale image's histogram. The binary image is then prospected for connected black regions having four corners as shown in Fig. 2. The candidate region which returns the smallest value related to subtract with the real binary image of the pattern and respects some predetermined threshold would be the pattern's region. That allows the evaluation of homography matrix H. Using it, it is possible to proceed directly with 2D augmentation or to compute the projection matrix's terms. For the next frames of the sequence, a tracking of localized pattern's corners or bounds is made in order to update the homography matrix from frame to frame.

3   Non-synthetic Object Projection

Most researchers use virtual objects as a 3D computer generated entities by using a graphical library, such as OpenGL. They are called synthetic. They are designed and arranged according to the camera viewpoint and then projected into image space using explained concepts [1] (Fig. 3). The use of real object's images is used by some researchers in 2D augmentation. An image will then appear mapped on the desired plan in the scene. Our approach is where virtual objects reflect real objects' images according to their different viewpoints. Thus, the augmentation will simulate a 3D real object using its different views in the form of 2D images (Fig. 4). This is what we call virtualized real objects.

The challenge to insert real pictured objects is important since a novice user is not able, otherwise difficult for her/him to have a graphical model of each used object. Also, this way has an advantage of suppressing the complicated programming of 3D models related to complex real objects. For example, art objects presented for sale have no evident underlying model.

Fig. 3. Projection of synthetic object

Fig. 4. Images of real objects associated to different views

4 Visual Realism Constraints

For the purpose to project different object's views, we have to acquire related images from a spherical 3D view space. Each taken image is linked to a property indicating the camera viewpoint. Then, during augmentation session, each frame is augmented with the image related to user's request orientation. Hence, obtained visual realism of an object in its movement is bind to the number of taken images and to their qualities.

4.1 Size Adaptation

To get such augmentation visual realism, the relative real size of object and printed pattern has to be respected; otherwise, the object's apparent size will be warped and consequently, scene realism too. This aspect ratio is translated to their images' size proportion during object's projection. Fig. 5 shows this problem.

Therefore, homography projection is used on a scaled detected pattern's position. Let us assume that S_o and S_p represent respectively object and pattern measured real sizes. The object's size is considered related to a chosen reference direction view which is pictured as a reference image (Fig. 6). S_o as well as S_p must either be given as an input session in order to compute the proportion real size $P_r = S_o/S_p$. Similarly, let us assume that the extracted object region from the reference image has its size equal to S_{io} and the image size is S_i. The scale of object's region in its image is $P_i = S_{io}/S_i$. This hypothesis remains true if all object's images have similar sizes. By taking into account that the size is made up of two components, width (W) and height (H), and placing the equation into matrix form, we obtain two constants:

$$P_r = \begin{bmatrix} W_{P_r} \\ H_{P_r} \end{bmatrix} = \begin{bmatrix} W_o/W_p \\ H_o/H_p \end{bmatrix} \ and \ P_i = \begin{bmatrix} W_{P_i} \\ H_{P_i} \end{bmatrix} = \begin{bmatrix} W_{io}/W_i \\ H_{io}/H_i \end{bmatrix} \tag{2}$$

Fig. 5. On the left, the two relative images' size, on the right the real proportion of the pattern and real objects (not projected)

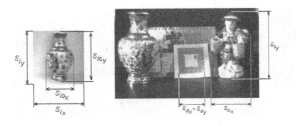

Fig. 6. Measurement principles

Fig. 7. Example of evaluated proportion in object projection

The use of these constants in a process session, each four detected corners will be scaled relatively to their estimated gravity centre $O(o_x, o_y)$. In other words, each detected point $p_i(x, y)$, where x and y are relative to frame origin, will be firstly expressed relatively to O as $p_{io}(x_o, y_o)$ and scaled using a proportion P_s. More over, the aspect ratio of the object's region in the reference image view, compared to the detected size of the pattern, remains constant, it is right to write $S_{o_s} = P_r \cdot S_{p_d}$, where S_{o_s} represents the scaled object's size to use in the current frame relatively to detected pattern's size S_{p_d}. Likewise, knowing that the aspect ratio of the object's region into the image's reference view remains constant after scaling (Fig. 7), the former should have as size, with respect to the detected pattern's size, $S_{i_s} = S_{o_s}/P_i = P_r \cdot S_{p_d}/P_i$. The current scale proportion is then expressed as $P_s = S_{i_s}/S_{p_d} = P_r/P_i$. Expressed into matrix form, we obtain:

$$P_s = \begin{bmatrix} W_s \\ H_s \end{bmatrix} = \begin{bmatrix} W_{p_r}/W_{p_i} \\ H_{p_r}/H_{p_i} \end{bmatrix} \tag{3}$$

Hence, each detected corner $p_{io}(x_o, y_o)$ will be translated to $p_{io_s}(x_{o_s}, y_{o_s})$ and expressed relatively to pattern's detected centre:

$$p_{io_s} = \begin{bmatrix} x_{o_s} \\ y_{o_s} \end{bmatrix} = \begin{bmatrix} W_s & 0 \\ 0 & H_s \end{bmatrix} \cdot \begin{bmatrix} x_o \\ y_o \end{bmatrix} \tag{4}$$

We indicate here that all these expressions are established under the hypothesis that the pattern is always being viewed front-facing the camera. If it is inclined, at least one side decreases in size due to the effect of the geometrical projection. At this time and as a primary solution, we require a square form of the pattern. Thus, the four lines connecting detected corners are evaluated. The longest one is then the closest to the camera video and will be used for the projection and aspect ratio computation. Generally, the associated errors have no effects on the visual aspect.

4.2 Projection Process

Therefore, the projection virtualised real object is done as a 2D augmentation and relatively to pattern's gravity centre. Firstly, a not oriented virtual square frame is built around the computed centre having its sides parallel to those of the image plane. Each side is scaled by using the factor P_s. After all, the selected object's image is projected after the user's manipulation requests application.

There are no possible geometrical rotations in x and y directions. The only possible one, in z direction, means the rotations in image plane. Rotations in x and y directions stand for the different real object's images to be projected.

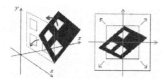

Fig. 8. VRO is mapped to the rearranged and scaled plan of the pattern's detected region front-facing the camera video

4.3 Images Choice

The images related to object's different views are taken from a spherical equidistant positions 'd' around and in direction of its gravity centre. The procedure consists in sweeping the object by fixed angles from the low towards the upper, following its horizontal axes and picturing consequent views. Each taken image forms a different view related to the camera position during its plug (Fig. 9). The reference view should have $(d, 0, 0)$ as polar coordinates. We notice that the quality of the obtained realism during the manipulation is good depending on the smallness of sweeping angle. However, a very small one would create very slow displacements despite the obtained visual aspect. On the other side, a great angle loses the manipulated object's visual realism. After tests, we found out that $\pi/9$ value gives an optimal augmentation.

Fig. 9. A sample of images related to views of an object having polar coordinates. From left to right, coordinates are: (d, 0, 0), (d, -π/4, 0), (d, -π/3, π/4), (d, -π/2, π/4).

Fig. 10. Objects' surrounding regions declared as transprente after internal region extraction

Fig. 11. Virtualized real object disposed by a user on a chair

Also, we notice that the chosen angle affects the number of images and consequently the size of the manipulated database containing them as well as the time of an image search. For example, for an angle of π/12, the total number of images to take for all views is 312. If each image size is 43.200 bytes, as an RGB bitmap 24 bits having a dimension of 120x120, the total size for images will be 13.478.400 bytes. Even so, some heuristics can be applied so as to optimize this total size. Objects having meaningless views or are symmetrical are an example. It is an open problem. Certainly, the most evident technical optimization is to use compressed images.

Each object's image is pre-processed before its storage. It consists of declaring object's external region as transparent in order to be ignored during augmentation; this means it is not projected. The pre-processing is a segmentation which delimits the internal region from the external one. This last is normally uniform. The internal region is assumed to be the object form (Fig. 10). The external one is set to white or black according to the object is whether dark or clear (Fig. 11).

5   Virtual Object Manipulation

The interest of the manipulation of virtual objects in an augmented scene is to give the possibility to place it somewhere in the scene according to the user's need and not in predefined position (Fig. 11). These adaptations consist of a set of applicable geometrical transformations to apply to an object; in the occurrence rotations and translations. The pattern's region is then used as a geometrical reference mark.

For a computer generated 3D virtual object, the theoretical detail is explained in [1]. As for virtualized real objects, rotations following x and y axes are used for image search. It must reflect the correspondent object's view when it is rotated. Their values serve as index value search expressing the current camera viewpoint. In case where the search could not match any image, the first one having the nearest coordinate parameters is used. This problem is related to initial database construction during real object's views acquisition, where the user is free to choose the value of the angle step. For example, in the acquisition of only six views: front, behind, left, right, top and down, the angle between each consecutive two views is $\pi/2$ and all searches for intermediary rotations will fail.

6 Conclusion and Perspectives

This paper presents a basis of a new method for an augmented reality application which superimposes real objects' images. We have shown how it is possible to augment a video sequence in real time. Virtual object is then simply the real object's different views. We call it: 'virtualized real object'. We have equally shown how it is possible to manipulate it and how an acceptable realism is obtained related to composition and user's different actions. The adopted principle is a video augmentation. It consists of an insertion of a planar pattern that allows us deducing the 3D aspects of the scene. This deduction gives principally the possibility of a 3D synthetic virtual objects insertion. Also, we have presented how just 2D aspects is used for augmentation of virtualized real object.

The major problem relative to scene augmentation with 3D computer generated virtual objects is their correct registration. The orientation is then to 3D modelling domain research. Virtualized real objects orient the problem of their incrustation. Proportion size of the real object and the printed pattern, search for the current image view, extraction of the object from its image and so on, are opened problems.

The manipulation of inserted objects strengthens the sentiment of the augmentation realism. For virtualized real objects orientations, it is reflected by several images linked to several views. The problem of the number of taken object's images, expecting realism in object's manipulation appearance, is an opened problem. If for a single object, the manipulated size is important, what about several objects? It is surely possible to import a number of solutions from other domains' research. The problem here is that we must remain in respect of real time augmentation constraint. It is for this objective that we have used a very simple and modest solution with low process time consuming.

In our work, some points have not been covered. The most important are related to visual aspect. They are related to virtualized real object translation following z axis. Indeed, this translation would make enlarge or narrow the appearance of the object following the perspective law. The second problem is that the view of the object does not change when the camera is moved around the scene. We notice in the same way the lack of controls giving natural effects to inserted objects. Especially, we have not studied the occlusion of real objects by virtual ones and their lighting.

Our future work is related mainly to above points and opened problems. The realistic effect relative to lighting, shading, rendering, as well as the correct occlusion of virtual objects by real ones will be equally some points of the objectives of our research. Obviously, our works make to improve current results.

References

1. Brahim Nini and Med Chaouki Batouche: Virtual Object Manipulation in Collaborative Augmented Reality Environment. IEEE ICIT December 8-10 (2004). Tunis
2. Gilles Simon and Marie-Odile Berger: Registration with a Zoom Lens Camera for Augmented Reality Applications. LORIA- INRIA Lorraine
3. Henrik Tramberend: Avocado: A Distributed Virtual Environment Framework. Bielefeld University, Doctoral thesis, Mars (2003)
4. Holger T. Regenbrecht, Michael T. Wagner: Interaction in a Collaborative Augmented Reality Environment. CHI 2002, April 20-25 (2002), Minneapolis, Minnesota, USA. ACM 1-58113-454-1/02/0004
5. Marcio S. Pinho, Doug A. Bowman, Carla M.D.S. Freitas: Cooperative Object Manipulation in Immersive Virtual Environments: Framework and Techniques. VRST'02, November 11-13 (2002), Hong Kong
6. Norbert Braun: Storytelling in Collaborative Augmented Reality Environments. WSGS'(2003), February 3-7. Pizen. CZech Republic
7. Oliver G. Staadt, Martin Näf, Edouard Lamboray, Stephan Würmlin: JAPE: A Prototyping System for Collaborative Virtual Environments. EUROGRAPHICS 2001 / A. Chalmers and T.-M. Rhyne. Volume 20 (2001), Number 3, pp. C-8–C-16
8. Pablo Alvarado, Axel Berner, Suat Akyol: Combination of high-level cues in unsupervised single image segmentation using Bayesian Belief Networks. Unknown reference
9. Peter Franz STRUM: Vision 3D non calibrée : Contribution à la reconstruction projective et étude des mouvements critiques pour l'auto-calibration. INPG Doctoral Theses (1997)
10. Raphaël Grasset, Xavier Decoret and Jean-Dominique Gascuel: Augmented Reality Collaborative Environment: Calibration and Interactive Scene Editing. VRIC, Virtual Reality International Conference, Laval Virtual (2001), May 16-18
11. R. Azuma: A Survey of Augmented Reality. Presence: Teleoperators and Virtual Environments. vol. 6, no. 4, Aug (1997), pp. 355-385
12. R. Azuma: Recent advances in Augmented Reality. 0272-1716/01/ IEEE Nov-dec (2001)
13. Shahzad Malik, Gerhard Roth, Chris McDonald: Robust 2D Tracking for Real-time Augmented Reality. In Proceedings of Vision Interface (2002), Calgary, Alberta, Canada
14. Xiao Wei Zhong, Pierre Boulanger and Nicolas D. Georganas, "Collaborative Augmented Reality: A Prototype for Industrial Training". Multimedia Communications Research Laboratory. School of Information Technology and Engineering. University of Ottawa

Dominant Plane Detection Using Optical Flow and Independent Component Analysis

Naoya Ohnishi[1] and Atsushi Imiya[2]

[1] School of Science and Technology, Chiba University,
Yayoicho 1-33, Inage-ku, Chiba, 263-8522, Japan
`ohnishi@graduate.chiba-u.jp`
[2] Institute of Media and Information Technology, Chiba University,
Yayoi-cho 1-33, Inage-ku, Chiba, 263-8522, Japan
`imiya@media.imit.chiba-u.ac.jp`

Abstract. Dominant plane is an area which occupies the largest domain in an image. Estimation of the dominant plane is an essential task for the autonomous navigation and the path planning of the mobile robot equipped with a vision system, since the robot moves on the dominant plane. In this paper, we develop an algorithm for dominant plane detection using optical flow and Independent Component Analysis(ICA). Since the optical flow field is a mixture of flows of the dominant plane and the other area, we separate the dominant plane using ICA. Using the initial data as a supervisor signal, the robot detects the dominant plane. For each image in a sequence, the dominant plane corresponds to an independent component. This relation provides us a statistical definition of the dominant plane. Experimental results using real image sequence show that our method is robust against a perturbation of the motion speed of robots.

1 Introduction

In this paper, we aim to develop an algorithm for detection of a dominant plane using the optical flow observed through a vision system mounted on a mobile robot. The dominant plane is a planar area which occupies the largest domain in the image observed by a camera. Assuming that the robot moves on the dominant plane (e.g., floors and ground areas) and avoids collision to obstacles, dominant plane detection is an essential task for the autonomous navigation of the mobile robot.

Recently, mobile robots are widely used in various environments. If these robots can move autonomously, they are of great benefit for collaboration with human beings. However, a payload of mobile robots is restricted since a limited power supply are provided to mobile robots. Therefore, autonomous mobile robots are required to use simple mechanisms and devices.

For the autonomous navigation of mobile robots, vision sensors are low cost devices and provide a simple system for the robot navigation. Stationary vision sensors are difficult to obtain range information for detection of obstacles. However, vision sensors mounted on a mobile robot can obtain an image sequence

M. De Gregorio et al. (Eds.): BVAI 2005, LNCS 3704, pp. 487–496, 2005.

since a camera/cameras mounted on the robot moves/move with the robot. The image sequence provides the motion and structure from correspondences of points on successive images [1]. Additionally, vision sensors are fundamental devices for the understanding of the environment for the robot which collaborates with human beings.

There are many methods for the detection of obstacles or planar areas using vision systems [2]. For example, the edge detection of omni and monocular camera systems [3] and the observation of landmarks [4] are the classical ones. However, since these methods are dependent on the environment around a robot, they are difficult to apply in general environments without any specified features which are used as markings and targets for motion. If a robot captures an image sequence of moving objects, the optical flow [5] [6] [7], which is the motion of the scene, is obtained for the fundamental features in order to construct environment information around the mobile robot. Additionally, the optical flow is considered as fundamental information for the obstacle detection in the context of biological data processing [8]. Therefore, the use of optical flow is an appropriate method from the viewpoint of the affinity between the robot and human being.

The obstacle detection using optical flow is proposed in [9] [10]. Enkelmann [9] proposed an obstacle-detection method using the model vectors from motion parameters. Santos-Victor and Sandini [10] also proposed an obstacle-detection algorithm for a mobile robot using the inverse projection of optical flow to ground floor, assuming that the motion of the camera system mounted on a robot is pure translation with a uniform velocity. However, even if a camera is mounted on a wheel-driven robot, the vision system does not move with uniform velocity due to mechanical errors of the robot and unevenness of the floor.

Independent Component Analysis(ICA) [11] provides a powerful method for texture analysis, since ICA extracts dominant features from textures as independent components [12][13]. Optical flow is a texture yielded on surfaces of objects in an environment observed by a moving camera. Therefore, it is possible to extract independent features from flow vectors on pixels dealing with flow vectors as textons. Consequently, we use ICA to separate the dominant plane and the other area from a sequence of images observed by moving camera.

Our algorithm is separated into two phases; learning phase and navigation phase. In the learning phase, ICA employs input values for the computation of features. In this scene, our algorithm is a statistical version of Santos-Victor's algorithm. However because of the adaption of statistical method, our algorithm is stable against a perturbation of the motion speed of robots.

2 Separation of Texture by ICA

In this section, we briefly present ICA, and we show that ICA can separate optical flow vectors in an image sequence.

ICA [11] is a statistical technique for the separation of original signals from mixture signals. Assume that the mixture signals $x_1(t)$ and $x_2(t)$ are expressed as a linear combination of the original signals $s_1(t)$ and $s_2(t)$, that is,

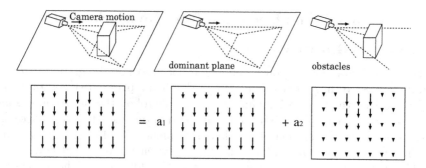

Fig. 1. Top: Example of camera displacement and the environment. Bottom-left: Optical flow observed through the moving camera. Bottom-middle: The motion field of the dominant plane. Bottom-right: The motion field of the other objects. The optical flow(bottom-right) is expressed as the linear combination of the bottom middle one and the bottom right one. a_1 and a_2 are scale coefficients.

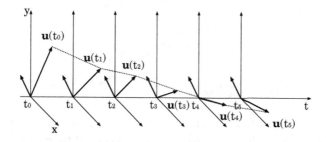

Fig. 2. Dominant vector detection in a sequence of images. $u(t_i)$ corresponds to the dominant vector which defines the dominant plane at time t_i.

$$x_1(t) = a_{11}s_1(t) + a_{12}s_2(t), \tag{1}$$
$$x_2(t) = a_{21}s_1(t) + a_{22}s_2(t), \tag{2}$$

where a_{11}, a_{12}, a_{21}, and a_{22} are weight parameters of the linear combination. Using only the recorded signals $x_1(t)$ and $x_2(t)$ as an input, ICA can estimate the original signals $s_1(t)$ and $s_2(t)$ based on the statistical properties of these signals.

We apply ICA to the optical flow observed by a camera mounted on a mobile robot for the detection of a feasible region on which the robot can move. The optical-flow field are suitable for the input signals to ICA, since the optical flow observed by the moving camera is expressed as the linear combination of the motion field of the dominant plane and the other objects, as shown in Fig. 1. Assuming that the motion field of the dominant plane and the other objects are spatially independent components, ICA enables us to detect the dominant plane on which robot can moves. For each image in a sequence, we assume that optical flow vectors in the dominant plane corresponds to an independent component. as shown in Fig. 2.

3   Dominant Plane Detection from Image Sequence

3.1   Camera Geometry

When the camera mounted on the mobile robot moves on the ground plane, we obtain successive images which include a dominant plane area and obstacles. Assuming that the camera is mounted on a mobile robot, the camera moves parallel to the dominant plane. Since the computed optical flow from the successive images describes the motion of the dominant plane and obstacles on the basis of the camera displacement, the difference between these optical flow vectors enables us to detect the dominant plane area. The difference of the optical flow is shown in Fig.3.

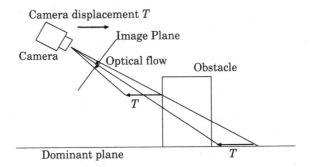

Fig. 3. The difference of the optical flow between the dominant plane and obstacles. If the camera moves in the distance T parallel to the dominant plane, optical flow vector at the obstacles area in the image plane shows that the obstacle moves in the distance T, or optical flow vector at the dominant plane area in the image plane shows that the dominant plane moves in the distance T. Therefore, the camera observes difference optical flow vector between the dominant plane and obstacles.

3.2   Learning Supervisor Signal

We capture image sequence $\hat{I}(x, y, t)$ at time t without obstacles and compute optical flow $\hat{u}(t) = (\frac{dx}{dt}, \frac{dy}{dt})$ as

$$\hat{u}(t)^\top \nabla \hat{I}(x, y, t) + \hat{I}_t = 0, \tag{3}$$

where x and y are the pixel coordinates of a image. For the detail of the computation of this equation, see references [5], [6], and [7].

After the optical flow $\hat{u}(t)$ for frame $t = 0, \ldots, n-1$ are computed, supervisor signal $\hat{u}$,

$$\hat{u} = \frac{1}{n-1} \sum_{t=0}^{n} \hat{u}(t). \tag{4}$$

is created.

3.3 Dominant Plane Detection Using ICA

We capture image sequence $I(x, y, t)$ with obstacles and compute optical flow $\boldsymbol{u}(t)$ in the same way.

The optical flow $\boldsymbol{u}(t)$ and the supervisor signal $\hat{\boldsymbol{u}}$ are used as an input signal for ICA. Setting $\boldsymbol{v}_1$ and $\boldsymbol{v}_2$ to be the output signals of ICA, $\boldsymbol{v}_1$ and $\boldsymbol{v}_2$ are ambiguity of the order of the each components. We solve this problem using the difference between the variance of the length of $\boldsymbol{v}_1$ and $\boldsymbol{v}_2$. Setting l_1 and l_2 to be the length of $\boldsymbol{v}_1$ and $\boldsymbol{v}_2$,

$$l_j = \sqrt{v_{xj}^2 + v_{yj}^2}, \quad (j = 1, 2) \tag{5}$$

where v_{xj} and v_{yj} are arrays of x and y axis components of output v_j, respectively, the variance σ_j^2 are

$$\sigma_j^2 = \frac{1}{xy} \sum_{i \in xy} (l_j(i) - \bar{l}_j)^2, \quad \bar{l}_j = \frac{1}{xy} \sum_{i \in xy} l_j(i), \tag{6}$$

where $l_j(i)$ is the ith data of the array l_j. Since the motions of the dominant plane and obstacles in the image is different, the output which expresses the obstacle-motion has larger variance than the output which expresses the dominant plane motion. Therefore, if $\sigma_1^2 > \sigma_2^2$, we detect dominant plane using output signal l as $l = l_1$, else we use output signal $l = l_2$.

Since the dominant plane occupies the largest domain in the image, we compute the distance between l and the median of l. Setting m to be the median value of the elements in the vector l, the distance $\boldsymbol{d} = (d(1), d(2), \ldots, d(xy))^\top$ is

$$d(i) = |l(i) - m|. \tag{7}$$

We detect the area on which $d(i) \approx 0$, as the dominant plane. Our algorithm is separated into two phases, say learning phase and navigation phase.

3.4 Procedure for Dominant Plane Detection

Learning phase is described as:

1. Robot moves on a plane without any obstacles in the small distance.
2. Robot captures a image $\hat{I}(u, v, t)$ of the plane.
3. Compute the optical flow $\hat{u}(t)$ between the images $\hat{I}(u, v, t)$ and $\hat{I}(u, v, t-1)$.
4. If time $t > n$, compute the supervisor signal $\hat{\boldsymbol{u}}$ using Eq.(4), else go to step 1, where n is number of images for creation of the supervisor signal.

Next, dominant plane recognition phase is described as,

1. Robot moves in the environment with obstacles in the small distance.
2. Robot captures a image $I(u, v, t)$.
3. Compute the optical flow $\boldsymbol{u}(t)$ between the images $I(u, v, t)$ and $I(u, v, t-1)$.

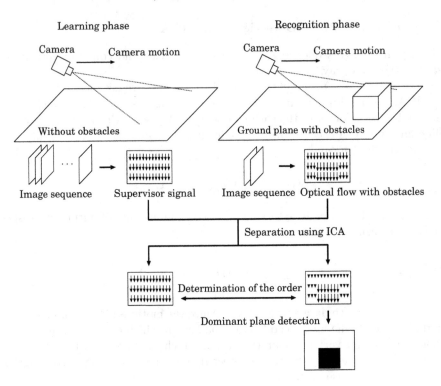

Fig. 4. Procedure for the dominant plane detection using optical flow and ICA

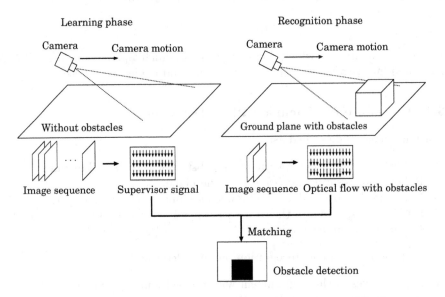

Fig. 5. Procedure for the obstacle detection using optical flow and matching

4. Input the optical flow $u(t)$ and the supervisor signal $\hat{u}$ to ICA, and output the signal v_1 and v_2.
5. Determine the output's order using the variance of output signals.
6. Detect the dominant plane using the median value of flow vector.

Figure 4 shows the procedure for dominant plane detection using optical flow and ICA. The left part of Fig.4 is learning phase and the right part of Fig.4 is recognition phase using the supervisor signal obtained in learning phase. Figure 5 shows the procedure for obstacle detection used in [8], [9], and [10]. This algorithm detects obstacles using matching operation between the flow images in database and the observed flow fields, though our algorithm separates the obstacles region using ICA.

4   Experiment

We show experiment for the dominant plane detection using the procedure in Section 3.

First, the robot equipped with a single camera moves forward with uniform velocity on the dominant plane and capture the image sequence without obstacles until $n = 20$. For the computation of optical flow, we use the Lucas-Kanade method with pyramids [14]. Using Eq.(4), we compute the supervisor signal $\hat{u}$. Figure 6 shows the computed supervisor signal $\hat{u}$.

Next, the mobile robot moves on the dominant plane toward the edge of the table, and the captured image sequence is shown in Fig.7.

In order to demonstrate that our method is robust against the non-unique velocity of the mobile robot, we compute the optical flow $u(t)$ between the image sequence $I(x, y, 0)$ and $I(x, y, t)$ $(t = 1, 2, 3)$. Computed optical flow $u(t)$ is shown in the first rows in Fig.8. The optical flow $u(t)$ and supervisor signal $\hat{u}$ are used as an input signal for fast ICA. We use the *Fast ICA package for MATLAB* [15] for the computation of ICA. The output signal $v(t)$ of ICA and the detected dominant plane are shown in the second, third, and fourth rows in Fig.8, respectively. In images of the dominant plane, the white region is the dominant plane, and the black area is the other area. The results show that

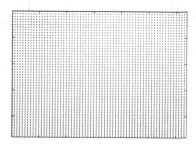

Fig. 6. Optical flow $\hat{u}$ used for the supervisor signal

Fig. 7. Image sequence $I(x,y,t)$. Starting from the left image, the image is $I(x,y,0)$, $I(x,y,1)$, $I(x,y,2)$, and $I(x,y,3)$, respectively.

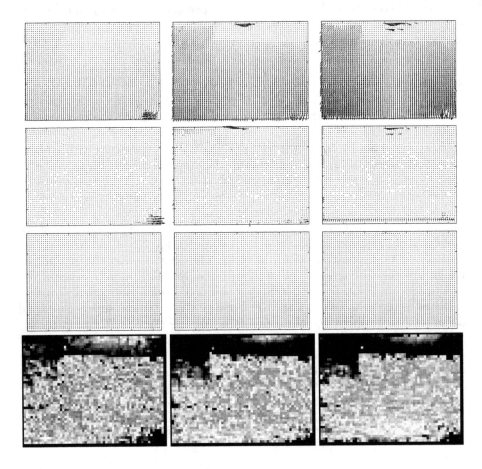

Fig. 8. The first, second, third, and fourth rows show computed optical flow $u(t)$, output signal $v_1(t)$, output signal $v_2(t)$, and image of the dominant plane $D(x,y,t)$, respectively. In the image of the dominant plane, the white areas are the dominant planes and the black areas are the obstacle areas. Starting from the left column, $t = 1, 2,$ and 3.

the dominant plane area can be correctly detected comparing with the original image of Fig.7. Furthermore, we our method is robust against the non-unique velocity of the mobile robot.

5 Conclusion

We developed an algorithm for the dominant plane detection from a sequence of images observed through a moving uncalibrated camera. The use of the ICA for the optical flow enables the robot to detect a feasible region in which robot can move without requiring camera calibration. These experimental results support the application of our method to the navigation and path planning of a mobile robot with a vision system. For each image in a sequence, the dominant plane corresponds to an independent component. This relation provides us a statistical definition of the dominant plane.

The future work is autonomous robot navigation using our algorithm of dominant plane detection. As shown in Fig. 9, if we project the dominant plane of the image plane onto the ground plane using a camera configuration, the robot detects a feasible region for a robot motion in front of the robot in an environment. Since we can obtain the sequence of the dominant plane from optical flow, the robot can move the dominant plane in a space without collision to obstacles.

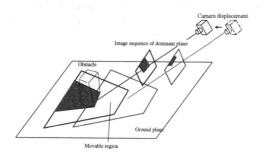

Fig. 9. Projection of the dominant plane onto the ground plane

References

1. Huang, T. S. and Netravali, A. N., Motion and structure from feature correspondences: A review, Proc. of the IEEE, **82**, 252-268, (1994).
2. Guilherme, N. D. and Avinash, C. K., Vision for mobile robot navigation: A survey IEEE Trans. on PAMI, **24**, 237-267, (2002).
3. Kang, S.B. and Szeliski, R., 3D environment modeling from multiple cylindrical panoramic images, *Panoramic Vision: Sensors, Theory, Applications*, 329-358, Ryad Benosman and Sing Bing Kang, ed., Springer-Verlag, (2001).
4. Fraundorfer, F., A map for mobile robots consisting of a 3D model with augmented salient image features, 26th Workshop of the Austrian Association for Pattern Recognition, 249-256, (2002).

5. Barron, J.L., Fleet, D.J., and Beauchemin, S.S., Performance of optical flow techniques, International Journal of Computer Vision, **12**, 43-77, (1994).
6. Horn, B. K. P. and Schunck, B.G., Determining optical flow, Artificial Intelligence, **17**, 185-203, (1981).
7. Lucas, B. and Kanade, T., An iterative image registration technique with an application to stereo vision, Proc. of 7th IJCAI, 674-679, (1981).
8. Mallot, H. A., Bulthoff, H. H., Little, J. J., and Bohrer, S., Inverse perspective mapping simplifies optical flow computation and obstacle detection, Biological Cybernetics, **64**, 177-185, (1991).
9. Enkelmann, W., Obstacle detection by evaluation of optical flow fields from image sequences, Image and Vision Computing, **9**, 160-168, (1991).
10. Santos-Victor, J. and Sandini, G., Uncalibrated obstacle detection using normal flow, Machine Vision and Applications, **9**, 130-137, (1996).
11. Hyvarinen, A. and Oja, E., Independent component analysis: algorithms and application, Neural Networks, **13**, 411-430, (2000).
12. van Hateren, J., and van der Schaaf, A., Independent component filters of natural images compared with simple cells in primary visual cortex, Proc. of the Royal Society of London, Series B, 265, 359-366, (1998).
13. Hyvarinen, A. and Hoyer, P., Topographic independent component analysis, Neural Computation, 13, 1525-1558, (2001).
14. Bouguet, J.-Y., Pyramidal implementation of the Lucas Kanade feature tracker description of the algorithm, Intel Corporation, Microprocessor Research Labs, OpenCV Documents, (1999).
15. Hurri, J., Gavert, H., Sarela, J., and Hyvarinen, A., The FastICA package for MATLAB, website: http://www.cis.hut.fi/projects/ica/fastica/

Algorithm That Mimics Human Perceptual Grouping of Dot Patterns

G. Papari and N. Petkov

Institute of Mathematics and Computing Science,
University of Groningen,
P.O.Box 800, 9700 AV Groningen, The Netherlands

Abstract. We propose an algorithm that groups points similarly to how human observers do. It is simple, totally unsupervised and able to find clusters of complex and not necessarily convex shape. Groups are identified as the connected components of a Reduced Delaunay Graph (RDG) that we define in this paper. Our method can be seen as an algorithmic equivalent of the gestalt law of perceptual grouping according to proximity. We introduce a measure of dissimilarity between two different groupings of a point set and use this measure to compare our algorithm with human visual perception and the k-means clustering algorithm. Our algorithm mimics human perceptual grouping and outperforms the k-means algorithm in all cases that we studied. We also sketch a potential application in the segmentation of structural textures.

1 Introduction

One of the remarkable properties of the human visual system is its ability to group together bits and pieces of visual information in order to recognize objects in complex scenes. In psychology, there is a long tradition of research devoted to perceptual grouping. This tradition has been largely formed and is still very much influenced by gestalt laws that name factors, such as proximity or similarity in orientation, colour, shape, or speed and direction of movement which play a role in perceptual grouping (see e.g. [1-4]). The sole naming of these factors, however, is not sufficient for a quantitative analysis of an image aimed at grouping features together automatically, i.e. without the involvement of a human observer. Such automatic grouping is essential for the computerized recognition of objects in digital images.

In the current paper we describe an algorithm for the grouping of points (Section 2) and demonstrate that this algorithm delivers results that are in agreement with human visual perception (Section 3). To quantify the degree of agreement we introduce a measure of dissimilarity between two possible groupings of the points of one set. We also compare the performance of our algorithm in mimicking human visual perception with the performance of the k-means clustering algorithm, commonly used in computer vision (Section 4). Our algorithm is closely related to the gestalt law of proximity but it goes beyond that law in that it has predictive power. In Section 5 we refer to some related previous work, draw conclusions and outline future work on possible applications in computer vision.

M. De Gregorio et al. (Eds.): BVAI 2005, LNCS 3704, pp. 497–506, 2005.

2 Grouping Algorithm

2.1 Voronoi Tessellation and Delaunay Graph

Given a set $S = \{p_1, \ldots, p_N\}$ of N points in the plain, we partition the plain in cells $C_1, \ldots, C_N$ (bound or unbound) such that the points which belong to cell C_j, associated with point $p_j \in S$, are closer to p_j than to any other point $p_k \in S$, $k \neq j$:

$$q \in C_j \quad \Leftrightarrow \quad d(q, p_j) \leq d(q, p_k), \quad \forall q, \quad \forall p_j, p_k \in S . \qquad (2.1)$$

Such a partition of the plain is called the *Voronoi Tessellation* (VT) or *Voronoi diagram* related to S. The dual of the Voronoi tessellation, called the *Delaunay Graph* (DG), is obtained by connecting all pairs of points of S whose Voronoi diagram cells share a boundary (Fig. 1). More details about Voronoi tessellation and Delaunay graph can be found in the standard literature (see for example [5]).

Fig. 1. Voronoi tessellation and Delaunay graph of a set of points

2.2 Reduced Delaunay Graph

Perceptually, a *group* of points in S is a subset of points, which are much closer to each other than to the other points of S. However, the concept of "much closer" is subjective and it is not well defined mathematically. We propose an algorithm which partitions S in disjoint subsets, and show that this partitioning corresponds to human visual perception of groups. We compute the Delaunay Graph DG of the set S and eliminate some edges from it to obtain a new graph that we call the Reduced Delaunay Graph; then, we regard the connected components of that graph as groups. This is illustrated by Fig. 2. In order to choose which edges must be removed, for each edge pq of the DG we first compute the distance $d(p, q)$ (Fig. 2a); then we normalize it with the distances of p and q to their respective nearest neighbours:

$$\xi(p,q) = \frac{d(p,q)}{\min\limits_{x \in S}\{d(p,x)\}}; \quad \xi(q,p) = \frac{d(q,p)}{\min\limits_{x \in S}\{d(q,x)\}} . \qquad (2.2)$$

Note that in general $\xi(p, q) \neq \xi(q, p)$. In this way, we assign two ratios, $r_1(e) = \xi(p, q)$ and $r_2(e) = \xi(q, p)$, to each edge e of the DG (Fig.2b).

Next, we reduce the two above mentioned numbers to a single quantity, computed as their geometric average:

$$r(e) = \sqrt{r_1(e) \cdot r_2(e)} . \qquad (2.3)$$

and remove from the DG every edge e for which $r(e)$ is larger than a fixed threshold r_T. We call the remaining graph *Reduced Delaunay Graph (RDG)*.

More precisely, RDG $= (V_{RDG}, E_{RDG})$ is a graph whose vertex set V_{RDG} is the same as the vertex set of the DG, and whose edge set E_{RDG} contains those edges $e \in E_{DG}$ for which $r(e)$ is less than or equal to a given threshold vlaue r_T:

$$V_{RDG} = V_{DG}; \qquad E_{RDG} = \left\{ e \in E_{DG} \middle| r(e) \le r_T \right\}. \qquad (2.4)$$

Finally, we regard the connected components of the RDG as *groups*.

This is illustrated in Fig. 2, where the value chosen for r_T is 1.65. The two normalized distances assigned to edge $p_1 p_2$, for instance, are $\xi(p_1, p_2) = 4.95$ and $\xi(p_2, p_1) = 2.48$. Their geometrical average is 3.5, larger than r_T, so $p_1 p_2$ must be removed. The other edges that must be removed are shown in dashed line in Fig.2c. The remaining edges (shown in solid line) produce two connected components, $\{p_1 p_3 p_4\}$ and $\{p_2 p_5 p_6\}$, which we regard as groups.

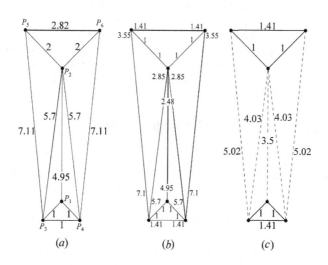

(a)   (b)   (c)

Fig. 2. (*a*) A set of points and its Delaunay graph. The numbers assigned to the edges are equal to the distances between the corresponding vertices. (*b*) A pair of normalized distances is assigned to each edge of the DG. (*c*) The pair of normalized distances assigned to an edge is replaced by a single number, computed as their geometric mean. The dash lines represent the edges removed from the DG; these are the lines that are assigned numbers larger than the threshold (1.65). The vertices and the remaining edges define the reduced Delaunay graph; its connected components are regarded as groups.

3   Results

In this section we apply our algorithm to several sets of points (see Figures 3-5); in all these examples we take a threshold value $r_T = 1.65$ that is empirically chosen.

In the cases shown in Fig.3*a-b* the RDG is connected and all points are grouped together in one single group; this corresponds to the human visual perception of these dot patterns; the examples of Fig.3c-f are point configurations in which distinct groups, arranged both regularly and randomly, are formed. In the case shown in Fig.4a the points arranged in a circle and the points inside that circle form separate groups. Fig.4b-c present examples of sets in which there are isolated points. Fig. 4d-f illustrate the ability of our algorithm to find clusters of complex shape that are not necessarily convex.

Fig.5a-b show examples of point sets in which groups of points are immersed in a group that covers the whole image. In Fig.5a, for instance, we perceive a set of crosses immersed in a square grid, and it is exactly what the RDG reveals. Similarly, in Fig.5b we perceive small squares surrounded by a grid of octagons and big squares. In Fig.5c the RDG reveals the lines traced by the points. This example has a certain relation to the gestalt law of good continuation. The arcs of the RDG not only allow identifying groups but also reveal the order of continuation.

4 Quantitative Comparison to Human Observers

We claim that our algorithm mimics the grouping properties of the human visual system. To quantify this claim, we now compare the grouping results obtained with this algorithm with the groupings defined by human observers. For this purpose we first introduce a measure of dissimilarity between two possible groupings of the points of one set.

4.1 Dissimilarity Between Two Partitions of a Point Set

Let $C_1 = \{U_1, \ldots, U_N\}$ be a collection of disjoint subsets of a point set S, such that the union of these subsets is identical with S. Each such subset defines a group of points, and C_1 defines a possible grouping or partitioning of the points of S into different groups. Let $C_2 = \{W_1, \ldots, W_M\}$ be another such grouping of S. We introduce the following quantities:

$$\alpha_{i,k} = \frac{\text{card}(U_i \cap W_k)}{\text{card}(S)}; \quad u_i = \frac{\text{card}(U_i)}{\text{card}(S)}; \quad w_k = \frac{\text{card}(W_k)}{\text{card}(S)}. \tag{4.1}$$

In analogy with probability theory, we call α_{ik} *joint probability* and u_i and w_k marginal probabilities; we also say that C_1 and C_2 are independent if $\alpha_{ik} = u_i w_k$. We also define the following *formal entropies* [6]:

$$H(C_1) = -\sum_i u_i \ln u_i; \quad H(C_2) = -\sum_k w_k \ln w_k; \quad H(C_1, C_2) = -\sum_{i,k} \alpha_{i,k} \ln \alpha_{i,k}. \tag{4.2}$$

We now define the dissimilarity coefficient $\rho(C_1, C_2)$ between the two partitions C_1 and C_2 as follows:

$$\rho(C_1, C_2) = \frac{H(C_1, C_2) - \min\{H(C_1), H(C_2)\}}{\max\{H(C_1), H(C_2)\}}. \tag{4.3}$$

Fig. 3. Six point sets (first and third rows) and their corresponding RDGs (second and fourth rows). In cases (*a-b*) the RDGs are fully connected and all points belong to the same group. In cases (*c-f*) the points are clustered in groups, both regularly and randomly arranged, which are correctly detected by the respective RDGs.

Fig. 4. Other six point sets (first and third rows) and their corresponding RDGs (second and fourth rows). In case (*a*) the points that form a circle belong to a different group than the point inside that circle. Cases (*b-c*) are examples of RDGs that have isolated points; in examples (*d-f*) the shape of the clusters is complex and not necessarily convex.

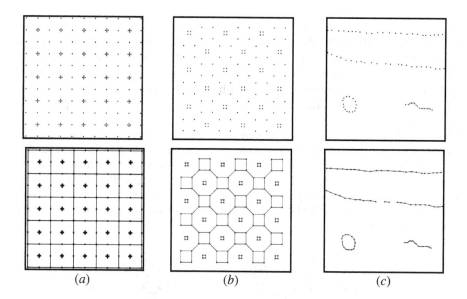

Fig. 5. Point sets (above) and their corresponding RDGs (below). (*a-b*) A system of groups is immersed in a group that covers the whole image. (*c*) A case related to the gestalt principle of good continuation. The edges of the RDG reveal the connectivity of that continuation.

It can easily be shown that ρ is symmetric, positive, equal to zero iff $C_1 = C_2$, and that it satisfies the triangular inequality; therefore, it defines a metrics in the space of the groupings. ρ has also the property to be always between 0 and 1, with $\rho = 1$ if and only if the two concerned groupings are independent. Fig.6 illustrates that the concept of dissimilarity between two groupings is related to their correlation.

4.2 Results

We used the dissimilarity coefficient defined above to compare the results of our grouping algorithm with the perceptual grouping as done by human observers. For each of the images named in the first column of Table 1, we asked eight human observers (male, age varying between 25 and 48) to group the points of the corresponding set. Originally, we used a larger number of point sets but then we excluded sets for which the observers produced different groupings; the set shown in Fig. 4d is one such case that is included here for illustration; the maximum dissimilarity coefficient of two groupings produced by two observers for this set was 0.026. For all other point sets included here the groupings produced by different observers are identical.

In all the cases but the ones presented in Fig.4d and Fig.5c our algorithm produces groupings that are identical with the groupings defined by the human observers. Consequently, the dissimilarity coefficients of the groupings obtained by the algorithm and by perceptual grouping are 0 in these cases, Table 1. One case in which a difference arises is shown in Fig.7. As can be seen, this difference is small which is well reflected in the small value of the corresponding dissimilarity coefficient. For the case shown in Fig.4d the dissimilarity coefficient is computed as the average of the dissimilarity coefficients between the algorithmic grouping on one hand and each of the human perceptual groupings on the other hand. The average value obtained in this way is smaller than the maximum value of dissimilarity between the perceptual groupings by two different observers.

Table 1 shows also the results achieved by another algorithm - the k-mean clustering [7]. Since this algorithm requires a number of clusters to be specified, this number has been selected to be equal to the number of groups drawn by the human observers. In all cases, the RDG algorithm outperforms the k-means algorithm in its ability to mimic human perception. The performance difference is especially large for point sets in which the groups (as defined by human visual perception) are not convex and have complex form, Fig.7.

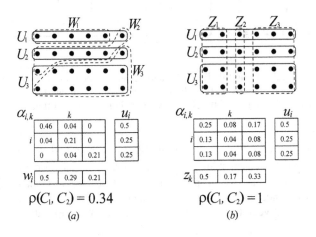

Fig. 6. (a) The groupings/partitions $C_1 = \{U_1, U_2, U_3\}$ and $C_2 = \{U_1, U_2, U_3\}$ defined by the continuous and dashed lines, respectively, are strongly correlated and consequently their dissimilarity $\rho(C_1, C_2)$ is small. (b) The partitions C_1 and $C_3 = \{U_1, U_2, U_3\}$ are totally uncorrelated and their dissimilarity coefficient is maximal.

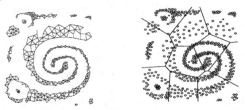

Fig. 7. (left) The RDG grouping algorithm mimics human perception while (right) the k-means algorithm clusters points in a very different way

Table 1. Dissimilarity coefficient values between perceptual grouping by humans and two grouping algorithms, RDG and k-means

Point set	ρ (*RDG* to human)	ρ (k-mean to human)
Fig. 3c	0	0.08
Fig. 3d	0	0.04
Fig. 3e	0	0.05
Fig. 3f	0	0.05
Fig. 4a	0	0.24
Fig. 4d	0.007	0.48
Fig. 4e	0.21	0.85
Fig. 4f	0	0.68
Fig. 5c	0.17	0.30

5 Summary and Conclusion

Attempts to identify perceptually meaningful structure in a set of points have been made in previous works. Voronoi neighbourhood is used in [8]. A discussion in [9] motivates a graph-approach to detect Gestalt groups. In [10] the following concept is introduced: two points p and q of a set S are considered *relatively close* if $d(p,q) <$ $\max\{d(p,x), d(q,x)\}$, $\forall x \in S$; linking all points of S which are relatively close, we obtain what is called the Relative Neighbourhood Graph [11]. In [11] it is shown by some examples that points are linked in a way that is perceptually natural for human observers. However, this algorithm cannot be used to find groups of points, which is the goal of the current paper. A nice algorithm, presented in [12], repeatedly splits the convex hull of the point set, until clusters are found; but it is unable to find clusters which are one inside the other.

We introduced the concept of a RDG that we use to group points. We demonstrated that this algorithm mimics human visual perception. For this purpose we introduced a quantitative measure of dissimilarity between two possible groupings of the points of a set. The dissimilarities between groupings produced by our algorithm and perceptual groupings done by human observers are zero or very small for a number of point sets that we studied. In contrast, the popular k-means clustering algorithm groups points in a way that is quite different from visual perception. Our algorithm is very simple, totally unsupervised, and is able to find groups of complex shape.

In future work we will apply this algorithm to computer vision problems, such as segmentation of structural textures. Such textures cannot be treated adequately with traditional filter based approaches (see e.g. [13]). Our idea is to first reduce a texture (Fig.8a) to one or more sets of points that indicate the positions of structural elements, using morphological filters, and to group them using the RDG approach, Fig.8b-c.

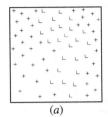   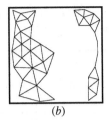   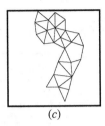

(a)   (b)   (c)

Fig. 8. (*a*) A texture in which the regions are defined by different structural elements. (*b*) The positions of the + elements are identified by a morphological filter selective for the + shape, and the points are connected in a RDG to identify regions of + elements. (*c*) The regions that contain L elements are identified in a similar way using another morphological filter.

References

1. Moore, P., Fitz, C.: Gestalt Theory and Instructional Design. *J. Technical Writing and Communication*, Vol. 23, No.2 (1993) 137-157.
2. Wertheimer, M.: Untersuchungen zur Lehere von der Gestalt II. *Psychologische Forschungen*, Vol. 4 (1923) 301-350.
3. Koffka, K.: Principles of Gestalt Psychology. R. & K. Paul London (1935).
4. Koheler, W.: Gestal Psychology. Mentor Books New York (1947).
5. De Berg, M.: Computational Geometry. Springer (2000).
6. Cover, T. M., Thomas, J. A..: Elements of Information Theory, Wiley series in Telecommunication. Wiley and Son New York (1991).
7. Hartigan, J. A.: Clustering Algorithms. Wiley & Sons New York (1975).
8. Ahuja, N.: Dot pattern processing using Voronoi neighborhoods, *IEEE Trans. on Pattern Analysis and Machine Intelligence*, Vol. 4, No 3 (1982) 336-343.
9. Zhan, T. C.: Graph-theoretical methods for detecting and describing gestalt clusters, *IEEE Trans. On Computers*, Vol C-20, No 1 (1971) 68-86.
10. Lackford, P. A.: Regionalization, Theory and alternative algorithms. *Geographical Analysis*, Vol. 1 (1969) 196-212.
11. Toussaint, G. T.: The relative neighbourhood graph of a finite planar set, *Pattern Recognition*, Vol. 12 (1980) 261-268.
12. Garai, G., Chaudhuri, B. B.: A Split and merge procedure for polygonal border detection of dot pattern, *Image and Vision Computin,* Vol.17 (1999) 75-82.
13. Grigorescu, S.E., Petkov, N., Kruizinga, P.: Comparison of texture features based on Gabor filters, *IEEE Trans. on Image Proc.*, Vol. 11, No. 10 (2002) 1160-1167.

Heuristic Algorithms for Fast and Accurate Tracking of Moving Objects in Unrestricted Environments[*]

Elena Sánchez-Nielsen[1] and Mario Hernández-Tejera[2]

[1] Departmento de E.I.O. y Computación. 38271 Universidad de La Laguna, Spain
[2] IUSIANI, Campus Universitario de Tafira, 35017 Gran Canaria, Spain
enielsen@ull.es, mhernandez@iusiani.ulpgc.es

Abstract. Tracking of objects is a basic process in computer vision. This process can be formulated as exploration problems and thus can be expressed as a search into a states space based representation approach. However, these problems are hard of solving because they involve search through a high dimensional space corresponding to the possible motion and deformation of the object. In this paper, we propose a heuristic algorithm that combines three features in order to compute motion efficiently: (1) a quality of function match, (2) Kullback-Leibler measure as heuristic to guide the search process and (3) incorporation of target dynamics for computing promising search alternatives. Once target 2D motion has been calculated, the result value of the quality of function match computed is used in other heuristic algorithm with the purpose of verifying template updates. Also, a short-term memory subsystem is included with the purpose of recovering previous views of the target object. The paper includes experimental evaluations with video streams that illustrate the efficiency for real-time vision based-tasks.

1 Introduction

Tracking of moving objects in video streams [1] is a critical task in many computer vision applications such as vision-based interface tasks [2], visual surveillance or perceptual intelligence applications.

In this paper, it is proposed a template-based solution for fast and accurate tracking of moving objects. The main contributions are focused on: (1) an A* search algorithm for computing shape motion, (2) dynamic update of the search space in each image whose corresponding dimension is determined by target dynamics, (3) updating templates only when the target object has evolved to a new shape change significantly dissimilar with respect to the current template and (4) representation of the most illustrative views of the target evolution through a short-term memory subsystem. As a result, the two first contributions provide a fast algorithm to apply over a transformations space for computing target 2D motion and the other two contributions provide robust tracking because accurate template updating can be performed. In addition to these contributions, the paper contains experimental evaluations with

---

[*] This work has been supported by the Spanish Government and the Canary Islands Autonomous Government under projects TIN2004-07087 and PI20003/165.

M. De Gregorio et al. (Eds.): BVAI 2005, LNCS 3704, pp. 507–516, 2005.
© Springer-Verlag Berlin Heidelberg 2005

indoor and outdoor video streams of number of nodes explored, average runtime and comparison of the proposed search approach with conventional search strategies, demonstrating that A* heuristic search based approach is faster and the computational time requirements are under the time restriction on real-time situations. Also, the experimental results reveal that updating templates using combined results focused on the value of the quality of function match and the use of a short-term memory subsystem leads to accurate template tracking.

This paper is organized as follows: Section 2 illustrates the problem formulation. In Section 3, the heuristic algorithm for computing target position is described. The updating reference template problem is detailed in Section 4. Experimental results are presented in Section 5 and Section 6 concludes the paper.

2   Problem Formulation

The template tracking problem of objects in 3D space from 2D images proposed in this paper is formulated in terms of decomposing the transformations induced by moving objects between frames into two parts: (1) a 2D motion, corresponding to the change of the target position in the image space, which is referred to as template position matching problem and (2) a 2D shape, corresponding to an actual change of shape in the object, which is referred to as template updating problem.

2.1   Template Position Matching

Let $T = \{t_1, ..., t_r\} \subseteq \Re^2$ be a set of points that represents a template, let $I = \{i_1, ..., i_s\} \subseteq \Re^2$ be another set of points that denotes an input image, let a bounded set of translational transformations $\mathbf{G}(.)$ be a set of transformations $G : \Re^2 \to \Re^2$, and let a bounded error notion of quality of match $Q(G;T,I,\varepsilon)$ be a measurement for computing the degree of match between a template T and a current input image I, where the dependence of Q on T, I and/or ε is omitted for sake of simplicity but without lost of generality. That is, the quality of match assigned to a transformation G is represented by the allowed error bound, ε, when template points are brought to point's image using a transformation G. This quality of match function assigned to a transformation G is expressed as:

$$Q(G) = \sum_{t \in T} \max_{i \in I} \|G(t) - i\| < \varepsilon \tag{1}$$

Given a template T, an input image I and an error bound ε, template position matching problem can be viewed as the search process in the space of transformations in order to find the transformation, G_{max}, that maximizes the quality of match $Q(G)$ between the transformed template $G(T)$ and the current image I:

$$G_{\max}(T,I,\varepsilon) = \arg \max_{G \in G} Q(G;T,I,\varepsilon) \tag{2}$$

2.2 Template Position Updating

Once the new position of the target has been computed, the template is updated to reflect the change in its shape. Since, template matching position problem determines translational motion between consecutive frames, all the non-translational transformations are considered to be a change in the 2D shape of the object. New 2D shape change between successive frames is computed as the measure of the discrepancy between $G_{max}(T_k)$, which denotes the translated points set of template T_k by the translation G_{max}, and the given input image in step time k, denoted as I_k, under a certain error bound δ. That is, the new template T_{k+1} is represented by all those points of input image I_k that are within distance δ of some point of $G_{max}(T_k)$ according to the following expression:

$$T_{k+1} = \sum_{i \in I} \left\| G_{max}(T_k) - i \right\| < \delta \tag{3}$$

3 Heuristic Search Algorithm for Template Position Matching

Formulation of problem solving under the framework of heuristic search is expressed through a *state space-based representation approach* [3], where the possible problem situations are considered as a *set of states*. The *start state* corresponds to the initial situation of the problem, the *final state*, *goal* or *target state* corresponds to problem solution and the transformation between states can be carried out by means of *operators*. Next, the elements of the problem are described in order to formalize the heuristic search framework:

- *State:* each state n is associated with a subset G_k of the space of transformations $G(.)$. Each state is represented by the transformation that corresponds to the center of the partial set of transformations, G_k, which is referred to as G_c.
- *Initial state:* is represented by a bounded set of translational transformations, which allow matching the current template position in the current scene.
- *Final state:* is the transformation that best matches the current template in the current scene, according to $Q(G)$. The quality of function match assigned to a transformation G is expressed in terms of the partial directed Hausdorff distance (see appendix) between the transformed template T and the current image I:

$$Q(G) = h_k(G(T), I) < \varepsilon \tag{4}$$

Where the parameter k represents the kth quartile value selected according to expression 10 and ε denotes that each point of $G(T)$ must be within distance ε of some point of I.

- *Operators*: are the functional elements that transform one state to another. For each current state n, the operators A, and B are computed:

  - *Function A.* The current state is partitioned into four regions by vertical and horizontal bisections, that is, four new states.

- *Function B.* The quality of function match (equation 4) is computed for each one of the new states generated. It is referred to as $h_k(G_c(T), I)$, where $G_c(T)$ represents the transformation of template points by the central translation of the corresponding state.

Splitting each current state into four new states leads to the representation of the search tree to be a quaternary tree structure; where each node is associated to a $2^i \times 2^j$ region. The splitting operation is finished when the quadrisection process computes a translational motion according to the quality of function match $Q(G)$ or all the regions associated with the different nodes have been partitioned in cells of unit size. Figure 1 illustrates the search process. Each one of the four regions computed is referred to as *NW, NE, SE* and *SW* cells. The best node to expand from these cells at each tree-level *l* is computed using an A* approach [3], which combines features of uniform-cost and heuristic search. The corresponding value assigned to each state *n* is defined as:

$$f(n) = c(n) + h*(n) \qquad (5)$$

Where $c(n)$ is the estimated cost of the path from the initial node n_0 to current node *n*, and $h*(n)$ is the heuristic estimate of the cost of a path from node *n* to the goal.

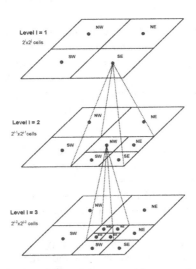

Fig. 1. Search tree: hierarchical partition of the space of states using a quadrisection process. The nodes at the leaf level define the finest partition.

3.1 Heuristic Evaluation Function h*(n) and Estimated Cost Function c(n)

The heuristic value $h*(n)$ is estimated by means of evaluating the quality of the best solution reachable from the current state *n*. Desirability of the best state is estimated measuring the similarity between the distribution functions P and Q that respectively characterize the current and goal state. The definition of both functions is based on the quality of function match assigned to the target transformation G_{max}. Since the quality of function match is denoted by the partial directed Hausdorff distance, the distribution function P can be approximated by a histogram of distances $\{H_{Gc}\}_{i=1...r}$, which contains the number of template points T at distance d_j with respect to the points of I, when the transformation G_c of the current state n is applied on T and the distribution function Q can be modelled by approximating $\{H_{Gc}\}_{i=1...r}$ by an exponential distribution function $f(n) = ke^{-an}$, which represents the highest number of distance values d_j near to zero values and lower than error bound ε, when the transformation G_{max} corresponds to the transformation G_c.

Given the distribution functions P and Q, and let R be the number of template points, the Kullback-Leibler distance (KLD) between the two distributions is defined as:

$$D(P \| Q) = \sum_{i=1}^{R} p_i \log \frac{p_i}{q_i} \tag{6}$$

According to [4], $D(P \| Q)$ has two important properties: (1) $D(P \| Q) \geq 0$; and (2) $D(P \| Q) = 0$ iff $P = Q$. These properties show that when the template points do not match to the input image points, the values of KLD will be non-zero and positive because the distributions are not similar, $P \neq Q$. On the other hand, if the template points match to the input image points, then the value of KLD is equal or near to zero.

An estimated cost function $c(n)$ is added to the $f(n)$ function (expression 5) for generating a backtracking process when the heuristic function leads the search process towards no promising solutions. This depth term is based on the number of operators A type applied from the initial state to the current state n.

3.2 Initial State Computation

The initial dimension MxN of $\mathbf{G}(.)$ is computed by means of incorporating an alpha-beta predictive filtering [5] into the search algorithm. The parameters estimated by the filtering approach are represented by the 2D opposite coordinates of the bounding box that encloses the target shape and are expressed as a *four*-dimensional vector $\theta = [\theta_1, \cdots, \theta_4]^T$. The location and velocity vector are jointly expressed as a state vector $x = [\theta^T, \dot{\theta}^T]^T$. The state vector estimation using a constant velocity model is formulated as:

$$\hat{x}(k+1|k+1) = \hat{x}(k+1|k) + v(k+1)\left[\alpha \, \frac{\beta}{\Delta T}\right]^T \tag{7}$$

Since $v(k)$ represents the residual error between the predicted value at time step k-1 and the current measurement $z(k)$, a decision rule focused on this uncertainty measurement can be obtained in order to compute the dimension of $\mathbf{G}(.)$. Two main criteria are considered in the decision rule design. The first one is that small values of the residual factor indicate low uncertainty about its estimate and therefore, a reduced size of $\mathbf{G}(.)$. The second criterion is that the definition of MxN must be a $2^p \times 2^q$ value in order to assure that each terminal cell of $\mathbf{G}(.)$ will contain a single transformation after the last quadrisection operation had been applied. Assuming these requirements, the dimension $M \times N$ of $\mathbf{G}(.)$ is computed as:

$$M = \begin{cases} 2^{\min}, & \text{if } \omega + 2^{\min} \leq v_M(k) \\ 2^{\max}, & \text{if } \omega + 2^{\min} > v_M(k) \end{cases} \qquad N = \begin{cases} 2^{\min}, & \text{if } \omega + 2^{\min} \leq v_N(k) \\ 2^{\max}, & \text{if } \omega + 2^{\min} > v_N(k) \end{cases} \tag{8}$$

Where $v(k) = (v_M(k), v_N(k))$, 2^{min}, 2^{max} represent the nearest values to $v(k)$ and ω is calculated according to the expression: $\omega = \phi(2^{max} - 2^{min})$, where ϕ weights the influence of the difference between 2^{min} and 2^{max}. The figure 2 and 3 show respectively the computation of MxN and the heuristic search algorithm.

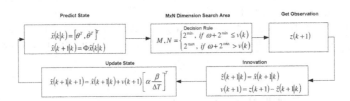

Fig. 2. Alpha-beta filtering stages and computation of MxN dimension of $G(.)$

Input
G(.): initial set of transformations.
ε: distance error bound allowed when template points are brought to point's image using a transformation G.
$D(P \| Q)$: value of Kullback-Leibler distance.
η: number of operators of type A applied from the initial search state to current state n.

Algorithm
Step 1) Compute MxN dimension of $G(.)$:
Step 2) Find G_{max} that verifies $Q(G) = h_k(G(T), I) < \varepsilon$:
    While ($Q(G) > \varepsilon$) **Do**
    2.1) Split current state n into four new states $\{n\}_{i=1...4}$
    2.2) Compute $Q(G_c) \leftarrow h_k(G_c(T), I)$ for each new n_i
    2.3) Expand the best state n_i according to the evaluation function $f(n) = c(n) + h*(n)$:
        2.4.1) $h*(n) \leftarrow D(P \| Q)$
        2.4.2) $c(n) \leftarrow c(n-1) + \eta$
    End While

Fig. 3. Heuristic algorithm for computing template motion

4   Template Update Approach

The new template is only updated when the target object has evolved significantly to a new shape. Since, heuristic search computes only 2D motion component and the best matching between the current template T and the input image I is expressed through the error bound distance ε of the quality of function match, a low error bound ε will denote that the target is moving according to a translational motion. However, the target object will have evolved towards a new shape when a large value of the error bound ε is computed. In order to detect an appreciable shape change, we define a minimum and maximum boundary for ε from the analysis of different processed sequence images that represent deformable and rigid objects. Let ε_{min} be the minimum distance value that does not denote shape changes and let ε_{max} be the maximum distance value that is acceptable for a tolerable matching. Thus, all the solutions values computed between $\varepsilon_{min} \leq Q(G) \leq \varepsilon_{max}$ will denote a 2D shape change.

At the same time, in certain situations, the target will show previous views that are not represented by the current template. Recovery of previous views is achieved by means of a short-term memory subsystem (*STMS*). The different templates that compose *STMS* must be represented by the more common views of the object. With the purpose of minimizing redundancies, the problem about what *representative* templates must be stored is addressed as a dynamic approach that removes the less distinctive templates according to leave space to the new ones when the capacity of the visual memory is achieved and a new template must be inserted in *STMS*. In order to determinate the weight of every template, we introduce a *relevance index*, which is associated to every template. This index is defined according to the following expression:

$$R(k,i) = \frac{T_p(k)}{1+k-T_s(k)} \tag{9}$$

Where k represents the time step, i corresponds to identification symbol template, $T_p(i)$ characterizes the *persistent* parameter of the ith template and represents the frequency of use as current template. $T_s(i)$ denotes the *obsolescence* parameter and corresponds to the time from the last instant it was used as current template. A new template is inserted into *STMS*, when the value of $Q(G_{max})$ between the current template T and input image I ranges from ε_{min} to ε_{max}. On the other hand, a template is removed of *STMS* when the stack of templates is full and a new template must be added into the short-term memory, removing the template that has the less index of relevance and inserting the new template.

4.1 Template Updating Algorithm

According to the value of $Q(G_{max})$, every template T_k is updated as T_{k+1} based on one of the steps of the following heuristic algorithm:

Step 1) If $Q(G_{max}) \leq \varepsilon_{min}$, the new template in time step $k+1$, T_{k+1}, is equivalent to the best matching of T_k in I. That is, the edge points of I that are directly overlapping on some edge point of the best matching, $G_{max}(T_k)$, represents the new template T_{k+1}:

$$T_{k+1} \leftarrow \left\{ i \in I_k \, / \min_{t \in T_k} \left\| G_{max}(t) - i \right\| = 0 \right\}$$

Step 2) If some template of *STMS* computes the best matching when the current template T_k cannot match the target object with an inferior or equivalent distance value ε_{min}, $Q(G_{max}) > \varepsilon_{min}$, this template of *STMS* is selected as the new template T_{k+1}. Otherwise, the current template, T_k is updated by incorporating the shape change by means of the partial directed Hausdorff distance measure [see appendix]. In this context, we denote $STMS = \{T(STMS)_i\}_{i=1}^{N}$ as the different templates that integrate the iconic visual memory subsystem, $Q(G;\ T(STMS)_i,I,\varepsilon)$ as the best error bound distance ε computed for the ith template of $STMS$, where this template is referred to as $T(STMS)_i$. The updating process is expressed as:

$$T_{k+1} \leftarrow \begin{cases} \left\{i \in I_k \,/\, \min_{t \in T_k} \|G_{max}(t) - i\| \leq \delta \right\} & \text{if } Q(G_{max};T_k,I,\varepsilon) \leq Q(G_{max};T(STMS)_i,I,\varepsilon) \\ T(STMS)_i, & \text{if } Q(G_{max};T(STMS)_i,I,\varepsilon) < Q(G_{max};T_k,I,\varepsilon) \end{cases}$$

Step 3) If the best matching computed using the current template T_k and all templates of $STMS$ is superior to the error bound distance ε_{max}, no template is updated:

$$T_{k+1} \leftarrow \{\phi \quad \text{if } Q(G_{max};T_k,I,\varepsilon) \geq \varepsilon_{max} \text{ and } Q(G_{max};T(STMS)_i,I,\varepsilon) \geq \varepsilon_{max}\}$$

5 Experiments and Results

Diverse experiments have been carried out with 24 different sequences that contain 800 frames as average rate, with deformable and rigid objects, achieving the same behaviour for all of them on a P-IV 3.0 GHz. Particularly, indoor and outdoor video streams, "*People*" (855 frames) and "*Motorcycle*" (414 frames) are illustrated. The average size of each frame is 280x200 pixels and average size of templates is 170x149 pixels. The first reference template is computed from initial image areas that exhibit coherent movement among the two first frames. Initial states evaluated correspond to: (1) *Fixed search area (A1):* a 64x64 pixels 2D translations set ranging from (-32, -32) to (32, 32); (2) *Fixed search area with motion prediction (A2):* a 64x64 pixels 2D translations set computed from the predicted target position and (3)

Fig. 4. *People* and *Motorcycle* Sequence (frames 150, 200 and 250 are shown)

Adjustable search area (A3): the dimension of each initial state is computed according to expression 8. The goal state is defined as the translation G that verifies that 80% (parameter $k = 0.8$) of template points are at maximum 2 pixels distance ($\varepsilon = 2.0$) from I. Heuristic thresholds ε_{min}, ε_{max} and δ are respectively settled up to 2, 10 and 8. The dimension of *STMS* is settled up to 6. Figure 4 illustrates three sample frames of the sequences mentioned above. First and third column show original frames; second and fifth column depict edge image using Canny approach [7]; third and sixth column show edge located template.

5.1 Computation of Initial Search State and Comparative Analysis

The performance of the approaches for computing initial search state is measured by means of nodes to be explored and the time required for processing each sequence. The results of Figure 5 show that the number of nodes to be explored and the temporal cost are reduced considerably by incorporating a filtering approach into the search algorithm.

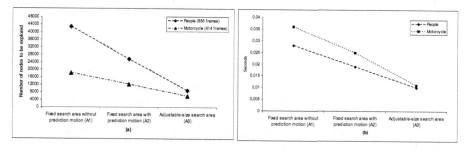

Fig. 5. Computation of initial search state: Nodes explored and total time required for processing each frame of the sequences *People* and *Motorcycle*

In order to compute the robustness of template updating algorithm, we evaluate the number of template updates for each sequence, testing: (1) our approach based on updating templates only when the target has evolved to a new shape and the use of a short-term memory and (2) the template updating approach used in [6] based on continuous updating at every frame using the directed Hausdorff measurement. Results reported in Table 1 for the sequences illustrated in this paper show that the number of required updates is minimized in relation to other updating approaches [6]. This situation leads to minimize the *drift* risk. Concretely, no target was *drifted* using the proposed approach; however, templates were *drifted* using continuous updating approach in every frame. On the other hand, templates of STMS were used when the current template did not reflect the target object in the next frame. These situations corresponded to: an imprecision error of the edge detection process in the current frame, and disappearance and reappearance conditions of the target in the video stream. In order to evaluate the average runtime behaviour of both algorithms, the motion computation and the update of templates, we compute runtime in seconds. Average time measured for processing each frame for the 24 sequences is 0.028 seconds using general purpose hardware, which is lower than real-time requirements.

Table 1. Results of Template Updating

Sequence	People (855 frames)	Motorcycle (414 frames)
Number of updates	430	196
Number of different templates stored in *STMS*	84	10
Number of templates used of *STMS*	16	3
Number of frames where the target was retrieved using *STMS*	10	5

6 Conclusions

This paper is concerned with fast and accurate tracking of objects. The heuristic search proposed to compute shape motion is faster than previous search strategies [6] in an average rate three times better. Dynamic update of templates minimizes the drift risk. However, the target evolution in the spatial-temporal domain, introduces in certain situations of disappearance and appearance of the object from scenes, views represented by a reduced set of sparse edge points that cannot be matched. In these situations, the use of colour cue is required in order to avoid the loss of the target.

References

[1] Spengler, M., Schiele, B. "Towards robust multi-cue integration for visual tracking". In *Journal of Machine Vision and Applications*, Springer-Verlag 14:50-58, 2003.

[2] Matthew Turk. "Computer Vision in the Interface". In *Communications of the ACM*, 47(1):61-67, January 2004.

[3] J. Pearl. Heuristics. Intelligent Search Strategies for Computer Problem Solving. *Addison-Wesley Series in Artificial Intelligence*, 1984.

[4] T. Cover and J. Thomas. Elements of Information Theory. *John Wiley & Sons Incs*, 1991.

[5] Bar-Shalom, Y., Xiao-Rong Li. Estimation and Tracking: Principles, Techniques, and Software. Artech House, 1993.

[6] W. Rucklidge. "Efficient computation of the minimum Hausdorff distance for visual recognition". *Lecture Notes in Computer Science, 1173, Springer*, 1996.

[7] Canny, J. "A computational approach to edge detection". In *IEEE Transactions on Pattern Analysis and Machine Intelligence*, 8(6):679-698, 1986.

Appendix. Partial Directed Hausdorff Distance

The *partial directed Hausdorff* distance between two sets of points A and B ranks each point of A based of its distance to the nearest point in B and uses the kth quartile value ranked point as the measure of distance. It is defined as:

$$h_k(A, B) = K_{a \in A}^{th} \min_{b \in B} \|a - b\| \tag{10}$$

Single Image Estimation of Facial Albedo Maps

William A.P. Smith and Edwin R. Hancock

Department of Computer Science, The University of York
{wsmith, erh}@cs.york.ac.uk

Abstract. This paper describes how a facial albedo map can be recovered from a single image using a statistical model that captures variations in surface normal direction. We fit the model to intensity data using constraints on the surface normal direction provided by Lambert's law and then use the differences between observed and reconstructed image brightness to estimate the albedo map. We show that this process is stable under varying illumination and use the process to render images under novel illumination.

1 Introduction

Shape-from-shading provides an alluring yet somewhat elusive route to recovering 3D surface shape from single 2D intensity images [1]. This has been partially motivated by psychological evidence of the role played by shape-from-shading in human face perception [2]. In addition, the accurate recovery of facial shape would provide an illumination and viewpoint invariant description of facial appearance which may be used for recognition. Unfortunately, the method has proved ineffective in recovering realistic 3D face shape because of local convexity-concavity instability due to the bas-relief ambiguity [1]. This is of course a well known effect which is responsible for a number of illusions, including Gregory's famous inverted mask [3]. The main problem is that the nose becomes imploded and the cheeks exaggerated [4]. It is for this reason that methods such as photometric stereo [5] have proved to be more effective.

One way of overcoming this problem with single view shape-from-shading is to use domain specific constraints. Several authors [6,7,8,4,9] have shown that, at the expense of generality, the accuracy of recovered shape information can be greatly enhanced by restricting a shape-from-shading algorithm to a particular class of objects. For instance, both Prados and Faugeras [9] and Castelan and Hancock [4] use the location of singular points to enforce convexity on the recovered surface. Zhao and Chellappa [7], on the other hand, have introduced a geometric constraint which exploited the approximate bilateral symmetry of faces. This 'symmetric shape-from-shading' was used to correct for variation in illumination. They employed the technique for recognition by synthesis. However, the recovered surfaces were of insufficient quality to synthesise novel viewpoints. Moreover, the symmetry constraint is only applicable to frontal face images. Atick et al. [6] proposed a statistical shape-from-shading framework based on a

M. De Gregorio et al. (Eds.): BVAI 2005, LNCS 3704, pp. 517–526, 2005.

low dimensional parameterisation of facial surfaces. Principal components analysis was used to derive a set of 'eigenheads' which compactly captures 3D facial shape. Unfortunately, it is surface orientation and not depth which is conveyed by image intensity. Therefore, fitting the model to an image equates to a computationally expensive parameter search which attempts to minimise the error between the rendered surface and the observed intensity. This is similar to the approach adopted by Samaras and Metaxas [8] who incorporate reflectance constraints derived from shape-from-shading into a deformable model.

A desirable feature of such models is the ability to separate the underlying shape and reflectance properties of the observed face from the imaging and illumination conditions, which combine to produce the observed image. There has been a considerable effort in the computer vision literature aimed at developing generative statistical models that can be used to learn the modes of appearance variation [10,11,12,13]. This is, of course, a complex problem where the devil resides in the detail. The appearance of a face is determined by a number of complex factors. The first of these is the three-dimensional shape of the face [14]. The second is the albedo map which captures effects such as local variations in skin pigmentation and the distribution of facial hair [15]. Finally, there is the process by which light is reflected from the skin. Skin reflectance is a complex process, which is thought to be governed by subsurface scattering processes and is strongly affected by blood flow beneath the skin [16]. In particular, the pattern of reflectance is strongly non-Lambertian [17]. For these reasons, much of the effort here has been aimed at developing generative statistical models that can be used to learn the modes of appearance variation [10,13], and then subsequently used to synthesise face appearance. Statistical methods are used since they are usually robust, have well understood parameter estimates and can be used in a flexible way [18,19]. Moreover, they allow the complex physical processes which give rise to variable face appearance to be subsumed into a parametrically efficient model [11]. Although this can be viewed as a merit from the computational standpoint, it circumvents the direct modelling of the underlying shape and reflectance effects that give rise to variable appearance.

In this paper we focus on one aspect of this problem and develop of means of estimating the albedo map of a face from a single image. Albedo estimation from a single image is an under-constrained problem. Previous approaches have been based on the assumption that reflectance changes lead to much stronger image gradients than shading effects [20] or, in the case of faces, that albedo is piecewise constant [7]. Neither approach has yielded results of sufficient quality to allow realistic image-based rendering or to allow useful information to be drawn from the estimated albedo map.

Our approach is based on two observations. First, that facial albedo is fairly constant across much of a face's surface. Second, that facial shape is sufficiently constrained that it may be captured by a low-dimensional space [6]. We choose to model facial shape using a statistical model which captures variations in surface normal directions. This allows us to estimate the field of normals using shape from shading and simplifies the imposition of data closeness locally at each point in the image. We train the model on range data. We begin by iteratively fitting the model to an image using the hard constraint of the image irradiance equation assuming constant albedo. Since albedo is constant across much of a face's surface, the imposition of data closeness in areas of actual albedo variation does not overly disrupt the parameter estimate. We also use an image based reflectance estimation process [21] to remap Lambertian reflectance onto the input face to reduce the effect of specularities. After the fitting process converges, the best fit field of surface normals satisfies data-closeness except in areas of actual variation in albedo. We may then use the differences between observed and reconstructed image brightness to account for albedo variations.

We begin by summarising how we construct the statistical model of surface normal variation. We describe how the model is fitted to intensity images and how this process is used to estimate facial albedo. Finally, we apply the technique to real world images and show that the albedo map is stable under varying illumination and that the process may be used for realistic reilluminations under novel lighting.

2   A Statistical Surface Normal Model

A "needle map" describes a surface $z(x,y)$ as a set of local surface normals $\mathbf{n}(x,y)$ projected onto the view plane. Let $\mathbf{n}_k(i,j) = (n_k^x(i,j), n_k^y(i,j), n_k^z(i,j))^T$ be the unit surface normal at the pixel indexed (i,j) in the kth training image. If there are T images in the training set, then at the location (i,j) the mean-surface normal direction is $\hat{\mathbf{n}}(i,j) = \frac{\bar{\mathbf{n}}(i,j)}{\|\bar{\mathbf{n}}(i,j)\|}$ where $\bar{\mathbf{n}}(i,j) = \frac{1}{T}\sum_{k=1}^{T}\mathbf{n}_k(i,j)$.

On the unit sphere, the surface normal $\mathbf{n}_k(i,j)$ has elevation angle $\theta_k(i,j) = \frac{\pi}{2} - \arcsin n_k^z(i,j)$ and azimuth angle $\phi_k(i,j) = \arctan\frac{n_k^y(i,j)}{n_k^x(i,j)}$, while the mean surface normal at the location (i,j) has elevation angles $\hat{\theta}(i,j) = \frac{\pi}{2} - \arcsin\hat{n}^z(i,j)$ and azimuth angle $\hat{\phi}(i,j) = \arctan\frac{\hat{n}^y(i,j)}{\hat{n}^x(i,j)}$.

To construct the azimuthal equidistant projection we commence by constructing the tangent plane to the unit-sphere at the location corresponding to the mean-surface normal. We establish a local co-ordinate system on this tangent plane. The origin is at the point of contact between the tangent plane and the unit sphere. The x-axis is aligned parallel to the local circle of latitude on the unit-sphere. Under the equidistant azimuthal projection at the location (i,j), the surface normal $\mathbf{n}_k(i,j)$ maps to the point with co-ordinate vector $\mathbf{v}_k(i,j) = (x_k(i,j), y_k(i,j))^T$. The transformation equations between the unit-sphere and the tangent-plane co-ordinate systems are

$$x_k(i,j) = k'\cos\theta_k(i,j)\sin[\phi_k(i,j) - \hat{\phi}(i,j)]$$

$$y_k(i,j) = k'\left\{\cos\hat{\theta}(i,j)\sin\phi_k(i,j) - \sin\hat{\theta}(i,j)\cos\theta_k(i,j)\cos[\phi_k(i,j) - \hat{\phi}(i,j)]\right\}$$

where $\cos c = \sin\hat{\theta}(i,j)\sin\theta_k(i,j) + \cos\hat{\theta}(i,j)\cos\theta_k(i,j)\cos[\phi_k(i,j) - \hat{\phi}(i,j)]$ and $k' = \frac{c}{\sin c}$.

The equations for the inverse transformation from the tangent plane to the unit-sphere are

$$\theta_k(i,j) = \sin^{-1}\left\{ \cos c \sin \hat\theta(i,j) - \frac{1}{c} y_k(i,j) \sin c \cos \hat\theta(i,j) \right\}$$

$$\phi_k(i,j) = \hat\phi(i,j) + \tan^{-1} \psi(i,j)$$

where

$$\psi(i,j) = \begin{cases} \dfrac{x_k(i,j)\sin c}{c\cos\hat\theta(i,j)\cos c - y_k(i,j)\sin\hat\theta(i,j)\sin c} & \text{if } \hat\theta(i,j) \neq \pm\frac{\pi}{2} \\ -\dfrac{x_k(i,j)}{y_k(i,j)} & \text{if } \hat\theta(i,j) = \frac{\pi}{2} \\ \dfrac{x_k(i,j)}{y_k(i,j)} & \text{if } \hat\theta(i,j) = -\frac{\pi}{2} \end{cases}$$

and $c = \sqrt{x_k(i,j)^2 + y_k(i,j)^2}$.

For each image location the transformed surface normals from the T different training images are concatenated and stacked to form two long-vectors of length T. For the pixel location indexed (i,j), the first of these is the long vector with the transformed x-co-ordinates from the T training images as components, i.e. $\mathbf{V}_x(i,j) = (x_1(i,j), x_2(i,j), ..., x_T(i,j))^T$ and the second long-vector has the y coordinate as its components, i.e. $\mathbf{V}_y(i,j) = (y_1(i,j), y_2(i,j), ..., y_T(i,j))^T$. Since the equidistant azimuthal projection involves centering the local co-ordinate system, the mean long-vectors over the training images are zero. If the data is of dimensions M rows and N columns, then there are $M \times N$ pairs of such long-vectors. The long vectors are ordered according to the raster scan (left-to-right and top-to-bottom) and are used as the columns of the $T \times (2MN)$ data-matrix $\mathbf{D} = (\mathbf{V}_x(1,1)|\mathbf{V}_y(1,1)|\ \mathbf{V}_x(1,2)|\mathbf{V}_y(1,2)|\ ...|\mathbf{V}_x(M,N)|\mathbf{V}_y(M,N))$. The covariance matrix for the long-vectors is the $(2MN) \times (2MN)$ matrix $\mathbf{L} = \frac{1}{T}\mathbf{D}^T\mathbf{D}$.

We follow Atick et al. [6] and use the numerically efficient method of Sirovich [22] to compute the eigenvectors $\mathbf{L}$. Accordingly, we construct the matrix $\hat{\mathbf{L}} = \frac{1}{K}\mathbf{D}\mathbf{D}^T$. The eigenvectors $\hat{\mathbf{e}}_i$ of $\hat{\mathbf{L}}$ can be used to find the eigenvectors $\mathbf{e}_i$ of $\mathbf{L}$ using $\mathbf{e}_i = \mathbf{D}^T\hat{\mathbf{e}}_i$.

We deform the equidistant azimuthal point projections in the directions defined by the $2MN \times K$ matrix $\mathbf{P} = (\mathbf{e}_1|\mathbf{e}_2|...|\mathbf{e}_K)$ formed from the leading K principal eigenvectors. This deformation displaces the transformed surface normals on the local tangent planes in the directions defined by the eigenvectors $\mathbf{P}$. If $\mathbf{b} = (b_1, b_2, ..., b_K)^T$ is a vector of parameters of length K, then since the mean-vector of co-ordinates resulting from the equidistant azimuthal projection is zero, the deformed vector of projected co-ordinates is $\mathbf{v}_b = \mathbf{Pb}$. Suppose that $\mathbf{v}_o$ is the vector of co-ordinates obtained by performing the azimuthal equidistant projection on an observed field of surface normals. We seek the parameter vector $\mathbf{b}$ that minimises the squared error $\mathcal{E}(\mathbf{b}) = (\mathbf{v}_o - \mathbf{P}^T\mathbf{b})^T(\mathbf{v}_o - \mathbf{P}^T\mathbf{b})$. The solution to this least-squares estimation problem is $\mathbf{b}^* = \mathbf{P}^T\mathbf{v}_o$. The best fit field of surface normals allowed by the model is $\mathbf{v}_o^* = \mathbf{PP}^T\mathbf{v}_o$. The deformed vector of azimuthal equidistant projection co-ordinates can be transformed back into a surface normal on the unit sphere using the inverse azimuthal equidistant projection equations given above.

3   Fitting the Model to an Image

We may exploit the statistical constraint provided by the model in the process of fitting the model to an intensity image and thus help resolve the ambiguity in the shape-from-shading process. We do this using an iterative approach which can be posed as that of recovering the best-fit field of surface normals from the statistical model, subject to constraints provided by the image irradiance equation.

If $I(i,j)$ is the measured image brightness at location (i,j), then $I(i,j) = \rho(i,j)\,[\mathbf{n}(i,j).\mathbf{s}]$ according to Lambert's law, where $\mathbf{s}$ is the light source direction and ρ is the albedo. We begin by assuming constant and unit albedo (the Lambertian remapping process [21] normalises the brightest point to unity) and return to this in the next section. In general, the surface normal $\mathbf{n}$ can not be recovered from a single brightness measurement since it has two degrees of freedom corresponding to the elevation and azimuth angles on the unit sphere.

In the Worthington and Hancock [23] iterative shape-from-shading framework, data-closeness is ensured by constraining the recovered surface normal to lie on the reflectance cone whose axis is aligned with the light-source vector $\mathbf{s}$ and whose opening angle is $\alpha = \arccos I$. At each iteration the surface normal is free to move to an off-cone position subject to smoothness or curvature consistency constraints. However, the hard irradiance constraint is re-imposed by rotating each surface normal back to its closest on-cone position. This process ensures that the recovered field of surface normals satisfies the image irradiance equation after every iteration. The framework is initialised by placing the surface normals on their reflectance cones such that they are aligned in the direction opposite to that of the local image gradient.

Our approach to fitting the model to intensity images uses the fields of surface normals estimated using the geometric shape-from-shading method described above. This is an iterative process in which we interleave the process of fitting the statistical model to the current field of estimated surface normals, and then re-enforcing the data-closeness constraint provided by Lambert's law by mapping the surface normals back onto their reflectance cones. The algorithm can be summarised as follows:

1. Initialise the field of surface normals $\mathbf{n}$.
2. Each normal in the estimated field $\mathbf{n}$ undergoes an azimuthal equidistant projection to give a vector of transformed coordinates $\mathbf{v}$.
3. The vector of best fit model parameters is $\mathbf{b} = \mathbf{P}^T\mathbf{v}$.
4. The vector of transformed coordinates corresponding to the best-fit parameters is $\mathbf{v}' = \mathbf{P}\mathbf{P}^T\mathbf{v}$.
5. Using the inverse azimuthal equidistant projection find $\mathbf{n}'$ from $\mathbf{v}'$.
6. Find $\mathbf{n}''$ by rotating each normal in $\mathbf{n}'$ back to their closest on-cone position.

7. Test for convergence. If $\sum_{i,j} \cos^{-1}[\mathbf{n}(i,j).\mathbf{n}''(i,j)] < \epsilon$, where ϵ is a predetermined threshold, then stop and return $\mathbf{b}$ as the estimated model parameters and $\mathbf{n}''$ as the recovered needle map.
8. Make $\mathbf{n} = \mathbf{n}''$ and return to step 2.

4   Albedo Estimation

The fitting process typically converges within 20 to 25 iterations. We find that the constraint provided by the model is sufficiently strong that the constant albedo assumption does not overly disrupt the fitting process. Our claim is that the final best fit needle map in the model space ($\mathbf{n}'$) satisfies the image irradiance equation except in areas of true albedo variation. Moreover, the model allows recovery of the shape of these areas based on the statistical information contained in the rest of the needle map. To demonstrate this in Figure 1 we show the angular change as data-closeness is restored to a typical final best fit needle map, i.e. the angular difference between $\mathbf{n}'$ and $\mathbf{n}''$.

Fig. 1. Angular difference between final $\mathbf{n}'$ and $\mathbf{n}''$

From the plot it is clear that the changes are almost solely due to the variation in albedo at the eyes, eye-brows and lips. Aside from these regions there is very little change in surface normal direction. We therefore assume $\mathbf{n}'$ represents the true underlying shape.

We can now use the differences between observed and reconstructed image brightness to estimate the albedo map. If the final best-fit field of surface normals is reilluminated using a Lambertian reflectance model, then the predicted image brightness is given by $I(i,j) = \rho(i,j)[\mathbf{s}.\mathbf{n}'(i,j)]$. Since I, $\mathbf{s}$, and $\mathbf{n}'$ are all known we can estimate the albedo at each pixel using the formula:

$$\rho(i,j) = \frac{I(i,j)}{\mathbf{s}.\mathbf{n}'(i,j)}. \tag{1}$$

The technique puts no constraint on the albedo being piecewise constant and is estimated on a per-pixel basis. The combination of the final best-fit needle map and estimated albedo map allows for near photo-realistic reilluminations under novel illumination. The process also shows considerable stability under varying illumination.

5   Experiments

We commence by building a "ground truth" model using fields of surface normals extracted from range data. This allows us to show the utility of the model in capturing facial shape in a compact manner when trained on relatively 'clean' data. We used the 3DFS dataset [24] which consists of 100 high resolution scans of subjects in a neutral expression. The scans were collected using a *Cyberware*^{TM}

3030PS laser scanner. The database is pre-aligned, registration being performed using the optical flow correspondence algorithm of Blanz and Vetter [25]. Fields of surface normals were extracted by orthographically projecting the 3 surface normal components onto a view plane positioned fronto-parallel to the aligned faces.

We begin by examining the principal modes of variation for a model trained on fields of surface normals derived from range images of faces. In Figure 2 we show the first 5 modes of variation of this model. In each case we deform the points under azimuthal equidistant projection by ± 3 standard deviations along each of the first 5 principal axes. We then perform the inverse azimuthal equidistant projection before reilluminating the resulting needle maps with a point light source situated at the viewpoint and Lambertian reflectance. The modes encode shape only, since the needle maps are invariant to illumination conditions and the training set contained no variation in expression. The modes clearly capture distinct facial characteristics. For example, mode 1 encodes head size and also seems to be correlated with gender. This is manifested in the broader jaw, brow and nose in the negative direction, all of

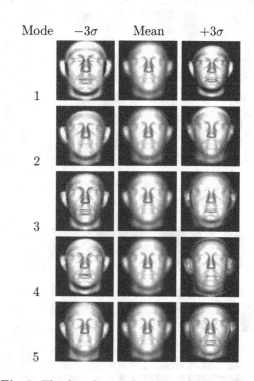

Fig. 2. The first five modes of variation of a statistical surface normal model trained on a set of facial needle maps extracted from range data

which are masculine features. The third mode encodes the difference between long, narrow faces and short, wide faces, whereas the second mode encodes the difference between a pointy and a rounded chin.

We apply the albedo estimation method described above to real world face images drawn from the Yale B database [26]. In Figure 3 we begin by demonstrating the stability of the process under variable lighting. The first row shows the input images of a single subject under varying illumination. The subject is a challenging choice due to the large albedo variations caused by facial hair. The light source is moved in an arc along the horizontal axis to subtend an angle of $-50°$, $-25°$, $0°$, $25°$ and $50°$ with the viewing direction. In the second row

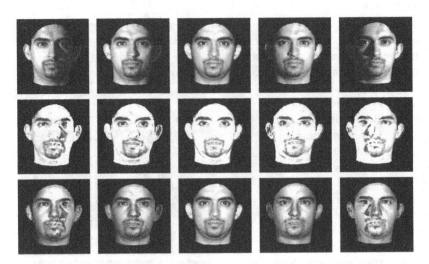

Fig. 3. Top row: input images, second row: estimated albedo maps, third row: synthesised images under frontal illumination

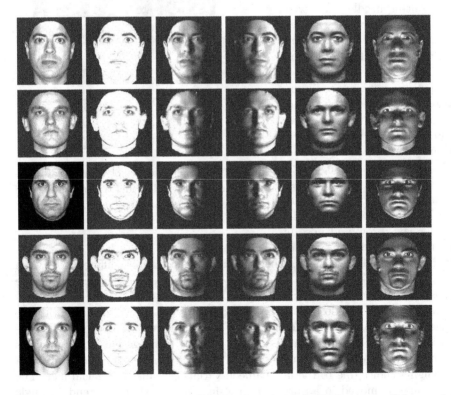

Fig. 4. Column 1: input images, Column 2: estimated albedo maps, Columns 3-6: synthesised views of the subjects under novel illumination. The light source directions are $[-1\ 0\ 1]^{T}$, $[1\ 0\ 1]^{T}$, $[0\ 1\ 1]^{T}$ and $[0\ -1\ 1]^{T}$ respectively.

we show the estimated albedo maps. The results of the albedo estimation process appear intuitively convincing. For instance, the albedo map identifies the eyes, eyebrows, facial hair, nostrils and lips. Moreover, there are no residual shading effects in the albedo map, for example the nose is given constant albedo. The albedo maps are consistent under varying illumination apart from the obvious errors caused by cast shadows as the lighting direction becomes more extreme. In columns 1 and 5, the shadows cast by the nose have been erroneously interpreted as albedo variations. This problem may be overcome by integrating the estimated field of normals to recover a surface. Using a ray-tracer, areas in shadow may be identified. Without a statistical model of albedo distribution, we could assume unit albedo in these shadow regions. The third row of Figure 3 shows the recovered normals rendered with the estimated albedo map and frontal illumination, effectively correcting for lighting variation. Apart from the errors caused by cast shadows, these synthesised images are of a good quality, even under large changes in illumination.

In Figure 4 we apply the albedo estimation process to 5 subjects from the Yale B database illuminated by a light source coincident with the viewing direction. The first column shows the input images and the second shows the estimated albedo maps. As in the previous figure, the estimated albedo maps are qualitatively convincing. In columns 3 to 6 we show the recovered fields of surface normals rendered with the estimated albedo map under varying illumination. The images are near photo-realistic in quality under fairly large changes in illumination.

6 Conclusions

In this paper we presented a statistical approach to estimating the albedo map of a face from a single image. The results are qualitatively convincing and the process is stable under varying illumination apart from the misclassification of cast shadows. The process has a number of potential applications. The estimated albedo map allows realistic reilluminations of the input face under novel illumination. In addition, the albedo map decouples subject identity from illumination conditions and may thus prove more useful for face recognition than raw image intensity. In future work we intend to address the issue of cast shadows. We also plan to improve the fitting process and develop ways of aligning the model with images which are not in a frontal pose.

References

1. Zhang, R., Tsai, P.S., Cryer, J.E., Shah, M.: Shape-from-shading: a survey. IEEE Trans. PAMI **21** (1999) 690–706
2. Johnston, A., Hill, H., Carman, N.: Recognising faces: effects of lighting direction, inversion, and brightness reversal. Perception **21** (1992) 365–375
3. Gregory, R.L.: Knowledge in perception and illusion. Phil. Trans. R. Soc. Lond. B **352** (1997) 1121–1128

4. Castelán, M., Hancock, E.R.: Acquiring height maps of faces from a single image. In: Proc. 3DPVT. (2004) 183–190
5. Georghiades, A., Belhumeur, P., Kriegman, D.: From few to many: Illumination cone models for face recognition under variable lighting and pose. IEEE Trans. PAMI **23** (2001) 643–660
6. Atick, J.J., Griffin, P.A., Redlich, A.N.: Statistical approach to SFS: Reconstruction of 3D face surfaces from single 2D images. Neural Comp. **8** (1996) 1321–1340
7. Zhao, W.Y., Chellappa, R.: Illumination-insensitive face recognition using symmetric SFS. In: Proc. CVPR. (2000) 286–293
8. Samaras, D., Metaxas, D.: Illumination constraints in deformable models for shape and light direction estimation. IEEE Trans. PAMI **25** (2003) 247–264
9. Prados, E., Faugeras, O.: A rigorous and realistic shape from shading method and some of its applications. Technical Report RR-5133, INRIA (2004)
10. Cootes, T.F., Edwards, G.J., Taylor, C.J.: Active appearance models. In: Proc. ECCV. (1998) 484–498
11. Costen, N.P., Cootes, T.F., Edwards, G.J., Taylor, C.J.: Automatic extraction of the face identity-subspace. Image and Vision Computing **20** (2002) 319–329
12. Turk, M., Pentland, A.: Face recognition using eigenfaces. In: IEEE Conf. CVPR. (1991) 586–591
13. Xiao, J., Baker, S., Matthews, I., Kanade, T.: Real-time combined 2D+3D active appearance models. In: Proc. IEEE Conf. CVPR. (2004) 535–542
14. Bruce, V., Coombes, A., Richards, R.: Describing the shapes of faces using surface primitives. Image and Vision Computing **11** (1993) 353–363
15. Marschner, S.R., Guenter, B., Raghupathy, S.: Modeling and rendering for realistic facial animation. In: Proc. 11th Eurographics Workshop on Rendering. (2000) 231–242
16. van Gemert, M.J.C., Jacques, S.L., Sterenborg, H.J.C.M., Star, W.M.: Skin optics. IEEE Transactions on Biomedical Engineering **36** (1989) 1146–1154
17. Marschner, S., Westin, S., Lafortune, E., Torrance, K., Greenberg, D.: Reflectance measurements of human skin. Technical Report PCG-99-2, Program of Computer Graphics, Cornell University (1999)
18. Lanitis, A., Taylor, C.J., Cootes, T.F.: Towards automatic simulation of ageing effects on face images. IEEE Trans. PAMI **24** (2002) 442–455
19. Matthews, I., Cootes, T.F., Bangham, J.A.: Extraction of visual features for lipreading. IEEE Trans. PAMI **24** (2002) 198–213
20. Blake, A.: Boundary conditions for lightness computation in mondrian world. Computer Vision, Graphics and Image Processing **32** (1985) 314–327
21. Smith, W., Robles-Kelly, A., Hancock, E.R.: Reflectance correction for perspiring faces. In: Proc. ICIP. (2004) 1389–1392
22. Sirovich, L.: Turbulence and the dynamics of coherent structures. Quart. Applied Mathematics **XLV** (1987) 561–590
23. Worthington, P.L., Hancock, E.R.: New constraints on data-closeness and needle map consistency for shape-from-shading. IEEE Trans. PAMI **21** (1999) 1250–1267
24. USF HumanID 3D Face Database, Courtesy of Sudeep. Sarkar, University of South Florida, Tampa, FL.
25. Blanz, V., Vetter, T.: A morphable model for the synthesis of 3d faces. In: Computer Graphics Proc. SIGGRAPH. (1999) 187–194
26. Belhumeur, P.N., Hespanha, J., Kriegman, D.J.: Eigenfaces vs. fisherfaces: Recognition using class specific linear projection. IEEE Trans. PAMI **17** (1997) 711–720

Optical Flow Computation for Compound Eyes: Variational Analysis of Omni-Directional Views

Akihiko Torii[1], Atsushi Imiya[2], Hironobu Sugaya[1], and Yoshihiko Mochizuki[1]

[1] School of Science and Technology, Chiba University
[2] Institute of Media and Information Technology, Chiba University,
Yayoi-cho 1-33, Inage-ku, Chiba 263-8522, Japan

Abstract. This paper focuses on variational optical flow computation for spherical images. It is said that some insects recognise the world through optical flow observed by their compound eyes, which observe spherical views. Furthermore, images observed through a catadioptric system with a conic mirror and a fish-eye-lens camera are transformed to images on the sphere. Spherical motion field on the spherical retina has some advantages for the ego-motion estimation of autonomous mobile observer. We provide a framework for motion field analysis on the spherical retina using variational method for image analysis.

1   Introduction

It is said that some insects, for instance dragon flies, observe spherical images through their compound eyes [1,2]. Furthermore, the compound eye systems of insects detect moving objects using optical flow computed as the difference of neighbouring ommateum in the compound eyes. Compound eyes collect light rays from the world to a spherical retina. Spherical camera captures images on a sphere by collecting light rays from the objects to the centre of the spherical retina. Therefore, it is possible to consider images captured by compound eyes as spherical images.

Motion analysis and tracking of obstacles and targets are fundamental requirements for robot vision. Spherical motion field on the spherical retina has some advantages for ego-motion estimation of an autonomous mobile observer [3,4]. In this paper, we introduce a mathematical model for optical flow computation [5,6,7] of spherical images using variational method for image analysis [8,9,10,11]. A catadioptric omni-directional vision system captures omni-directional views using a conic mirror and a pin-hole camera [12,13,14,15]. The fish-eye-lens camera systems, which are dioptric, capture omni-directional images which are similar to images observed by the eyes of a fish. Images captured by these omni-directional imaging systems are geometrically equivalent to images captured on the spherical retina. Since the omni-directional imaging system is widely used as imaging system of mobile robots, image analysis on a sphere is required in robot vision. Therefore, both in robot vision and in biological vision, spherical views are fundamental tools for studies on ego-motion estimation of cameras and eyes mounted on robots and animals.

M. De Gregorio et al. (Eds.): BVAI 2005, LNCS 3704, pp. 527–536, 2005.

2   Optical Flow Computation on the Sphere

Setting $x = (x, y, z)^\top$ to be a point on a space $\mathbf{R}^3$, for $0 \leq \theta \leq \pi$ and $0 \leq \phi < 2\pi$, a point on the unit sphere is parameterised as $x = \cos\phi\sin\theta$, $y = \sin\phi\sin\theta$, and $z = \cos\theta$. Therefore, a function on the unit sphere S^2 is parameterised as $I(\theta, \phi)$. The vector expressions of the spatial and spatio-temporal gradients on the unit sphere are $\nabla_S = \left(\frac{\partial}{\partial\theta}, \frac{1}{\sin\theta}\frac{\partial}{\partial\phi}\right)^\top$ and $\nabla_{St} = \left(\frac{\partial}{\partial\theta}, \frac{1}{\sin\theta}\frac{\partial}{\partial\phi}, \frac{\partial}{\partial t}\right)^\top$, respectively. For temporal image $I(\theta, \phi, t)$ on the unit sphere S^2, the total derivative is

$$\frac{d}{dt}I = \boldsymbol{q}^\top(\nabla_S I) + I_t = \boldsymbol{s}^\top(\nabla_{St}I). \tag{1}$$

The solution $\boldsymbol{q} = (\dot\theta, \dot\phi)^\top$ of the equation $\boldsymbol{s}^\top(\nabla_{St}I) = 0$, for $\boldsymbol{s} = (\boldsymbol{q}^\top, 1)^\top = (\dot\theta, \dot\phi, 1)^\top$, is optical flow of image I on the unit surface S^2. The computation of optical flow from $\boldsymbol{s}^\top(\nabla_{St}I) = 0$, is an ill-posed problem. Horn-Schunck criterion for the computation of optical flow [5,7] on the unit sphere is expressed as the minimisation of the functional

$$J(\dot\theta, \dot\phi) = \int_{S^2}\left(|\boldsymbol{s}^\top(\nabla_{St}I)|^2 + \alpha(\|\nabla_S\dot\theta\|_2^2 + \|\nabla_S\dot\phi\|_2^2)\right)\sin\theta d\theta d\phi, \tag{2}$$

where L_2 norm on the unit sphere is defined by

$$\|f(\theta, \phi)\|_2^2 = \int_{S^2}|f(\theta, \phi)|^2\sin\theta d\theta d\phi. \tag{3}$$

The Euler-Lagrange equations of this minimisation problem are

$$\nabla_S^\top\cdot\nabla_S\dot\theta = \frac{1}{\alpha}\frac{\partial I}{\partial\theta}\left(\frac{\partial I}{\partial\theta}\dot\theta + \frac{1}{\sin\theta}\frac{\partial I}{\partial\phi}\dot\phi + \frac{\partial I}{\partial t}\right),$$

$$\nabla_S^\top\cdot\nabla_S\dot\phi = \frac{1}{\alpha\sin\theta}\frac{\partial I}{\partial\phi}\left(\frac{\partial I}{\partial\theta}\dot\theta + \frac{1}{\sin\theta}\frac{\partial I}{\partial\phi}\dot\phi + \frac{\partial I}{\partial t}\right). \tag{4}$$

From this system of equations, we have the system of diffusion-reaction equations on the sphere,

$$\frac{\partial}{\partial\tau}\dot\theta = \nabla_S^\top\cdot\nabla_S\dot\theta - \frac{1}{\alpha}\frac{\partial I}{\partial\theta}\left(\frac{\partial I}{\partial\theta}\dot\theta + \frac{1}{\sin\theta}\frac{\partial I}{\partial\phi}\dot\phi + \frac{\partial I}{\partial t}\right),$$

$$\frac{\partial}{\partial\tau}\dot\phi = \nabla_S^\top\cdot\nabla_S\dot\phi - \frac{1}{\alpha\sin\theta}\frac{\partial I}{\partial\phi}\left(\frac{\partial I}{\partial\theta}\dot\theta + \frac{1}{\sin\theta}\frac{\partial I}{\partial\phi}\dot\phi + \frac{\partial I}{\partial t}\right) \tag{5}$$

for the computation of optical flow. For numerical computation, setting the right-hand-side equations of this system of equation to be $\frac{\boldsymbol{q}^{n+1} - \boldsymbol{q}^n}{\Delta\tau}$ and digitised the right-hand-side equation for the step $(n + 1)$, we have the system of linear equations

$$\begin{pmatrix} \Delta\tau\frac{1}{\alpha}\left(\frac{\partial I}{\partial\theta}\right)^2 + 1 & \Delta\tau\frac{1}{\alpha\sin\theta}\frac{\partial I}{\partial\phi}\frac{\partial I}{\partial\theta} \\ \Delta\tau\frac{1}{\alpha\sin\theta}\frac{\partial I}{\partial\phi}\frac{\partial I}{\partial\theta} & \Delta\tau\frac{1}{\alpha\sin^2\theta}\left(\frac{\partial I}{\partial\phi}\right)^2 + 1 \end{pmatrix}\begin{pmatrix} \dot\theta^{n+1} \\ \dot\phi^{n+1} \end{pmatrix}$$

$$= \begin{pmatrix} \dot\theta^n + \Delta\tau\nabla_S^\top\nabla_S\dot\theta^n - \Delta\tau\frac{1}{\alpha}\frac{\partial I}{\partial\theta}\frac{\partial I}{\partial t} \\ \dot\phi^n + \Delta\tau\nabla_S^\top\nabla_S\dot\phi^n - \Delta\tau\frac{1}{\alpha\sin\theta}\frac{\partial I}{\partial\phi}\frac{\partial I}{\partial t}, \end{pmatrix}, \tag{6}$$

for $q^n := \dot{\theta}^n, \dot{\phi}^n$, where

$$
\Delta\tau \nabla_S^\top \nabla_S q^n(\theta, \phi)
$$

$$
\begin{aligned}
& \quad q^n(\theta + \Delta\theta, \phi - \Delta\phi, t) \quad +q^n(\theta + \Delta\theta, \phi, t) \quad +q^n(\theta + \Delta\theta, \phi + \Delta\phi, t) \\
&= +q^n(\theta, \phi - \Delta\phi, t) \quad\quad -8q^n(\theta, \phi, t) \quad\quad +q^n(\theta, \phi + \Delta\phi, t) \\
& \quad +q^n(\theta - \Delta\theta, \phi - \Delta\phi, t) +q^n(\theta - \Delta\theta, \phi, t) +q^n(\theta - \Delta\theta, \phi + \Delta\phi, t)
\end{aligned} \tag{7}
$$

is the discrete Laplacian of 8-neighbourhood on the sphere.

Since q is a function of the time t, we accept the smoothed function

$$
q(t) := \int_{t-\tau}^{t+\tau} w(\tau)q(\tau)d\tau, \quad \int_{t-\tau}^{t+\tau} w(\tau)d\tau = 1, \tag{8}
$$

as the solution. Furthermore, instead of the M-estimator [1] in the form, for $s = (q^\top, 1)^\top = (\dot{\theta}, \dot{\phi}, 1)^\top$

$$
J_\rho(q) = \int_{S^2} \left(\rho(|s^\top \nabla_{St} I|^2) + \alpha(||\nabla_S \dot{\theta}||_2^2 + ||\nabla_S \dot{\phi}||_2^2) \right) \sin\theta d\theta d\phi, \tag{9}
$$

where $\rho(\cdot)$ is an appropriate weight function, we adopt an operation Θ, such that

$$
J_\Theta(q) = \Theta\left(J(\dot{\theta}, \dot{\phi}) \right). \tag{10}
$$

This operation allows us to achieve the minimisation operation before statistical operation. As an approximation of the operation Θ, we achieve the operation

$$
q^* = \text{argument}\left(\text{median}_{\Omega(q)} \{ |q| \le T | \text{median}_M(\min J(q)) | \} \right), \tag{11}
$$

which we call the double median operation [16,17].

3   Sphere Image Transform

3.1   Catadioptric System

As illustrated in Figure 1 (a), the focal point of the hyperboloid S_h is located at the point $F = (0, 0, 0)^\top$. The centre of the pinhole camera is located at the point $C_h = (0, 0, -2e)$. The hyperbolic-camera axis l_h is the line which connects C_h and F. We set the hyperboloid

$$
S_h : \frac{x^2 + y^2}{a^2} - \frac{(z+e)^2}{b^2} = -1, \tag{12}
$$

---

[1] For the estimation of $y = f(x)$ from noisy data $(x_i, y_i)^\top$, for $1 \le i \le n$ in the interval $[a, b]$, the function f, which minimises the criterion

$$
J_\rho(f) = \sum_{i=1}^n \rho(y_i - f(x_i)) + \alpha \int_a^b |f_{xx}(x)|^2 dx,
$$

where $\rho(x)$ is an appropriate convex function of x, is called M-estimator.

where $e = \sqrt{a^2 + b^2}$. A point $\boldsymbol{X} = (X, Y, Z)^\top$ in a space is projected to the point $\boldsymbol{x}_h = (x_h, y_h, z_h)^\top$ on the hyperboloid S_h according to the formulation,

$$\boldsymbol{x}_h = \lambda \boldsymbol{X}, \quad \lambda = \frac{\pm a^2}{b\sqrt{X^2 + Y^2 + Z^2} \mp eZ}. \tag{13}$$

This relation between $\boldsymbol{X}$ and $\boldsymbol{x}_h$ is satisfied, if the line, which connects the focal point $\boldsymbol{F}$ and the point $\boldsymbol{X}$, and the hyperboloid S_h have at least one real common point. Furthermore, the sign of parameter λ depends on the geometrical position of the point $\boldsymbol{X}$. Hereafter, we assume that the relation of equation (13) is always satisfied. Setting $\boldsymbol{m}_h = (u_h, v_h)^\top$ to be the point on the image plane π, the point $\boldsymbol{x}_h$ on S_h is projected to the point $\boldsymbol{m}_h$ on π according to the equations

$$u_h = f \frac{x_h}{z_h + 2e}, \quad v_h = f \frac{y_h}{z_h + 2e}, \tag{14}$$

where f is the focal length of the pinhole camera. Therefore, a point $\boldsymbol{X} = (X, Y, Z)^\top$ in a space is transformed to the point $\boldsymbol{m}_h$ as

$$u_h = \frac{fa^2 X}{(a^2 \mp 2e^2)Z \pm 2be\sqrt{X^2 + Y^2 + Z^2})},$$
$$v_h = \frac{fa^2 Y}{(a^2 \mp 2e^2)Z \pm 2be\sqrt{X^2 + Y^2 + Z^2})}. \tag{15}$$

For the hyperbolic-to-spherical image transform, setting $S_s : x^2 + y^2 + z^2 = r^2$, the spherical-camera centre $\boldsymbol{C}_s$ and the the focal point $\boldsymbol{F}$ of the hyperboloid S_h are $\boldsymbol{C}_s = \boldsymbol{F} = \boldsymbol{0}$. Furthermore, the axis connecting $\boldsymbol{C}_s$ and north pole of the spherical surface is $\boldsymbol{l}_s$. For the axis $\boldsymbol{l}_s$ and the hyperbolic-camera axis $\boldsymbol{l}_h$, we set $\boldsymbol{l}_s = \boldsymbol{l}_h = k(0, 0, 1)^\top$ for $k \in \mathbf{R}$, that is, the directions of $\boldsymbol{l}_s$ and $\boldsymbol{l}_h$ are the direction of the z axis. The spherical coordinate system expresses a point $\boldsymbol{x}_s = (x_s, y_s, z_s)$ on the unit sphere as

$$x_s = \sin \theta \cos \varphi, \ y_s = \sin \theta \sin \varphi, \ z_s = \cos \theta \tag{16}$$

where $0 \leq \theta < 2\pi$ and $0 \leq \varphi < \pi$. For the configuration of the spherical camera and the hyperbolic camera which share axes $\boldsymbol{l}_s$ and $\boldsymbol{l}_h$ as illustrated in Figure 1 (b), the point $\boldsymbol{m}_h$ on the hyperbolic image and the point $\boldsymbol{x}_s$ on the sphere satisfy

$$u_h = \frac{fa^2 \sin \theta \cos \varphi}{(a^2 \mp 2e^2) \cos \theta \pm 2be}, \quad v_h = \frac{fa^2 \sin \theta \sin \varphi}{(a^2 \mp 2e^2) \cos \theta \pm 2be}. \tag{17}$$

Setting $I(u_h, v_h)$ and $I_S(\theta, \varphi)$ to be the hyperbolic image and the spherical image, respectively, these images satisfy the equation

$$I(u_h, v_h) = I\left(\frac{fa^2 \sin \theta \cos \varphi}{(a^2 \mp 2e^2) \cos \theta \pm 2be}, \frac{fa^2 \sin \theta \sin \varphi}{(a^2 \mp 2e^2) \cos \theta \pm 2be}\right) = I_S(\theta, \varphi). \tag{18}$$

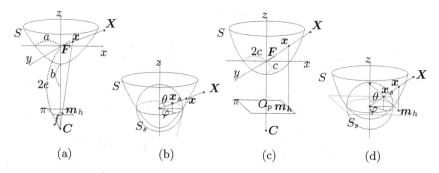

(a)   (b)   (c)   (d)

Fig. 1. Transforms between hyperbolic- and spherical-camera systems and parabolic-and spherical-camera systems. (a) illustrates a hyperbolic-camera system. The camera C_h generates the omnidirectional image π_h by the central projection, since all the rays corrected to the focal point F are reflected to the single point. A point X in a space is transformed to the point x_h on the hyperboloid and x_h is transformed to the point m_h on image plane. (b) illustrate the geometrical configuration of hyperbolic- and spherical-camera systems. In this geometrical configuration, a point x_s on the spherical image and a point x_h on the hyperboloid lie on a line connecting a point X in a space and the focal point F of the hyperboloid. (c) illustrates a parabolic-camera system. The camera C_p generates the omnidirectional image π_p by the orthogonal projection, since all the rays corrected to the focal point F are orthogonally reflected to the imaging plane. A point X in a space is transformed to the point x_p on the paraboloid and x_p is transformed to the point m_p on image plane. (d) illustrate the geometrical configuration of parabolic-and spherical-camera systems. In this geometrical configuration, a point x_s on the spherical image and a point x_p on the paraboloid lie on a line connecting a point X in a space and the focal point F of the paraboloid.

As illustrated in Figure 1 (c), the focal point of the paraboloid S_p is located at the point $F = (0,0,0)^\top$. The parabolic-camera axis l_p is the line which connects F and the centre of the parabolic image O_p. We set the paraboloid

$$S_p : z = \frac{x^2 + y^2}{4a} - a, \tag{19}$$

where a is the parameter of the paraboloid. A point $X = (X, Y, Z)^\top$ in a space is projected to the point $x_p = (x_p, y_p, z_p)^\top$ on the paraboloid S_p according to the formulation,

$$x_p = \lambda X. \tag{20}$$

This relation between X and x_p is satisfied, if the line, which connects the focal point F and the point X, and the paraboloid S_p have at least one real common point. Furthermore, the λ has two solutions. The geometrical configuration of the space point and the paraboloid leads that the solution is always positive expressed as

$$\lambda = \frac{2f}{\sqrt{x^2 + y^2 + z^2} - z}. \tag{21}$$

Setting $\boldsymbol{m}_p = (u_p, v_p)^\top$ to be the point on the parabolic image plane π_p, the point $\boldsymbol{x}_p$ on S is orthogonally projected to the point $\boldsymbol{m}_h$ on π expressed by the equations

$$u_p = x_p, \quad v_p = y_p. \tag{22}$$

Therefore, a point $\boldsymbol{X} = (X, Y, Z)^\top$ in a space is transformed to the point $\boldsymbol{m}_p$ as

$$u_p = \frac{2aX}{\sqrt{X^2 + Y^2 + Z^2} - Z}, \quad v_p = \frac{2aY}{\sqrt{X^2 + Y^2 + Z^2} - Z}. \tag{23}$$

For the parabolic-to-spherical image transform, setting $S_s : x^2 + y^2 + z^2 = r^2$, the spherical-camera centre $\boldsymbol{C}_s$ and the the focal point $\boldsymbol{F}$ of the paraboloid S_p are $\boldsymbol{C}_s = \boldsymbol{F} = \boldsymbol{0}$. Furthermore, the axis connecting $\boldsymbol{C}_s$ and north pole of the spherical surface is $\boldsymbol{l}_s$. For the axis $\boldsymbol{l}_s$ and the parabolic-camera axis $\boldsymbol{l}_p$, we set $\boldsymbol{l}_s = \boldsymbol{l}_p = k(0, 0, 1)^\top$ for $k \in \mathbf{R}$, that is, the directions of $\boldsymbol{l}_s$ and $\boldsymbol{l}_h$ are the direction of the z axis. The spherical coordinate system expresses a point $\boldsymbol{x}_s = (x_s, y_s, z_s)$ on the unit sphere as

$$x_s = \sin\theta\cos\varphi, \quad y_s = \sin\theta\sin\varphi, \quad z_s = \cos\theta \tag{24}$$

where $0 \le \theta < 2\pi$ and $0 \le \varphi < \pi$. For the configuration of the spherical camera and the parabolic camera which share axes $\boldsymbol{l}_p$ and $\boldsymbol{l}_h$ as illustrated in Figure 1 (b), the point $\boldsymbol{m}_p = (u_p, v_p)^\top$ on the hyperbolic image and the point $\boldsymbol{x}_s$ on the sphere satisfy the equations

$$u_p = 2a\frac{\sin\theta\cos\varphi}{1 - \cos\varphi}, \quad v_p = 2a\frac{\sin\theta\sin\varphi}{1 - \cos\varphi}. \tag{25}$$

Setting $I(u_p, v_p)$ and $I_S(\theta, \varphi)$ to be the parabolic image and the spherical image, respectively, these images satisfy the equation

$$I(u_p, v_p) = I(2a\frac{\sin\theta\cos\varphi}{1 - \cos\varphi}, 2a\frac{\sin\theta\sin\varphi}{1 - \cos\varphi}) = I_S(\theta, \varphi). \tag{26}$$

3.2   Dioptric System

Fish-eye-lens camera generates an image on the basis of stereographic, equisolid angle, orthogonal, and equidistance projection as shown in Figure 2.

Setting $\boldsymbol{x} = (x, y)^\top$ to be a point on an image acquired by fish-eye-lens camera, the point on the fish-eye-lens camera image is transformed to a point $(\theta, \varphi)^\top$ on an image on a sphere as

$$\theta = \tan^{-1}(y/x), \quad \varphi = 2\tan^{-1}(|\boldsymbol{x}|/2f), \tag{27}$$

$$\theta = \tan^{-1}(y/x), \quad \varphi = 2\sin^{-1}(|\boldsymbol{x}|/2f), \tag{28}$$

$$\theta = \tan^{-1}(y/x), \quad \varphi = \sin^{-1}(|\boldsymbol{x}|/f), \tag{29}$$

$$\theta = \tan^{-1}(y/x), \quad \varphi = |\boldsymbol{x}|/f. \tag{30}$$

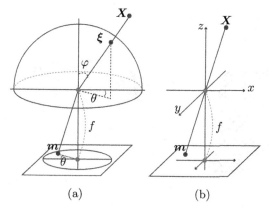

Fig. 2. Imaging geometry of the dioptric system and the pinhole systme. (a) In dioptric system, the light ray from point X is imaged on a plane after passing through fish-eye-lens. Images on imaging plane is transformed to images on the sphere. (b) A pin-hole system collects light rays which pass through a point in a space to the imaging plane. The pin-hole system collects light rays in a narrow area around the north pole of the sphere, although the dioptric systems collect light rays in a wide area using a lens system as shown in (a).

4   Numerical Examples

In this section, we show examples of optical flow detection for omni-direction images to both synthetic and real world image sequences. We have generated synthetic test pattern of image sequence for the evaluation of algorithms on the flow computation of omni-directional images. Since a class of omni-directional camera using catadioptical systems observes images on middle latitude images on the sphere. we accept direct numerical differentiation for numerical computation of the system of diffusion reaction equations [2].

We show numerical results of both synthetic and real world images for the Horn-Schunck criterion on the sphere. In these examples, the algorithm first computed optical flow vectors of each point for successive three intervals using the successive four images, second computed the weighted average at each point selecting weight as $1/4$, $1/2$, and $1/4$, and third applied non-linear statistic analysis selecting $T = 4$.

We set the parameters as shown in the table 2. For Figure 3 (e), every two frame images are accepted for the optical flow computation. Figure 3 (b) shows the the ideal patterns of optical flow on the imaging plane of the catadioptic camera for the camera translation with synthetic patterns in Figure 3 (a). Specially,

---

[2] In meteology [18], to avoid the pole problem in the discritization of partial differential equations on the sphere, the discrete spherical harmonic transform [19] and the quasi-equi-areal domain decomposition are common [20]. However, in our problem, imaging systems do not capture images in the neighborhood of pole, since the pole on the sphere is the dead-view regin to a class of catadioptical imaging systems.

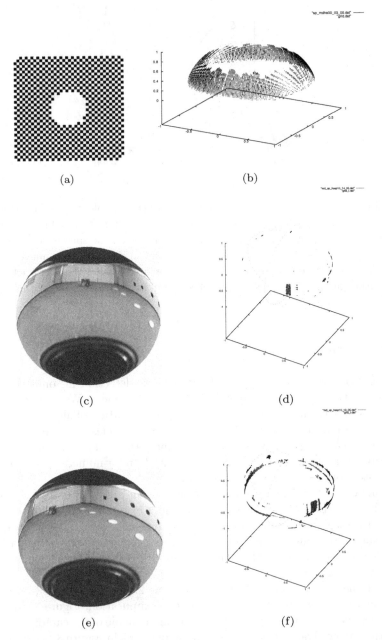

Fig. 3. Optical flow of synthetic and real world images. (a) A regular chess-board. A catadioptica system translates along a line parallel to an axis of pattern. The central circle is the invisible region of the camera system. (b) Optical flow on the imaging plane computed the image sequence of the patten (a). (c) A image observed from the translating robot. (d) Optical flow when the robot translates. (e) A image observed from the rotating robot. (f) Optical flow when the robot rotates.

Table 1. Discritization Parameters

Synthetic Data		
Iteration time		2000
Grid length	$\Delta\tau$	0.002
Parameter	α	1000
Grid pitch	$\Delta\theta$	0.25°
Grid potch	$\Delta\phi$	0.25°
Image size on the Sphere	$(\phi \times \theta)$	1440 × 360
Real World Images		
Iteration times		2000
Grid length	$\Delta\tau$	0.002
Parameter	α	1000
Grid pitch	$\Delta\theta$	0.20°
Grid pitch	$\Delta\phi$	0.20°
Image Size	$(\phi \times \theta)$	1800 × 900

the patten formed by the translation of the imaging system shows the direction on the translation of the camera system mounted on a mobile robot. Figure 3 (d) and (f) show optical flow images of real world images both for the case that objects move around stationary camera and that the camera system moves in the stationary environment. These results show objects in the environment and markers for the navigation yield typical flow patterns with these observed in the synthetic patterns. These results lead to the conclusion flow vectors computed by our method is suitable for the navigation of mobile robot with a catadioptic imaging system which captures omni-directional images.

5   Conclusions

We have introduced some examples for image analysis on the sphere, which are required from the context of robot vision. Since, the Hamiltonian-minimisation-based variational methods for image analysis provide a coordinate-free expression for the image analysis, our idea and extension of image analysis are applicable to wide ranges of new problems, which would be interested in robot vision and image analysis.

References

1. Neuman, T. R., Modeling insect compound eyes: Space-vriant spherica vision LNCS, **2525**, 360-367, 2002.
2. Dahmen, H.-J., Franz, M. O., Krapp, H. G., Extracting egmotion from optical flow: Limits of accuracy and nural matched filters, *in Zanker, J. M., Zeil, J., eds, Motion Vision-Computational Neural, and Ecological Constraints,* 143-168, Springer Verlag, 2001

3. Nelson, R. C., Aloimonos, J., Finding motion parameters from spherical flow fields (or the advantage of having eyes in the back of your head), Biological Cybernetics, **58**, 261-273, 1988.

4. Fermüller, C., Aloimonos, J., Ambiguity in structure from motion: sphere versus plane, IJCV. **28**, 137-154, 1998.

5. Horn, B. K. P. and Schunck, B. G., Determining optical flow, Artificial Intelligence, **17**, 185-204, 1981.

6. Nagel, H.-H., On the estimation of optical flow:Relations between different approaches and some new results, Artificial Intelligence, **33**, 299-324, 1987.

7. Barron, J. L. Fleet, D. J., Beauchemin, S. S.,
Performance of optical flow techniques,
International Journal of Computer Vision, **12**, 43-77, 1994.

8. Morel, J.-M., Solimini,.S., *Variational Methods in Image Segmentation*, Rirkhaäuser, 1995.

9. Aubert, G., Kornprobst, P., *Mathematical Problems in Image Processing:Partial Differencial Equations and the Calculus of Variations*, Springer-Verlag, 2002.

10. Sapiro, G., *Geometric Partial Differencial Equations and Image Analysis*, Cambridge University Press, 2001.

11. Osher, S., Paragios, N., eds., *Geometric Level Set Methods in Imaging, Vision, and Graphics* , Springer-Verlag 2003.

12. Benosman, R., Kang, S.-B. eds., *Panoramic Vision, Sensor, Theory, and Applications*, Springer-Verlag, New York, 2001.

13. Baker, S. Nayer, S., A theory of single-viewpoint catadioptric image formation, International Journal of Computer Vision, **35**, 175-196, 1999.

14. Geyer, C., Daniilidis, K., Catadioptric projective geometry, International Journal of Computer Vision, **45** 223-243, 2001.

15. Svoboda, T., Pajdla, T., Epipolar geometry for central catadioptric cameras, International Journal of Computer Vision, **49**, 23-37, 2002.

16. Imiya, A., Torii, A., Sugaya, H., Optical flow computation of omni-directional images, submitted.

17. Imiya, A., Iwawaki, K., Voting method for subpixel flow detection, Pattern Recognition Letters, **24**, 197-214, 2003.

18. Zdunkowski, W., Bott, A., *Dynamics of the Atmosphere*, Cambridge University Press, 2003.

19. Freeden, W., Schreiner, M., Franke, R., A survey on spherical spline approximation, Surveys on Mathematics for Industry, **7**, 1997.

20. Randol, D. *et al*, Climate modeling with spherical geodesic grids, IEEE Computing in Science and Engineering, **4**, 32-41, 2002.

Latent Semantic Description of Iconic Scenes

Filippo Vella[1], Giovanni Pilato[2], Giorgio Vassallo[1], and Salvatore Gaglio[1,2]

[1] DINFO – Dipartimento di Ingegneria INFOrmatica,
Università di Palermo, Viale delle Scienze - 90128 Palermo - Italy
vella@csai.unipa.it
{gvassallo, gaglio}@unipa.it
[2] ICAR - Istituto di CAlcolo e Reti ad alte prestazioni,
Italian National Research Council,
Viale delle Scienze - 90128 Palermo - Italy
pilato@pa.icar.cnr.it

Abstract. It is proposed an approach for the automatic description of scenes using a LSA–like technique. The described scenes are composed by a set of elements that can be geometric forms or iconic representation of objects. Every icon is characterized by a set of attributes like shape, colour and position. Each scene is related to a set of sentences describing their content. The proposed approach builds a data driven vector semantic space where the scenes and the sentences are mapped. A new scene can be mapped in this created space accordingly to a suitable metric. Preliminary experimental results show the effectiveness of the procedure.

1 Introduction

Many approaches in literature try to define the linguistic categories for the representation of spatial objects [3][4][7][10]. The reason could be found considering that spatial location is often expressed by closed-class forms and the concepts gained from this representation can act as fundamental structure in organizing conceptual material of different nature [7] [10].

The description of visual scenes can be viewed as a form of *language grounding*[8] [10] that is the connection of symbols in the language domain to their referents in the language user's environment. Furthermore categorization of space can be considered as the foundation for successive levels of abstraction in the concept hierarchy[8]. The system proposed in this paper aims to capture the basic relation between language and spatial displaced entities. Natural language descriptions are used as atomic values and no a priori hypothesis about the structure of language is assumed.

This work aims to verify the thesis that as Latent Semantic Analysis (LSA) allows to extract semantic relationship among terms and documents also in this domain the semantic links among scene and sentences could be caught by the Singular Value Decomposition (SVD) approach.

A set of artificial scenes has been created. Each scene is composed by objects chosen among ten different shapes. Each object can be modified changing color, size and orientation.

M. De Gregorio et al. (Eds.): BVAI 2005, LNCS 3704, pp. 537–544, 2005.

Scenes are represented by a set of sentences describing the contained objects and their properties. The relationship among sentences and scenes is described in matrix form, sentences being associated to the rows and columns being associated the scenes. The generic i,j-th element of the matrix is set to one if the i-th sentence can be applied to the j-th scene, otherwise the i,j-th element is set to zero.

SVD is applied to this matrix to extract the latent relationship among entities in the two domains and to create a semantic vector space where are represented, in a subsymbolic way, both sentences and scenes. Subsequently, a new scene is mapped in the semantic space according to a suitable metric. After the mapping, its description in terms of sentences, which have been already codified in the generated semantic space, is automatically obtained.

The remainder of paper is organized as follows: in Section 2 related works in the field of visual entities description are reported, in Section 3 a background about LSA is given. Section 4 describes the proposed system and the procedure to extract the semantic relationships between scenes. In section 5 the results of experiments and in section 6 the conclusions are reported.

2   Related Works

The task of describing visual entities with natural language sentences have been tackled in different way in the attempt to link visual objects with their description in linguistic form.

Feldman et al. address the problem to learn a subset of natural language, called *Miniature Language* for the description of picture-sentences pairs. The problem is described not considering the methodology to be used and authors' intention is to propose a well defined problem to be a *touchstone* for the cognitive science in this field[3]. In [2] are described the update of the project developed with main attention to language acquisition and induction of the grammar. The proposed solution is based on bayesian inference and model merging to build a probabilistic model of the grammar. The linguistic categorization of space allows to characterize the domain in a cross-linguistic environment to capture the conceptualization above the linguistic structure.

Representation of spatial terms has been also studied by Regier[7] conceiving a set of psychologically motivated perceptual features that are present in a wide range of spatial expressions in different languages.

The approach of Regier is based on connectionist learning of the acquired spatial terms. Input for experiments are synthetic images of pair of objects and their single word labels. His work aims to create a system able to adapt itself to the structuring of space in different languages.

The Visual Translator(VITRA)[4] is a knowledge-based system created by Herzog and Wazinski to integrate computer vision and natural language and in particular to address the task of description of images and image sequences. The system has been applied to complex real word domain as automobile traffic and soccer games and is based on a detailed representation of the objects of domain with their spatial relation. High level proposition are formed from these representations and expressed in natural language by a rule-based text planner.

Roy in [8] and [9] describes a system for the generation of spoken language for the task of describing objects in computer-generated visual scenes. The system is trained with a "show and tell" procedure, giving as input to the system, scenes coupled with their visual description. No prior knowledge is given about lexical semantics, word classes or syntactic structures. The DESCRIBER learns to generate natural language sentences through the creation of a probabilistic structure encoding the visual semantic of the phrase structure.

Monay and Gatica-Perez in [5] use LSA [11][12] for the task of images annotation. The purpose is to give labels to images accordingly to the subject of the photo or image. Images are represented in a vector space gathering keywords referred to content and visual information from quantitative properties of the photo. Images are divided in three parts and for each part the RGB color histogram is evaluated. An image is represented as a vector containing the visual features and the correct keywords. The union of all the vectors is used to form a matrix and then LSA is applied. Images, without annotation, are characterized by the histogram values and are projected in the created space to get the annotations from near vectors.

3   Latent Semantic Analysis

Latent Semantic Analysis (LSA) [12] is a paradigm to extract and represent the meaning of words by statistical computations applied to a large corpus of texts. LSA is based on the *vector space method*: given a text corpus of M words and N documents, it is represented as a matrix $\mathbf{W}$ where rows are associated to words and columns are associated to documents. The content of the *i,j-th* cell of $\mathbf{W}$ is a function of the *i-th* word frequency in the *j-th* text. The matrix W is replaced with a low-rank (R-dimension) approximation generated by the truncated singular-value decomposition (SVD) technique [11]:

$$\mathbf{W} \approx \hat{\mathbf{W}} = \mathbf{U}\mathbf{\Sigma}\mathbf{V}^{T} \tag{1}$$

where $\mathbf{U}$ is the (MxR) left singular matrix, $\mathbf{\Sigma}$ is (RxR) diagonal matrix with decreasing values $\sigma_1 \geq \sigma_2 \geq ... \geq \sigma_R > 0$ and $\mathbf{V}$ is the (NxR) right singular matrix. $\mathbf{U}$ and $\mathbf{V}$ are column-orthogonal and so they both identify a basis to span the R dimensional space.

Terms (represented as $\mathbf{u}_i\mathbf{\Sigma}$) are projected on the basis formed by the column vectors of the right singular matrix $\mathbf{V}$ and documents (represented as $\mathbf{v}_j\mathbf{\Sigma}$) are projected on the basis formed by the column of the matrix $\mathbf{U}$ to create their representation in the R-dimensional space.

In [1] Bellegarda uses this methodology to extrapolate from a corpus of documents the latent relations between words and between documents. The semantic relationship among words (as synonymy) and among documents (topic covering) can be evaluated with distance assessment. In particular, words that are in documents describing the same contents will have a shorter distance than term found in uncorrelated documents. On the other side documents containing words with the same context will convey information on the same topic.

4   The Proposed Approach

The target of the system is to automatically characterize scenes accordingly to the contained objects and the relationships among them.

Our work goes in the same direction of Feldman[3] to tackle the problem of scene description but starts from a different approach. As difference from Feldman[2] and from Roy [8][9], there is no characterization of the language and the information of domain is not integrated in the system as in[4]. The work is based on the holistic connection among language and visual information. Our work differs from Monay [5] because his work is aimed to image annotation and starts from a hybrid representation of images by vector with quantitative values and keyword. Our approach tends to make the semantic link emerge only from the space of co-occurrences.

In our work, scenes contain a variable number of objects chosen from a fixed set. Objects can be geometric shapes (circle, triangle, square, rectangle, etc.) or iconic representation of more complex objects as table, chair, bottle, house, hammer. Objects are displaced in the scene, without overlapping each other and they are characterized by the following properties: colour, orientation, size. An example of scene is presented in Fig. 1. The following objects are present in the scene: two chairs, a tree, a rhombus and a house. The house is pink coloured, the rhombus is on the right of the scene, the tree is below the house. A chair is under the rhombus and the other is near the tree.

A training set of scenes is built. Each scene is described by a set of sentences stating the presence of an object and its predicates or relations between couple of objects.

Fig. 1. An example of a typical scene

Considering a fixed order for all the sentences, a vector **p** is associated to each scene. If the sentence in position i is suitable for describing the scene, the i-th component of **p** is set to 1 otherwise it is set to 0. The set composed by all these vectors, considering to have N sentences and M scenes, is therefore a (NxM) matrix, called **W** in the remainder of the paper.

The i-th column of the matrix **W** is the representation of the i-th scene in the N dimensional vector space and, at the same time, the j-th sentence is represented in the M dimensional vector space by the j-th row (in analogy to the representation words-documents in LSA[12]). Truncated SVD is then applied to the matrix **W**, generated with the training set of scenes and sentences and the R-dimensional vector space is created.

The created semantic space is used to represent both scenes and sentences. If $\mathbf{v_i}$ is the i-th row of the matrix V, the vector $\mathbf{v_i}\Sigma$ is the representation of the scene in the R-dimensional space and is projected on the orthonormal basis formed by the column vectors of the left singular matrix **U**. The vector $\mathbf{u_i}\Sigma$ is the representation of the *i-th* sentence in the R-dimensional space and it is projected in the basis formed by the column vectors of the left singular matrix **V**.

In fig. 2 an example of Semantic Space created by the proposed approach is shown. The axes are represented by the columns of the matrix **U** when R is set to 3. The axes are orthogonal and can be labelled accordingly to the values of the vectors $\mathbf{U_1}$, $\mathbf{U_2}$, $\mathbf{U_3}$ for each sentence (i.e. $\mathbf{U_1}(i)$ is referred to the *i-th* sentence). Labels are associated filtering the lower values and picking the sentences connected to the highest values.

The rows of **V** represent the components of scenes and taking into account their belonging to one of the clusters identified by the axes they can be labelled with textual information associated with **U** axes. Two scenes with similar contents have little variation of components on these three axes so their representations are two near vectors in the semantic space.

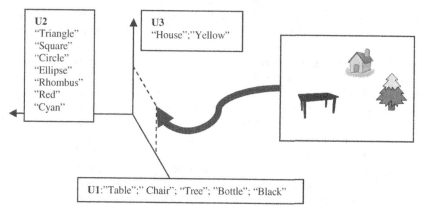

Fig. 2. The Semantic Space with automatically labeled axes

To "fold-in" a new scene in the semantic space some consideration must be drawn. In traditional LSA documents are represented as decomposition on the set of words composing the vocabulary. If a new document has to be mapped in the semantic space, its representation can be easily found as weighted vector of words components (i.e. counting the occurrences of each word in the new document). If $\tilde{d}_z$ is this vector of words occurrences in the document z, which does not belong to the training set, it can be considered as a column of the matrix **W** and accordingly to eq. 1 can be written:

$$\tilde{\mathbf{d}}_z = \mathbf{U}\mathbf{\Sigma}\tilde{\mathbf{v}}_z^T \qquad (2)$$

where $\tilde{\mathbf{v}}_z^T$ is a R-dimensional row vector representing this new document in the same form of the row of matrix $\mathbf{V}$. The representation in the semantic space can be derived as:

$$\tilde{\tilde{\mathbf{v}}}_z^T = \tilde{\mathbf{v}}_z^T \mathbf{\Sigma} = \tilde{\mathbf{d}}_z \mathbf{U} \qquad (3)$$

$\tilde{\tilde{\mathbf{v}}}_z^T$ is called *pseudodocument vector*[8] and is a good approximation of the document if the semantic space is generic enough to represent this new vector. If the insertion of this vector in the space would bring structural changes in the space the representation could be sensibly wrong [8].

The aim pursued in this paper is, given a new scene, automatically obtaining its description in terms of sentences which have already codified in the semantic space. Starting from a new image, to retrieve its description a representation in the space must be assessed considering the distance between the new scene and the other scenes in the starting set of images. The vector considered is the weighted sum of the most similar scene found in the semantic space.

The metric among scenes has been devised considering that distance between scenes cannot be calculated as differences of pixel but taking into account the objects present in the scene. For example the distance between two scenes containing the same objects (e.g. a tree and an house) but placed in different position, should have a value which reflects this similarity.

For these reason distances between objects have been settled considering the type of the object, its color, its size and its position. The distances of all the objects of a scene with all the objects of another scene constitute a matrix having as its *i,j-th* element, the distance between the i-th element of the first scene and the j-th element of the second scene. To evaluate the distance between two scenes the best assignment among the objects of the scene must be calculated. The best matching among the object is evaluated in a polynomial time using Munkres' assignment algorithm[6].

The most similar scenes, according to this metric contribute to the building of the vector representing the new scene in the semantic space. Each vector is weighted with the coefficient α_i inversely proportional to the distance between the scene represented and the new scene:

$$\alpha_i = \frac{\sum_{N_s} r_i - r_i}{(N_s - 1)\sum_{N_s} r_i} \qquad (4)$$

where N_s is number of nearest scene considered and r_i is the distance between the new scene and the *i-th* most similar scene.

Description of the new scene is evaluated accordingly to eq. 2 where $\tilde{\mathbf{v}}_z^T$ is replaced with the new generated vector. The vector $\tilde{\mathbf{d}}_z$ is replaced with the set of attivation values for the sentences allowing to describe the external scene.

5 Results

To evaluate the effectiveness of the proposed approach, an artificial set of 150 scenes has been created. 100 scenes, with their associated sentences have been used as a training set, while 50 scenes have been used to test the system generalization capabilities.

The experiments have been aimed to verify the representation capabilities in the semantic space of heterogeneous objects with the same meaning, the kind of connections emerging from data and the description of new scene not used for the generation of the semantic space.

The set of 150 scenes has been created with rules for the colours of objects related to the presence or not of objects of the same type. After the application of the proposed technique, experiments show that a trade-off must be found between the precision in retrieving correct sentences suitable for a new scene and the regularities discovery

The set of scene not contributing to the creation of the semantic space have been processed with the described method. For each scene the describing sentences are retrieved and the percentage of correctness has been calculated. The column "Correctly Associated Sentences" reports the percentage of sentences correctly describing the scene which have been retrieved by the procedure. The column "False Positive Sentences" reports the number of sentences, activated by new scenes but not belonging to the original images. The column "False Negative Sentences" reports the percentage of sentences describing the scene but not retrieved by the system.

Table 1. New scene sentences association results

R	Correctly Associated Sentences	False Positive Sentences	False Negative Sentences
5	51,1%	32,3%	16,6%
10	58,9%	24,7%	16,4%
15	58,1%	25,7%	16,1%

6 Conclusions and Future Works

An approach has been presented for the description of new scenes with natural language sentences. Experimental trials show interesting results obtained for the task of mapping new scenes in an automatically, data driven, created semantic space.

Future works will regard the extension of the approach on real images where visual characteristic are described with features tightly connected to pixel distribution. The new experiments will be aimed to find the connection of verbal information with sets of computable features of real objects.

References

1. J. R. Bellegarda. Exploiting latent semantic information in statistical language modeling. *In Proceedings of the IEEE*, volume 88 No.8, pages 1279–1296, 2000.
2. J.A. Feldman, G. Lakoff, D. Bailey, S. Narayanan, T. Regier, and A. Stolcke. L0 - the first five years of an automated language acquisition project. In *Artificial Intelligence Review*, volume 10(1-2), pages 103–129, 1996.
3. J.A. Feldman, G. Lakoff, A. Stolcke, and S.Weber. Miniature language acquisition: A touchstone for cognitive science. In *Proceedings of the 12th Annual Conference of the Cognitive Science Society*, pages 686–693, 1990.
4. G. Herzog and P. Wazinski. Visual translator: linking perception and natural language description. In *Artificial Intelligence Review*, volume 8, pages 175–187, 1994.
5. F. Monay and D. Gatica-Perez. On image auto-annotation with latent space models. In *Proc. ACM Int. Conf. on Multimedia* (ACM MM), pages 275 – 278, 2003
6. M. Munkres. Algorithms for the Assignment and Transportation Problems, *Journal of the Society for Industrial and Applied Mathematics*, vol. 5, no. 1, pages 32-38, 1957
7. T. Regier. A model of the human capacity for categorizing spatial relation. In Cognitive Linguistics, volume 6-1, pages 63–88, 1998.
8. D. K. Roy. Grounded spoken language acquisition: Experiments in word learning. In *IEEE Transaction on Multimedia*, pages 197-209, 2001.
9. D. K. Roy. Learning visually-grounded words and syntax for a scene description task. In *Computer Speech and Language*, pages 353–385, 2002.
10. L. Talmy. How language structures space. In Herbert Pick and Linda Acreolo, editors, In Spatial Orientation: Theory, Research and Application. Plenum Press, 1983.
11. S.T. Dumais, T.K. Landauer. A solution to Plato's problem: the latent semantic analysis theory of acquisition, induction and representation of knowledge. *Psychological Review*, 104, pages 211-240, 1997.
12. P.W. Foltz, T.K. Landauer and D. Laham. An introduction to latent semantic analysis. *Discourse Processes*, 25:259–284, 1998.

Pose-Invariant Face Recognition Using Deformation Analysis

Taeg-Keun Whangbo[2], Jae-Young Choi[1], Murlikrishna Viswanathan[2], Nak-Bin Kim[2], and Young-Gyu Yang[2]

[1] Dept. of Computer Science, University of California, Los Angeles
jaeyoung@cs.ucla.edu
[2] Dept. of Computer Science, Kyungwon University
{murli,tkwhangbo,ykyang,nbkim}@kyungwon.ac.kr

Abstract. Over the last decade or so, face recognition has become a popular area of research in computer vision and one of the most successful applications of image analysis and understanding. In addition, recognition of faces under varied poses has been a challenging area of research due to the complexity of pose dispersion in feature space. This paper presents a novel and robust pose-invariant face recognition method. In this approach, first, the facial region is detected using the TSL color model. The direction of face or pose is estimated using facial features and the estimated pose vector is decomposed into X-Y-Z axes. Second, the input face is mapped by a deformable template using these vectors and the 3D *CANDIDE* face model. Finally, the mapped face is transformed to the frontal face which appropriates for face recognition by the estimated pose vector. Through the experiments, we come to validate the application of face detection model and the method for estimating facial poses. Moreover, the tests show that recognition rate is greatly boosted through the normalization of the poses.

1 Background

Person identification is a challenging problem which has received much attention during the recent years due to its many applications in different fields such as banking, law enforcement, security applications and others. Although extremely reliable techniques of biometric personal identification exist, e.g., fingerprint analysis and retinal or iris scans, these methods rely on the cooperation of the participants, whereas an identification system based on facial analysis could function without such a need. Thus research in this area, especially face recognition, has gained prominence with results being spontaneously incorporated into application systems. In this paper we focus on the issues in face recognition.

Face recognition approaches on still images can be broadly grouped into geometric and template matching techniques. In the first case, geometric characteristics of faces to be matched, such as distances between different facial features, are compared. This technique provides limited results although it has been used extensively in the past. In the second case, face images represented as a two-dimensional array of pixel intensity values are compared to a single or several templates representing the whole face. In

M. De Gregorio et al. (Eds.): BVAI 2005, LNCS 3704, pp. 545–554, 2005.
© Springer-Verlag Berlin Heidelberg 2005

most studies that have employed full frontal facial photos the rate of recognition has been hampered due to the effects of illumination and variation of facial poses [1].

In order to overcome the insufficiency of the existing facial recognition methods, this paper proposes a pose-invariant face recognition system. Assessing and analyzing the ever-changing facial poses (external feature) we transform the face into a normalized form that can also be recognized by the existing face recognition systems. This approach boosts the accuracy of facial recognition and substantially reduces the FAR (False Acceptance Rate) and FRR (False Rejection Rate).

2 Face Detection

Tint-Saturation-Luminance (TSL) color model has been known to be efficient in extracting facial region on image since its T-S space is classified densely and independent from illumination [2]. Sometimes, however, T-S color model detects spurious regions when the background has a similarity with the facial color. In this case, we find the final facial region using labeling.

Irregular illumination sometimes causes different facial colors, and these are classified as a different region [3, 4]. In order to reduce the effects of illumination we analyze the effects of brightness based on the facial angle. Then, after compensating the intensity value for the effected region we finally detect the facial color.

3 Pose Estimation Using Geometrical Relationship

Facial poses are then calculated using the relative position of facial features: two eyes, and mouth. Generally, geometrical and template-based techniques use edge detection methods in pre-processing while detecting facial features since most facial features are horizontal shapes. However, facial features may not be horizontal shapes when input faces are angularly dispersed. Facial features in this paper are detected using their geometric relationship such as the line connecting two ends of the mouth being parallel to the line connecting the centers of two eyes and the length of two lines are almost same, etc.

Provided the facial features (two eyes, mouth) are detected correctly, connecting the center of each feature makes a triangle. With the exact frontal pose, the center of the triangle coincides with the center of the facial region. As the pose varies, there is the offset between two centers, a direction vector. As Figure (1) indicates, the direction of vector v gives indication of facial pose; the length of vector is shift offset from center of facial region. We can estimate the values of yaw and tilt after analyzing this vector. $A(x_1, y_1)$ is the gravity center of the facial region and $B(x_1, y_1)$ is the midpoint of the triangle made by facial features. It is possible to decompose $v = \overrightarrow{AB}$ into v_{yaw} and v_{tilt} using Eqn. (1)-(3). The formulas (1)-(3) are represented in degrees. In addition, $half_{face\_width}$ and $half_{face\_height}$ imply a radius of major and minor axis on the momentum of facial region, respectively.

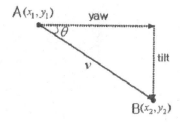

Fig. 1. Analyzing vector for estimation of angle

$$\angle v_{yaw} = \frac{v \cdot \cos \theta}{half_{face\_width}} \cdot 90 \qquad , where \quad \theta = \arctan \left(\frac{\mid y_2 - y_1 \mid}{\mid x_2 - x_1 \mid} \right) \tag{1}$$

$$\angle v_{tilt} = \frac{v \cdot \sin \theta}{half_{face\_height}} \cdot 90 \tag{2}$$

$$\angle roll_{face} = \arctan \left(\frac{\mid y_{R_{eye}} - y_{L_{eye}} \mid}{\mid x_{R_{eye}} - x_{L_{eye}} \mid} \right) \times 180 / \pi \tag{3}$$

4 Synthesizing Deformable Face and Pose Normalization

This paper uses the *CANDIDE*-3 3D wire frame model for input face mapping [6]. The process of pose normalization finds additional features including facial features for mapping the 3D wire frame model with the input image. The mapped face is normalized by transformation of texture using inverse value of the estimated pose vector for frontal face.

4.1 Mapping Input Image to Facial Model Using Extracted Features

This paper uses template matching for finding facial features since it is known to be more accurate than other geometrical techniques and although it is a slower technique the speed of searching can be increased if positions of eye, nose, and mouth are roughly acquainted [7]. However, a problem with template matching is that the mask has to be similar with the object. And in our case the need to match a proper mask to image in real time becomes difficult as the input data has varying poses thus requiring many templates. Therefore, this study suggests a deformable template which transforms one template mask to special template by estimated geometrical value in advance (as in Fig. 3).

Mapping implies overlapping between input image and facial model using extracted features. In this case, we use additional features of face in order to map more accurately as in Fig 2.

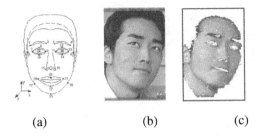

(a)   (b)   (c)

Fig. 2. Facial features for mapping. (a) Total features, (b) Features by deformable template, (c) Features by facial region we detected previous.

Three dimensions decompose rotation $\Re = R(r_x, r_y, r_z)$ into rotation of x-axis, y-axis, and z-axis. We use the homogeneous form in rotation and translation. Moreover, scale vectors use equal transformation matrix to apply different scales to x, y, and z-axis respectively. So we can deform a model through calculating parameters $P = [r_x, r_y, r_z, s, t_x, t_y, \sigma]^T$ using Eqn. (4)-(5) where $\bar{g}$ is original model, σ is parameter for shape, S is shape, t is translation matrix, R is rotation, and s is scale.

$$g = sR(\bar{g} + \sigma S) + t \tag{4}$$

$$\min \left\| g - f_{features} \right\|^2 \tag{5}$$

(a) Test image

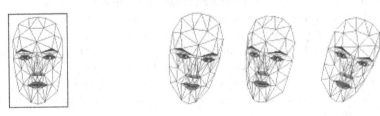

(b) Original template and   (c) Deformation of template

Fig. 3. Deformation of facial model using estimated angle

4.2 Input to Frontal Face Transformation

Facial template consists of a phase model and texture. Therefore, total transformation of the facial template synthesizes a new model by transforming the coordinates of points and the textures of the triangle which comprises of these points. Generally, the pixel coordinates are always integers. But, in our approach, sometimes the coordinates of transformed texture can be non-integral. In this case we use a reverse direction warping which interpolate the points using adjacent four points before translation as shown in figure 4 [8]. Figure 4 shows how the transformed pixel q_b is calculated from pixel q_a which is located in $p_{a,i}$ ($0 \le i \le 3$) on original image f_a using rate of α and β as $f_b(q_b) = \sum_{i=0}^{3} w_i(\alpha, \beta) f_a(p_{a,i})$.

Fig. 4. Compensation of pixel value using a reverse direction warping

The example of the complete process is presented in Fig. 5. The original template is deformed by estimated pose vector and mapped on to the input face. The texture is then transformed to normal value as shown in Fig. 5(e). The pose of the eyes is not rectified as it is not essential.

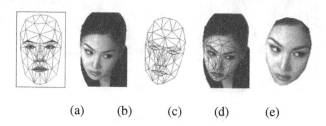

(a)   (b)   (c)   (d)   (e)

Fig. 5. Face mapping and pose normalization. (a) Original template, (b) Input image, (c) Deformation of template, (d) Mapping frame, (e) Mapping texture.

5 Experimental Study

Fig. 6 outlines the experimental framework and process. The experimentation consists of two processes; Ex1 is face recognition without compensation while Ex2 is with compensating pose. Fig. 7 presents a sampling of input faces from a total of 45 used in the empirical analysis.

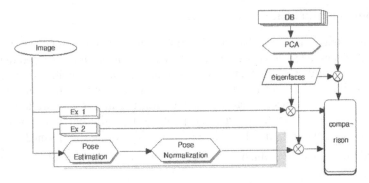

Fig. 6. Flowchart of face recognition experiment

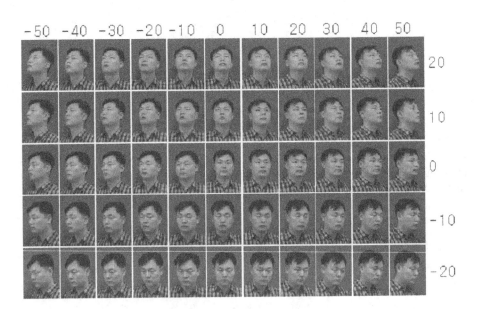

Fig. 7. A variety of poses

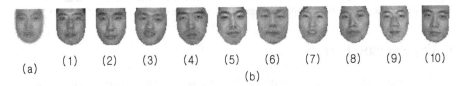

Fig. 8. Face examples for PCA; (a) Mean face, (b) Learning faces

Principle Component Analysis (PCA) is used for comparing the two processes Ex1 and Ex2, and we analyze the Euclidean distance for rate of recognition [9,10]. For PCA, the face of ten people is used as learning data as shown in Fig. 8 [11].

This paper measures Euclidean distance error ε_k for each component between the normalized and DB faces using Eqn. (6) where f_k represents the learning faces and f_i, the input faces. In these experiments the hair is also eliminated for an accurate measurement of face like in Fig. 9.

$$\varepsilon_k = \|y_i - y_k\|$$
$$y_k = \Omega^T * f_k, \qquad y_i = \Omega^T * f_i, \tag{6}$$

Fig. 9. Examples of extracting facial region for PCA

5.1 Analysis of Results

Fig. 10 shows estimated angle of input images from Fig. 7 using our proposed method. There is no bar where it fails calculation of angle. The reason of failure implies that it is difficult to extract the opposite eye if the angle of yaw is large.

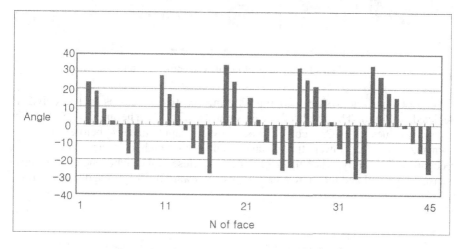

Fig. 10. Angle of face through estimated poses (yaw)

Almost of facial models are transformed in the same direction. However, as we can observe from Fig. 3, the error is large when the pose is upward facing. This is due to the ambiguity between the jaw and forehead region. The estimated pose value is used to normalize face as well as map input face to facial model such as Fig. 11.

In case that the angle of face is large, the mirroring process is needed due to the lack of facial information the region that is located on the other side of camera view [11]. For the mirroring process the visible half of face detected by the camera is duplicated and put it on the other side lacking information after transformation (see Fig. 11).

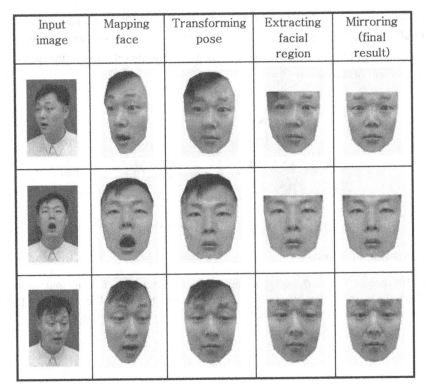

Input image	Mapping face	Transforming pose	Extracting facial region	Mirroring (final result)

Fig. 11. Examples of facial pose normalization

We test input faces shown in Fig. 7 using the two processes Ex1 and Ex2 as depicted in Fig. 6. The result of test is shown in Fig. 12. The graph represents the distance values of PCA coefficients between input images before and after normalization. The lower the distance value, the higher is accuracy of face recognition. Naturally, when the angle of face is close to the center the distance error measured is small and the more a face points downward the larger the distance error.

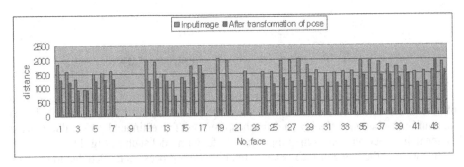

Fig. 12. Difference of principle vector from normalized face

Fig. 13 presents the result of recognition where the x-axis and y-axis of graph imply the number of faces in Fig. 7 and Fig. 8, respectively. No. 6 on the y-axis is a face that we want to detect. After normalization, more input faces on x-axis are recognized as a No. 6 on the y-axis.

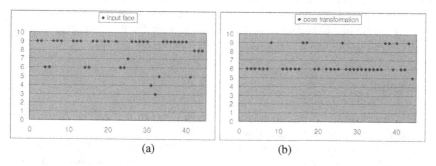

(a)   (b)

Fig. 13. Results of recognition; (a) Before normalization, (b) After normalization

To judge the accuracy of face recognition we use minimum Euclidean distance between input face in Fig.7 and learning face in Fig. 8. Although face recognition generally uses a threshold value for reducing FAR(false acceptance rate), in our case a face satisfying a minimum distance is considered as similar for reducing FRR(false rejection rate) because it just confirms the recognition. Fig. 14 shows a proportion of results from Fig.13. Face No. 6 is our target face and its rate of recognition can be seen to increase from 13% to 76%.

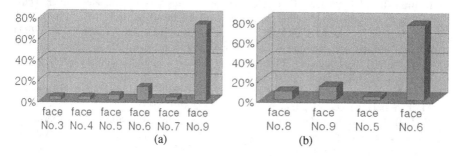

(a)   (b)

Fig. 14. Improvements in recognition rate - (a) Before normalization, (b) After normalization

6 Conclusions

There are many challenges to face recognition including pose variation, illumination conditions, scale variability, low quality image acquisition, partially occluded faces, etc. In general, varying facial poses create problems with acquisition, analysis, and recognition. Thus most studies showing plausible performance are restricted to frontal face and normalized face without rotation. In order to overcome this insufficiency of existing face recognition methods this paper proposes a novel pose-invariant face recognition system by using a normalized algorithm in preprocessing.

Numerous tests have been experimented categorically to evaluate proposed algorithm and many facial images which have various poses, and used to experiment on normalization. Through the experiments, we come to validate the rationale of our face detection model and method for estimating facial poses. Moreover, the tests show that recognition rate is greatly boosted through the normalization of poses by 76%. The accuracy is improved six-fold than prior to pose transformation. In the future we would like to solve problems associated with distortion by large angles and design a facial model that it is optimized to warp the facial features.

References

[1] G. Yongsheng, "Face recognition using line edge map," IEEE Trans. on Pattern Analysis and Machine Intelligence, vol. 24, no. 6, pp. 764-779, 2002.
[2] J. C. Terrillon and S. Akamatsu, "Comparative performance of different chrominance spaces for color segmentation and detection of human faces in complex scene images," Proc. of the 4th IEEE Int'l Conf. on Automatic Face and Gesture Recognition, pp. 54-60, 2000.
[3] H. Yao and W. Gao, "Face locating and tracking method based on chroma transform in color images," Proc. Int'l Conf. on Signal Processing, vol. 2, pp. 1367-1371, 2000.
[4] K. K. Sung and T. Poggio, "Example based learning for view-based human face detection," IEEE Trans. on Pattern Recognition and Machine Intelligence, vol. 20, pp. 39-51, 1998.
[5] J. Ahlberg, "Model-based Coding : Extraction, Coding, and Evaluation of Face Model Parameters," Dissertations, Dept. of Electrical Engineering, Linköping University, Sweden, 2002.
[6] R. Brunelli and T. Poggio, "Face Recognition: Features versus Templates," IEEE Trans. on Pattern Analysis and Machine Intelligence, vol. 15, no 10, pp. 1042-1052, 1993.
[7] D. J. Beymer, "Pose-Invariant Face Recognition Using Real and Virtual Views," Ph.D. Thesis, Massachusetts Institute of Technology, Cambridge, MA, 1995.
[8] M. Turk and A. Pentland, "Eigenfaces for face recognition," Journal of Cognitive Neuroscience, vol. 3, no. 1, pp. 71-86, 1991.
[9] A. M. Martinez and A. C. Kak, "PCA versus LDA," IEEE Trans. on Pattern Analysis and Machine Intelligence, vol. 23, no. 2, pp. 228-233, 2001.
[10] V. I. Belhumeur, J. P. Hespanha, and D. J. Kriegman, "Eigenfaces vs. fisherfaces : Recognition using class specific linear projection," IEEE Trans. on Pattern Analysis and Machine Intelligence, vol. 19, no. 7, pp. 711-720, 1997.
[11] S. H. Hwang, J. Y. Choi, N. B. Kim, "A Study on Face Reconstruction using Coefficients Estimation of Eigen-Face," Proc. of Korean Society for Internet Information, vol. 4, no. 1, pp. 505-509, 2003.

Author Index

Lecture Notes in Computer Science

For information about Vols. 1–3650

please contact your bookseller or Springer

Vol. 3696: W. Duch, J. Kacprzyk, E. Oja, S. Zadrożny (Eds.), Artificial Neural Networks: Biological Inspirations – ICANN 2005, Part I. XXXI, 703 pages. 2005.

Vol. 3695: M.R. Berthold, R. Glen, K. Diederichs, O. Kohlbacher, I. Fischer (Eds.), Computational Life Sciences. XI, 277 pages. 2005. (Subseries LNBI).

Vol. 3694: M. Malek, E. Nett, N. Suri (Eds.), Service Availability. VIII, 213 pages. 2005.

Vol. 3693: A.G. Cohn, D.M. Mark (Eds.), Spatial Information Theory. XII, 493 pages. 2005.

Vol. 3692: R. Casadio, G. Myers (Eds.), Algorithms in Bioinformatics. X, 436 pages. 2005. (Subseries LNBI).

Vol. 3691: A. Gagalowicz, W. Philips (Eds.), Computer Analysis of Images and Patterns. XIX, 865 pages. 2005.

Vol. 3690: M. Pěchouček, P. Petta, L.Z. Varga (Eds.), Multi-Agent Systems and Applications IV. XVII, 667 pages. 2005. (Subseries LNAI).

Vol. 3688: R. Winther, B.A. Gran, G. Dahll (Eds.), Computer Safety, Reliability, and Security. XI, 405 pages. 2005.

Vol. 3687: S. Singh, M. Singh, C. Apte, P. Perner (Eds.), Pattern Recognition and Image Analysis, Part II. XXV, 809 pages. 2005.

Vol. 3686: S. Singh, M. Singh, C. Apte, P. Perner (Eds.), Pattern Recognition and Data Mining, Part I. XXVI, 689 pages. 2005.

Vol. 3685: V. Gorodetsky, I. Kotenko, V. Skormin (Eds.), Computer Network Security. XIV, 480 pages. 2005.

Vol. 3684: R. Khosla, R.J. Howlett, L.C. Jain (Eds.), Knowledge-Based Intelligent Information and Engineering Systems, Part IV. LXXIX, 933 pages. 2005. (Subseries LNAI).

Vol. 3683: R. Khosla, R.J. Howlett, L.C. Jain (Eds.), Knowledge-Based Intelligent Information and Engineering Systems, Part III. LXXX, 1397 pages. 2005. (Subseries LNAI).

Vol. 3682: R. Khosla, R.J. Howlett, L.C. Jain (Eds.), Knowledge-Based Intelligent Information and Engineering Systems, Part II. LXXIX, 1371 pages. 2005. (Subseries LNAI).

Vol. 3681: R. Khosla, R.J. Howlett, L.C. Jain (Eds.), Knowledge-Based Intelligent Information and Engineering Systems, Part I. LXXX, 1319 pages. 2005. (Subseries LNAI).

Vol. 3679: S.d.C. di Vimercati, P. Syverson, D. Gollmann (Eds.), Computer Security – ESORICS 2005. XI, 509 pages. 2005.

Vol. 3678: A. McLysaght, D.H. Huson (Eds.), Comparative Genomics. VIII, 167 pages. 2005. (Subseries LNBI).

Vol. 3677: J. Dittmann, S. Katzenbeisser, A. Uhl (Eds.), Communications and Multimedia Security. XIII, 360 pages. 2005.

Vol. 3676: R. Glück, M. Lowry (Eds.), Generative Programming and Component Engineering. XI, 448 pages. 2005.

Vol. 3675: Y. Luo (Ed.), Cooperative Design, Visualization, and Engineering. XI, 264 pages. 2005.

Vol. 3674: W. Jonker, M. Petković (Eds.), Secure Data Management. X, 241 pages. 2005.

Vol. 3673: S. Bandini, S. Manzoni (Eds.), AI*IA 2005: Advances in Artificial Intelligence. XIV, 614 pages. 2005. (Subseries LNAI).

Vol. 3672: C. Hankin, I. Siveroni (Eds.), Static Analysis. X, 369 pages. 2005.

Vol. 3671: S. Bressan, S. Ceri, E. Hunt, Z.G. Ives, Z. Bellahsène, M. Rys, R. Unland (Eds.), Database and XML Technologies. X, 239 pages. 2005.

Vol. 3670: M. Bravetti, L. Kloul, G. Zavattaro (Eds.), Formal Techniques for Computer Systems and Business Processes. XIII, 349 pages. 2005.

Vol. 3669: G.S. Brodal, S. Leonardi (Eds.), Algorithms – ESA 2005. XVIII, 901 pages. 2005.

Vol. 3668: M. Gabbrielli, G. Gupta (Eds.), Logic Programming. XIV, 454 pages. 2005.

Vol. 3666: B.D. Martino, D. Kranzlmüller, J. Dongarra (Eds.), Recent Advances in Parallel Virtual Machine and Message Passing Interface. XVII, 546 pages. 2005.

Vol. 3665: K. S. Candan, A. Celentano (Eds.), Advances in Multimedia Information Systems. X, 221 pages. 2005.

Vol. 3664: C. Türker, M. Agosti, H.-J. Schek (Eds.), Peer-to-Peer, Grid, and Service-Orientation in Digital Library Architectures. X, 261 pages. 2005.

Vol. 3663: W.G. Kropatsch, R. Sablatnig, A. Hanbury (Eds.), Pattern Recognition. XIV, 512 pages. 2005.

Vol. 3662: C. Baral, G. Greco, N. Leone, G. Terracina (Eds.), Logic Programming and Nonmonotonic Reasoning. XIII, 454 pages. 2005. (Subseries LNAI).

Vol. 3661: T. Panayiotopoulos, J. Gratch, R. Aylett, D. Ballin, P. Olivier, T. Rist (Eds.), Intelligent Virtual Agents. XIII, 506 pages. 2005. (Subseries LNAI).

Vol. 3660: M. Beigl, S. Intille, J. Rekimoto, H. Tokuda (Eds.), UbiComp 2005: Ubiquitous Computing. XVII, 394 pages. 2005.

Vol. 3659: J.R. Rao, B. Sunar (Eds.), Cryptographic Hardware and Embedded Systems – CHES 2005. XIV, 458 pages. 2005.

Vol. 3658: V. Matoušek, P. Mautner, T. Pavelka (Eds.), Text, Speech and Dialogue. XV, 460 pages. 2005. (Subseries LNAI).

Vol. 3657: F.S. de Boer, M.M. Bonsangue, S. Graf, W.-P. de Roever (Eds.), Formal Methods for Components and Objects. VIII, 325 pages. 2005.

Vol. 3656: M. Kamel, A. Campilho (Eds.), Image Analysis and Recognition. XXIV, 1279 pages. 2005.

Vol. 3655: A. Aldini, R. Gorrieri, F. Martinelli (Eds.), Foundations of Security Analysis and Design III. VII, 273 pages. 2005.

Vol. 3654: S. Jajodia, D. Wijesekera (Eds.), Data and Applications Security XIX. X, 353 pages. 2005.

Vol. 3653: M. Abadi, L. de Alfaro (Eds.), CONCUR 2005 – Concurrency Theory. XIV, 578 pages. 2005.

Vol. 3652: A. Rauber, S. Christodoulakis, A.M. Tjoa (Eds.), Research and Advanced Technology for Digital Libraries. XVIII, 545 pages. 2005.

Vol. 3651: R. Dale, K.-F. Wong, J. Su, O.Y. Kwong (Eds.), Natural Language Processing – IJCNLP 2005. XXI, 1031 pages. 2005. (Subseries LNAI).